Successful Writing at Work

Successful Writing at Work

ELEVENTH EDITION

Philip C. Kolin

University of Southern Mississippi

CENGAGE
Learning·

Australia • Brazil • Mexico • Singapore • United Kingdom • United States

CENGAGE
Learning®

**Successful Writing at Work,
Eleventh Edition**
Philip C. Kolin

*For Kristin, Eric, and Theresa
Evan Philip and Megan Elise
Erica Marie
Julie and Loretta
Ethlyn
and
MARY*

Product Director: Monica Eckman

Product Team Manager: Nicole Morinon

Product Manager: Kate Derrick

Content Developer: Ed Dodd

Managing Content Developer:
Cara Douglass-Graff

Senior Content Developer: Jessica Badiner

Associate Content Developer: Erin Bosco

Product Assistant: Mario Davila

Marketing Director: Stacey Purviance

Associate Marketing Manager:
Jameson Walsh

Senior Content Project Manager:
Michael Lepera

Senior Art Director: Marissa Falco

Manufacturing Planner: Betsy Donaghey

IP Analyst: Ann Hoffman

IP Project Manager: Farah Fard

Production Service/Compositor:
MPS Limited

Text and Cover Designer:
Liz Harasymczuk Design

Cover Image: Jose Luis Pelaez Inc/Blend
Images/Getty Images

For product information and technology assistance, contact us at
Cengage Learning Customer & Sales Support, 1-800-354-9706

For permission to use material from this text or product,
submit all requests online at **www.cengage.com/permissions.**
Further permissions questions can be emailed to
permissionrequest@cengage.com.

Library of Congress Control Number: 2015947469

Student Edition:
ISBN-13: 978-1-305-66761-7

Loose-leaf Edition:
ISBN-13: 978-1-305-67173-7

Cengage Learning
20 Channel Center Street
Boston, MA 02210
USA

Cengage Learning is a leading provider of customized learning solutions with employees residing in nearly 40 different countries and sales in more than 125 countries around the world. Find your local representative at **www.cengage.com.**

Cengage Learning products are represented in Canada by Nelson Education, Ltd.

To learn more about Cengage Learning Solutions, visit **www.cengage.com.** Purchase any of our products at your local college store or at our preferred online store **www.cengagebrain.com.**

Printed in the United States of America
Print Number: 01 Print Year: 2015

Contents

PART II: Correspondence   114

Chapter 4: E-Communications at Work:
Email, Blogs, Messaging, and Social Media   116

Chapter 5: Writing Letters:
Some Basics for Communicating with Audiences Worldwide   152

Preface

Successful Writing at Work, Eleventh Edition, is a practical, comprehensive introductory text for business, technical, professional, and occupational writing courses. Regardless of a student's career choice, writing is a vital part of virtually every job, and as readers of earlier editions have learned, *Successful Writing at Work* can help them become better writers while they also learn to develop and design effective workplace documents for multicultural, global audiences. *Successful Writing at Work*, Eleventh Edition, is organized to take students step-by-step from the basic concepts of audience analysis, purpose, message, style, and tone to the processes of researching, drafting, revising, formatting/designing, and editing. Students will learn to write a variety of job-related documents, from emails, social media posts, and correspondence to more complex instructions, proposals, reports, websites, and presentations.

BUILDING ON PAST EDITIONS

Benefiting from the feedback of instructors, students, and employers over many editions, this revised Eleventh Edition continues to give students detailed, clear guidelines for preparing well-organized and readable business documents. Moreover, because effective models are critical for learning new skills, students will find a wide range of realistic, up-to-date, and rhetorically diverse examples (all of them annotated and visually varied) demonstrating the function, scope, format, and organization of numerous documents for audiences with differing needs. Each of these model documents focuses directly on practical issues in the world of work and portrays employees as successful writers, either individually or as part of a collaborative writing group. Furthermore, this new edition fully covers a broad spectrum of current workplace technologies and considerations, such as social media, messaging, Google Docs, professional networking sites, Skype, and Prezi.

VERSATILITY OF NEW ELEVENTH EDITION

As in past editions, this Eleventh Edition is as versatile as it is comprehensive. Full enough for a sixteen-week semester, it can also be easily adapted to shorter six-, eight-, or ten-week courses. *Successful Writing at Work*, Eleventh Edition, is designed to go beyond classroom applications: It is a ready reference that students can easily carry with them as they begin or advance in the workplace. As students will discover, this edition maintains the reputation of former editions by including numerous practical applications in each book chapter and also in the MindTap Reader version of the text. It can be as useful to readers with little or no job experience as to those with years of experience in one or several fields. This edition also addresses the needs of students re-entering the job market or changing careers.

DISTINCTIVE APPROACH OF *SUCCESSFUL WRITING AT WORK*

The distinctive approach that in the past has made *Successful Writing at Work* a student-friendly text in the contemporary workplace continues to be emphasized and expanded in this Eleventh Edition. This approach, stressing up-to-date strategies for teaching business, technical, and professional writing, can be found throughout this new edition.

- **Analyzing audiences.** The Eleventh Edition focuses on the importance of audience analysis and the writer's obligation to achieve the "you attitude" in every workplace document. In addition, the concept of audience extends to readers worldwide, as well as to non-native speakers of English, whether as co-workers, employers, clients, or representatives of various agencies and organizations. Memos, emails, social media posts, letters, résumés, reports, presentations, and other documents are written, designed, organized, and introduced with the intended audience(s) in mind.

- **Seeing writing as a problem-solving activity.** The Eleventh Edition continues to approach writing not merely as a set of rules and formats but as a problem-solving activity in which employees meet the needs of their employers, co-workers, customers, clients, community groups, and vendors worldwide by getting to the bottom line. This approach to writing, introduced in Chapter 1 and carried throughout the text, helps students to think through the writing process by asking the key questions of *who* (who is the audience?), *why* (why do they need this document?), *what* (what is the message?), and *how* (how can the writer present the most appropriate style, tone, and format?). As in earlier editions, this Eleventh Edition teaches students how to develop the critical skills necessary for planning, drafting, revising, editing, and formatting a variety of documents. To help them, numerous case studies and figures demonstrate how writers answer these key questions to solve problems in the world of work.

- **Being an ethical employee.** Companies expect their employees to behave and write ethically. As in earlier editions, the Eleventh Edition reinforces and expands discussions of ethical writing practices in almost every chapter. Beginning with enhanced coverage of ethical writing and solving ethical dilemmas at work, Chapter 1 further stresses "Ethical Writing in the Workplace." Subsequent chapters offer practical guidelines on and numerous examples of documents that illustrate the types of ethical choices workers must make in the business world. Special attention is given to editing to avoid sexism and biased language in Chapter 2; working cooperatively with a collaborative writing team in Chapter 3; making ethical choices when writing e-communications, including email, messages, blogs, and social media posts in Chapter 4; drafting diplomatic letters in Chapters 5 and 6; preparing honest, realistic résumés and webfolios in Chapter 7; conducting truthful, objective, and carefully documented research in Chapter 8; using and constructing unbiased visuals and ethical websites in Chapters 10 and 11; preparing safe, legal instructions and procedures in Chapter 12; writing honest proposals and reports in Chapters 13 to 15; and making clear and accurate presentations in Chapter 16.

- **Writing for the global marketplace.** Effective employees must write for a variety of readers, both in the United States and across the globe. Consequently, this new Eleventh Edition throughout emphasizes writing for international readers and non-native speakers of English. The needs and expectations of these international audiences receive special attention in the Eleventh Edition, starting in "Writing for the Global Marketplace" in Chapter 1 and continuing with coverage of writing letters for international speakers of English in Chapter 5, designing appropriate visuals and documents for this audience in Chapter 10, preparing clear instructions in Chapter 12, and making presentations for global audiences in Chapter 16. Especially important is the long report in Chapter 15 on the role international workers play in a corporation that must meet their needs and those of their clients worldwide.

- **Viewing student readers as business professionals.** To encourage students in their job-related writing, this new Eleventh Edition treats them as professionals seeking success at different phases of their business. Students are asked to place themselves in the workplace setting (or, in the case of Chapter 7, in the role of job seekers) as they approach each topic, to understand the differences between workplace and academic writing better. Chapter 1 gives them an orientation to the kinds of corporate culture and protocols that they might find in the early days of their employment. Students are then asked to see themselves as members of a collaborative team drafting and developing an important workplace document in Chapter 3; in Chapters 4 to 6 they write to fellow employees and superiors and represent their company through routine e-communications and respectful and diplomatic correspondence; in Chapters 10 and 11 they are co-workers designing documents, visuals, and websites; in Chapters 12 through 15 they are employees designing and writing more complex documents, such as instructions, proposals, and reports; and in Chapter 16 they are company representatives making presentations before co-workers and potential clients worldwide.

- **Using the latest workplace technologies.** This new edition offers the most current coverage of communication technologies for writing successfully in the rapidly changing world of work, including social media (such as Facebook, Twitter, LinkedIn, Pinterest, Instagram, Flickr, YouTube, and Yelp), email, messaging, wikis, document tracking systems, Google Docs, business blogs, tablets, smartphones, videoconferencing tools, and presentation software such as PowerPoint and Prezi. Coverage of these technologies is integrated into each chapter through Tech Notes, Case Studies, sample documents, and text discussion, and Chapter 4 illustrates many of these new technologies in action. Easy-to-understand explanations and annotated models throughout this edition assist students in discovering the hows as well as the whys of writing and using visuals for the digital world of work.

- **Commitment to ecology.** The Eleventh Edition continues to stress environmental issues and greening the workplace though a section in Chapter 1 ("Thinking Green: Making Ethical Choices About the Environment"), instructions on fixing a leaky faucet and installing solar panels in Chapter 12, a progress report emphasizing the use of solar energy in Chapter 14, and several other sample documents and Exercises throughout the text.

OVERVIEW OF MAJOR CHANGES IN THE ELEVENTH EDITION

In response to reviewer feedback and that of instructors and their students, the new Eleventh Edition has undergone some major changes to make it more useable and effective:

- This new edition has been streamlined, shortened, updated, and redesigned to provide essential and current coverage of major communication strategies with real-world examples that students need to succeed in today's e-world of work. Chapter 8, for example, has been thoroughly revised to make it even more student-friendly, retaining only the most important information students need to conduct research and properly evaluate and document sources in the workplace. The discussion of memos has been moved to Chapter 6 to show how letters and memos work together in the business world.
- The new edition features a strong emphasis on and integration of social media throughout, including a new section on cyberbullying in Chapter 1, a section on ethical guidelines to follow when writing for social media and other e-communications in Chapter 4, a new section in Chapter 4 that highlights how to write effectively in the medium and includes examples of Facebook and Twitter posts, examples of Facebook and LinkedIn profiles and a list of social media "do's and don'ts" when looking for a job in Chapter 7, an extended example showing how social media can help rent units in a new apartment complex in the updated business report in Chapter 8, examples of how social media can help shape proposals in Chapter 13, and a discussion of how it can influence the findings in a long report in Chapter 15.
- The use of tablets and smartphones in the workplace has been included and addressed throughout the text, including a discussion of their use in e- and m-communications in Chapter 4. The rise of m-commerce is also addressed in proposals in Chapter 13 and a short report in Chapter 14. Additionally, many exercises have been revised throughout the text to showcase the importance of these communication tools.

- Many new Tech Notes and exercises have been added, as well as new Case Studies tied to technology. All existing Tech Notes have been updated with the latest information and technological advances.
- **Now available with MindTap!** MindTap is the digital learning solution that helps instructors engage and transform today's students into critical thinkers, communicators, and writers. Numerous real-world examples and strong visuals come to life in the MindTap Reader, where students can search, highlight, and take notes, right on the text. Students build grammar, mechanics, and writing skills with interactive activities and apply those skills to project and writing assignments. A variety of writing and research apps allow students to collaborate and improve their research. Instructors can customize the course by blending their own materials with curated content, and incorporate additional examples and models, as desired. An easy-to-use paper management system allows for submission, grading, peer review, and plagiarism prevention. With MindTap for *Successful Writing at Work*, Eleventh Edition, students reveal mastery of the text's skills and strategies to find their voice as professional writers.

CHAPTER-BY-CHAPTER UPDATES

Here, then, chapter-by-chapter, are the specific new additions and features of the Eleventh Edition.

Chapter 1 Getting Started: Writing and Your Career

- Revised case study on adapting technical information to meet the needs of diverse audiences within a corporate setting
- Revised section, "Employers Insist on and Monitor Ethical Behavior"
- Expanded discussion in "Ethical Requirements on the Job"
- *New* section, "Cyberbullying"
- Further attention to solving ethical dilemmas in the workplace
- Revised Tech Note, "Know Your Computer at Work"
- Revised section, "Using International English" with expanded guidelines

Chapter 2 The Writing Process at Work

- Enhanced coverage of drafting, revising, and editing on the job
- Revised, updated case study, "A 'Before' and 'After' Revision of a Short Report"
- Revised Tech Notes on "Drafting," "Revising," and "Editing"
- Updated advice on avoiding stereotypical language, including eliminating sexism

Chapter 3 Collaborative Writing and Meetings in the Workplace

- Increased emphasis on being a team player in the world of work
- Greater attention to collaborative communication technologies

- Heavily revised Case Study on collaboratively written documents
- Revised sections, case studies, and figures illustrating the use of Track Changes in Microsoft Word and Google Docs for collaborative writing
- *New* Tech Note, "Virtual Meetings"
- Revised Tech Note, "Videoconferencing with Skype"
- *New* coverage on using social media with collaboration (including office collaboration software like Yammer, FB@Work, and Slack)
- *New* section on preparing for and conducting a meeting at work—setting an agenda, taking notes, summarizing ethically, and writing the minutes

Brand New Chapter 4 E-Communications at Work: Email, Blogs, Messaging, and Social Media

- Discusses the importance of and differences between business and personal emails, messages, blogs, and social media posts
- Revised section, "Legal/Ethical Guidelines to Follow in Writing E-Communications"
- Substantially revised sections on email in the workplace, including a revised "Guidelines for Using Email on the Job" with up-to-date, practical advice
- Revised "Messaging" section focusing on both using a networked company system and texting on smartphones.
- Expanded discussion of business blogs
- *New* section, "Writing for Social Media in the Workplace"
- New figures showcasing business social media posts on Facebook and Twitter
- Includes new exercises related to writing for social media in the workplace

Chapter 5 Writing Letters: Some Basics for Communicating with Audiences Worldwide

- Further emphasis on the importance of letters in the Internet Age
- Strengthened discussions of the business contexts for correspondence
- Revised section, "Essential Advice on Writing Effective Letters"
- *New* section on "Different Ways to Send Letters"
- Revised section on "The Appearance of Your Letter," reflecting contemporary document designs
- Expanded sections on writing different correspondence
- Greater attention to needs of international readers with an enhanced Case Study on adapting letters to international readers
- Revised exercises on up-to-date topics reflecting international readers' needs

Chapter 6 Types of Business Letters and Memos

- Revised "Preliminary Guidelines" section for sales letters
- *New* Tech Note, "Mail Merge"
- Revised section, "Getting the Reader's Attention"
- Revised section, "Showing the Customer the Product's or Service's Application"
- Revised section on "Adjustment Letters"

- Heavily revised section on "Memos"
- Thirteen redesigned letters and memos
- Revised exercises with up-to-date topics and subjects

Chapter 7 How to Get a Job: Searches, Networking, Dossiers, Portfolios/Webfolios, Résumés, Transitioning to a Civilian Job, Letters, and Interviews

- Revised section on identifying and emphasizing marketable job skills
- Updated coverage on where to look for a job, with further examples of and advice on using job-posting sites
- *New* section, "Transitioning to the Civilian Workforce," aimed at helping veterans prepare successful job applications; *new* sample résumé
- Updated section on "Looking in the Right Places for a Job"
- Revised section on "Using Online Social and Professional Networking Sites in Your Job Search"
- *New* sample LinkedIn profile page; updated discussion of using Facebook as part of your job search
- Revised and updated "Do's and Don'ts When Creating Your Online Profile"
- Updated and redesigned letters and résumés throughout
- Chapter now includes ten print and digital résumés
- Revised section on "The Digital Résumé"
- Revised Case Study on creating a digital résumé for a job search
- *New* section with tips on "Being Ready for a Phone Interview"
- Revised Tech Note, "Skype Interviews"
- Revised and updated section on "Questions to Expect at Your Interview"
- New information on "What Interviewer(s) Can't Ask You"
- Updated, practical advice inquiring about salary and salary ranges
- *New* section, "Keep a Job Search Record"

Streamlined Chapter 8 Doing Research, Evaluating Sources, and Preparing Documentation in the Workplace

- Useful, updated section on "Use of Social Networking Sites as a Recruiting Tool"
- *New* section on "Online Survey Builders"
- Revised and updated Tech Note, "Intranets"
- Revised and updated sections on searching online catalogs, e-libraries, and reference materials
- Revised Tech Note, "Gray Literature"
- *New* section, "How to Conduct Keyword Searches: Some Guidelines"
- Coverage of latest Modern Language Association (MLA) and American Psychological Association (APA) documentation styles, including for podcasts, blogs, emails, tweets, and Facebook posts
- Updated and reformatted business report, marketing a large real estate project (written in MLA style)
- *New* exercises with current business topics

Chapter 9 Summarizing Information at Work

- In response to user and reviewer feedback, the chapter has been streamlined and shortened to make it more reader-friendly and applicable to the needs of today's students
- Thoroughly revised section, "Summaries in the Information Age"
- Updated Case Study with annotated summary of an article on virtual reality and law enforcement
- *New* advice on "What Managers Want to See in an Executive Summary"
- Revised section, "Writing Successful News Releases"
- *New* figure of a news release posted on the Web
- *New* article on security considerations for mobile app developers in exercises

Chapter 10 Creating Clear Visuals

- Revised section, "Using Appropriate Visuals for International Audiences"
- *New* examples of bar graphs, line graphs, flow charts, photographs, and pictographs
- Revised and updated advice in "Choosing Effective Visuals" and "Insert Your Visuals Appropriately"
- *New* Tech Note, "Using Photoshop"
- *New* section on using infographs
- Greater attention to creating ethical visuals

Chapter 11 Designing Successful Documents and Websites

- Revised section on "The ABCs of Print Document Design"
- Updated discussion on differences between writing for a print source versus a Web source
- Revised section on "Desktop Publishing"
- *New* Case Study on designing a company newsletter
- Greatly enhanced, updated Case Study on the differences between print document design organization and website organization
- *New* Tech Note, "Website Accessibility"

Chapter 12 Writing Instructions and Procedures

- Updated coverage of preparing legally and ethically proper instructions and procedures
- *New*, annotated examples of online and print instructions
- Revised section on "Using Word-Processing Software to Help You Design Instructions"
- *New* case study on meeting your audience's needs, including new figure
- Revised section on "Warnings, Cautions, and Notes," with more attention to needs of international readers

- Enhanced discussion of workplace procedures, including a revised Case Study
- Seven new exercises

Chapter 13 Writing Winning Proposals

- Updated examples of sales and internal proposals
- Revised Tech Note, "Online RFPs"
- Heavily revised Case Study on drafting an internal proposal to create a mobile app for a health food store
- *New*, fully annotated internal proposal on purchasing inventory tracking software
- Revised figure of a sales proposal responding to a request from a company
- *New* figure of a student proposal on writing a report on the ethical issues involved in using apps in m-commerce
- Additional coverage of researching and collaborating in preparing proposals
- Six *new* exercises

Chapter 14 Writing Effective Short Reports

- Heavily revised and expanded coverage of guidelines for writing short reports
- *New* Case Study on preparing a periodic report
- Revised section on "How to Write the Body of a Progress Report"
- Expanded discussion of how and why different audiences read a report
- Revised progress report for a student research report
- Revised section on "Common Types of Trip/Travel Reports"
- Six revised exercises

Chapter 15 Writing Careful Long Reports

- Revised guidelines on the process of writing a long report
- Revised discussion of transmittal letters
- Revised coverage of developing and documenting conclusions and recommendations
- Completely revised, updated model long report (written in APA style) on cultural sensitivity for multinational workers

Chapter 16 Making Successful Presentations at Work

- Enhanced section on informal briefings with a new figure instructing bank employees how to detect and report counterfeit currency
- Revised advice and slides for a PowerPoint presentation
- Revised section on "Presentation Software," including a discussion of web-based software such as Prezi and new presentation technologies such as SMART boards

- Revised section, "Delivering the Presentation"
- Revised discussion on evaluating a presentation

ADDITIONAL RESOURCES

MindTap® English for Kolin's *Successful Writing at Work*, Eleventh Edition engages your students to become better thinkers, communicators, and writers by blending your course materials with content that supports every aspect of the writing process.

- Interactive activities on grammar and mechanics promote application in student writing.
- Easy-to-use paper management system helps prevent plagiarism and allows for electronic submission, grading, and peer review.
- A vast database of scholarly sources with video tutorials and examples supports every step of the research process.
- Professional tutoring guides students from rough drafts to polished writing.
- Visual analytics track student progress and engagement.
- Seamless integration into your campus learning management system keeps all your course materials in one place.

MindTap lets you compose your course, your way.

Online Instructor's Resource Manual. Streamline and maximize the effectiveness of your course preparation using such resources as teaching suggestions, sample course schedules, assignments, chapter test banks, and many other classroom support materials. This password-protected Instructor's Resource Manual is easily downloadable by accessing www.cengagebrain.com.

ACKNOWLEDGMENTS

In a very real sense, *Successful Writing at Work*, Eleventh Edition, has profited from my collaboration with various reviewers. I am, therefore, honored to thank the following individuals who have helped me improve this edition significantly with their helpful comments: Karen Cristiano, *Drexel University*; Michelle Davidson, *The University of Toledo*; Glenn Deutsch, *Albion College*; Julie Gard, *University of Wisconsin–Superior*; Teresa Henning, *Southwest Minnesota State University*; Todd Kennedy, *Nicholls State University;* Elizabeth Shelley, *Aquinas College*; Allen Shepard, *University of Wisconsin–Superior*; Suzanne Smith, *The University of Toledo*; Jennifer Thompson, *Columbia College Chicago*; Ellen Tsagaris, *St. Ambrose University*; Julie Vick, *University of Colorado at Denver*.

I also want to thank the reviewers of the last edition: Etta Barksdale, *North Carolina State University;* Jonathan Lee Campbell, *Valdosta State University*; Don Cunningham, *Radford University*; Linda Eicken, *Cape Fear Community College*; Wolfgang Lepschy, *Tallahassee Community College*; Sabrina Peters-Whitehead,

University of Toledo; Mary E. Shannon, *California State University–Northridge*; and Pinfan Zhu, *Texas State University*.

Reviewers of previous editions also helped guide this revision: Jenny Billings Beaver, English Division Chair, *Rowan-Cabarrus Community College*; Ann E. Biswas, *University of Dayton*; William Carney, *Cameron University*; Darin Cozzens, *Surry Community College*; Terry Dale, *King Fahd University of Petroleum & Minerals, Saudi Arabia*; Carlos Evia, Director of Professional Writing at *Virginia Polytechnic Institute and State University*; Traci HalesVass, *San Juan College*; and Suba Subbarao, *Oakland Community College*.

My thanks also go to the following individuals at the University of Southern Mississippi for their help—Linda Allen, Jeremy DeFatta, Nikita Core, Anna Beth Williams, chair Eric Tribunella (Department of English); David Tisdale (University Communications), Mary Lux (Department of Medical Laboratory Science), Cliff Burgess (Department of Computer Science), and Daniel Miles (Department of Biochemistry). I am also grateful to Steven R. Moser, Dean of the College of Arts and Letters, for his continued appreciation of my work. My special thanks go to Danielle Sypher-Haley, web designer for the College of Arts and Letters, for her help with my discussions of social media and writing for the Internet.

My gratitude also goes to Terri Smith Ruckel, Jianqing Zheng at Mississippi Valley State University, Erin Smith at the University of Tennessee–Knoxville, Billy Middleton at Stevens Institute in New Jersey, Ed Parecki at Marylhurst University, Terry Dale at King Fahd University of Petroleum & Minerals, Saudi Arabia, and Sandra Leal at Harris-Stowe State University.

Several individuals from the business world also gave me wise counsel, for which I am deeply grateful—Sally Eddy at Georgia Pacific; Kirk Woodward at Visiting Nurses Services of New York; Jimmy Stockstill at Petro Automotive; Carrie Logan and Nancy Steen from Adelman & Steen, LLP; Teresa Rogers and Rachel Sullivan at Regents Bank, Inc.; Rick Leal; Debbie Yates, RN; and Brig. General Steve Parham, U.S. Army. Cecile Douglas and Kari Sapsis at the Center for Disease Control and Prevention helped me to obtain two new figures in Chapter 1, for which I am thankful.

I am also especially grateful to Father Michael Tracey for his counsel and contributions to Chapter 11 on document and website design.

My thanks go to the team at Cengage Learning for their assistance, encouragement, and friendship—Nicole Morinon, product team manager; Kate Derrick, product manager; Erin Bosco, associate content developer; Mario Davila, product assistant; Jessica Badiner, senior content developer; Michael Lepera, senior content project manager; and Stacey Purviance, marketing director and to content developer Ed Dodd for his always helpful assistance and friendship. I want to thank Ed Dionne at MPS Limited for his cooperation through the painstaking production cycle. I am also grateful to Farah Fard at Cengage, and Manojkiran Chander and Kanchana Vijayarangan at Datamatics Ltd., who handled the image and text permissions, respectively, for *Successful Writing at Work*, Eleventh Edition.

I thank my extended family—Margie and Al Parish, Sister Carmelita Stinn, SFCC, and Sister Annette Seymour, RSM, and Mary and Ralph Torrelli—for their prayers and love.

Finally, I am deeply grateful to my son, Eric, and my daughter-in-law, Theresa, for their enthusiastic and invaluable assistance as I prepared this edition; to my grandson, Evan Philip, and granddaughters, Megan Elise and Erica Marie, for their love and encouragement. My daughter, Kristin, also merits loving praise for her help throughout this new edition by doing various searches and revisions and by offering her knowledgeable, practical advice on successful writing at work. And, finally, I thank Ethlyn Dorrington for her love and kindness.

P.C.K.
January 2016

Getting Started

Writing and Your Career

WRITING—AN ESSENTIAL JOB SKILL

Writing is a part of every job, from your initial letter of application conveying first impressions to memos, emails, tweets, texts, blogs, letters, websites, proposals, instructions, and reports. Writing keeps businesses moving. It allows employees to communicate with one another, with management, and with the customers, clients, and agencies a company must serve to stay in business. The average office worker receives 80 emails daily, and that means that most [people] are receiving at least one email message every 6 or 7 minutes while at work.[1] A survey conducted by the McKinsey Global Insitute found that workers spend more than 2½ hours a day just reading and answering their emails.

How Writing Relates to Other Skills

Almost everything you do at work is related to your writing ability. Deborah Price, a human resource director with thirty years of experience, stresses that "Without the ability to write clearly an employee cannot perform the other duties of the job, regardless of the company he or she works for." Here is a list of the common tasks you will be expected to perform in the workplace that will require clear and concise writing to get them done well.

- Assess a situation, a condition, a job site, etc.
- Research and record the results accurately.
- Summarize information concisely and identify main points quickly.
- Work as part of a team to collect, to share, and to evaluate information.
- Tackle and solve problems and explain how and why you did.

[1]Stephens, M. (2012, January 10). Volume of email reaching a tipping point. *SME: Small and Medium-Sized Enterprises.* Retrieved from http://www.smeweb.com/technology /features/4639-volume-of-email-reaching-tipping-point

Backgrounds

Part Opening Image: fotog/Tetra/Corbis

PART I

Successful Writing at Work

- Display cultural sensitivity in the workplace.
- Network with individuals in diverse fields outside your company and across the globe.
- Answer customer questions and meet their needs.
- Make a post to your company's social media site to get information out about its brand.
- Prepare and test instructions and procedures.
- Justify financial, personnel, or other actions and decisions.
- Make persuasive presentations to co-workers, employers, and clients.

To perform each of these essential workplace tasks, you have to be an effective writer—clear, concise, accurate, ethical, and persuasive.

The High Cost of Effective Writing

Clearly, then, writing is an essential skill. According to Don Bagin, a communications consultant, most people need an hour or more to write a typical business letter. If an employer is paying someone $30,000 a year, one letter costs $14 of that employee's time; for someone who earns $50,000 a year, the cost for the average letter jumps to $24. The National Commission on Writing estimates that American businesses spent $3.1 billion annually in training employees to write.[2]

Unfortunately, as the Associated Press (AP) reported in a recent survey, "Most American businesses say workers need to improve their writing . . . skills." Yet that same report cited a survey of more than 400 companies that identified writing as "the most valuable skill employees can have." In fact, the employers polled in that AP survey indicated that 80 percent of their workforce needed to improve their writing. Beyond a doubt, your success as an employee will depend on your success as a writer. The higher you advance in an organization, the more and better writing you will be expected to do. Promotions, and other types of job recognition, are often based on an employee's writing skills.

How This Book Will Help You

This book will show you, step by step, how to write clearly and efficiently the job-related communications you need for success in the world of work. Chapter 1 gives you some basic information about writing in the global marketplace and raises major questions you need to ask yourself to make the writing process easier and the results more effective. It also describes the basic functions of on-the-job writing and introduces you to one of the most important requirements in the business world—writing ethically.

WRITING FOR THE GLOBAL MARKETPLACE

The Internet, teleconferencing, digital communications, social media, and m-commerce have shrunk the world into a global village. Many companies are multinational corporations with offices throughout the world. In fact, many U.S. businesses are branches

---

[2]Combest, T. What is the importance of business letters? *eHow*. Retrieved from http://www.ehow.com/facts_5595243_importance-business-letters_.html

of international firms. A large, multinational corporation may have its equipment designed in Japan; built in Bangladesh; and sold in Detroit, Atlanta, and Los Angeles. Its stockholders may be in Mexico City as well as Saudi Arabia—in fact, anywhere.

Competing for International Business

Companies must compete for international sales to stay in business. Every business, whether large or small, has to appeal to diverse international markets to be competitive. Each year a larger share of the U.S. gross national product (GNP) depends on global markets. Some U.S. firms estimate that 50 to 60 percent of their business is conducted outside of the United States. Walmart, for example, has opened hundreds of stores in mainland China, and General Electric has plants in more than fifty countries. In fact, estimates suggest that 75 percent of the global Internet population lives outside the United States. If your company, however small, has a website, then it is an international business.

Communicating with Global Audiences

To be a successful employee in our highly competitive global market, you have to communicate clearly and diplomatically with a host of readers from different cultural backgrounds. Notice how the ad for Digital World Technologies emphasizes diversity (see Figure 1.1). Adopting a global perspective on business will help you communicate and build goodwill with the customers you write to, no matter where they live—across town, in another state, or on other continents, miles and time zones away.

   As a result, don't presume that you will be writing only to native speakers of American English. You may communicate with readers in Singapore, Jamaica, and South Africa, for example, who speak varieties of English quite different from American English. You will also very likely be writing to readers for whom English is not their first (or native) language. Your international readers will have varying degrees of proficiency in English, from a fairly good command (as with many readers in India and the Philippines, where English is widely spoken), to little comprehension without the use of a foreign language dictionary and a grammar book. Non-native speakers, who may reside either in the United States or in a foreign country, will constitute a large and important audience for your work.

Seeing the World Through the Eyes of Another Culture

Writing to international readers with proper business etiquette means first learning about their cultural values and assumptions—what they value and also what they regard as communication taboos. They may not conduct business exactly the way it is done in the United States, and to think they should is wrong. Your international audience is likely to have different expectations of:

- how they want communications addressed to them
- whether they allow you to use their first name

FIGURE 1.1 How a Company Appeals to a Global Audience

- how they wish a business meeting to be conducted
- how they think questions should be asked and agreements reached
- concepts of time, family, money, the world, and the environment; they may be nothing like those in the United States
- visuals, including icons; those easily understood in the United States may be baffling elsewhere in the world

If you misunderstand your audience's culture and inadvertently write, create, or say something inappropriate, it can cost your company a contract and you your job.

Cultural Diversity at Home

Cultural diversity exists inside as well as outside the company you work for. Don't conclude that your boss or co-workers are all native speakers of English, either, or

TECH NOTE

Know Your Computer at Work

A major part of any job is knowing your workplace technology, which now can include smartphones and tablets. You need to know not just how to use the applications installed on your computer or other device but also what to do if there is a computer emergency.

Given the kinds of security risks businesses face today, employees have to be especially careful. As Kim Becker cautions in *Nevada Business*, "With malware, spyware, adware, viruses, Trojans, worms, phishing, and server problems, it's time for every business to review its IT strategy and security before a loss occurs."*

Here are some guidelines on how to use your computer effectively on the job:

- **Understand how to use the software programs required for your job.** Your office will most likely require employees to use many different kinds of software—not just the word-processing application, but also the filing, formatting, spreadsheet, presentation, and tables/graphics programs. They will also expect you to be adept at using many different kinds of social media platforms, such as Facebook and Twitter.
- **Get training on how to use company-specific applications.** You will be expected to know how to use company-created databases, templates, and other customized applications on the job. If your company offers classes on how to use these programs, take them. Otherwise, ask for the advice of a co-worker or someone in your company's information technology (IT) department who knows the programs.
- **Learn how to back up your files.** You will save yourself, your boss, your co-workers, and your clients time and stress by backing up your essential files regularly.

*Kim Becker, "Security in the Workplace: Technology Issues Threaten Business Prosperity," *Nevada Business*, July 2008.

that they come from the same cultural background that you do. In the next decade, as much as 40 to 50 percent of the U.S. skilled workforce may be composed of international workers who bring their own traditions and languages with them. These are highly educated, multicultural, and multinational individuals who have acquired English as a second or even a third language.

For the common good of your company, you need to be respectful of your international colleagues. In fact, multinational employees can be tremendously important for your company in making contacts in their native country and in helping your firm understand and appreciate ethical and cultural differences among customers. The model long report in Chapter 15 (Figure 15.3, pages 607–621) describes ways a company can both acknowledge and respect the different cultural traditions of its international employees. Businesses want to emphasize their international commitments. A large corporation such as Citibank, for instance, is eager to promote its image of helping customers worldwide, as Figure 1.2 shows.

FIGURE 1.2 A Company's Dedication to Globalization

How Citigroup Meets Banking Needs Around the World

WITH A BANKING EMPIRE that spans more than 100 countries, Citigroup is experienced at meeting the diverse financial services needs of businesses, individuals, customers, and governments. The bank is headquartered in New York City but has offices in Africa, Asia, Central and South America, Europe, the Middle East, as well as throughout North America. Live or work in Japan? You can open a checking account at Citigroup's Citibank branch in downtown Tokyo. How about Mexico? Visit a Grupo Financiero Banamex-Accival branch, owned by Citigroup. Citigroup owns European American Bank and has even bought a stake in a Shanghai-based bank with an eye toward attracting more of China's $1 trillion in bank deposits. Between acquisitions and long-established branches, Citigroup covers the globe from the Atlantic to the Pacific and the Indian Oceans.

AP Photo/Greg Baker

Citigroup is active in communities around the world through . . . financial literacy seminars, volunteerism, and supplier diversity programs. This financial services giant strives for the best of both worlds, wielding its global presence and resources to meet banking needs locally, one customer at a time.

Source: From William M. Pride, Robert J. Hughes, and Jack R. Kapoor, *Business*, 8th ed. (Boston: Houghton Mifflin, 2005), 587.

Using International English

Whether your international readers are customers or colleagues, you need to adapt your writing to respect their language needs and cultural protocols. To communicate with non-native speakers, use "international English," a way of writing that is easily understood, culturally appropriate, and diplomatic. International English is user friendly in terms of the words, sentences, formats, and visuals you choose. The global use of social networking makes it essential that international English plays a role in effective communication.

To write international English means you re-examine your own writing. The words, idioms, phrases, and sentences you select instinctively for U.S. readers may not be appropriate for an audience for whom English is a second, or even a third, language. If you find the set of instructions accompanying your software package confusing, imagine how much more intimidating such a document would be for non-native speakers of English. You can eliminate such confusion by making your message clear, straightforward, and appropriately polite for readers who are not native speakers.

Here are some basic guidelines to help you write international English:

- Use clear, easy-to-understand sentences, not rambling, complex ones. That does not mean you write insultingly short and simple sentences but that you take into account that readers will find your message easier to translate if your sentences do not exceed 15 to 20 words.
- Do not try to pack too much information into a single sentence; consider using two or more sentences instead (see "Editing Guidelines for Writing Lean and Clear Sentences," pages 59–62)
- Avoid punctuation difficult to translate, for example, dashes, parentheses, and slashes meaning and/or.
- Avoid jargon, idioms (such as "to line one's pockets"), and abbreviations ("FEMA" instead of "Federal Emergency Management Agency") that international readers may not know.
- Do not use slang, acronyms, or cliches. And stay away from using compound verb phrases ("fill in", "file away") for simple active verbs.
- Choose clear, commonly used words that unambiguously translate into the non-native speaker's language. Avoid symbols such as an ampersand (&), Latin abbreviations (for example, "c.f.," "e.g.," and "i.e.") or flowery or pretentious language ("amend" instead of "change").
- Select visuals and icons that are free from cultural bias and that are not taboo in the non-native speaker's country. (For more on this, see "Using Appropriate Visuals for International Audiences," pages 438–441).
- When in doubt, consult someone from the native speaker's country — a co-worker or an instructor, for example.

Because it is so important, international English is discussed in greater detail in "International Business Correspondence" on pages 169–180. Later chapters of this book will also give you additional practical guidelines on writing correspondence, instructions, proposals, reports, websites, PowerPoint presentations, and other work-related documents suitable for a global audience.

FOUR KEYS TO EFFECTIVE WRITING

Effective writing on the job is carefully planned, thoroughly researched, and clearly presented. Its purpose is always to accomplish a specific goal and to be as persuasive as possible. Whether you send a routine email to a co-worker in Cincinnati or Shanghai or a commissioned report to the president of the company, your writing will be more effective if you ask yourself these four questions:

1. Who will read what I write? (Identify your audience.)
2. Why should they read what I write? (Establish your purpose.)
3. What do I have to say to them? (Formulate your message.)
4. How can I best communicate? (Select an appropriate style and tone.)

The questions *who, why, what,* and *how* do not function independently; they are all related. You write (1) for a specific audience (2) with a clearly defined purpose in mind (3) about a topic your readers need to understand (4) in language appropriate for the occasion. Once you answer the first question, you are off to a good start toward answering the other three. Now let's examine each of the four questions in detail.

Identifying Your Audience

Knowing *who* makes up your audience is one of your most important responsibilities as a writer. Keep in mind that you are not writing for yourself but for a specific reader or group of readers. Expect to analyze your audience throughout the composing process.

Look at the public safety messages in Figures 1.3, 1.4, and 1.5. The main purpose of all three messages is the same—to discourage people from smoking. The underlying message in each poster—smoking is dangerous to your health—is also the same. But note how the different details—words, photographs, situations—have been selected to appeal to three different audiences.

The poster in Figure 1.3 is aimed at fathers who smoke. As you can see, it shows an image of a father smoking next to his son, who is reaching for his pack of cigarettes. Note how the headline "Will your child follow in your footsteps?" plays on the fact that the father and son are both literally sitting on steps, but at the same time it implies that the son will imitate his father's behavior as a smoker. The statistic at the bottom of the advertisement reinforces both the headline and the image, hitting home the point that parental behavior strongly influences children's behavior. The child in the photograph already is following his father by showing a clear interest in smoking, picking up his father's pack of cigarettes.

The advertisement in Figure 1.4, however, is aimed at an audience of pregnant women and shows a new mother with a photo of her premature baby in an incubator. The headline addresses both the act of quitting smoking and smoking's effects on a newborn child. The headline, the photo of a mother unable hold her child, and

FIGURE 1.3 No-Smoking Advertisement Aimed at Fathers Who Smoke

Peter Poulides/Getty Images

FIGURE 1.4 No-Smoking Advertisement Directed at Pregnant Women

United States Department of Health and Human Services, Centers for Disease Control, Office on Smoking and Health's Health Communication Branch (OSH/HCB)

FIGURE 1.5 No-Smoking Advertisement Appealing to Young Athletes

United States Department of Health and Human Services, Centers for Disease Control, Office on Smoking and Health's Health Communication Branch (OSH/HCB)

the background information provided are designed to appeal to a mother's sense of responsibility and to encourage pregnant women to stop smoking to avoid harming their unborn children.

Figure 1.5 is directed toward another audience: young athletes. The appeal here is direct and to the point (no background or supplemental information is needed or provided, in contrast to the messages in Figures 1.3 and 1.4). It appeals to a young person's sense of being able to achieve two goals: (a) winning at soccer and (b) quitting smoking.

The copywriters who created these public service messages have chosen approriate details—words, pictures, captions, and so on—to persuade each audience not to smoke. With their careful choices, they successfully answered the question "How can we best communicate with each audience?" Note that details relevant for one audience (athletes, for example) could not be used as effectively for another audience (such as mothers).

The three posters in Figures 1.3, 1.4, and 1.5 illustrate some fundamental points you need to keep in mind when identifying your audience:

- Members of each audience differ in their backgrounds, experiences, and needs.
- How you picture your audience will determine what you say to them.
- Viewing something from the audience's perspective will help you to select the most relevant details for that audience.

Some Questions to Ask About Your Audience

You can form a fairly accurate picture of your audience by asking yourself key questions before you write. For each audience you need to reach, consider the following questions:

1. **Who is my audience?** What individual(s) will most likely be reading my work?

   If you are writing for colleagues or managers at work:

   - What is my reader's job title? Is he or she a co-worker? Immediate supervisor? Vice president?
   - What kinds of job experience, education, and interests does my reader have?

   If you are writing for clients or consumers (a very large, often diverse audience):

   - How can I find out about their interest in my product or service?
   - How much will this audience know about my company? About me?
   - Does my company have data or statistics that might help inform my writing? Can my company's social media sites provide any relevant information about the audience I'm writing for—what they like and what they tell others about my company and its products?

2. **How many people will make up my audience?**

   - Will just one individual read what I write (the nurse on the next shift, the production manager), or will many people read it (all the consumers of my company's product or service, those viewing my company's Facebook page or Twitter feed)?
   - Will my boss want to see my work (say, an email or social media post to a consumer in response to a complaint) to approve it?
   - Will I be sending my message to a large group of people sharing a similar interest in my topic?

3. **How well does my audience understand English?**

   - Are all my readers native speakers of English?
   - Will I be communicating with people around the globe?
   - Will some of my readers speak English as a second or even a third language and thereby require extra sensitivity on my part to their needs?
   - Will some of my readers speak no English and instead use an English grammar book, a foreign language dictionary, or perhaps an online translator, such as Google Translate (**translate.google.com**)?

4. **How much does my audience already know about my topic?**

   - Will my readers know as much as I do about the particular problem or issue, or will they need to be briefed, be given background information, or be updated?
   - Are my readers familiar with, and do they expect me to use, technical terms and descriptions, or will I have to provide definitions and easy-to-understand, nontechnical wording and visuals?

CASE STUDY

Writing to Different Audiences in a Large Corporation

Jan Melius works in the Communication Department of GrandCo, a firm that designs and produces large heavy-duty equipment. As a regular part of her job, Melius has to prepare documents for several different audiences, including the management and staff at GrandCo, current and potential customers, and the greater community of Fairfield where the company is located. Each group of her readers has different requirements and expectations, and she has to understand those differences if she wants to meet their needs. Often the documents that she prepares are a result of collaborations with individuals (accountants, engineers, safety and security) at GrandCo as well as at other companies (vendors) and community leaders. Melius also has to decide on the right type of document (e.g., email, memo, report, blog, social media post) to send to her readers.

Below is a list of the audiences that Melius writes for or to, along with the kinds of documents they need with examples of appropriate information found in these documents.

Audience	Types of Information/Documents to Supply
Customer	Ads, websites, proposals urging customers to buy a GrandCo model, stressing its state-of-the-art advantages over the competition's and the specific benefits GrandCo offers (cost, service, quality, efficiency)
Owner or Principal Executive	Short and long reports on sales, cash flow, productivity, market trends; research about potential competition
Production Engineer	Reports on design and manufacturing models, including spec sheets, diagrams, etc., on transmissions, strength of materials; status reports following Environmental Protection Agency (EPA) or Occupational Safety and Health Administration (OSHA) guidelines
Production Supervisor	Service reports about schedules, staffing needs, and employee activity reports; availability of parts from vendors
Operator	Instructions in manuals on operating equipment safely and responsibly; warnings about any type of precautions; information on necessary special training
Maintenance Worker	Reports and guidelines about maintenance procedures; schedules; checklists of items to be inspected; troubleshooting procedures
Community Residents	News releases about GrandCo's sponsoring events, offering tours or demonstrations; blogs and social media posts on how the company is greening the workplace; articles on GrandCo's dedication to community environment and safety; hiring notices

As these examples show, to succeed in the world of work, give each reader the details he or she needs to accomplish a given job.

5. **What is my audience's reason for reading my work?**

- Is my communication part of their routine duties, or are they looking for information to solve a problem or make a decision?
- Am I writing to describe benefits that another writer or company cannot offer?
- Will my readers expect complete details, or will a short summary be enough?
- Are they looking at my work to make an important decision affecting a co-worker, a client, a community, government agency, or the environment?
- Are they reading something I write because they must (a legal notification or an incident report, for instance)?

6. **What are my audience's expectations about my written work?**

- Do they want a response via social media, an email, or will they expect a formal letter?
- Will they expect me to follow a company format and style?
- Are they looking for a one-page memo or for a comprehensive report?
- Should I use a formal tone or a more relaxed and conversational style?

7. **What is my audience's attitude toward me and my work?**

- Will I be writing to a group of disgruntled and angry customers or vendors about a sensitive issue (a product recall, the discontinuation of a service, a refusal of credit, or a shipment delay)?
- Will I have to be sympathetic while at the same time give firm, convincing reasons for my company's (or my) decision?
- Will my readers be skeptical, indifferent, or accepting about what I write?
- Will my readers feel guilty that they have not answered an earlier message of mine, not paid a bill now overdue, or not kept a commitment?

8. **What do I want my audience to do after reading my work?**

- Do I want my readers to purchase something from me, approve my plan, or send me additional documentation?
- Do I expect my readers to acknowledge my message, save it for future reference, or review and email it to another individual or office?
- Do my readers have to take immediate action, or do they have several days or weeks to respond?
- Do I simply want my readers to get my message and not respond at all?

As your answers to these questions will show, you may have to communicate with many different audiences on your job. Each group of readers will have different expectations and requirements; you need to understand those audience differences if you want to supply relevant information.

Establishing Your Purpose

By knowing *why* you are writing, you will communicate better and find the writing process itself to be easier. The reader's needs and your goal in communicating will help you to formulate your purpose. It will guide you in determining exactly what you can and must say.

Make sure you follow the most important rule in occupational writing: *Get to the point right away*. At the beginning of your message, state your goal clearly. Don't feel as if you have to entertain or impress your reader.

> I want new employees to know how to log on to the company server.

Think over what you have written. Rewrite your purpose statement until it states precisely why you are writing and what you want your readers to do or to know.

> I want to teach new employees the security code for logging on to the company server.

Since your purpose controls the amount and order of information you include, state it clearly at the beginning of every email, memo, letter, and report.

> This email will acquaint new employees with the security measures they must take when logging on to the company server.

In the opening purpose statement that follows, note how the author clearly informs the reader what the report will and will not cover.

> As you requested at last month's organizational meeting, I have conducted a survey of how well our websites advertise our products. This survey describes users' responses but does not prioritize them.

Formulating Your Message

Your message is the sum of the facts, responses, and recommendations you put into writing. A message includes the scope and details of your communication.

- **Scope** refers to how much information you give readers about key details.
- **Details** are the key points you think readers need to know.

Some messages will consist of one or two phrases or sentences: "Do not touch; wet paint." "Order #756 was sent this afternoon by express shipment. It should arrive at your office on March 22." At the other extreme, messages may extend over many pages. Messages may carry good news or bad news. They may deal with routine matters, or they may handle changes in policy, special situations, or problems.

Keep in mind that you will need to adapt your message to fit your audience. For some audiences, such as engineers or technicians, you may have to supply a complete report with every detail noted or contained in an appendix. For other readers—busy executives, for example—include only an abstract or quick summary of financial or managerial significance. See Figure 8.10 (page 350) and Figure 15.3 (page 609) for examples of an abstract.

Selecting Your Style and Tone

Style

Style refers to *how* something is written rather than what is written. Style helps to determine how well you communicate with an audience and how well your readers understand and receive your message. It involves the choices you make about

- the construction of your paragraphs
- the length and patterns of your sentences
- your choice of words

You will have to adapt your style to take into account different messages, different purposes, and different audiences. Your words, for example, will certainly vary with your audience. If all your readers are specialists in your field, you may safely use the technical language and symbols of your profession. Nonspecialists, however, will be confused and annoyed if you write to them in the same way. The average consumer, for example, will not know what a potentiometer is; but if you write "volume control on a radio" instead, you will be using words that the general public can understand. And as we saw, when you write for an international audience you have to take into account their proficiency in English and choose your words and sentences with their needs in mind (see "Writing for the Global Marketplace," pages 5–11).

CASE STUDY

Adapting a Description of Heparin for Two Different Audiences

In the workplace you will often be faced with the problem of presenting the same information to two completely different audiences. To better understand the impact that style and tone can have when you have to solve this problem, read the following two descriptions of heparin, a medication used to prevent blood clots. In both descriptions, the message is basically the same. Yet because the audiences differ, so do the style and the tone.

The first description of heparin appears in a reference work for physicians and other health care providers and is written in a highly technical style with an impersonal tone appropriate for the contexts in which this medicine is discussed.

The writer has made the appropriate stylistic choices for the audience, the purpose, and the message. Health care providers understand and expect the jargon and the scientific explanations, which enable them to prescribe or administer heparin correctly. The writer's authoritative, impersonal tone is coldly clinical, which, of course, is also appropriate because the purpose is to convey the accurate, complete scientific facts about this medication, not the writer's or reader's personal opinions or beliefs. The writer sounds both knowledgeable and objective.

Technical Description

Heparin Sodium Injection, USP Sterile Solution

Description: Heparin Sodium Injection, USP is a sterile solution of heparin sodium derived from bovine lung tissue, standardized for anticoagulant activity.

Each ml of the 1,000 and 5,000 USP units per ml preparations contains heparin sodium 1,000 or 5,000 USP units; 9 mg sodium chloride; 9.45 mg benzyl alcohol added as preservative. Each ml of the 10,000 USP units per ml preparations contains heparin sodium 10,000 units; 9.45 mg benzyl alcohol added as a preservative.

When necessary, the pH of Heparin Sodium Injection, USP was adjusted with hydrochloric acid and/or sodium hydroxide. The pH range is 5.0–7.5.

Clinical pharmacology: Heparin inhibits reactions that lead to the clotting of blood and the formation of fibrin clots both *in vitro* and *in vivo*. Heparin acts at multiple sites in the normal coagulation system. Small amounts of heparin in combination with antithrombin III (heparin cofactor) can inhibit thrombosis by inactivating activated Factor X and inhibiting the conversion of prothrombin to thrombin.

Dosage and administration: Heparin sodium is not effective by oral administration and should be given by intermittent intravenous injection, intravenous infusion, or deep subcutaneous (intrafrat, i.e., above the iliac crest or abdominal fat layer) injection. **The intramuscular route of administration should be avoided because of the frequent occurrence of hematoma at the injection site.**[3]

The second description of heparin below, however, is written in a nontechnical style and with an informal, caring tone. This description is similar to those found on information sheets given to patients about the medications they are receiving in a hospital.

The writer of this patient-centered description has also made appropriate choices for nonspecialists, such as patients or their families, who do not need elaborate descriptions of the origin and composition of the medicine. Using familiar words and adopting a personal, friendly tone help to win the patients' confidence and enable them to understand why and how they should take the drug.

Nontechnical Description
Patient Information Sheet

Your doctor has prescribed a medicine called *heparin* for you. It will prevent any new blood clots from forming in your body. Since heparin cannot be absorbed from your stomach or intestines, you can not receive it in a capsule or tablet. Instead, it will be given into a vein or the fatty tissue of your abdomen. After several days, when the danger of clotting is past, your dosage of heparin will be gradually reduced. Then another medication you can take by mouth will be started.

Tone

Tone in writing, like tone of voice, expresses your attitude toward a topic and toward your audience. Your tone can range from formal and impersonal (a scientific report) to informal and personal (an email to a friend or a how-to article for consumers). Your tone can be unprofessionally sarcastic or diplomatically agreeable.

---

[3]*Source: Physicians' Desk Reference®* 45th edition, 1991, published by Medical Economics, Montvale, NJ 07645.

Tone, like style, is indicated in part by the words you choose. For example, saying that someone is "concerned about details" conveys a more positive tone than saying the person is a "nitpicker." The word *economical* is more positive than *stingy* or *cheap*.

The tone of your writing is especially important in occupational writing because it reflects the image you project to your readers and thus determines how they will respond to you, your work, and your company. Depending on your tone, you can appear sincere and intelligent or angry and uninformed. Of course, in all your written work, you need to sound professional and knowledgeable. The wrong tone in a letter or a proposal might cost you a customer. Sarcastic or hostile language will alienate you from your readers, as the letter in Figure 5.5 demonstrates (see page 165).

CHARACTERISTICS OF JOB-RELATED WRITING

Job-related writing characteristically serves six basic functions: (1) to provide practical information, (2) to give facts rather than impressions, (3) to supply visuals to clarify and condense information, (4) to give accurate measurements, (5) to state responsibilities precisely, and (6) to persuade and offer recommendations. These six functions tell you what kind of writing you will produce after you successfully answer the *who, why, what,* and *how.*

1. Providing Practical Information

On-the-job writing requires a practical "here's what you need to do or to know" approach. One such practical approach is **action oriented**. You instruct the reader to do something—assemble a ceiling fan, test for bacteria, perform an audit, or create a website. Another practical approach of job-related writing is **knowledge oriented**. You explain what you want the reader to understand—why a procedure was changed, what caused a problem or solved it, how much progress was made on a job site, or why a new piece of equipment should be purchased.

The following description of the Energy Efficiency Ratio combines both the action-oriented and knowledge-oriented approaches of practical writing.

> Whether you are buying window air-conditioning units or a central air-conditioning system, consider the performance factors and efficiency of the various units on the market. Before you buy, determine the Energy Efficiency Ratio (EER) of the units under consideration. The EER is found by dividing the BTUs (units of heat) that the unit removes from the area to be cooled by the watts (amount of electricity) the unit consumes. The result is usually a number between 5 and 12. The higher the number, the more efficiently the unit will use electricity.[4]

2. Giving Facts, Not Impressions

Occupational writing records what can be seen, heard, felt, tasted, or smelled. The writer uses **concrete language** and specific details. The emphasis is on facts rather than on the writer's feelings or guesses.

---

[4]*Source:* New Orleans Public Services, Inc.

The discussion below, addressed to a group of scientists about the sources of oil spills and their impact on the environment, is an example of writing with objectivity. It describes events and causes without anger or tears. Imagine how much emotion would have been packed into a paragraph by the residents of the coastal states who have watched massive spills come ashore.

> The most critical impact results from the escapement of oil into the ecosystem, both crude oil and refined fuel oils, the latter coming from sources such as marine traffic. Major oil spills occur as a result of accidents such as blowout, pipeline breakage, etc. Technological advances coupled with stringent regulations [can] reduce the chances of such major spills; however, there is [still] a chronic low-level discharge of oil associated with normal drilling and production operations. Waste oils discharged through the river systems and practices associated with tanker transports dump more significant quantities of oils into the ocean, compared to what is introduced by the offshore oil industry. All of this contributes to the chronic low-level discharge of oil into world oceans. The long-range cumulative effect of these discharges is possibly the most significant threat to the ecosystem.[5]

3. Supplying Visuals to Clarify and Condense Information

Visuals are indispensable partners of words in conveying information to your readers. On-the-job writing makes frequent use of visuals—such as tables, charts, photographs, infographs, flow charts, diagrams, and drawings—to clarify and condense information. Thanks to various software packages, you can easily create and insert visuals into your writing. Visuals are discussed in detail in Chapters 10 and 11, and PowerPoint and Prezi presentations are covered in Chapter 16.

Visuals play an important role in the workplace. Note how the photograph in Figure 1.6 can help employees to better understand and follow the accompanying written ergonomics guidelines. A visual like this, reproduced in an employee handbook or displayed on a website, can significantly reduce physical stress and increase a worker's productivity.

The following graphic devices in your letters, reports, and websites can also make your writing easier to read and follow:

- headings, such as "Four Keys to Effective Writing" or "Characteristics of Job-Related Writing"
- subheadings to divide major sections into parts, such as "Providing Practical Information" or "Giving Facts, Not Impressions"
- numbers within a paragraph, or even a line, such as (1) this, (2) this, and (3) also this
- different types of s p a c i n g
- CAPITALIZATION (use sparingly only when necessary)
- *italics* (easily made by a word processing command or indicated in typed copy by underscoring)
- **boldface** (darker print for emphasis)
- symbols (visual markers such as →)
- hypertext (Internet links, often presented underscored, in boldface, or in a different color)

---

[5]*Source:* The Offshore Ecology Investigation.

FIGURE 1.6 Use of a Visual to Convey Information

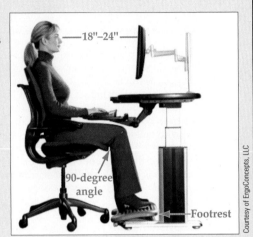

Using Your Computer Safely

By following the bulleted guidelines below, illustrated in the photo to the right, you can avoid workplace injuries when you are at your computer.

- To reduce the possibility of eye damage, make sure you stay 18 to 24 inches from the computer screen and always make sure your work area is well lit.

- To minimize neck strain, position your computer screen so that the top of the screen is at or just below your eye level.

- To avoid back and shoulder strain, sit up straight at a right angle in your chair with your shoulders relaxed and your lower back firmly supported (with a cushion, if necessary).

- To lessen leg and back strain, adjust your chair height so that your upper body and your legs form a 90-degree angle and that your feet are flat on the floor or on a footrest.

18"–24"

90-degree angle

Footrest

Courtesy of ErgoConcepts, LLC

© Cengage Learning

- asterisks (*) to separate items or to note key information
- lists with bullets (like those before each entry in this list)

Keep in mind that graphic devices should be used carefully and in moderation, not to decorate a letter or report. When used properly, they can help you to

- organize, arrange, and emphasize your ideas
- make your work easier to read and to recall
- preview and summarize your ideas, for example, through boldface headings
- list related items to help readers distinguish, follow, compare, and recall them—as this bulleted list does

4. Giving Accurate Measurements

Much of your work will depend on measurements—acres, bytes, calories, kilometers, centimeters, degrees, dollars and cents, grams, percentages, pounds, square feet, and so on. Numbers are clear and convincing. However, you must be sensitive to which units of measurement you use when writing to international readers. Not every culture computes in dollars or records temperatures in degrees Fahrenheit.

The following discussion of mixing colored cement for a basement floor would be useless to readers if it did not supply accurate quantities:

Including permanent color in a basement floor is a good selling point. One way of doing this is by incorporating commercially pure mineral pigments in a topping mixture placed to a 1-inch depth over a normal base slab. The topping mix should range in volume between 1 part portland cement, 1¼ parts sand, and 1¼ parts gravel or crushed stone and 1 part portland cement, 2 parts sand, and 2 parts gravel or crushed stone. Maximum size gravel or crushed stone should be ⅜ inch.

Mix cement and pigment before aggregate and water are added and be very thorough to secure uniform dispersion and the full color value of the pigment. The proportion varies from 5 to 10 percent of pigment by weight of cement, depending on the shade desired. If carbon black is used as a pigment to obtain grays or black, a proportion of from ½ to 1 percent will be adequate. Manufacturers' instructions should be followed closely; care in cleanliness, placing, and finishing are also essential. Colored topping mixes are available from some suppliers of ready mixed concrete.[6]

5. Stating Responsibilities Precisely

Your job-related writing should make it absolutely clear what you expect from, or can do for, a specific audience. Misunderstandings waste time, cost money, and can result in injuries. Directions on online order forms, for example, should indicate how and where information is to be listed and how it is to be routed and acted on. The following directions show readers how to perform different tasks:

- Enter agency code numbers in the message box.
- Items 1 through 16 of this form should be completed by the injured employee (or by someone acting on his or her behalf), whenever an injury is sustained on the job. The term *injury* includes occupational disease caused by the employment. The form should be given to the employee's official superior within one week following the injury. The official superior is that individual having responsible supervision over the employee.

Other kinds of job-related writing deal with the writer's responsibilities rather than the reader's, for example, "Tomorrow I will meet with the district sales manager to discuss (1) July's sales, (2) the opportunities of expanding our market, and (3) next fall's production schedule. I will send a PDF of our presentation by August 3."

6. Persuading and Offering Recommendations

Persuasion is a crucial part of writing on the job. In fact, it is one of the most valuable skills you need in the business world. Persuasion means trying to convince your reader(s) to accept your ideas, approve your recommendations, or order your products. Convincing your reader to accept your interpretation or ideas is at the heart of the world of work, whether you are writing to someone outside or inside your company.

Writing Persuasively to Clients and Customers

Much of your writing in the business world will promote your company's image by persuading customers and clients (a) to buy a product or service, (b) to adopt a plan of action endorsed by your employer, or (c) to support a particular cause or campaign that affects a community. You will have to convince readers that you (and your company)—your products, technologies, and services—can save them time and money,

---

[6]*Source: Concrete Construction Magazine,* World of Concrete Center, 426 S. Westgate, Addison, IL 60101.

increase efficiency, reduce risks, or improve their image and that you can do this better than your competitors can. Communicating effectively through social media sites, for example, can help a company persuade customers about a new product or policy.

Expect also to be called on to write convincingly about your company's image, as in the case of product recalls (see Figure 4.11, page 143), customer complaints (see Figure 4.12, page 146), or damage control after a corporate mistake affecting the environment. You may also have to convince international customers that your company respects cultural diversity and upholds specific ethnic values.

A large part of being a persuasive writer is supporting your claims with evidence. You will have to conduct research; provide logical arguments; supply appropriate facts, examples, and statistics; and identify the most relevant information for your particular audience(s). Notice how the advertisement in Figure 1.7 offers a bulleted list of persuasive reasons—based on cost, time, efficiency, safety, and convenience—to convince corrections officials that they should use General Medical's services rather than those of a hospital or clinic.

Writing Persuasively to In-House Personnel

As much as 70 percent of your writing may be directed to individuals you work with and for. In fact, your very first job-related writing will likely be a persuasive resume and letter to land an interview with a potential employer.

FIGURE 1.7 An Advertisement Employing Persuasive Arguments to Convince Potential Customers to Use a Service

General Medical Services Corp.
A subsidiary of

Federal Medical Industries, Inc. O.T.C.
950 S.W. 12th Avenue, 2nd Floor Suite, Pompano, Florida 33069
(305) 942-1111   FL WATS: 1-800-654-8282

GENERAL MEDICAL WILL STOP THE UNNECESSARY TRANSPORTING OF YOUR INMATES.

- We'll bring our X-ray services to your facility, 7 days a week, 24 hours a day.
- We can reduce your X-ray costs by a minimum of 28%. X-ray cost includes radiologist's interpretation and written report.
- Same-day service with immediate results telephoned to your facility.
- Save correctional officers' time, thereby saving your facility money.
- Avoid chance of prisoner's escape and possible danger to the public.
- Avoid long waits in overcrowded hospitals.
- Reduce your insurance liabilities.
- Other Services Available: Ultrasound, Two-Dimensional Echocardiogram, C.T. Scan, EKG, Blood Lab and Holter Monitor.

General Medical Is Your On-Site Medical Problem Solver

Visual stresses the need for a more efficient way to transport prisoners for medical attention

Bulleted list conveniently and persuasively uses factual data to convince

Encourages readers to use this service

© Cengage Learning

On the job, you may have to persuade a manager to buy a new technology or lobby for a change in your office or department. To be successful, you will have to evaluate various products or options by studying, analyzing, and deciding on the most relevant one(s) for your boss. Your reader will expect you to offer clear-cut, logical, and convincing reasons for your choice, backed up with persuasive facts.

As part of your job, too, you will be asked to write convincing memos, emails, letters, blogs, and websites to boost employee morale, encourage them to be more productive, and compliment them on a job well done.

Figure 1.8 is a persuasive email from an employee to a manager reporting a payroll mistake and persuading the reader to correct it. The email contains many of the other characteristics of job-related writing we have discussed. Note how the

FIGURE 1.8 A Persuasive Email from an Employee to a Business Manager

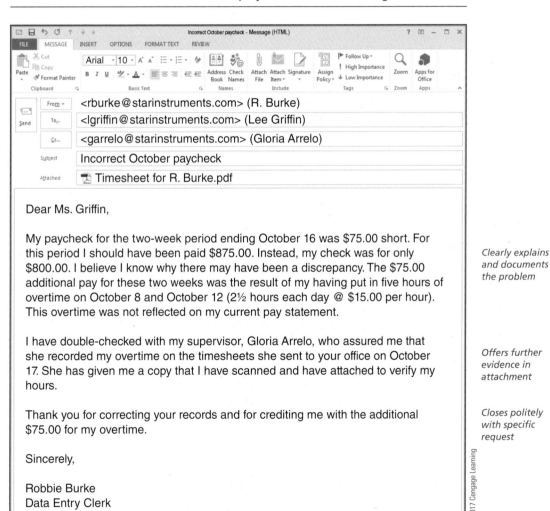

Dear Ms. Griffin,

My paycheck for the two-week period ending October 16 was $75.00 short. For this period I should have been paid $875.00. Instead, my check was for only $800.00. I believe I know why there may have been a discrepancy. The $75.00 additional pay for these two weeks was the result of my having put in five hours of overtime on October 8 and October 12 (2½ hours each day @ $15.00 per hour). This overtime was not reflected on my current pay statement.

Clearly explains and documents the problem

I have double-checked with my supervisor, Gloria Arrelo, who assured me that she recorded my overtime on the timesheets she sent to your office on October 17. She has given me a copy that I have scanned and have attached to verify my hours.

Offers further evidence in attachment

Thank you for correcting your records and for crediting me with the additional $75.00 for my overtime.

Closes politely with specific request

Sincerely,

Robbie Burke
Data Entry Clerk

© 2017 Cengage Learning

writer provides factual, not subjective, information; attaches a PDF of his timesheet (a type of visual); gives accurate details; and identifies her own and her immediate supervisor's responsibilities. The writer's tone is suitably polite yet direct.

ETHICAL WRITING IN THE WORKPLACE

One of your most important job responsibilities is to ensure that your writing and behavior are ethical. Writing ethically means choosing language that is right and fair, honest, and complete in all the documents you prepare for your employer, co-workers, customers, and vendors. Your reputation and character plus your employer's corporate image will depend on your following an ethical course of action. It takes a long time to build trust, and only a second to destroy it.

Many of the most significant phrases in the world of business reflect an ethical commitment to honesty and fairness: *accountability, public trust, equal opportunity employer, core values, global citizenship, good-faith effort, truth in lending, fair play, honest advertising, full disclosure, high professional standards, fair trade, community involvement,* and *corporate responsibility.*

Unethical business dealings, conversely, are stigmatized in *cover-ups, dodges, stonewalling, shady deals, spin-doctoring, foul play, bid rigging, employee raiding, misrepresentations, kickbacks, hostile takeovers, planned obsolescence, insider trading, price rigging,* and *unfair advantage.* Those are the activities that make customers angry and that local, state, and federal agencies may investigate.

Employers Insist on and Monitor Ethical Behavior

Ethical behavior is crucial to your success in the workplace. Your employer will insist that you are honest, adhere to professional standards, show integrity, and exhibit loyalty in your relationships with clients, co-workers, supervisors, and vendors. You will be expected to know, honor, and comply with your company policies and procedures, as outlined in the employee or agency handbook (see "Writing Procedures for Policies and Regulations," pages 510–513), and you will also have to follow your profession's codes, regulations, and methods.

On the job, employers can legally monitor their employees' work—electronically, through cameras, or by personal visits. Some of these visits are not announced (such as the "secret shoppers" who report on the customer service they receive). How many times have you made a call to an organization and heard, "This call may be monitored for quality assurance"? According to a survey conducted by the American Management Association, monitoring employees has risen 45 percent in the past few years and extends to their voicemail, email, social media, and other Internet uses.

Employers monitor the behavior of their employees for several reasons:

- to determine if a worker is doing his or her job properly
- to identify employee wrongdoing
- to make sure all calls are returned, emails answered, and information provided promptly and accurately

- to improve service, production, communication, or transportation
- to ensure compliance with federal, state, and municipal codes
- to limit company liability
- to adhere to and even strengthen security measures

Monitoring gives management solid facts about employee training, performance reviews, and evidence about promotions. But working with integrity means doing the right thing—even when no one is watching.

Ethical Requirements on the Job

In the workplace, you will be expected to meet the highest ethical standards by fulfilling the following eight requirements:

1. Be professionally competent. Know your job. Your company will expect you to be well prepared through your education, internships, experience, in-house training, continuing education units (CEUs), professional conferences, discussions with co-workers, and reading. You need to use equipment safely and efficiently, produce high-quality products, deliver up-to-date and accurate service, and represent your company as a knowledgeable professional. Adhere to your profession's code or standard of ethics, internal audits, licenses, and certificate requirements.

2. Be honest. Never misrepresent yourself on a résumé, at an interview, or on a networking site such as LinkedIn (see Figure 7.2, pages 246–249), by lying about your background, inflating a job title, or exaggerating your responsibilities at a previous job. The résumé and your portfolio/webfolio (see "Career Portfolio/Webfolio," pages 252–254) are two places where you must make ethical decisions about your qualifications for a job. At work, honesty is equally crucial. You need to acknowledge and correct all mistakes and make sure you submit complete, accurate, and truthful reports. Never falsify a document by padding an expense account, covering up a problem, taking a company vehicle or computer or smartphone for personal use, or wrongly accusing a co-worker. Inventing or falsifying information is fraud (the government website stopfraud.gov is dedicated to uncovering such false claims). In your dealings with customers, honor all guaranties and warranties and respond to customer requests promptly and fairly. Refuse to use language that makes false claims or tries to deceive readers with ambiguous words, jargon, or misleading statistics and visuals (see "Writing Ethically on the Job," pages 35–37 and "Using Visuals Ethically," pages 433–438). It would be neglectful and dishonest to allow an unsafe product to stay on the market just to spare your company the expense and embarrassment of a product recall.

3. Maintain confidentiality. You violate your employer's trust by telling others about your company's sensitive or confidential research, financial business, marketing strategies, sales records, personnel decisions, customer interactions, or by not properly disposing of company documents (via shredding or other secure and environmentally safe methods). Always keep in mind that nothing is confidential when posted on a social media site, so be careful. In fact, your employer may rightfully insist that you sign a binding confidentiality agreement when you are hired.

You also must respect an individual's right to privacy. For example, according to Health Insurance Portability and Accountability Act (HIPAA) guidelines, health care professionals are not allowed to share a patient's records with unauthorized individuals.

4. Be loyal. Follow your company's policies and procedures. Be faithful to its goals, mission, and image. Your employer has every right to expect you to be a team player striving for the good of the company; its products, service, and image; your department; and your co-workers. Cooperate fully, fairly, and on a timely basis with your collaborative team (see "Collaboration is Crucial to the Writing Process," pages 75–76, and "Ten Proven Ways to Be a Valuable Team Player," pages 80–81). Working secretly for a competitor or doing outside work that interferes with your normal duties is a clear conflict of interest (for instance, running a consulting business during office hours). Also, criticizing a boss, product, service, or event, or engaging in malicious gossip at work are examples of disloyalty that companies will not tolerate.

5. Follow the chain of command. You need to know and follow your company's or department's chain of command—for example, whom you report to, who gets copies of your written work and who does not, how work is to be submitted and routed, and whom you need to go to with problems. Always direct your correspondence to the appropriate person(s) in the company. Be careful not to speak on behalf of or about your company on social media or in interviews without first securing permission. To help you identify the proper chain of command at work, find or construct an organizational chart (see "Organizational Charts," pages 418–420).

6. Respect your employer, co-workers, customers, and suppliers. Avoid intimidation, bullying (see "Cyberbullying," pages 30–31), spreading rumors, discrimination, defamation, or any other unfair, unprofessional action that would harm someone or tarnish his or her reputation. It is unethical and illegal to use language that excludes others on the basis of gender, race, national origin, religion, age, physical ability, or sexual orientation (see "Editing Guidelines to Eliminate Sexist Language," pages 65–66). Never use racial slurs or obscene language.

7. Research and document your work carefully. Your boss will expect you to provide the hard evidence he or she needs. Study codes, specifications, agency handbooks, and websites. Keep up to date with professional literature found in trade journals, websites, and manuals in your field, confer with experts in your company, interview clients, make a site visit, conduct a survey, and so on. (See "Two Types of Research: Primary and Secondary," pages 306–307, for a description of the different types of research you will be expected to do on the job.) You are also ethically obligated to admit when you did not do the work by yourself. Respect all copyright obligations and privileges. Always give credit to your sources—whether print or Web sources or individuals whose discussions contributed to your work. Just because something is on the Internet or on social media does not mean you can paraphrase, copy, or republish it without crediting the source. Not documenting your sources makes you guilty of plagiarism (see "Documenting Sources," pages 337–347).

8. Maintain accurate and current records. Remember, "If it isn't written, it didn't happen." You have a responsibility to your employer to prepare and store documents, keep backup files, and submit your work by the deadline. Disregarding a deadline or not doing your **due diligence** (professional competence and due care) when appraising a business situation or assessing a legal requirement could jeopardize your group's effort or prevent your company from making an important sale, receiving a key permit, or getting a license or a government contract. Comply with all local, state, and federal regulations, especially those ensuring a safe, healthy work environment, products, and/or services, for example, following the Department of Labor guidelines for the number of hours an employee can work in a given day or week.

Online Ethics

Online ethics are essential in the world of e-commerce. A good rule to follow is never to do anything online that you wouldn't do offline. For instance, never use a company computer for any activity not directly related to your job. Moreover, it would be grossly unethical to erase a computer program intentionally, violate a software licensing agreement, or misrepresent (by fabrication or exaggeration) the scope of a database. Also, posting anything that attacks a competitor, a colleague, your boss, or your company is considered unethical. Follow the Ten Commandments of Computer Ethics prepared by the Computer Ethics Institute listed in Figure 1.9.

You are also ethically bound to protect your computer, tablet, or smartphone at work from security risks and possible system malfunctions. Never be afraid to ask for advice from a co-worker or someone in your firm's IT department who knows what to do if there is a computer emergency.

FIGURE 1.9 The Ten Commandments of Computer Ethics

1. Thou shalt not use a computer to harm other people.
2. Thou shalt not interfere with other people's computer work.
3. Thou shalt not snoop around in other people's computer files.
4. Thou shalt not use a computer to steal.
5. Thou shalt not use a computer to bear false witness.
6. Thou shalt not copy or use proprietary software for which you have not paid.
7. Thou shalt not use other people's computer resources without authorization or proper compensation.
8. Thou shalt not appropriate other people's intellectual output.
9. Thou shalt think about the social consequences of the program you are writing or the system you are designing.
10. Thou shalt always use a computer in ways that ensure consideration and respect for your fellow humans beings.

Source: Computer Ethics Institute, London.

Here are some other specific guidelines to follow when using your computer at work:

- Protect passwords that allow access to your company's documents as well as its proprietary databases, templates, and other customized applications. Do not share your password, and never use a password belonging to someone else.
- Always save sensitive emails, texts, social media postings, blogs, memos, letters, and so on, that you or your employer may need to document decisions.
- Protect your computer from viruses, spyware, and malware by making sure the most recent updates to your antivirus programs are installed on your computer. Report any viruses immediately to your IT department.
- Be especially careful in opening attachments or anything you suspect may be infected, such as spam. Never forward a document you think may have a virus.
- Do not use your work email account for personal emails (see "Guidelines for Using Email on the Job," pages 120–124). Instead, use an alternate email address (for example, Yahoo!, Gmail).

Cyberbullying

Cyberbullying is a term referring to one of the worst violations of online ethics (see pages 29–30). It refers to using the Internet, email, your cell phone, or social media (Facebook, Twitter, Instagram, etc.) to post harassing or threatening messages or embarrassing pictures or videos. Cyberbullying can also involve spreading gossip and rumors, posting sexually explicit photos, or attacking someone for age, race, gender, sexual orientation, religious practices, political affiliation, culture, or disabilities. Whether subtle or overtly offensive, cyberbullying is not tolerated in the workplace and can turn it into a battleground, demoralizing employees, thwarting group projects (see "Collaborative Writing and the Writing Process," pages 77–79), and can damage an employee's or a company's reputation. It is always smart to follow your employer's policies on social media; specific guidelines are often available through your HR department.

What You Can Do to Prevent Cyberbullying

There are several steps you can take to help prevent cyberbullying:

1. Be careful what you post on social media. Never give personal, confidential information thinking it will be harmless and read only by your friends. It can easily be leaked, forwarded, and can compromise your reputation and job.
2. Don't "add a friend" or communicate with people you don't know. Anybody can send Facebook friend requests or post comments.
3. Check your security settings on the social media site and make sure information you want "private" remains visible only to your intended audience.

What You Can Do if You Become a Target

1. Resist the temptation to lash back with an insulting, angry email, tweet, or posting. Remain calm and be professional. You do not want to jeopardize your position or reputation in the workplace.

2. If the bullying continues, gather evidence by downloading posts and screenshots; keep a record of when they were sent and how often.
3. Block any further messages from the bully.
4. Report the bully to your supervisor, your HR or IT department, and supply documentation of the offenses. If the bully is your superior at work, or someone you report to, communicate with your HR department. If possible, speak directly to the bully, explain why you do not welcome such posts, and insist that he/she stop sending them.
5. If the bully is someone outside your company, file a complaint with the social media site or cell phone provider. Every site has an option to do this. Your complaint will thereby be on record in case the bullying continues or escalates. If the bully stalks you or threatens you physically, file a report with your local police department.

"Thinking Green": Making Ethical Choices About the Environment

Be respectful of the environment—whether at the office, at a work site, in the community, or in the global marketplace. This means doing nothing to jeopardize the safety, ecology, economy, or quality of life of your community or the larger global world. Many companies are proud of their ethical commitments to the environment. Starbucks, for example, tells customers that its "10 percent post-consumer recycled . . . paper cups helped conserve enough energy to supply your homes for a year and save approximately 110,000 trees."

Like Starbucks, companies around the globe have adopted a green philosophy, encouraging their employees to avoid polluting the environment, save energy, and protect endangered species.

Note how in Figure 1.10 the Southern Company and its employees are proud of their ethical commitment to the environment, the community, and the country. The company projects an image of itself as being concerned about reducing pollution, preserving and protecting the environment, and ensuring a sustainable future.

You can "think green" in several ways. At your office, conserve energy by and reduce your company's carbon footprint by turning off all computers, copiers, and other machines when you leave work; replace incandescent lightbulbs with energy-efficient ones; recycle paper; copy and print your documents on both sides of paper; view documents on your computer screen instead of printing them; adjust thermostats when you are gone for the day or weekend, and car pool to and from work. You can also reduce toxic chemicals in the atmosphere by using soy-based ink, by inspecting vehicles regularly, and by maintaining them properly to reduce or eliminate pollution.

International Readers and Ethics

Communicating in the world of multinational corporations places additional ethical demands on you as a writer. You have to make sure that you respect the ethics of all of the countries where your firm does business. Some behaviors regarded as normal or routine in the United States might be seen as highly unethical elsewhere, and vice versa. In many countries, accepting a gift to initiate or conclude a business

FIGURE 1.10 A Company's Commitment to Ethical Responsibility

Our Environmental Responsibility

Emphasizes corporate commitment to ethical conduct

Southern Company is not only a leader in the energy market, but also a leader in protecting the environment. We believe our environmental initiatives and our strong compliance record will give us a competitive advantage.

The Southern Company's environmental policy spells out each company's commitment to protecting the environment. The first and foremost goal is to meet or exceed all regulatory requirements for domestic and international operations. To do that, we're using a combination of the best technologies and voluntary pollution-prevention programs. We also set aggressive environmental goals and make sure employees are aware of their individual environmental responsibilities. We are good citizens wherever we serve.

Links good business practices with good ethical behavior

As an affiliate of Southern Company, Mississippi Power's environmental issues are business issues. In addition to regulatory obligations, our employees carry out a most active grassroots environmental program. It's this employee involvement and strong environmental commitment that gives our commitment life and promises future generations a healthy environment.

Praises employees for their contributions to both the community and the company

For example, one employee's concern that motor oil is properly discarded led to the founding of a countrywide annual household hazardous waste collection program. Thousands of tons of waste have been collected, including jars of DDT, mercury, paint, batteries, pesticides, and other poisons.

Scores of employees participate in island, beach, and river cleanups throughout Mississippi Power's 23-county service area. More than 30 employees compiled "The Wolf River Environmental Monitoring Program."

Assures readers that corporate ethical behavior extends to the entire community

This report is the first-ever historical, biological assessment completed on the Wolf River by scientists and engineers. Employees volunteered countless hours to compile the statistical data. Today, Mississippi Power employees continue to support the Wolf River Project by producing photographs and slides as an educational and community awareness project.

Our commitment to the environment goes beyond our business. By sponsoring a variety of programs, we're helping to teach the public, students, and teachers about environmental responsibility.

Source: Reprinted by permission of Mississippi Power Company.

agreement is considered not only proper but also honorable. This is not the case in the United States where a "bribe" is seen as bad business or, worse, illegal. Moreover, you should be on your ethical guard not to take advantage of a host country, such as allowing or encouraging poor environmental control because regulatory and inspection procedures are not as strict as those of the United States, or by using pesticides or conducting experiments outlawed in the United States. It would also be unethical to conceal something risky about a product from international clients that you would disclose to U.S. customers.

Some Guidelines to Help You Reach Ethical Decisions

The workplace presents conflicts over who is right and who is wrong, what is best for the company and what is not, and whether a service or product should be changed and why. You will be asked to make a decision and justify it. While this chapter cannot cover all kinds of ethical problems, here are a few guidelines to help you respond ethically on the job.

1. Follow your conscience and "to thine own self be true." You cannot authorize something that you believe is wrong, dangerous, unfair, contradictory, or incomplete. But don't be hasty. Leave plenty of room for diplomacy and for careful questioning and researching. Don't blow a small matter out of proportion.

2. Be suspicious of convenient (and false) appeals that go against your beliefs. Watch out for red flags that anyone places in the way of your conscience: "No one will ever know." "We never had this conversation." "It's OK to cut corners every once in a while." "We got away with it last time." "Don't rock the boat." "No one's looking." "Don't put this down in writing." "As long as the company makes money, who cares?" These rationalizations are traps you must avoid.

3. Meet your obligations to your employer, your co-workers, your customers, and the global community. Keeping information from a co-worker who needs it, omitting a fact, slanting evidence, justifying unnecessary expenses, concealing something risky about a product or service from an international customer that you otherwise would disclose to a U.S. consumer—all of these are unethical acts.

4. Take responsibility for your actions. Saying "I do not know" when you do know can constitute a serious ethical violation. Keep your records up-to-date and accurate, sign and date your work, and never backdate a document to delete information or to fix an error that you made. Failing to test a set of instructions thoroughly, for example, might endanger readers in other countries.

5. Keep others in the loop. Confer regularly with your boss and collaborative writing team (see "Some Guidelines for Successful Group Writing," pages 79–80) and report to your boss as often as you are instructed to give progress reports and to alert him or her about problems. If you experience a problem at work, don't wait until it gets worse to tell your supervisor and/or co-workers. Prompt and honest notifications are essential to the safety, security, morale, progress, and success of a company. Also, never keep a co-worker, customer, or vendor waiting; call in advance if you are going to be delayed.

6. Treat company property respectfully. Use company supplies, networks/computers, equipment, technology, and vehicles responsibly and only for work-related business. Taking supplies home, using a company vehicle for non-business reasons, charging non–work-related expenses (meals, clothes, travel) on a company credit card, using company letterhead to solicit donations for a charity or political party, surfing the Internet when you are at work—these are just a few instances of unethical behavior.

7. Weigh all sides before you commit to a conclusion. Research what you write and communicate orally. Do your homework by conferring with co-workers, checking the history of a transaction or other corporate decision, and familiarizing yourself with company policies. Don't rely on office gossip or create problems where there are none. Give people the benefit of the doubt until you have hard evidence (for example, dates, costs, names, frequency, etc.) to the contrary.

Ethical Dilemmas: Some Scenarios

Sometimes in the workplace you will face situations where there is no clear-cut right or wrong choice. Here are a few scenarios, similar to ones in which you may find yourself, that are gray areas, ethically speaking, along with some possible solutions.

- You work with an office bully who often intimidates co-workers, including you, by talking down to them, interrupting them, or insulting them for their suggestions. At times, this bully has even sent sarcastic emails, texts, and tweets. You are upset that this behavior has not been reported to management. But you are concerned that if the bully finds out that you have reported the situation the entire office may suffer. How should you handle the problem?

  You cannot allow such rude, insulting behavior to go unreported. But first you need to provide documentation about where, when, and how often the bullying has occurred. You may want to speak directly to the bully, but if you feel uncomfortable doing this, go directly to your boss, report how the bully's actions have negatively affected the workplace, and ask for assistance. You may also get help from your company's employee assistance program or from someone in human resources. In accordance with state and federal laws, companies must provide a safe work environment, free from intimidation, harassment, or threats of dismissal for reporting bullying.

- You work very closely with an individual who takes frequent extended lunch breaks, often comes in late and leaves early, and even misses deadlines. Sometimes you cover for him when he is not at the office to answer questions. But your department is under minimal supervision from an off-site manager, so there is no boss looking over your colleague's shoulder. You like your co-worker and do not want him to be fired, but he is taking advantage of your friendship and unfairly expecting you to cover for him. What should you do?

  The best route is to take your co-worker aside and speak with him before informing management. Let him know you value working with him, but firmly explain that you no longer will cover for him or take on his workload. If he does not agree with you, let him know that you will be forced to discuss the problem with your manager. If the problem persists, and you go to your boss, bring documentation—dates, duties not performed, and so on—with you.

- You see an opening for a job in your area, but the employer wants someone with a minimum of two years of field experience. You have just completed

an internship and had one summer's experience, which together total almost seven months. Should you apply for the job, describing yourself as "experienced"?

Yes, but honestly state the type and the extent of your field experience and the conditions under which you obtained it.

- You work for a company that usually assigns commissions to the salesperson for whom the customer asks. One afternoon a customer asks for a salesperson who has the day off. You assist the customer all afternoon and even arrange to have an item shipped overnight so that she can have it in the morning. When you ring up the sale, should you list your employee number for the commission or the off-duty employee's?

  You probably should defer crediting the sale to either of you until you speak to the absent employee and suggest a compromise—splitting the commission, for instance.

- A piece of IT equipment, scheduled for delivery to your customer the next day, arrives with a damaged part. You decide to replace it at your store before the customer receives it. Should you inform the customer?

  Yes, but assure the customer that the equipment is still under the same warranty and that the replacement part is new and also under the same warranty. If the customer protests, agree to let him or her use the computer until a new unit arrives.

As these brief scenarios suggest, sometimes you have to make concessions and compromises to be ethical in the world of work (see "Collaboration is Crucial to the Writing Process," pages 75–76).

Writing Ethically on the Job

Ethical writing is clear, accurate, fair, and honest. These are among the most important goals of any workplace communication. Because ethics is such an important topic in writing for the business world, it will be emphasized throughout this book.

Your writing as well as your behavior must be ethical. Words, like actions, have implications and consequences. If you slant your words to conceal the truth or to gain an unfair advantage, you are not being ethical. False reporting and advertising are unethical. Bias and omission of facts are wrong. Strive to be fair, reliable, and accurate in reporting products, services, events, environmental issues, statistics, and trends.

Unethical writers are usually guilty of one or more of the following faults, which can conveniently be listed as the three *M*'s: misquotation, misrepresentation, and manipulation. Here are nine examples:

  1. Plagiarism is stealing someone else's words and ideas (or even the results of a study) and claiming them as your own without documenting the source. Do not think that by changing a few words of someone else's writing here and there you are not plagiarizing. Give proper credit to your source, whether in print, in person (through an interview), or online. The penalties for plagiarism are

severe—a reprimand or even the loss of your job. See "Documenting Sources," pages 337–347 for further advice on how to avoid plagiarism.

2. Selective misquoting deliberately omits damaging or unflattering comments to paint a better (but untruthful) picture of you or your company. By picking and choosing only a few words from a quotation, you unethically misrepresent what the speaker or writer originally intended.

Selective Misquotation: I've enjoyed . . . our firm's association with Advanced Computer Services, Inc. The quality of their service was . . . excellent.

Full Quotation: I've enjoyed at times our firm's association with Advanced Computer Services, Inc., although I was troubled by the uneven quality of their service. At times, it was excellent while at others it was far less so.

The spaced dots, called **ellipses**, unethically suggest that only extraneous or unimportant details were omitted.

3. Skewing numbers unethically misrepresents, by increasing or decreasing percentages or other numbers, statistical or other information. It is unethical to stretch the differences between competing plans or proposals to gain an unfair advantage or to express accurate figures in an inaccurate way.

Embellishment: An overwhelming majority of residents voted for the new plan.
Ethical: The new plan was passed by a vote of 53 to 49.
Embellishment: Our competitor's sales volume increased by only 10 percent in the preceding year, while ours doubled.
Ethical: Our competitor controls 90 percent of the market, yet we increased our share of that market from 5 to 10 percent last year.

4. Omitting key information, service, or location, or omitting articles, studies, or research that contradicts your ideas or challenges what you propose intentionally deprives readers of the facts they need to reach a decision.

Omitting Information: You will save thousands of dollars when buying the Model 2400T, the least expensive four-wheeler on the market.
Key Information Supplied: Although the model 2400T is the least expensive four-wheeler you can purchase, it is the most expensive to operate and to repair, making it the most costly four-wheeler to choose.

5. Manipulating information or context, which is closely related to the embellishment of numbers, is the misrepresentation of events, usually to put a good face on a bad situation. The writer here unethically uses slanted language and intentionally misleading euphemisms to misinterpret events for readers.

Manipulation: Looking ahead to 2018, the United Funds Group is exceptionally optimistic about its long-term prospects in an expanding global market. We are happy to report steady to moderate activity in an expanding sales environment last year. The United Funds Group seeks to build on sustaining investment opportunities beneficial to all subscribers.

Ethical: Looking ahead to 2018, the United Funds Group is optimistic about its long-term prospects in an expanding global market. Though the market suffered from inflation this year, the United Funds Group hopes to recoup its losses in the year ahead.

The writer who manipulates information minimizes the negative effects of inflation by calling it "an expanding sales environment."

6. Using fictitious benefits to promote a product or service seemingly promises customers advantages but delivers none. Saying a product is environmentally safe when that claim is unproven is unethical, as is neglecting to point out that results may vary greatly when advertising a weight-loss program or home care product.

False Benefit: Our bottled water is naturally hydrogenated from clear underground springs.
Truth: All water is hydrogenated because it contains hydrogen.
False Benefit: All our homes come with construction-grade fixtures.
Truth: Construction-grade fixtures are the least expensive and least durable a builder can use.

7. Exaggerating or minimizing hiring or firing conditions is unethical.

Unethical: One of the benefits of working for Spelco is the double pay you earn for overtime.
Truth: Overtime is assigned on the basis of seniority.
Unethical: Our corporate restructuring will create a more efficient and streamlined company, benefiting management and workers alike.
Truth: Downsizing has led to 150 layoffs this quarter.

Companies faced with laying off employees want to protect their corporate image and maintain their stockholders' good faith, so they often put the best face on such an action.

8. Misleading international readers by adopting a condescending view of their culture and economy is unethical.

Unethical: Since our product has appealed to U.S. customers for the last sixteen months, there's no doubt that it will be popular in your country as well.
Fair: Please let us know if any changes in product design or construction may be necessary for customers in your country.

9. Using a distorted or slanted visual is one of the most common types of unethical writing. Making a visual appear bigger, smaller, or more or less favorable is all too easy with graphics software. Printing warning or caution statements the same size and type font as ingredients or directions or enlarging advertising hype ("Double Your Money Back") is also unethical if major points are then reduced to small print. (See "Using Visuals Ethically," pages 433–438 in Chapter 10 for guidelines on how to prepare ethical visuals.)

SUCCESSFUL EMPLOYEES ARE SUCCESSFUL WRITERS

As this chapter has stressed, being a successful employee means being a successful writer at work. The following ten guidelines, which summarize the key points of this chapter, will help you to be both:

1. Know your job—assignments, roles, responsibilities, goals, what you need to write, and what you *shouldn't*.
2. Analyze your audience's needs and what they will expect to find in your writing.
3. Be a team player and be prepared to give and to receive feedback from co-workers, managers, vendors, government inspectors, and customers.
4. Work toward and meet all deadlines.
5. Be sensitive to the needs of a international audience.
6. Be sure your written work is accurate, relevant, and practical, and include culturally appropriate visuals to help readers understand your message.
7. Document, document, document. Submit everything you write with clear-cut evidence based on factual details and persuasive, logical interpretations.
8. Use your work-issued computer, tablet, or smartphone only for company business. Never share your password, and protect your computer from viruses.
9. Follow your company's policies, and be loyal to your company's or organization's image, culture, and traditions.
10. Be ethical in what you say, write, illustrate, and do.

✓ REVISION CHECKLIST

At the end of each chapter is a checklist you should review before you submit the final copy of your work, either to your instructor or to your boss. The checklists specify the types of research, planning, drafting, editing, and revising you should do to ensure the success of your work. Regard each checklist as a summary of the main ideas in the chapter as well as a handy guide to quality control. You may find it helpful to check each box as you verify that you have performed the necessary revision and review. Effective writers are also careful editors.

- ☐ Showed respect for and appropriately shaped my message for a global audience.
- ☐ Identified my audience—background, knowledge of English, reason for reading my work, and likely response to my work and me.
- ☐ Tailored my message to my audience's needs and background, giving them neither too little nor too much information.
- ☐ Pushed to the main point right away; did not waste my readers' time.
- ☐ Selected the most appropriate language, technical level, tone, and level of formality.
- ☐ Did not waste my readers' time with unsupported generalizations or opinions; instead gave them accurate measurements, facts, and carefully researched material.

☐ Selected appropriate visuals to make my work easier for my audience to understand and follow.

☐ Used persuasive reasons and data to convince my readers to accept my plan or work.

☐ Ensured that my writing and visuals are ethical—accurate, fair, honest, a true reflection of the situation or condition I am explaining or describing, for U.S. as well as global audiences.

☐ Followed the Ten Commandments of Computer Ethics.

☐ Adhered to the ethical codes of my profession as well as the policies and regulations set down by my employer.

☐ Gave full and complete credit to any sources I used, including resource people.

☐ Avoided plagiarism and unfair or dishonest use of copyrighted materials, both written and visual, including all electronic media.

EXERCISES

1. Write a memo (see "Memos," pages 220–227 for format) addressed to a prospective supervisor to introduce yourself. Your memo should have four headings: **Education**—including goals and accomplishments; **Job Information**—where you have worked and your responsibilities; **Community Service**—volunteer work, church work, youth groups; and **Writing Experience**—your strengths and weaknesses as a writer, the types of writing you have done, your knowledge of and experience in writing e-communications, and the audiences for whom you have written.

2. Bring to class a set of printed instructions, a memo, a sales letter, a brochure, or the printout of a company's or organization's home page. Comment on how well the example answers the following questions:

   a. Who is the audience?
   b. Why was the material written?
   c. What is the message?
   d. Are the style and tone appropriate for the audience, the purpose, and the message? Explain.
   e. Discuss the use of any visuals and color in the document. For instance, how does color (or the lack of it) affect an audience's response to the message?

3. Find an advertisement in a print source or online that contains a drawing or photograph. Bring the ad to class along with a paragraph of your own (75–100 words) describing how the message of the ad is directed to a particular audience and commenting on how the drawing or photo is appropriate for that audience.

4. Select one of the following topics, and write two descriptions of it. In the first description, use technical details and vocabulary. In the second, use language and details suitable for the general public.

   a. iPad
   b. blood pressure cuff
   c. flash drive
   d. energy drinks

e. Bluetooth headset
f. legal contract
g. electric sander
h. firewalls
i. muscle
j. protein
k. smartphone
l. cloud computing
m. bread
n. money

o. all-in-one printer
p. soap
q. blogging
r. computer virus
s. Ebola
t. thermostat
u. trees
v. mobile app
w. earthquake
x. recycling

5. Select another topic from Exercise 4, and write two more descriptions as a collaborative writing project.

6. Select one article from an online newspaper and one article from a professional, trade, e- or print journal in your major field or from one of the following journals: *Advertising Age, American Journal of Nursing, Business Marketing, Bloomberg Businessweek, Computer, Computer Design, Construction Equipment, Criminal Justice Review, E-Commerce, Food Service Marketing, Journal of Forestry, Journal of Soil and Water Conservation, National Safety News, Nutrition Action, Park Maintenance, Scientific American.* State how the two articles you selected differ in terms of audience, purpose, message, style, and tone.

7. Assume that you work for Appliance Rentals, Inc., a company that rents TVs, microwave ovens, stereo components, and the like. Write a persuasive letter to the members of a campus organization or civic club urging them to rent an appropriate appliance or appliances. Include details in your letter that might have special relevance to members of this specific organization.

8. Read the article, "The Mouse That Knows You" (see below), and identify its audience (technical or general), purpose, message, style, and tone.

The Mouse That Knows You: A device that recognizes your grip highlights Raytheon's cyber innovation

The idea dawned on Glenn Kaufman one day in the lab. His computer was running a pattern-recognition biometrics program—a piece of software that measured how hard and fast he typed, then used it like a fingerprint to confirm his identity the next time he logged on.

Amid the clicking and clacking of keys, he remembered seeing something on the news about "smart guns" that know their owner's grip and won't fire for anybody else. He got to thinking: If that sort of thing works on computer keyboards and guns, it must work on other things too.

"I thought that maybe if there was a pattern to gripping a gun grip, maybe there was a pattern to gripping a mouse," he said.

Kaufman, a Raytheon cybersecurity engineer, got to work. Four years later, he was awarded U.S. Patent No. 8,762,734 for the "Biometric Pressure Grip" — a sensor that measures how hard and how tightly someone holds a mouse, then uses that information as part of a multi-step login process.

Kaufman's invention is among hundreds of innovations company engineers are developing as Raytheon's cybersecurity business surges in an age of larger and increasingly destructive computer-system breaches.

A culture of creation

"Raytheon is a technology leader across all aspects of the cyber domain," said Jeff Snyder, vice president of Raytheon's cyber programs. "If we see a gap that we have in cyber technology, we will either invest internally to develop it . . . or we'll find the right partner. And our leadership believes in this technology area as it is so critical to protect our products, Raytheon's infrastructure, and our important cyber clients."

Major Raytheon cybersecurity innovations include:

SureView — Software that guards against "insider threats" or abuses of computer systems by people authorized to access them. The system alerts IT security to warning signs – such as employees downloading files at unusual times — and also provides a detailed, video-quality recording of computer users' activity.

Advanced Threat Protection (formerly RShield) — An advanced malware detection system that, for example, segregates incoming emails and downloads, putting them through a battery of tests to root out any malicious code. Raytheon announced at the 2014 Black Hat cybersecurity conference in Las Vegas that it is developing a major upgrade to the system.

High Speed Guard — Software that provides fast, secure and automated transfer of complex data such as video between multiple classified networks. High Speed Guard has been shown to transfer data at rates of more than nine gigabits per second.

Net Maneuver Commander — A "moving target" system that protects a network by constantly rearranging it through the use of randomization algorithms. The technique keeps weak spots on the move, forcing hackers to relearn the entire system and rebuild their malware every time the system redraws the network.

Kaufman's mouse is not yet part of any specific security system. But inventions like his could have potential as part of a "layered" security system that uses a security token and a password or a passphrase.

Kaufman's research showed a person's mouse grip is a surprisingly effective biometric identifier. It turns out only about one in 10,000 people place their fingers in exactly the same spot and exert precisely the same amount of pressure.

"It's not only a reliable identifier, but it's also harder to defeat," Kaufman said. "I can defeat fingerprints, because I can take it from something else like a glass . . . once I've done that, all I have to do is override the system by using a mockup of your fingerprint. Because this is a pattern-recognition biometric, it's harder to defeat."

Inventions like Kaufman's smart mouse show Raytheon engineers are gearing up to meet the growing demands of cybersecurity, Snyder said. Private companies such as retailers and utility providers are realizing they need military-style protection for their data and networks, and Snyder said building that protection — assessing a client's needs, designing a system and monitoring it around the clock — is something Raytheon already does for government agencies.

"That continuum, that delivery continuum, applies in the federal and commercial marketplace exactly the same," he said. "No different—it's all the same."

Source: Raytheon Company/870 Winter Street, Waltham, MA 02451

9. How do the visuals and the text of the Digital World Technologies advertisement in Figure 1.1 on page 7 stress to current (and potential) employees, customers, and stockholders that the company is committed to diversity in the workplace? Also explain how the ad illustrates the functions of on-the-job writing as defined on pages 20–26 ("Characteristics of Job-Related Writing").

10. Write an email or a social media post to a cell phone provider that has mistakenly billed you for a data plan that you never ordered, received, or needed.

11. The following statements contain embellishments, selected misquotations, false benefits, omitted key information, and other types of unethical tactics. Revise each statement to eliminate the unethical aspects. Make up details as needed.

    a. Storm damage done to water filtration plant #3 was minimal. While we had to shut down temporarily, service resumed to meet residents' needs.
    b. All customers qualify for the maximum discount available.
    c. "The service contract . . . on the whole . . . applied to upgrades."
    d. We followed the protocols precisely with test results yielding further opportunities for experimentation.
    e. All our costs were within fair-use guidelines.
    f. Customers' complaints have been held to a minimum.
    g. All the lots we are selling offer relatively easy access to the lake.
    h. Factory-trained technicians respond to all our calls.

12. You work for a large international company, and a co-worker tells you that he has no plans to return to his job after he takes his annual two-week vacation. You know that your department cannot meet its deadlines shorthanded and that your department will need at least two or three weeks to recruit and hire a qualified replacement. You also know that it is your company's policy not to give paid vacations to employees who do not agree to work for at least three months following their return. What should you do? What points would you make in a confidential email to your boss? What points would you raise to your co-worker?

13. Your company is regulated and inspected by the Environmental Protection Agency (EPA). In 90 days, the EPA will relax a regulation about dumping occupational waste. Your company's management is considering cutting costs by relaxing the standard now, before the new, less demanding regulation is in place. You know that the EPA inspector probably will not return before the 90-day period elapses. What do you recommend to management?

14. You and your co-workers have been intimidated by an office bully, a twelve-year employee who has seniority. As a collaborative writing project (see "Collaboration is Crucial to the Writing Process," pages 75–76), draft a letter to the head of your human resources department documenting instances of the bully's actions and asking for advice on how to proceed.

15. Write a memo to your boss about being passed over for promotion. Diplomatically and ethically compare your work with that of the individual who did receive the promotion.

16. Write a 50- to 200-word email to your boss about one of the following unethical activities you have witnessed in your workplace. Your email must be carefully documented, fair, and persuasive—in short, ethical.

a. cyberbullying

b. surfing pornography websites

c. using workplace technology for personal matters (shopping, dating, buying stocks)

d. falsifying compensatory or travel time

e. telling sexist, off-color jokes

f. concealing the use of company funds for personal gifts for fellow employees

g. misdating or backdating company records

h. sharing privileged information with individuals outside your department or company

i. fudging the number of hours worked

j. lying about family illnesses

k. exaggerating a workplace-related injury

l. not reporting a second job to avoid scheduled weekend work

m. misrepresenting, by minimizing, a client's complaint

fotog/Tetra/Corbis

The Writing Process at Work

In Chapter 1, you learned about the different functions of writing for the world of work and also explored some basic concepts all writers must master. To be a successful writer, you need to

- identify your audience's needs
- determine your purpose in writing to that audience
- make sure your message meets your audience's needs
- use the most appropriate style and tone for your message
- format your work so that it clearly reflects your message to your audience

Just as significant to your success is knowing how effective writers actually create their work for their audiences. This chapter gives you practical information about the strategies and techniques careful writers use when they work. These procedures are a vital part of what is known as the **writing process**. This process involves such matters as how writers gather information, how they transform their ideas into written form, and how they organize and revise what they have written to make it relevant for their audiences.

WHAT WRITING IS AND IS NOT

As you begin your study of writing for the world of work, it might be helpful to identify some notions about what writing is and what it is not.

What Writing Is

- **The writing process is dynamic; it is not static.** It enables you to discover and evaluate your thoughts as you draft and revise.
- **A piece of writing changes as your thoughts and information change and as your view of the material changes.**

- **Writing takes time.** Some people think that revising and polishing are too time consuming. But poor writing actually takes more time and costs more money in the end. It can lead to misunderstandings, lost sales, product recalls, and even damage to your reputation and that of your company.
- **Writing means making a number of judgment calls.**
- **Writing grows sometimes in bits and pieces and sometimes in great spurts.** It needs many revisions; an early draft is never a final copy.

What Writing Is Not

- **Writing is not a mysterious process, known only to a few.** Even if you have not done much writing before, you can learn to do it effectively.
- **Writing is not simply following a magical formula.** Successful writing requires hard work and thoughtful effort, not simply following a formula, as if you were painting by numbers. Writing does not proceed in some predictable way, in which introductions are always written first and conclusions last.
- **Writing is not completed in a first attempt.** Just because you put something down on paper or on a computer screen does not mean it is unchangeable. Writing means *re*writing, *re*vising, and *re*thinking. The better a piece of writing is, the more the writer has reworked it.

THE WRITING PROCESS

The writing process we have just discussed is something fluid, not static. Think of it as a back and forth process rather than following a formula—do this, then do that. To move from a blank sheet of paper or computer screen to a successful piece of writing, you need to follow a process. The parts of that process include researching, planning, drafting, revising, and editing.

RESEARCHING

Before you start to compose any email, memo, letter, report, proposal, or website, you'll need to do research. Research is crucial because it enables you to obtain the right information for your audience. The world of work is based on conveying correct and relevant information—the logical presentation and sensible interpretation of facts. Chapter 8 will introduce you to the variety of research strategies and tools you can expect to use in the world of work.

Don't ever think you are wasting time by doing some research before starting to write any document. Actually, you will waste more time and risk doing a poor job if you do not find out as much as possible about your topic (and your audience's interest in it). Find out about your readers' needs and how to meet them.

Then you can determine the kind of research you must do to gather and interpret the information your audience needs. Depending on the length and scope of your written work and on your audience's needs, your research may include

- interviewing people inside and outside your company
- reviewing similar or related company documents
- consulting notes from conferences or meetings
- collaborating in person, by email, or by messaging
- doing Internet searches
- locating and evaluating websites and social media posts
- reading current periodicals, trade journals, reports, and other documents
- evaluating reports, products, and services
- conferring with co-workers, customers, or vendors
- surveying customers' views
- visiting a work site

Keep in mind that research is not confined to just the beginning of the writing process; it is an ongoing process.

PLANNING

At this stage in the writing process your goal is to get something—anything—down on paper or on your computer screen. For most writers, getting started is the hardest part of the job. But you will feel more comfortable and confident once you begin to see your ideas written down before your eyes. It is always easier to clarify and criticize something you can see.

Getting started is also easier if you have researched your topic, because you have something concrete to say and to build on. Each part of the process relates to and supports the next. Careful research prepares you to begin writing.

Still, getting started is not easy. Take advantage of a number of widely used strategies that can help you to develop, organize, and tailor the right information for your audience. Use any one of the following techniques, alone or in combination.

1. **Clustering**. In the middle of a sheet of paper, write the word or phrase that best describes your topic, and then start writing other words or phrases that come to mind. (It is also possible to do this on your computer screen using a "mind mapping" software program such as FreeMind, XMind, or iMindMap to create clusters.) As you write, circle each word or phrase and connect it to the word from which it sprang. Note the clustered grouping in Figure 2.1 (page 47) for a report encouraging a manager to switch to flextime—a system in which employees can work on a flexible time schedule within certain limits. The resulting graphic gives the writer a rough sense of some of the major divisions of the topic and where they may belong in the report.

2. **Brainstorming**. At the top of a sheet of paper or your computer screen, describe your topic in a word or phrase and then list any information you know or

FIGURE 2.1 Clustering of Ideas to Prepare a Report on Flextime

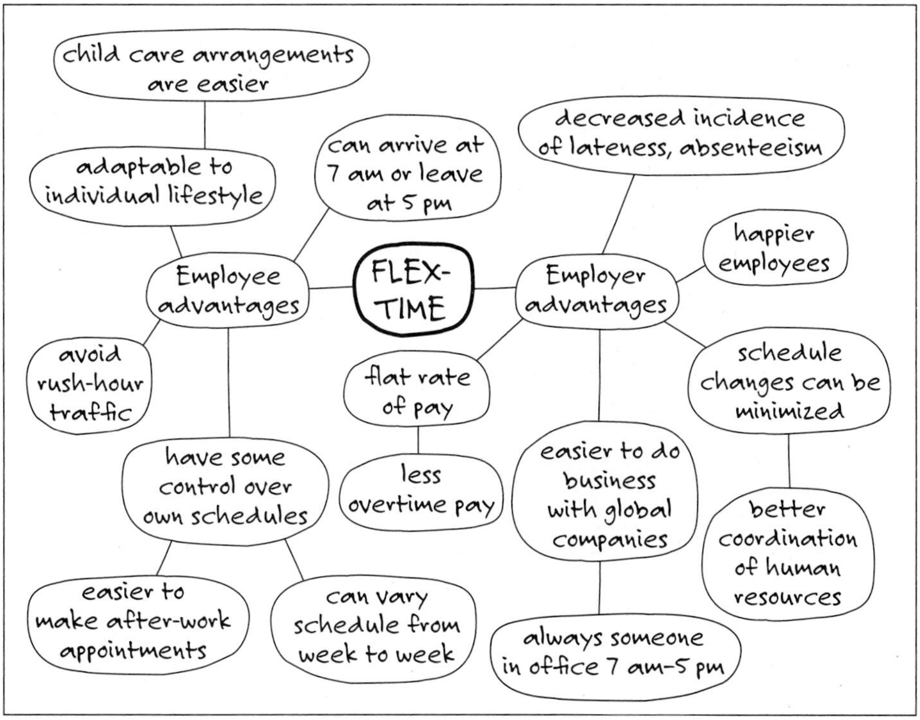

© Cengage Learning

found out about that topic—in any order and as quickly as you can. Brainstorming is like thinking aloud except that you are recording your thoughts.

- Don't stop to delete, rearrange, or rewrite anything, and don't dwell on any one item.
- Don't worry about spelling, punctuation, grammar, or whether you are using words and phrases instead of complete sentences at this point.
- Keep the ideas flowing. The result may well be an odd assortment of details, comments, and opinions.
- After stepping away from the list for a few minutes (or hours) and returning with fresh eyes, expect to add and delete some ideas or combine or rearrange others as you start to develop your topic in more detail.

Figure 2.2 (page 48) shows Marcus Weekley's initial brainstormed list for a report to his boss on purchasing a new color laser all-in-one printer. After he began to revise it, he realized that some items were not relevant for his audience (6, 8, and 13). He also recognized that some items were repetitious (1, 2, and 11). Further investigation revealed that his company could purchase a printer for far less than his initial high guess (17). As Weekley continued to work on his list and the overall topic became clearer to him, he added and deleted points.

FIGURE 2.2 Marcus Weekley's Initial, Unrevised Brainstormed List

List is not organized but simply records writer's initial ideas about possible topics

1. combines four separate pieces of equip—printer, copier, fax, and scanner

2. more comprehensive than our current configuration of four pieces of equip

3. would coordinate with office furniture

4. energy efficiency increased due to fewer machines being used

5. more scalable fonts

1, 2, and 11 are repetitious

6. one machine interfaces with all others in same-case housing

7. scanner makes photographic-quality pictures

6, 8, and 13 are not relevant for audience or purpose

8. print capabilities are a real contribution to technology

9. increased communication abilities through fax machine

10. new scanner picture quality better than current scanner

11. only have to buy one machine as opposed to four

4, 9, 12, and 14 are of special interest to decision makers concerned about costs

12. speed of fax allows quick response time

13. stock is doing better on Wall Street compared to other equities

14. reducing our advertising costs through use of color printer

15. increased work area available

16. would help us do our work better

Research will show cost estimate is too high

17. top-of-line models can be bought for $4,500

© Cengage Learning

3. Outlining. This process may be the easiest and most comfortable way to begin or to continue planning a report or letter. Outlines can go through stages, so don't worry if your first attempt is brief and messy. It does not have to be formal (with lots of Roman and Arabic numerals), complete, or pretty. It is intended for no one's eyes but yours. Use your preliminary outline as a quick way to sketch in some ideas, a convenient container into which you can put information. You might simply jot down a few major points and identify a few subpoints. Note how Weekley organized his revised brainstormed list into an outline seen below in Figure 2.3.

FIGURE 2.3 Marcus Weekley's Early Outline After Revising His Brainstormed List

I. Convenience/capabilities of all-in-one laser printer

    A. Would reduce number of machines having to be serviced

    B. Can be configured easily for our network system

    C. Easy to install and to operate

    D. 33.6 Kbps fax machine would increase our communication

    E. 2,400 × 1,200 dpi copier means better copy quality

    F. 4,800 × 4,800 dpi scanner means higher quality pictures than current scanner provides

Outline form helps writer group ideas/ topics and go to next step in the process

II. Time/efficiency

    A. 40 ppm color printer is nearly twice as fast as current printer

    B. 33.6 Kbps fax allows quick response time

    C. Greater graphics capability—130 scalable fonts

    D. Scanner compatible with our current PhotoEdit imaging/graphics software

    E. 100,000-page monthly duty cycle means less maintenance

Headings correspond to major sections of report

III. Money

    A. Costs less overall for multitasking printer than combined four machines

    B. Reduced monthly power bill by using one machine rather than four

    C. Wi-fi capability means no need to buy new software to network office computers

    D. Save on service costs

    E. Reduced advertising costs through printer's 50–400% enlargement/ reduction options, which allow for more in-house advertising

Outline reflects scope and details of writer's research

Last section of outline also functions as a conclusion

DRAFTING

If you have planned carefully, it will be easier to start your first draft. When you draft, you convert the words and phrases from your outline, brainstormed list, or clustered grouping into paragraphs. During drafting, as elsewhere in the writing process, you will see some overlap as you look back over your list or outline to shape your text.

Don't expect to wind up with a polished, complete version of your letter or report after working on only one draft. In most cases, you will have to work through many drafts, but each draft should be less rough and more focused than the preceding one.

Key Questions to Ask as You Draft

As you work on your drafts, ask yourself the following questions about your content and organization:

- Am I giving my readers too much or too little information?
- Do I need to do more research—where and why?
- Should I confer further with my boss or co-workers?
- Does this point belong where I have it, or would it more logically follow or precede something else?
- Is this point necessary and relevant?
- Am I repeating or contradicting myself?
- Have I ended appropriately for my audience?

To answer the questions successfully, you may have to continue researching your topic and reexamining your audience's needs. But, in the process, new and even better ideas may come to you, and the ideas you originally thought were essential may in time appear to be unworkable and unnecessary.

Guidelines for Successful Drafting

Following are some suggestions to help your drafting go more smoothly and efficiently.

- In an early draft, write the easiest part first. Some writers feel more comfortable drafting the body (or middle) of their work first. See the differences between the short report in Figures 2.6 and 2.7 (pages 57–58).
- As you work on a later draft, write straight through. Do not worry about spelling, punctuation, or the way a word or sentence sounds. Save those concerns for later stages.
- Allow enough time between drafts so that you can evaluate your work with fresh eyes and a clear mind.
- Get frequent outside opinions. Show or email a draft to a co-worker or a supervisor for comment. A new pair of eyes will see things you missed. As we'll see, collaboration is essential in the workplace (see "Collaboration Is Crucial to the Writing Process," pages 75–76).

TECH NOTE

Drafting

Here are a few tips to make the process go more smoothly when you draft your document, no matter what device you use (a computer, a tablet, a smartphone, etc.):

- Get your thoughts down on the screen as quickly as possible, without stopping to worry about spelling, punctuation, or spacing. If you stop to correct these small errors, you may forget to write down larger points.
- Save your document regularly (every few minutes) so that you do not lose valuable work and time in the event of a power outage or computer malfunction. Back up your document at the end of each day.
- If you run into trouble completing a point or writing a transition, or if you know you will need to add documentation later, do not lose momentum by stopping. Instead, add notes to yourself (in parentheses, in italics, or in a different color) reminding you to "add transition," "back up this point," "clarify," "check with boss," or "add documentation."
- Use the Save As option to save each draft of your document. That way, you will be able to salvage versions of sentences or paragraphs from one draft and incorporate them into another. Give each draft a clear title, such as "Office Equipment, 3rd draft," so you can tell at a glance which version is which.
- If you intend to share your document with others for collaborative editing, use cloud computing tools like Google Docs (see Figure 3.10, page 101) or Adobe Buzzword to create your draft. These applications will allow you to save a complete revision history of your document, add comments and notes to your work, share your work with others for their review, and create presentation-ready documents.

- Consider whether visuals would enhance the quality of your work and, if so, decide on what types and where best to insert them.

Figure 2.4 (page 52) shows one of the several drafts that Marcus Weekley prepared. Because he wisely recognized that his outline was not final, he continued to work on it during the drafting stage. Note that he added an introduction and a conclusion, which were not part of his original outline (Figure 2.3), to convince Melissa Hill to purchase a new all-in-one laser printer. Even so, Weekley recognized that this draft was still not ready for his boss to see, so he showed it to co-workers for suggestions.

From discussions with co-workers and vendors, and after further work on his draft, Weekley realized that he had placed one of the most important considerations for his audience (savings) last. In his final version, shown in Figure 2.5 (page 53), he moved that section to the beginning of his report. Weekley thus paid attention to his audience's priorities and needs. He also added headings and bulleted lists to help his reader find information. The format of his earlier draft (Figure 2.4) did not assist his readers in finding information quickly, nor did it reflect a convincing organizational plan.

FIGURE 2.4 Intermediate Draft of Marcus Weekley's Report

To: Melissa Hill, Office Manager
From: Marcus Weekley
Date: May 25, 2015
Subject: Improving Efficiency

Vague subject line

As you requested, I have been researching what to do about improving our office efficiency. One of the most beneficial and immediate solutions I have found is to replace our current laser printer with a new all-in-one color laser printer. More and more businesses today are incorporating multifunction printers into their information technology systems because of ease and efficiency. With the advances in printer technology in the past three years, it makes good business sense to replace our Van Eisen 4200 laser printer with a Lightech 520 multifunction printer. This printer would reduce business costs and increase business efficiency at a total cost significantly lower than the combined price of a laser printer, fax machine, copier, and scanner.

Wordy opening paragraph takes too long to get to the point

The printer, fax machine, copier, and scanner in the Lightech 520 is compatible with our operating systems. The addition of a 33.6 Kbps fax machine to our office, as opposed to our current 20.5 Kbps, would increase operating efficiency by allowing quicker response times. With the new multifunction color printer, our office can print up to 40 high-resolution color pages per minute, compared with our current printer's 20 color ppm. And the new printer's 5 GB of memory helps to manage multiple jobs easily. The Lightech 520 printer also holds 3,100 sheets of paper, as opposed to our current printer's 500-page capacity.

No headings or bullets make information hard to find

The multifunction printer would provide higher quality printing through a 4,800 dpi printer, whereas our current Image 4200 laser printer only has 900 dpi. The new printer also offers over 130 scalable type fonts, whereas our current printer only offers 60. Also, our current scanners scan images in at 1,200 × 1,200 dpi, whereas the new scanner operates at 4,800 × 4,800 dpi, so scanned images will be of an even better quality.

Does not supply source of research

The greatest benefit a multifunction printer would provide our company is monetary. The price of a new multifunction business printer ranges from $3,000 to $9,000 depending on the model. Lightech's 520 multifunction color laser printer (including 2,400 × 1,200 dpi copier, 4,800 × 4,800 dpi scanner, and 33.6 Kbps fax) costs only $3,175 not including shipping and handling purchased from Computerbuyers.com. This cost nearly equals the price of our own Van Eisen 4200 printer and West 400 scanners, but combines the equipment into one more efficient machine. Purchasing the multifunction printer would not only save our business money on the initial purchase, but use of a multitasking unit that combines four machines into one would also save on subsequent servicing and maintenance, as well as decreasing our monthly electric bill by $50–$150 per month. Use of the multifunction printer's 50–400% enlargement/reduction options should also save us an additional $300–$500 each month by enabling us to generate advertising brochures in-house. Computerbuyers.com also offers a two-year warranty on all products sold through its website. What better way to begin improving business efficiency than through the purchase of a new multifunction color printer?

Includes most important point for reader—costs—too late

Paragraph is long and hard to follow. Break into 2 or 3 paragraphs

Ends with question rather than plan for how to make change

© Cengage Learning

FIGURE 2.5 Final Version of Marcus Weekley's Report

To: Melissa Hill, Office Manager
From: Marcus Weekley
Date: June 12, 2015
Subject: Advantages of Purchasing a New All-in-One Printer

As you requested, I have investigated some ways to improve office efficiency. The best solution I have found is to replace our current Van Eisen 4200 laser printer, two West 400 scanners, and XL290 fax machine with a new-generation laser all-in-one color laser printer, the Lightech 520.

With advances in printer technology over the last two years (enclosed is a copy of a review article "New Technology Means Office Efficiency" from *Computer World* [**http://www.computerworld.com/article/2912897/new-technology -means-office efficiency.html**]), it makes good business sense to replace our less-efficient laser printer with a Lightech 520 all-in-one color laser printer. Our laser printer does only one task, while the Lightech will give us higher-resolution color printing, a high-speed fax machine, a copier, and a scanner all in one. This new unit is economical and more efficient and will significantly improve the transmission and design of our documents.

Cost
The greatest benefit of the all-in-one Lightech 520 is cost. We can purchase this printer for only $3,175, plus shipping and handling, totaling $3,298 when ordered through **Computerbuyers.com**. Purchasing a Lightech 520 would allow us to recoup that cost easily in just a few months because we would

- realize a savings in the purchase price—one Lightech costs less than the four current machines combined
- receive ScanText and WordPort software free with the printer
- decrease our monthly electricity bill by $50–$150 by reducing four pieces of office equipment to one
- have less maintenance, saving at least $150 per month in service calls
- receive a two-year warranty with guaranteed overnight service, which should decrease downtime
- be able to trade in our current printer for $375 and our two scanners for $200 each
- save an additional $300–500 each month by not having to use outside advertising thanks to Lightech's 50–400% enlargement/reduction capabilities

More precise subject line

Introduction gets to the point quickly

Documentation shows research on subject

Excellent use of headings and bulleted lists

Cites specific model and costs

Justification for new purchase clearly and persuasively laid out

FIGURE 2.5 (Continued)

Page 2

Efficiency

This all-in-one printer accomplishes all four tasks—printing, faxing, scanning, copying—simultaneously, and each task is compatible with our current networking system. Other key features include

Gives reader appropriate amount and type of detail

- allows quicker faxing (3 seconds per page) with 33.6 Kbps and greater storage (600 pages)
- prints twice as fast—40 high-resolution color pages per minute as opposed to our current printer's 20
- enhanced memory of 5 GB manages multiple jobs easily
- expanded paper capacity (3,100 sheets) to handle our heavy quarterly mailings easily
- 100,000-page monthly duty cycle means less maintenance
- all four tasks compatible with our PhotoEdit software

Contrasts current equipment with new model

Quality

The Lightech 520 prints and processes higher quality and quantity of work because it

- has a 4,800 dpi printer, whereas our current printer offers only 900 dpi
- exhibits same color density on the 1,000th copy as on the first; solid ink sticks ensure no toner spills
- offers a 2,400 × 1,200 dpi high-resolution copier
- would increase the quality of manipulated scanned images with a 4,800 × 4,800 dpi, whereas our current scanner is only 1,200 × 1,200
- offers over 130 scalable fonts, as opposed to the 60 we now have, which will give our publications a more varied and professional appearance

Selects only most relevant points for reader

I recommend that we purchase a Lightech 520 laser printer from **Computerbuyers.com.** It will unquestionably save us money, improve office efficiency, and help us to integrate our office systems to better project our corporate image.

Recommendation ends report persuasively, highlighting benefits to employer

© Cengage Learning

REVISING

Revision is an essential stage in the writing process. It requires more than giving your work another quick glance. Do not be tempted to skip the revision stage just because you have written the required number of words or sections or because you think you have put in too much time already. Revision is done *after* you produce a draft that you think conveys the appropriate message for your audience. The quality of your memo, letter, or report depends on the revisions you make now.

Allow Enough Time to Revise

Like planning or drafting, revision is not done well in one big push. It evolves over a period of time. Make sure you budget enough time to do it carefully.

- Avoid drafting and revising in one sitting. If possible, wait at least a day before you start to revise. (In the busy work world, waiting a couple of hours may have to suffice.)
- Ask a co-worker or friend familiar with your topic to comment on your work.
- Plan to read your revised work more than once.

Revision Is Rethinking

When you revise, you *resee*, *rethink*, and *reconsider* your entire document. You ask questions about the major issues of content, organization, tone, and format (see "The ABCs of Print Document Design," pages 449–459). Revision involves going back and repeating earlier steps in the writing process.

Revision means asking again the questions you have already asked and answered during the planning and drafting stages. During the process, you will discover gaps to fill, points to change, and errors to correct in your draft. Revision gives you a second (or third or fourth) chance to get things right for your audience. Take advantage of the document tracking options (see "Document Tracking Software," page 97) such as *Track Changes* and *Edit* that allow you to see your additions, cuts, and moves in a different color.

Key Questions to Ask as You Revise

By asking and successfully answering the following questions as you revise, you can discover gaps or omissions, points to change, and errors to correct in your draft.

Content

1. Is it accurate? Are my facts (figures, names, addresses, dates, costs, references, warranty terms, statistics) correct?
2. Is it relevant for my audience and purpose? Have I included information that is unnecessary, too technical, concrete or inappropriate?
3. Have I given enough concrete evidence to explain things adequately and to persuade my readers? (Too little information will make readers skeptical about what you are describing or proposing.) Have I left anything out?

Organization

1. Have I clearly identified my main points and shown readers why those points are important?

TECH NOTE

Revising

Here are some suggestions on how you can effectively revise a document on your computer, tablet, or smartphone:

- During this part of the writing process, respond to the notes you left yourself when you were drafting the document. Move sentences and paragraphs to more appropriate places, add clarifications and transitions, insert parenthetical documentation, create headers, or add visuals. At this stage, do not worry about spelling and punctuation, which are fine-tuning matters you can resolve during the editing stage.
- As you did when you drafted, save your document regularly (every few minutes) so that you do not lose your work if there's a power outage or your computer malfunctions. (Some word processing programs and apps can be set to save your document automatically at set time intervals.) Back up your document at the end of each day.
- Use the Save As option for each revision of your document, and give each revision a clear title, such as "Office Equipment, Revision #1."
- Take advantage of change-tracking options (see "Document Tracking Software," page 97) that allow you to see your edits (additions, cuts, and moves) in a different color, rather than deleting existing text. Use the Comment option to insert notes to yourself that will appear in the margin or at the bottom of your document.
- Choose the Print Preview option to see the final version of your document. Check to see if your document is too long or too short or if some sections of your document appear to be too dense with text. If your text is too dense, you may need to make deletions, add headings or headers, or include visuals to make your document attractive and easy to read and follow. (See "The ABCs of Print Document Design," pages 449–459).
- If you are using collaborative editing tools like Google Docs and Adobe Buzzword, share the document with the colleagues, managers, vendors, and so on, who can best help you to revise it. Then inform your collaborating team about how you want them to use this technology.

2. Is everything in the right, most effective order? Should anything be switched or moved closer to the beginning or the end of my document?
3. Am I spending too much (or too little) effort on one section? Do I repeat myself? What can be cut? Where and why?
4. Have I grouped related items in the same part of my report or letter, or have I scattered details that need to appear in one paragraph or section?

Tone

1. How do I sound to my readers—professional and sincere, or arrogant and unreliable? What attitude/tone do my words or expressions convey?
2. How will my readers, native speakers as well as an international audience, think I perceive them—honest and intelligent or unprofessional and uncooperative?

A "Before" and "After" Revision of a Short Report

Mary Fonseca, a staff member at Seacoast Labs, was asked by her supervisor to prepare a short report for the general public on the Labs's most recent experiments. Conferring with her supervisor, Fonseca learned that the report was intended to attract favorable publicity for the Labs's commitment to conserving energy and lowering marine fuel costs.

When she began to revise her first draft (seen in Figure 2.6), Fonseca realized that it lacked focus. It jumped back and forth between drag on ships and drag on airplanes. Because Seacoast Labs did not work on planes, she wisely decided to drop that idea. She also understood that the information on the effects of drag was so important it deserved a separate paragraph. In light of this key idea, she knew that her explanation of molecules, eddies, and drag needed to be made more reader-friendly, and so she added the analogy about spoons/ships and honey/drag. Researching further, she decided to add a new paragraph on the causes and effects of drag, which became paragraph 2 in her second draft (seen in Figure 2.7 on page 58).

Yet by pulling ideas about drag and its effects from the long first paragraph in Figure 2.6, Fonseca had to find an opening for this section of her report. Buried in her original opening paragraph was the idea that we cannot always see the forces of nature, but we can feel them.

FIGURE 2.6 Unorganized Opening Paragraphs of Mary Fonseca's "Before" Draft

Drag is an important concept in the world of science and technology. It has many implications. Drag occurs when a ship moves through the water and eddies build up. Ships on the high seas have to fight the eddies, which results in drag. In the same way, an airplane has to fight the winds at various altitudes at which it flies; these winds are very forceful, moving at many knots per hour. All these forces of nature are around us. Sometimes we can feel them, too. We get tired walking against a strong wind. The eddies around a ship are the same thing. These eddies form various barriers around the ship's hull. They come from a combination of different molecules around the ship's hull and exert quite a force. Both types of molecules pull against the ship. This is where the eddies come in.

Information hard to follow and not relevant for audience

Does not explain process very well

Scientists at Seacoast Labs are concerned about drag. Dr. Karen Runnels, who joined Seacoast about three years ago, is the chief investigator. She and her team of highly qualified experts have constructed some fascinating multilevel water tunnels. These tunnels should be useful to ship owners. Drag wastes a ship's fuel.

Important point not developed

© Cengage Learning

(Continued)

FIGURE 2.7 The "After" Draft—a Revision of Mary Fonseca's "Before" Draft in Figure 2.5

Effective use of headings and definition

What Is Drag?

We cannot see or hear many of the forces around us, but we can detect their presence. Walking or running into a strong wind, for example, requires a great deal of effort and often quickly leaves us feeling tired. When a ship sails through the water, it also experiences these opposing forces known as **drag**. Overcoming drag causes a ship to reduce its energy efficiency, which leads to higher fuel costs.

How Drag Works

Describes cause and effect of drag in concise, easy to understand terms

It is not easy for a ship to fight drag. As the ship moves through the water, it drags the water molecules around its hull at the same rate the ship is moving. Because of the cohesive force of those molecules, other water molecules immediately outside the ship's path get pulled into its way. All the molecules become tangled rather than simply sliding past each other. The result is an **eddy**, or small circling burst of water around the ship's hull, which intensifies the drag. Jorge Fröes, a highly respected structural engineer, explains the process using this analogy: "When you put a spoon in honey and pull it out, half the honey comes out with the spoon. That's what is happening to ships. The ship is moving and at the same time dragging the ocean with it."

Ways to Reduce Drag

Supplies an easy-to-follow analogy for her audience

Clearly explains the Labs' research and its importance for readers concerned about the economy and environment

At Seacoast Labs, scientists are working to find ways to reduce drag on ships. Dr. Karen Runnels, the principal investigator, and a team of researchers have constructed water tunnels to simulate the movement of ships at sea. The drag a ship encounters is measured from the tiny air bubbles emitted in the water tunnel. To reduce the drag, Runnel's team developed the use of polymers, or long carbon chain molecules. These polymers act like a slimy coating for the ship's hull to help it glide through the water more easily. When asbestos fibers were added to the polymer solutions, the investigators achieved a 90 percent reduction in drag. The team has also experimented with an external pump attached to the hull of a ship, which pushes the water away from a ship's path, saving even more energy and time.

She thought this comparison of walking against the wind and fighting drag would work better for her audience than the original wooden remarks she had started with.

Although her organization and ideas were far better in her second draft than in her "before" draft in Figure 2.6, she concluded she had said very little about her employer, Seacoast Labs, and the image it wanted to project through its experiments. Doing more research, she found additional information about Seacoast's experiments and why they were so important in conserving fuel and saving money. This information was far more significant and relevant than saying that Dr. Runnels had been at Seacoast for three years.

Through revision and further research, then, Mary Fonseca transformed two poorly organized and incomplete paragraphs into three separate yet logically connected ones that highlighted her employer's work. In her revision (Figure 2.7), she came up with three very helpful headings—"What Is Drag?," "How Drag Works," and "Reducing Drag"—to help organize information for her nonspecialist readers.

EDITING

Editing is the equivalent of quality control for your reader. This last stage in the writing process might be compared to detailing an automobile—the preparation a dealer goes through to ready a new car for prospective buyers. Editing is done only after you are completely satisfied that you have made all of the big decisions about content, organization, and format—that you have said what you wanted to, where and how you intended, for your audience.

When you edit, you will check your work to make sure it is readable and correct. At this stage, pay close attention to

- sentences
- word choices
- punctuation
- spelling
- grammar and usage
- tone

As with revising, don't skip or rush through the editing process, thinking that once your ideas are down, your work is done. If your work is hard to read or contains mistakes in spelling or punctuation, readers will think that your ideas and your research are also faulty.

The following sections will give you basic guidelines about what to look for when you edit your sentences and words. "A Writer's Brief Guide to Paragraphs, Sentences, and Words," found in the Appendix on pages A-1–A-19, also contains helpful suggestions on using correct spelling and punctuation.

Editing Guidelines for Writing Lean and Clear Sentences

Here are four of the most frequent complaints readers voice about poorly edited writing in the world of work:

- **The sentences are too long.** I could not follow the writer's ideas easily.
- **The sentences are too complex,** making it hard to understand what the writer meant the first time I read the work; I had to reread it several times.

TECH NOTE

Editing

Word-processing programs available on tablets, smartphones, and computers make editing easy and efficient. These programs flag errors in spelling, punctuation, word choice, subject-verb agreement, wordiness, and sentence construction. But keep the following guidelines in mind when you use these programs. Be aware of what your computer can and cannot do for you.

- Customize your spell-checker. You can set your spell-checker to flag words that you frequently misspell and to ignore words that aren't in its dictionary (such as proper names, brand names, technical terms or concepts, etc.).
- Don't accept everything your spell-checker or grammar-checker tells you. While these tools are helpful, do not rely on them exclusively. For instance, a grammar-checker may fail to recognize homonyms (their/there or its/it's), and a spell-checker may highlight a proper name or industry jargon that is spelled correctly but is not included in your spell-checker's dictionary. When in doubt, use a dictionary or consult the Appendix of this book to verify the accuracy of your spelling and grammar. Popular online dictionaries include Dictionary.com (**dictionary.reference.com**) and Merriam-Webster (**www.merriam-webster.com**).
- Use global find and replace for unique character strings only. For example, trying to change the word "on" to "at" will also change "only" to "atly," "once" to "atce," and "content" to "cattent." If your spell-checker spots a word that is in fact misspelled or used incorrectly in one place, don't assume that all occurrences of the word are misspelled. For instance, if your spell-checker tells you to capitalize the word "South" (as in "South Carolina") in one instance, the word may not need to be capitalized elsewhere (e.g., "south of the highway"). Check each correction individually.
- To avoid having to make time-consuming repetitive changes to style for such things as paragraph indents or heading style, set up your document using autoformatting for accuracy and consistency throughout your document.
- Non-standard punctuation that may be necessary for a Works Cited or References list (see "Documenting Sources," pages 337–347) or a company name may cause your grammar-checker to mark as erroneous writing that is correct. Check any such writing carefully.

- **The sentences are unclear.** Even after I reread them, I was not sure I understood the writer's message.
- **The sentences are too short and simplistic.** The writing felt "dumbed down."

Writing clear, readable sentences is not always easy. It takes effort, but the time you spend editing will pay off in rich dividends for you and your readers. The seven guidelines that follow should help with the editing phase of your work.

   1. Avoid needlessly complex or lengthy sentences. Do not pile words on top of words. Instead, edit one overly long sentence into two or even three more manageable ones.

Too long: The planning committee decided that the awards banquet should be held on March 15 at 6:30, since the other two dates (March 7 and March 22) suggested by the hospitality committee conflict with local sports events, even though one of those events could be changed to fit our needs.

Edited for easier reading: The planning committee has decided to hold the awards banquet on March 15 at 6:30. The other dates suggested by the hospitality committee—March 7 and March 22—conflict with two local sports events. Although the date of one of those sports events could be changed, the planning committee still believes that March 15 is our best choice.

2. Combine short, choppy sentences. Don't shorten long, complex sentences, only to turn them into choppy, simplistic ones. When you find yourself looking at a series of short, blunt sentences, as in the following example, combine them where possible and use connective words similar to those italicized in the edited version.

Choppy: Medical transcriptionists have many responsibilities. Their responsibilities are important. They must be familiar with medical terminology. They must listen to dictation. Sometimes physicians talk very fast. Then the transcriptionist must be quick to transcribe what is heard. Words could be missed. Transcriptionists must forward reports. These reports have to be approved. This will take a great deal of time and concentration. These final reports are copied and stored properly for reference.

Edited: Medical transcriptionists have many important responsibilities. *These* include transcribing physicians' orders using correct medical terminology. *When* physicians dictate rapidly, transcriptionists have to keyboard accurately *so* that no words are omitted. *Among their most demanding* duties are keyboarding and forwarding transcriptions *and then*, after approval, storing copies properly for future reference.

3. Edit sentences to tell who does what to whom or what. The clearest sentence pattern in English is the subject-verb-object (s-v-o) pattern.

s   v   o

Sue booted the computer.

s   v   o

Our website contains a link to key training software programs.

Readers find this pattern easiest to understand because it provides direct and specific information about the action. Hard-to-read sentences obscure or scramble information about the subject, the verb, or the object. In the following unedited sentence, the subject is hidden in the middle rather than being placed in the most crucial subject position.

Unclear: The control of the ceiling limits of glycidyl ethers on the part of the employers for the optimal safety of workers in the workplace is necessary. *(Who is responsible for taking action? What action must they take? For whom is such action taken?)*

Edited: Employers must control the ceiling limits of glycidyl ethers for workers' safety.

4. Use strong, active verbs rather than verb phrases. In trying to sound important, many bureaucratic writers avoid using simple, graphic verbs. Instead, these writers use a weak verb phrase (for example, *provide maintenance of* instead of *maintain, work in cooperation with* instead of *cooperate*). Such verb phrases imprison the active verb inside a noun format and slow readers down. Note how the edited version here rewrites the weak verb phrases.

> Weak: The city provided the employment of two work crews to assist the strengthening of the dam.

> Strong: The city employed two work crews to strengthen the dam.

5. Avoid piling modifiers in front of nouns. Putting too many modifiers (words used as adjectives) in the readers' path to the noun is confusing for readers, who will have trouble deciphering how one modifier relates to another modifier or to the noun.

> Crowded: The vibration noise control heat pump condenser quieter can make your customer happier.

> Readable: The quieter on the condenser for the heat pump will make your customer happier by controlling noise and vibrations.

6. Replace wordy phrases or clauses with one- or two-word synonyms.

> Wordy: The college has parking zones for different areas for people living on campus as well as for those who do not live on campus and who commute to school. (*Twenty-one words of the original sentence—everything after "areas for"—have been reduced to four words: "resident and commuter students."*)

> Edited: The college has different parking zones for resident and commuter students.

7. Combine sentences beginning with the same subject or ending with an object that becomes the subject of the next sentence.

> Wordy: Homeowners want to buy low-maintenance bushes. These low-maintenance bushes include the ever-popular holly and boxwood varieties. These bushes are also inexpensive.

> Edited: Homeowners want to buy low-maintenance and inexpensive bushes such as holly and boxwood. (*This revision combines three sentences into one, condenses twenty-four words into fourteen, and joins three related thoughts.*)

Editing Guidelines for Cutting Out Unnecessary Words

Too many people in business think the more words, the better. Nothing could be more self-defeating. Your readers are busy; unnecessary words slow them down. Make every word work. Cut out any words you can from your sentences. If the sentence still makes sense and reads correctly, you have eliminated wordiness.

1. Replace wordy phrases with precise ones. See how in Table 2.1 wordy phrases on the left are replaced with their much more concise equivalents on the right. Many of these wordy phrases have slowed business writing down for decades.

2. Use concise, not redundant, phrases. Another kind of wordiness comes from using redundant expressions—saying the same thing a second time, only in different words. "Fellow colleague," "component parts," "corrosive acid," and "free gift" are phrases that contain this kind of double speech; a fellow *is* a colleague, a component

TABLE 2.1 Wordy Phrases and Their Concise Equivalents

Wordy	Concise	Wordy	Concise
at a slow rate	slowly	in connection with	about
at an early date	soon	in the event that	if
at this point in time	now	in the month of May	in May
based on the fact	because	in the neighborhood of	approximately, about
be in agreement with	agree	it is often the case that	often
bring to a conclusion	conclude, end	look something like	resemble
come to terms with	agree, accept	of the opinion that	think
due to the fact that	because	on the grounds that	because
during the course of	during	until such time as	until
express an opinion that	affirm	with reference to	regarding, about
for the period of	for	with the result that	so

© 2015 Cengage Learning

is a part, acid *is* corrosive, and a gift *is* free. In the following examples, the suggested changes on the right are preferable to the redundant phrases on the left.

Redundant	Concise
absolutely essential	essential
advance reservations	reservations
basic necessities	necessities, needs
close proximity	proximity, nearness
end result	result
final conclusions/final outcome	conclusions/outcome
first and foremost	first
full and complete	full, complete
personal opinion	opinion
tried-and-true	tried, proven

© 2015 Cengage Learning

3. Watch for repetitious words, phrases, or clauses within a sentence. Sometimes one sentence or one part of a sentence needlessly duplicates another.

Redundant: To provide more room for employees' cars, the security department is studying ways to expand the employees' parking lot.

Edited: The security department is studying ways to expand the employees' parking lot. (*Because the first phrase says nothing that the reader does not know from the independent clause, it can be cut.*)

4. Avoid unnecessary prepositional phrases. Adding a prepositional phrase can sometimes contribute to redundancy. The italicized words in the following list are unnecessary. Be on the lookout for these phrases and delete them.

audible *to the ear*	light *in weight*	short *in duration*
bitter *in taste*	loud *in volume*	soft *in texture*
fly *through the air*	orange *in color*	tall *in height*

hard *to the touch*	rectangular *in shape*	twenty *in number*
honest *in character*	second *in sequence*	visible *to the eye*

Figure 2.8 shows an email that Trudy Wallace wants to send to her boss, Lee Chadwick, about issuing tablets to the sales force. Her unedited work is bloated with unnecessary words, expendable phrases, and repetitious ideas.

FIGURE 2.8 A Wordy, Unedited Email

Wordy and unfocused subject

One long, unbroken paragraph is hard to follow

Repeats same idea in two or three sentences

Uses awkward and wordy sentences

Does not specify what writer will do about problem

Dear Lee,

Due to the inescapable reliance on technology, specifically on email and Internet communications, within our company, I believe it would be beneficial to look into the possibility of issuing tablets to our employees. Issuing these devices would have a variety of positive implications for the efficiency of our company. Unlike smartphones, tablets have many more capabilities that will help our employees in their daily work since these tablets expand the technological features of a smartphone and a laptop's ability to transfer documents. On the road their portability would assist the sales staff to participate in online meetings both locally and at distant sites. It should be pointed out, too, that the tablet's screens are two and one-half to three times bigger than a smartphone's, so our employees could actually make better presentations to clients on these devices. With a tablet, employees would also benefit by having access to more extensive business documents such as manuals, contracts, and invoices, even when they are out on the road traveling or at our local office. By means of tablets, I feel quite certain that our company's correspondence would be dealt with much more speedily, since not only will these devices allow our employees to access their email and full documents at all times, it will enable them to actually create documents in a more efficient manner because of the size of the virtual keyboard. I think it would be absolutely essential for the satisfaction of our customers and to the ongoing operation of our company's business today to respond fully and completely to the possibility such a proposal affords us. It would, therefore, appear safe to conclude that with reference to issuing tablets every means at our disposal would be brought to bear on aiding our sales staff.

Thanks,

Trudy

After careful editing, Trudy Wallace streamlined her email (see Figure 2.9). She pruned wordy expressions and combined sentences to cut out duplication. The revised version is only 127 words, as opposed to the 299 words in the draft. Not only has Wallace shortened her message, but she has also made it easier to read.

Editing Guidelines to Eliminate Sexist Language

Editing involves far more than just making sure that your sentences are readable. It also reflects your professional style—how you see and characterize the world of work, your co-workers and customers, not to mention how you want your readers to see you. Your words should reflect a high degree of ethics and honesty, free from bias, offense, and stereotype. They need to be sensitive to the needs of your

FIGURE 2.9 A Concise Version of the Wordy Email in Figure 2.8

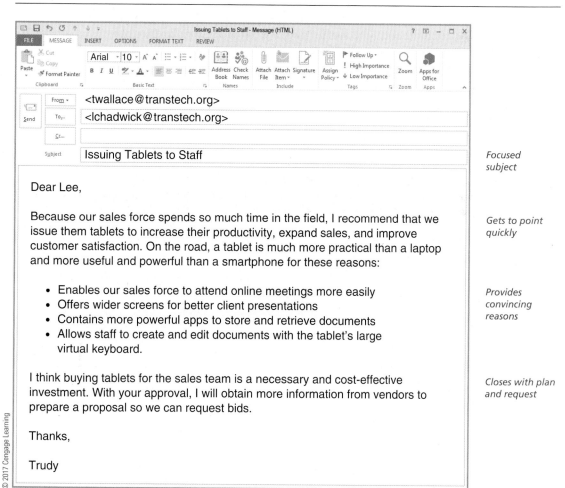

Subject: Issuing Tablets to Staff — *Focused subject*

Dear Lee,

Because our sales force spends so much time in the field, I recommend that we issue them tablets to increase their productivity, expand sales, and improve customer satisfaction. On the road, a tablet is much more practical than a laptop and more useful and powerful than a smartphone for these reasons: — *Gets to point quickly*

- Enables our sales force to attend online meetings more easily
- Offers wider screens for better client presentations
- Contains more powerful apps to store and retrieve documents
- Allows staff to create and edit documents with the tablet's large virtual keyboard.

Provides convincing reasons

I think buying tablets for the sales team is a necessary and cost-effective investment. With your approval, I will obtain more information from vendors to prepare a proposal so we can request bids. — *Closes with plan and request*

Thanks,

Trudy

international audience as well (see "Ten Guidelines for Communicating with International Readers," pages 169–173).

Sexist language in particular offers a distorted and unethical view of a job force and discriminates in favor of one sex at the expense of another, usually women. It portrays men as having more powerful, higher-paying jobs than women do. Using sexist language offends and demeans female readers by depriving them of their equal rights and it may cost your company business as well. You can avoid gender bias by using inclusive language for women and men alike, treating them equally and fairly.

Sexist language is often based on stereotypes that depict men as superior to women. For example, calling politicians *city fathers* or *favorite sons* follows the stereotypical picture of seeing politicians as male. Such phrases discriminate against women who do or could hold public office at all levels of government. Never assume or imply a person's gender is based on his or her profession.

Sexist Language and Professional Titles

As the above examples show, such language prejudiciously labels some professions as masculine and others as feminine. Keep in mind that sexist phrases assume engineers, physicians, and pilots are male (*he*, *his*, and *him* are often linked with these professions in descriptions), while social workers, nurses, administrative assistants, and secretaries are often portrayed as female (*she*, *her*), although members of both sexes work in all these professions. Sexist language also wrongly points out gender identities when such roles do not seem to follow biased expectations — *lady lawyer*, *male secretary*, *female surgeon*, or *male nurse*. Such offensive distinctions reflect prejudiced attitudes that you should eliminate from your writing.

Always prune the following sexist phrases: *every man for himself, gal Friday, little woman, lady of the house, old maid, women's intuition, the best man for the job, to man a desk* (or *post*), *the weaker sex, woman's work, working wives, a manly thing to do,* and *young man on the way up.*

Finally, don't assume all employees are male. Instead of writing, "All staff members and their wives are invited to attend," simply say, "All staff members and their guests are invited to attend."

Ways to Avoid Sexist Language

Here are four ways you can eliminate sexist writing from your work.

1. Replace sexist words with neutral ones. Neutral words do *not* refer to a specific sex; they are genderless. The sexist words on the left in the following list can be replaced by the neutral nonsexist substitutes on the right.

Sexist	Neutral	Sexist	Neutral
alderman	representative	chairman	chair, chairperson
assemblyman	representative	common man	average citizen
businessman	businessperson	congressman	representative
cameraman	photographer	craftsman	skilled worker

Sexist	Neutral	Sexist	Neutral
fireman	firefighter	manmade	synthetic, artificial
foreman	supervisor	manpower	strength, power
housewife	homemaker	man to man	candidly
janitress	custodian	policeman	police officer
landlord, landlady	owner	salesman	salesperson
maiden name	family name	spokesman	spokesperson
mailman, postman	mail carrier	weatherman	meteorologist
man-hours	work-hours	women's intuition	intuition
mankind	humanity	workman	worker

2. Watch masculine pronouns. Avoid using the masculine pronouns (*he, his, him*) when referring to a group that includes both men and women.

> *Every worker must submit his travel expenses by Monday.*

Workers may include women as well as men, and to assume that all workers are men is misleading and unfair to women. You can edit such sexist language in several ways.

a. Make the subject of your sentence plural and thus neutral.

> *Workers must submit their travel expenses by Monday.*

b. Replace the pronoun *his* with *the* or *a* or drop it altogether.

> *Every employee is to submit a travel expense report by Monday.*
> *Every worker must submit travel expenses by Monday.*

c. Use *his or her* instead of *his.*

> *Every worker must submit his or her travel expenses by Monday.*

d. Reword the sentence using the passive voice.

> *All travel expenses must be submitted by Monday.*

Moreover, in some contexts exclusive use of the masculine pronoun might invite a lawsuit. For example, you would be violating federal employment laws prohibiting discrimination on the basis of gender if you wrote the following in a help-wanted notice for your company.

> *Each applicant must submit his transcript with his application. He must also supply three letters of recommendation from individuals familiar with his work.*

The language of such a notice implies that only men can apply for the position.

Keep in mind that international readers may find these guidelines on avoiding masculine pronouns confusing because many languages (e.g., French, Spanish) follow grammatical gender instead of natural gender. In French, the word for *doctor* is masculine, for example.

3. Avoid using sexist words that end in -ess or -ette. Use gender-neutral alternatives for words like *stewardess* (*flight attendant*), *poetess* (*poet*), *waitress* (*server*).

4. Eliminate sexist salutations. Never use the following salutations when you are unsure of who your readers are:

- Dear Sir
- Gentlemen
- Dear Madam

Any woman you write to would surely be offended by the first two greetings and may also be unhappy with the pompous and obsolete *madam*. It is usually best to write to a specific individual, but if you cannot do that, direct your letter to a particular department or group: *Dear Warranty Department* **or** *Dear Selection Committee.*

Be careful, too, about using the titles *Miss, Mr.,* and *Mrs.* Sexist distinctions are unjust and insulting. It is preferable to write *Dear Ms. McCarty* rather than *Dear Miss or Mrs. McCarty.* A woman's marital status should not be an issue. Try to find out if the person prefers *Ms.* to another courtesy title (e.g., *Editor Hawkins, Supervisor Jones*). If you are in doubt, write *Dear Indira Kumar.* Chapter 5 provides acceptable salutations to use in your letters (see "Salutation," pages 159–160).

Avoiding Other Types of Stereotypical Language

In addition to sexist language, avoid any references that stereotype an individual because of race, color, national origin, age, disability, sexual orientation, or gender identity. Not only are such references almost always irrelevant in the workplace (except for Equal Employment Opportunity Commission reports or health care documentation, where you still need to respect an individual's identity), they are discriminatory, culturally insensitive, and ethically wrong.

To eliminate biased language in your workplace writing, follow these guidelines.

1. Do not single out an individual because of race or national origin or stereotype him or her because of it. Be especially sensitive when referring to someone's ethnic identity.

Wrong: Bill, who is African American, is one of the company's top sales reps.
Right: Bill is one of the company's top sales reps.

Wrong: The Chinese computer whiz was able to find the problem.
Right: The programmer was able to find the problem.

2. Identify members of an international community accurately. Not every native Spanish speaker is Latin American or Hispanic. Be sensitive to significant cultural differences among groups (Cuban Americans and Mexican Americans, for example).

3. Avoid words or phrases that discriminate against an individual because of age. For example, do not use *elderly, up in years, geezer, old-timer, over the hill, senior moment,* or the adjectives *spry* or *frail* when they are applied to someone's age: "a spry sixty-seven." Also avoid phrases like *baby engineer* or *middle-aged supervisor.*

Wrong: Jerry Fox, who will be fifty-seven next month, comes up with obsolete plans from time to time.
Right: Some of Jerry Fox's plans have not been adopted.

4. Respect individuals who may have a disability. Do not discriminate against someone who has a disability. Keep in mind that the Americans with Disabilities Act (1990) prohibits employers from asking if a job applicant has a disability. Avoid derogatory words such as *amputee, crippled, handicapped, impaired,* or *lame* (physical disabilities) or *retarded* or *slow* (mental disabilities). Stay away from terms such as these because they identify the entire individual rather than just the aspects that the disability affects. Emphasize the individual instead of the physical or mental condition as if it solely determined that person's abilities.

> Wrong: Tom suffers from MS.
> Right: Tom is a person living with MS.

> Wrong: Sarah, who is crippled, still does an excellent job of keyboarding.
> Right: Sarah's disability does not prevent her from keyboarding.

Also, do not use such phrases as *wheelchair-bound* or *confined to a wheelchair*, which wrongly and unfairly imply that a person in a wheelchair cannot move around on his or her job. Avoid using discriminatory expressions in your writing, such as a *crippled economy, lame excuse, mentally challenged,* or *mental midget.*

5. Don't stereotype based on sexual orientation or gender identity. It is wrong and a violation of human rights to discriminate against someone because of sexual orientation or gender identity. The workplace has zero tolerance for insensitive and unethical language.

> Wrong: Paula Smith, a lesbian, hosts a successful daytime talk show.
> Right: Paula Smith hosts a successful daytime talk show.

In addition, avoid derogatory innuendos, comments, or jokes about gay men, lesbians, bisexuals, or transgender people (e.g., "That's so gay"), and don't assume that all of your readers are heterosexual.

THE WRITING PROCESS: SOME FINAL THOUGHTS

To make sure that your writing process at work—all your researching, planning, drafting, revising, and editing—is successful, follow these final guidelines:

1. Be sure that your document focuses clearly and consistently on your audience's needs—that is, meets their expectations and answers their questions.
2. Verify that all the information you have used in your document is current, accurate, ethical, and relevant.
3. Ensure you successfully completed the drafting, revising, and editing stages of your writing and did not skip any of the steps.
4. Confer with any co-workers, members of your collaborative writing team, your supervisor, etc., who prepared the document with you to make sure everyone agrees with the final version.
5. Proofread the final version of your document, paying close attention to spelling, punctuation, formatting, and factual content, including names, dates, models, costs, and places. Misspelled words, comma splices, inconsistent dates,

or incorrect costs can seriously undermine all your hard work in developing your document.

6. Make sure that you send the final revised, edited, and proofread version—and not an earlier draft or revision.

7. Send the document in the correct format—hard copy, Word file, PDF, and so on.

✓ REVISION CHECKLIST

☐ Investigated the research, planning, drafting, revising, and editing benefits of my computer software.

☐ Researched my topic carefully to obtain enough information to answer all my readers' questions—online searches, interviews, questionnaires, personal observations.

☐ Before writing, determined the amount and kinds of information needed to complete my writing task.

☐ Spent enough time planning—brainstorming, outlining, clustering, or a combination of these techniques. Produced substantial material from which to shape a draft. Documented sources.

☐ Prepared enough drafts to decide on the major points in my message to readers. Made major changes and deletions where necessary in my drafts to strengthen the document.

☐ Revised drafts carefully to successfully answer readers' questions about content, organization, and tone. Formatted the text to make it easy to follow.

☐ Made time to edit my work so that the style is clear and concise and the sentences are readable and varied. Checked punctuation, sentences, and words to make sure they are spelled correctly and are appropriate for my audience.

☐ Eliminated sexist and other biased language that unfairly stereotypes individuals because of race, color, ethnicity, disability, sexual orientation, or gender identity.

☐ Made sure final edited copy was carefully proofread and transmitted.

EXERCISES

1. Following is a writer's initial brainstormed list for a report on stress in the workplace. Revise the brainstormed list, eliminating repetition and combining related items.

—leads to absenteeism

—high costs for compensation for stress-related illnesses

—proper nutrition

—numerous stress-reduction techniques

—good idea to conduct interviews to find out levels, causes, and extent of stress in the workplace

—low morale caused by stress

—higher insurance claims for employees' physical ailments

—myth to see stress leading to greater productivity

—various videos used to teach relaxation

—environmental factors—too hot? too cold?

—teamwork intensifies stress
—counseling
—work overload
—setting priorities
—wellness campaign
—savings per employee add up to
  $6,150 per year
—skills to relax
—learning to get along with co-workers

—need for privacy
—interpersonal communication
—employee's need for clear policies
  on transfers, promotion
—stress management workshops very
  successful in California
—physical activity to relieve stress
—affects management
—breathing exercises

2. Prepare a suitable outline from your revised list in Exercise 1 for a report to a decision maker on the problems of stress in the workplace and the necessity of creating a stress-management program.

3. From the revised brainstormed list in Exercise 1, write a one-page memo to a decision maker about how the problems of stress negatively affect workplace production.

4. You have been asked to write a short report (two to three pages) to the manager of the small company you work for on a topic of your choice. Prepare a cluster diagram similar to that on flextime in Figure 2.1. Add, delete, or rearrange anything in the diagram to complete your outline. Submit your final outline along with your report to your instructor.

5. Compare the draft of Marcus Weekley's report in Figure 2.4 with the final copy of his report in Figure 2.5. What kinds of changes did he make? Were they appropriate and effective for his audience and purpose? Why or why not?

6. Assume you have been asked to write a short report (two to three pages) to a decision maker (the manager of a business you work for or have worked for; the director of your campus union, library, or security; a city official) about one of the following topics:

a. recruitment of more specialists in your field	**f.** public transportation
b. Internet resources	**g.** sporting events/activities
c. security lighting	**h.** team building/morale
d. food service	**i.** greening the workplace/community
e. health care plans	**j.** hiring more part-time student workers

Then do relevant research and planning about one of those topics and the audience for whom it is intended by answering the following questions:

- What is my precise purpose in writing to my audience?
- What do I know about the topic?
- What information will my audience expect me to know?
- Where can I obtain relevant information about my topic to meet my audience's needs?

7. Using one or more of the planning strategies discussed in this chapter (clustering, brainstorming, outlining), generate a group of ideas for the topic you chose in Exercise 6. Work on your planning activities for about 15–20 minutes or until you have about ten to fifteen items. At this stage, do not worry about how appropriate your ideas are or even if some of them overlap. Just get some thoughts down on paper.

8. Go through the list you prepared in Exercise 7, and eliminate any entries that are inappropriate for your topic or audience or that overlap. Try to see how many entries you might expand or rearrange into categories or subcategories. Then create an outline similar to the one in Figure 2.3.

9. Using your outline from Exercise 8, prepare three drafts of your memo report. Submit at least two drafts to your instructor.

10. Revise your drafts in Exercise 9 as much as necessary to create your final report.

11. In a few paragraphs, explain to your instructor the changes you made between your early drafts and your final revision in Exercise 10. Explain why you made them. Concentrate on major changes—adding and moving paragraphs—as well as matters of style, tone, and even format.

12. In an email to your instructor, describe any problems you encountered while working on your report in Exercises 6-10. Also point out any planning, drafting, and revising strategies that worked especially well for you.

13. The following paragraph is wordy and full of awkward, hard-to-read sentences. Edit these paragraphs to make them more readable and user friendly by using clear and concise words and sentences.

It has been verified conclusively by this writer that our institution must of necessity install more bicycle holding racks for the convenience of students, faculty, and staff. These parking modules should be fastened securely to walls outside strategic locations on the campus. They could be positioned there by work crews or even by the security forces who vigilantly and constantly patrol the campus grounds. There are many students in particular who would value the installation of these racks. Their bicycles could be stationed there by them, and they would know that safety measures have been taken to ensure that none of their bicycles would be apprehended or confiscated illegally. Besides the precaution factor, these racks would afford users maximized convenience in utilizing their means of transportation when they have academic business to conduct, whether at the learning resource center or in the instructional facilities.

14. Following are very early drafts of memos that businesspeople have sent to their bosses or co-workers. Revise and edit each draft, referring to the Revision Checklist on page 70. Turn in your revision and the final, reader-ready copy. As you revise, keep in mind that you may have to delete and add information, rearrange the order of information, and make the tone suitable for your readers. As you edit, make sure your sentences are clear and concise.

   a. TO: All workers
      FROM: B. J. Blackwell
      DATE: February 3, 2016
      RE: Parking

   The parking violations around here have gotten very, very bad. And the administration is provoked and wants some action taken. I don't blame them. I have been late for meetings several times in the last month because inconsiderate folks from other divisions have parked their cars in our zone. That just is not fair, and so we in our department must not be the only ones who are upset. No wonder the management finds things so bad they have asked me to prepare this memo.

A big part of the problem it seems to me is that employees just cannot read signs. They park in the wrong zones. They also park in visitors' spots. The penalties are going to be stiff. The administration, or so I was led to believe, is thinking of fining any employee who does not obey the parking policies. I know for a fact that I saw someone from the research department pull right into a visitor parking area last week just because it was 8:55 and he did not want to be late for work. That gives our business a bad name. People will not want to do business with us if they cannot even find a parking spot in the area that the company has reserved for them.

Vice President Watson has laid the law down to me about all this and told me to let each and every one of you know that things have to improve. One of the other big problems around here is that some employees have even parked their cars in loading zones, and security had to track them down to move.

As part of the administration's new policy, each employee is going to be issued a company parking policy and will have to come in and sign for it verifying that he received it. I think things really have gotten out of hand and that some drastic action has to be taken. We will all have to shape up around here.

b. TO: All Employees
FROM: George Holmes
DATE: October 19, 2015
RE: Travel

Every company has its policies regarding travel and vouchers. Ours strike me as important and fairly straightforward. Yet for the life of me I cannot fathom why they are being ignored. It is in everyone's best interest. When you travel, you are on company time, company business. Respect that, won't you. Explain your purpose, keep your receipts, document your visits, keep track of meals. Do the math.

If you see more than one client per day, it should not be too hard or too much to ask you to keep a log of each, separate, individual visit. After all, our business does depend on these people, and we will never know your true contributions on company trips unless you inform us (please!) of whom you see, where, why, and how much it costs you. That way we can keep our books straight and know that everything is going according to company policy.

Please review the appropriate pages (I think they are pages 23–25) about travel procedures. Thanks. If you have questions, give me a call, but check your employee handbook or with your office/section manager, first. That will save everyone more time. Good luck.

15. Find a piece of writing—email, memo, blog, brochure, short report, or website—that you believe was not carefully drafted or revised. In a short memo or email, point out to your instructor what is wrong with the piece of writing—for example, it is not logically organized, it uses an inappropriate tone, it is incomplete, or the information is too technical. Attach a copy of the poor example to your memo or email.

16. Revise the piece of poor writing you analyzed in Exercise 15. Submit your improved version to your instructor.

17. The following sentences contain sexist and other biased language. Edit them to correct these errors.

   a. Every intern had to record his readings daily for the spokesman.
   b. Although Marcel was an amputee, he still could hunt and peck at the keyboard.
   c. She saw a woman doctor, who told her to take an aspirin every day.
   d. Our agency was founded to help mankind.
   e. Even though John is a diabetic, he has an excellent attendance record.
   f. Every social worker found her schedule taxing—not enough days in the week to help out man-to-man.
   g. Maria, who is Cuban, always adds spice to company events.
   h. To be a policeman, each applicant had to pass a rigorous physical and prove himself in the manly art of self-defense.
   i. It's a wise man who can rise to the top in this cutthroat, volatile stock market.
   j. Sandy Frain, a middle-aged Irish-born woman, came by this morning wanting an appointment to discuss the new policies on energy efficiency.
   k. Mrs. Johnson is in charge of safety issues.
   l. He made his PowerPoint presentation as emphatically as an Italian opera singer on stage.
   m. Team B tried to disable our proposal by introducing irrelevant references to the many foreigners living on the north side.
   n. The average consumer spends at least two to three hours a week on her computer looking for coupons and other bargains.
   o. How many of our customers don't speak English well?
   p. Our office installed new power doors to assist employees who are unable to leave their wheelchairs.
   q. More mentally retarded individuals are being hired to do menial tasks on the job.

fotog/Tetra/Corbis

Collaborative Writing and Meetings in the Workplace

In the world of work, writing skills, such as researching, planning, drafting, revising, and editing are vital for your success. But you will often communicate as part of a team (including managers and co-workers) to write a set of instructions, a report, a proposal, or even a letter successfully. A major survey estimates that 90 percent of all businesspeople spend some time writing as part of a collaborative team. Being a team player is one of the most prized skills you can possess in the world of work.

In this chapter, we'll explore the advantages of the collaborative writing process, guidelines for effective group writing, and ways to help resolve conflicts in the group-writing process. Because an overwhelming majority of workplace collaborative writing takes place online, we'll also investigate how technology furthers the collaborative writing process and see how a document can be collaboratively created online.

COLLABORATION IS CRUCIAL TO THE WRITING PROCESS

Collaboration is essential for success within the world of work. Being a part of a writing team is a major responsibility in a world where each employee is connected to co-workers, managers, vendors, and customers around the globe. Collaboration is networking, and collaborative writing is a vital part of the global network in which individuals depend on one another's expertise, experience, and viewpoints.

Successful collaboration hinges on being a team player, one of the most highly valued skills in the workplace. Being a team player means you

- interact successfully on an interpersonal level
- network to access and archive information

FIGURE 3.1 A Collaborating Team at Work

- participate and provide feedback
- give and take constructive criticism
- raise important and relevant questions
- get assistance from resource experts in other departments and fields
- put the good of your company above your ego
- work toward consensus
- contribute to customer service and satisfaction

Collaboration builds teamwork as it helps get writing done more easily and more efficiently. Figure 3.1 shows a collaborating team at work, planning and interacting on a company project.

Keep in mind that collaboration must always reflect your employer's corporate image, goals, and politics. Your employer determines the subject that your group will discuss and the formats in which your work will appear. Moreover, everything your team does is subject to review and revision by your boss. Viewing collaboration in this broader corporate context will get you off to a good start in the world of work.

ADVANTAGES OF COLLABORATIVE WRITING

Collaborative writing teams benefit both employers and employees. Here are some specific advantages of collaboration:

1. It builds on collective talents.
2. It allows for productive feedback and critiques.

3. It increases productivity and saves time and money.

4. It ensures overall writing effectiveness.

5. It accelerates decision-making time.

6. It reduces corporate risk.

7. It boosts employee morale and confidence while decreasing stress.

8. It contributes to customer service and satisfaction.

9. It provides greater opportunities to understand global perspectives.

COLLABORATIVE WRITING AND THE WRITING PROCESS

The writing process described in Chapter 2 also applies to collaborative writing. Groups use the same strategies and confront the same problems that individual writers do. Like the individual writer, a team must move through the writing process, going back and forth as necessary between the various stages. But although the essential steps in the writing process are the same, there are some differences you need to know about. Below is a rundown of how collaborative groups tackle the process of preparing a document.

1. Groups must plan before they write. As in individual writing, the planning phase includes brainstorming and outlining (see "Planning" and "Drafting," pages 46–54), as well as identifying the audience, purpose, format, and scope of a document. Unlike individual writers, though, the group must also set ground rules for the collaborative process to work, select a leader or moderator, assign individual responsibilities within the group, and create a schedule that respects individual group members' schedules.

2. Groups must do research. Using a variety of research methods to gather data, as discussed in Chapter 8, the group documents the findings of the report. Insufficient or incorrect research can jeopardize the success of a collaborative document just as easily as it can derail the efforts of an individual writer. In a group context, the responsibility of researching is usually shared by several individuals who must share and coordinate the results of their research prior to the group drafting process.

3. Groups must prepare drafts. Based on research and company goals, the drafting process in group writing can be done in two ways. The first way is similar to individual writing in that only one complete draft of the document is prepared at a time, benefiting from the feedback and critiques of several individuals. The second, more common, way is to have individual members of the group draft separate portions of the document, later to be combined and edited by the entire group.

4. Groups must revise and edit. The revising and editing processes in group writing are also similar to what an individual would do. But group writing offers the added benefit of multiple writers being involved, each of whom may spot organizational problems, inconsistencies in format and tone, as well as grammatical and mechanical mistakes. Groupware (see "Types of Groupware," pages 96–101). is an invaluable tool in helping writing teams access, share, and comment on one another's files.

Collaborative Writing and Editing

Figure 3.2 contains an email written to a listserv by Tara Barber, the Documentation Manager of CText, Inc., a large firm in Ann Arbor, Michigan, that develops software for the publishing industry. Barber describes the writing process followed by her team of collaborative writers. Her approach sheds light on the practical, day-to-day process of group writing and editing. Group harmony is essential to completing documents successfully and on time.

Study Barber's approach. She effectively works *with* and *not against* her staff. She manages the collaborative effort without being heavy-handed or suppressing individual creativity. Her strategy offers a good model to follow.

FIGURE 3.2 Collaborative Editing: Advice from a Pro

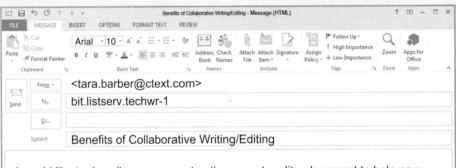

I would like to describe some constructive ways to edit a document to help new writers improve their skills.

I agree that the more projects you make collaborative, the better results you will get. Here's how we do it in my department. Although all my writers are experienced, they come from different backgrounds, which means I have to coordinate editing activities similar to the ways I interact with new writers. It's my job to make sure all the pieces fit.

When I first took this job, several documentation styles were used for the company's manuals, but the department was small, and so the senior writer and I prepared a consistent style manual. We experienced some tension, but by compromising, we ironed out our differences. We developed a style guide and a set of manual conventions that gave writers precise guidelines to follow. The new manual helped us eliminate glaring editing problems such as inconsistencies in spelling, capitalization, use of formats, headings, and documentation.

But the department has grown since that time, and on at least two occasions all of us have reassessed the content and format of the style guide and manual. By doing this, we are able to get input from everyone and to allow for new ideas. When a problem arises now, we are comfortable addressing it as a group.

FIGURE 3.2 (Continued)

In addition to the usual reviews by subject-matter experts, all of us read each other's materials. This collaborative review helps us to become familiar with each other's projects, homogenizes our writing styles, and keeps our documentation consistent. It's also a great way to get a good "clean-eyes edit."

In my role as documentation manager, I try to edit early and late, but not in the middle. Our materials usually go through several edits before they're ready. I try to look over early material found in outlines and first drafts to make sure everything follows our house style and procedures. I edit final drafts because I am responsible for the work my department does. Peer review works best during this intermediate phase, and I don't want to step on individual creativity.

If I have to make comments, I make them at various levels.

a) I point out problems, or sections that seem confusing, but then let the writer suggest fixes.

b) I make suggestions and provide examples—more than one if I can.

c) I actively work with the writer to develop new ways around a problem, such as finding another way of approaching the documentation. This issue is then addressed at our next style meeting, which involves the rest of the department in a brainstorming session.

d) If nothing else works, I play the heavy manager and say, "Do it this way because I say so." I try to avoid this, however, if I possibly can.

Working as a collaborative team, we rarely have editing problems that we can't solve, with the result that everyone is happy with the final document. And, even more important, our customers find the documents usable and valuable. You can't really ask for more than that.

Tara Barber
CText, Inc.
<tara.barber@ctext.com>

SOME GUIDELINES FOR SUCCESSFUL GROUP WRITING

To be successful, a collaborative writing team should observe the following seven helpful guidelines.

1. Understand and agree on the purpose, audience, scope, organization, and deadlines for the report. Everyone needs to be on the "same page" from start to finish.

2. Establish group rules early on and stick to them. Decide when and where the group will meet, how and when members are to communicate with each other (face-to-face, telephone, email, other online technologies).

3. Put the good of the group ahead of individual egos. Group harmony and productivity are essential if the report or proposal is to get done on time. Adopt a "we can get this done together" attitude.

4. Agree on the group's organization. The group can appoint a leader who keeps the team on task by being a coordinator, cheerleader, a scheduler, and a peacemaker who can resolve conflicts quickly, as well as a referee who knows when to call time-out.[1]

5. Identify each member's responsibilities precisely. There should be a fair distribution of labor so that each member can use his or her particular and proven skills. The entire group, however, needs to share responsibility for the overall preparation, design, writing, and proofing of the report.

6. Provide clear and positive feedback at each meeting and for each part of the report the group prepares. Members need to come to meetings prepared, raise important questions, and make thoughtful recommendations.

7. Follow an agreed-on timetable, but leave room for flexibility. The group should estimate a realistic time frame necessary to complete the various stages of their work—when drafts and revisions are due or when editing must be concluded. But remember: Projects always take longer than initially planned. New information may surface or you may need to do additional research.

TEN PROVEN WAYS TO BE A VALUABLE TEAM PLAYER

As we saw, being a team player is one of the most highly prized skills in the world of work. By following the ten guidelines below, many of which Tara Barber's team follows in Figure 3.2, you can contribute to your writing team and earn the respect of your colleagues and supervisor:

1. Think collectively. Adopt a "we can get this done together" attitude. Do not treat some team members as favorites and ignore others. Both actions nurture resentment.

2. Participate. Avoid being a passive observer. Recognize that you have valuable ideas to contribute to the group.

3. Be clear and precise. Express your ideas clearly and appropriately. Avoid veering off the point, being vague, or making unsupported generalizations. Do not be afraid to ask for clarification of anything you don't understand.

4. Set aside your ego. Do not view the group as a battleground or contest in which someone wins and someone else loses. Put the team ahead of self.

---

[1]Adapted from Hendrie Wesigner, *Emotional Intelligence at Work* (New York: Jossey-Bass, 1997).

5. Be enthusiastic. Avoid sounding uninterested in or inconvenienced by the group process. Replace cynicism with a "can do" spirit, and your team will value you as a vital player.

6. Listen. Give everyone a chance to be heard. Pay attention to what others say when they are speaking, and avoid monopolizing the conversations. Develop a "third ear" to discern the meanings behind group members' words.

7. Be open-minded. Be receptive to other points of view. Give serious consideration to each member's suggestions and ideas. Weigh the pros and cons before firing off a question or an objection.

8. Follow company and group protocols. Adhere to company and group protocols regarding the organization, style, and format of the document. Follow the group's rules about meeting times, places, and order of business.

9. Compromise. After ample discussion and deliberation, you may need to compromise for the overall benefit of the group.

10. Go with group consensus. Don't be a lone ranger. Accept the group's decisions as final. Stubbornness only leads to delay and hard feelings.

SOURCES OF CONFLICT IN GROUP DYNAMICS AND HOW TO SOLVE THEM

The success of collaborative writing depends on how well the team interacts. They have to meet and plan before they can even begin researching, set ground roles, decide on responsibilities, and work together on solving problems and come up with solutions. Discussion and criticism are essential to the process of creating any successful document—report, proposal, etc. "Conflict" in the sense of conflicting opinions—a healthy give-and-take—can be positive if it alerts the group to problems (inconsistencies, redundancies, incompleteness) and provides ways to resolve them. A conflict can even help the group generate and refine ideas, leading to a better organized and more carefully written document.

But when conflict translates into ego tripping and personal attacks, nothing productive emerges. Everyone in the group must agree beforehand on three iron-clad working policies of group dynamics: (1) individuals must seek and adhere to group consensus; (2) compromise may be advisable, even necessary, to meet a deadline; and (3) if the group decides to accept compromise, the group leader's final decision on resolving conflicts must be accepted.

Common Problems, Practical Solutions

Following are some common problems in group dynamics, with suggestions on how to avoid or solve them.

1. Resisting constructive criticism. No one likes to be criticized, yet criticism can be vital to the group effort. Be open to suggestions. Individuals who insist on "their way or no way" can become hostile to any change or revision, no matter how small.

> Solution: When emotions become heated, the group leader may wisely move the discussion to another section of the document or to another issue to allow for some cooling-off time. Negotiation is an essential job skill.

2. Giving only negative criticism. Do not saturate a meeting with nothing but negatives. You will block communication if you start criticizing the group's efforts with words such as "Why don't you try . . . ," "What you need is . . . ," "Don't you realize that . . . ," or "If you don't. . . ."

> Solution: When you criticize an idea, diplomatically remind the individual of the team's goals and point to ways in which revision (criticism) furthers those goals. Explain the problem, and offer a helpful, relevant revision. Never attack a group member. Mutual respect is everyone's right and obligation. For the sake of group harmony, be objective, constructive, and cooperative.

3. Dominating a meeting. The group process should stress sharing and responding to ideas, not about taking over. When one member dominates the discussion and becomes aggressive and territorial, the group process suffers.

> Solution: The leader should let the group know that the participation of all members is valued but then say, "We need to hear from the rest of the group." Some groups follow a three-minute rule—each member has three minutes to make comments and does not get the floor again until everyone has had a chance to speak. If one group member still continues to dominate, the leader may (in private) have to speak to him/her.

4. Refusing to participate. Withholding your opinions hurts the group efforts; identify what you believe are major problems, and give the group a chance to consider them.

> Solution: If you don't feel sure of yourself or your points, talk to another member of the group, a listening partner, before a meeting to "test" your ideas or to write down your suggestions before a meeting to share them with the group.

5. Interrupting with incessant questions. Some people interrupt a meeting so many times with questions that all group work stops. The individual may simply be unprepared or may be trying to exercise his or her control of the group.

> Solution: When that happens, a group leader can remark, "We appreciate your interest, but would you try an experiment, please, and attempt to answer your own questions?" or if the person claims not to know, the leader might then say, "Why don't you think about it for a while and then get back to us?"

6. Inflating small details out of proportion. Nitpickers can derail any group. Some individuals waste valuable discussion and revision time by dwelling on relatively insignificant points (e.g., an optional comma, the choice of a single word, etc.) or steer the group away from larger, more important issues (e.g., costs, schedules, etc.).

> Solution: If there is consensus about a matter, leave it alone and turn to more pressing issues. The leader should remind the group (without singling anyone out) about the bigger picture and caution them to stay on track.

7. Being overly deferential to avoid conflict. This problem is the opposite of that described in guideline 1 (page 81). You will not help your group by being a "yes person" simply to appease a strong-willed member of the group.

> Solution: Feel free to express your opinions politely; if tempers begin to flare, call in the group leader or seek the opinions of others on the team. The leader needs to promote and protect meetings as a safe place to express ideas.

8. Not respecting cultural differences. You may have individuals from different countries or cultures on your team. Disregarding or misjudging the way they interact with the group can seriously threaten group success and harmony. Moreover, discrimination of any type—based on race, age, religious beliefs, sexual orientation, or nationality, for example—is unacceptable in a collaborative group or workplace.

> Solution: Some companies offer employees seminars on cultural sensitivity in the workplace. But a group leader must also ensure that diversity is honored and, if anyone does not, he/she may write that person up.

9. Violating confidentiality. Leaking confidential information about a personal issue, product, research, procedure, or operation is a serious violation in the world of work. Some meetings are closed except for those who are a part of the group.

> Solution: Violating confidentiality is often grounds for dismissal. At a preliminary meeting, and periodically during the writing process, the leader should emphasize the whys, hows, and whens of confidentiality.

10. Not finishing on time or submitting an incomplete document. Meeting established deadlines is the group's most important obligation. When some members are not involved in the planning stages or when they skip meetings or ignore group communications, deadlines are invariably missed. If you miss a meeting, get briefed by an individual who was there.

> Solution: The group leader can institute networking through email or other web-based systems to announce meetings, keep members updated, or provide for ongoing communication and questions. See "Web-Based Collaboration Systems" (pages 97–101).

MODELS FOR COLLABORATION

There are as many types of collaborative writing methods as there are companies. The process can range from relatively simple phone calls or emails to a much more extensive use of groupware (see "Types of Groupware," pages 96–98).

The scope, size, and complexity of your document as well as your company's organization will determine what type of (and how much) collaboration is necessary. A shorter assignment (say, a field report, for instance) may not require the same type of group participation as would a policy handbook, a proposal, or a long report. At some large companies, for example, a staff of professional editors (such as Tara Barber's team in Figure 3.2) revises the final draft prepared by a departmental team. The more important and more detailed a document is, the more extensive collaboration will be.

The following sections describe four models for collaboration used in the world of work: (1) Cooperative model, (2) Sequential model, (3) Functional model, and (4) Integrated model.

Cooperative Model

The **cooperative model** is one of the simplest and most expedient ways to write collaboratively in the business world. An individual writer is given an assignment and then goes through the writing process to complete it (see Chapter 2). Along the way, he or she may show a draft to a colleague to get feedback or to a supervisor for a critique. That is what Randy Taylor did in Figure 3.3. He shared a draft of a letter to a potential client with his boss, Felicia Krumpholtz, who made changes in content, wording, and format and then sent it back to Taylor. Following his boss's suggestions, Taylor then created the revised letter in Figure 3.4.

If Taylor had sent his first draft, the customer would hardly have been impressed with his company's professionalism and might not have placed an order. If Terry Tatum were a woman, she might have been offended by being addressed as "Sir." But thanks to Krumpholtz's revisions, Taylor's letter is much more effective. Even though Krumpholtz helped Taylor improve his work, strictly speaking it was not a case of group writing. Although the two interacted, they did not share the final responsibility for creating the letter. Even so, Servitron profited from their interaction.

Sequential Model

In the **sequential model**, each individual is assigned a specific, nonoverlapping responsibility—from brainstorming to revising—for a section of a proposal, report, or other document. There is a clear-cut, rigid division of labor. If four people are on the team, each will be responsible for his or her part of the document. For example, one employee might write the introduction; another, the body of the report; another, the conclusion; and the fourth, the group's recommendation.

Team members may discuss their individual progress and even exchange their work for group review and commentary. They may also choose a coordinator to oversee the progress of their work. When each team member finishes his or her section, the coordinator then assembles the individual parts to form the report. While this model can work well for groups where certain members cannot fully participate, it can lead to a document with an inconsistent style and tone.

FIGURE 3.3 A Draft of Randy Taylor's Letter, Edited by His Supervisor, Felicia Krumpholtz

servitron

4083 Randolph Street
Houston, TX 77016
(713) 555-6761

————————————————————————————————— November 16, 2015

Terry Tatum
Manager
i Consoloodated Solutions
Houston, TX *add zip code*

Dear ~~Sir~~, *Terry Tatum:*

Thank you for asking
~~I am taking the opportunity of answering your request~~ for a price list of
Servitron products. Servitron has been in business in the Houston area for
22 more than ~~twenty-two~~ years and we offer unparalleled equipment and
Consolidated service to ~~any customer.~~ Using a Servitron product will give you both
Solutions efficiency and economy.   *can*

boldface   *boldface*
Whatever Servitron model you choose carries with it a full one-year
warranty on all parts and labor. After the expiration date of your warranty
you ~~should~~ purchase our service contract for $75,000 a year.
       might

~~Here are the models Servitron offers~~

Model Name	Number	Price
Zephyr	81072	$759.95 — *wrong price*
Colt	86085	$929.95
Meteor	88096	$1069.95

Depending on your needs, one of these models should be right for you.

If I might be of further assistance to you, please call on me. Our brochure
is available at **www.servitron.com/brochure** and will give you more
information, including specifications, on these Servitron products.

~~Truly,~~ *Sincerely yours,*   *add phone number*   *reverse*
                                                 and email   *the order*
                                                                             of these
Servitron — *leave 4 spaces*   *two*
Randy Taylor *sign your name*   *sentences*
Sales Associate

www.servitron.com

FIGURE 3.4 The Edited, Final Copy of Figure 3.3

servitron

4083 Randolph Street
Houston, TX 77016
(713) 555-6761

November 16, 2015

Terry Tatum
Manager
Consolidated Solutions
Houston, TX 77005-0096

Dear Terry Tatum:

Thank you for asking for a price list of Servitron products. Servitron has
been in business in the Houston area for more than 22 years and we can
offer unparalleled equipment and service to Consolidated Solutions. Using
a Servitron product will give you both **efficiency** and **economy**.

Depending on your needs, one of these models should be right for you.

Model Name	Number	Price
Zephyr	81072	$789.95
Colt	86085	$929.95
Meteor	88096	$1069.95

Whatever Servitron model you choose carries with it a full **one-year
warranty** on all parts and labor. After your warranty expires, you can
purchase our service contract for only $75.00 a year.

Our brochure is available at **www.servitron.com/brochure** and will give
you more information, including specifications, on these Servitron
products. If I can help you further, please call me at (713) 555-6761 or
email me at **rtaylor@servitron.com**.

Sincerely yours,

SERVITRON

Randy Taylor

Randy Taylor
Sales Associate

www.servitron.com

Functional Model

The division of labor in the **functional model** is assigned not according to parts of a document but by skill or job function of the members. For example, a four-person team may be organized as follows:

- The **leader** schedules and conducts meetings, issues progress reports to management, and generally coordinates everyone's efforts to keep the project on schedule.
- The **researcher** collects data, conducts interviews, searches the literature, administers tests, classifies the information, and then prepares notes on the work.
- The **designated writer/editor**, who receives the researcher's notes, prepares outlines and drafts and circulates them for corrections and revisions.
- The **graphics expert** obtains and prepares all graphics/illustrations, specifying why, how, and where visuals should be placed, and might even suggest that visuals replace certain sections of text. The graphics expert may also be responsible for the design (layout) and production of the document (see Chapter 11).

This organizational scheme fosters much more group interaction than the sequential model does. It also allows each member to do what he or she knows best.

Figure 3.5 illustrates how a functional model works. It describes the behind-the-scenes joint effort that went into Joycelyn Woolfolk's proposal for her boss to authorize a new journal, which would incorporate a newsletter her office currently prepares. A publications coordinator for a large, regional health maintenance organization (HMO), Woolfolk supervises a small staff and reports directly to the public affairs manager, who in turn is responsible to the vice president of the regional office.

As you will see from Woolfolk's functional approach, collaboration can move up and down the chain of command, with participation at all levels. Often, individual employees will pull together information from their separate functional areas (such as finance, information systems, marketing, and sales), and someone else will put that information into a draft that others read and revise until the document is ready to send to the boss. By the time the boss reviews the document, it has been edited and revised many times (and by many individuals) to ensure accuracy and consistency. (Review Figure 3.2.) This is a common business practice.

Integrated Model

In the **integrated model**, all members of the team are engaged in planning, researching, and revising. Each shares the responsibility of producing the document. Members participate in every stage of the document's creation and design, and the group goes back to each stage as often as needed. This model offers intense group interaction. Even though individual writers on the team may be asked to draft different sections of the document, all share in drafting, revising, and editing that document (see "Case Study," pages 89–95). Depending on the scope of the document and company policy, the group may also go outside the team to solicit reviews and evaluations from experts—both inside and outside the company.

FIGURE 3.5 How a Proposal Is Collaboratively Written

Status Report: Coordinating Regional Magazine Project

The idea to start a regional magazine was first expressed in passing by our vice president, who is interested in getting more and higher-level visibility for our regional office. Several other regional offices in our company have created fairly attractive magazines, and one office in particular has earned a lot of good publicity.

The public affairs manager (my boss) and I quickly picked up on the vice president's hint and began to formulate ways to justify the need for such a publication and ways to substantiate our recommendation. For several weeks the public affairs manager and I discussed the kind of documentation our proposal would need, what our resources for researching the question were, what our capabilities would be for producing such a publication, and so on. We were guided by the twofold goal of getting the vice president's approval and, ideally, meeting a genuine market need.

After discussions with my boss, I met with members of my staff to ask them to do the following tasks:

1. Review existing HMO publications and report on whether there was already a regional magazine for the Northwest

2. Develop, administer, and analyze a readership survey for current subscribers to our newsletter, which would potentially be incorporated into the new magazine

3. Formulate general design concepts for the magazine in print and online that we can implement without increasing staff, while still producing the quality magazine the vice president wants

4. Prepare a detailed budget for projected costs

5. Consult with experts on our staff (actuaries, physicians, nurses) about topics of interest

6. Confer with IT about online designs and problems

I requested emails, Web sources, and other documentation from my staff members about most of these tasks, and then I used that information to draft the proposal that eventually would go to the vice president, and perhaps even to the president's office. And I communicated with my staff often, through emails, messages, blogs, personal meetings, and group sessions, both face-to-face and online.

(Continued)

FIGURE 3.5 (Continued)

> After I revised my draft several times, I asked my staff to look over each draft for their feedback. Based on their comments, I made further revisions and did careful editing. My boss also reviewed my proposal, revising and editing it several times. Ultimately, the proposal will go out as a memo from me to my boss, who will then send it under her name to the vice president.

CASE STUDY

Evolution of a Collaboratively Written Document

Figures 3.6, 3.7, and 3.8 show the evolution of a memo that follows an integrated model of collaboration. This memo informed employees that their company was enhancing its recycling program. Alice Schuster, the vice president of Fenton Companies, which manufactures appliances, asked two employees in the human resources department—Abigail Chappel and Manuel Garcia—to prepare a memo ("a few paragraphs" is how Schuster put it) to be sent to all Fenton employees.

Schuster had an initial conference with Chappel and Garcia, at which she stressed that their memo had to convey Fenton's renewed commitment to the environment and greening the workplace and that, as part of that commitment, the employees had to intensify their recycling efforts. Chappel and Garcia thus shared the responsibility of convincing co-workers of the importance of recycling and educating them about practicing it.

Chappel and Garcia also had the difficult job of writing for several audiences simultaneously— the boss, whose name would not appear on the memo, other managers at Fenton, and the Fenton workforce itself.

First Draft

Figure 3.6 is the first draft that Chappel and Garcia collaborated on and then presented to the manager of the human resources department—Wells McCraw—for his comments and revisions. As you can see from McCraw's remarks, written in ink, he was not especially pleased with their first attempt and asked them to make a number of revisions. As a careful reader (conscious of the document's audience), McCraw found Chappel and Garcia's paragraphs to be rambling and repetitious—the writers were unable to stick to the point. Specifically, he pointed out that they included too much information in one paragraph and not enough in others.

As a good editor/manager, McCraw also directed their attention to factual mistakes, irrelevant and even contradictory comments, and essential information they had omitted. Finally, McCraw offered some advice on using visual devices (see "Supplying Visuals to Clarify and Condense Information," pages 21–22) to make their information more accessible to readers.

(Continued)

FIGURE 3.6 Early Draft of the Chappel and Garcia Collaborative Memo, with Revisions in Blue Suggested by Wells McCraw, Their Manager

FENTON COMPANIES

TO: All Employees
FROM: Abigail Chappel; Manuel Garcia
DATE: February 4, 2016
RE: Our Recycling Program

Vague— "Improving"

This ¶ is too long. Too many topics—costs, protecting the environment. Keep it short—say what we are doing and why

An in-house study has shown that Fenton sends approximately 48,000 pounds of paper to the landfill. The landfill charge for this runs about $2,160, which we could save by recycling. Fenton Companies is conscious of our commitment to sustainability and our responsibility to save and protect the environment. Accordingly, starting March 1 we will begin a more intensive paper recycling program.
    Our program, like many others nationwide, will use the latest degradable technology to safeguard the air, trees, and water in our community. It has been estimated that of the 250 million tons of solid waste, three-quarters of goes to landfills. These landfills across the country are becoming dangerously overcrowded. Such a practice wastes our natural resources and endangers our air and drinking water. For example, it takes 10 trees to make 1 ton of paper, or roughly the amount of paper Fenton uses in two weeks. If we could recycle that amount of paper, we could save those trees. Recycling old paper into new paper involves less energy than making paper from new trees. Moreover, waste sent to landfills can, once broken down, leach, seep into our water supply, and contaminate it. The dangers are great.

Start off with this key idea

Check your facts; I think it is closer to 16–17

Word "it" left out

Delete — not relevant to our purpose

No cap

By enhancing our recycling, we will not be sending so much to the Springfield Landfill and so help alleviate a dangerous condition there. We will keep it from overflowing. Fenton will also be contributing to transforming waste products into valuable reusable materials. Recycling paper in our own office shows that we are concerned about the environmental clutter. By having an improved paper recycling program, we will establish our company's reputation as an environmentally conscious industry and enhance our company's image.

Add the fact about our saving trees in this ¶

Delete — makes us look bad

Start ¶ with this point

Fenton is primarily concerned with recycling paper. The 600 old phone books that otherwise would be tossed away can get our recycling program off to a good start.

When? How? Implications for saving/costs?

Give some examples

We encourage you to start thinking about the additional kinds of paper around your office/workspace that needs to be earmarked for recycling. When you start to think about it, you will see how much paper we as a company use.

FIGURE 3.6 (Continued)

↑ not into your wastebaskets

Starting the last week of February, paper bins will be placed by each office door inside the outer wall. These bins will be green—not unsightly and blending with our decor. Separate your waste paper (white, colored, and computer) and put it into these bins. You do not need to remove paper clips and staples, but you must remove rubber bands, tape, and sticky labels. They will be emptied each day by the clean-up crew. There will also be large bins at the north end of the hallway for you to deposit larger paper products. The crucial point is that you use these specially marked bins rather than your wastebasket to deposit paper.

Delete — repetitious

¶ lacks effective "call to action" and incentives

Fenton Companies will deeply appreciate your cooperation and efforts. Thanks for your cooperation.

This memo needs more work
— add at least one ¶ on how recycling will save us money
— insert headings to separate sections

— make directions clearer and easier to follow; try using numbered steps

— end on a more upbeat note; tell employees about the benefits coming to them for recycling — i.e., a bonus/our contribution to their favorite charity

—why don't we say something about America Recycles Day, Nov. 15

© 2017 Cengage Learning

Subsequent Drafts

Figure 3.7 shows the next stage in the collaboration. In this version of the memo, prepared through several revisions over a two-day period, the authors incorporated McCraw's suggestions as well as several changes of their own. It was this revision that they submitted to Vice President Schuster, who also made some comments on the memo. Schuster's suggestions—all valid—show how different readers can help writing teams meet their objectives.

Note that in the process of revising their memo Chappel and Garcia had to make major changes from the first draft in Figure 3.6. Their work went through several versions to arrive at the document in Figure 3.7. Those changes—shortening and expanding paragraphs, adding and deleting information, and refocusing their approach to meet the needs of their audience—are the essential revisions a collaborative writing team, like an individual writer, would expect to make.

Final Copy

With McCraw's further input and their own revision, Chappel and Garcia submitted the final, revised memo found in Figure 3.8 (page 94) to the vice president a few days later. This final copy received Schuster's approval and was then routed to the Fenton staff.

Thanks to an integrated model of collaboration and careful critiques by McCraw and Schuster, Chappel and Garcia successfully revised their work. Effective team effort and shared responsibility were at the heart of Chappel and Garcia's assignment.

(Continued)

FIGURE 3.7 Revision of the Chappel and Garcia Memo, with Changes Suggested by Vice President Schuster

FENTON COMPANIES

TO: All Employees
FROM: Abigail Chappel; Manuel Garcia
DATE: February 9, 2016
RE: Improving Our Recycling Program

Make all headings more precise in next draft

To save money and protect our environment, Fenton Companies will begin a more intensive waste paper recycling program on March 1. Three-quarters of the 250 million tons of solid waste dumped annually in America could be recycled. Our program will still use the latest recycling technology to safeguard trees, air, and water.

New Program

¶ needs more information

Say strengthen or continue

This new program will establish Fenton's reputation as an environmentally conscious company committed to sustainability. Fenton now uses two tons of paper every four weeks. This represents 34 trees that can be saved just by recycling our paper waste. Recycling also means we will send less waste to the landfill, alleviating problems of overfill and reducing the potential for contamination of the water supply. Waste sent to large landfills can leach and seep into water systems. By recycling paper, Fenton will also reduce the risk of long-term environmental pollution.

Add that we no longer use Styrofoam and that our suppliers use only biodegradable products

Saving Money

Indicate how much we save

Increased recycling would save us money. Right now Fenton pays $180 per month to dump 4,000 pounds (two tons) of paper waste at the landfill. However, increased recycling will eliminate the $180 dumping expense.

Put in itemized bulleted list to stand out.

Ultimately, the success of our project depends on renewed awareness of the variety of office paper suitable for recycling. Paper products that can be recycled include newspapers, scrap paper, computer printouts, letters, envelopes (without windows), shipping cartons, old phone books, and uncoated paper cups.

Do not start new ¶ here; keep as part of previous ¶

Recycling 600 or so old phone books each year alone will save 2,400 pounds of landfill space (or close to $108). The old 2015 phone books, which will be replaced by new 2016 ones on March 1, will give us an excellent opportunity to intensify our recycling.

FIGURE 3.7 (Continued)

Directions

Here are some easy-to-follow directions to make our recycling efforts even more effective:

Boldface these words

1. Starting the last week in February, <u>paper bins will be placed inside each office door.</u> Put all waste paper into these bins, which will be emptied by maintenance.
2. Place <u>larger paper products</u>—such as cartons or phone books—in the <u>green</u> bigger paper bins at the end of each main corridor.
3. Put white, colored, computer printout, and newspapers into separate marked bins. Remove all rubber bands, tape, and sticky notes.

Thanks for your cooperation. To show our appreciation for your help, 50 percent of the savings from recycling paper will go toward employee bonuses and the other 50 percent will be given to the office's favorite charity. The benefits of our new recycling program will more than outweigh the inconvenience it may cause. We will conduct another study in time for America Recycles Day on November 15 to determine how our company has improved in this area.

End with the incentive for emphasis

Add another sentence to this ¶ on how a safer environment will benefit our company and the employees, too

FIGURE 3.8 Final Copy of the Memo Prepared by Chappel and Garcia Using an Integrated Model of Collaboration

FENTON COMPANIES

TO: All Employees
FROM: Abigail Chappel; Manuel Garcia
DATE: February 12, 2016
RE: Improving Our Recycling Program

Why We Need to Increase Recycling Efforts

To save additional money and to protect the environment, Fenton will begin a more intensive waste paper recycling program on March 1. For the new program to succeed, we need to increase our paper recycling efforts. Three-quarters of the 250 million tons of solid waste dumped annually in America could be recycled. Our program will continue to rely on the latest recycling technology for better greening of the workplace and to safeguard trees, air, and water.

Recycling has already saved us money. Right now Fenton pays $180 per month to dump 4,000 pounds (two tons) of paper waste at the landfill, compared to 6,000 pounds (three tons) and $270 per month last year. However, increased recycling will eliminate the $180 monthly dumping expense.

Fenton's Image as a Green Company

Even more important, this new, intensive program will further strengthen Fenton's reputation as an environmentally conscious company committed to sustainability. Three years ago, we stopped using Styrofoam products and asked suppliers to use biodegradable materials for all our shipping containers. Our efforts have proved successful, but Fenton still uses two tons of paper every four weeks. This paper represents 34 trees that can be saved just by recycling our paper waste. We need to send even less waste to the landfill, alleviating problems of overfill and reducing the potential for contamination of the water supply. Waste sent to large landfills can leach and seep into water systems.

Paper Products to Recycle

Ultimately, the success of this project depends on our being aware of the variety of office paper suitable for recycling. A list of paper products that can be recycled includes

- newspapers
- letters
- envelopes (without cellophane windows)
- phone books
- uncoated paper cups
- scrap paper
- computer printouts
- junk mail (only black print on white paper)
- shipping cartons

FIGURE 3.8 (Continued)

The old 2015 phone books, which will be replaced by new 2016 ones on March 1, will give us an excellent opportunity to launch our intensified recycling program.

Steps to Follow

Here are some easy-to-follow directions to make our recycling efforts even more effective:

1. Starting the last week in February, put all waste paper into the **paper bins** that will be placed **inside each office door.** These bins will be emptied by maintenance.

2. Place **larger paper products**—such as bulky cartons—in the **green bigger paper bins** at the end of the main corridor.

3. Remove all rubber bands, tape, and sticky notes and put white, colored, computer printout, and newspapers into separate marked bins.

We will conduct another study in time for America Recycles Day on November 15 to determine how our company has improved in this area. The benefits of our new recycling program will more than outweigh the inconvenience it may cause. A safer environment—and a more cost-effective way to run our company—benefits us all.

Thanks for your cooperation. To show our appreciation for your increased efforts, 50 percent of the savings from recycling paper will go into an annual employee bonus fund and the other 50 percent will be given to the office's favorite charity.

COMPUTER-SUPPORTED COLLABORATION

While you will sometimes collaborate on drafts using handwritten notes and comments, as we just saw in Figures 3.6 and 3.7, to be successful writers, employees must also be proficient in using multiple types of collaborative software systems, otherwise known as **groupware.** You will be expected to know—or at least be adaptable to learning—not only how to use email for collaborative coomunications but also how to navigate document tracking systems (such as Microsoft Word's Track Changes feature or Adobe Acrobat) as well as web-based collaboration systems (wikis, Google Docs).

Advantages of Computer-Supported Collaboration

Computer-supported collaboration offers significant advantages to both employers and workers. Here are some of those benefits:

1. **Increased opportunities to "meet."** Today's meeting-heavy and travel-filled work environments often make collaborating in person difficult and costly. Various types of groupware provide a virtual shared workplace where team members can ask questions, share information, make suggestions and revisions, and troubleshoot.

2. **Improved feedback and accountability.** Because it is accessible and easy to use, groupware helps team members participate actively in the collaboration process. Groupware encourages team members to get to the point and make sure other members understand their message clearly and quickly. Because each member's contributions are documented, everyone's participation becomes a matter of record.

3. **Enhanced possibility of complete and clear information.** Groupware allows everyone involved in the team to truly be "on the same page." It provides a running record, thus saving all information and preventing misinterpretation.

4. **Reduced stress in updating new group members.** Groupware can efficiently and quickly bring new team members into the ongoing conversation, saving time and effort and reducing the stress of face-to-face meetings.

5. **Expanded options for communicating worldwide.** Groupware ensures the flexibility to contact group members anywhere—at a home office (telecommuters, freelancers), on the road, at another office, or in another country.

Groupware and Face-to-Face Meetings

Groupware does not, of course, completely eliminate the need for a group to meet in person to discuss priorities, clarify issues, or build team spirit. But face-to-face communications, although sometimes essential, are frequently accompanied by computer-supported collaboration via groupware. In fact, groupware can enhance meetings by allowing people to draft and discuss documents online *before* they arrive at a meeting, thus saving time and increasing efficiency. It also allows teams to extend their collaboration beyond the confines of the workplace, whether at an off-site location or at a telecommuting employee's home. For instance, you and your colleagues might use Microsoft Word's Track Changes to revise a progress report after an important meeting, or you might use Google Docs to help your supervisor make last-minute edits to a presentation before an important trade show.

Types of Groupware

There are essentially three types of groupware commonly used to produce collaboratively written documents in today's workplace: email, document tracking software, and web-based collaboration systems.

Email

Email is used for many jobs in the world of work, as you will see in Chapter 4. It has an important role to play in collaborative writing online as well. While email is not the

place to create or revise a collaboratively written document (because edits and other changes are hard to incorporate and track), email nevertheless makes online collaboration possible for the following reasons:

1. It is used to send collaboratively written documents as text files or PDF files. Team members in the same office or from around the globe can then access the same document and share their feedback.
2. It can ensure that every member of the team is working on the same document by identifying each document by name and number in the "subject field" (*Report on Parking, Rev. 4* or *Proposal on Recycling, Draft 2*).
3. It saves the group time by decreasing the number of face-to-face meetings it must have. Email cannot take the place of a face-to-face exchange, however.

Document Tracking Software

Document tracking software, such as Microsoft Word's Track Changes feature or Adobe Acrobat, provides another way for collaborative writing teams to share, comment on, and revise their work online. Figure 3.9 (page 98) shows an example of a collaboratively written document using Microsoft Word—the first draft of a section of a report on increasing parking spaces at a hospital—and how it has been revised and edited by several team members using the Track Changes feature.

Sent as an email attachment to every team member, Figure 3.9 uses the Track Changes feature in Word to preserve all the original text of Draft 1 while automatically showing and identifying comments from each individual. Team members can ask for and even supply new text, insert headings, clarify and verify factual data, and call for visuals. They can also edit sentences in the document, and Word will automatically track these changes.

When a group member revises the next version of this section of the report, he or she can then accept or reject the tracked changes. But keep in mind that all changes must be agreed on by the group. This is where the dynamics of collaborative writing works for the good of the entire group in order to produce a careful document on time.

Web-Based Collaboration Systems

You can also use a wide variety of web-based applications to write collaboratively at work. These include wikis and online word-processing applications like Google Docs. With these systems, the text/report is automatically shared between you and your various collaborators—no emails or attachments are required. You and your collaborators can post revised drafts, meet to review one another's work, offer suggestions, and store files and revisions.

Web-based collaboration systems also make communication among more than two people much more efficient. Most systems consolidate all team communications into a single site on the Web for each team member to view. These systems help employees manage complicated editing projects and receive feedback from co-workers at different branches of a company. Office collaboration software like Yammer, FB@Work, or Slack also make it easier to collaborate with colleagues who are not in the same office.

FIGURE 3.9 Collaborative Editing Using a Document Tracking System

Draft 1 — Proposal to Expand Hospital Parking Facilities ~~How We Can Expand the Hospital's Parking~~

~~CGH~~ Community General Hospital needs to expand its parking facilities. Right now there is just too little room for visitors, staff, and patients. These inadequate parking facilities are a ~~detrime~~ detriment to the overall growth of pt. care. They have been an important talking point since the inception of this committee. Maybe they were ok when the hospital opened its doors in 1973, but not today. ~~CGH is a good place to work and t~~The new parking facilities would definitely benefit the present staff and visitors from walking ~~long distances~~ two blocks in the rain and ice.

The exact number of new spots is hard to estimate now but I am thinking around 500 might be just right. The problem is the traffic flow around the hospital. While the new parking facilities would alleviate it, it also raises a central question about how to get it done. Perhaps Wentworth Avenue, East to West, might be turned into a one-way street. That way we could add up to 11 new spots in the front of the ER and thus resolve the congestion that has hampered easy ~~egress~~ entrance and ~~ingress~~ exit. Another possibility worth considering is changing Taylor Street—right now it is a two-way street and we could make it one-way West to East.

At any rate, the traffic flow is a key issue the hospital needs to solve if it is to expand its parking facilities. But there are other important engineering problems that must be solved. Eleanor Yi, the hospital engineer, has studied the stress points, pre-cast concrete, and the slope of vehicular access ramps that would accommodate increased traffic flow. As you can see, she believes that the hospital does not have the space to locate all the new parking spots in one plane area. She recommends a two-story structure and believes the North side of the ER might be the best place.

KT 5/5/15 8:58 AM
Comment: Let's use the full name of the hospital here.

MM 5/5/15 11:28 AM
Comment: We should cite source and statistics. See hospital report CGH-GR-2010

KT 5/5/15 9:00 AM
Comment: We need to take out abbreviations in the final copy.

LB 5/5/15 10:15 AM
Comment: We must be precise. It was 417, according to the engineering proposal.

MM 5/5/15 11:38 AM
Comment: I think it might be best to start a new section here and title it "Increased Traffic Flow."

LB 5/5/15 10:17 AM
Comment: Let's put her documentation in an appendix.

MM 5/5/15 11:40 AM
Comment: That's a good idea; her solution appears workable and falls within our budget.

KT 5/5/15 9:04 AM
Comment: I don't understand this terminology. Should we use a different phrase here?

LB 5/5/15 10:19 AM
Comment: We have to provide further information about the number of ramps and perhaps confirmation from engineering consulting firm to corroborate Yi's findings.

© Cengage Learning

Wikis

Wikis are similar to document-tracking systems, but they have a few crucially different characteristics:

- Wikis are websites to which team members are given passwords, enabling them to check documents in and out of the site.
- They typically do not show tracked changes directly on the document as Microsoft Word does. Rather, each edited version is assigned a new version number. The team members can then easily compare different versions of the document, but these differences will not show up within a single version.

The advantage of wikis over tracked documents is that each wiki version is a clean document free of complicated tracked edits. When team members revise, they need to proofread only the latest draft rather than going through the time-consuming process of accepting or rejecting changes, deleting comments, or troubleshooting inconsistencies.

The disadvantage of wikis the lack of quality control. Because each group member's changes are not clearly tracked, it can be difficult for members to keep up with the number of changes. When using wikis, then, the team needs to establish a clear protocol outlining who may make changes to the document and when. To see an example of a wiki, go to http://en.wikipedia.org/wiki/Main_Page (the main English-language Wikipedia page).

Online Word-Processing Systems

Another popular web-based collaboration tool are online word-processing systems. Applications like Google Docs, Microsoft Office 365, Adobe Buzzword, and Zoho Writer help collaborative teams share and edit a variety of documents easily on the Web. These systems are essentially online word processors that bundle file-sharing, online collaboration, word-processing, and document design features. Like wikis, writing and editing are done on websites. Unlike wikis, though, these systems also allow for tracking changes and document design.

One of the most widely used online systems is Google Docs, seen in Figure 3.10 (page 101). This free application can be accessed and used through the Google site by anyone with a Gmail password. Google Docs offers the following benefits:

- It functions like a word processor, so the user can build publishable documents with it (a feature most wikis do not include).
- It safely stores documents in a secure space online, accessible from any computer.
- Is available free-of-charge.
- It allows team members to create, comment on, share, and revise documents on the Web.
- It records a complete revision history of any changes made to the document.
- It provides a chat window in the interface for real-time collaboration online.

Google Docs is used frequently in the workplace as a collaborative tool because it streamlines the editing process and bundles all revisions into a shared and secured space. Google Docs and other online word processors are especially helpful when you need a fast turnaround on collaboratively written and edited documents.

CASE STUDY

Using Google Docs as a Collaboration Tool

Allen Knutz is the inventory manager for Lightofmylife.com, a company that specializes in designer lights and in a popular line of "green" lighting fixtures, lamps, and lightbulbs. The company has grown recently because of greater customer demands for environmentally friendly products and for compact fluorescent bulbs and LEDs. As the company expanded, it needed more floor space for their inventory and additional forklifts to accommodate an accelerated delivery schedule. To make sure the company had enough inventory on hand, the CEO of Lightofmylife.com has asked Knutz to write a proposal about expanding their warehouse space.

Writing proposals has always been a collaborative project at Lightofmylife.com, with teams of four or five employees under the direction of a primary supervisor who manages the process. This proposal was particularly challenging because the CEO wanted it in less than a week to take advantage of available storage options. In the past, Knutz collaborated with his colleagues using the Track Changes feature in Word, but he knew that this process generates numerous email exchanges as well as multiple versions of the same document that everyone must open and read.

Why Use Google Docs

Google Docs allowed Knutz's team to create, share, revise, and comment on an evolving document quickly and efficiently and produce the final version—all using the same web-based groupware application. Since some team members would be off-site for sales visits or at trade shows and another member was telecommuting, Knutz decided that his team would have to meet online at least three or four times during the week to participate in real-time editing through the chat room feature, rather than through a back-and-forth email exchange that would take much longer.

How to Set Up and Use Google Docs

Knutz set up the proposal on Google Docs and then was ready to share the document to be created with his colleagues. He keyed in their Gmail addresses in the "share" window. Figure 3.10 shows what the "problem" portion of the proposal looked like in Google Docs. Before collaboration began, however, Knutz established some guidelines. Each team member could comment on the document, but Knutz was the only editor who could actually make the revisions. Using a sequential model for collaboration, he stressed that each team member would write a different section of the proposal but that everyone was responsible for suggesting changes through the comments feature for the entire document at various stages. Though his team was working at different locations, they were able to complete a successful proposal in time for the CEO's deadline.

FIGURE 3.10 Using Google Docs to Collaborate on a Document

Similar with Track Changes in MS Word, Google Docs highlights specific revisions made to the document. This is an earlier version of the document in the document window above. Notice how Google Docs has recorded the changes to the document.

Google Docs records a revision history of all changes made to the document in a chronological list, allowing you to easily access different versions.

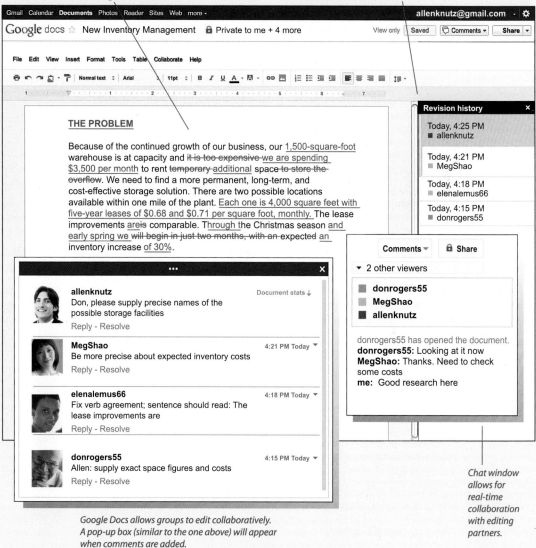

Google Docs allows groups to edit collaboratively. A pop-up box (similar to the one above) will appear when comments are added.

Chat window allows for real-time collaboration with editing partners.

Models for Computer-Supported Collaboration

Employees using groupware will find that the *integrated model* (see below) and the *sequential model* (see below) are the most effective models for computer-supported collaboration.

The Integrated Model

1. All members of the team work on the entire document—developing, expanding, revising, and editing it. The original draft is saved so that it is accessible to all team members who will work on it. When using email, the team should be careful not to lose sight of the original draft. But when employing a document tracking system, writers/revisers need to look at the original draft and continue to edit it. When using a wiki, the original draft will remain available separately as subsequent versions are uploaded.

2. Each member of the team keeps the rest of the team in the loop when he or she makes changes to the document. When using email, the team member making the change should copy all other members of the team on the email. But when using a document tracking system, each team member should inform the others while he or she is making changes so that two writers aren't working on the tracked document at once. With a wiki, however, only the person currently making changes will be able to access the document, since wikis automatically lock out other users when one team member has the document checked out.

3. Each team member looks at each draft of the document as it is edited. When using email, team members should comment on each draft when it is emailed to the entire team. Editing through a document tracking system, each subsequent reader/writer should insert comments, noting where he or she agrees or disagrees with the previous editor's comments. With a wiki, though, each member of the team should look at each draft as it is uploaded and provide comments or express concerns to the rest of the group, which can be either fixed by the most recent editor or passed on to the next editor.

4. The team agrees on the final draft. If the steps above for email, document tracking systems, or wikis are followed, the final draft can be produced relatively smoothly. When editing via email or a document tracking system, the team must select one or more members to consolidate their various drafts. When using a wiki, the team has to agree to the second-to-last draft so that any changes to it will become the final draft version. In any instance, the final draft should be proofread one more time by all members of the team, to resolve any loose ends.

The Sequential Model

1. Each member of the team is responsible only for drafting his or her assigned section of the document. At this point, the writer is simply word processing, not using groupware. The team should choose a team leader, however, who can act as an overall editor (see step 4).

2. Each team member sends his or her completed section to everyone else in the group. Since the sections will remain separate for the time being, email should be used (it would be premature to use a document tracking system or wiki).

3. All members of the group edit the individual sections and return the revised sections to their respective authors. Email continues to be the most appropriate medium to convey these edits.

4. Each team member revises his or her section based on team comments and sends the revised version to the team leader. The team leader then combines the reviewed and edited sections into a single document, reads through the entire document for consistency of style and format within each section, and, if additional group feedback is necessary, sends the complete document to the entire group via email (in which case everyone can respond at once), as a tracked document (then each member would need to make edits and add comments in turn), or posted on a wiki (where only one member at a time will be able to check out the document and make changes).

5. The team leader finalizes the document. Now that all team members have not only written and revised their sections but also had a chance to edit and comment on the complete document, the team leader has all of the information he or she needs to finalize and submit the document.

Avoiding Problems with Online Collaboration

Regardless of the online collaborative method your team uses, it must establish ground rules by which documents are created, posted, revised, protected, and submitted. By following these guidelines, your team can avoid common problems in any online collaboration:

1. Be sure that all team members have access and authorization.
2. Everyone in the group must be "in the loop."
3. Save the original draft and subsequent ones in separate files to refer to earlier drafts.
4. Link each revision with the individual who made it.
5. Require all team members to agree to the final document.
6. Maintain confidentiality to protect the document from unauthorized users.

MEETINGS

One of the most frequent ways to collaborate is through meetings, which can be small group discussions or large, formal conferences. Whether regularly scheduled (a weekly staff meeting) or a special, unscheduled one, a meeting requires teamwork. Collective energy and goodwill will bear much fruit. To succeed in the workplace, you need to know how to plan a meeting, create an agenda, and write minutes for your group.

Planning a Meeting

As with a collaboratively written document, meetings have to be carefully planned. They need to be organized, specifying when and how the meeting will take place (in-person, face-to-face via Skype, a virtual meeting, etc.), a focus provided for the meeting, and guidelines set for how it will be conducted. If you have the responsibility of planning a meeting, be sure you can answer the following questions:

1. **What is the purpose of the meeting?** Determine why the meeting is necessary, what essential topics need to be discussed, and what results or outcomes the meeting hopes to accomplish.

2. **Who should attend the meeting?** Identify key people who need to be involved, e.g., managers, co-workers, colleagues from other departments, clients, vendors, etc.

3. **What specific responsibilities do individuals in your group have?** Determine who will take minutes (see "Writing the Minutes," pages 105–109), introduce the meeting, or deliver a PowerPoint or Prezi presentation, for example.

4. **When should the meeting take place?** There are good times and bad times to hold a business meeting, as the following schedule shows:

Good times	Bad times
1. Mid-morning or mid-afternoon	1. Early in the morning or late in the afternoon
2. Any time during the week except Monday morning or Friday afternoon, or immediately before or after a major holiday	2. Monday morning or Friday afternoon
	3. Immediately before or after a major holiday
3. After a major company celebration when morale is high	4. Same day as a long training session or long meeting

© 2015 Cengage Learning

5. **Where should the meeting take place?** Select an appropriate space, one equipped with all the technology your group plans to use (e.g., speakerphones, SMART Boards, web-based conferencing systems).

TECH NOTE

Virtual Meetings

While face-to-face meetings are still very frequent in the workplace, technology has made virtual meetings a useful alternative. They allow a group to meet online no matter where team members are located. Virtual meetings in the world of work facilitate communication and save money on travel costs.

Here are three ways technology can help you conduct a virtual meeting:

1. **Teleconferencing** allows for conference calls in which multiple participants at one's office, across the country, or around the globe can communicate with one another. But note that participants have to be notified of the call and given a password to participate in the conversation.

2. **Web conferencing** (such as Cisco's WebEx) combines the audio component of teleconferencing with the face-to-face interaction of a traditional meeting. The greatest advantage of web conferencing over teleconferencing is that individuals attending a web conference can view presentations and share documents electronically during a meeting.

3. **Dedicated videoconferencing** systems are primarily used for group-to-group conferences or one-way seminars in large rooms and auditoriums, bringing large groups of people together to share information without the expense and time of traveling.

Creating an Agenda

Out of your planning will come your **agenda,** a list of the topics to be covered at the meeting. An agenda is a one- or sometimes two-page outline of the main points to be covered at the meeting. The agenda should list only those items that your group, based on its work and interaction, regards as most crucial. Prioritize your action items so that the most important ones come first.

Observing Courtesy at a Group Meeting

To show your team members the courtesy they deserve during a meeting (whether face-to-face or virtually), observe the following guidelines:

1. **Be on time.** Coming in late can disrupt a meeting and cause further delays if you have to be brought up-to-date.

2. **Silence your cell phone.** Set your phone on vibrate if you are expecting an important business call.

3. **Do not send text messages.** Sending text messages during a meeting is as rude as playing a video game on a smartphone.

4. **Avoid side conversations.** Talking to others around you while the meeting is in progress shows poor manners and can distract from the business and progress of the meeting.

5. **Avoid interrupting.** If you need to interject a comment, raise your hand or wait for the meeting planner to ask for comments from the group.

6. **Be an active listener.** Pay attention to what is being said at the meeting and also try to discern the message behind those words.

7. **Participate; don't dominate.** Give everyone a chance to speak. Contribute to the discussion, but don't monopolize it.

8. **Be a focused speaker.** If you are called on or choose to speak to the group, get to the point quickly, be clear, and avoid straying from your topic.

9. **Do not record the meeting or take photographs.** Unless you have permission, do not bring an audio recorder or video camera to a meeting, and do not take photographs.

Writing the Minutes

The **minutes** are a summary of what happened at the meeting (see Figure 3.12, pages 107–108). Copies of minutes are kept on file—they are the official, permanent record of the group's deliberations and are regarded as legal documents. Minutes need to be clear, accurate, and impartial. If you are asked to take minutes, don't inject your own opinions of how well or poorly the meeting went; for example, "Once more Hicks got off the topic" is not appropriate. Plan on transmitting minutes 24 to 48 hours after the meeting has adjourned.

TECH NOTE

Videoconferencing with Skype

Skype allows individuals in the world of work to conduct videoconferences over the Internet without purchasing expensive videoconferencing systems. Skype can be used for one-on-one meetings (see Tech Note: Skype Interviews, page 289) or for video-conferences with a small group (up to ten participants). Skype functions like a telephone call but it uses a webcam to send video to your partner(s) (see Figure 3.11). You can download the free software from **www.skype.com**.

Like other business meetings, you have to prepare for a Skype conference. You need to do your homework—planning, sharing information, and taking notes. Here are five guidelines to help make your Skype videoconference productive:

- Collaboration works best in Skype videoconferences when everyone has a compatible fast Internet connection.
- Always test your webcam to make sure it is working (and is in focus) before making a Skype call, and ask the other participants to check theirs, too. In your Skype contact list, click on "Echo/Sound Test Service" to test your audio settings.
- Look directly into your computer's webcam (and not at the keyboard) so that the participants can see you clearly.
- Be sure that any files you share during the meeting through Skype are relevant.
- Do not try to carry on another conversation on your cell phone or tweet or text during your Skype conversation.

FIGURE 3.11 Multiple people Engaged in a Skype Conversation

Andrey Popov/Dreamstime.com

FIGURE 3.12 Minutes from a Business Meeting

NewTech, Inc.   **www.newtech.com**
● ● ●   4300 Ames Boulevard, Gunderson, CO 81230-0999
303.555.9721

Minutes for Environmental Safety Committee (ESC) meeting on August 12, 2015, in Room 203 of Lab Annex at 10:00 a.m.

Members Present:

Thomas Baldanza, Grace Corlee (President), Virginia Downey, Victor Johnson, Roberta Koos, Kent Leviche (Secretary), Ralph Nowicki, Barbara Poe-Smith, Williard Ralston, Asah Rashid, Morgan Tachiashi, and Carlos Zandrillia

Members Absent:

Paul Gordon (family leave); Marty Wagner

Old Business:

The minutes from the previous meeting on July 8, 2015, were approved as read.

Reports:

(1) Morgan Tachiashi reported on the progress the Site Inspection Committee is making in getting the plant ready for the August 28 visit of the State Board of Examiners. All preparations are on schedule.

(2) The proposal to study the use of biometric identification in place of employee ID badges is nearly complete, according to Asah Rashid.

New Business:

(1) Virginia Downey and Ralph Nowicki voiced concern about a computer virus that may strike the plant—Monkey. Disguised as a familiar email, the virus is contained in an attachment that destroys files. Barbara Poe-Smith moved, and Virginia Downey seconded, that management upgrade its antivirus protection software. The vote carried by 9 to 3.

Supplies essential information on attendance, date, and place of meeting

Refers to previous meeting to provide continuity

Concisely summarizes progress on ongoing business

Identifies key speakers

Records only main points of discussion and votes

© 2017 Cengage Learning

(Continued)

FIGURE 3.12 (Continued)

Includes other business to be continued

Excellent morale builder

Signals end of meeting and date of next one

Page 2

(2) Concerned about computer downtime in the plant during the month of July—5 outages totaling 7.5 lost working hours—Kent Leviche asked the ESC to address this problem. After discussion, the ESC unanimously agreed to appoint a subcommittee to investigate the outages and determine solutions. Roberta Koos and Thomas Baldanza will chair the subcommittee and then present a survey report at next month's meeting.

(3) Personnel in the Environmental Testing Lab were commended for their extra effort in ensuring that their department maintained the highest professional standards during the month of July.

(4) Grace Corlee adjourned the meeting at 11:41 a.m.

Next Meeting:

The next meeting of the ESC will be on September 9 at 1:00 p.m. in Room 203 of the Lab Annex Building.

© Cengage Learning

What to Include in Your Minutes

Minutes of a meeting should include the following information:

- date, time, and place of the meeting
- name of the group holding the meeting and why
- name of the person chairing the meeting
- names of those present and those absent
- the approval or amendment of the minutes of the previous meeting
- for each major point—the action items—indicate what was done:
  - what was discussed, suggested, or proposed
  - what was decided and the vote, including abstentions
  - what was continued (tabled) for a subsequent study, report, or meeting
  - the time the meeting officially concluded

Guidelines on Writing Minutes

To be effective, minutes must be concise and to the point. Here are a few guidelines to help you:

- Make sure of your facts; spell all names, products, and tests correctly.
- Concentrate on the major facts surrounding action items. Condense lengthy discussions, debates, and reports given at the meeting.
- Do not report verbatim what everyone said; readers will be more interested in outcomes—what the group did.
- List each motion (or item voted on) exactly as it is worded and in its final form.
- Avoid words that interpret (negatively or positively) what the group or anyone in the group did or did not do.

Figure 3.12 (pages 107–108) containing minutes of a meeting shows how these parts fit together.

CONCLUSION

This chapter has emphasized the importance of collaboration in the world of work and explained the various collaborative models you may need to follow. It has also given you detailed guidelines on creating, editing, and revising a collaborative document, using the most current types of web-based applications. Working successfully as part of a team, whether at face-to-face meetings or online, is one of the most valuable skills you can develop, and one that your employer will expect you to use successfully as a vital part of your job.

✔ REVISION CHECKLIST

Being a Responsible Team Member

☐ Succeeded in being a team player by putting the success of my group over the needs of my own ego.

☐ Followed the necessary steps of the writing process to take advantage of team effort and feedback.

☐ Attended all group meetings and understood and agreed to the responsibilities of the group and my own obligations.

☐ Finished the research, planning, and/or drafting expected of me as a group member.

☐ Conducted necessary interviews and conferences to gather, clarify, and verify information.

☐ Shared my research, ideas, and suggestions for revision through constructive criticism.

☐ Participated honestly and politely in discussions with colleagues.

☐ Treated members of my team with respect and courtesy.

☐ Was open to criticism and suggestions for change.

☐ Read colleagues' work and gave specific and helpful criticism and suggestions.

☐ Kept matters in proper perspective by not being a nitpicker and by not interrupting with extraneous points or unnecessary questions.

☐ Sought help when necessary from relevant subject matter experts and from co-workers.

☐ Secured responses and approval from management.

Using Computer-Supported Collaboration

☐ Took advantage of email, instant messaging, and groupware applications (e.g., document tracking systems, wikis, Google Docs) to communicate with my collaborative team.

☐ Investigated the research, drafting, revising, and editing benefits available with computer software.

☐ Answered questions and responded to requests promptly from the team leader and collaborative team members.

☐ Attached pertinent documents in emails to the collaborative team.

☐ Avoided technical problems with online collaboration by adhering to established policies.

☐ Respected confidentiality and used computer-assisted editing technologies responsibly and ethically.

Preparing for and Participating at a Meeting

☐ Prepared a clear agenda for the meeting and distributed it to members ahead of time.

☐ Wrote minutes that objectively reported what happened.

☐ Took notes that highlighted main points of the meeting for my collaborative team and boss.

☐ Participated in virtual meetings through teleconferencing, web conferencing, or videoconferencing.

EXERCISES

1. Assume you belong to a three- or four-person editing team that functions the way Tara Barber's does, as described in Figure 3.2. Each member of your team should bring in four copies of a paper written for this course or for another one. Exchange copies with the other members of your team so that each team member has everyone else's papers to review and revise. For each paper you receive, comment on the style, organization, tone, and discussion of ideas as Wells McCraw did in Figure 3.6.

2. With the members of your collaborative team, select four different brands of the same product (such as a software package, a Web browser, a smartphone, a wireless router, a Blu-Ray player, or a power tool). Each member of your team should select one of the brands and prepare a two-page memo report for your instructor (see "Memos," pages 220–227), evaluating the product according to the following criteria:

   - convenience
   - performance
   - technical capabilities or capacities
   - reviews
   - adaptability
   - price
   - warranties
   - comparisons with competitors' models

   Each team member should then submit a draft to the other members of the team to review. At a subsequent group meeting, the group should evaluate the four brands based on the team's drafts and then together prepare one final recommendation report for your instructor.

3. Your company is planning to construct a new office, and you, together with other employees, have been asked to serve on a committee to make sure that plans for the new building adhere to the Americans with Disabilities Act, passed in 1990. According to that act, it is against the law to discriminate against anyone with disabilities that limit "major life activities," such as walking, seeing, speaking, hearing, or working.

The law is expressly designed to remove architectural and physical barriers and to make sure that plans are modified to accommodate those protected by the law (for example, wider hallways to accommodate wheelchairs). Other considerations include choosing appropriate floor surfaces (reducing the danger of slipping), placing water fountains low enough for use by individuals in wheelchairs, and installing doors that require minimal pressure to open and close.

After studying the plans for the new building, you and your team members find several problem areas. Prepare a group-written report advising management of the problems and what must be done to correct them to comply with the law. Divide your written work according to areas that need alteration—doors, floors, water fountains, restroom facilities. Each team member should bring in his or her section for the group to edit and revise. The group should then prepare the final report for management.

4. A new manager will be coming to your office park in the next month, and you and five other employees have been asked to serve on a committee that will submit a report about safety problems at your office park and what should be done to solve them. You and your team must establish priorities and propose guidelines that you want the new manager to put into practice. After two very heated meetings, you realize that what you and two other employees have considered solutions, the other half of your committee regards as the problems. Here is a rundown of the leading conflicts dividing your committee:

- **Speed bumps.** Half the committee likes the way they slow traffic down in the office park, but the other half says there are too many of them and are a menace because they damage a car's shock absorber system.
- **Sound pollution.** Half your team wants Security to enforce a noise policy preventing employees from playing loud music while driving in and out of the office park, but the other half insists that policy violates employee rights.
- **Van and sport utility vehicle parking.** Half the committee demands that vans and sport utility vehicles park in specially designated places because they block the view of traffic for any vehicle parked next to them; the other members protest saying that people who drive these vehicles will be singled out and be given less desirable parking places.

Clearly your committee has reached a deadlock and will be unproductive as long as those conflicts go unresolved. Based on this scenario, do the following:

a. Have each person on the committee email the other five committee members suggesting a specific plan on how to proceed—how the group can resolve their conflicts. Prepare your email message and send it to the other five committee members and to your instructor. What's your plan to get the committee moving toward writing the report to the incoming manager?

b. Assume that you have been asked to convince the other half of the committee to accept your half's views on the three areas of speed bumps, noise control, and parking. Send the three opposition committee members an attachment via email persuading them to your way of thinking. Your message must assure them that you respect their point of view.

 c. Assume that the committee members reach a compromise after seeing your plan put forth in part (a). Collaboratively draft a three-page report to the new manager.

5. You work for a hospital laboratory, and your lab manager, under pressure from management to save money, insists that you and the three other medtechs switch to a different brand of vacuum blood-drawing tubes. You and your colleagues prefer the brand of tubes you have been using for years. Moreover, the price difference between the two brands is small. As a group project, prepare a memo to the business manager of the hospital explaining why the switch is unnecessary, unwise, and unpopular. Focus especially on the cost difference and its effect on the laboratory's budget. Then prepare another collaboratively written memo to your lab manager. Be sensitive to each reader's needs as you diplomatically explain the group's position.

PART II

Part opening image: Murat Taner/Flirt/Corbis

Correspondence

CHAPTER

4

E-Communications at Work:

Email, Blogs, Messaging, and Social Media

A large and routine share of your writing at work will be through e-communications—emails, blogs, messaging, and mushrooming social media such as Facebook, Twitter, Instagram, Flickr, and LinkedIn. These forms of e-communications are used for various purposes and messages in the world of work, including

- communicating within the company
- promoting your company's brand
- receiving and responding to consumer views
- tracking trends
- searching for and finding a job
- enhancing networking and collaboration around the globe
- assuring and expanding interactive communication
- enabling you to do research

Businesses depend on e-communications to manage the large flow of information they need to be competitive, to stay connected to customers and employees, and to remain on the cutting edge. Later chapters will discuss specific uses of e-communication. But this chapter will give you practical information on (a) the benefits and differences among these various e-technologies, (b) when and how to write them, and (c) the ethical and legal obligations you have when you communicate in the digital workplace.

THE FLOW OF INFORMATION THROUGH E-COMMUNICATIONS

Because each of these e-communications is vital to the operation of any business, expect to use them—often in combination—in the course of the business day. It is common for information to flow from one type of e-communication to another because these mediums are often used collectively to develop, edit, or send information to people both internally and externally. One method of e-communication drives another. Links to a company's Facebook page and Twitter feed are included on their corporate website, while a tweet could include a link back to a specific company website page. Your reader's needs and the type of message will dictate which e-communication you use. How carefully you manage your emails and messaging, for instance, gives your employer a very good idea of how well you do your job. See how an employee's monthly activity report (see Figure 14.7, pages 574–575) reflects, in part, the quality and quantity of work he/she has done through these various e-tools.

DIFFERENCES AMONG E-COMMUNICATIONS

While e-communications are the workhorse of business communication, there are key differences among them you need to know. Essentially, your workplace circumstances will determine which one is the most practical. For example:

- When you need to write a longer message, or send documents to co-workers across the country or the globe, send an email with an attachment.
- When you want to communicate in more detail with customers about a new product, service, or your company's views on a topic, write a blogpost.
- If your team members (or your boss) need to see brief information right away because of a looming deadline, and they work in the same office, use your company's messaging system.
- When a team member is out in the field and away from the office/his or her desk, a text is an expedient way to ask or answer a question.
- When you want to quickly share news, information, or promote your products visually to your customers or the general public, a tweet or social media posting may be appropriate.

E-COMMUNICATIONS ARE LEGAL RECORDS

Employers own their e-communications systems as well as the computers, smartphones, and tablets that employees use. As we saw in Chapter 1 ("Employers Insist on and Monitor Ethical Behavior," pages 26–27), employers have the right to monitor what you write and to whom. Any e-communication sent over a company server can be copied, archived, forwarded, and, most significantly, intercepted. For instance, emails can never really be deleted. Moreover, you can be fired for writing an angry or abusive email, blogpost, message, text, tweet, or social media posting. Your communications can easily be converted into an electronic paper trail. You never know who will receive and then forward them—to your boss, a customer, an attorney, a licensing board. Many companies issue disclaimers to protect themselves from legal action because of an employee's offensive workplace communication. In court, an email, message, text, message, tweet, social media post, or blog can carry the same weight as a printed letter or memo.

Legal/Ethical Guidelines to Follow in Writing E-Communications

Here are some guidelines to help you write and send ethical/legal business e-communications.

1. **Do not use them for personal messages.** Write emails, messages, texts, tweets, and social media and blog postings only to conduct appropriate company business.

2. **Take your time.** Don't dash off a hasty, unedited, or unrevised draft of your email, text, or social media post. When sending an email, for example, double-check all the addresses you're sending it to, as you may have accidentally included someone or entered a wrong address.

3. **Always project your company's best image.** Do not make your employer look bad by undermining management or criticizing a vendor, customer, or even a competitor. And, of course, never attack a boss or co-worker.

4. **Be accurate.** Double-check your facts—contracts, prices, warranties, guarantees, model numbers, delivery dates, safety features, etc. If you give customers wrong or misleading information, your company can be legally liable.

5. **Respect your employer's confidentiality.** Guard company trade secrets. Do not send an e-communication about ongoing research, developing new or updated products and services, sales figures, marketing plans, or personnel issues.

6. **Never write any e-communication about a raise, a grievance, or a complaint about a co-worker.** Meet with your supervisor in person to discuss these issues.

7. **Be professional and conscientious.** Avoid posting stories or pictures unrelated to your company's business. Moreover, don't spread office gossip or rumors, comment on company policies, or make political statements—all of which may be grounds for your dismissal.

8. **Deliver what you promise.** Answer e-communications promptly and courteously. Clear your in box at the end of every business day. If you tell someone that you will respond later, don't fail to do so. And always do the necessary research to give your reader(s) the information they need.

9. **Be familiar with and follow your company's policies on e-communication and on any company-specific apps or social media sites.** Know your company handbook.

10. **Protect your business records from viruses, spam, worms, Trojan horses, and hackers by following your company's security procedures.** Review your firm's IT strategies about identifying and reporting cyberspace problems. Install and use virus protection software as your company instructs.

11. **Always follow company policy.** Find out what your company rules are about texting, formats, screen names, contact information, whether you can download documents or software, etc.

"Promoting Your Best Image—Some Do's and Don'ts" (pages 245–250) will give you advice on how to avoid ethical and legal problems when using social network sites.

EMAIL: ITS IMPORTANCE IN THE WORKPLACE

Email continues to be one of the most common forms of e-communication in the workplace. It is the lifeblood of every business or organization because it expedites communication within a firm as well as outside it. On their tablets, computers, notebooks, or mobile devices, professionals in the world of work may receive between forty and one hundred emails each day from supervisors, co-workers, clients, and vendors worldwide. Email allows you to send short messages about routine matters that make business function smoothly. It also enables the quick dissemination of longer documents (such as memos or reports) by way of file attachments.

Some of the information you convey (or is conveyed to you) via email may need to be sent via your company's messaging system, texts, or blog or social media posts; an important skill employers look for is the ability to move information across these media platforms without losing its meaning or coherence.

Using an email program such as Microsoft Office 365, Outlook, or Gmail, you can expedite workplace communication in many ways:

- Send and receive information quickly; delete it, forward it, or archive it
- Set up your business calendar and keep track of your appointments
- Synchronize your address book, email, and calendar functions, including across multiple devices
- Share Calendars, so you can see your colleagues' schedules and plan meetings accordingly
- Group or "bundle" emails according to subject line, sender, or customized topic, for easy searching, reference, and archiving
- Organize and archive emails in folders according to date, sender, subject line, or other topic area
- Use the Search function to help you to find specific emails or email threads, documents, or attachments quickly and easily
- Identify and delete spam
- Send attachments, including documents, visuals, video and audio clips, tables, lists, and statistical files
- Enhance all phases of your collaborative work (see "Computer-Supported Collaboration," pages 95–103).
- Communicate anytime, all the time, 24 hours a day, 7 days a week

Email is an informal, relaxed type of business correspondence, far more informal than a printed memo, letter, short report, or proposal, though it is more complex than instant messaging or an Instagram or Facebook post (see "Messaging," pages 135–139). Think of your workplace email as a polite, informative, and professional conversation. It should always be to the point and accessible, as in Figure 4.1. Yet even though business email is a way of communicating, this does not mean you can forget about your responsibilities as a courteous and ethical employee, co-worker, and writer. Figure 4.2 (page 121) exemplifies an email used to communicate diplomatically with a collaborative team.

Business Email Versus Personal Email

The email you write on the job will require more effort than your personal email will. Don't assume you can write to your employer or a customer the way you would a text message or a Facebook response to an old friend. In the world of work, you don't just dash off an email. You have to revise and review it before you click and send it. That means proofreading carefully and following all the rules of proper spelling (avoid text-message spellings), punctuation, capitalization, and word choice, as well as the "Guidelines for Using Email on the Job" (pages 120–124). The tone of your business email should also be much more professional than the instant messaging you may do with friends or the e-conversations you have in chat rooms.

FIGURE 4.1 An Email Sent to a Co-worker

Header contains all necessary information

Gives all necessary details concisely

Indicates follow-up

Uses informal yet professional tone

Gives contact information

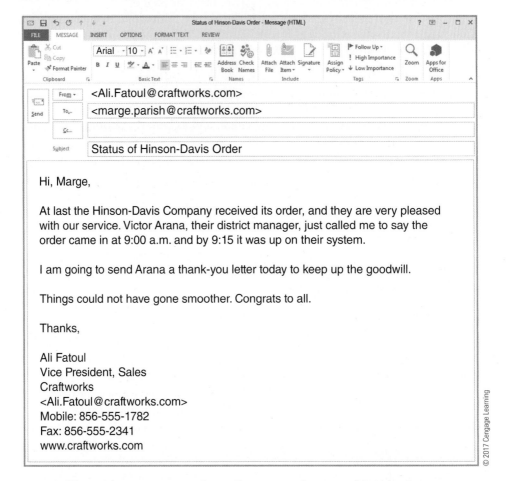

From <Ali.Fatoul@craftworks.com>

To <marge.parish@craftworks.com>

Cc...

Subject Status of Hinson-Davis Order

Hi, Marge,

At last the Hinson-Davis Company received its order, and they are very pleased with our service. Victor Arana, their district manager, just called me to say the order came in at 9:00 a.m. and by 9:15 it was up on their system.

I am going to send Arana a thank-you letter today to keep up the goodwill.

Things could not have gone smoother. Congrats to all.

Thanks,

Ali Fatoul
Vice President, Sales
Craftworks
<Ali.Fatoul@craftworks.com>
Mobile: 856-555-1782
Fax: 856-555-2341
www.craftworks.com

Unlike with your personal email, you need to consider the impact your business email will have on your company and on your career. When you send a business email, you are representing more than yourself and your preferences, as in a personal email. You are speaking on behalf of your employer. Because your email must reflect your company's best image, make sure it is businesslike, free from grammatical mistakes, carefully researched, and polite. Sarcasm, slang, an aggressive tone, name-calling, and inappropriate clip art do not belong in a company email. As we saw, Figures 4.1 and 4.2 illustrate effectively written business email. Notice that these emails are cordial without being unprofessional.

Guidelines for Using Email on the Job

When you prepare and organize your email message, always consider your reader's specific needs as well as those of your company. The guidelines set out here will help you to write effective business emails.

FIGURE 4.2 Email Sent to a Distribution List of Co-workers

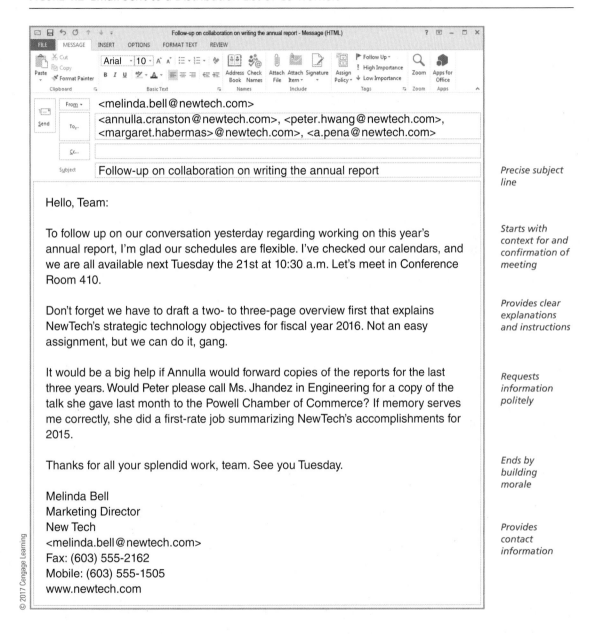

Precise subject line

Starts with context for and confirmation of meeting

Provides clear explanations and instructions

Requests information politely

Ends by building morale

Provides contact information

© 2017 Cengage Learning

1. **Make sure your email is confidential and ethical.**

   ● Avoid **flaming**, that is, using strong, angry language that mocks, attacks, or insults your employer, a colleague, a customer, a government agency, or a company, as in Figure 4.3 (see page 125). Abusive, obscene, or racially or culturally offensive language in an email constitutes grounds for dismissal.

- Send nothing through email that you would not want to see on your company's website or that of your local newspaper.
- Do not forward a co-worker's or an employer's email without that person's approval.
- Do not change the wording of a message that you are expected to read and forward.
- Never send an objectionable file, photo, or video.

2. **Make your email easy to read.**

- **Always provide a clear, precise subject line.** Avoid one-word subjects like "Report" or "Meeting." Instead, write "Meeting to boost declining April sales." A subject line like "Bill" leaves readers wondering if your email is about a person or an unpaid account.
- **Try to limit your emails to one screen.** Messages longer than four or five short paragraphs are better sent in an attachment rather than in the body of an email.
- **Do not send emails written in all capital or all lowercase letters.** All capital letters look as if you are shouting. Conversely, emails in all lowercase imply you do not know how to capitalize, or may be seen as spam.
- **Break your message into short paragraphs.** A screen filled with one dense block of text is intimidating. Make each paragraph no more than three to four lines long and always double-space between paragraphs. Do not indent your paragraphs.
- **Provide hyperlink URLs for all websites you reference.** Do not make your reader look them up.
- **Use plain text.** Because different email programs can garble your message, avoid overusing typefaces like italic, script, or decorative fonts, colored wallpaper, or complex formatting (such as long numbered and bulleted lists), and symbols (monetary, accents, etc.) within the body of an email. Use a simple typeface such as Arial or Times New Roman.
- **Avoid long strings of emails.** Delete strings of previously answered emails when you reply.

3. **Observe the rules of "netiquette"** (*Internet* + *etiquette*).

- **Respond promptly to an email.** Don't let emails pile up in your in-box. Check for new messages three to four times each day. If you will be offline for an extended period, use the out-of-office assistant to let readers know politely you are not available and when you will return. You can also have your emails forwarded to your mobile device.
- **Give your readers reasonable time to respond.** Consider time zone differences between you and your reader. It may be 2:00 a.m. when your email arrives for an international recipient.
- **Do not keep sending the same email over and over.** This is discourteous and will only antagonize your recipient.
- **Proofread and revise before you send an email.** Hold off filling in the "To" line until you have double-checked all facts, spelling, and grammar.
- **Avoid unfamiliar abbreviations, jargon, and emoticons.** Don't use abbreviations common in personal emails (*btw*, *lol*) or that are used in text

messaging. Include only those abbreviations and jargon that your recipients will understand (e.g., *fyi*). Also, stay away from emoticons (smiley faces, sad faces, etc.) in your professional communications.

- **Don't use red flag words unnecessarily**. Stay away from words like "Urgent," "Crucial," or "Top Priority," along with accompanying exclamation marks, in your subject line just to get your reader's attention. Your tactic will backfire, potentially upsetting readers or, worse yet, causing them to ignore any genuinely urgent messages you may send in the future. Instead, utilize your email system's method of indicating prioritization of an email, which is a more professional approach.

- **Include a signature block**. A signature block, found at the end of your message, includes your name, title, and contact information (see Figures 4.1 and 4.2). Make it easy for others to contact you. Such information is crucial when you are part of a large organization.

4. **Adopt a professional business style.**

- **Use a salutation (greeting), but always follow your company's policy.** Use a comma before the party's name in a direct address.
  - — to a colleague—Hi, Hello
  - — to a customer—Dear Ms. Pietz, Dear Bio Tech

- **Get to the point right away**. Because readers receive a lot of email, they may look only at the first few lines you write. Start by briefly reminding readers why you are writing. Refer to a previous email. Fill in the background that explains the purpose of your message.

- **Keep your message concise**. Cut wordy phrases, and send only the information your reader needs. Exclude unnecessary details and chatter.

- **Don't turn your email into a telegram**. "Send report immediately; need for meeting" is rude, as is a reply only with "Yes," "No," or "Sure." Save words like "Nope," "Yeah," and "Huh" for your personal emails and texts.

- **Never send an attachment without a cover email that politely and concisely tells readers what you are attaching and why it is important.** Because of the fears of viruses and malware, many business people don't open email attachments, especially ones sent with no explanation.

- **End politely**. Let readers know in your last sentence that you appreciate their help or cooperation and look forward to their reply (see Figure 4.2).

- **Use a complimentary close, but always follow your company's policy.**
  - — to a colleague—Thanks, Later, Take care,
  - — to a customer—Sincerely yours, Sincerely, Best regards,

- **Do not include your favorite quotation** at the bottom of your email. Your boss or customer may not agree with you. Remember, your email represents your company.

- **Proofread and spell-check** your email before you send it.

5. **Respect your international readers.**

- Use international English, which calls for short sentences, common words, and so on (see "Using International English," pages 10–11).

- Avoid using abbreviations, symbols, or measurements your reader may not know.
- Respect your reader's cultural traditions. Don't be too informal or chatty. For example, do not use first names unless the reader approves. Use the reader's title and last name. Some cultures (East Asian, for instance) regard the use of abbreviations as discourteous.
- Always spell your reader's name, address, and country correctly, including the use of hyphens, accents, and capital letters.
- Be careful about sending photographs or other graphics which may not be appropriate in your reader's culture.
- Avoid humor; it might be misinterpreted.

6. **Ensure that your email is safe and secure.**

- **Use email antivirus software**. Always consult with your company's information technology (IT) department.
- **Don't be a victim of identity theft, or "phishing."** Companies you do business with will never ask for personal information, such as your bank account or Social Security number.
- **Create an email password that is not easy to guess.** Do not use a password such as "ABCDE" or "123456." Change your password regularly, and do not use the same password for all your accounts.
- **Back up important files, including emails.** Save your most important and current files in case your computer contracts a virus or crashes.

Figure 4.3 shows an example of a poorly written email that violates many of the preceding guidelines. Figure 4.4 contains an effective revision that reflects the professional and courteous way the writer and his company conduct business.

When Not to Use Email

Although email is convenient, easy to use, and appropriate for routine business correspondence, be careful not to use it in the following situations:

- Send a formal letter rather than an email when you apply for a job and for any follow-up communication.
- When you make a new business contact or welcome a new client, write a formal letter, not an email. International readers, in particular, will expect this.
- Always acknowledge a business gift or courtesy by sending a handwritten thank-you note or formal letter rather than dashing off an email.
- Never send an email in place of a letter for any type of legal notification or financial statement.
- When a situation involving a client or vendor is too complex to handle in a short email, a phone call may be more productive and provide the chance for "real time" discussion and feedback that is difficult to capture in a series of emails.

FIGURE 4.3 A Poorly Written Email Guilty of Flaming

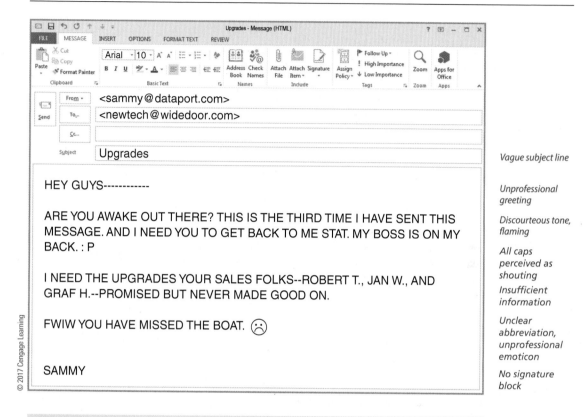

Vague subject line

Unprofessional greeting

Discourteous tone, flaming

All caps perceived as shouting

Insufficient information

Unclear abbreviation, unprofessional emoticon

No signature block

BLOGS

Like emails, blogs (*web + logs*) are important e-communications for employees, managers, and customers alike. Think of a blog as an evolving website, or a newspaper for which managers and employees write regular short articles, or posts. Blogposts are short, conversational articles giving readers current and relevant news and commentary on a variety of issues important for your company, your brand, your organization and your profession. Posts are generally a few paragraphs long and are often written two to three times a week, although some bloggers post their work more frequently, sometimes daily. Written in chronological order, blogs are dated, titled, and frequently archived. Figures 4.5 (page 128), 4.6 (pages 130–131), and 4.7 (pages 134–135) show examples of blogs.

Blogs Are Interactive

A blog includes more than the blogger's views. Blogs are highly interactive, allowing for a two-way or often group conversation between the author and his or her online audience. In the blogosphere, readers write comments in response to blog posts, and the blogger and other readers can reply. This interaction is the key to

FIGURE 4.4 A Revised, Effective Version of the Poorly Written Email in Figure 4.3

Uses email address of specific person

Precise subject

Polite salutation

Gets to the point concisely but diplomatically

Provides explanation and documentation

Ends with clear-cut directions

Professional close

Includes signature block

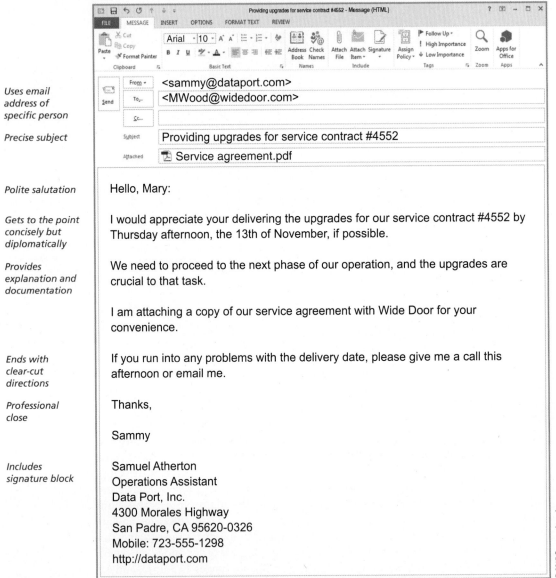

© 2017 Cengage Learning

a blog's success. In fact, bloggers often post the number of visitors who have left comments at the site. To write a successful business blog, you have to

1. attract readers
2. build relationships with them
3. promote and market products, services, or ideas
4. respond to comments and suggestions

Blog Sponsors

Blogs carry different types of messages, depending on who sponsors them and why. It is impossible to estimate the number of blogs in the blogosphere. Individuals can host their own blogs to express their opinions on any subject, from world affairs to technologies, community affairs, or even their families. Organizations host blogs, too. For instance, the Sierra Club, which is devoted to preserving the environment, has blogged on protecting endangered species, funding nature trails, and making and selling eco-friendly furniture. Almost every government agency has its own blog, or multiple blogs. The Food and Drug Administration (FDA), for instance, uses its blogs to keep consumers up to date about potential health risks, such as an outbreak of influenza or the spread of botulism from contaminated meat or dairy products. And every type of business, from major international corporations to small, local firms, blogs about its products, services, workforce, and commitment to customers and community. The following sections will show you how to blog successfully about work-related activity.

Two Types of Blogs

Blogs can be either internal or external, depending on their audience and use in the workplace.

Internal Blogs

Internal blogs are among the most versatile forms of workplace correspondence. They are designed exclusively to be used on the company network (or intranet) by in-house management and by employees to post their comments and questions, their views on new policies, announce events, introduce new staff, and generally to communicate up and down the corporate ladder. But some internal blogging is directed only to individuals in a given department or area, such as engineers tackling an energy problem or nurses in a large health care organization discussing new treatments for burn patients. Every internal blog, though, is aimed at making the workplace safer, more productive, and professionally and personally more satisfying.

Internal blogging serves many functions, including these:

- Informing employees about vital company news
- Helping employees to better understand and perform their jobs
- Conducting virtual meetings without having to make arrangements for face-to-face gatherings
- Enhancing collaboration through the interaction of blog posts and comments
- Providing a forum for workplace discussions
- Improving employee participation and morale by inviting suggestions and questions

Note how the internal blog in Figure 4.5 (page 128) fulfills many of these functions.

Always follow your company's blogging policies, but be especially careful that you do not divulge information that may be confidential or sensitive. Your employer will expect you to observe the same guidelines whether posting your own blogs or commenting on others' (see "Guidelines for Writing Business Blogs," pages 129–133). What you say on your own blog can reflect positively or negatively

FIGURE 4.5 An Internal Blog

	HMC Hong, McCarson, and Steinway, LLC

Blog topics clearly differentiated

Topic: New antivirus software
(comments: 6)

Topic: Importing HMS logo into memos, letters, etc.
(comments: 7)

Uses clear and concise title

Chooses an informal yet professional tone

Acknowledge responses to blog

Keeps the blog post brief and chunks text

Lets readers know IT is responsive to their needs

Tone is conversational but professional

Offers practical help for employees

Invites further responses

"Comments" link allows for further discussion

Topic: Using the new binding machines
2/8/16, 10:43 a.m. (mschwartz): Hi, this is Maxine in IT. Congratulations to those of you who have completed our training workshops on the new binding equipment, and I look forward to working with individuals in the marketing and legal departments, who are scheduled for a session next week.

Overall, I think the sessions have gone well. However, a number of questions have come up about the new binding machines, and so I thought the best thing to do would be to post the most frequently asked ones here, with answers:

1. Why are the binding machines located only on the 6th floor? We're just waiting for three additional machines to arrive from the supplier within the next two weeks. We will put two of the new machines in the 5th floor copy room (5-204) for legal services and one in the 3rd floor copy room (3-122) for marketing and facilities.

2. Where are the supplies for the binding machines located? You can find the supplies in each of three copy rooms. IT apologizes about the shelf locations not being more clearly labeled. We fixed that problem. Thanks for letting us know about it. Also, to help our employees, IT has emailed all employees a detailed sheet for supplies and procedures for the new machines.

3. Why can't I get the laminated insert pages to line up properly? Here's a tip to help you: Make sure that the rounded edges of the inserts are facing out and that the squared edges are lined up with the inside edges of the paper.

4. How do I avoid damaging legal documents when using the machines? To be on the safe side, insert a few pages of scrap paper into the machine and do a test bind before inserting original documents. You'll then be sure that the machine is aligned properly.

I hope these answers help everyone out. If you have further comments or questions, please email or call me at Extension 304.
(comments: 14)

Topic: What is the company policy on maternity/paternity leaves?
(comments: 7)

Topic: Prezi presentations — is there a specialist in-house to help?
(comments: 3)

on your employer. Finally, don't let internal blogging take up so much of your time that you neglect your other duties.

External Blogs

External, or business, blogs are essential marketing and public relations tools in the world of e-commerce. They allow a company to share information about its brand, mission, achievements, and activities, as in Figures 4.6 (pages 130–131) and 4.7 (pages 134–135). They also allow companies to express their side of the story—their interpretation of events and their clarification of the issues—quickly and publicly. A carefully designed and persuasively written business blog can announce and sell new products, services, or technology; share information about employee accomplishments; and describe the company's contributions to the community or the environment, as in Figure 4.6. It can provide updates about corporate changes in personnel, locations, benefits, and so on. Moreover, a business blog can be used to announce and respond to consumer/community concerns, such as environmental problems, product recalls, or the discontinuation of a service, brand, or model, as shown in Figure 4.7.

Guidelines for Writing Business Blogs

To post a successful blog, follow all the guidelines for writing a business email. Always be ethical and honest, and document what you say. Also, your writing cannot be sloppy or careless; you have to use proper spelling and punctuation. Be diplomatic, whether you are writing to co-workers, as Maxine Schwartz does in Figure 4.5, or customers, as the blogs in Figures 4.6 and 4.7 do. Avoid sounding curt, condescending, or arrogant. Keep in mind, too, that an external blog is your employer's official, and many times daily, publication, as we see in Figure 4.6. Your employer may require you to get your post approved by a blog administrator to make sure it meets your company's expectations. The guidelines that follow will also help you to write appropriate business blog posts.

Use the Right Tone to Attract Readers

Essential to any business blog's success is getting information from readers—their views, concerns, and feedback. Whether you are a manager or an employee, your business blog needs to reveal the personal side of your company and its brand. Your blog needs to sound sincere and friendly, welcoming readers to your site. As we saw, every blogger's goal is to attract visitors to his or her site and to keep them coming back to read more. Using the interactive features of a blog, you can make it easy for readers to contact you. A friendly and inviting tone will let readers know you want to hear their views and will take them into account. In subsequent posts, you can address their views and concerns, as Clay Denton-Tyler does in Figure 4.7.

Follow Company Protocol

- **Project your company's best image.** Keep your company's history, mission, brand, and reputation in mind when you prepare your blog. Be enthusiastic about its products, services, workforce, company mission, and commitment to the environment. Do not make your company look bad by undermining management or criticizing a vendor or a competitor. And never attack a boss or co-worker.

FIGURE 4.6 An External Blog on Choosing an Eco-Friendly Product

WFM HOME   STORES   PRODUCTS   RECIPES   HEALTH STARTS HERE   VALUES   COMPANY   FORUMS   SUBSCRIBE VIS RSS

WHOLE STORY
the official whole foods market® blog

SEARCH

Attention-grabbing headline

Get to Know Your Tilapia

by Carrie Brownstein, January 4th, 2011 | Permalink | Email this

Convinces readers right away about the safety of the product

Unlike conventional grocers who may source tilapia from any old place as long as the price is right, Whole Foods Market sources all seafood, including tilapia, according to our Quality Standards. In the case of tilapia, we source from just three supplier partners, all of whom have passed a third-party audit to ensure that they meet our rigorous quality standards.

Provides essential jargon-free background information for readers

Our primary supplier partner, Tropical Aquaculture Inc., brings us tilapia from Santa Priscila, located in beautiful Ecuador. Santa Priscila practices polyculture by raising shrimp and tilapia together in the same ponds. This helps reduce waste and water pollution, as tilapia consume feed that the shrimp leave behind and help get rid of organic matter that otherwise could end up in the environment. The farm also recirculates its water, which further helps to protect water quality surrounding the farm.

Addresses the reader directly but sincerely; uses a friendly conversational tone

And you'll be glad to know that our Quality Standards for Aquaculture prohibit the common industry practice of using the hormone methyl testosterone to reverse the sex of tilapia. Conventional tilapia producers prefer to raise only male fish so that the fish put their energy into growth rather than reproduction and grow to a larger, more marketable size. Our farmer partners, however, grow fish the old fashioned way: they let the fish reproduce naturally. Then they separate the males and females by hand and raise them in separate ponds.

Documents the rigorous standards consumers expect from Whole Foods

And as always, Whole Foods Market prohibits slaughterhouse by-products from avian or mammalian species in feed. Fortunately, tilapia are naturally omnivorous fish that don't require a lot of fishmeal in their feed, which helps our tilapia suppliers meet our goal of reducing pressure on wild populations of fish that are used to produce animal feed, but are also important species in marine food webs. In fact, Santa Priscila's feed (as well as other supplier partners' feed), uses trimmings from other fish species processed for seafood, which also reduces wastes.

Provides hyperlink for easy reference

We launched our Quality Standards for Aquaculture in 2008 and they still remain the toughest quality standards for farmed seafood in the industry. Fish farmers who want to partner with us must complete a lengthy application detailing all of their farming practices. And it's more than just words; third-party auditors verify that the farm is meeting our standards before any of their fish makes its way to our stores. Not only that, but suppliers must continue to pass annual inspections for as long as they partner with us.

Includes logo within blog to show consumers exactly what to look for when purchasing ecofriendly tilapia

So, how do you know you're purchasing farmed seafood that meets Whole Foods Market's strict standards? Look for our aquaculture logo — Responsibly Farmed — at Whole Foods Market stores. That symbol means that the fish has been third-party verified to meet our standards.

FIGURE 4.6 (Continued)

8 Responses to "Get to Know Your Tilapia"

Tricia: I just purchased some tilapia at WFM last night specifically for this reason. I don't shop at WFM for everything, but I think it's important to purchase items in industries that can be unsafe. The fish was reasonably priced and tasted great!
January 4th, 2011 at 3:55 pm

dining room table: I have heard of this fish before and they told me that this is really something so delicious.
January 5th, 2011 at 7:02 am

Lynda Reynolds: Tilapia are a freshwater fish, not seafood. And how did the prison system in Colorado go about getting a contract with Whole Foods to sell? . . . is this something I can start in California or do we already have the same program?
January 5th, 2011 at 1:36 pm

Sharon Miracle: I commend you for taking these steps to protect the aquaculture, and for helping protect us humans from ingesting more unnecessary hormones which may have negative consequences on our bodies over time.
January 5th, 2011 at 3:06 pm

Kat: Thank you for this info about tilapia. I just starting eating it but I did not know that hormones are added to it by certain suppliers.
January 5th, 2011 at 5:34 pm

Ellie: Most tilapia is grown in such conditions that it is gross, if not unhealthy, to eat. It is wonderful to hear yours is worth eating. Thanks!
January 5th, 2011 at 9:30 pm

Ryan: But what are they fed? Most tilapia are fed corn, resulting in an extremely high omega 6 to omega 3 ratio.
January 8th, 2011 at 10:30 pm

Bev Baker: Just checking to ensure that the tilapia are not fed GMO corn???
January 10th, 2011 at 8:44 pm

ON THE WEB

Whole Foods Market photos on Flickr

Whole Foods Market on Facebook

Whole Foods Market updates on Twitter

VIDEOS & PODCASTS

View our growing library of video content.

BE GOOD TO YOUR
WHOLE BODY

Audio podcast all about natural body care and supplements.

CATEGORIES

Back to School (23)
Best Meal of the Week (15)
Cheese (27)
Community – Local and Global (20)
Farm to Market (67)
South (2)
Field Reports (20)
Floral (20)
Food & Recipes (357)
Food Issues (45)
Food Podcasts (68)
Food Safety (11)
Grass-fed Beef (12)
Green Action (115)
Grocery (30)

Blog posts always provide links to the company's other social media sites

Comments from customers on the blog post will help the author refine future postings and alert the company to possible new trends/ issues that are important to its clientele

Questions posed in the comments section provide a further way the company can interact with its customer base (through future posts or with responses to direct questions)

Courtesy of Whole Foods Market. "Whole Foods Market" is a registered trademark of Whole Foods Market IP, L.P.

- **Respect your employer's confidentiality.** Guard your company's trade secrets. Do not blog about anything that might reveal confidential, restricted, or otherwise off-limits information. Topics to stay away from include any ongoing research and development of products and services, sales and marketing plans, financial matters including stocks, and personnel matters.
- **Avoid making your company liable for false or misleading information.** Don't make promises, offer guarantees, or provide additional warranties unless they have been approved by upper management. Be careful about using the pronoun *we*, which implies you are speaking for your employer.
- **Be professional.** Avoid posting stories and pictures unrelated to your work on the company's blog. Don't comment on company policies or make political comments, all of which may be grounds for dismissal.

Target Your Audience

- **Know what your audience cares about.** Track the number of page views for each blog post (as well as the number of overall visitors your blog gets on a weekly or monthly basis). Make sure your comments are relevant to their questions and needs. Be aware of their attitudes, likes, and dislikes. Read replies to previous blog posts, be open to suggestions, and acknowledge readers' insights. Tell readers how and why your blog will help them.
- **Write an attention-grabbing headline.** Attract readers with a title that tells them how and why they can profit from reading your blog, and encourage them to respond to your post; for example, "Getting to Know Your Tilapia" in Figure 4.6 and "A Power Tool Even Better Than the PH-450?" in Figure 4.7. Avoid vague, boring headlines, such as "Important News," "Something You Need to Know," and "Any Further Ideas?"
- **Determine if your blog will attract an international audience** as well as native English speakers (see "Communicating with Global Audiences," page 6). To accommodate global readers, avoid jargon and unclear abbreviations.
- **Date every blog post so readers can follow a conversation.** Update your blog to make sure the information you give readers is current and accurate.
- **Make it easy for readers to respond to your post.** Welcome feedback. Consider your blog a place where you want to listen to readers' comments. Tell them where and how to reply. Like the blog in Figure 4.7, refer to customer posts to show how concerned you and your company are about readers' opinions.

Make Your Blog Persuasive

- **Structure your blog so that your first paragraph comes to the point at once and tells readers what you are blogging about and why.** For example, in Figure 4.6, Carrie Brownstein reassures readers that Whole Foods still faithfully follows its tough quality standards for aquaculture. In Figure 4.7, Clay Denton-Tyler clearly states he has information on "why the PH-450 will not be available," a question his audience is eager to see him answer.
- **Provide firsthand information that shows readers you are knowledgeable and sincere.** Observe how, in Figure 4.7, Denton-Tyler expresses his views

as an owner of the popular, but discontinued, PH-450 without in any way compromising his company's position or decision.

- **Highlight any new, improved, or special features.** Note how Denton-Tyler points to the benefits the new power tool offers customers. See how his blog post gives his readers an incentive to buy the new model.
- **Use facts and statistics to develop your message or point of view.** Honest numbers sell products and services. Include units sold, costs, and so on. Note how Denton-Tyler wisely cites a lower price to promote the new model SHP-1000 in Figure 4.7.

Write Concisely and Sincerely

- **Keep your posts short and easy to read.** Your blog needs to be simple and practical. Most blogs are no more than a few paragraphs. Don't turn yours into a report or a compilation of technical data.
- **Adopt a casual, conversational style.** Be personable and friendly. Sound authentic and upbeat. Emphasize your interest in your readers. Don't weigh them down with long, windy paragraphs that can bore or confuse your audience.

Document Your Sources, Including Visuals

- If you use someone else's statistics, surveys, illustrations, or ideas, get permission first from the individual or the company that owns the copyright.
- Quote accurately, but do not include an extended quote without obtaining permission.
- Include relevant documentation (and permission) if you use a visual you or your company did not create.

CASE STUDY

Writing a Blog to Keep Customer Goodwill

Clay Denton-Tyler is an assistant sales manager for PowerHouse Inc., a company that sells a large line of power tools. The company recently decided to discontinue one of its most popular models, the PH-450, which had enjoyed wide brand recognition and high consumer ratings. Customers had been blogging PowerHouse to complain about the company's decision, and Denton-Tyler faced the difficult challenge of responding to customer posts. His blog in Figure 4.7 does that.

To respond successfully, he had to consider his audience's needs, as voiced in their posts to the PowerHouse blog. Because his readers were loyal customers, he did not want to lose their business and goodwill. But he had to acknowledge that they were understandably disappointed that a well-received product was being taken off the market. He also had to be credible, honest, and diplomatic in addressing their needs and expressing his company's continuing gratitude to its customers. He also had to convince them that the replacement model Power-House was offering was better and cheaper than the discontinued PH-450.

But in the interactive world of blogging, he recognized that he was also writing to potential customers, and he realized that his post would be a part of an ongoing public discussion about the new model and his company. He wanted to answer as many questions as he could while keeping the conversation going—all in a positive direction—and, ideally, attracting new customers around the globe.

(Continued)

FIGURE 4.7 An External Blog

Search engine and navigation links help readers find information

Additional links aid site navigation

Provides a clear and concise title and date

Writes to a general audience and avoids jargon

Thanks customers for feedback

Uses a conversational but professional tone

Acknowledges customers' disappointment

Attempts to persuade customer to switch to a new model

PowerHouse, Inc.

About Us | Products | International | Jobs | Mobile | RSS

⊙ PowerBlog   ○ All of Powerhouse, Inc.   🔍 Search this site   Go

PowerBlog

| All | Company News | Product News | Distribution | Manufacturing |

<< Previous Post   >> Next Post

Today's Post (August 14, 2015):

>> **A Power Tool Even Better than the PH-450?**
by Clay Denton-Tyler, District Manager

© iStockPhoto.com/
Prill Mediendesign &
Fotografie

Many of our loyal customers have disagreed with PowerHouse's decision to discontinue manufacturing the PH-450 All-in-One Power Tool. It is always great to hear from our customers and to receive their feedback, even when they believe we've done something wrong. To help our customers better understand our perspective, let me fill in some of the background about why the PH-450 will not be available.

Discontinuing the PH-450 was not an easy decision. After all, this was the product that first brought our company to national attention and widespread customer acceptance. Also, I know from many complimentary emails and replies to earlier posts, as well as from my personal experience as a proud owner of the PH-450, that customers have always applauded its price, compact design, durability, and all-weather usability. As one of you put it, "Why kill a popular product that has worked so well for 20 years?"

While all of these responses are helpful, the good news is that even though the PH-450 is being discontinued, our customers will now have a very similar but improved alternative. Recently, our parent company, International Dyanamics, SE, acquired a new multipurpose tool from Swiss

Recent Posts:

International Dyanamics, SE CFO announces retirement.

PowerHouse announces the discontinuation of the PH-450.

FIGURE 4.7 (Continued)

Home Products. The SHP-1000 is not only just as compact, durable, and weather-friendly as the PH-450, but it offers several additional features, such as a nail gun attachment and a lifetime limited warranty. And due to an excellent distribution deal negotiated between International Dyanamics, SE, and Swiss Home Products, we can sell it at less than 30 percent of the retail cost of the PH-450.

I know it is hard to say goodbye to a reliable helper, but like many products in our increasingly technical age, the PH-450 is being replaced by a more efficient model. I will miss the old PH-450, but I have found that the SHP-1000 is even more effective in my home shop. Adapting to a new model has never come easier for me. Why not give it a try? Thanks. I would like to hear from you.

Comments: (21)
- Sign in to add a comment
- First time users, please register first, in order to add a comment

PowerHouse opens new retail outlets in Dunedin, New Zealand and Tianjin, China.

International Dyanamics, SE acquires quality Swiss Home Products.

PowerHouse goes international.

More

Describes benefits of new model and why it is being marketed

Sympathizes with readers but offers personal endorsement characteristic of bloggers at same time

Tone is sincere and friendly

Link allows for further discussion

© 2017 Cengage Learning

MESSAGING

Messaging is a real-time conversation that can take place either online over a computer network or through a wireless network on a tablet or mobile device. Messaging in the workplace can involve either a networked messaging system or text messaging (and, often, both); what follows are important considerations when you are called upon to write in either medium.

Messages

Think of messages (or, as they are sometimes still called, *instant messages*) as somewhere between a phone call and an email, or a chat with a colleague in the hallway of your office. Message conversations are almost as instantaneous as phone conversations, but at the same time they provide written records of communications just as emails do. Keep in mind, though, that messages are not just used for communication with your friends; they are also a important part of workplace e-correspondence. In fact, researchers estimate that 90 percent of all businesses have used or will use messaging systems for routine workplace correspondence. Figure 4.8 (page 136) is an example of a professional workplace messaging conversation.

FIGURE 4.8 A Message Exchange Between Co-workers

IM user names are informal but appropriate	**DanielleS** 9:14 AM I'm working on the second draft of the environmental impact report today.
Messages are kept to 1–2 lines each	**JuanB** 9:15 AM So am I; let's talk.
Message exchange sticks to a single topic	**DanielleS** 10:01 AM I just emailed my revision--OK or not?
	JuanB 10:19 AM Looks good, but not enough detail on the cost of implementation.
Clear language avoids "text speak"	**DanielleS** 10:24 AM I'll take another stab at it later today.
Time stamp accompanies each message	**JuanB** 10:31 AM FYI, I'll fax you a copy of a similar short report so you have an idea of what they're looking for.
Style is informal but polite	**DanielleS** 10:34 AM Got it!
Writer lets co-worker know there will be a delay in responding so he can obtain the information	**JuanB** 10:49 AM Let's confer after you've had a chance to read it over.
	DanielleS 1:10 PM I've just read the report. Do you have the latest figures on the expected implementation costs? Mine are from last quarter.
	JuanB 1:18 PM I don't have them either, but let me call Florence Ng; she should have them.
Writer confirms the necessary information has been received, signaling the end of the exchange	**JuanB** 1:25 PM Florence said she'd send you the latest cost figures in an email.
	DanielleS 1:36 PM Got the cost figures, thanks. Great! They're just what we need.

© 2015 Cengage Learning

Exchanges through messaging reflect the way people in the world of work connect and communicate with one another. Messages allow you to communicate with one or several co-workers and managers in the same office, at remote sites, or around the globe, all using the same system. Crossing time zones, messages give you access to anyone around the world who is online and connected to the same service.

When to Use Messages Versus Emails

Like emails, messages promote collaboration, provide a written record, and further global communication. But they are used for very different kinds of messages. Emails are more detailed than messages. By answering the following questions, you will be better able to determine when to send a message or an email:

1. **How quickly does my message need to be answered?** If you need information right away, use a message rather than an email because recipients will most likely reply at once if they are online.
2. **How long or complex is my message?** If you need to transmit a message that is, say, more than a line or two or that contains multiple points, send an email. But you can also use a message to send attachments for immediate discussion.
3. If your message requires more time than a few brief back-and-forth communications, start an email exchange that can extend over several hours or days.

Guidelines for Using Messages in the Workplace

Messages may be instantaneous and informal, but that does not mean that you can send them with little thought about their content, tone, and punctuation. Again, keep in mind that your company can monitor, trace, record, and archive your message conversations just as it can with emails. In addition to the guidelines for writing workplace emails (pages 120–124), observe these rules for your messages:

1. **Stay connected.** Always indicate your status—"Away," "Busy," "Offline." "Please email me at tjones@comcast.com." If you are away, tell individuals on your contact list when you will be back or give them alternate contact information, as in the preceding example.
2. **Always ask if the other person is available for messaging.** He or she may be in a meeting, on the road, etc. Don't keep sending messages if you haven't received a response. It is discourteous to have your query keep popping up on the reader's screen. If the person is busy, inquire about a better time to chat.
3. **Keep your message short.** Get to the point right away. A sentence, or two at most, is enough for your message. Ask your question and then wait for a reply. Don't inject unnecessary pleasantries; for example, "How was your weekend?"
4. **Write about one topic at a time.** Don't include information about two or three different subjects in one message exchange. Keep the conversation flowing in one direction, not three.
5. **Avoid textspeak.** That may be acceptable in your personal texting, but avoid acronyms and abbreviations such as "CUL8R" for "See you later" or "B4" for "before," especially when writing to an international reader who may not understand them. Moreover, your boss might not appreciate a textspeak IM such as "np gtg ttyl" for "No problem. Got to go. Talk to you later."
6. **Be professional.** Make sure the style and tone of your message are polite and business-like. Your boss will expect you to be courteous to co-workers as well as management and customers.
7. **Choose an appropriate screen name, not "Go-Getter Pete" or "PartyAnimal."** Select one that is professional and reflects your job title and responsibilities.
8. **Use correct spelling and punctuation.** Just because IMs are streamlined, don't assume you can use slang, misspell words, or forget about punctuation.
9. **Don't bombard co-workers or your boss with messages.** Send them only for brief, necessary work-related communications.

10. **Organize your contact lists into separate groups,** such as clients, co-workers, friends/family, and so on, so you do not embarrassingly send someone the wrong message.

Text Messages

Texting is the most casual, and among the shortest, form of business communication. Even so, text messaging plays an important role in the world of work:

- It is a quick and quiet way to send and receive information.
- It keeps employees who travel or telecommute in the loop.
- Used ethically, texting can be a valuable marketing tool, informing established clients about new services, product upgrades, etc.
- A text can be crucial for safety alerts and/or maintenance reminders.

Because individuals carry their mobile devices with them, texting makes it easier to reach a co-worker or client than emailing or even calling them. Because emails can be forwarded to your smartphone, you do not need a laptop or tablet to wait to use a PC to read and respond to them. Texting programs also make it possible to share multiple files, photos, videos, and graphics. A number of mobile apps will also help you to search, retrieve, send, and post information, and several (such as GroupMe) allow you to easily send a text to all the individuals in your office (for example, notifying staff that an employee will be out sick for two to three days or that the date of a meeting has been changed).

But the text messages you send from a company smartphone are very different from those that you write to a friend or family member. As with business emails and IMs, your texts must be ethical and legal (see "E-Communications Are Legal Records," pages 117–118). Again, pay close attention to tone, context, and spelling and always remember that what you write needs to reflect positively on you and your employer (see Figure 4.9).

Guidelines for Texting

While the guidelines for sending a text message and networked messaging (see "Guidelines for Using Messages in the Workplace," pages 137–138) are similar, here are a few especially relevant to texting:

1. Never text while driving a car or operating machinery. In many states texting while driving is illegal.
2. Put your mobile phone on vibrate to avoid disturbing co-workers or clients.
3. Never text when you are at a business meeting or a class or when talking to a client, co-worker, or manager. It is unprofessional and discourteous.
4. Send texts only when they convey company business; never use them for personal conversations.
5. Avoid textspeak, which often disregards proper spelling and punctuation.
6. Make sure any photos/videos you send are ethical and relevant to your job.
7. Textual harassment (for example, sending or forwarding sexual images or jokes; bullying a fellow employee) is grounds for being fired and maybe even prosecution. Again, don't put something in a text you would not put in an email or say in a business call.

FIGURE 4.9 An Example of a Text Message Exchange Between Ali and Thomas, Two Public Works Employees

WRITING FOR SOCIAL MEDIA IN THE WORKPLACE

Your employer will expect you to represent your company professionally on a variety of social media sites reaching audiences worldwide. These social media can be accessed through websites or mobile apps. In 2015, over 2 billion individuals used social media. As of this writing, Facebook (the world's largest marketing social media site) claimed 864 million daily fans. Twitter, Pinterest, Instagram, and Tumblr together had over 347 million active accounts. With a global audience this massive, large and small companies alike can create their own pages, posts, and pins to reach current and potential customers. Monitoring and responding quickly to your company's target audience on social media generates better customer interaction and drives sales.

As with your business email (see "Business Email Versus Personal Email," pages 119–120), you will be expected to project a positive and professional image of your company. You cannot post messages about your company on social media the same way you use social media for your personal use to communicate with friends and family. You need to recognize how the corporate world regards social media as a networking and marketing tool, and not as a way to exchange personal views. There is a big difference between expressing your own opinions on social media and representing your company's brand. You have to choose your words carefully before posting company information and responses to the public. Again, keep in mind your posts represent your employer.

How Social Media Helps Business

Having a presence on Facebook, Pinterest, Instagram, Twitter, Flickr, YouTube, or other social media is mandatory in today's global economy. As we saw, almost every business has a presence on a variety of social media that can be used in conjunction with each other. In fact, Facebook and Pinterest currently generate the most traffic as marketing tools drawing people to a website. Here are some ways social media can help a business:

- Provides current information about a company's brand, its products, and services to both present and potential customers. Pep Boys, on its Facebook "About" page (see Figure 4.10) explains the company's position on integrity and ethics and also its corporate mission to both customers and the environment.
- Builds customer loyalty and encourages feedback and interaction. Note how Pep Boys provides its "Community Guidelines" in Figure 4.10, explaining what kinds of comments and language will not be tolerated on their Facebook page.
- Boosts sales and knowledge of your brand.
- Answers customer questions and resolves complaints to counter negative images.
- Furnishes corporate news—what's going on in your company that affects visitors, marketing plans, and new products.
- Shares information with and/or about other companies (e.g., repinning, providing links, etc.) and thus increases your exposure to a target audience and enhances networking.

Technology changes rapidly. It is impossible to predict what new forms of social media may develop in the future, but no matter what online media are created, the following guidelines in this section will always apply.

FIGURE 4.10 A Company's Description of Its Values and Mission on Social Media

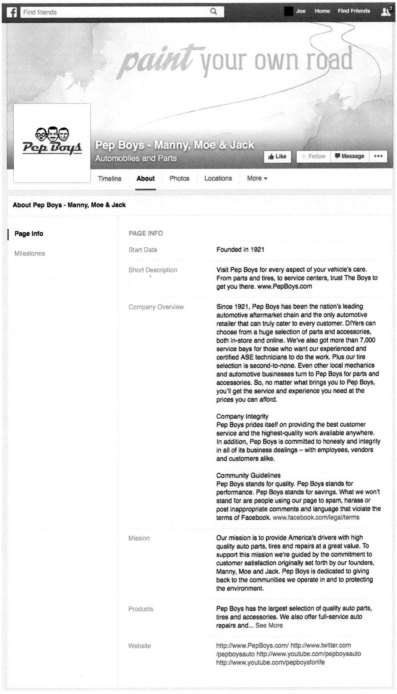

Source: Pep Boys

Staying Connected on Social Media Sites

Above all, social media is interactive; it's about building and sustaining relationships. Think of your posts, tweets, and pins as part of an ongoing conversation with customers who want information about your products but who also want to share information with you about their experiences—both good and bad. Your goal is to keep the conversation about, and interest in, your company strong through a global dialogue with potentially millions of readers.

To let fans and potential customers know you are available and eager to share information with them, follow these guidelines:

- Make it easy for fans to connect with and follow your company's platforms. Embed links to all the social media sites your company has. Link your Facebook page to your Twitter feed and your Pinterest, Flickr, and Instagram pages as well. And link everything to your company website. (Note how Pep Boys in Figure 4.10 provides links to its corporate website as well as its Twitter and YouTube sites on its Facebook page.) But do not simply repeat the same posts across various media; fans have different loyalties and expectations for each of the social media they use.

- Include social media logos on brochures, letterheads, company websites, and blogs alerting customers where they can find out about you, your products, and services, etc. Let fans know about the different ways they can learn about your brands. For example, you can insert a hover pin on your Pinterest board linked to websites, blogs, videos, and so on.

- Insert your URL in your posts and tweets to make getting in touch with you easier and accessing your company quicker. Notice how Amazon includes a link in the Facebook post in Figure 4.11 so its followers can easily find the page where they can share their favorite road trip read.

- Drive traffic to your site with attention grabbing titles—"The Top Ten Work Sites for Women in Technology"; "Understanding How New Pain Sensitive Protein Can Lead to Better Pain Meds."

- Motivate customers to visit your sites by sharing valuable tips and other practical, money-saving information with them.

- Strive to keep a conversation going by asking fans for input, and always thank readers for their feedback through posts, pins, FAQs, and surveys (see "Guidelines for Writing Business Blogs," pages 129–133). In Figure 4.11, Amazon encourages Kindle users to share feedback either via their corporate website, a hashtag that could be used on Twitter, or a comment left on their Facebook post.

- Track followers and use analytics across all your social media platforms to find out where your message is being most widely read and successfully received.

- Do not overload your page/post with keywords. Although they can help customers find your product or service, stuffing your posts or tweets with keywords will actually thwart the reception of your message. Search engines like Google will not list sites that overuse keywords.

- Keep track of your competitors' posts and pages to see what their customers like, share, tweet, and review to see what your competitors are doing to

FIGURE 4.11 A Model Post on Facebook

Source: Amazon Kindle

win customers or to turn them off. That way, you gather valuable marketing intelligence for your employer (see "Characteristics of Effective Workplace Research," page 305).

Know Your Customers and What They Like

- Keep track of visitors to your site(s). Facebook, for instance, provides help to tell you the age, gender, location, educational level, etc., of those who come to your site. With Facebook and other sites, you can monitor visitors' "likes," retweets, repins. Visiting these sites allows you to determine your company's strengths, shortcomings, and trends.
- Promise readers a reward for visiting your site. The most successful social media sites offer readers something they can get only online—giveaways, contests, prizes, discount sales, previews, exclusive promotions, infographics, etc.
- Ask for readers' favorite image, story, product, and so forth to give them a strong sense of having participated in your marketing plan to better serve them. Encouraging Kindle users to share their favorite road trip read (Figure 4.11) helps foster a shared sense of community among Amazon's customer base.

Choose Your Content Carefully

- Make sure your company's posts are current. Post new content on a regular basis, which may be twice a day or four or five times a week. But be careful that you do not overwhelm readers. Post news only when it is new or important for your target audience.
- Exclude your views about religion, politics, sports, or the latest movie or popular song. Save those posts for your personal social media sites.
- Write ethically (see "Legal/Ethical Guidelines to Follow in Writing E-Communications," pages 117–118). If you post unethical, erroneous, or indiscreet information or images, you could be jeopardizing your employer by causing a public relations catastrophe, and that could cost you your job.
- Be careful about using humor; it could be seen as offensive or misunderstood.
- Keep your sites personable; do not turn them into hard sell messages. Steven D. Strauss, the author of *The Small Business Bible*, advises wisely, "Eighty percent of your tweets or posts should be about your customers. The other twenty percent can be about your business—but make sure it is worthwhile content your customers will want to share." Even if your employer asks you to have an identity on, say, Twitter or Facebook, so customers get to know you, you have to walk a fine line between being too personal and chatty and representing your company. Note how the blog entry on power tools (see Figure 4.7, pages 134–135) translates the writer's experience with the product into a professional setting without injecting a lot of personal information.
- Watch out for clutter. You cannot say everything you want to about your company on a social media site. Keep in mind that Twitter has a 140 character limit; Facebook, too, has limits for both companies and individuals. You have only 200 words on Pinterest. Make them count. Include essential information about your business—location, contact details, the way you help customers, testimonials.
- Adapt your message to a particular site. Different sites emphasize different communication strategies (e.g., Facebook is a blend of weblogs and messaging).

Style

- Keep posts short. Remember that first impressions online are made in 3–5 seconds; many social media posts are now usually not much longer than a tweet (140 characters). An audience will read your post on a social media site quickly and move on if you do not grab their attention quickly. Notice how the Facebook post in Figure 4.11 is only 126 characters, well under the limit for a tweet.
- Write concise, simple, and informative sentences. Strive for between 100–125 characters in your tweets; some experts recommend keeping a tweet under 90. Keep in mind that Twitter is a "microblog." Note how Facebook emphasizes text but keeps it consumer-friendly and easy to read. Recognize that by being brief and to the point, you win points with your readers.

- Be sure your posts are grammatically flawless and that they do not contain spelling or punctuation errors. Such embarrassing mistakes can be shared around the globe in a matter of seconds.
- Avoid textspeak (see "Guidelines for Using Messages in the Workplace," pages 137–138). Instead, write clear, easy-to-understand sentences in international English (see "Using International English," pages 10–11).
- Do not insert excessive hashtags, which makes your post look unprofessional.
- Make sure your tone is friendly, engaging, and shows your readiness for a profitable and pleasurable conversation with customers, or prospective ones, worldwide. Note the even tone and professional responses of Nation Airlines to an irate customer in Figure 4.12 (page 146).

How to Respond to Criticism

- Don't ignore complaints; respond to them promptly. But make sure you are professional and calm. Don't post anything in anger, and keep your reply simple and to the point. Be courteous, and thank followers for their posts, comment, or question. Nothing infuriates a customer more than feeling his/her complaints are not being taken seriously. The opening tweet in Figure 4.12 by Adam Kinney starts out as overwhelmingly negative (even including a derogatory hashtag aimed at Nation Airlines), but the airline is quick to respond to the criticism and to help the process of satisfying the customer.
- When many customers express a similar complaint about your company, you must respond to each individually (as Nation Airlines does in Figure 4.12). In addition to personalized responses, a strategic Facebook post about a widespread complaint can ensure that your larger customer base is aware of your company's commitment to addressing the issue.
- Track user review sites such as Yelp, TripAdvisor, and Angie's List and respond to any negative reviews with sensitivity and diplomacy. Suggest that the customer contact you directly (through private email or a phone call) to discuss the issues. You do not want to encourage a negative back-and-forth on a social media site where potentially millions of customers can see and/or hear it. Be careful not to violate company policy by giving out personal names, email addresses, or phone numbers. Keep in mind that it may take several follow-up emails or phone calls to resolve the problem.
- Don't be afraid to admit a mistake. Again, your goal is to build customer trust and faith in you and your company.

Visuals

Visuals are essential to success by enhancing a company's appeal on social media. They are eye-catching and reinforce the message that you want customers to take away about your brand. Note how the photo in Figure 4.11 reinforces the language of the post by incorporating both relaxation (the reclined pose of the person holding the Kindle) and a sense of being "on the road" (because the subject is located in

FIGURE 4.12 Responding to Criticism on Social Media

Photo by Jason Stitt/Shutterstock.com

a car). Facebook posts containing images are the most often shared, with an 87 percent interaction rate. Tweets that feature an image are retweeted 35 percent more often than those that use text alone. Instagram and Pinterest are photoimage sites with a minimum amount of text. But by clicking on an image, a Pinterest fan can gain access to videos, statistics, your resume, a report.

Regardless of the site, follow these guidelines about including visuals.

- Make sure your images or videos are relevant. Connect them to your message and brand. They need to tell a story about your product or service and how they relate to one another. Visuals should emphasize a major or continuing theme and/or corporate image; note how the Kindle is located in the middle of the frame of the photo shown in Figure 4.11.
- Be sure they are properly sized, clear, and have enough resolution to look professional on a screen. A fuzzy picture says your company does poor work.
- Give each image, or pin, a title.
- Do not keep using the same image with each post. Vary your image to arouse online interest.
- Never steal images from other websites or post them on your own social media sites. This is a violation of the owner's copyright and could get your company into legal trouble. Instead, use images that are in the public domain (i.e., those not subject to copyright protection), from websites (such as creativecommons.org) where images are free provided you give proper credit, or from an online stock agency such as shutterstock.com.
- Be careful when you take an image for your employer with your phone or tablet. Make sure you get your boss's approval and that the photos are clear, relevant, and not offensive.

CONCLUSION

E-communications—emails, blogs, instant and text messages, and social media posts—are a routine yet important part of every employee's job. These basic types of business communication keep crucial information flowing among co-workers, management, vendors, and others, so that a company can meet its day-to-day obligations. In addition, the information contained in these short messages often helps you to write longer documents.

By following the guidelines in this chapter, you will be better able to write clear, concise, and ethical e-communications for your audience. Your annual evaluations may in part depend on how well you research, draft, revise, and how promptly you send and respond to e-communications.

✓ REVISION CHECKLIST

☐ Understood the reader's need and the information that had to be transferred, and determined which e-communication to use.

☐ Distinguished the various types of e-communications and how they relate to one another.

Email

☐ Did not send unsolicited or confidential email.

☐ Sent to reader's correct address.

☐ Formatted email with acceptable margins and spacing.

☐ Observed netiquette; avoided flaming.

☐ Wrote a separate message rather than returning sender's message with a short reply.

☐ Kept paragraphs short but used full—not telegraphic—sentences.

☐ Avoided unfamiliar abbreviations or terms that would confuse a reader.

☐ Received permission to repeat or incorporate another person's email.

☐ Observed all legal obligations in using email.

☐ Safeguarded employer's confidentiality and security by excluding sensitive or privileged information.

☐ Included enough information and documentation for reader's purpose.

☐ Honored reader by observing proper courtesy.

☐ Began with friendly greeting; ended politely.

☐ Considered needs of international audience.

☐ Used antivirus program, did not forward or reply to spam.

Blogs

☐ Posted nothing critical of employer or co-workers and nothing embarrassing, offensive, or confidential.

☐ Made posts conversational and informal, yet professional.

☐ Dated every blog post.

☐ Targeted my audience.

☐ Included attention-grabbing headline.

☐ Posted only current and relevant information.

☐ Provided a place for readers to give feedback.

Messaging

☐ Used messaging only for professional, job-related communications.

☐ Kept messages short—not over a line or two.

☐ Avoided "textspeak" in business messages.

☐ Notified readers when your messaging system was offline and back online.

☐ Did not send anything confidential through a message exchange.

☐ Used text messages only for necessary business communications.

☐ Made sure text was courteous and professional.

☐ Kept text messages short, but used correct spelling and punctuation.

☐ Took advantage of apps to communicate more efficiently on the job.

Social Media

☐ Posted new content on a regular basis but did not overwhelm followers with an excessive number of posts.

☐ Projected a positive and professional image of your company or organization and excluded any personal views on topics such as religion or politics.

☐ Provided current information about your company's brand, products, and services.

☐ Encouraged feedback and interaction to build customer loyalty and always thanked readers for their input.

☐ Addressed customer complaints and questions promptly in a professional and courteous manner.

☐ Cross-linked to your company's other social media platforms and included relevant URLs in posts to allow customers direct access to information.

☐ Did not use textspeak or overload posts with keywords and hashtags.

☐ Avoided posting unethical, erroneous, or indiscrete messages or images.

☐ Kept posts as brief as possible while still communicating your company's message effectively.

☐ Made sure any images or videos used connected directly to your company's message or brand.

EXERCISES

1. Write an email requesting information from one of the following types of businesses. Submit a copy of your email request, along with the response, to your instructor.

   a. From an airline: an up-to-date schedule along a certain route and information about any bonus-mile or discount programs

   b. From a stock brokerage firm: free quotes or research about a particular stock

   c. From a resort: special rates for a given week

   d. From a professional organization to which you belong about any conferences to be held in your city or state

2. Write an email with one of the following messages, observing the guidelines discussed in "Guidelines for Using Email on the Job" (pages 120–124).

   a. You have just made a big sale, and you want to inform your boss.

   b. You have just lost a big sale, and you have to inform your boss.

   c. Inform a co-worker about a union or national sales meeting.

   d. Notify a company to cancel your subscription to one of its publications because you find it to be dated and no longer useful in your profession.

   e. Request help from a listserv about research for a major report you are preparing for your employer.

   f. Advise your district manager to discontinue marketing one of the company's brands because of low customer acceptance.

   g. Write to a friend studying finance at a German, Korean, or South American university about the biggest financial news in your town or neighborhood in the last month.

3. Rewrite the following email to your boss to make it more professional.

   Hi—

   This new territory is a pain. Lots of stops; no sales. Ughhhh. People out here resistant to change. Could get hit by a boulder and still no change. Giant companies ought to be up on charges. Will sub. reports asap as long as you care rec.

   The long and short of it is that market is down. No news = bad news.

4. As a collaborative venture, join with three or four classmates to prepare one or more of the email messages for Exercise 2. Send each other drafts of your messages for revision. Email the final draft to your instructor.

5. Email your instructor about a project you are now working on for class, outlining your progress and describing any difficulties you are having.

6. You have just missed work or a class meeting. Email your employer or your instructor explaining the reason and telling how you intend to make up the work.

7. As a collaborative project, write three or four external blog posts about some aspect of your current job or a previous job. Share with readers news about your company's products or services, technology you are using, professional travel, community service, work with international colleagues, and so forth. Be sure that your posts show your company, department, or agency in a good light.

8. Send a short post (200–300 words) to your company's blog administrator about a recent accomplishment you or your office, department, or section achieved. Include a link to a relevant site for readers to visit for further information.

9. As a group activity, message two or three other members of your collaborative writing team on a project you are working on. Print out your message exchanges during this time, and submit them to your instructor.

10. Revise the following unethical or poorly worded text messages.

    a. Y r u not here yet? Mtg starts in 5.
    b. If u don't have reprt on my desk by 5 heads will roll!!!!
    c. U rocked tht mtg thx 4 cing this thru ttyl
    d. GMAB u need 2 GOWI and meet the client F2F by COB 2moro

11. Contact a larger local business that has a social media coordinator and interview that person about the challenges they face in that role and where they see the role of creating content for social media going in the next few years.

12. Collaborate with classmates to create a fictitious company. Chose the line of business the company engages in and what its business philosophy and ideals are. Then create a fictitious social media presence for the company on three of the social media platforms discussed in this chapter. Follow the guidelines in "Staying Connected on Social Media Sites" (pages 142–143) as well as the tips provided in "Choose Your Content Carefully" (page 144) and "Style" (pages 144–145). Prepare screen shots of the home pages of the final versions to share with other groups and to discuss what improvements you might make.

13. Imagine that you are introducing a new product line for the company created in Exercise 12. Explain in detail how you would roll out the announcement of and then the unveiling of the product line across three social media platforms so as to maximize customer interest and excitement. Then execute your plan and prepare screen shots of the final result in each platform so that other groups can discuss where you might be able to improve on what you've done.

14. Select a *Fortune* 500 company and evaluate their presence on social media platforms. Which of the guidelines in "Staying Connected on Social Media Sites" (pages 142–143) have they followed? Which have they ignored? (And can you assess if there is a philosophy behind why they've ignored them?)

15. Explore the social media presence of a business that primarily operates in another country and in a language other than English. Compare that company's mix of words, images, and video to that of a company from the United States that works primarily in English. What different strategies does the non-American company use on their sites, and why might they have chosen to use them? Are there strategies they use that you can imagine incorporating into the U.S.–based company's social media sites?

16. Find a local business on Yelp that has a few negative reviews. Select one of them and map out what your strategy would be to interact with the dissatisfied customer, including both your initial contact with the reviewer and a longer follow-up message.

Murat Taner/Flirt/Corbis

CHAPTER

5

Writing Letters

Some Basics for Communicating with Audiences Worldwide

Letters are among the most important writing you will do on your job. While emails remain the most frequent type of communication in the world of work because they are a quick and easy way to send a message to one person or to many, formal business letters are still prized as a way of communicating. Businesses worldwide take letter writing very seriously, and employers will expect you to prepare and respond to your correspondence promptly and diplomatically. Your signature on a letter tells readers that you are accountable for everything in it.

Learning to write effective letters is not some lost art but a skill you need to be successful in the workplace. The higher up the corporate ladder you climb, the more letters you will be expected to write. Because letter writing is so significant to your career, this chapter introduces you to the entire process and provides guidelines and problem-solving strategies. It also shows you how to write for international readers. Chapter 6 will then help you to prepare the most common types of letters you will be expected to write on your job.

ESSENTIAL ADVICE ON WRITING EFFECTIVE LETTERS

To write effective letters, keep in mind the guidelines from Chapter 1 (see "Four Keys to Effective Writing," pages 11–18). You need to identify and analyze your **audience** and their needs (whether that audience is one person or many); clearly and quickly establish your **purpose** in sending your letter (see "Organizing a Standard Business Letter," page 164); formulate your **message** by including the key facts, recommendations, and details readers need; and select the appropriate **style** and **tone** so that your letters are reader-friendly and persuasive (see "Making a Good Impression on Your Reader," pages 164–168). Of course, your letters must follow your company's protocols, policies, and chain of command and be ethical (see "Ethical Writing in the Workplace," pages 26–37).

LETTERS IN THE AGE OF THE INTERNET

Even in this age of the Internet, letters are vital in the world of work. A professional-looking letter is one of the most significant symbols in the business world for the following reasons:

  1. **Letters represent your company's public image and your competence.** A firm's corporate image is on the line when it sends a letter. Its name and logo will appear on the company's letterhead (see "Letter Formats," pages 155–157). Carefully written letters create goodwill and make a positive impression on readers. Poorly written letters can anger customers, cost your company business, and project an unfavorable image of you.

  2. **Letters are far more formal—in tone and structure—than other types of business communication.** Letters adhere to far more conventions than do e-communications. Emails, messages, texts, tweets, and other social media posts (whether on Facebook or Instagram) are a much less formal way to communicate. A full discussion of the different types of letter formats (pages 155–157) and the parts of a letter (pages 158–162) can be found in this chapter.

  3. **Letters constitute an official legal record of an agreement.** They state, modify, or respond to a business commitment. A signed letter constitutes a legally binding contract (and will often be scanned to create an electronic record). They provide legal evidence where there is a dispute over a business matter. Letters also provide a reference, a stable record for any problems that come up. Be absolutely sure that what you put in a letter about prices, guarantees, warranties, equipment, delivery dates, and/or other issues is accurate. Your readers can hold you and your company accountable for such written commitments.

  4. **Unlike emails, many businesses require that letters are routed through channels before they are sent out.** Because they convey how a company looks and what it offers to customers, letters often need to be approved by your boss and others in the company. Depending on the content, a company's legal, finance, human resources, purchasing, planning, or IT departments may need to review and authorize a business letter.

  5. **Letters are more substantial and secure than emails.** They are a vital record of a company's business, and provide a documented hard copy and paper trail that is not as easily deleted as emails. Letters are often logged in, filed, and bear a handwritten, authorized signature.

  6. **A letter is the official and expected medium through which important hard copy documents and enclosures (contracts, specifications, proposals) are sent to readers.** Letters often convey official changes in policy or organization; accompany key materials submitted to outside vendors, partners, or companies; or notify customers about adjustments to their account.

7. **Because readers receive far fewer letters than emails, letters often get higher priority; readers tend to pay more attention to them.** A letter commands attention because of its formal elements (see "Parts of a Letter," pages 158–162). It is a physical, tangible document whereas an email can be missed or confused with spam. All the physical components of a letter—envelope, letterhead/stationery, mailing label, etc.—convey a far different impression than an email.

8. **Letters are far more personable than emails or other e-communications.** They are addressed to a specific person whose name and address are typed on the envelope. Letters, moreover, show readers that the writer has taken time to send them a personalized message. Unlike an email which might be sent to hundreds of individuals, a letter shows specific customer appreciation.

9. **A letter is still the most formal and approved way to conduct important business with many international audiences.** These readers see a letter as more polite and honorable than an email for initial contacts and even for subsequent business communications.

10. **A hard copy letter is confidential.** Emails are sent over the Internet, which is far less secure than letters, which come sealed in a stamped envelope. Unlike an email, which can be easily opened, copied, deleted, and resent, a letter is more permanent and more likely to be delivered to *only* the proper recipient and less likely to be forwarded to unintended readers (as an email might be).

DIFFERENT WAYS TO SEND LETTERS

Sending a hard copy letter continues to be the most formal way to communicate with your audience (and is the required way in certain legal situations; see "Letters in the Age of the Internet," pages 153–154). But it is not the *only* way; your company may ask you to use one of the following options to send a letter *in addition to* the hardcopy version you send out:

- **As an attachment to an email.** You can create a digital copy of your letter (such as a PDF file), either directly from your word processing program or by scanning your signed copy. Because a PDF file preserves exactly the format and style of your letter, sending it as an attachment is a quick, direct way to announce a change in policy or other corporate news.
- **Through posting on the company's website or social media platforms.** This method is often used for letters that are considered **open letters**, that is, addressed to a company's own employees or to their customers. Posting an open letter will usually accompany sending the hardcopy version to intended readers.
- **In the body of an email.** This is just as direct as sending a letter as an attachment to an email and has the same benefit of timeliness. Sending a letter in the body of an email assures recipients that a computer virus will not be unloosed when opening an attachment, and most software programs can retain the necessary formatting of a hardcopy letter. It can be used as an additional way of ensuring a message is delivered to a specific individual.

- **By fax.** Though far less common now than, say, ten or fifteen years ago, some organizations and businesses still communicate by fax. Sending a letter by fax is both fast and an additional way of ensuring the message is delivered, because it is sent to a recipient's specific fax number. It also is a useful method to use when sending a cover letter for original documents that cannot to be mailed (and which are being sent via fax).

No matter how you send your letter, you still must follow the guidelines on the format, parts of, and appearance discussed below.

LETTER FORMATS

Letter format refers to the way your letter looks on the page (whether in print on on a screen)—where you indent and where you place certain kinds of information. Several letter formats exist. The most formal, preferred, and frequently used business letter format in the world of work is the **full-block**, but you should also be familiar with the **modified-block** and the **semi-block**. Format conveys message; know your company's preference. Above all, no matter what format you use, your letter should not look *lopsided, crowded,* or *spread out.*

Full-Block Format

In full-block format all information is flush against the left margin, double-spaced between paragraphs. Figure 5.1 (page 156) shows a full-block letter. Many employers prefer this format when your letter is on **letterhead stationery** (specially printed paper giving a company's name and logo; business, web, and social media addresses; phone and fax numbers; and sometimes the names of its executives).

Modified-Block Format

In modified-block format (see Figure 5.2 on page 157), the writer's address (if it is not imprinted on a letterhead), the date, the complimentary close, and the signature are positioned at the center point and then keyed toward the right side of the letter. The date aligns with the complimentary close. The inside address, the salutation, and the body of the letter are flush against the left margin. Though used less frequently than the full-block format, the modified-block is a format an employer may ask you to utilize.

Semi-Block Format

The semi-block format (see Figure 6.1, page 190) looks just like the modified-block format in terms of aligning the date line with the complimentary close, signature, and any enclosures at the center point of the letter. But the paragraphs in the semi-block format are always indented five to seven spaces. Though, again, not as frequently used as the full-block format, the semi-block format is a template you may be called upon to use in the world of work.

FIGURE 5.1 Full-Block Letter Format with Appropriate Margins

Letterhead with company name and logo	**NIRA** Nevada Insurance Research Agency 7500 South Maplewood Drive, Las Vegas, NV 89152-0026 (702) 555-9876 **www.NIRA.org** ⬛ **www.facebook.com/nira/** 🐦 **@nira**

1"–1.25" → |April 7, 2016   ← 1"–1.25"

2 lines

All text aligned on the left-hand margin

Ms. Molly Georgopolous, C.P.A.
Business Manager
Meyers, Inc.
3400 South Madison Road
Reno, NV 89554-3212

2 lines

Uses professional, businesslike font

Dear Ms. Georgopolous:

2 lines

As I promised in our telephone conversation earlier this afternoon, I am enclosing a study of the Nevada financial responsibility law. I hope that it will help you prepare your report.

2 lines

Text of letter balanced on the page

Let me emphasize again that probably 95 percent of all individuals who are involved in an accident obtain reimbursement for medical bills and for damages to their automobiles. If individuals have insurance, they can receive reimbursement from their own carrier. If they do not have insurance and the other driver is uninsured and judged to be at fault, the Nevada Bureau of Motor Vehicles revokes that party's driver's license until all costs and damages are paid.

Generous margins on all sides of the letter

2 lines

Please call me again if I can help you.

2 lines

Sincerely yours,

Signature written in black ink and not squeezed in between the complementary close and typed signature

4 lines

Carmen Tredeau

Carmen Tredeau, President

2 lines

Enclosure

Names of agency's executives

Bradley Fuller, CPCU	Carmen Tredeau, CPCU	Theodore Kendrick	Iping Li, CPCU	Dora Salinas-Diego, CPCU
Chairperson	President	Vice President Public Affairs	Vice President Research	Vice President Actuary

© 2017 Cengage Learning

FIGURE 5.2 Modified-Block Letter Format

7239 East Daphne Street
Mobile, AL 36608-1012

September 30, 2015

Mr. Travis Boykin, Manager
Scandia Gifts
703 Hardy St.
Hattiesburg, MS 39401-4633

Dear Mr. Boykin:

I am writing to see if you currently stock the Crescent pattern of
model 5678 and how much you charge per model number. I would
also like to know if you offer special prices for multiple-box orders.

Your store has been highly recommended to me by several
colleagues, who have praised your service and the excellent quality
of your products.

I look forward to working with you.

Sincerely yours,

Arthur T. McCormack

Arthur T. McCormack

*Date is indented
at center point
of letter*

*Inside address is
single-spaced*

*Paragraphs can
be indented or
not indented*

*Complimentary
close and
writer's name
are indented
and aligned
under date line*

© 2017 Cengage Learning

Continuing Pages

Do not number a one-page letter. To indicate subsequent pages if your letter runs beyond one page, use one of these two conventions. Note the use of the recipient's name.

| Jorge Vargas | 2 | April 7, 2016 |

$1\frac{1}{4}$" above the continuing text of the letter

2
Bo Yates
September 30, 2015

$1\frac{1}{4}$" above the continuing text of the letter

© 2017 Cengage Learning

PARTS OF A LETTER

A letter contains many parts, each of which contributes to your overall message. The parts and their placement in your letter form the basic conventions of effective letter writing. Readers look for certain information in key places.

The parts of a letter discussed in the following sections will appear in every letter you write. Figure 5.3 is a sample letter containing all of the parts discussed here. Note where each part is placed in the letter.

FIGURE 5.3 A Sample Letter, Full-Block Format, with All Parts Labeled

Heading (letterhead)	**M+Σ Madison and Moore, Inc.** *Professional Architects* 7900 South Manheim Road Crystal Springs, NE 71003-0092 Phone 402-555-2300 **www.mmi.com** **f** **www.facebook.com/mmi/** **@mmi**
Date line	July 14, 2016
Inside address with correct state abbreviation and zip code	Ms. Paula Jordan Systems Consultant Broadacres Development Corp. 12 East River Street Detroit, MI 48001-0422
Salutation	Dear Ms. Jordan:
Body of letter	Thank you for your letter of July 7, 2016. I have discussed your request with the staff in our planning department and have learned that the design modules we used for our Vestavia project are no longer available.
Left margin justified and single spaced except between paragraphs which are double spaced	In searching the Internet, however, I came across some designs from a California firm that might be helpful to you. California Concepts offers plans very similar to the ones you are interested in, as you can tell from the design featured here: **www.californiaconcepts.com/officemodule.** I hope this will help you, and I wish you every success in your project.
Complimentary close	Sincerely yours,
Company name	MADISON AND MOORE, INC.
Signature	*William Newhouse*
Writer's name and title	William Newhouse Design Coordinator
Copy notation	cc: Planning Department

Heading

The heading of a letter may be either your company's letterhead or your full return address. (See Figure 5.2 for an example of a full return address when letterhead is not used.)

Date Line

Try to leave four lines below the letterhead before the date line. Spell out the name of the month in full—"September" or "March" rather than "Sept." or "Mar." The date line is usually keyboarded this way: November 11, 2016. Different cultures express dates in different ways. Most countries, including those in Europe, list the day first, then the month, and then the year. See Figure 5.9 (page 175) for an example of how to correctly provide a date for international readers.

Inside Address

The inside address, the address of the recipient, is always placed against the left margin, two lines below the date line. It contains the name, title (if any), company, street address, city, state, and zip code of the person to whom you are writing. Single-space the inside address, and do not use any punctuation at the end of the lines.

Dr. Mary Petro
Director of Research
Midwest Laboratories
1700 Oak Drive
Rapid City, SD 56213–3406

Always try to write to a specific person rather than just "Sales Manager" or "President." To find out the person's name, check previous correspondence, email lists, or the company's or individual's website, or call the company. Make sure you use an abbreviated courtesy title (Ms., Mr., Dr., Prof.) before the recipient's name for the inside address (e.g., Capt. María Torres; Mr. A. T. Ricks; Rev. Siam Tau). Use Ms. when writing to a woman unless she has expressly asked to be called Miss or Mrs.

The last line of the inside address contains the city, state, and zip code.

Salutation

Two spaces below the inside address includes your salutation, or greeting. Begin with *Dear*, and then follow with a courtesy title, the reader's last name (unless you are on a first-name basis), and a colon (Dear Mr. Brown:). *Never use a comma for a formal letter*. Avoid the sexist "Dear Sir," "Gentlemen," or "Dear Madam" and the stilted "Ladies and Gentlemen" or "Dear Sir or Madam." (For a discussion of sexist language and how to eliminate it, see "Editing Guidelines to Eliminate Sexist Language," pages 65–66.)

Sometimes a first name does not reveal whether the reader is male or female. There are women named Stacy, Robin, and Lee, and men named Leslie, Kim, and Kelly. If you aren't certain, you can use the reader's full name: "Dear Terry Jones." Similarly, if your recipient uses just initials, write "Dear S.K. Holmes." Or if you know the person's title, you might write "Dear Credit Manager Jones."

Avoid casual salutations such as "Hello," "Hi," "Good Morning," "Greetings," or "Happy Tuesday"; these are best reserved for emails or messages. And never begin a letter with "To Whom It May Concern," which is old-fashioned, impersonal, and trite.

Body of the Letter

The body of the letter, two spaces after the salutation, contains your message. Some of your letters will be only a few lines long, while others may extend to three or more paragraphs. Keep your sentences concise, and try to hold your paragraphs to less than seven lines. (Refer to "Editing," pages 59–69.)

Complimentary Close

A close, two lines below the last line of your message, is the equivalent of a formal goodbye. For most business correspondence, use one of these standard closes:

> Sincerely,
> Respectfully,
> Sincerely yours,

Capitalize only the first letter of the first word. The entire close is followed by a comma. If you and your reader know each other well, as in Figure 5.4, you can use

> Cordially,
> Best wishes,
> Regards,

But avoid flowery closes, such as

> Forever yours,
> Devotedly yours,
> Faithfully yours,

These belong in a romance novel, not in a business letter.

Signature

Allow four spaces between the complimentary close and your typed name and title so that your signature will not look squeezed in. Always sign your name in black ink. An unsigned letter indicates carelessness or, worse, indifference toward your reader. A stamped signature tells readers you could not give them personal attention.

Some firms prefer using their company name along with the employee's name in the signature section. If so, type the company name in capital letters two line spaces below the complimentary close and then sign your name. Add your title underneath your typed name. Here is an example:

> Sincerely yours,
> THE FINELLI COMPANY
>
> *Helen Stravopoulos*
>
> Helen Stravopoulos
> Web Coordinator

FIGURE 5.4 Careful Organization of a Business Letter

Office Property Management Associates
2400 South Lincoln Highway
Livingston, NJ 07040-9990
(201) 555-3740   www.opma.com

Clear, professional letterhead with contact information

April 11, 2016

Mr. W. T. Albritton
Albritton & Sharp, CPA
Suite 400
Suburban Office Complex
Livingston, NJ 07038-2389

Accurate inside address

Dear Mr. Albritton:

Thank you for your recent suggestions on improving security at the Suburban Office Complex. You will be pleased to learn that OPMA will be making the following improvements in services, to go into effect within 45 days.

Introduction comes to point quickly and cordially by referencing reader's earlier request

Starting May 2, an on-site manager, Thomas Vasquez, will be available to answer any questions you may have about the Complex and help you with any problems you may encounter. His ten years of experience in managing commercial office parks will benefit you and other businesses at the Suburban Office Complex.

Body describes changes with specific details

The new outdoor security system you asked for will be installed by May 16. It will give you and your employees greater protection through seven additional security cameras around the perimeters of the parking lot while movement sensors will monitor every outside door.

I want to reassure you that none of these changes will inconvenience the operation of your firm or interfere with your employees entering the office complex. We are honored to have Albritton & Sharp as residents. I welcome your comments as these changes are implemented as well as additional suggestions you may have.

Conclusion builds goodwill by promising reader what will be done and how

Best wishes,

Cheryl Hu

Cheryl Hu
Vice President

Four spaces left between complimentary close and typed name

Enclosure Line

The enclosure line informs the reader that additional materials (such as a brochure, diagram, form, contract, or proposal) accompany your letter.

> Enclosure (only one item is enclosed)
> Enclosures (2)
> Encl.: Spring Quarter Sales Report

Copy Notation

The abbreviation **cc:** —two c's followed by a colon—informs your reader that a copy of your letter has been sent to one or more individuals.

> cc: Service Dept.
> cc: Hannah Pittman-Jarzelski
>   Ivor Vas

Letters are copied and sent to third parties for two reasons: (1) to document a paper trail and (2) to indicate that other readers need the information contained in the letter. Unless your employer instructs you otherwise, tell your reader if others will receive a copy of your letter.

THE APPEARANCE OF YOUR LETTER

The way your letter looks can determine how readers will respond to your message. Here are some tips on how to format and produce professional-looking letters:

- If you are printing your letter, use a high-quality printer, and check ink or toner cartridge levels to avoid sending a fuzzy, faint, or messy letter.
- Stay away from fancy fonts and scripts. Use the business-like Times New Roman or Arial. (See "Typography," pages 454–456 for a further discussion of this topic.)
- Consider using templates to help format and design your letters. Most word-processing programs, such as Microsoft Word or Google Docs, have them. Some organizations, however, may prefer you not to use a template. Always check with your company before you start your letter.
- Leave generous margins of at least 1 to 1¼ inches all around your message. For a shorter letter, as in Figure 5.6 (page 166), don't expand your margins to 2 inches or increase the font size, which will only make your letter look unprofessional.
- Leave double line spaces between key parts of a letter—the date line, the salutation, copy notation, and enclosure—but leave four lines between the letterhead and date as well as the complimentary close and your typed signature. Do *not* try to squeeze in a handwritten signature; it projects a bad professional image.
- Single-space within each paragraph, but double-space between paragraphs. The white space enhances the professional look of your letter and makes it easier to read.

- Avoid crowding too much text onto one page. Squeezing too many characters on a line by using overly small fonts will make your letter look cramped and be hard to read. Also, don't cram a long letter onto one page; instead, allow your letter to flow to a second page.
- Be careful about lopsided letters. Don't start a brief letter at the top of the page and then leave the lower three-fourths blank. Begin a shorter message near the center of the page.
- Use Print Preview to see an image of your letter before you print a hard copy or create a digital version of it, so that you can make any necessary changes or corrections. Never print over your company's letterhead or any addresses or company logos printed across the bottom of the letter.
- If making a hard copy of your letter, always print your letter on high-quality white bond paper (20-pound, 8½ × 11) and matching standard-size (#10) business envelopes (see "Envelopes" below). Avoid colored paper.

ENVELOPES

The way your envelope looks says a great deal about your message. Most companies have envelopes with their name, contact information, and logos that they will expect you to use. There are many different kinds of envelopes, including ones that have a window where the recipient's name an address would normally go. If you have to supply your own, use #10 envelopes, which are 9½ inches long and hold an 8½ × 11 sheet of paper. There are word-processing programs that have envelope addressing templates you can use. Center and single-space your recipient's name and address (which must match the inside address in your letter), and put your name and address in the upper left-hand corner of the envelope. A mailing label is less personable than directly typing the recipient's name and address on the envelope. The U.S. Postal Service recommends that all information be in all capital letters with no punctuation, to ensure that it scans effectively.

FELIX MARTIN-ROCHA
2314 SOUTH 14TH STREET
CHICAGO IL   60608-5037

*All capital
letters used*

MS. THERESA ROOKER
ASSISTANT MANAGER
PREWITT & FIDDLER
4800 TRUMAN AVENUE NORTH
SPRINGDALE MN   55439-0480

*Used full
addresses*

No punctuation

© Cengage Learning

ORGANIZING A STANDARD BUSINESS LETTER

A standard business letter can be divided into an introduction, a body, and a conclusion, each section responding to or clarifying a specific issue for your recipient. These three sections can each be one paragraph long, as in Figures 5.1, 5.2, and 5.3, or the body of your letter can be two or more paragraphs, as in Figure 5.4.

To help readers grasp your message clearly and concisely, follow this simple plan for organizing your business letters:

- In your first paragraph start with a friendly opening and explain why you are writing and why your letter is important to the recipient. Acknowledge any relevant previous meetings, correspondence, or telephone calls early in the paragraph (as in Figures 5.1 and 5.3).
- Put the most significant point of each paragraph first to make it easier for the reader to find. Never bury important ideas in the middle or at the end of a paragraph.
- In the second (or subsequent) paragraph, develop the body of your message with factual support, key details, and descriptions your reader needs. For instance, note how Figure 5.4 refers to the specific changes to improve security that the reader had requested.
- In your last paragraph, thank readers and be very clear and precise about what you want them to do or what you will do for them. Let them know what will happen next, what you or they need to do (Figure 5.4), or any combination of these messages. Don't leave your readers hanging. End cordially and professionally.

MAKING A GOOD IMPRESSION ON YOUR READER

You have just learned about formatting and organizing your letters. Now we turn to the content of your letters—what you say (your message) and how you say it (your style and tone). Writing letters means communicating to influence your readers, not to alienate or antagonize them. Keep in mind that writers of effective letters are like successful diplomats; they represent both their company and themselves. You want readers to see you as courteous, well informed, and professional.

First, put yourself in the reader's position. What kinds of letters do you like to receive: vague, impersonal, sarcastic, pushy, and condescending; or polite, businesslike, and considerate? If you have questions, you want them answered honestly, courteously, and fully.

To send such effective letters, adopt the **"You Attitude,"** in other words, signal to readers that they and their needs are of utmost importance. Incorporating the "you attitude" means you should be able to answer "Yes" to these two questions:

1. Will my readers receive a positive image of me?
2. Have I chosen words that convey both my respect for the readers and my concern for their questions and comments?

The first question deals with your overall view of the reader. Do your letters paint readers as dedicated or unprofessional, practical managers or spendthrifts?

FIGURE 5.5 A Letter Lacking the "You Attitude"

Brown County • **Office of the Tax Assessor**

County Building, Room 200, Ventura, Missouri 56780-0101

712-555-3000

 www.facebook.com/browncountymo/

February 5, 2016

Mr. Ted Ladner
451 West Hawthorne Lane
Morris, MO 64507-3005

Dear Mr. Ladner:

You have written to the wrong office here at the County Building. There is no way we can attempt to verify the kinds of details you are demanding from Brown County.

Simply put, by carefully examining the 2015 tax bill you said you received, you should have realized that it is the Tax Collector's Office, not the Tax Assessor's, that will have to handle the problem you claim exists.

In short, call or write the Tax Collector of Brown County.

Thank you!

Tracey Kowalski

Tracey Kowalski

Tone is sarcastic and uncooperative

Use of "you" alone does not signal a positive image of reader

Insulting and curt ending and complimentary close

Does not list writer's job title or specific contact information

© 2017 Cengage Learning

www.browncounty.gov

The second question concerns the language and tone conveying your message to the reader. Words can burn or soothe. Choose them carefully. As you revise your letters, you will become more aware of and concerned about the ways readers will respond to you and your message.

Figures 5.5 and 5.6 (page 166) contain two versions of the same letter. Which one would you rather receive?

FIGURE 5.6 A You-Centered Revision of Figure 5.5

Brown County • Office of the Tax Assessor

County Building, Room 200, Ventura, Missouri 56780-0101

712-555-3000

 www.facebook.com/browncountymo/

February 5, 2016

Mr. Ted Ladner
451 West Hawthorne Lane
Morris, MO 64507-3005

Dear Mr. Ladner:

Thanks reader and gives polite explanation

Thank you for writing about the difficulties you encountered with your 2015 tax bill. I wish I could help you, but it is the Tax Collector's Office that issues your annual property tax bill. Our office does not prepare individual homeowners' bills.

Helps reader solve problem with specific information

If you will kindly direct your questions to Paulette Sutton at the Brown County Tax Collector's Office, County Building, Room 100, Ventura, Missouri 56780-0100, I am sure that she will be able to assist you. Should you wish to call her, the number is 712-555-3455, extension 212. Her email address is **psutton@bctc.gov**. I hope this helps you.

Uses appropriate complimentary close

Respectfully,

Tracey Kowalski

Tracey Kowalski
Assistant Tax Assessor

Lists specific job title and contact information to personalize the letter

712-555-3455 Ext. 232
tracey_kowalski@browncounty.gov

www.browncounty.gov

© 2017 Cengage Learning

Achieving the "You Attitude": Four Guidelines

As you draft and revise your work, pay special attention to the following four guidelines for making a good impression on your reader.

1. Never forget that your reader is a real person. Avoid writing cold, impersonal letters that sound as if they were clinical reports or voicemail instructions. Let the readers know that you are writing to them as individuals. The following letter violates every rule of personal and personable communications.

> It has come to our attention that policy number 342q–765r has been delinquent in payment and is in arrears for the sum of $302.35. To keep the policy in force for the duration of its life, a minimum payment of $50.00 must reach this office by the last day of the month. Failure to submit payment will result in the cancellation of the aforementioned policy.

The example above displays no sense of one human being writing to another, of a customer with a name, personal history, or specific needs. Revised, this letter contains the necessary personal (and human) touch.

> We have not yet received your payment for your insurance policy (342q–765r). By sending us your check for $50.00 within the next two weeks, you will keep your policy in force and can continue to enjoy the financial benefits and emotional security it offers you.

Here the benefits to a specific policy holder are stressed, and the reader is addressed directly as a valued customer.

Don't be afraid of using "you" in letters. Readers will feel more friendly toward you and your message. Of course, no amount of "yous" will help if they appear in a condescending context, such as the letter in Figure 5.5.

2. Keep the reader in the forefront of your letter. Make sure the reader's needs control the tone, message, and organization of your letter—the essence of the "you attitude." Stress the "you," not the "I" or the "we." Below you can see a paragraph from a letter that forgets about the reader:

I-Centered Draft

> I think that our rug shampooer is the best on the market. Our firm has invested a lot of time and money to ensure that it is the most economical and efficient shampooer available today. We have found that our customers are very satisfied with the results of our machine. We have sold thousands of these shampooers, and we are proud of our accomplishment. We hope that we can sell you one of our fantastic machines.

3. Be courteous and tactful. Refrain from turning your letter into a punch through the mail. Don't inflame your letter or email audience; review Figures 4.3 and 4.4 (pages 125 and 126). When you capture the reader's goodwill, your rewards will be great. The following negative words can leave a bad taste in the reader's mouth.

it's defective	unprofessional (job, attitude, etc.)
I demand	your failure
I insist	you contend
we reject	you allege
that's no excuse for	you should have known
totally unacceptable	your outlandish claim

Compare the following discourteous sentences with the courteous revisions.

Discourteous	Courteous
We must discontinue your service unless payment is received by the date shown.	Please send us your payment by November 4 so that your service will not be interrupted.
You are sorely mistaken about the contract.	We are sorry to learn about the difficulty you experienced over the service terms in your contract.
The new iPad you sold me is third-rate and you charged first-rate prices.	Because the iPad is still under warranty, I hope you can make the repairs easily and quickly.
It goes without saying that your suggestion is not worth considering.	It was thoughtful of you to send me your suggestion, but, unfortunately, we are unable to implement it right now.

© Cengage Learning

The last discourteous example begins with a phrase that frequently sets readers on edge. Avoid using "*It goes without saying*"—it can quickly set up a hostile barrier between you and your reader.

    4. Don't sound pompous or bureaucratic. Write to your reader as if you were carrying on a professional conversation. Your tone should be polite but natural and to the point. Make your letters reader-friendly and believable, not stuffy and overbearing. To do that, don't resort to using phrases that remind readers of **legalese**—language that some writers use to make themselves sound important, but that only alienates readers. It smells of contracts, deeds, and stuffy rooms.

    In the following list, the words and phrases on the left are pompous expressions that have crept into letters for years; the ones on the right are contemporary equivalents.

Pompous	Contemporary	Pompous	Contemporary
aforementioned	previously mentioned	herewith; heretofore; hereby	(drop these three *h*'s entirely)
as per your request	as you requested	immediate future	soon
I am in receipt of	I have received	in lieu of	instead of
attached herewith	enclosed	pursuant	concerning
be advised that	for your information	remittance	payment
due to the fact that	because	under separate cover	I'm also sending you
endeavor	try	this writer	I
henceforth	after this	we regret to inform you that	we are sorry that

© Cengage Learning

International Business Correspondence

After emails, letters are the most frequent type of communication you are likely to have with international readers. Being able to write a formal letter to these readers will be an important part of your job. But as we saw in Chapter 1 (see "Writing for the Global Marketplace," pages 5–11), you cannot assume that people in every culture write letters the way we do in the United States. The conventions of letter writing—formats, inside addresses, salutations, dates, complimentary closes, signature lines—are as diverse as international audiences are.

Sometimes your international client may reside in the United States. Then you have to exercise the same diplomacy as you would when communicating with audiences living in other countries. For example, in Figure 5.7 (page 170) restaurant owner Patrice St. Jacques writes an effective sales letter by zeroing in on his reader's (Etienne Abernathy's) ethnic pride and heritage. Although Abernathy's company is located in the United States, St. Jacques persuasively sees him from a much broader cultural perspective.

It would be impossible to provide information about how to write letters to each international audience. There are at least five thousand major languages representing diverse ethnic and cultural communities around the globe. But here are some of the most important culturally sensitive questions you need to ask about writing to readers whose cultures are different from yours:

- What is your relationship to your reader(s) (client, vendor, salesperson, or international colleague)?
- How should you format and address your letter?
- What is an appropriate salutation?
- How should you begin and conclude your letter?
- What types and amount of information will you have to give?
- What is the most appropriate tone to use?

To answer these and similar questions about proper letter protocol for your international readers, you need to learn about their culture by consulting a source such as www.international-business-etiquette.com or www.vayama.com/etiquette.

Ten Guidelines for Communicating with International Readers

The following ten guidelines will help you communicate more successfully with an international audience and significantly reduce the chances of readers' misunderstanding you.

1. Use common, easily understood vocabulary. Write in basic, simplified English. Choose words that are widely understood. Whenever you have a choice, use the simpler word. For example, use *stop*, not *refrain*; *prevent*, not *forestall*; *happy*, not *exultant*.

2. Keep your sentences simple and easy to understand. Short, direct sentences will cause a reader whose native language is not English the least amount of trouble.

FIGURE 5.7 A Sales Letter That Appeals to a Specific International Audience

Distinctive, functional letterhead and use of color

ISLAND JACQUES
4700 Cyprus Avenue
Philadelphia, PA 19172

www.islandjacques.com
www.facebook.com/islandjacques/
@islandjacq
215-555-3295

10 May 2016

Mr. Etienne Abernathy, President
Seagrove Enterprises
1800 S. Port Haven Road
Philadelphia, PA 19103-1800

Dear Mr. Abernathy:

Compliments reader on award

Congratulations on winning the Hanover Award for Community Service. We in the Port Haven area of Philadelphia are proud that a business with Caribbean roots has received such a distinguished honor.

Extends invitation

Appeals to reader's senses through art, music, and food

To celebrate your and Seagrove's success, as well as all your business entertaining needs (annual banquet, monthly meetings, etc.), I invite you to Island Jacques. We are a family-owned business that for 30 years has offered Philadelphia residents the finest Caribbean atmosphere and food west of the Islands. Our black pepper shrimp, reggae or mango chicken, and Steak St. Lucie—plus our irresistible beef and pork jerk—are the talk from here to Kingston. You and your guests will be surrounded by our original Caribbean art and enjoy our steel drum music.

Describes special features, such as flexible hours and dining options

Ties costs to benefits

Island Jacques can offer Seagrove a variety of dining options. With five separate dining rooms, we are small enough for an intimate party of 4 yet large enough to accommodate a group of up to 250 guests. We can do early lunches or late dinners, depending on your schedule. And we even cater, if that's your style. Our chefs—Diana Maurier and Emile Danticat—will prepare a special calypso menu just for you. Also a benefit, our prices are competitive for the Philadelphia area.

Ends by giving reader incentive to act soon

Please call me soon so you can savor Island Jacques's unique hospitality. For your convenience, I am enclosing a copy of this week's menu delights. Check out our website, too, for a taste of Caribbean sound. We would love to feature Seagrove as Island Jacques's "Guest of the Week!"

Stay Cool, Mon.

Patrice St. Jacques

Uses an appropriate close for reader

Patrice St. Jacques
Event Coordinator

A good rule of thumb is that the shorter and less complicated your sentences, the easier and clearer they will be for a reader to process. Long (more than fifteen to twenty words) and complex (using many clauses) sentences can be so difficult for readers to unravel that they may skip over them or simply guess at your message. Do not, however, be insultingly childish, as if you were writing to someone in kindergarten. Also, always try to avoid the passive voice. It is one of the most difficult sentence patterns for a non-native speaker to comprehend. Stick to the common subject-verb-object pattern as often as possible. See "Editing Guidelines for Cutting Out Unnecessary Words" (pages 62–65) and the "Writer's Brief Guide to Paragraphs, Sentences, and Words" (pages A-1–A-19).

3. Avoid ambiguity. Words that have double meanings force non-native readers to wonder which one you mean. For example, "We fired the engine" would baffle your readers if they were not aware of the multiple meanings of *fire.* Unfamiliar with the context in which *fire* means "start up," a non-native speaker of English might think you're referring to "setting on fire or inflaming," which is not what you intend. Or because *fire* can also mean "dismiss" or "let go," a non-native speaker of English might even suspect the engine was replaced by another model. Such misinterpretations are likely because most bilingual dictionaries list only a few meanings.

Be especially careful of using synonyms just to vary your word choice. For example, do not write *quick* in one sentence and then, referring to the same action, describe it as *rapid.* Your reader may assume you have two different things in mind instead of just one.

4. Be careful about technical vocabulary. While a reader who is a non-native speaker may be more familiar with technical terms than with other English words, make sure the technical word or phrase you include is widely known and not a word or phrase used only at your plant or office. Double-check by consulting the most up-to-date manuals and websites in your field, but steer clear of technical terms in fields other than the one with which your reader is familiar. Be especially careful about using business words and phrases that an international reader may not know, such as *reverse mortgages, best practices, toxic assets, granular, pain point,* and so forth.

5. Watch idiomatic expressions. Idioms are the most difficult part of a language for an audience of non-native speakers to master. As with the example of *fire,* the following colorful idiomatic expressions will confuse and may even startle a non-native reader:

I'm all ears	think outside the box
throw cold water on it	sleep on it
hit the nail on the head	give a heads-up
new blood	land in hot water
easy come, easy go	touch and go
get a handle on it	pushed the envelope
right under your nose	it was a rough go

The meanings of those and similar phrases are not literal but figurative, a reflection of our culture, not necessarily your reader's. A non-native speaker of English will

approach such phrases as combinations of the separate meanings of the individual words, not as a collective unit of meaning.

A non-native speaker of English—a potential customer in Asia or Africa, for example—might be shocked if you wrote about a sale concluded at a branch office this way: "Last week we made a killing in our office." Substitute the idiomatic expression with a clear, unambiguous translation easily understood in international English. "We made a big sale last week." For "Sleep on it," you might say, "Please take a week to make your decision."

6. Delete sports and gambling metaphors. These metaphors, which are often rooted in U.S. popular culture, do not translate word for word for non-native speakers and so can interfere with your communication with your readers. Here are a few examples to avoid:

out in left field	a ballpark figure
strike out	out of bounds
drop the ball	make a pass
long shot	beat the odds
be in left field	win by a nose

Use a basic English dictionary and your common sense to find nonfigurative alternatives for these and similar expressions.

7. Don't use unfamiliar abbreviations, acronyms, or contractions. While these shortened forms of words and phrases are a part of U.S. business culture, they might easily be misunderstood by a non-native speaker who is trying to make sense of them in context or by looking them up in a foreign language dictionary. Avoid abbreviations such as pharm., gov., org., pkwy., rec., hdg., hr., mfg., or w/o. The following acronyms can also cause your international reader trouble: ASAP, PDQ, p's and q's, IRA, SUV, RV, DOB, DOT, SSN. If you have to use acronyms, define them. Finally, contractions such as the following might lead readers to mistake them for the English words they look like: I've (ivy), he'll (hell), I'll (ill), we'll (well), can't (cant), won't (wont, want).

8. Watch units of measure. Do not fall into the cultural trap of assuming that your reader measures distances in miles and feet (instead of kilometers and meters as most of the world does), measures temperatures on the Fahrenheit scale (instead of Celsius), buys gallons of gasoline (instead of liters), spends dollars (rather than euros, pesos, rupees, or yen), tells time by a twelve-hour clock (many countries follow a twenty-four-hour clock), and records dates by month/day/year (most countries record dates by day/month/year).

9. Avoid culture-bound descriptions of place. For example, when you tell a reader in Hong Kong about the Sunbelt or a potential client in Africa about the Big Easy, will he or she know what you mean? When you write from California about the eastern seaboard, meaning the East Coast of the United States, the directional reference may not mean the same thing to a reader in India as it does to you. Moreover, referring to February as a winter month does not make sense to someone in New Zealand for whom it is a summer month.

10. **Use appropriate salutations, complimentary closes, and signature lines.** Find out how individuals in the recipient's culture are formally addressed in a salutation (e.g., Señor, Madame, Frau, Monsieur). Unless you are expressly asked to use a first name, always use your reader's surname and include proper titles and other honorifics (e.g., Doctor, Sir, Father). For a complimentary close, use an appropriately formal one, such as *Respectfully*, which is acceptable in almost any culture.

CASE STUDY

Writing to Readers from a Different Culture

In 2015, two IT firms—one American, the other Argentinian—merged. The manager of the American company asked her assistant, Frank Sims, to write a letter of introduction to Antonio Mosca-Guzman, the manager of the Argentinian company, Technologia Canderas, explaining how much Pro-Tech was looking forward to the merger and was seeking help with the transition. The early draft of Sims's letter in Figure 5.8 (page 174) violates the Ten Guidelines for Communicating with International Readers (pages 169–173) because it:

- used the incorrect format for the dateline
- misspelled the name of the reader's city
- left out important postal information
- contained U.S. idioms (e.g., *drop you a line*)
- included unclear, troubling abbreviations
- disregarded how the reader's culture records time and temperature

Even more disrespectfully, Sims's overall tone is condescending (*south of the border; olé*) and inappropriately casual (*before I take off*). At the end of the second paragraph, for instance, he tells Señor Mosca-Guzman that the U.S. firm is superior to the Argentine company.

But after consulting relevant cultural guides and asking a fellow worker, originally from Argentina, to critique his draft, Sims revised his letter. Note how the revised letter in Figure 5.9 (page 175),respects Señor Mosca-Guzman's cultural conventions because it

- spells and punctuates the reader's name and address correctly
- incorporates a clear date line
- uses an appropriate salutation and complimentary close
- is written in plain, international English
- recognizes that the reader uses a 24-hour clock
- identifies the writer and makes the reader feel welcome and honored
- courteously informs the reader how the merger will affect his relationship with the writer
- strives to develop a spirit of global cooperation and mutuality
- acknowledges the reader's position of authority in his company

Above all, though, Sims now honors his audience's culture and role in the business world and seeks to win the reader's confidence and respect, two invaluable assets in the global marketplace. Writing letters with the specific needs of your international audience in mind, as in Figure 5.9, is a crucial skill to have in today's international world of work.

(Continued)

FIGURE 5.8 Frank Sims's Inappropriately Written Letter to His International Reader

Pro-Tech, Ltd. 452 West Main St.   Concord, MA 01742   978-634-2756
www.protech.com
www.facebook.com/protechltd/   @protechltd

Misleading date line

5-8-15

Incorrect, misspelled address

Mr. Antonio Guzman
Canderas
Mercedes Ave.
Bunos Aires, ARG.

Salutation is too informal

Dear Tony,

Impolite opening disrespecting reader's status

I wanted to drop you a line before the merger hits and in doing so touch base and give you the lowdown on how our department works here in the good old U.S. of A.

Culturally condescending

None of us had a clue that Pro-Tech was going to go south of the border, but your recent meeting about the Smartboard T-C spoke volumes to the tech people who praised your operations to the hilt. So it looks like you and I both will be getting a new corp. name. Olé. I love moving from Pro-Tech, Ltd. to Pro-Tech International. We are so glad we can help you guys out.

Filled with American idioms and abbreviations

At any rate, I'm sending you an email with all the ins and outs of our department struc., layout, employees, and prod. eff. quotas. From this info, I'm hoping you'll be able to see ways for us to streamline, cooperate, and soar in the market. I understand that all of this is in the works and that you and I need to have a face-to-face and so I'd appreciate your reciprocating with all the relevant data stat.

Disregards time differences and reader's 24-hour clock

Consequently, I guess I'll be flying down your way next month. Before I take off, I would like to give you a ring. How does after lunch next Thursday (say, 1:00–1:30) sound to you? I hope this is doable.

Ignores differences between Fahrenheit and Celsius scales

We've had a spell of great weather here (can you believe it's in the low 70s today!). So, I guess I'll just sign off and wait 'til I hear from you further.

I send you felicitations and am keeping my fingers crossed that things go smoothly before the merger is a done deal.

Close sounds insincere

Adios,

Frank Sims

Frank Sims

FIGURE 5.9 Sims's Appropriately Revised Letter

Pro-Tech, Ltd. 452 West Main St. Concord, MA 01742 978-634-2756
www.protech.com
f www.facebook.com/protechltd/   @protechltd

8 May 2015

Señor Antonio Mosca-Guzman
Director, Quality Assurance
Tecnología Canderas, S.A.
Av. Martin 1285, 4° P.C.
C1174AAB BUENOS AIRES
ARGENTINA

Dear Señor Mosca-Guzman:

As our two companies prepare to merge, I welcome this opportunity to write to you. I am the manager for the Quality Assurance division at Pro-Tech, a title I believe you have at Tecnología Canderas. I am looking forward to working with you both now and after our companies merge in two months.

Allow me to say that we are very honored that your company is joining ours. Tecnología Canderas has been widely praised for the research and production of your Smartboard T-C systems. I know we have much to learn from you, and we hope you will allow us to share our systems analyses with you. That way everyone in our new company, Pro-Tech International, will benefit from the merger.

Later this week, I will send you a report about our division. It describes how our division is structured and the quality inspections we make. It will also give you a brief biography of our staff so that you can learn about their qualifications and responsibilities.

The director of our new company, Dr. Suzanne Nknuma, asked me to meet with you before the merger to see how we might help each other. I would very much like to travel to Buenos Aires in the next month to visit you and take a tour of your company.

Would you please let me know when it may be convenient for us to talk so we might discuss the agenda for our meeting? I am in my office at Extension 347 from 11:00 to 17:00 Buenos Aires time.

I look forward to working with and meeting you.

Respectfully,

Frank Sims

Frank Sims
Quality Assurance Officer

Clear date line

Includes appropriate title for reader

Complete and correct address

Uses courteous salutation

Clear and diplomatic opening

Respectful view of reader's company

Explains business procedures in plain English

Recognizes reader's time zone

Polite close

Gives business title

Respecting Readers' Nationality and Ethnic/Racial Heritage

In addition to following the Ten Guidelines for Communicating with International Readers (see pages 169–173), you need to always show respect for your reader. Do not risk offending any of your readers, whether they are native speakers of English or not, with language that demeans or stereotypes their nationality or ethnic and racial background. Here are some precautions to take.

1. **Respect your reader's nationality**. Always spell your reader's name and country properly, which may mean adding diacritical marks (e.g., accent marks) not used in English—e.g. Muñoz. If your reader has a hyphenated last name (e.g., Arana-Sanchez), it would be rude to address him or her by only part of the name (e.g., only Arana or only Sanchez). In addition, be careful not to use the former name of your reader's country or city, for instance, the Soviet Union (now Russia), Calcutta (now Kolkata), Czechoslovakia (now the Czech Republic), or Bombay (now Mumbai). Not only is it rude, but it also demonstrates a lack of interest about your reader's nationality.

2. **Observe your reader's cultural traditions**. Cultures differ widely in the way they send and receive information and how they prefer to be addressed, greeted, and informed in a letter. Culture plays a major role in how you word your message. What is acceptable in one culture may be offensive in another. A sales letter to an East Asian business person, for example, needs to employ a very different strategy from one intended for an American reader. The best strategy for an American audience would be hard-hitting and to the point, stressing your product's strengths versus the competitor's weaknesses. But the East Asian way of drafting such a letter would be more subtle, indirect, and complimentary.

American: Our Imaging 500 delivers much more extensive internal imaging than any of our competitors' models.

East Asian: One of the ways we may be able to serve you is by informing you about our new Imaging 500 MRI (Magnetic Resonance Imaging) equipment.

The hard sell in the American example would be a sign of arrogance, suggesting inequality for a reader in China, Japan, Malaysia, or Korea who is more comfortable with a compliment or a wish for prosperity.

3. **Honor your reader's place in the world economy**. Phrases such as "third-world country," "emerging nation," and "undeveloped/underprivileged area" are derogatory. Including such phrases signals that you regard your reader's country as inferior. Use the name of your reader's country instead. Saying that someone lives in the Far East implies that the United States, Canada, or Europe is the center of culture, the hub of the business community. The word "Oriental," is insulting. Simply say "East Asia."

4. **Avoid derogatory stereotypes.** Expressions such as "oil-rich Arabs" and "aggressive foreigners" unfairly characterize particular groups. Similarly, prune from your communications any stereotypical phrase that insults one group or singles it out for praise at the expense of another—"Mexican standoff," "Russian roulette," "Chinaman's chance," "Irish wake," "Dutch treat," "Indian giver." Also note that the word *Indian* refers to someone from India; use *Native American* to refer to the indigenous people of North America, who want to be known by their tribal affiliations (e.g., the Lakota).

5. Be sensitive to the cultural significance of colors. Do not offend your audience by using colors in a context that would be offensive. Purple in Mexico, Brazil, and Argentina symbolizes bad luck, death, and funerals. Green and orange have a strong political context in Ireland. In Egypt and Saudi Arabia, green is the color of Islam and is considered sacred. But in China, green can symbolize infertility or adultery. Also in some Asian countries, white does not symbolize purity and weddings but mourning and funerals. Similarly, in India if a married woman wears all white, she is inviting widowhood. While red symbolizes good fortune in China, it has just the opposite meaning in Korea.

6. Be careful, too, about the symbols you use for international readers. Triangles are associated with anything negative in Hong Kong, Korea, and Taiwan. Political symbols, may have controversial implications as well (e.g., the hammer and sickle, a crescent). Avoid using the flag of a country as part of your logo or letterhead for global audiences. Many countries see this as a sign of disrespect, especially Saudi Arabia, whose flag features the name of Allah.

CASE STUDY

Writing to a Client from a Different Culture: Two Versions of a Sales Letter

Let's assume that you have to write a sales letter to an Asian business executive. As we saw, you will have to employ a very different strategy in writing to this executive as opposed to an American reader. For an American audience, the best strategy is to take a direct approach—fast, hard-hitting, to the point, and stressing your product's strengths versus the opposition's weaknesses. Businesses in the United States thrive on the battle of the brands, the tactics of confrontation symbolized in the sports metaphors on page 172. A typical sales letter to an American reader would be polite but direct.

But such a strategy would be counterproductive in writing to an Asian reader. Business in East Asia is associated with courtesy and friendship and includes a great many social customs. In a sales letter to an Asian reader, you have to first establish a friendship before business details are dealt with. The Asian way of doing business, including writing and receiving letters, is far more subtle, indirect, and complimentary than it is in the United States. The U.S. style of directness and forcefulness would be perceived as rude or unfair in, say, Japan, China, Malaysia, or Korea. A hard-sell letter to an Asian reader would be a sign of arrogance, suggesting inequality for the reader.

To better understand the differences between communicating with a U.S. reader and an Asian one, study the two versions of the sales letter in Figures 5.10 and 5.11. The letters, written by Susan DiFusco for Starbrook Electronics, sell the same product, but Figure 5.10 is written to a U.S. executive, while Figure 5.11 adapts the same message for a businessperson in Seoul, South Korea. See how the two letters differ not only in content but also in the way each is formatted.

Format

The full-block style of the letter to the U.S. reader signals a no-nonsense, all-business approach. Everything is lined up in neat, orderly fashion. For the Korean reader, however, DiFusco

(Continued)

wisely chose the more varied pattern of indenting her paragraphs. For Asian readers, the visual effect suggests a much more relaxed and friendly, yet respectful, communication. Note the different typefaces, too.

Opening

Pay special attention to how the U.S. letter (Figure 5.10) starts off politely but much more directly, an opening the Korean reader would regard as blunt and discourteous. The sales letter written to the Korean audience (Figure 5.11) starts not with business talk but with a compliment to the reader and his company, praising them for trustworthiness and wishing them much prosperity in the future. DiFusco sought the advice of a Korean co-worker, Kim Ji, and from him she learned the Korean greeting that opens the letter. She knew that when addressing the Korean administrator she should not get to business right away but instead used her introductory paragraph to show respect for the company and the reader—the equivalent of East Asian business executives socializing before any mention of business is made.

The Body

Compare the second and third paragraphs of the letters in Figures 5.10 and 5.11. While the letter to the U.S. reader launches an aggressive campaign to get the reader's business, the letter to the Korean reader avoids the hard sell of U.S. business tactics. DiFusco knew that for her Korean reader she must not promote too strenuously. The more she boasted about Starbrook's work, the less likely it was that she would make a sale. She recognized, again from discussions with other Asian businesspeople over the years, that she had to supply key information—such as the application and the advantages of her product—without overwhelming or pressuring her audience. Yet DiFusco subtly reassures Kim Sun-Lim that her company is honorable and worthy to be recommended to his friends.

View of Competitors

Observe, too, how the letter to the U.S. executive (Figure 5.10) undermines the competition by stating how much better Starbrook's offer is. For most Asian readers, it would be considered impolite to claim that your product is better than another company's or that your firm is currently doing business with other firms in the reader's country. Asian audiences prefer to avoid anything that hints of boasting or assertiveness.

The Conclusion

Finally, contrast the conclusions of the two letters. Writing to a U.S. audience, DiFusco strongly urges her potential customer to get in touch with her. Such a call to action is customary in a sales letter to a U.S. firm. But in her concluding paragraph to Kim Sun-Lim, DiFusco adopts a more reserved and personal tone. Her use of such appropriate phrases as "kindly let me know" and "it would be a privilege" expresses the friendly sentiments of respect and esteem that would especially appeal to her reader. Note, too, that DiFusco has chosen a complimentary close ("Respectfully") much more in keeping with her reader's cultural sensitivities than the "Sincerely yours," which was more suitable for the letter in Figure 5.10.

 As these two letters show, writers need to know and respect their readers' cultures. In addressing an audience of non-native speakers of English, a writer must consider the readers' communication patterns, protocols, and cultural (or subcultural) traditions. The same guidelines apply whether you are writing to non-native speakers abroad or in this country. Your message and vocabulary should always be clear, understandable, and appropriate for the intended audience.

FIGURE 5.10 Sales Letter to a Native English Speaker in a U.S. Firm

Starbrook Electronic
Perry, TX 75432-3456
phone **(713) 555-2121** Email **info@starbrook.com**
www.starbrook.com

April 6, 2015

Mr. Ellis Fanner, Director
Morgan General Hospital
300 Oakland Drive
Morgan, OR 97342-0091

Dear Mr. Fanner:

How many times have your physicians asked when Morgan General would have an Open MRI? This state-of-the-art imaging equipment will help maintain your reputation as a leading health care provider in the Morgan River Valley.

As the world leader in designing and manufacturing MRI equipment, Starbrook can offer you the latest technology to save your patients time and improve the care you give them. With our Open Imaging 500, Morgan General can deliver more accurate and timely diagnoses. Within an hour you can determine whether a patient has had a stroke rather than having to wait with less powerful scanner technology.

Thanks to our Open Imaging 500 model, Morgan General can also improve diagnoses for orthopedic and cardiac problems. Our MRI delivers much more extensive internal imaging than any other of our competitors' equipment.

By obtaining the Open Imaging 500, you will surpass all other health care providers who do not offer this technology. By acting now, you will also receive Starbrook's unsurpassed guarantee of exceptional service plus free maintenance for a year by our team of expert technicians.

And we will even give you free upgrades to make sure your Open Imaging 500 continues to be state of the art. Since software updates change so often, no other MRI vendor dares make such an offer. We deliver what we promise. Ask any of our recent satisfied customers—Tennessee General, Grantsville Uptown Clinic, or Nevada Memorial Hospital.

We are hosting a demonstration on May 4 in Portland. Please call me today to arrange for your showing.

Sincerely yours,

Susan DiFusco

Susan DiFusco
Assistant Manager

Begins with an aggressive question and emphasis on hospital's competitive role

Hard-hitting appeal to sell reader on MRI features

Stresses MRI advantages over competitors' models

Urges reader to act to surpass competition

Praises own company

Asks for immediate response from reader

(Continued)

FIGURE 5.11 Sales Letter to a Non-Native Speaker of English in a Foreign Firm

---

✳ Starbrook Electronics
Perry, TX 75432-3456

phone (713) 555-2121   Email info@starbrook.com
www.starbrook.com

May 4, 2015

Mr. Kim Sun-Lim
Administrator
Tangki Hospital
Nowonku 427–1
Seoul, Korea 100–175

Dear Mr. Kim:

In your beautiful language I say *"Annyeonghaseyo hago insa"* on behalf of my firm Starbrook Electronics. I am honored to introduce myself to you through this letter and send you greetings at this beautiful flower season.

Please let us know how we might be of service to you. One of the ways we may be able to serve you is by informing you about our new Open Imaging 500 MRI (magnetic resonance imaging) equipment. This new model can offer you and your patients many advantages. It is far better than conventional scanner models. Your physicians can offer quicker diagnoses for patients with strokes, heart attacks, or orthopedic injuries. MRI pictures will also give you clearer and deeper pictures than any X-ray or scanner can.

It would be an honor to provide Tangki Hospital with one of our Open Imaging 500s. If you select the Open Imaging 500, we will be happy to give you all maintenance and software updates free for one year. Such service will provide the best in health care for the many people who come to you for help. Our firm is well known for its quality service.

Kindly let me know if I might send you information about the Open Imaging 500. It would be a privilege to meet you and to give you and your staff a demonstration of our Open Imaging MRI.

Respectfully,

Susan DiFusco

Susan DiFusco
Assistant Manager

Side annotations:

Font and format more appropriate for audience— more open and inviting—than in Figure 5.10

Opens with a compliment and subtle reference to business

Gives important equipment information without bashing competitors; appeals to the honor of reader's company

Ends with courteous invitation

© 2017 Cengage Learning

SENDING PROFESSIONAL-QUALITY LETTERS: SOME FINAL ADVICE TO SEAL YOUR SUCCESS

Here is some final advice to follow that will help you format, draft, and tailor the business correspondence you will be asked to write.

- **Identify your reader.** Are you writing to an individual, a group, a company or an agency, a new individual customer or a longtime one, a native or non-native speaker?
- **Pay special attention to an international reader's needs.** Research his or her cultural traditions and avoiding writing anything that may offend or confuse him or her.
- **Emphasize the "you attitude."** Keep the reader's needs in the forefront of your message. Consider how your reader will respond to your message.
- **Organize your information.** Make sure your letter has a clear introduction, body, and conclusion.
- **Include essential information:** schedules; dates; prices and expenses; personnel; explanation of services, warranties, and products; background.
- **Use an appropriate style and tone.** Be professional and courteous, concise and focused, and sensitive to your reader's needs, including his or her culture and traditions.
- **Make sure your letter looks professional.** Choose an appropriate format and font, but always follow your company's policies.

Planning your letter carefully—its purpose, organization, content, and format—will help you to make sure your message begins, continues, and ends professionally and successfully for readers in the United States and around the globe.

✔ REVISION CHECKLIST

Audience Analysis and Research

- [ ] Made sure reader's name and job title are correct.
- [ ] Researched something about my audience—interests and background, well informed or unfamiliar with topic, former client or new one.
- [ ] Determined whether audience will be friendly, hostile, or neutral about my message.
- [ ] Did necessary research—in print, through online sources, in discussions with colleagues—to give readers what they need.
- [ ] Acknowledged previous correspondence.
- [ ] Spent sufficient time drafting and revising letter before producing final copy.
- [ ] Determined what (if any) other means I needed to use in conjunction with sending my hardcopy letter.

Letter Format and Appearance

- [ ] Followed one letter format (full-block, modified-block, semi-block) and your company's policies consistently.

(Continued)

- ☐ Used templates with caution.
- ☐ Set left margins wide enough to make my letter look attractive and well proportioned.
- ☐ Included all the necessary parts of a letter for my purpose.
- ☐ Made sure that my letter looks neat and professional.
- ☐ Printed my letter on company letterhead or quality bond paper, or created an appropriately formatted e-version of the letter.
- ☐ Proofread my letter carefully and made sure each correction was made before printing or distributing electronically the final copy.
- ☐ Eliminated any grammatical and spelling errors.
- ☐ Signed my letter legibly in black ink.
- ☐ Informed reader that copies were sent to appropriate parties.
- ☐ Printed envelopes properly.

Content and Organization
- ☐ Clearly understood my purpose in writing.
- ☐ Put most important point first in my letter.
- ☐ Began each paragraph with the central idea of that paragraph.
- ☐ Answered all the reader's questions and concerns.
- ☐ Omitted anything offensive, irrelevant, or repetitious.
- ☐ Stated clearly what I want the reader to do.
- ☐ Used last paragraph to summarize and encourage the reader to continue cordial relations with me and my company.

Style: Words, Tone, Sentences, Paragraphs
- ☐ Emphasized the "you attitude" by seeing things from the reader's perspective.
- ☐ Avoided being too casual or colloquial.
- ☐ Chose words that are clear, precise, and friendly.
- ☐ Cut anything sounding flowery, stuffy, or bureaucratic.
- ☐ Ensured that my sentences are readable, clear, and not too long (less than fifteen to twenty words).
- ☐ Wrote paragraphs that are easy to read, flow together, and are formatted correctly.

Writing to International Readers
- ☐ Did appropriate research about the reader's culture—in print, through online sources, and with colleagues who are native speakers (as well as teachers)— especially about accepted ways of communicating.
- ☐ Adopted a respectful, not condescending, tone.
- ☐ Avoided anything offensive to my reader, especially references to politics, religion, or cultural taboos.
- ☐ Used plain and clear language that my reader would understand.
- ☐ Tested my sentences for length and active voice.
- ☐ Made sure nothing in my letter might be misinterpreted by my reader.
- ☐ Chose colors and symbols culturally appropriate for readers.
- ☐ Selected the right format, salutation, and complimentary close for my reader.
- ☐ Observed the reader's units of measurement for time, temperature, currency, dates, and numbers.

EXERCISES

1. Find two business letters and bring them to class. Be prepared to identify and comment on the various parts of a letter discussed in this chapter.

2. Find a form letter that is addressed to "Dear Customer," "Postal Patron," or "Dear Resident," and rewrite it to make it more personal.

3. Correct the following inside addresses:

   a. Dr. Ann Clark, M.D.
   1730 East Jefferson
   Jackson, MI. 46759

   b. To: Miss Tommy Jones
   Secretary to Mrs. Franks
   Donlevey labs
   Cleveland, O. 45362

   c. Debbie Hinkle
   432 Parkway
   N. Y. C. 10054

   d. Mr. Charles Howe, Acme Pro.
   P.O. Box 675
   1234 S. e. Boulevard
   Gainesville, Flor. 32601

   e. Alex Goings, man.
   Pittfield Industries
   Longview, TEXAS 76450

   f. ATTENTION: G. Yancy (Mrs.)
   Police Academy
   1329 Tucker
   N. O., La. 3410–70122

   g. David and Mahenny
   Lawyers
   Dobbs Build.
   L.A. 94756

   h. Barry Fahwd
   Man., Peninsular, Ltd.
   Arabia

4. Write appropriate inside addresses and salutations to (a) a woman who has not specified her marital status; (b) an officer in the armed forces; (c) a professor at your school; (d) an assistant manager at your local bank; (e) a member of the clergy; (f) a government worker.

5. Rewrite the following sentences to make them more personal.

   a. It becomes incumbent upon this office to cancel order #2394.
   b. Management has suggested the curtailment of parking privileges.
   c. ALL USERS OF HYDROPLEX: Desist from ordering replacement valves during the period of Dec. 20–30.
   d. The request for a new circuit board has been honored; it will be shipped to same address soon.
   e. Perseverance and attention to detail have made this writer important to company in-house work.
   f. The Director of Nurses hereby notifies staff that a general meeting will be held Monday afternoon at 3:00 p.m. sharp. Attendance is mandatory.
   g. Reports will be filed by appropriate personnel no later than the scheduled plans allow.

6. The following sentences are discourteous, boastful, excessively humble, vague, or lacking the "you attitude." Rewrite them to correct those mistakes.

   a. Something is obviously wrong in your head office. They have once more sent me the wrong model number. Can they ever get things straight?

    b. My instructor wants me to do a term paper on safety regulations at a small plant. Since you are the manager of a small plant, send me all the information I need at once. My grade depends heavily on all this.

    c. It is apparent that you are in business to rip off the public.

    d. I was wondering if you could possibly see your way into sending me the local chapter president's name and address—if you have the time, that is.

    e. I have waited for my confirmation for two weeks now. Do you expect me to wait forever, or can I get some action?

7. The following letter, filled with musty expressions and in old-fashioned language (legalese), buries key ideas. Rewrite and reorganize it to make it shorter, clearer, and more reader-centered.

Dear Ms. Granedi:

This is in response to your firm's letter of recent date inquiring about the types of additional services that may be available to business customers of the First National Bank of Bentonville. The question of a possible time frame for the implementation of said services was also raised in the aforementioned letter. Pursuant to these queries, the following answers, this office trusts, will prove helpful.

Please be advised that the Board of Directors at First National Bank has a continuing reputation for servicing the needs of the Bentonville community, especially the business community. For the last fifty years—half of a century—First National Bank has provided the funds necessary for the growth, success, and expansion of many local firms, yours included. This financial support has bestowed many opportunities on a multitude of business owners, residents of Bentonville, and even residents of surrounding local communities.

The Board is at this present writing currently deliberating, with its characteristic caution, over a variety of options suggested to us by our patrons, including your firm. These options, if the Board decides to act upon them, would enhance the business opportunities for financial transactions at First National Bank. Among the two options receiving attention by the Board at this point in time are the creation of a branch office in the rapidly growing north side of Bentonville. This area has many customers who rely on the services of First National Bank. The Board may also place a business loan department in the new branch.

If this office of the First National Bank of Bentonville might be of further helpful assistance, please advise. Remember, banking with First National Bank is a community privilege.

Soundly yours,

M. T. Watkins
Public Relations Director

8. Either individually or in a small group, write a business letter to one of the following individuals and submit an appropriate envelope with your letter.

    a. your mayor, asking for an appointment and explaining why you need one

    b. your college president, stressing the need for more parking spaces or for additional databases at the library

    c. the local water department, asking for information about fluoride supplements

    d. the editor of an online magazine, requesting permission to reprint an article in your company's blog and stating why

    e. the author of an article you have read recently, telling why you agree or disagree with the views presented

    f. the director of food services on campus asking for more ethnic meals

    g. a computer vendor, inquiring about costs and availability of a specific software package; explain your company's special needs

9. Rewrite the following letters, making them appropriate for a reader whose native language is not English. Identify the intended reader's cultural heritage. As you revise the letters, pay attention to the words, measurements, and sentence constructions you employ. Be sure to consider the reader's cultural traditions and avoid cultural insensitivity.

    a. Dear Mr. Wong,

    It's not every day that you have the chance to get in on the ground floor of a deal so good you can actually taste it. But Off-Wall Street Mutual can make the difference in your financial future. Give me a moment to convince you.

    By becoming a member of our international investing group for just under $250, you can just about ensure your success. We know all the ins and outs of long-term investing and can save you a bundle. Our analysts are the hot shots of the business and always look long and hard for the most propitious business deals. The stocks we select with your interests in mind are as safe as a bank and not nearly so costly for you. Unlike any of your undertrained local agents, we can save you money by investing your money. We are penny pinchers with our clients' initial investments, but we are King Midas when it comes to transforming those investments into pure gold.

    I am enclosing a brochure for you to study, and I really hope you will examine it carefully. You would be foolish to let a deal like Off-Wall Street Mutual pass you by. Go for it. Call me by 3:00 today.

    Hurriedly,

    b. Dear Mr. Bafaloukos,

    My firm is taking a survey of businesses in your part of the world to see if there is any likelihood of getting you on board our international computer network, and so I thought I would see if you might like to take the chance. In today's shaky world, business events can change overnight and without the proper scoop you could be left out in the cold. We can alleviate that mess.

    Not only do we interface with major exchanges all around the globe, but we make sure that we get the facts to you pronto. We do not sit on our hands here at Intertel. Check out our website on who and how we serve and I have no doubts that you will email or ring us up to find out about joining up.

    One last point: Can you really risk going out on a limb without first knowing that you have all the facts at your fingertips about worldwide business events? Intertel is there to save you.

    Fondly,

10. Interview a student at your school or a co-worker who was born and raised in a non-English-speaking country about the proper etiquette in writing a business letter to someone from his or her country. Collaborate with this individual to write a letter to an executive from that country—for example, a sales letter or a letter asking for information.

11. In a letter to your instructor, describe the kinds of adaptations you had to make for the international reader you wrote to in Exercise 10.

12. Assume you work for a large international corporation that has just opened a new office in one of the following cities:

   a. Dar es Salaam, Tanzania
   b. Istanbul, Turkey
   c. Caracas, Venezuela
   d. Manila, Philippines
   e. Kiev, Ukraine
   f. Beijing, China
   g. Warsaw, Poland
   h. Mexico City, Mexico
   i. Amman, Jordan
   j. Perth, Australia
   k. Lagos, Nigeria
   l. Prague, Czech Republic

   Write a short report (one to two pages; see Chapter 14) on the main points of letter etiquette that your boss will have to observe in communicating with the non-native speaker of English who is the manager at the new office. In researching your report, pay attention to such cultural differences such as those discussed in "Respecting Readers' Nationality and Ethnic/Racial Heritage" (pages 176–177).

13. As a collaborative project, team up with three other students in your class to write separate letters tailored to executives in each of the following cities:

   a. Riyadh, Saudi Arabia
   b. Tokyo, Japan
   c. Munich, Germany
   d. Nairobi, Kenya

   Assume you are selling the same product or service to each reader, but adapt your communication to the culture represented by the reader.

   Turn in the four letters, and explain to your instructor in an accompanying memo how you met the needs of those diverse cultural audiences in terms of style, tone, level of content, format, and sales tactics. Describe the research tools you used to find out about your reader's particular culture (and communication protocols) and how you benefited from using those tools.

Murat Taner/Flirt/Corbis

Types of Business Letters and Memos

As we saw in Chapter 5, letters can be the lifeblood of any company or organization. In this chapter, you will learn to write a variety of letters for different workplace occasions. But regardless of your message, every letter you send needs to

- establish or maintain good rapport with the reader
- protect and promote your company's and your own professional image
- continue or increase business sales, relationships, and opportunities

Letters can help or hurt your company as well as your career. You want to write letters that lead to promotions and greater professional opportunities.

You can also expect to write memos, a type of internal company correspondence that may announce a new policy, alert staff to a problem, or give instructions to team members. Memos are discussed on pages 220–227. Because business letters and memos are so significant to your career, this chapter will give you guidelines and problem-solving strategies to write effective letters and memos that will help you in your career.

FORMULATING YOUR MESSAGE

Writing effective, diplomatic letters can be challenging. Business correspondence places a great demand on your ability to formulate and organize a suitable message for your readers. You have to identify your audience, your purpose in writing to them, and their needs in wanting to hear from you. To communicate with your audience effectively, you have to determine

- what to say
- how to say it
- where to say it

The second and third points are just as important as the first. In fact, they may be even more crucial to your success as a letter writer. As we saw in

Chapter 5, the **tone** and **organization** of your letter will determine how your message is received. In the process of drafting and revising your letter, consider whether your reader will bristle at or welcome the words you use. Review the discussion of the "you attitude" (see "Making a Good Impression on Your Reader," pages 164–168).

You will also have to select the best communication strategy, which means taking into account where and how you give readers information. Some messages need to be direct and clear-cut; others require being indirect, holding off a bad news message until you prepare the reader for it. Consider the following two versions of sections from a letter that send the same message:

Insensitive Version

Your job is being outsourced next quarter. Corporate knows of your twelve years with the firm, but downsizing mandates this decision. The firm will try to place you in another job, but expect no guarantees.

Respectful Version

Thank you for your twelve years of excellent work. We appreciate your many contributions. Unfortunately, downsizing means that your position, like several others in the department, will be outsourced. However, I will try to arrange a transfer for you. I may not succeed, but I know you will in your career because of your skills and dedication.

Clearly, the first letter has no respect for the reader's feelings or contributions, while the second is a model of respect and sincerity.

Letter Writers Play Key Roles

To be a skilled letter writer means that you will have to play several key roles, sometimes all at once. Among them are

- researcher
- problem solver
- decision maker
- honest and ethical spokesperson
- team player

These are the assets of a valued employee and the characteristics that employers want in job applicants (see "Preparing a Resume," pages 254–266). In fulfilling these roles through your business letters, you demonstrate that you can work well with people, are sensitive to their needs, and represent your company with integrity.

Letters and Collaboration at Work

Like other types of workplace writing, letters can be collaborative documents. For instance, you may confer with specialists in IT to answer a complaint about one of your company's products, or you may work with individuals in the legal or marketing department to draft a sales letter. Possibly you may need to have your letter approved by your boss, who may edit your letter before you send it. Or you may be asked to write a letter for another person's signature.

Whatever the degree of your collaboration, this chapter gives you guidelines and strategies to write successful business letters. It will also show you how *not* to write these letters, an equally valuable lesson worth learning about the world of work.

THE FIVE MOST COMMON TYPES OF BUSINESS LETTERS

The following section of this chapter discusses the most frequently used types of business correspondence you will be expected to write on the job.

1. Inquiry letters
2. Cover letters
3. Special request letters
4. Sales letters
5. Customer relations letters

   - Follow-up letters
   - Complaint letters
   - Adjustment letters
   - Refusal-of-credit letters
   - Collection letters

These business letters can be classified as **positive, neutral**, or **negative**, depending on their message and the anticipated reactions of your audience. Inquiry and special request letters are examples of neutral, routine letters. Other business letters can be positive or negative, depending on your message.

   - Neutral letters request specific information about a product or service, place an order, or respond to some action or question.
   - Sales letters are positive, promoting a product to carry good news, according to the companies that spend millions of dollars a year preparing them.
   - Customer relations letters can be positive (responding favorably to a writer's request or complaint) or negative (e.g., refusing a request, saying no to an adjustment, seeking payment, denying credit or critiquing poor performance).

INQUIRY LETTERS

An inquiry letter asks for information about a product, service, or procedure. Businesses frequently exchange such letters. As a customer, you too may write a letter asking about a service or a special line of products, the price, the size, the color, delivery arrangements, or recent technological changes. The clearer your letter, the quicker and more helpful your answers are likely to be.

Figure 6.1 (page 190) shows an inquiry letter from Michael Ortega to a real estate office managing a large number of apartment complexes. Note that it follows these five rules for writing an effective inquiry letter:

   - states exactly what information the writer wants
   - indicates clearly why the writer requests the information

FIGURE 6.1 A Letter of Inquiry Written in Semi-Block Format

Ortega has
designed his
own letterhead
to use

Michael Ortega
403 South Main Street
Kingsport, TN 37721-0217
mortega@gmail.com
www.facebook.com/michaelortega

April 7, 2016

Mr. Fred Stonehill
Property Manager
Hillside Properties
701 South Arbor St.
Roanoke, VA 24015-1100

Dear Mr. Stonehill:

Explains need
for information

    My wife, one-year-old son, and I will be moving to Roanoke for the summer so I can take classes at Virginia Western Community College. Would you please let me know if you will have any two-bedroom furnished apartments available for rent during June, July, and August? I did not see any short-term vacancies on your website, but I know such openings are usually not announced months in advance. I am willing to pay up to $1,100 a month plus utilities.

States precise
request

Identifies area
of interest

    If possible, we would like to have an apartment that is within two or three miles of the college. We do not have any pets.

Specifies exact
date when a
reply is needed

    I would appreciate hearing from you within the next two weeks. My email address is **mortega@gmail.com**, or you can call me at home (606-555-8957) any evening from 6–10 p.m.

Offers to confer
with and then
thanks the
reader

    If you have any suitable vacancies, we would be happy to drive to Roanoke to look at them and give you a deposit to hold an apartment. Thanks for your help.

Sincerely yours,

Michael Ortega

Michael Ortega

- keeps questions short and to the point
- specifies when the writer must have the information
- thanks the reader

Had Michael Ortega simply written the following very brief letter to Hillside Properties, he would not have received information he needed about size, location, availability, and price of apartments: "Please send me some information on housing in Roanoke. My family and I plan to move there soon."

COVER LETTERS

A cover letter accompanies a document (e.g., a proposal, a report, a contract, a portfolio) that you send to your readers. It identifies the type of document you are sending and prepares your audience to read it. Adreienne Hong and her team (Figure 8.9, page 348) and Terri Smith Ruckel (Figure 15.2, page 606) both prepared cover letters to be sent with a copy of a long report. A cover letter should do the following:

- Provide a written record that you have transmitted a document.
- Tell readers why you are sending them the document.
- Briefly summarize what the document contains—number of sections, visuals, statistics, appendices, etc.
- Explain why the document is of interest to readers.
- Express a willingness to answer questions about the document.
- Thank readers for their time.

SPECIAL REQUEST LETTERS

Special request letters do not make a routine inquiry as Michael Ortega's did in Figure 6.1. For example, these letters can ask a company for information that you as a student will use in a paper, an individual for a copy of an article or a speech, or an agency for statistics or other information that your company needs to prepare a proposal or sell a product.

Make your request clear and easy to answer. Supply readers with an addressed, postage-paid envelope, a URL (if necessary), an email address, and fax and telephone numbers in case they have questions.

Follow these seven guidelines when asking for information in a special request letter.

1. Address your letter to the appropriate person.
2. State who you are and why you are writing—e.g., student doing a paper, employee compiling information for a report, and so on.
3. Indicate clearly your reason for requesting the information. Mention any individuals who may have suggested you write for help and information.
4. Precisely and succinctly state your questions; list and number them.
5. Specify exactly when you need the information. Allow sufficient time—at least three weeks. Be reasonable; don't ask for the impossible.

6. Offer to forward a copy of your report, paper, or survey in thanks of the anticipated help.

7. Thank the reader for helping.

Figure 6.2 gives an example of a letter that follows these guidelines.

SALES LETTERS

A sales letter is written to persuade the reader to buy a product, try a service, support some cause, or participate in some activity. No matter what profession you have chosen, there will always be times you have to sell a product, a service, a community or charitable program, a point of view, or yourself! In fact, an application letter for a job (see "Letters of Application," pages 280–288) or an introductory letter to a new or prospective customer is a sales letter. Study the sales letters in Figure 6.3 (page 195) and the one to an international reader in Figure 5.7 (page 170). (Companies will also put sales information found in sales letters on their website as well, so company websites can be a good resource for examples.)

Preliminary Guidelines

You have undoubtedly received numerous sales letters from large companies, local merchants, charitable organizations, and campus groups. Because of the great volume of sales letters like these in the business world, the ones you write face a lot of competition. To write an effective sales letter that stands out and does its job, you have to do the following:

1. Identify and limit your audience. Knowing who your target audience is and how to find them is crucial to your success. Companies often use previous customers' addresses, social media, and posts on their website or blogs to gather a list of possible customers. You will also have to determine how many people are in your audience. A sales letter may be written to just one person (Figure 5.7, page 170) or to hundreds of readers at different companies (Figure 6.3).

2. Use reader psychology. Think like your reader and ask: "What am I trying to do for the customer?" Ask that question before you begin writing and you will be using effective reader psychology. Appeal to readers' health, security, convenience, comfort, or finances by focusing on the right issues (for instance, inform buyers that your product research involves no animal testing). Note that Patrice St. Jacques appeals to the reader's ethnic and community values in Figure 5.7.

3. Send your sales letter at the right time. Back-to-school specials are best announced in August. Appealing to customers to use their tax refund checks to buy a product or service is most effective from February to early April.

4. Don't be a bore or boast. Save elaborate explanations about a product for after the sale. Put detailed documentation in instruction booklets, in warranties, or on your company's website. Further, do not turn your sales letter into a glowing commendation of your company or yourself. Figures 5.7 and 6.3 both avoid that.

FIGURE 6.2 A Special Request Letter

1505 West 19th Street • Syracuse, NY 13206
315-555-1214 • jkawatsu@webnet.com
 www.facebook.com/juliekawatsu
 www.linkedin.com/pub/julie-kawatsu

An example
of a student-
designed
letterhead

October 5, 2015

Ms. Sharonda Aimes-Worthington
Research Director
Creative Marketing Associates
198 Madison Ave.
New York, NY 10016-0092

Dear Ms. Aimes-Worthington:

I am a junior at Monroe College in Syracuse, and I am writing a report
entitled "E-commerce Strategies for the Finger Lakes Region of New York"
for my Marketing 340 class. Several of my professors have spoken highly of
Creative Marketing Associates, and in my own research I have learned a
great deal from reading your blogs that posted over the last few months.

*Explains reason
for letter and
how the writer
learned about
the firm*

Given your extensive experience in developing websites and apps to
promote regional businesses and tourism, I would be grateful if you would
share your responses to the following three questions with me:

*Proves writer
has done
research*

*Acknowledges
reader's
expertise*

1. What have been the most effective e-commerce strategies you have
   used for a regional marketplace such as the Finger Lakes?

2. How can area chambers of commerce and various municipalities help
   generate Web traffic to a regional marketplace website for the Finger
   Lakes area?

3. Which other regional area(s) do you see having the same or very similar
   marketing goals and challenges as the Finger Lakes?

*Lists specific,
numbered
questions on the
topic*

Your answers to these questions would make my report much more
authoritative and useful. I would be happy to send you a copy and will, of
course, be honored to cite you and Creative Marketing Associates in my work.

*As an incentive
offers to send
copy of report*

Because my report is due by December 2, I would greatly appreciate having
your answers within the next month so that I can include them. Would you
kindly send your responses, or any questions you may have, to my email
address listed above.

*Indicates when
information is
needed, and
makes contact
easy*

Many thanks for any help you can give me.

Thanks reader

Sincerely yours,

Julie Kawatsu

Julie Kawatsu

© 2017 Cengage Learning

TECH NOTE

Mail Merge

One way to help make your sales letters more personable (and to avoid, for example, the use of "Dear Consumer" or the like in the salutation) is the use of **mail merge.** This feature, available in many word-processing programs, allows you to personalize each of the letters you write by merging the content of a standard letter with unique information about a customer that you may need or want to highlight in your letter (such as their mailing address or other special information about their business or account). Mail merge allows you to produce multiple versions of a single letter, each one tailored to a specific customer. Such personalization can make your sales appeal stand out from other, more generic requests.

---

5. **Use words that appeal to the reader's senses.** Choose concrete words instead of abstract, vague ones. Find verbs that are colorful, that put the reader in the picture, so to speak. You will have a greater chance of selling readers if they can hear, see, taste, or touch your product in their mind. That way they can visualize themselves buying or using your product or service. Note how St. Jacques fills the sales letter in Figure 5.7 with Caribbean sights, sounds, and tastes to appeal to Etienne Abernathy and his company.

6. **Be ethical.** Avoid untruths, exaggerations, distortions, false comparisons, and unsupported generalizations. Honesty is the best way to make a sale. Never make false claims about the cost, safety, or adaptability of your product or service. You could be prosecuted for mail fraud or sued for misrepresentation. (Review "Writing Ethically on the Job," pages 35–37.) In addition, never attack a competitor and always get permission before you include an endorsement.

The Four A's of Sales Letters

Successful sales letters follow a time-honored and workable plan—what can be called the "Four A's":

1. It gets the reader's **attention**—with a question or a how-to statement (e.g., "We can show you how to save $100 on your next credit card purchase").
2. It highlights the product's or service's **appeal**—emotionally or financially, or both. Focus on benefits to the reader.
3. It shows the customer the product's or service's **application**—descriptions, special features, warranties.
4. It ends with a specific request for **action**—call, visit, participate, take advantage of a special sales price, register online. Motivate reader to act promptly. Provide any necessary order forms or information.

These four goals can be achieved in fewer than four or five paragraphs. Look at the sales letter in Figure 6.3 in which these parts are labeled.

FIGURE 6.3 A Sales Letter Sent to a Business Reader

Workwell Software
3700 Stewart Avenue Chicago IL 60637-2210
Phone: (312) 555-3720 Email: sales@workwell.com
www.facebook.com/workwell   @Workwell
www.workwell.com

August 13, 2015

Ali Jen, Office Manager
Circuit Systems, Inc.
7 Tyler Place
Oklahoma City, OK 73101-0761

Dear Ali Jen:

Do you know how much money your company loses from repetitive strain injury (RSI)? Each year employers spend millions of dollars on employee insurance claims because of back pains, fatigue, eye strain, bursitis, and carpal tunnel syndrome injuries.

Workwell can solve your problems with its easy-to-use Exercise Program Software, which automatically monitors the time employees spend at their computers and also measures their keyboard activity. After each hour (or the specified number of keystrokes), **Workwell** software will take your employees through a series of brief exercises that will help prevent carpal tunnel syndrome and muscle strains.

Workwell's Exercise Program Software will not interfere with your busy schedule. Each of the 27 exercises is demonstrated on screen with audio instructions. The entire program takes less than 3 minutes and is available for Windows 8, 8.1, and 10 as well as OS X 10.8 or higher. For only $1,499.00, you can provide a networked version of this valuable software to all of Circuit Systems' employees. To view a short demonstration of the software, please visit our website at **www.workwell.com/demo**.

To help your employees stay at peak efficiency in a safe work environment, please call us at 1-800-555-WELL or visit us at **www.workwell.com** to order your software today.

Thank you. I hope to hear from you soon.

Cory Soufas

Cory Soufas
Sales Representative

Relevant, distinctive letterhead.

*Gets reader's **attention** with a question*

*Emphasizes the product's **appeal** using precise language*

*Shows specific **application** of the product*

Links costs to benefits

*Ends with a call for prompt **action***

© 2017 Cengage Learning

Getting the Reader's Attention

Your opening sentence is crucial. That first sentence is bait on a hook. If you lose readers there, you will have lost them forever. A typical television commercial or website has about two to five seconds to catch the viewers' attention. Keep your opening short, one or two sentences at most. Show how your product or service will make your reader's life or job easier, save money, or make him or her safer (see Figure 6.3), happier, more productive, or get a job done more easily or quicker.

The following six techniques are a few of the many interest-grabbing ways to begin a sales letter. Adapt these techniques to your product or service.

1. Ask a question. Look, for example, at the opening question in Figure 6.3. Avoid such general questions as "Are you happy?" or "Would you like to make money?" Use more specific questions with concrete language. For instance, an ad for Air Force Reserve Nursing asks nurses, "Are you looking for something 30,000 feet out of the ordinary?"

2. Use a how-to statement. This is one of the most frequently used openers in a sales letter. Here are some effective how-to statements: "We can show you how to increase your plant growth up to 91%." "This is how to provide nourishing lunches for less than eighty cents a person." Note that the opening sentence of Cory Soufas's sales letter in Figure 6.3 combines both a how-to and a question approach.

3. Compliment your reader. Appeal to the reader's ego. But remember that readers are not naive; they will be suspicious of false praise. Patrice St. Jacques opens the sales letter in Figure 5.7 (page 170) with fitting and sincere praise.

4. Offer a gift or a buyer's protection plan. Often you can lure readers further into your letter by sending a coupon for a discount on their next purchase, telling them they are eligible for a rewards program, assuring them of getting a second product free or at half price, providing a guarantee that will make their purchase of your product or service a safe buy, and so on. A realtor tempts customers to see lots for sale with this opening: "Enclosed is a coupon worth $50 in gas after you tour Deer Trails Estates."

5. Introduce a comparison. Compare your product or service with conventional or standard ones. For instance, a clothing firm told police officers that if they purchased a particular jacket, they were really getting three coats in one because the product had a removable lining for winter or summer use and a visibility coating for nighttime use.

6. Announce a change. Link your sales offer to a current event that will affect your prospective buyer. For instance, when the sales tax on hybrid cars was about to be increased, a dealer sent sales letters to potential buyers, alerting them to the implications of delaying their purchase: "The sales tax on hybrids will jump a WHOPPING 4 percent effective next month. You may not think that 4 percent will mean that much money, but on a new 2017 model that increase could cost you an extra $1,500." The sales letter continued: "Couldn't you use that money for something else, say, those extras you've always wanted, like integrated Bluetooth connectivity or an extended warranty?"

Highlighting the Product's Appeal

Once you have aroused your reader's attention, introduce your product or service by making it so attractive, so necessary, and so profitable that the reader will want to buy or use it. In Figure 5.7 on page 170, the Island Jacques letter zeroes in on the reader's ethnic pride and heritage. In Figure 6.3, Workwell Software's mass mailing letter to office managers appeals to their desire for greater productivity and improved employee safety. Here is an appeal by the Gulf Stream Fruit Company:

> Can you, when you bite into an orange, tell where it was grown? If it tastes better than any you have ever eaten . . . full of rich, golden flavor, brimming with juice, sparkling with sunshine . . . then you know it was grown here in our famous Indian River Valley where we have handpicked it, at the very peak of its flavor, just for your order.[1]

Showing the Customer the Product's or Service's Application

In the third part of your sales letter, supply evidence of the value of what you are selling. Don't overwhelm readers with facts, statistics, detailed technical descriptions, or elaborate arguments. Keep the emphasis on the reader's beneficial use of the product and not on the company that manufactures or sells it.

  1. **Supply the right evidence.** What evidence best convinces readers about a product's or service's appeal?

  - Descriptions that emphasize state-of-the-art design and construction, efficiency, convenience, usefulness, and economy. Note how the letter in Figure 6.3 points out that the software will not interfere with the employees' busy schedule.
  - Special features or changes that make your product or service more attractive. For example, a greenhouse manufacturer stressed that in addition to using its structure for growing plants, customers would also find it to be a "perfect sun room enclosure for year-round 'outdoor' activities, gardening, or leisure health spa." A computer outlet store promised free IT support for a year.
  - Testimonials, or endorsements, from previous customers as well as from specialists.
  - Warranties, services, or special considerations that will make your customer's life easier or happier—a loaner car, free home delivery, a ten-day trial period, a year's free Internet access, or upgrades.

  2. **Do I mention costs?** As a general rule, do not bluntly state the cost. Instead, relate prices, charges, or fees to the benefits provided by the services or products you are selling. Let customers see how much they are getting for their money, as Cory Soufas does in paragraph 3 in Figure 6.3. Similarly, a dealer who installs steel shutters did not tell readers the exact cost of this product but stressed that they will save money by buying them: "Your Reel Shutters also offer substantial savings in energy costs by reducing your heat loss through radiation by as much as 65% . . . and that lowers your utility bills by at least 35%."

---

[1]From "Gifts from Gulf Stream," Gulf Stream Fruit Company, Ft. Lauderdale, Fla. Reprinted by permission.

Ending with a Specific Request for Action

The last section of your letter is vital. If the reader ignores your request for action, you have written your letter in vain. Tell readers exactly what you want them to do and by when. Make it easy for them to

- authorize a deduction
- visit your business (as in Figure 5.7, page 170)
- visit your website or blog (as in Figure 6.3)
- take a test drive
- participate in a meeting
- fill out a pledge card
- respond via the Internet (as in Figure 6.3)
- sign and return an order form (provide a stamped, addressed envelope)
- place an order through your company's safe and secure website

As with price, link the benefits the customers will receive to their responses. "Respond and be rewarded" is the basic message of the last section of your letter. Note that in Figure 6.3, the call to action is made in the last paragraph; the writer urges the reader to call a toll-free number immediately in order to increase employee safety and efficiency.

CUSTOMER RELATIONS LETTERS

Much business correspondence deals explicitly with establishing and maintaining friendly working relations. Customer relations letters show how you and your company regard the people with whom you do business. The letters should reveal your sensitivity to their needs. The first lesson to learn is that you cannot look at your letter only from your (the writer's) perspective. You have to see it from the reader's perspective and anticipate his/her needs and reactions. Customer relations letters send readers good news or bad news, acceptances or refusals. Good news tells customers one or more of the following:

- You agree with them about a problem they brought to your attention.
- You are solving their problem exactly the way they want.
- You are approving their loan or request for a refund.
- You are grateful to them for their business.

Thank you letters, congratulations letters, and adjustment letters saying "Yes" with these messages are all examples of good news messages.

Bad news messages, however, inform readers that:

- You do not like their work or the equipment/technology they sold you.
- You do not have the equipment or service they want or you cannot provide it at the price they want to pay.
- You cannot refund their purchase price or perform a service.
- You are raising their rent or not renewing their lease.
- You are denying a loan or a line of credit

Bad news messages often come to readers through complaint letters, adjustment letters that say "No," and collection letters.

Diplomacy and Reader Psychology

Writing effective customer relations letters requires skill in human relations and reader psychology. Regardless of the news—good or bad—you need to be a diplomatic and persuasive writer. In fact, customer relations letters, like other correspondence, call upon your most effective skills in persuasion (see "Persuading and Offering Recommendations," pages 23–26). To be at your best persuasively, do some research about your readers—their business needs, their schedules, their areas of authority in the chain of command, and even their grievances (if applicable).

The Customers Always Write

As you read this section on customer relations letters, keep in mind the two basic principles captured in the pun "The customers always write."

1. Customers will write about how they would like to be or have been treated—to thank, to complain, to request an explanation.
2. Customers have certain rights that you must respect in your correspondence with them. They deserve a prompt and courteous reply, whether or not you think they are correct. If you refuse their request, they deserve to know why and what you can or cannot do about it; if they owe you money, you should give them an opportunity to explain and a chance, up to a point, to set up a payment schedule. Always be ethical in responding—be fair, honest, undeniably legal, and professional. (Review "Ethical Writing in the Workplace," pages 26–37.)

Being Direct or Indirect

Not every customer relations letter starts by giving the reader the writer's main point, judgment, conclusion, or reaction. Whether you are sending good news or bad news, determine what to say and where. *Where you place your main idea is determined by the type of letter you are writing*. Good news messages require one tactic; bad news ones, another.

Good News Message

If you are writing a good news letter, use the direct approach. Start your letter with the welcome, pleasant news that the reader wants to hear. Begin by putting your reader in the right frame of mind and creating goodwill for your company. Then, provide any relevant supporting details, explanations, or commentary. Being direct is advantageous when you have good news to convey.

Bad News Message

If you have bad news to report, do *not* open your letter with it. Be indirect. Prepare your reader for the bad news; keep the tension level down. If you throw

the bad news at your reader right away, you jeopardize the goodwill you want to create and sustain. Consider how you would react to a letter that begins with these slaps:

- Your order cannot be filled.
- Your application for a loan has been denied.
- It is our unfortunate duty to report …

Having been denied, disappointed, or even offended in the first sentence or paragraph, the reader is not likely to give you his or her attentive cooperation thereafter.

We will discuss some specific types of good news/bad news letters in the next several sections: *follow-up letters, complaint letters, adjustment letters, refusal-of-credit letters,* and *collection letters.*

CASE STUDY

Two Versions of a Bad News Message

Figures 6.4 and 6.5 illustrate two versions of a letter written by A. J. Griffin, the business manager of a large mall, to one of her tenants, Daniel Sobol, notifying him about an increase in rent. Notice how Griffin's bad news letter in Figure 6.4 curtly starts off with the bad news. Receiving such a letter, the owner of Flowers by Dan certainly could not be blamed for looking for a new place of business. Griffin was too direct when she should have been diplomatically indirect. She did not consider her reader's reaction; all she was concerned about was delivering her message.

Compare the curt version of Griffin's letter in Figure 6.4 with her revised message in Figure 6.5. In the revised version, she begins tactfully with pleasant, positive words designed to put her reader in a good frame of mind. Then Griffin gives some background information that the owner of Flowers by Dan can relate to. Griffin makes one more attempt to encourage Sobol to recall his good feelings about the mall—last year they did not raise rents—before introducing the bad news of an increase.

Griffin softens the blow by saying that the River Road Mall knows it is not welcome news. Her tactic here is to defuse some of the anger that Sobol will inevitably feel. In fact, Griffin words the bad news so that the tenant sees the mall as acting in the best interest of his flower shop. The mall will not lower or compromise on the services that the tenant has enjoyed and profited from in the past. Griffin then ends on a positive, upbeat note: a prosperous future for Flowers by Dan.

FIGURE 6.4 An Ineffective Bad News Letter

River Road Mall

300 First Street
Canton, OH 44701
(216) 555-6700
www.RRMall.com
www.facebook.com/RRMall/
@RRMall

December 3, 2016

Mr. Daniel Sobol
Flowers by Dan
Lower Level 107
River Road Mall

Dear Mr. Sobol:

This is to inform you of a rent increase. Starting next month your new rent will be $3,500.00, resulting in a 15 percent increase.

Please make sure that your January rent check includes this increase.

Sincerely,

A.J. Griffin

A. J. Griffin
Business Manager
ajg@rrmall.com

Blunt opening disregards audience's needs and feelings

Ends with a discourteously written demand

No attempt to help audience understand or accept message

(Continued)

FIGURE 6.5 A Diplomatic Revision of the Bad News Letter in Figure 6.4

River Road Mall

300 First Street
Canton, OH 44701
(216) 555-6700
www.RRMall.com
www.facebook.com/RRMall/
@RRMall

December 3, 2016

Mr. Daniel Sobol
Flowers by Dan
Lower Level 107
River Road Mall

Dear Mr. Sobol:

Opens with positive association

It has been a pleasure to have you as a tenant at the mall for the past two years, and we look forward to serving you in the future.

Prepares reader for bad news to follow

Over these last two years we have experienced a dramatic increase in costs at River Road Mall for security, maintenance, landscaping, pest control, utilities, insurance, and taxes. Last year we absorbed those increases and so did not raise your rent. We

States bad news in most concise, upbeat way

wish we could do it again, but, unfortunately, we must increase your rent by 15 percent, to $3,500.00 a month, effective January 1.

Links bad news to reader benefits

Although no one likes a rent increase, we know that you do not want us to compromise on the quality of service that you and your customers expect and deserve from River Road Mall.

Does not apologize but ends respectfully

Please let us know how we can assist you in the future. We wish you a very successful and profitable 2017. If you have any questions, please call or visit my office.

Cordially,

Friendly complimentary close suitable for a long-term client

A. J. Griffin
Business Manager
ajg@rrmall.com

Follow-Up Letters

A follow-up letter is sent by a company after a sale to thank the customer for buying a product or using a service and to encourage the customer to buy more products and services. A follow-up letter is a combination thank-you note and sales letter. The letter in Figure 6.6 (page 204) shows how an income tax preparation service attempts to obtain repeat business by doing the following:

1. begins with a brief and sincere expression of gratitude
2. discusses the benefits (advantages) the customer already knows about and then transfers the firm's dedication to the customer to a continuing sales area
3. ends with a specific request for future business

Complaint Letters

Each of us, either as customers or businesspeople, at some time has been frustrated by a defective product, late or prolonged deliveries, inadequate or rude service, or incorrect billing. When we get no satisfaction from calling an 800 number and are routed through a series of prompts, our frustration level goes up. Usually our first response is to write a letter or dash off an email or tweet, dripping with juicy insults. But an angry letter, like a flaming email (see Figure 4.3, page 125), rarely gets positive results and can hurt your company's image.

A complaint letter is a delicate one to write. First off, avoid the following:

- name calling
- sarcasm
- insults

- threats
- unflattering clip art
- using all captial letters

The key thing to keep in mind is that you can disagree without being disagreeable. Be rational, not hostile. Just to let off steam, you might want to write an angry letter but then delete or tear it up, replacing all the heat with courteous and diplomatic language.

Establishing the Right Tone

A complaint letter is written for more reasons than just blowing off steam. You want some specific action taken. The "you attitude" is especially important here to maintain the reader's goodwill. Complaint letters that are professional and considerate are more likely to receive positive attention than letters bristling with angry words. An effective complaint letter can be written by an individual consumer or by a company. Figure 6.7 (page 205) shows Michael Trigg's complaint about a defective fishing reel; Figure 6.8 (page 206) expresses a restaurant's dissatisfaction with a commercial dishwasher.

Writing an Effective Complaint Letter

To increase your chances of receiving a speedy settlement, follow these seven steps in writing your letter of complaint. They will help you build your case.

FIGURE 6.6 A Follow-Up Letter to Encourage Repeat Business

Taylor Tax Service
Highway 10, North Jennings, TX 78326
(888) 555-9681 | taylortax@gmail.com
www.taylortax.com

December 3, 2015

Ms. Laurie Pavlovich
345 Jefferson St.
Jennings, TX 78326

Dear Ms. Pavlovich:

Links business goal to customer advantage

Thank you for using our services in February of this year. We were pleased to help you prepare your 2014 Federal income tax return. Our goal is to save you every tax dollar to which you are entitled. If you ever have questions about your return, we are open all year long to help you.

Stresses reasons for customer to return for service

We are looking forward to serving you again next year. There have been quite a number of changes for this year that you need to be aware of; most of them relate to the Affordable Care Act, which asks if members of your household had health coverage for all the months of 2015. Additionally, several new federal tax laws enacted this year will change the types of deductions you can declare. These changes might appreciably increase your refund. Our consultants know the new laws and are ready to apply them to your return.

Another important tax matter influencing your 2015 returns will be any losses you may have suffered because of the hailstorms and tornadoes that hit our area five months ago. Our consultants are specially trained to assist you in filing proper damage claims with your federal return.

Makes it easy and profitable for customer to act soon

Ends with commitment to customer convenience

To make using our services even more convenient, we file your tax return electronically to speed up any refund. Please call or email us as soon as you have received all your 2015 tax forms to set up an appointment. We are waiting to serve you seven days a week from 9:00 a.m. to 9:00 p.m.

Sincerely yours,

TAYLOR TAX SERVICE

Demetria Taylor

Demetria Taylor, CPA

Yuri Arcurs/ShutterStock.com

FIGURE 6.7 A Complaint Letter from a Consumer

17 Westwood Drive

Magnolia, MA 02171

mtrigg@roof.com

Identifies appropriate persons to resolve problem

October 9, 2015

Mr. Ralph Montoya
Customer Relations Department
Smith Sports Equipment
P.O. Box 1014
Tulsa, OK 74109-1014

Dear Mr. Montoya:

On September 21, 2015, I purchased a Smith reel, model 191, at the Uni-Mart Store on Marsh Avenue in Magnolia. The reel sold for $94.95 plus tax. The reel is not working effectively, and I am returning it to you under separate cover by first-class mail.

Documents all relevant details about the product

I had made no more than five casts with the reel when it began to malfunction. The button that releases the spool and allows the line to cast would not spring back into position after casting. In addition, the gears made a grinding noise whenever I tried to retrieve the line. Because of these problems, I was unable to continue my participation in the Gloucester Fishing Tournament last week.

Explains politely what is wrong

I request that a new reel be sent to me free of charge in place of the defective one I returned. I would also like to know what was wrong with the defective reel.

Clearly states what should be done

Thank you for processing my claim within the next two weeks.

Specifies an acceptable timeframe

Sincerely yours,

Michael Trigg

Michael Trigg

1. **Sending your letter to the right person further ensures your success.** But, as we saw, never address it "To Whom It May Concern." Do your homework—search the company's website or go to *Hoover's Business Directory* (www.hoovers.com) to get contact information. But don't send your letter to the CEO. Find the appropriate person or office that responds to customer problems.

FIGURE 6.8 A Complaint Letter from a Business

The Loft

Cameron and Dale
Sunnyside, California 91793-4116
213-555-7500

June 21, 2016

Writes to
specific reader

Ms. Priscilla Dubrow
Customer Relations Department
Superflex Products
San Diego, CA 93141-0808

Dear Ms. Dubrow:

Gives all
product's facts
and warranty
information

On September 15, 2015, we purchased a Superflex commercial dishwasher model 3203876, at the Hillcrest store at 3400 Broadway Drive in Sunnyside, for $41,296. In the last three weeks, our restaurant has had serious and repeated problems with this machine. Three more months of warranty remain on the unit.

Describes what
happened and
when

The machine does not complete a full cycle; it stops before the final rinsing and thus leaves the dishes dirty. It appears that the cycle regulators are not working properly because they refuse to shift into the next necessary gear. Attempts to repair the machine by the Hillcrest service team on June 4, 11, and 14 have been unsuccessful.

Documents
problem and
reason for
adjustment

The Loft has been greatly inconvenienced. Our kitchen team has been forced to sort, clean, and sanitize utensils, dishes, pans, and pots by hand, resulting in an additional overtime expense of $1,100. Moreover, our expenses for proper detergents have increased.

Provides clear
description of
how problem
should be solved

We want your main office to send another repair crew to fix this machine. If your crew is unable to do this, we want a discount worth the amount of the warranty life on this model to be applied to the purchase of a new Superflex dishwasher. This amount would come to $8,260, or 20 percent of the original purchase price.

Concludes
politely with
justification for
prompt action

So that our business is not further disrupted, we would appreciate your resolving this problem promptly within the next four to five business days.

Sincerely yours,

Emily Rashon

Emily Rashon
Co-Owner

Browse our menu, which changes daily, at www.theloft.com

2. Be concise. Keep your letter to one page. Your reader wants essential details, not a saga of your troubles.

3. Begin with a detailed description of the product or service. Give the appropriate model and serial numbers, size, quantity, color, and cost, as Emily Rashon does in Figure 6.8. Indicate when, where (specific address), and how (through a vendor, the Internet, at a brick-and-mortar store) you purchased it and also the time remaining on a warranty. If you are complaining about a service, give the name of the company, the date of the service, and the personnel providing it.

4. State exactly what is wrong with the product or service. Be factual. Precise information will help the reader to understand and act on your complaint.

- How many times did the product work before it stopped?
- What parts were malfunctioning?
- What parts of a job were not done or were done poorly?
- When did all this happen? How many times?
- Where and exactly how were you inconvenienced?
- Was the service late, incomplete, rude?

Stating that "the brake shoes were defective" tells very little about how long they were on your car, how effectively they may have been installed, or what condition they were in when they ceased functioning safely. Michael Trigg specifies "no more than five casts" in Figure 6.7.

5. Briefly describe the inconvenience you have experienced. Show that your problems were directly caused by the defective product or service. To build your case, give precise details about the time and money you lost. Don't just say you had "numerous difficulties." Did you have to pay a mechanic to fix your car when it was stalled on the road? Did you have to buy a new printer or wireless router? In Figure 6.8, Emily Rashon cites overtime her staff had to put in. Where appropriate, refer to any previous telephone calls, emails, or letters. Give the names of the people you have written to or spoken with and the dates.

6. Indicate precisely what you want done. Be realistic. Don't inflate costs or damages. And do not simply write that you "want something done." State precisely that you want one or more of the following:

- your purchase price refunded in full
- a credit made to your account
- a credit toward the purchase of another model (as in Figure 6.8)
- your exact model repaired or replaced (as in Figure 6.7)
- a new repair crew assigned to the job
- an apology from the company for discourteous or late service

If you are asking for damages, state your request in dollars and cents and always include copies of bills documenting your expenses related to the problem.

7. Ask for prompt handling of your claim. In your concluding paragraph, ask the reader to answer any question you may have (such as finding out where calls came from that you were billed for but did not make). Also specify a reasonable time by which you want to hear from the reader or need the problem fixed. Note how the writer does this in the last paragraph in Figure 6.8.

Adjustment Letters

Adjustment letters respond to complaint letters by telling customers dissatisfied with a product or service how their claim will be settled. Customer feedback, whether through letters or social media, is crucial to maintain and expand a business. You need to take these posts seriously and provide fast follow-up to ensure your customers that their comments are being heard and acted upon. Adjustment letters should reconcile the differences that exist between a customer and a company, restore the customer's confidence in that company, and encourage that customer to spread the good news about how your company or organization has treated him or her. Always treat your customers, regardless of their complaint, with respect and sincerity. Acknowledge that they are experiencing a problem with your product or service and that you have the customer's best interest in mind in wanting to respond.

How to (and Not to) Write an Adjustment Letter

An effective adjustment letter requires diplomacy. Be prompt, courteous, and decisive; do not brush the complaint aside in hopes that it will be forgotten. Respond quickly; the longer you wait, the more frustrated and angry your reader becomes. Investigate the complaint quickly, and determine its validity by checking previous correspondence, warranty statements, guarantees, and your firm's adjustment policies on merchandise and service, whether posted on the Web or in documents accompanying the product or service. In some cases you may even have to send returned damaged merchandise to your company's laboratory to determine who is at fault.

A noncommittal letter signals to the customer that you have failed to investigate the claim or are stalling for time. Do not resort to vague statements such as the following:

- We will do what we can to solve your problems as soon as possible.
- A company policy prohibits our returning your purchase price in full.
- Your request, while legitimate, will take time to process.
- While we cannot now determine the extent of an adjustment, we will be back in touch with you.
- We are sorry you are having this problem, but there is little we can do about it.
- Please get in touch with a customer service representative.

Customers want to be told that they are right; if they cannot get what they request, they will demand to know why. When you comply with a request, a begrudging tone will destroy the goodwill that your refund or replacement would have created.

At the other extreme, do not overdo an apology by agreeing that the company is "completely at fault" or that "such shoddy merchandise is inexcusable." If you make your company look too bad, you risk losing the customer permanently, and saying your company was negligent or that a product was defective may result in a lawsuit. Before you reply, therefore, always check your company's policies about what should and should not be said and promised in an adjustment letter.

Complaints are often made on social media; multiple complaints may justify an online response (such as the blog entry regarding the elimination of a popular product in Figure 4.7, page 134). In addition to checking your company's social media sites, you should also review sites such as Yelp, Zagat's, Angie's List, or TripAdvisor to see if an adjustment letter needs to be posted on your company's website.

Adjustment Letters That Tell the Customer "Yes"

It is easy to write a "Yes" letter if you remember a few useful suggestions. As with a good news message, start with the favorable news the customer wants to hear; that will put him or her in a positive frame of mind to read the rest of your letter. Let the customer know that you sincerely agree with him or her—don't sound as if you are begrudgingly honoring the request. Use a friendly, welcoming tone. Give readers contact information so they know how to reach you with questions or further comments.

The two examples of adjustment letters saying "Yes" show you how to write this kind of correspondence. The first example, Figure 6.9 (page 210), says "Yes" to Michael Trigg's letter in Figure 6.7. Reread the Trigg complaint letter to see what problems Ralph Montoya faced when he had to write to Mr. Trigg. The second example of an adjustment letter that says "Yes" is in Figure 6.10 (page 211). It responds to a customer who has complained about an incorrect billing.

Guidelines for Writing a "Yes" Letter

The following four steps will help you write a "Yes" adjustment letter.

1. Admit immediately that the customer's complaint is justified and apologize. Briefly and sincerely state that you are sorry and thank the customer for writing to inform you.

2. State precisely what you are going to do to correct the problem. Let the customer know that you will

- extend warranty coverage
- credit the account with funds, more air miles, or additional bonus points
- offer a discount on the next purchase
- cancel a bill or give credit toward another purchase
- repair damaged equipment
- enclose a free pass, coupon, or waiver
- upgrade a product or service

Do not postpone the good news the customer wants to hear. That way the rest of your letter will be much more appreciated and convincing. In Figure 6.9, Michael Trigg is told that he will receive a new reel; in Figure 6.10, Kathryn Brumfield learns she will not be charged for parts or service.

FIGURE 6.9 An Adjustment Letter Saying "Yes" to the Complaint Letter in Figure 6.7

Smith Sports Equipment
P.O. Box 1014
Tulsa, OK, 74109-1014
(918) 555-0164

www.smithsports.com
www.facebook.com/SmithSports/
@SmithSports

Responds within time frame specified in complaint letter

October 20, 2015

Mr. Michael Trigg
17 Westwood Drive
Magnolia, MA 02171

Dear Mr. Trigg:

Apologizes and announces good news

Thank you for alerting us in your letter of October 9 to your problems with one of our model 191 spincast reels. I am sorry for the trouble the reel caused you. A new Smith reel is on its way to you.

Explains what happened and why problem will not recur

We have examined your reel and found the difficulty. It seems that a retaining pin on the button spring was improperly installed by one of our new soldering machines on the assembly line. We have thoroughly inspected, repaired, and cleaned this machine to eliminate the problem from happening again.

Expresses respect for customer

Since we began making quality reels in 1955, we have taken pride in helping loyal customers like you who rely on a Smith reel. We hope that your new reel brings you years of pleasure and many good catches, especially next year at the Gloucester Fishing Tournament.

Closes with friendly offer to help again

Thank you for your business. Please let me know if I might help you again.

Respectfully,

SMITH SPORTS EQUIPMENT

Signed, not stamped, signature

Ralph Montoya
Ralph Montoya
Customer Relations Department

FIGURE 6.10 An Adjustment Letter Saying "Yes"

Brunelli Motors

- -

Route 3A, Giddings, KS 62034-8100 (913) 555-1521
www.brunellimotors.com

f www.facebook.com/BrunelliMotors/   🐦 @BrunelliMotors

August 6, 2015

Ms. Kathryn Brumfield
34 East Main
Giddings, KS 62034-1123

Dear Ms. Brumfield:

We appreciate your notifying us, in your letter of July 30, about the problem you experienced with warranty coverage on your new Phantom Hawk GT. The bills sent to you were incorrect, and I have canceled them. Please accept my apologies. You should not have been charged for a shroud or for repairs to the damaged fan and hose, since all those parts, and labor on them, are fully covered by your warranty.

The problem was the result of an error in the way the charges were listed. Our firm has begun using new billing software to give customers better service, and the technician apparently entered the wrong code for your account. We have since programmed our system to flag any bills for vehicles still under warranty. We hope that this new procedure will help us serve you and our other customers more efficiently.

Thank you for taking the time to write to us. We value you as a customer at Brunelli Motors. When you are ready for another Phantom Hawk GT, take a virtual test drive at **www.brunellimotors.com/phantom**. Please let me know if I can be of any further help to you. Happy motoring!

Sincerely yours,

Susan Chee-Saafir
Susan Chee-Saafir
Service Manager

- -
Experience virtual reality: Drive a new Phantom at
www.brunellimotors.com/phantom

*Responds
promptly*

*Thanks
customer and
complies with
request*

*Explains why
problem
occurred and
how it has been
resolved*

*Ends courteously
and leaves
reader with
good feeling
about the
dealership*

*Provides
company URL
so customer can
further explore
product line*

© 2017 Cengage Learning

3. Tell customers exactly what happened. They deserve an explanation for the inconvenience they suffered. Note that the explanations in Figures 6.9 and 6.10 (pages 210 and 211) give only the essential details; they do not burden the reader with side issues or petty remarks about who was to blame. But assure customers that the mishap is not typical of your company's operations.

4. End on a friendly—and positive—note. Don't remind customers about their trouble. Leave customers with a positive feeling about your company. You want them to purchase your product or service again.

Adjustment Letters That Tell the Customer "No"

Writing to tell customers "No" is obviously more difficult than agreeing with them. You are faced with the sensitive task of conveying bad news, while at the same time convincing the reader that your position is fair, logical, and consistent. You want them to do business again. Do not bluntly start off with a "No." Do not accuse or argue. Avoid remarks such as the following that blame, scold, or remind customers of a wrongdoing:

- You obviously did not read the instruction manual.
- Our records show that you purchased the equipment with no warranty left.
- The company policy plainly states that such refunds are not allowed.
- You were negligent in running the machine.
- You claim that our portable hard drive was poorly constructed.
- Your complaint is unjustified.

Guidelines for Saying "No" Diplomatically

The following five suggestions will help you say "No" diplomatically. Practical applications of these suggestions can be found in Figures 6.11 (page 213) and 6.12 (page 214). Contrast the refusal of Michael Trigg's complaint in Figure 6.11 with the favorable response to it in Figure 6.9.

1. Thank customers for writing. Open with a polite, respectful comment, called a **buffer,** to soften your reader's response before he or she sees your "No." Don't put them on the defensive by beginning with "We regret to inform you." The letter writers in Figures 6.11 and 6.12 use buffers to thank the customers for bringing the matter to their attention and sympathize with them about their inconvenience. As with other bad news letters, never begin with a refusal. Telling them "No" in the first sentence or two will negatively color their reactions to the rest of your letter. Use the indirect approach discussed earlier in this chapter (see "Being Direct or Indirect," pages 199–200), and avoid these reader-hostile openings:

- I was surprised to learn that you found our product unsatisfactory.
- We have been in business for years and nothing like this has ever happened.
- There is no way we could give you what you demand.

FIGURE 6.11 An Adjustment Letter Saying "No" to the Complaint Letter in Figure 6.7

Smith Sports Equipment
P.O. Box 1014
Tulsa, OK, 74109-1014
(918) 555-0164

www.smithsports.com
[f] www.facebook.com/SmithSports/
[tw] @SmithSports

October 20, 2015

Mr. Michael Trigg
17 Westwood Drive
Magnolia, MA 02171

Dear Mr. Trigg:

Thank you for writing to us on October 9 about the trouble you experienced with our model 191 spincast reel. We are sorry to hear about the difficulties you had with the release button and gears.

Buffer—thanks and sympathizes with reader

We have examined your reel and found the difficulty. It seems that a retaining pin in the button spring was pushed into the side of the reel casing thereby making the gears inoperable. The retaining pin is a vital yet delicate part of your reel. In order to function properly, it has to be pushed gently. Since our warranty does not cover pushing the pin forcibly, we cannot send you a replacement.

Explains problem without directly blaming the reader; gives firm decision

However, we want you to have many more hours of fishing pleasure, and so we would be happy to repair your reel for $49.98 and return it to you within 5–7 days. Please let us know your decision.

Turns a "No" into a "Yes" for customer

I look forward to hearing from you. Thank you for writing to us.

Ends politely without any reference to the problem

Respectfully,

SMITH SPORTS EQUIPMENT

Ralph Montoya

Ralph Montoya
Customer Relations Department

© 2017 Cengage Learning

FIGURE 6.12 Another Adjustment Letter Saying "No"

Eye-catching and appropriate logo

Health**AIR**

4300 Marshall Drive
Salt Lake City, Utah 84113-1521
(801) 555-6028
www.healthair.com

August 28, 2015

Inside address and salutation list reader's title

Denise Southby, Director
Bradley General Hospital
Bradley, IL 60610-4615

Dear Director Southby:

Professional you-centered opening with buffer

Thank you for your letter of August 20 explaining the problems you encountered with our Puritan MAII ventilator. We were sorry to learn that you were unable to get the high-volume PAO_2 alarm circuit to work.

Justifies firm decision by explaining causes of problem and conditions of sale

Our ventilator is a high-volume, low-frequency unit that can deliver up to 40 cm of water pressure. The ventilator runs with a center of gravity attachment on the right side of the diode. The trouble you had with the high oxygen alarm system is due to an overload on your piped-in oxygen. Our laboratory inspection of the ventilator you returned indicated that the high-pressure system had blown a vital adapter in the MAII. An overload in an oxygen system is not covered by the warranty on the ventilator, and so we cannot replace it free of charge.

Provides practical alternative with financial incentive to keep customer's business

We would, however, be pleased to send you another model of the adapter, which would be more compatible with your system, as soon as we receive your order. The price of the adapter is $600, but because you are a valued customer, our service representative will install it at no charge to you.

Ends with goodwill and specific contact information

Please let me know your decision. I look forward to hearing from you. You can reach me at my email RPG@healthair.com, or at (801) 555-6028, extension 318.

Sincerely yours,

R. P. Gifford

R. P. Gifford
Systems Coordinator

2. State the problem carefully to reassure the customer that you understand the complaint. You thereby prove that you are not trying to misrepresent or distort what the customer has told you.

3. Explain what happened with the product or service before you give the customer a decision. Provide a factual explanation to show the customer that he or she is being treated fairly. Rather than focusing on the customer's misunderstanding the instructions or a failure to observe details of a service contract, state the proper ways of handling a piece of equipment.

> Poor: By reading the instructions on the side of the paint can, you would have avoided the streaking condition that you claim resulted.
>
> Revised: Hi-Gloss Paint requires two applications, four hours apart, for a clear and smooth finish.

The revision reminds the customer of the right way to apply the paint without pointing an accusing finger. Note how the explanations in Figures 6.11 and 6.12 emphasize the appropriate way of using the product or equipment.

4. Give your decision without hedging. Do not say, "Perhaps some type of restitution could be made later" or "Further proof would have been helpful." Indecision will infuriate customers who believe that they have already presented a sound, convincing case. Never apologize for your decision.

5. Leave the door open for better and continued business. Whenever possible, help customers solve their problem by offering to send them a new product or part, or installing or repairing a product free of charge or at a discount. Note how the second-to-last paragraphs in Figures 6.11 and 6.12 do that diplomatically.

Refusal-of-Credit Letters

A special type of bad news letters deals with a company's refusing credit to an individual or another company. Like other bad news correspondence, writing such a letter requires a great deal of sensitivity. You want to be clear and firm about your decision; at the same time, you do not want to alienate the reader and risk losing his or her future business.

How to Say "No"

Follow these guidelines when saying "No" in a refusal-of-credit letter:

1. Begin on a positive—not a negative—note. Find something to thank the reader for; make the bad news easier to take. Compliment the reader's company or previous good credit achievements (if known), and certainly express gratitude to the individual for wanting to do business with your company.

2. In a second paragraph, provide a clear-cut explanation of why you must refuse the request for credit, but base your explanation on facts, not personal shortcomings or liabilities. Appropriate reasons to cite for a refusal of credit include

- a lack of business experience or prior credit
- being "overextended" or needing more time to pay off existing obligations (Figure 6.13, page 216)

FIGURE 6.13 An Effective Letter Refusing Credit

WEST COAST
SAVINGS & LOAN

4800 Ridge Road
Los Angeles, CA 91666
Phone (714) 555-3500
Fax (714) 555-4323
www.wcsl.com
 www.facebook.com/WCSL/   **@WCSL**

March 18, 2016

Mr. Otto L. King
Sunshine Interiors
8235 Mimosa Highway
Vinedale, CA 92004-0318

Dear Mr. King:

Begins on a positive note

We appreciate your interest in doing business with West Coast Savings & Loan. It is always gratifying to see a store like yours open in an expanding community like Vinedale.

Denies credit but explains precisely why in factual terms

In reviewing your credit application, we checked into the business history and credit references you supplied. We also called your local credit bureau and while there was nothing negative in your credit profile we did determine that for a business of your size you have already reached a maximum level of indebtedness. For that reason, we believe that this would not be the best time to extend your line of credit.

Ends encouragingly by urging reader to reapply

We would, however, encourage you to visit our website and fill out the credit survey. This site is periodically reviewed and evaluated and will give you up-to-date information on your credit availability. In the meantime, we wish you every success in your new business.

Cordially,

B. Rimes-Assante

B. Rimes-Assante
Supervisor

- current unfavorable or unstable financial conditions
- an order that is too large to process without prepayment
- a lack of equipment or personnel for the company to do the business for which they are seeking credit
- demographics-too many competitors in the marketplace; too little traffic, etc.

3. End on a positive note. Encourage the reader to reapply when business conditions have improved or when the reader's firm is in a better financial position. One of your goals is to keep the reader as a potential customer, as in Figure 6.13.

Collection Letters

Collection letters require the same tact and fairness as do complaint and adjustment letters. Each nonpayment case needs to be evaluated separately. A nasty collection letter sent to a customer who is a good credit risk after only one month's nonpayment can send that customer elsewhere. Three easygoing letters to a customer who is a poor credit risk may encourage that individual to postpone payment, perhaps indefinitely.

Types of Collection Letters

Many businesses send several letters to customers before turning matters over to a collection agency. But if you are asked to send a series of letters, know you will be employing different techniques, ranging from giving compliments and offering flexible credit terms to issuing demands for immediate payment and threatening legal consequences. One hospital uses the collection letters illustrated in Figures 6.14 and 6.15 (pages 218 and 219) to encourage patients to pay their bills. Figure 6.14 is a letter sent early in the collection process when a client is only a month or two late. The collection letter in Figure 6.15, however, is sent much later to a client who has ignored earlier notices.

The tone of Figure 6.14 is cordial and sincere—now is not the time to say "Pay up or else." Instead, the letter stresses how valuable the patient is and underscores how pleased the hospital is to have provided the care he needed. The second-to-last paragraph makes a request for payment, offering: (1) a flexible payment schedule and (2) an escape from the inconvenience (or embarrassment) of receiving past due notices. The bottom of the letter conveniently lists payment options available to the patient. The last paragraph leaves the door open for cordial communication with the hospital.

The late collection letter in Figure 6.15, however, points out that the time for concessions is over and reminds the patient of all the efforts that the hospital has expended to collect its bills. Appealing to the reader's need to maintain his good credit record, the last paragraph then announces what unfortunate consequences will result if he still does not pay.

FIGURE 6.14 A First, or Early, Collection Letter

SABINE MEMORIAL HOSPITAL

7200 MEDICAL BLVD.
SABINE, TX 77231-0011
(512) 555-6734
WWW.SABINEMEMORIAL.ORG

May 16, 2016

Re: Inpatient Services
Date of Hospitalization: March 11–12, 2016
Balance Due: $6,725.48

Mr. Cal Smith
24 Mulberry Street
Valley, TX 77212-3160

Dear Mr. Smith:

We are honored that we were able to serve your health care needs during your recent stay at Sabine County Hospital. It is our continuing goal to provide the best possible care for residents of Sabine County and its vicinity. To do so, we must keep our finances up-to-date.

Our records indicate that your account is now 30 days overdue and that we have not received a payment from you for two months. If you have recently sent one in, kindly disregard this letter and accept our thanks.

If for any reason you are unable to pay the full amount at this time, we would be happy to set up a convenient payment schedule. Just fill in the appropriate blanks below, and return this letter to me. That will enable us to avoid billing you on a "Past Due" basis. Thank you for your cooperation.

Please call me if you have any questions about our billing options.

Sincerely,

Morris T. Jukes

Morris T. Jukes
Accounts Department
(512) 555-6734, Ext. 721
morris_t_jukes@sabinememorial.org

( ) I will pay $ _____ ( ) monthly ( ) quarterly on my account.

( ) Enclosed is a check for full payment in the amount of $ _____.

Signature

_____

Important dates to remind reader of outstanding bill

Links hospital mission to patient's payment

Diplomatic reminder to pay now

Offers options to maintain goodwill

Closes with offer of assistance if customer cannot pay now

Personalizes letter with the writer's contact information

Makes it easy for reader to respond

Photo, mikecphoto/Shutterstock.com

FIGURE 6.15 A Final Collection Letter

SABINE MEMORIAL HOSPITAL

7200 MEDICAL BLVD.
SABINE, TX 77231-0011
(512) 555-6734
WWW.SABINEMEMORIAL.ORG

September 21, 2016

Mr. Cal Smith
24 Mulberry Street
Valley, TX 77212-3160

Re: Inpatient Services
Date of Hospitalization: March 11–12, 2016
Balance Due: $6,725.48

Dear Mr. Smith:

During the past few months we have written to you several times about your balance of $6,725.48 for hospital services you received on March 11 and 12. Your account is more than 190 days overdue, and we cannot allow any further extensions in receiving a payment from you.

As you will recall, we have tried to help you meet your obligations by offering several options for paying your bill. You could have arranged for installment payments that would be due each month, or even each quarter, whichever would be more convenient. Because you have not replied, we must ask for full payment now.

If we do not hear from you within the next ten days, we will have no alternative but to turn your account over to our collection agency, which will seriously hurt your credit rating. Neither of us would find this a welcome alternative. I look forward to receiving your payment.

Sincerely,

Morris T. Jukes

Morris T. Jukes
Accounts Department
(512) 555-6734, Ext. 721
morris_t_jukes@sabinememorial.org

Documentation of important dates and balance due appears on all correspondence

Direct opening about history and current status of the account

Reminds patient of goodwill and insists on payment

States final option in a respectful yet firm tone

© 2017 Cengage Learning

Photo, mikecphoto/Shutterstock.com

MEMOS

In addition to business letters you write to customers, you will be expected to write frequent memos to co-workers and employees. **Memorandum**, usually shortened to **memo**, is a Latin word for "something to be remembered." The Latin meaning points to the memo's chief function: to record information of immediate importance and interest in the busy world of work. Memos are often internal business communications, short and to the point, clearly stating what must be done or not. They provide a record that serves a variety of functions, including

- making an announcement
- giving instructions
- clarifying a policy, procedure, or issue
- changing a policy or procedure
- alerting staff to a problem

- sending recommendations
- providing a legal record of an important matter
- calling a meeting
- reminding employees of corporate history, policy, procedures

Memos are important documents invaluable for audits, outlining employee responsibilities, and announcing company policies. They provide an opportunity for employees (or even customers) to ask questions, make comments, or express concerns. Memos can be sent as printed hard copy documents or as e-copies.

Although memos are usually written for an in-house audience, the memo format can be used for documents sent outside a company, such as descriptions accompanying proposals (see Chapter 13) or short reports (see Chapter 14), or for cover notes for longer reports (see Chapter 15).

Memos keep track of what jobs are done where, when, and by whom; they also report on any difficulties, delays, or cancellations and what your company or organization needs to do about correcting or eliminating them. Memos are the workhorses of business.

Memo Protocol and Company Politics

As with other business correspondence, memos reflect a company's image and therefore must follow the company's **protocol**—accepted ways in which in-house communications are formatted, organized, written, and routed. In addition to following your company's protocol, use these commonsense guidelines when writing memos:

1. Be timely. Don't wait until the day of the meeting or change in policy to announce it.

2. Be professional. Just because a memo is an in-house piece of correspondence does not mean you can dash off a poorly organized, poorly written, or factually inaccurate document. Notice that in Figure 6.16 (page 223), the memo to Lucy from Roger is professionally written, clearly organized, and properly spelled and punctuated.

3. Be tactful. Be polite and diplomatic, not curt and bossy. For example, in Figure 6.17 (page 225), Janet Hempstead adopts a firm tone regarding an important safety issue, yet she does not blame or talk down to her readers—the machine shop employees. Politeness and diplomacy count a lot at work.

4. **Send memos to the appropriate individuals**. Don't send copies of a memo (either via hard copy or as an attachment) to people who don't need to read them. It wastes time and energy. Moreover, don't send a memo to high-ranking company personnel in place of your immediate supervisor, who may think you are going over his or her head. For instance, in Figure 6.17, Janet Hempstead has sent her memo only to the machine shop workers, not to the upper management of the Dearborn Company.

Keep in mind, though, that memos are often sent up and down the corporate ladder. Employees send memos to their supervisors, and workers send memos to one another. Figure 6.16 shows a memo sent from one worker to another. Figure 6.17 contains a memo sent from the top down, and Figure 6.18 (page 227) illustrates a memo sent from an employee to management.

Sending Memos: Email or Hard Copy?

Similar to letters (see "Different Ways to Send Letters," pages 154–155), a memo can be sent as printed hard copy, as an email attachment, in the body of an email, or—if appropriate—posted to a company's website or social media platforms. Find out your company's policies and follow them. Increasingly, email distribution is replacing printed memos, but there are times when a hard copy memo is preferred.

Consider the level of importance and confidentiality of your memo. If your memo is an official document, such as the policy outlined in Figure 6.17, you will likely draft it on company letterhead or send it as an attachment. Printing your memo on company letterhead signals that a formal policy now in place. If your memo on company letterhead is confidential (e.g., an evaluation of a co-worker or vendor, or a message containing sensitive financial or medical information), you may not want to send it as an email because it could easily be forwarded to someone other than for whom it was intended. But when you send a routine message that must reach your readers quickly, use email (see "Email: Its Importance in the Workplace," pages 118–125).

Memo Format

Memos vary in format and the way they are sent. Some companies use standard, printed forms (as in Figure 6.16), while others have their names (letterhead) printed on their memos (as in Figures 6.17 and 6.18). You can also create a memo by including the necessary parts in an email, as in Figures 4.1 (page 120) and 4.2 (page 121).

As you can see from looking at Figures 6.16, 6.17, and 6.18, memos look different from letters. Because they are often sent to individuals within your company, memos do not need the formalities necessary in business letters, such as an inside address, a formal salutation or complimentary close, or a signature line, as discussed in "Parts of a Letter" (see pages 158–162).

Memo Parts

Basically, the memo consists of two parts: the **header**, or the identifying information at the top, and the **message** itself. This identifying information includes four easily recognized parts: *To, From, Date,* and *Subject* lines. (If a memo is sent in the

body of an email, including these parts would not be necessary, as they are automatically included in the email's heading.)

TO:	Aileen Kelly, Chief Computer Analyst
FROM:	Stacy Kaufman, Operator, Level II
DATE:	January 28, 2016
SUBJECT:	Progress report on the fall marketing schedule

You can use a memo template, which automatically formats headers such as the following, to save time.

TO:	[Enter name]
FROM:	Linda Cowan
DATE:	[Enter date]
RE:	[Enter subject here.]

On the **To** line, write the name and job title of the individual(s) who will receive your memo. If you are sending your memo to more than one reader, make sure you list your readers in the order of their status in your company or agency, as Mike Gonzalez does in Figure 6.18 (according to company policy, the vice president's name appears before that of the public relations director). If you are on a first-name basis with the reader, use just his or her first name, as in Figure 6.16. Otherwise, include the reader's first and last names. Don't leave out anyone who needs the information.

On the **From** line, insert your name (use your first name only if your reader refers to you by it) and your job title (unless it is unnecessary for your reader). Some companies ask employees to handwrite their initials after their typed name to verify that the message comes from them and that they are certifying its contents, as in Figures 6.17 and 6.18.

On the **Date** line, do not simply name the day of the week. Give the full calendar date (June 2, 2016).

On the **Subject** line, key in the purpose of your memo. The subject line serves as the title of your memo; it summarizes your message. Vague subject lines, such as "New Policy," "Operating Difficulties," or "Software," do not identify your message precisely and may suggest that you have not restricted or developed it sufficiently. Note how Mike Gonzalez's subject line in Figure 6.18 is so much more precise than just saying "Ramco's Community Involvement."

Questions Your Memo Needs to Answer for Readers

Here are some key questions your audience may ask and your memo needs to answer clearly and concisely:

1. When? When did it happen? Is it on, ahead of, or behind schedule? When does it need to be discussed or implemented? *When* is answered in Figures 6.16 ("November 12," "in the next day or two"), 6.17 ("during the past two weeks," "after each use"), and 6.18 ("in early February," "before the end of the month").

2. Who? Who is involved? Who will be affected by your message? How many people are involved? *Who* is answered in Figures 6.16 (Jackie Wei), 6.17 (all machine shop employees), and 6.18 (Ramco Technologies as a whole).

FIGURE 6.16 Standard Memo Format

MEMO

TO: Lucy
FROM: Roger
DATE: November 11, 2016
SUBJECT: Review of "Successful Website" Seminar

As you know, I attended the "How to Build a Successful Website" seminar on November 10 and learned the "rules and tools" we can use to redesign our site.

Here is a review of the major topics covered by the presenter, Jackie Wei:

1. Keep your website content-based—identify your target audience.
2. Visualize and "map out" your site ahead of time.
3. Keep the design of your website simple and elegant; "busy" websites drive potential customers away.
4. Be sure your site is easy to navigate, especially for international readers.
5. Use keywords to maximize your website's search engine exposure.
6. Create hot links and image maps to move users from page to page.
7. Encourage customer interaction by including a comments section.
8. Complete your site with appropriate, professional sound and animation.
9. Keep your site updated on a regular (weekly) basis.

Could we meet in the next day or two to discuss recreating our website in light of these guidelines? I appreciate your suggestions about this project and how we can best proceed.

Thanks.

Memo parts

Introduction provides background and tells reader what memo will do

Preview

Numbered list in body helps readers follow information quickly

Conclusion asks for comments

© 2017 Cengage Learning

3. Where? Where did it take place or will it take place? *Where* is answered in Figures 6.16 (the website seminar), 6.17 (the brake shop), and 6.18 (the Mayfield facility).

4. Why? Why is it an important topic? *Why* is clearly answered in Figures 6.16 (because the website is being redesigned), 6.17 (because it's a safety issue), and 6.18 (because favorable publicity will help the company's image and mission).

5. Costs? How much will it cost? Will the costs be lower or higher than a competitor's costs? Not every memo will answer financial questions, but in Figure 6.17, the injuries discussed cost the company money, and in Figure 6.18, the specific cost of an individual scholarship ($21,000) is an important issue.

6. Technology? What technology (software, equipment, infrastructure) is involved? Is the technology current, able to be upgraded, safe for the environment?

Note that Figures 6.16, 6.17, and 6.18 all especially refer to technological issues—website design, equipment safety, education, robots.

7. What's next? What are the next steps that should be taken as a result of the issues discussed in the memo? What are the implications for the product, service, budget, staff? A good example of this is in Figure 6.18 (the company needs to decide on how to implement the suggestions before the new plant opens).

Memo Style and Tone

The audience within your company will determine your memo's style and tone (see "Identifying Your Audience," pages 11–13). When writing to a co-worker whom you know well, you can adopt a casual, conversational tone. You want to be seen as friendly and cooperative. In fact, to do otherwise would make you look self-important, stuffy, or hard to work with. Consider the friendly tone appropriate for one colleague writing to another as in Roger's memo to Lucy in Figure 6.16. Note how he ends in a polite but informal way.

When writing a memo to a manager, though, you will want to use a more formal tone than you would when communicating with a co-worker. Your boss will expect you to show a more respectful, even official, posture. See how formal yet conversationally persuasive Mike Gonzalez's memo to his bosses is in Figure 6.18. His tone and style are a reflection of his hard work as well as his respect for his employers. Here are two ways of expressing the same message, the first more suitable when writing to a co-worker and the second more appropriate for a memo to the boss.

> Co-worker: I think we should go ahead with Marisol's plan for reorganization. It seems like a safe option to me, and I don't think we can lose.
>
> Boss: I think that we should adopt the organizational plan developed by Marisol Vega. Her recommendations are carefully researched and persuasively answer the questions our department has about solving the problem.

When an employer writes to workers informing them about policies or procedures, as Janet Hempstead does in Figure 6.17, the tone of the memo needs to be official and straightforward. Yet even so, Hempstead takes into account her readers' feelings (she does not blame) and safety, which are at the forefront of her rhetorical purpose.

Finally, remember that your employer and co-workers deserve the same clear and concise writing and attention to the "you attitude" (see "Making a Good Impression on Your Reader," pages 164–168) that your customers do. Memos, like letters, require the same care and should follow the same rules of effective writing discussed in Chapter 1 (see "Four Keys to Effective Writing," pages 11–20).

Strategies for Organizing a Memo

Before you start writing, take a few minutes to outline and draft what you need to say and to decide in what order it needs to be presented. Organize your memos so that readers can find information quickly and act on it promptly. For longer, more complex communications, such as the memos in Figures 6.17 and 6.18, your message might be divided into three parts: (1) **introduction**, (2) **discussion**, and (3) **conclusion**. Regardless

FIGURE 6.17   Memo on Letterhead with a Clear Introduction, Discussion, and Conclusion

Dearborn Equipment Company

To: Machine Shop Employees
From: Janet Hempstead, Shop Supervisor   *JH*
Date: September 25, 2015
Subject: Cleaning Brake Machines Safely

During the past two weeks I have received several reports that the brake machines are not being cleaned properly after each use. Through this memo I want to explain and emphasize the importance of keeping these machines clean for the safety of all our employees.

When the brake machines are used, the cutter chops off small particles of metal from brake drums. These particles then settle on the machines and create a potentially hazardous situation for anyone working on or near the machines. If the machines are not cleaned routinely before being used again, these metal particles could easily fly into an individual's face or upper body when the brake drum is spinning.

To prevent accidents like this from occurring, please make sure you vacuum the brake machines after each use.

You will find vacuum cleaners for this purpose in two places—
    (1) In work area 1-A
    (2) In the storage area

Vacuuming break machines is quick and easy: It should take you no more than a few seconds, a small amount of time to make the shop safer for all of us.

Thanks for your cooperation. If you have any questions, please call or text me at (609) 555-9899, email me at jhemp@dearco.com, or come by my office.

204 South Mill St., South Orange, NJ 02341-3420 (609) 555-9848 www.dec.com

Writer's initals verify message

Introduction explains purpose and importance of memo

Discussion states why problem exists and how to solve it

Safety message is boldfaced for emphasis

Conclusion builds goodwill and asks for questions

of how short or long your memo is, recall the three **P's** for success: **plan** what you are going to say; **polish** your writing before you send it; and **proofread** everything.

Introduction

The introduction of your memo should do the following:

- Tell readers why you are writing to them about a problem, procedure, or other issue.
- Explain briefly any background information the reader needs to know.
- Be specific about what you are going to accomplish in your memo.

Do not hesitate to come right out and say, "This memo summarizes the action taken in Evansville to reduce air pollution." See how clearly this is done in Figure 6.16.

Discussion

In the discussion section (the body) of your memo, help readers in these ways:

- State why a problem or procedure is important, who will be affected by it, and what caused it and why.
- Indicate why and what changes are necessary.
- Give precise dates, times, locations, and costs.

Notice how Janet Hempstead's memo in Figure 6.17 carefully describes an existing problem and explains the proper procedure for cleaning the brake machines, and how Mike Gonzalez in Figure 6.18 offers carefully researched evidence about Ramco increasing its favorable publicity in the community.

Conclusion

In your conclusion, state specifically how you want the reader to respond to your memo. To get readers to act appropriately, you can do one or more of the following:

- Ask readers to call you if they have any questions, as in Figure 6.17.
- Request a reply—in writing, over the telephone, via email, or in person—by a specific date, as in Figure 6.18.
- Provide a list of recommendations that the readers are to approve, follow, revise, or reject, as in Figures 6.16 and 6.18.

Organizational Markers

Throughout your memo, use the following organizational markers, where appropriate:

- Headings organize your work and make information easy for readers to follow, as in Figure 6.18.
- Numbered or bulleted lists help readers see comparisons and contrasts readily and thereby comprehend your ideas more quickly, as in Figure 6.16.
- Underlining or boldfacing emphasizes key points (see Figure 6.17). But do not overuse this technique; draw attention only to main points and those that contain summaries or draw conclusions.

Organizational markers are not limited to memos; you will find them in email, letters, reports, and proposals as well. (See "The ABCs of Print Document Design," pages 449–459.)

FIGURE 6.18 A Memo That Uses Subheads to Organize Content

RAMCO TECHNOLOGIES
Where Technology Shapes Tomorrow
marketing@Ramco.com   www.Ramco.com

TO: Rachel Mohler, Vice President
             Harrison Fontentot, Public Relations
FROM: Mike Gonzalez MG
DATE: March 3, 2016
SUBJECT: Three Ways to Increase Ramco's Community Involvement

At our planning session in early February, our divisional managers stressed the need to generate favorable publicity for our new Ramco facility in Mayfield. Knowing that such publicity will highlight Ramco's visibility in Mayfield, I think the company's image might be enhanced in the following three ways.

CREATE A SCHOLARSHIP FUND
Ramco would receive favorable publicity by creating a scholarship at Mayfield Community College for any student interested in a career in technology. A one-year scholarship would cost $21,000. The scholarship would be awarded by a committee of Ramco executives and staff. Such a scholarship would emphasize Ramco's enthusiastic support for the latest technical education at a local college.

OFFER SITE TOURS
Guided tours of the Mayfield facility would introduce the community to Ramco's innovative technology. These tours might be organized for academic, community, and civic groups. Individuals would then see the care we take in protecting the environment in our production and equipment choices and the speed with which we ship our products. Of special interest to visitors would be Ramco's use of industrial robots working alongside our employees. Since these tours would be scheduled in advance, they should not conflict with our production schedules.

PROVIDE GUEST SPEAKERS
Many of our employees would be excellent guest speakers at civic and educational meetings in the Mayfield area. Possible topics include the advances Ramco has made in designing and engineering and how these changes have helped consumers as well as boost the local economy.

Thanks for sending your comments in the next few days. If we are going to put one or more of these suggestions into practice before the facility opens in mid-April, we'll need to act before the end of the month.

Company logo

Header

Introduction supplies background and rationale

Body offers concrete evidence (costs, personnel, location) that plan can work

Boldfaced headings reflect organization

Relates plan to company mission and image

Closing emphasizes the plan's feasibility

Ends with request for feedback and authorization

WRITING BUSINESS LETTERS AND MEMOS THAT MATTER: A SUMMARY

As we saw, letters and memos are important in workplace writing. Your employer will expect you to respond to and send a variety of them. This chapter has introduced you to five different types of letters you can expect to write on the job, as well as the basic formats, parts, and strategies used to draft effective memos. Although you will send many more emails and texts than letters or memos, every job will require you to write this workplace correspondence.

Regardless of the type of letter or memo you have to write, follow these six guidelines:

1. **Analyze your audience and their needs.** Anticipate the types of information readers are expecting to receive from you and how they will use it.
2. **Determine your reason for writing.** Are you writing to make a routine or special request, offer an explanation, file a complaint, apologize, sell a product or service, build goodwill, express thanks, refuse credit, or collect a debt?
3. **Organize your information.** Would a direct or an indirect approach be best? Begin with good news or a buffer, and save negative messages for the middle of the letter.
4. **Draft your letter or memo carefully.** Be clear, concise, and diplomatic. Select the most appropriate language for your reader. Letters sent to international readers should respect their cultural traditions.
5. **Revise your letter or memo.** Double-check all facts; make sure you left nothing out.
6. **Proofread, proofread, proofread.**

✓ REVISION CHECKLIST

Planning Correspondence

☐ Made sure reader's name, job title, and address are correct.
☐ Wrote to a specific individual.
☐ Determined if audience will be friendly, hostile, or neutral about my message.
☐ Did sufficient research—in print, through online sources, in discussions with colleagues and, when necessary, with my boss—to meet my reader's needs.
☐ Proved to reader that I am knowledgeable, professional, and easy to work with.
☐ Followed my company protocol in choosing the format, organization, style, tone, and content of my letter.
☐ Ensured that my correspondence was timely. Answered all correspondence both from people in my company and from customers promptly and reasonably.

Inquiry Letters
- [ ] Explained why I am writing and what information I need and why.
- [ ] Researched and formulated specific questions that are brief and to the point; put them in easy-to-read format.
- [ ] Indicated when information is needed.
- [ ] Thanked reader for reply.
- [ ] Offered to share a copy of my report with reader.

Cover Letters
- [ ] Told reader what I am transmitting.
- [ ] Concisely summarized contents of document.
- [ ] Explained why document is important for reader.

Special Request Letters
- [ ] Stated why I am writing.
- [ ] Explained reasons for writing and how I will use the requested information.
- [ ] Numbered questions to make them easy to answer.
- [ ] Allowed reader enough time to reply; indicated by what date information is needed; supplied stamped, addressed envelope or email address.
- [ ] Offered to cite reader's help and share a copy of my work.

Sales Letters
- [ ] Identified and convinced my targeted audience.
- [ ] Got reader's **attention** with question or with attention-capturing statement.
- [ ] **Appealed** to the reader's senses.
- [ ] Emphasized how product/service **applies** to solving reader's problem or ensures competitor cannot offer benefits.
- [ ] Asked reader to take **action**.
- [ ] Was honest and ethical and did not attack the competition.

Customer Relations Letters
- [ ] Began my correspondence with reader-effective strategies. If reporting good news, told the reader right away. If reporting bad news, was diplomatically indirect and considerate of my reader's reactions.

Follow-Up Letters
- [ ] Thanked reader for his or her patronage.
- [ ] Courteously stressed benefits to reader for his or her continuing business.
- [ ] Promised to resolve any problems or answer any questions.
- [ ] Requested future business.

Complaint Letters
- [ ] Wrote promptly using a courteous, professional tone free from name-calling, insults, or threats.

(Continued)

☐ Described the problem with product or service in detail, including necessary documentation (invoices, model numbers, dealer's name and address).

☐ Specified exactly what I wanted done and by when; was reasonable and objective.

☐ Ended politely.

Adjustment Letters Saying "Yes"

☐ Started off with good news reader wants to hear.

☐ Apologized sincerely for problem.

☐ Told reader what was wrong and how problem will be corrected; did not blame or make excuses.

☐ Ended on a friendly note without referring to the problem but encouraging further business.

Adjustment Letters Saying "No"

☐ Did not begin with a "No." Instead, followed the indirect approach and used a neutral buffer.

☐ Acknowledged reader's point of view but provided clear and direct explanation for denial of claim.

☐ Concluded by giving or suggesting an alternative to keep customer's goodwill.

Refusal-of-Credit Letters

☐ Began positively by thanking reader for letter.

☐ Gave appropriate factual reasons for refusal that did not lay personal blame on reader.

☐ Encouraged further inquiries or applications.

☐ Took special care to meet the needs of non-native speakers of English in both tone and message.

Collection Letters

☐ Tailored letter according to audience, time, and circumstances of overdue account.

☐ Tried to maintain goodwill.

☐ Followed all legal guidelines in informing reader about past due account and payment policies.

Memos

☐ Used appropriate and consistent format.

☐ Followed employer's policy regarding routing memos.

☐ Announced purpose of memo early and clearly.

☐ Organized memo according to reader's need for information, putting main ideas up front, giving documentation, and supplying conclusion.

☐ Kept reader's need for key information and considered his/her background in the forefront of writing memos.

☐ Wrote clearly and concisely.

☐ Included bullets, lists, boldfacing, and underscoring where necessary to reflect logic and organization of memo.

☐ Refrained from overloading reader with unnecessary details.

EXERCISES

1. Write a letter of inquiry to a utility company, a safety or health care agency, or a business in your town requesting information on how its services to the community protect the environment. Give specific reasons why you are requesting the information.

2. In which courses are you or will you be writing a report? Write to an agency or company that could supply you with helpful information, and request its aid. Indicate why you are writing, precisely what information you need, and why you need it. Offer to share your report with the company.

3. Choose one of the following, and write a sales letter addressed to an appropriate reader on why he or she should

   a. work for the same company you do
   b. move to your neighborhood
   c. be happy taking a vacation where you did last year
   d. dine at a particular restaurant
   e. use a particular app
   f. have their cars repaired at a specific garage
   g. give their real estate business to a particular agency
   h. use your company's new e-commerce software when constructing its website

4. Rewrite the following sales letter to make it more effective. Add any details you think are relevant.

   Dear Pizza Lovers:

   Allow me to introduce myself. My name is Rudy Moore and I am the new manager of Tasty Pizza Parlor in town. The Parlor is located at the intersection of North Miller Parkway and 95th Street. We are open from 10 a.m. to 11 p.m., except on the weekends, when we are open later.

   I think you will be as happy as I am to learn that Tasty's will now offer free delivery to an extended service area. As a result, you can get your Tasty Pizza hot when you want it.

   Please see your newspaper or newspaper's website for our ad. We also are offering customers a coupon. It is a real deal for you.

   I know you will enjoy Tasty's pizza and I hope to see you. I am always interested in hearing from you about our service and our fine product. We want to take your order soon. Please come in.

   Hungry for your business,
   Rudy

5. Send a follow-up letter to one of the following:

   a. a customer who informs you that she will no longer do business with your company because your prices are too high
   b. a family of four who stayed at your motel for a week last summer
   c. a wedding party or professional organization that used your catering services last month

    d. a customer who returned a coat for the purchase price

    e. a customer who purchased a used car from you and who has not been happy with your service

    f. a company that bought a piece of equipment from you nine months ago, alerting them about a recall

6. Write a bad news letter based on an experience at your workplace—rejecting an applicant for a job, notifying tenants of an increase in parking rates, or denying a request for funding, for example.

7. Write a bad news letter to an appropriate reader about one of the following situations:

    a. Your company has to discontinue Saturday deliveries because of rising labor and fuel costs.

    b. You are the manager of an insurance company writing to tell one of your customers that, because of a reckless driving citation, his or her rates will increase.

    c. You have to refuse to send a bonus gift to a customer who sent in an order after the promotion period ended.

    d. You have discontinued a model that a business customer wants to reorder.

    e. You have to notify residents of a community that a bus route or hours of operation are being discontinued.

    f. You represent the water department and have to tell residents of a community that they cannot water their lawns for the next month because of a serious water shortage in your town.

    g. You cannot repair a particular piece of equipment because the customer still owes your company for three previous service visits.

8. Write a good news letter about the opposite of one of the situations listed in Exercise 7.

9. Write a complaint letter about one of the following:

    a. an error in your utility, mobile phone, credit card, or Internet provider bill

    b. discourteous service you received on an airplane, train, or bus

    c. frustratingly long waits or prompts to speak to a company's representative

    d. a shipment that arrived late and damaged

    e. an insurance payment to you that is $357.00 less than it should be

    f. a public television station's decision to discontinue a particular series

    g. junk mail or spam that you have been receiving

    h. equipment that arrived with missing or defective parts

    i. misleading representation by a salesperson

    j. incorrect or misleading information given on a website

10. This exercise might be done as a collaborative project. You are a section manager at e-Tech. Your company has a service contract with Professional Office Cleaners (POC). However, each morning when you arrive at work you are disappointed with what they've done. POC has overlooked some essential tasks and done a poor job on others. Your staff is also disappointed and has emailed or spoken to you about problems with POC. Write the following:

    a. a memo or email to your boss, the vice president, about POC's shoddy work

    b. a complaint letter to POC that the vice president has asked you to write and to sign his name to

    c. a letter to the vice president from the manager of POC, apologizing for the problem and offering a solution

    d. a letter from POC to the vice president taking issue with the complaint made against the cleaning company and offering proof that the work was done according to contract specifications

    e. an email you send to your staff about what's happened with POC

11. Write the complaint letter that prompted the adjustment letter in Figure 6.10.

12. Write the complaint letter that prompted the adjustment letter in Figure 6.12.

13. Rewrite the following complaint letter to make it more precise, less emotional, and more persuasive.

Dear Sir:

We recently purchased a machine from your Albany store and paid a great deal of money for it. This machine, according to your website, is supposedly the best model in your line and has caused us nothing but trouble each time we use it. Really, can't you do any better with your technology?

We expect you to stand by your products. The warranties you give with them should make you accountable for shoddy workmanship. Let us know at once what you intend to do about our problem. If you cannot or are unwilling to correct the situation, we will take our business elsewhere, and then you will be sorry.

Sincerely yours,

14. Write an adjustment letter saying "Yes" to the manager of The Loft, whose letter is in Figure 6.8.

15. Write an adjustment letter saying "No" to the customer who received the "Yes" adjustment letter in Figure 6.10.

16. Rewrite the following ineffective adjustment letter saying "Yes."

Dear Mr. Smith:

We are extremely sorry to learn that you found the suit you purchased from us unsatisfactory. The problem obviously stems from the fact that you selected it from the rack marked "Factory Seconds." In all honesty, we have had a lot of problems because of this rack. I guess we should know better than to try to feature inferior merchandise along with the name-brand clothing that we sell. But we originally thought that our customers would accept poorer quality merchandise if it saved them some money. That was our mistake.

Please accept our apologies. If you will bring your "Factory Second" suit to us, we will see what we can do about honoring your request.

Sincerely yours,

17. Rewrite the following ineffective adjustment letter saying "No."

Dear Customer:

Our company is unwilling to give you a new toaster or to refund your purchase price. After examining the toaster you sent to us, we found that the fault was not ours, as you insist, but yours.

Let me explain. Our toaster is made to take a lot of punishment. But being dropped on the floor or poked inside with a knife, as you probably did, exceeds all decent treatment. You must be careful if you expect your appliances to last. Your negligence in this case is so bad that the toaster could not be repaired.

In the future, consider using your appliances according to the guidelines set down in their warranties. That's why they are written.

Since you are now in the market for a new toaster, let me suggest that you purchase our new heavy-duty model, number 67342, called the Counter-Whiz. I am taking the liberty of sending you some information about this model. I do hope you at least go to see one at your local appliance center.

Sincerely,

18. You are the manager of a computer software company, and one of your salespeople has just sold a large order to a new customer whose business you have tried to obtain for years. Unfortunately, the salesperson made a mistake writing out the invoice, undercharging the customer by $229. At that price, your company would not break even, and so you must write a letter explaining the problem so that the customer will not assume all future business dealings with your firm will be offered at such "below market" rates. Decide whether you should ask for the $229 or just "write it off" in the interest of keeping a valuable new customer.

   a. Write a letter to the new customer, asking for the $229 and explaining the problem while still projecting an image of your company as accurate, professional, and very competitive.
   b. Write a letter to the new customer, not asking for the $229 but explaining the mistake and emphasizing that your company is both competitive and professional.
   c. Write a letter to your boss explaining why you wrote the letter in **a**.
   d. Write a letter to your boss explaining why you wrote the letter in **b**.
   e. Write a letter to the salesperson who made the mistake, asking him or her to take appropriate action with regard to the new customer.

19. You just found out that a business that applied for credit has missed its mortgage payment. You have to refuse credit to this local firm, which has been in business successfully for eight years. Write a refusal letter without jeopardizing future business dealings.

20. Write an appropriate collection letter to one of the following:

   a. a loyal customer who has not responded to a first notice letter
   b. a new business customer who placed a large order with you last quarter and paid for it promptly but who has ignored two notices you have already sent about an order filled this quarter

    c. a customer who has just placed an order over the Internet but has not responded so far to any of your notices for payment for previous purchases

    d. a customer who has been continually late but has always paid eventually

    e. an international customer who has sent in only partial payment

21. Write a memo to your boss saying that you will be out of town two days next week and three days the following week for one of the following reasons: (a) to inspect some land your firm is thinking of buying, (b) to investigate some claims, (c) to look at some new office space for a branch your firm is thinking of opening in a city 500 miles away, (d) to attend a conference sponsored by a professional society, or (e) to pay calls on customers. In your memo, be specific about dates, places, times, and reasons.

22. Write a memo to two or three of your co-workers on the same subject you chose for Exercise 21.

23. Send a memo to your public relations department informing it that you are completing a degree or work for a certificate. Indicate how the information could be useful for your firm's publicity campaign.

24. Write a memo to the director of your school's library asking for one of the following. Be sure you include specific reasons for such a change.

    a. extended weekend hours

    b. more vending machines

    c. more computers

    d. more group study rooms

    e. increased journal subscriptions in your field of study

25. Write a memo notifying the human resources department that there is a mistake in an insurance claim you filed. Explain exactly what the error is, and give precise figures.

26. Select some change (in policy, schedule, or personnel assignment) you encountered in a job you held in the last two or three years and write an appropriate memo describing that change. Write the memo from the perspective of your former employer explaining the change to employees.

27. You are the manager of a major art museum. Write a memo to various department heads at your museum giving them the following information. Use proper memo format.

Old hours:	Mon.–Fri. 9–5; closed Sat. except during July and August, when you are open 9–12
New hours:	Mon.–Th. 8:30–4:30; Fri.–Sat. 9–9
Old rates:	Adults $12.00; senior citizens $5.00; children under 12 $3.00
New rates:	Adults $15.00; senior citizens $7.00; children under 12 $5.00
Added features:	Paintings by Thora Horne, local artist; sculpture from West Indies in display area all summer; guided tours available for parties of six or more; lounge areas will offer patrons sandwiches and soft drinks during May, June, July, and August

28. How would the memos in Exercises 21 to 27 have to be rewritten to make them suitable as an email message? Rewrite one of them as an email.

Murat Taner/Flirt/Corbis

How to Get a Job

Searches, Networking, Dossiers, Portfolios/ Webfolios, Résumés, Transitioning to a Civilian Job, Letters, and Interviews

Obtaining a job in today's tough market involves a lot of hard work. Before your name is added to a company's payroll, you will have to do more than simply walk into the human resources office and fill out an application form or send a résumé online. Finding the *right* job takes time in this highly competitive job market. And finding the right person to fill that job also takes time for the employer.

STEPS AN EMPLOYER TAKES WHEN HIRING

From the employer's viewpoint, the stages in the search for a valuable employee include the following:

1. Deciding what duties and responsibilities go with the job and determining the qualifications the future employee should possess
2. Advertising the job on the company's website and social media, on online job-posting sites, in newspapers, and in professional publications
3. Reviewing and evaluating résumés and letters of application
4. Having candidates complete application forms
5. Requesting further proof of candidates' skills (letters of recommendation, transcripts, portfolios/webfolios)
6. Interviewing selected candidates
7. Doing further follow-ups and selecting those to be interviewed again
8. Offering the job to the best-qualified individual

Sometimes the steps are interchangeable, especially steps 4, 5, and 6, but generally speaking, employers go through a long and detailed process to select employees. Step 3, for example, is among the most important for employers (and the most crucial for job candidates). At that stage employers often classify job seekers into one of three groups: those they definitely want to interview, those they may want to interview, and those in whom they have no interest.

STEPS TO FOLLOW TO GET HIRED

Whether you are searching for your first job after college or looking to change careers, you will have to know how and when to give prospective employers the kinds of information the preceding eight steps require. You will also have to follow a definite schedule in your search for a job. Expect to go through the following eight procedures:

1. analyzing your strengths and restricting your job search
2. enhancing your professional image
3. looking in the right places for a job
4. assembling a dossier and a portfolio
5. preparing a résumé tailored for each job you apply for
6. writing a letter of application and filling out a job application
7. going to an interview
8. accepting or declining a job offer

Your timetable should match that of your prospective employer. This chapter shows you how to begin your job search, design an effective portfolio, prepare appropriate résumés, write a persuasive letter of application, and prepare for an interview. It also contains information to help individuals to transition from their military assignment to the civilian workforce (see "Transitioning to the Civilian Workforce," pages 266–271).

ANALYZING YOUR STRENGTHS AND RESTRICTING YOUR JOB SEARCH

Job counselors advise students to start planning for their careers several years before they graduate. The more you find out about what career path you want to take ahead of graduation, the better you will be able to target the jobs that are right for you. Individuals changing careers or transitioning from the military to the civilian sector also need to assess their experiences, skills, and job goals.

Before you apply for jobs, analyze your job skills, career goals, and interests. Here are some points to consider:

1. Make an inventory of your most significant accomplishments in your major or on the job—writing and speaking, working with people, organizing, and troubleshooting, making presentations managing money, speaking a second language, designing websites, working for a health care agency.
2. Decide which specialty within your chosen career appeals to you the most. If you are in a nursing program, do you want to work in a large teaching hospital, for a home health or hospice agency, or in a physician's office?

3. What types of working conditions most appeal to you—small groups, traveling, telecommuting, relocating overseas?
4. What most interests you about a position—travel, technology, international contacts, on-the-job training, helping people, being creative?
5. What are some of the greatest challenges you face in your career today—or will face in five years?
6. Which specific companies or organizations have the best track record in hiring and promoting individuals in your field? What qualifications will such firms insist on from prospective employees?

Once you answer these questions, you can avoid applying for positions for which you are either overqualified or underqualified. If a position requires ten years of related work experience and you are just starting out, you will only waste the employer's time and your own by applying. However, if a job requires a certificate or license and you are in the process of obtaining one, go ahead and apply.

ENHANCING YOUR PROFESSIONAL IMAGE

Whether you are looking for your first job in your career field, re-entering the job market, changing careers or transitioning to a civilian job, you can take several steps to help improve your chances of getting hired.

- Attend job fairs and interviewing workshops on campus as well as those sponsored by municipal, state, and federal agencies.
- Go to trade shows to learn about the latest products, services, and technologies in your profession and to meet contacts and even potential employers.
- Use social media/networking sites to learn more about your profession.
- Join and participate in student and professional organizations and societies in your area of interest.
- Apply for relevant internships and training programs to gain real-world experience and increase your networking contacts.
- If available, take a temporary job in your profession to gain some experience.
- Confer with your academic adviser regularly, not just once a semester.
- Find a mentor—someone in a field you might want to join.
- Do volunteer work to gain or enhance experience working in a group setting, preparing documents, and so on.
- Find out if your school or university offers **job shadowing** opportunities, where you can follow someone during his/her daily work routine to gauge whether or not a particular position or profession matches your skills and interests.
- Follow companies or individuals in the field you are interested in on Twitter, Facebook, or other forms of social media (see "Writing for Social Media in the Workplace," pages 139–147).
- Establish a profile on a professional networking site such as LinkedIn (see Figure 7.2, pages 246–249) and connect to other people in your desired field.

LOOKING IN THE RIGHT PLACES FOR A JOB

One way to search for a job is simply to send out a batch of letters and résumés to companies you want to work for. But how do you know what jobs, if any, those companies have available, what qualifications they are looking for, and what deadlines they might want you to meet? You can avoid these uncertainties by consulting the following resources for a wealth of job-related information. Use as many of them as you can.

1. Personal (face-to-face) networking. One of the most successful ways to land a job is through networking. In fact, most jobs come through consulting with other people. John D. Erdlen and Donald H. Sweet, experts on job searching, cite the following as a primary rule of job hunting: "Don't do anything yourself you can get someone with influence to do for you." Let your professors, co-workers, friends, classmates, neighbors, relatives, and even your clergy know you are looking for a job. They may hear of something and can notify you or, better yet, recommend you for the position. See how the job seekers in Figures 7.15 and 7.16 (pages 285 and 286) have successfully networked with people they know.

2. Your campus placement office. Counselors know about current available positions, and they can also make your résumé available to recruiters when they come on campus. Placement offices have recruiting databases, allowing students access to a broad range of contacts and interview information. Counselors can also help you find summer and part-time positions that might lead to full-time jobs. Most important, they will give you sound advice on your job search, including strategies for finding the right job, salary ranges, and interview tips. Many placement offices also sponsor career fairs to bring job seekers and employers together in specific professional fields. Finally, your placement office will help you set up and archive your dossier, or credentials (see "Dossiers and Letters of Recommendation," pages 251–252).

3. Online job-posting sites. A majority of jobs can be found on the Internet. You can learn about jobs at a specific company or organization by visiting its website to see what vacancies it has and what the qualifications are for them. (Many companies also list job openings through social media postings on Facebook, Twitter, and other sites.) Also consult the *Riley Guide: Employment Opportunities and Job Resources* on the Internet (www.rileyguide.com). This invaluable resource surveys and classifies job openings on the Web by field, location, and category (private or public). In addition, you might want to explore many of the job-posting sites, such as those in Table 7.1.

4. Newspapers. Look at local newspapers as well as the Sunday editions of large city papers with a wide circulation, such as *The New York Times* (http://jobmarket .nytimes.com). The Careers section of *The Wall Street Journal* also lists jobs in different areas, including technical and managerial positions (online.wsj.com/public /page/news-career-jobs.html).

5. Federal and state employment offices. The U.S. government is one of the biggest employers in the country. Counselors at federal and state employment centers

TABLE 7.1 Job-Posting Sites on the Web

Website	URL	Description
After College	www.aftercollege.com	Lists more than 400,000 entry-level jobs and internships; connects students, alumni and employers through faculty and career networks across the country
Career One Stop	www.careeronestop.com	Sponsored by the Department of Labor; this site includes *America's Job Bank* (www.ajb.dni.us) and lists employment services, job search sites, vocational trends, and help for military transitions
Career Builder	www.careerbuilder.com	Hosts the career sites for more than 1,000 partner companies, including 140 newspapers
College Recruiter	www.collegerecruiter.com	Leading job board for college students searching for internships and recent graduates hunting for entry-level jobs and other career opportunities
College Grad	www.collegegrad.com	Targets college students and recent grads exclusively. Provides more entry-level job search content to job seekers and linked to more colleges and universities than any other career site
Craigslist	www.craigslist.com	Classified ads website includes regionalized job postings in a wide variety of fields
Diversity Employers	www.diversityemployers.com	Largest database of equal-opportunity employers committed to workplace diversity. Dedicated to providing career- and self-development information on careers, job opportunities, graduate/professional schools, internships/co-ops, and study-abroad programs
Indeed	indeed.com	A metasearch employment website that collects job listings from a wide variety of sources
Monster	www.monster.com	Biggest commercial online job board; lists hundreds of thousands of openings; includes global postings; offers advice on the job-search process
Monster College	college.monster.com	Jobs posted for college students and recent college graduates.
Net Temps	www.net-temps.com	Postings for temporary, temp-to-perm, and full-time employment through the staffing industry
Simply Hired	www.simplyhired.com	Job listings from thousands of websites, including newspapers, social media, and company career sites
Snagajob	www.snagajob.com	Claims to be the largest website dedicated specifically to hourly based jobs (for both employers and potential employees)
TweetMyJobs	www.tweetmyjobs.com	This social recruiting website helps job seekers to find job listings through Facebook and Twitter, and also enables them to receive targeted job recommendations by email or mobile notifications

also help job seekers find career opportunities. Consult USAJOBS (www.usajobs .gov) for listings of government jobs. Figure 7.1 shows the home page of USAJOBS, a U.S. government website. Veterans can take advantage of My Next Move for Veterans (http://www.mynextmove.org/vets/) or the National Resource Directory run by the Veteran's Administration and the Department of Defense (www.ebenefits .va.gov/ebenefits/nrd). The *Occupational Outlook Handbook* (www.bls.gov/ooh) provides information (including projections for job growth and salary ranges) for hundreds of occupations.

6. Professional and trade journals and associations in your major. Identify the most respected periodicals in your field and search their ads. For example, *CIO Magazine—Information Technology Professional Research Center* (itjobs.cio.com/a /all-jobs/list) can help you find jobs in the computer industry, engineering, and technology. Consulting *WEDDLE's Association Directory* (http://www.weddles.com /associations) is one way to find out about professional organizations and the journals they publish in your field.

FIGURE 7.1 USAJOBS Website

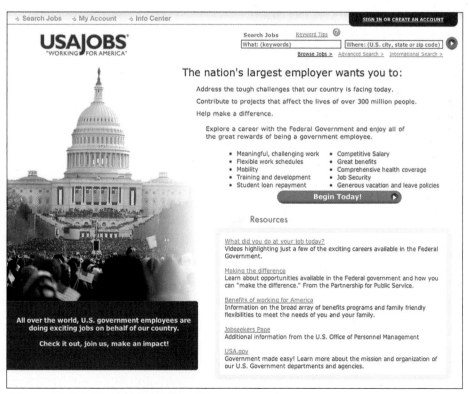

Courtesy of the United States Office of Personnel Management

7. **The human resources department of a company or an agency you would like to work for.** Often you will be able to fill out an application online even if there is not a current opening.

8. **A résumé database service.** A number of online services will put your résumé in a database and make it available to prospective employers, who scan the database regularly to find suitable job candidates. Check to see if a professional society to which you belong (or might join) offers a similar service.

But be careful about posting personal information, such as your social security number. You never know who can gain access to this information. If your current boss finds out you are looking for another job, you risk being fired. (See "Should You Ask Your Current Boss," page 252).

9. **Professional employment agencies.** Some agencies list jobs you can apply for free of charge (because the employer pays the fee), while others charge a stiff fee, usually a percentage of your first year's salary. Be sure to ask who pays the fee for this service. Because employment agencies often find out about jobs through channels already available to you, speak to someone at your campus placement center first.

USING ONLINE SOCIAL AND PROFESSIONAL NETWORKING SITES IN YOUR JOB SEARCH

Social networking sites (e.g., Facebook, Twitter, LinkedIn, and Google+) are essential tools to help you find a job and advance your career. Do not think of them only as personal media sites where you exchange news and photos with friends and family. These sites contain valuable information about the companies that might hire you. Companies also explore these sites to recruit potential employees.

Finding Jobs Through Networking Sites

Companies routinely post job openings on Facebook, Twitter, LinkedIn, and other social media. Following companies, organizations or events related to your job search on social media can alert you to job openings. You can then reference the social media site in the first paragraph of your application letter (see Figure 7.14, page 283) as the place where you learned of the job. Facebook and Twitter also allow you to post links to your blog and/or your portfolio/webfolio (see "Career Portfolios/Webfolios," pages 252–254) to attract potential employers.

Keep in mind that employers also search social media to do background checks to see if a candidate is a good fit with their corporate culture. Consequently, you want to make sure that you project a professional image on any social media site you post on. See the list of errors to avoid in Table 7.2 (page 250).

Also, you want to demonstrate your writing and organization ability with thoughtful posts that showcase your professionalism. But don't come across as overly stiff or cold or too casual. Employers will pay special attention to your language—avoid slang, textspeak, insults, jokes, and inappropriate pictures and images.

And don't turn your social media comments into posts about your personal details or your friends. Instead focus on professional issues in your field. Write about your career achievements, as Maria Lopez does in her Facebook "About Me" section below:

ABOUT ME

I will graduate from Miami-Dade Community College in May, 2016 with an A.S. degree in Dental Hygiene (GPA: 3.58) and will take the Dental Assisting National Board Exams in early June. During my clinical training I received intensive practical instruction from several Miami dentists and researched my major project on proper nutrition and dental care for preschoolers.

Prior to my pursuit of a degree, I worked for over two years as a unit assistant on the pediatric unit at St. Francis Hospital in Miami Beach, FL. There I greeted patients, transcribed medical orders and surgical notes, and assisted the nursing staff.

I am fluent in Spanish and also have experience using DentiMax Advanced, Dentrix Ascend, and Maxident 6.

Post comments about any interests or events that support your job application, including those about community affairs that show you are interested in building relationships or how you can help a prospective employer, and also any interests (such as creating a safer, green environment) that express your ethical values and dedication.

Using Facebook to Start Your Network

Facebook can help you start your professional networking (see "Writing for Social Media in the Workplace," pages 139–147). If you already have a Facebook account to socialize with friends, consider creating a separate account for professional networking and be sure to adjust the privacy settings on your personal account (see Table 7.2, page 250).

In creating your Facebook network of contacts, begin with former employers or co-workers who know your work and who will say good things about your education, skills, and previous experience in your chosen career. As you prepare to enter the job market, contact these people through Facebook and ask if they would notify you of any relevant job openings and if they would write a letter of reference for you. Also be sure to "friend" former professors through Facebook, especially in your area of study and those who liked your work. Your teachers are important professional contacts because many of them are plugged into professional networks themselves. Contact them to see if they have heard of any jobs in your field. Moreover, with their permission, your instructors can become some of your most important professional references. You can also expand your network by "Liking" professional organizations, companies, or related societies; this will help you as a job candidate by making you look career-oriented.

LinkedIn

LinkedIn (www.linkedin.com) is the most important social network for your job search. As the name implies, its purpose is to link, or connect, you to people who can help you professionally. As job counselors repeatedly advise, the best way to land a job is through networking—that is, one person helping another. LinkedIn is all about networking, making contacts who have inside information at a company and who may introduce (and maybe even recommend) you to the individual who makes the decision to interview applicants and eventually hire. More than 300 million companies and individuals belong to LinkedIn, including executives from every *Fortune* 500 company, giving you valuable information about the company and allowing you to target people whom you may want to contact.

Benefits of Joining LinkedIn

Joining LinkedIn is easy and free. Not only will belonging to LinkedIn help you find a job, it will enhance your professional image and signal that you value teamwork. But networking entails more than someone helping you. You need to be prepared to help others through your contacts. Joining LinkedIn tells prospective network contacts and employers you are ready to do that.

Five Ways LinkedIn Can Help Your Job Search

LinkedIn can help you find a position in five key ways.

1. **LinkedIn allows you to search for a specific type of job by targeting a particular specialized field, company, job title, or even zip code.** LinkedIn includes thousands of classified posts, helping you to search the wider Internet more efficiently.

2. **LinkedIn gives you valuable information about a company, such as its mission statement, the names of the CEO and directors, its products and services, its locations, its awards, and even its competitors.** Company profiles on LinkedIn provide the names and contact information for hiring managers and human resource professionals, the very individuals you want to reach and have reach you.

3. **LinkedIn helps you become part of a network and expand your list of contacts.** The working principle behind LinkedIn is to assist you in joining a network and then finding out if someone in your network knows someone at the company you want to work for.

4. **LinkedIn improves your search by including short recommendations from people in your network.** Recommendations praising your work will enhance your profile on LinkedIn (see Figure 7.2, pages 246–249), and give potential employers proof that you are a qualified, conscientious, and respected worker.

5. **LinkedIn allows you to create a public profile that shows you are a professional.** This profile shows your writing and organizational skills, and will be one

of the first pages that come up in a Google search when someone looks for you by name.

Establishing Your LinkedIn Network

When establishing your LinkedIn network, the first thing you need to do is identify as many individuals as possible who might be able to help you in your job search. Look for people who know you and like your work. Here are some of the individuals you might consider asking to be possible members of your network:

- Current and former instructors who have complimented your work
- Former bosses, managers, or co-workers who are willing to write a recommendation on your behalf—for example, "I have worked with Agnes Delancy for two years and always found her cooperative and efficient."
- Individuals who belong to a professional association or organization that you have joined, such as the National Society of Black Engineers, the National Student Nurses Association, or the Society of Marketing Specialists
- Community leaders you have worked for and who value what you have done
- Individuals in the military to whom you reported and can comment on your technical skills, cooperation, leadership ability, and so on
- People you do business with on a regular basis and who may have a wide circle of connections (e.g., current and former customers, suppliers)
- Alumni of schools you attended

A Sample LinkedIn Profile

Figure 7.2 (pages 246–249) contains the LinkedIn profile of Daniel Ricks Solter. Created using LinkedIn's helpful prompts and drop-down menu options in many sections, the profile lists such job-relevant categories such as experience, certifications, organizations, languages, education, and a brief summary of his accomplishments. It provides a list of the relevant skills that Solter has acquired and indicates that he is interested in job inquiries, reference requests, expertise requests, and getting back in touch. And it includes important recommendations about him.

Promoting Your Best Image—Some Do's and Don'ts

Used effectively, social media and professional networking sites allow you to publicize your qualifications through text, photographs, audio, and video images. As we saw, hiring managers and recruiters check these social networks for potential job candidates as well as to screen applicants to interview and eventually hire. In fact, more than a million hiring managers, recruiters, and human resource professionals look for qualified candidates on LinkedIn alone. These individuals scout other social networking sites, too, such as Facebook and Google+, and ask colleagues and other professionals to alert them to qualified job candidates.

But when you use these networks, make sure you enhance and don't jeopardize your chances with prospective employers. You have to be careful about your digital

FIGURE 7.2 LinkedIn Profile

Includes recent, professional-looking photo

"Connections" are people in Solter's network, many of whom are in a position to help his career

Concisely describes job responsibilities emphasizing technical leadership, and communication skills

Uses incomplete sentences, the standard style for LinkedIn profiles; chooses strong active verbs

Supplies information about work history

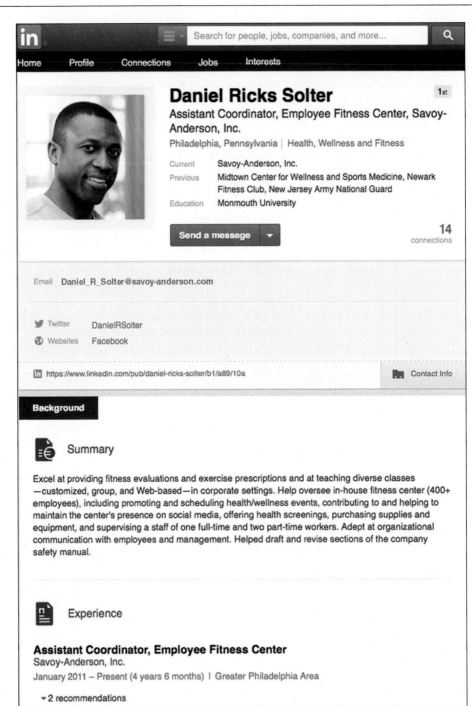

Dan Vallero. Photo, iStockPhoto.com/ranplett

FIGURE 7.2 (Continued)

Buddy Rirerson
Client Relations Director at Savoy-Ander...

Daniel is dynamic and knowledgeable. He can build rapport and relationships quickly and is always available for individual... View↓

Jennifer Keller
Human Resources Director at Savoy-An...

I have worked with Daniel for the last two years and he consistently ranks among the very best of Savoy-Anderson's staff.... View↓

Secured recommendations from current and former supervisors and co-workers praising his expertise, team spirit, and cooperative attitude, all qualities that hiring managers prize

Fitness Instructor
Midtown Center for Wellness and Sports Medicine

September 2008 – December 2010 (2 years 4 months) | Greater Philadelphia Area

▾ 1 recommendation

Joyce Hwang
Assistant Director at Midtown Center for Wellness and Sports Medicine

Daniel was a supportive and effective spokesperson for MCWSM. His group classes were among the most popular ones we offered, and he knows fitness programs extremely well. Above all, he is a team player. View↓

Personal Trainer
Newark Fitness Club

May 2006 – September 2008 (2 years 5 months) | Newark, DE

▾ 1 recommendation

Jorge Almodovar
Director at Newark Fitness Club

Daniel was a highly effective trainer with our wide cross section of clients, but excelled in his work with our senior population. He always went the extra mile to coordinate care with primary physicians. View↓

Specialist, 50th Infantry Brigade Combat Team
New Jersey Army National Guard

September 2002 – June 2006 (3 years 10 months) | Trenton, NJ

Provides information about military background

Intern
Cardiac Rehabilitation Program, St. Catherine's Hospital

January 2006 – May 2006 (5 months) | Trenton, NJ

🗎 Certifications

Personal Trainer Certification
National Academy of Sports Medicine (NASM)

Cardiopulmonary Resuscitation (CPR) Certification
American Red Cross

Lists professional certifications

Automated External Defibrillator) (AED) Certification
American Red Cross

Dan Vallero

FIGURE 7.2 (Continued)

Sports Management Certificate
United States Sports Academy

 Organizations

Groups from which Solter has built his network

ASEP (American Society of Exercise Physiologists)

Certified Personal Trainers of Trenton

Volunteer Experience & Causes

Strong link between job goals and community service

Coached 9th Grade Soccer
Boys and Girls Clubs of America
June 2004 – June 2006 (2 years 1 month)

Volunteer work shows professional commitment

Physical Fitness Trainer, Football
South Trenton High School
September 2006 – June 2010 (3 years 10 months)

Opportunities Daniel is looking for:

- Skills-based volunteering (pro bono consulting)

Skills

Uses LinkedIn's helpful drop-down menus to create a comprehensive list of job-related skills

2	Fitness Instruction
2	Employee Wellness
2	Fitness Consulting
2	Personal Training
2	Team Building
2	Wellness
2	Managing Facilities
2	Cardiac Rehabilitation

Dan Vallero

FIGURE 7.2 (Continued)

 Languages

English
Native or bilingual proficiency

Spanish
Limited working proficiency

Includes accurate and ethical assessment of language skills

 Education

Monmouth University
Bachelor's Degree, Kinesiology and Exercise Science
2004 – 2006

Raritan Valley Community College
Associate's Degree
2002 – 2004

Describes educational background

Additional Info

• **Personal Details**

Birthday   February 19

• **Advice for Contacting Daniel**

Interested in:

- job inquiries
- reference requests
- expertise requests
- getting back in touch

Identifies areas in which Solter wants to exchange information to further expand his network of professional contacts.

Dan Vallero

footprint (e.g., presence) and your online reputation. Success is all about how you look online, including your social networking profile and what you post on your page and in your portfolio (see "Career Portfolios/Webfolios," pages 252–254), in a blog, or on a website, whether it is your own or someone else's. To project your best professional image, employ the same care as you would in preparing other job-related documents, such as memos, letters, reports, and proposals.

In Table 7.2 (page 250), you will find some Do's and Don'ts when you create your profile on a social networking site.

TABLE 7.2 Do's and Don'ts When Creating Your Online Profile

Do's	Don'ts
Supply a current, professional picture showing how you want employers to see you at an interview.	Never use a profile photo taken at a party, a sports event, or on your vacation. Exclude photos with revealing clothing or compromising poses or gestures.
Choose appropriate "likes" and "activities" relating to your professional, community service, or charitable work. Mention the titles of current books related to your major or articles in *Time, The New York Times,* or *Bloomberg Business.*	Make sure that the hobbies or activities you list do not detract from your professional profile (e.g., playing computer games, gambling, etc.).
Highlight your strongest career accomplishments to demonstrate your knowledge of the industry where you want to work.	Do not give out someone's personal information (such as email addresses, phone numbers, or names) without first obtaining that person's permission.
Ensure that your tone, words, and comments are ethical.	Never use sexist, racist, or obscene language online. Steer clear of sensitive or inflammatory topics, such as politics and religion.
Respect all the ethical guidelines of your current or former employer (see "Ethical Requirements on the Job," pages 27–29).	Refrain from giving out any privileged company information (e.g., names of clients, financial details, marketing plans, etc.). Never use your company email address when registering for social networking sites, and do not log onto them via your office computer.
Check other websites where you may appear or may be quoted to make sure you look and sound professional. Google yourself to find these and other links.	Avoid posting anything that makes you look unprofessional in dress, actions, or words.
Be careful when blogging; exclude anything embarrassing or damaging to your job search.	Avoid criticizing a former or current co-worker, employer, client, vendor, competitor, instructor, or government official or agency.
Keep all information up-to-date.	Do not bombard a potential employer with repeated small posts, queries, or updates.
Verify that all images and video clips are clear and professional.	Eliminate background noise or unnecessary background images.
Check your privacy/security settings to ensure that information is available only to those you authorize.	Because social media sites have a "default" mode allowing anyone to access and post on your page, be sure to exclude any embarrassing posts or comments on your page.
Contact website administrators if anything abusive has been posted about you and request that the material be removed.	Don't forget that your profile is never as private as you think. Your current network of friends may include someone who has some type of connection to a prospective employer.

DOSSIERS AND LETTERS OF RECOMMENDATION

Dossiers play a major role in the job search. A **dossier**, French for "bundle of documents," provides a file of information about you and your work—recommendations and so on—that others have supplied.

Basically, your dossier contains the following documents:

- letters of recommendation
- letters that awarded you a scholarship, gave you an academic honor, or acknowledged your community service
- letters that praised your work on the job, notified you of a merit raise, promotion, or recognition ("Employee of the Month")
- your academic transcript(s)

A dossier collects important information about you that prospective employers will want to see to decide whether to interview you. You may ask your placement office to send your dossier to an employer, or employers may request it themselves if you have listed the placement office address on your résumé.

Obtaining Letters of Recommendation

Should You See Your Letters?

You have a legal right to see your recommendation letters, but some employers believe that if candidates read them, their references may be overly complimentary and more inclined to withhold information. Also, some of your references may refuse to write a letter of recommendation if they know you will read it. However, you may feel more comfortable knowing what your recommendation letters contain. But before you make any decisions about seeing your recommendation letters, get the advice of your instructors and placement counselors.

Whom Should You Ask?

Be careful about whom you ask. Whether your recommendation letters are confidential or not, they can sell you or sink your chances, so select your references carefully. Ask the following individuals to be your references and to write enthusiastically about your work qualifications and skills:

- previous employers (even for summer jobs or internships) who commended you and your work
- two or three of your professors who know and like your work, have graded your papers, or have supervised you in fieldwork or laboratory activities
- supervisors who evaluated and praised your work in the military
- community leaders or officials with whom you have worked successfully on civic projects

Recommendations from such individuals, whether in a letter or via comments left on your LinkedIn profile page (see Figure 7.2, pages 246–249), will be regarded as more objective—and more relevant—than letters from friends, neighbors, or members of the clergy.

Whoever you ask, make sure he or she is a strong supporter of yours, someone who has sincerely and consistently complimented your work and encouraged you in your career. Find out by asking if this person is willing to write a strong, enthusiastic letter on your behalf. Stay clear of individuals who are lukewarm about your work or who might be reluctant to recommend you for another reason. Figure 7.3 shows a letter requesting a letter of recommendation.

Should You Ask Your Current Boss?

Asking your current boss can be tricky. If your present employer is already aware that you are looking for work elsewhere (for instance, if your job is temporary or if your contract is about to run out) or you are working at a part-time job, by all means ask for a letter of recommendation. However, if you are employed full time and are looking for professional advancement and/or for a better salary elsewhere, you may not want your current employer to know that you are searching for another job. You may want to speak to a job counselor.

CAREER PORTFOLIOS/WEBFOLIOS

Like dossiers, career portfolios/webfolios play a major role in the job search. The documents they contain work together to support and supplement your résumé. Increasingly, job seekers are providing both a dossier and portfolio/webfolio to prospective employers. Unlike a dossier, which provides information about you and your work that others have written, a portfolio (or **webfolio** if it is submitted electronically) contains documents you have created or produced yourself.

For example, a portfolio would contain samples of your professional work—written or visual (reports, plans, paintings, photos, graphics)—to show to prospective employers.

Following is a sampling of the kinds of documents you might include in your career portfolio/webfolio.

- a mission statement (two or three paragraphs) that outlines your career goals and work skills
- an additional copy of your résumé
- scans of diplomas, certificates, licenses, internships, papers
- copies of awards (academic and job-related), promotion letters, or commendations (e.g., for protecting the environment)
- impressive examples of written work you did for college courses, such as reports or proposals (include any positive comments provided by instructors)
- newspaper or newsletter stories about your academic, community, or on-the-job successes
- pertinent examples of media presentations you have done, PowerPoint or Prezi presentations you have created, or a USB flash drive containing the files for a website you designed
- a list of your references with contact information

FIGURE 7.3 Request for a Letter of Recommendation

TADEUS MAJESKI • 5432 South Kenneth Avenue • Chicago, IL 60651

312-555-7733 tmajeski@gatenet.com www.facebook.com/tadeusmajeski @TadeusMajeski

March 29, 2016

Mr. Sonny Butler, Manager
Empire Supermarket
4000 West 79th Street
Chicago, IL 66052-4300

Dear Mr. Butler:

I was employed at your store from September 2014 through August 2015. During my employment, I worked part time as a stock clerk and relief cashier, and during the summer I was a full-time employee in the produce department, helping to fill in while Bill Dirksen and Vivian Ho were on vacation.

I enjoyed my work at Empire, and I learned much about the latest inventory tracking systems such as Blue Link ERP, ordering stock, calculating and helping to prevent merchandise shrinkage, and assisting customers.

This May, I will receive my A.A. degree from Moraine Valley Community College in retail merchandising and I have already begun preparing for my job search for a position in retail sales. Would you be willing to write an enthusiastic letter of recommendation for me describing what you regard as my greatest strengths as one of your employees? Having your endorsement would be a great help to me.

To assist you, I can send you a letter of recommendation form from the Placement Office at Moraine Valley via either email or regular mail. Your letter would then become part of my permanent placement file.

I look forward to hearing from you. I thought you might like to see the enclosed résumé, which shows what I have been doing since I left Empire. Thank you for the opportunity to work at your store.

Sincerely yours,

Tadeus Majeski

Tadeus Majeski

Encl.: Résumé

Student-designed letterhead

Reviews employment history

Emphasizes skills learned on the job

Diplomatically requests strong letter of recommendation

Explains how letter will be used

Encloses copy of résumé and thanks reader

What Not to Include in a Career Portfolio/Webfolio

Be highly selective about what you include. Never include anything that would contradict or call into question information in your résumé or letter of application. Exclude the following types of documents from your career portfolio/webfolio:

- documents or scans of documents that show your memberships in clubs, fraternities/sororities, sports teams, and so on, unless directly relevant to the job (e.g., applying for a job at the national office for Sigma Sigma Kappa or with the Professional Golfers Association of America)
- links to personal webpages, including Facebook, Twitter, and Pinterest pages, if these contain inappropriate personal information or portray you as unprofessional; see "Promoting Your Best Image-Some Do's and Don'ts," pages 245–250).
- pictures of your family, friends, pets, and the like
- scans of newspaper or newsletter stories about you that are not directly related to your job search, such as your winning a cruise or playing on a bowling team

Career Portfolio/Webfolio Formats

When you provide a prospective employer with your career portfolio, you can either mail it or provide it electronically via hyperlinks as a webfolio. If you submit a hard-copy portfolio, always make high-quality copies of each document. Never include originals. If you provide a webfolio, make sure that any images posted are at the highest resolution possible (see "Ineffective Visuals: What *Not* to Do," page 406). In addition, you can add hyperlinks to parts of your webfolio on your résumé, as Anthony Jones does in Figure 7.4 (page 258), making it easy for a job recruiter or prospective employer to find evidence of your qualifications.

PREPARING A RÉSUMÉ

The résumé, sometimes called a **curriculum vitae** (*cv*), may be the most important document you prepare for your job search. It merits doing some careful homework. A résumé is not your life history or your emotional autobiography, nor is it a transcript of your college work. It is a factual and concise summary of your qualifications, convincing a prospective employer that you have the education and experience to do the job you are applying for. Regard your résumé as a persuasive ad for your professional qualifications. It is a billboard advertising you.

What you include—your key details, the wording, the ordering of information, and the formatting—are all vital to your campaign to sell yourself and land an interview. Employers want to see the most crucial and current details about your qualifications quickly. Accordingly, keep your print résumé short (preferably one page, never longer than two) and hard-hitting. The same thing goes for your digital résumés. See Figures 7.10 to 7.13 for examples of digital résumés. Everything on your résumé needs to convince an employer you have the exact skills and background he or she is looking for.

What Employers Like to See in a Résumé

Prospective employers will judge you and your work by your résumé; it is their first view of you and your qualifications. They will expect an applicant's résumé to be

- **Honest.** Be truthful about your qualifications—your education, experience, and skills. Distorting, exaggerating, or falsifying information about yourself in your résumé is unethical and could cost you the job. If you were a clerical assistant to an attorney, don't describe yourself as a paralegal. Always tell the truth.
- **Attractive.** The document should be pleasing to the eye, with generous margins, consistent punctuation, and suitable spacing, typeface, and use of boldface and italics; it shows you have a sense of proportion and document design and that you are visually smart. The print should be clear and dark, not faded, on high-quality paper, and not so small it would be hard to read. Do not use gimmicks like clip art or excessive capitalization.
- **Carefully organized.** Arrange information so that it is easy to follow, logical, and consistent; the way you organize information shows you have the ability to process information and to summarize. Employers prize analytical thinking. Include plenty of white space to separate major sections, and use bullets to list and highlight key facts within each section, as in Figures 7.4 and 7.5 (pages 258–259).
- **Concise.** Make sure your résumé is to the point. Generally, keep your résumé to one page, as in Figure 7.4. However, depending on your education or your job experience, you may want to include a second page. Résumés are written in short sentences that omit "I" and that use action-packed verbs, such as those listed in Table 7.3 on page 256.
- **Accurate.** Make sure your grammar, spelling, dates, names, titles, and programs are correct; typos, inconsistencies, and math errors say you didn't check your facts and figures.
- **Current.** All information needs to be up-to-date and documented, with no gaps or sketchy areas about previous jobs or education. Missing or incorrect dates or leaving key information out are red flags.
- **Relevant.** The information on your résumé must be appropriate for the job description and level, documenting that you have the necessary education and experience, and confirm that you can be an effective team player. Tailor your résumé using keywords from the job posting to help your résumé stand out if it is scanned by an applicant tracking system (ATS); see "Things to Keep in Mind When Preparing a Digital Résumé," page 272.
- **Quantifiable.** Emphasize your accomplishments, not just responsibilities. Include specifics about how much revenue you generated for an employer (or how much money you saved, or how many times you performed a complex job).

Your goal is to prepare a résumé that shows the employer you possess the sought-after job skills. A résumé that is unattractive, difficult to follow, poorly written, filled with typos and spelling mistakes or that is sketchy, vague, boastful, or not relevant for the prospective employer's needs will not make the first cut.

Create Several Versions of Your Résumé

It is critical to prepare several versions of your résumé and then adapt each one you send out to the specific job skills a prospective employer is looking for. It pays to customize your résumé based on information you may have gathered about the job

TABLE 7.3 Action Verbs to Use in Your Résumé

accommodated	converted	generated	operated	served
accomplished	coordinated	guided	organized	settled
achieved	created	handled	oversaw	sold
acquired	customized	headed	performed	solved
adapted	dealt in	hired	persuaded	spearheaded
adjusted	delivered	implemented	planned	streamlined
administered	designed	improved	posted	succeeded
advocated	determined	increased	prepared	supervised
analyzed	developed	informed	presented	surveyed
applied	devised	initiated	programmed	taught
appraised	directed	inspected	protected	teamed up
arranged	discovered	installed	provided	tested
assembled	drafted	instituted	purchased	tracked
assisted	earned	instructed	ranked	trained
attended	economized	interpreted	reappraised	transcribed
awarded	edited	judged	received	translated
bridged	elected	launched	reconciled	tutored
budgeted	enforced	learned	recorded	updated
built	established	led	reduced	upgraded
calculated	estimated	logged	re-evaluated	validated
chaired	evaluated	maintained	reported	verified
coached	excelled	managed	researched	visualized
collaborated	expanded	mapped	restored	volunteered
collected	explored	mastered	reviewed	weighed
communicated	fashioned	met	saved	wired
compiled	figured	monitored	scanned	won
completed	formulated	motivated	scheduled	worked
composed	fostered	navigated	searched	wrote
computed	founded	negotiated	secured	
conducted	fulfilled	observed	selected	

from researching the company (see "Preparing for an Interview, pages 288–290), through networking (see "LinkedIn," pages 244–245), and from analyzing and using keywords both common to the industry and included by the employer in the job description. Keywords in your résumé are critical to having it stand out. Following the process detailed in the next section will help you prepare any résumé.

The Process of Writing Your Résumé

To write an effective résumé, ask the following important questions:

1. What classes did you excel in?
2. What papers, reports, surveys, or presentations earned you your highest grades?
3. What computer skills have you mastered—languages, software, e-commerce, blog or website design, collaborative online editing?
4. What other technical skills or professional licenses and certifications have you earned?
5. What language(s) do you speak, write, or have limited proficiency in?
6. What relevant jobs have you had? For how long and where? What were your primary duties and accomplishments? Did you supervise other employees?
7. How did you open or expand a business market? Increase a customer base? Improve customer feedback?
8. What did you do to earn a raise or a promotion in a previous or current job?
9. Do you work well with people? What skills do you possess as a member of a team working toward a common job goal (e.g., finishing a report)?
10. Can you organize complicated tasks or identify and solve problems quickly?
11. Have you had experiences or responsibilities managing money—collecting fees or receipts, preparing payrolls, conducting nightly audits, and so on?
12. Have you won any awards or scholarships or received a commendation or other recognition at work?

Pay special attention to your four or five most significant, job-worthy strengths, and work especially hard on listing them concisely and persuasively.

Although not everything you have done relates directly to a particular job, indicate how your achievements are relevant to the employer's overall needs. For example, supervising staff in a convenience store points to your ability to perform the same duties in another business context.

Balancing Education and Experience

If you have years of experience, don't flood your prospective employer with too many details. You cannot possibly include every detail of your jobs for the last ten or twenty years.

- Emphasize only those skills and positions most likely to earn you the job.
- Eliminate early jobs that do not relate to your present employment search.
- Combine and condense skills acquired over many years and jobs.
- Include relevant military schools or service.

Figures 7.6 (page 262) and 7.7 (page 267) show the résumés of two individuals who have a great deal of experience to offer prospective employers.

Many job candidates who have spent most of their lives in school are faced with the other extreme: not having much job experience to list. The worst thing to do is to write "None" for experience. Any part-time, summer, or other seasonal jobs, as well as volunteer work, apprenticeships, workshops attended, and internships, show an employer that you are responsible and knowledgeable about the obligations of being an employee. Figure 7.4 contains a résumé from Anthony Jones, a student with little job experience; Figure 7.5 shows María López's résumé, a student with a few years of experience.

FIGURE 7.4 Résumé from a Student with Little Job Experience

Headlines major achievements and gives contact details, including social media and professional networking sites

Anthony H. Jones

WEBSITE DEVELOPER
DESIGNER
GRAPHIC ARTIST

73 Allenwood Boulevard   www.plat.com/users/ajones/resume.html
Santa Rosa, CA 95401-1074   f www.facebook.com/anthonyhjones
707-555-6390   @AnthonyHJones
ajdesigner@plat.com   in www.linkedin.com/pub/anthony-h-jones

CAREER OBJECTIVE

Offers precise, convincing objective

Full-time position as a layout artist with a commercial publishing house with responsibilities including website design, page composition, and graphics creation.

EDUCATION

Starts with most important qualification— education

Santa Rosa Junior College, 2014–2016, A.S. degree to be awarded in 2016

Dean's List in 2015; GPA 3.25

Major: Commercial Graphics Illustration, with specialty in design layout

Related courses included:

Lists relevant software programs studied

- Digital Photography
- Graphics Programs: Adobe Illustrator CC, Adobe Dreamweaver CC, CorelDRAW Graphics Suite X7, Adobe Photoshop CC
- Desktop Publishing: Adobe InDesign CC, QuarkXPress 2015

Stresses job-related activities of internship

Internship, 2015–2016, McAdam Publishers

Major projects included:

- Assisting layout editors with page composition and photo archiving.
- Writing detailed assessment reports on digital photography, designs, and artwork used in *Living in Sonoma County* (www.sonomacounty.com) and *Real Estate in Sonoma County* (www.resc.net) magazines.

EXPERIENCE

Includes part-time work experience

Salesperson (part-time), 2013–2015, Buchman's Department Store

Serving customers in sporting goods and appliance departments, designing custom window displays each month for the main entrance, and helping to manage the inventory database.

COMPUTER SKILLS

Again demonstrates skills in graphic and web design software; names programs to maximize the number of keyword "hits"

Adobe InDesign CC, QuarkXPress 2015, Adobe Illustrator CC, Adobe Dreamweaver CC, XML, HTML, CorelDRAW Graphics Suite X7, Adobe Photoshop CC

RELATED ACTIVITIES

Relevant volunteer work

Designed website and developed and maintained a Facebook page for the Santa Rosa Humane Society's 2015 fund drive; helped raise $5,600.

WEBFOLIO

Webfolio documents accomplishments

A webfolio containing designs, photographs, illustrations, graphics, and graphic designs is available at www.plat.com/users/ajones/resume.html

FIGURE 7.5 Résumé from a Student with Some Job Experience

MARÍA LÓPEZ

1725 Brooke Street
Miami, FL 32701-2121
(305) 555-3429
mlopez@gmail.com
 www.linkedin.com/pub/maria-lopez

Provides easy-to-find contact information, including LinkedIn profile

CAREER OBJECTIVE

Position working in dental clinic specializing in pedodontics.

Objective tailored for a particular employer

QUALIFICATIONS

- Will be certified by the Dental Assisting National Board (DANB) as of June 2, 2016.
- Completed final project for dental hygiene major on proper nutrition and dental health for preschoolers
- Worked on a pediatric medical unit for over two years.
- Experienced with procedures and instruments used with oral prophylaxis techniques
- Bilingual in Spanish

Emphasizes skills that benefit employer and patients

EDUCATION

A.S. in Dental Hygiene, Miami-Dade Community College
August 2014–May 2016
GPA: 3.58 (Ranked in the top 10 percent of class)

Major courses:

- Oral pathology
- Dental materials and specialties
- Periodontics
- Community dental health

Lists courses required for the job

Minor: Psychology (12 hours in child and adolescent psychology)

St. Francis Hospital
(Miami Beach, FL) April 2012–July 2014
Unit assistant on pediatric unit. Maintained medical supply levels using inventory tracking software, keyboarded all medical records into hospital-wide database, transcribed medical orders and surgical notes, greeted and assisted visitors

Highlights previous job responsibilities in health care setting

Murphy Construction Company
(Miami, FL) June 2011–April 2012
Office assistant-receptionist. Did data entry and filing, and assisted with billing and creating project schedules in a small office (5 employees)

PROFESSIONAL MEMBERSHIPS

American Dental Hygienists Association (ADHA)
National Dental Hygienists Association (NDHA)

Uses both the name and the acronym for the professional associations, to increase keyword "hits"

COMPUTER SKILLS

DentiMax Advanced, Dentrix Ascend, Maxident 6, Microsoft Office 365, Filemaker Pro 13

Includes career-relevant computer skills

LANGUAGE SKILLS

Fluent in Spanish

Calls attention to bilingual skills of value to employer and patients

What to Exclude from a Résumé

Knowing what to exclude from a résumé is as important as knowing what to include. Because federal employment laws prohibit discrimination on the basis of age, sex, race, national origin, religion, marital status, or disability, do not include such information on your résumé. Here are some other details best left off your résumé:

- salary demands, expectations, or ranges
- preferences for work schedules, days off, or overtime
- comments about fringe benefits
- travel restrictions
- reasons for leaving your previous job
- your photograph (unless you are applying for a modeling or acting job)
- your Social Security number
- information about your family, spouse, or children
- height, weight, hair or eye color
- sexual orientation, religious and political affiliations
- hobbies, interests (unless relevant to the job you are seeking)

Save comments about salary and schedules for your interview (see "Going to an Interview," pages 288–294). The résumé should be written to earn you that interview.

Parts of a Résumé

As with memos, letters, and reports, most résumés consist of specific parts shown in boldface headings on the following pages. These parts—contact information, career objective, qualifications, credentials (education and experience), related skills and achievements, and references/portfolios—are critical building blocks to consider for any résumé.

Contact Information

At the top of your résumé, provide your full name (do not use a nickname), address including your zip code, home and mobile telephone numbers, and email address. If your academic address is different from your home address, list and identify both. The contact information can either be centered, flush left or right, or some combination of these approaches (note how María López uses a combination of flush left and right in Figure 7.5). Avoid unprofessional email addresses such as toughguy @netfield.com or sassygirl@techscape.com. Make sure your voice mail message is straightforward and professional as well. You may also want to include links to a Facebook, Twitter, or LinkedIn professional profile (see "Promoting Your Best Image—Some Do's and Don'ts," pages 245–250). And don't forget to include a URL for your website or webfolio (see "Career Portfolios/Webfolios," pages 252–254).

Career Objective

One of the first things a prospective employer will read is your career objective. It specifies the job you are looking for, and in what ways you are qualified to hold it. Create an objective that precisely dovetails with the prospective employer's requirements. Incorporating precise keywords from the job listing/description the employer posts can be crucial in getting your résumé past the applicant tracking systems that many companies now use.

Career objective statements should be the result of your focused self-evaluation and your assessment of the job market. Depending on your background and the types of jobs you are qualified for, you might formulate many different career or employment objectives to use with different versions of your résumé as you apply for various positions. Your career objective must be tailored for the particular job you are applying for. María López, for example, adapted her career objective listed in Figure 7.5 when she applied for jobs at dental offices where general dentistry or cosmetic dentistry was emphasized.

To write an effective career objective statement, ask yourself five basic questions:

1. What kind of job do I want?
2. What kind of job am I qualified for?
3. What capabilities do I possess?
4. What kinds of skills do I want to learn?
5. What keywords from the employer's job listing should I include?

Avoid trite, vague, or self-centered goals, such as "Looking for professional advancement," or "Seeking high-paying job that brings personal satisfaction." These are so general, a prospective employer may conclude you don't have the background to do the job. Compare the vague objectives on the left with the more precise ones on the right.

Unfocused	Focused
Job in sales to use my aggressive skills in expanding markets	Regional sales representative using my proven skills in e-commerce and communication to develop and expand a customer base.
Full-time position as staff nurse	Full-time position as staff nurse on cardiac step-down unit to offer excellent primary care nursing and patient/family teaching.
Position in cable industry	Position as part of a service team to provide efficient cable repair service.

© 2017 Cengage Learning

While inclusion of the career objective is important in many employment situations, some job counselors advise leaving an objective off a résumé if you either need the space or have lots of education or work experience you need to include.

Credentials

The order of the next two categories—Education and Experience—can vary. Generally, if you have lots of work experience, list it first, as Anna Cassetti does by including her realtor license information at the top of her résumé in Figure 7.6 (page 262). However, if you are a recent graduate short on job experience, list education first, as Anthony Jones does in Figure 7.4. María López (Figure 7.5) also decided to place her education before her job experience because the job she was applying for required the formal training she recently received at Miami-Dade Community College.

FIGURE 7.6 Résumé from an Individual with Significant Job Experience

Provides home, work, and social networking contact information, as well as her realtor license number

ANNA C. CASSETTI
6457 Blackstone Avenue
Fort Worth, TX 76321-6733
(817) 555-5657
acassetti@netdor.com

Licensed Texas Realtor—756a2737
MacMurray Real Estate
1700 Ross Boulevard
Haltom City, TX 77320-1700
(817) 555-7211

www.facebook.com/annaccassetti • **@AnnaCassetti**
www.linkedin.com/pub/anna-c-cassetti

OBJECTIVE
Full-time sales position with large real estate office in the Phoenix or Tucson area with opportunities to use proven skills in real estate appraisal and tax counseling.

Begins with the most important job qualification first—experience

EXPERIENCE
MacMurray Real Estate, Haltom City, Texas, 2012–present
Real estate agent. Excelled in small suburban office (five salespersons plus broker) with limited listings; sold individually over $3 million in residential property; appraised both residential and commercial listings.

Job history focuses on sales achievements, promotion, and responsibilities

Dallman Federal Savings and Loan, Inc., Fort Worth, Texas 2005–2011
Chief Teller. Responsible for supervising, training, and coordinating activities of six full-time and two part-time tellers. Promoted to Chief Teller, Mar. 2007, with bonus.

H&R Block, Westover Hills, Texas, 2005 (Jan.–Apr.)
Tax Consultant. Prepared personal and business returns.

Cruckshank's Hardware Store, Fort Worth, Texas, 2002–2004
Salesperson.

Gives related military experience

U.S. Navy, 1995–2001
Honorably discharged with rank of Petty Officer, Third Class.
Served as stores manager; earned three commendations.

Documents education; cites specific skills

EDUCATION
Texas Christian University, Fort Worth, Texas, 2004–2009
Awarded B.S. degree in Real Estate Management. Completed thirty-three hours in business and real estate courses with a concentration in finance, appraising, and property management. Also took twelve hours in programming and Web design. Wrote reports on appraisal procedures as part of supervised training program.

Includes computer and communication skills

H&R Block, Westover Hills, Texas, 2004 (Sept.–Dec.)
Earned diploma in Basic Income Tax Preparation after completing ten-week course.

U.S. Navy, 1995–2001
Attended U.S. Navy's Supply Management School
Applied principles of stores management at Newport Naval Base

Provides examples of community service

COMMUNITY SERVICE
Chair, Financial Committee, Grace Presbyterian Church, Fort Worth
Adviser, Junior Achievement

Education Begin with your most recent education first, then list everything significant since high school. For each school, give the name, the dates you attended, and the degree, diploma, or certificate you earned. Don't overlook relevant military experience or major training programs (EMT, court reporter), institutes, internships, or workshops you have completed. Because he had little relevant work experience, Anthony Jones emphasized his internship in his résumé (Figure 7.4).

Remember, however, that a résumé is not a transcript. Simply listing a series of required courses will not set you apart from hundreds of other applicants taking similar courses across the country. Focus on courses that have specifically prepared you for the job. Avoid vague titles such as Science 203 or Nursing IV. Instead, concentrate on describing the specific skills you learned.

> 30 hours in planning and development courses specializing in transportation, land use, and community facilities; 12 hours in field methods of gathering, interpreting, and describing survey data in reports.

> Completed 28 hours in major courses in business marketing, management, and materials in addition to 12 hours in information science, including web design and publishing.

Mention any special projects, experiments, or reports that bear directly on the job you are seeking. Note how María López (Figure 7.5) briefly references her major project on preschoolers' nutrition and dental health, a topic sure to interest her potential employer.

List your grade point average (GPA) only if it is 3.0 or above; otherwise, indicate your GPA in just your major or during your last year or term, again if it is above 3.0.

Experience Your job history is the key category for many employers. It shows them that you have held jobs before and that you are responsible. Here are some guidelines about listing your experience.

1. Begin with your most recent position and work backward—in reverse chronological order. List the company or agency name, location (city and state), your job title, and dates of employment. Do not mention why you left a job.

2. For each job or activity, provide a short description (one or two lines) of your duties and achievements. Quantify your achievements whenever possible; for example, you helped set up a chemistry laboratory and established protocols that reduced the breakage rate of glasswear by 45 percent. Instead of simply saying you were an administrative assistant, indicate that you maintained the company's social media presence, prepared schedules for part-time help in an office of twenty-five people, or assisted the manager in preparing minutes, accounts, and presentations.

3. Prospective employers are interested in your leadership abilities, teamwork, financial responsibility, tact in dealing with the public, and communications skills. Always emphasize any responsibilities that involve:

- handling money (such as assisting customers, filing insurance claims, or preparing payrolls)
- managing other employees

- working with customer accounts, services, and programs
- writing letters and reports

They will also be favorably impressed by earning or saving money for your company, commendations like "Earned Highest Sales Record," recognized for "Exceptional Clinical Care" in serving geriatric patients, and promotions you have earned.

4. Include any relevant volunteer work you have done, as Anthony Jones did for an animal shelter in Figure 7.4. Note how Dora Cooper Bolger's volunteer work translates into marketing skills an employer wants to see in a prospective employee's résumé in Figure 7.7 (page 267).

5. You might also note community or civic service, or any relevant skills you developed as a full-time parent or caregiver for a family member or friend. Anna Cassetti noted her involvement with her local church and with Junior Achievement (Figure 7.6). Dora Cooper Bolger, in her résumé in Figure 7.7 (page 267) skillfully related her role as a full-time parent and community organizer to the job she seeks.

Related Skills and Achievements

Not every résumé will have this section, but the following are all employer-friendly things to include:

- certificates or licenses you hold
- memberships in professional associations (e.g., American Society of Safety Engineers, National Black Law Students Association, National Hispanic Business Association, Texas Executive Women)
- memberships in community service groups (e.g., Habitat for Humanity, Salvation Army, Big Brothers/Big Sisters); list any offices you held
- second or third languages you speak or write

Computer Skills

Knowledge of both common (such as Microsoft Office) and specialized software packages (such as Adobe InDesign CC in Figure 7.4 or Maxident 6 in Figure 7.5) is extremely valuable in the job market. Note how Anthony Jones and María López both inform prospective employers about their relevant technical competencies in Figures 7.4 and 7.5.

Honors/Awards

List any civic honors (mayor's award, community service award, cultural harmony award) and academic honors (dean's list, department awards, scholarships, grants, honorable mentions), and military awards or medals you have won. Memberships in honor societies in your major and technical/business associations also demonstrate that you are professionally accomplished and active.

References

You can list "References available upon request," but employers generally assume these will be readily available. Never list the names of your references on a résumé. Instead, prepare a list of references, either to forward to an employer upon request or to bring with you to an interview (see "Going to an Interview," pages 288–294).

Here is where networking can help you. Ask your instructors, previous employer, or individuals who have supervised your work. Give the person providing the reference a copy of your current résumé, as Tadeus Majeski did in Figure 7.3. But always ask for permission before you list an individual as a reference. You could jeopardize your chances for a job if a prospective employer called one of your references and that person did not even know you were looking for a job or, worse yet, said that you did not have the courtesy to ask to use his or her name.

Organizing Your Résumé

There are two primary ways to organize your résumé: chronologically and by function or skill area. You may want to prepare two versions of your résumé—one chronological and one by function or skill area—to see which sells your experience and your talents better. Don't hesitate to seek the advice of a placement counselor or instructor about which may work best for you.

Chronologically

The résumés in Figures 7.4 and 7.5 are organized chronologically, with most recent education and experience listed first. This is the traditional (and generally more common) way to organize a résumé. It is straightforward and easy to read, and employers find it acceptable. The chronological sequence works especially well when you can show a clear continuity toward progress in your career through your employment and schoolwork or when you want to apply for a similar job with another company.

A chronological résumé is also appropriate for students who want to emphasize recent educational achievements.

By Function or Skill Area

Depending on your experiences and accomplishments, you might organize your résumé according to function or skill area. According to this plan, you would *not* list your information chronologically in the categories "Experience" and "Education." Instead, you would sort your achievements and abilities—whether from course work, jobs, extracurricular activities, military service, or technical skills—into two to four key skill areas, such as

- Sales/Customer Service
- Public Relations
- Training/Teaching
- Management
- Safety/Security
- Counseling
- Leadership
- Communication
- Network Operations
- People Skills
- Teamwork
- Troubleshooting
- Opening New Markets
- Multicultural Experiences
- Information Technology
- Problem-Solving Skills

Under each area you would list three to five points illustrating your achievements in that area. Functional and skills résumés are often called **bullet résumés** because they itemize the candidate's main strengths in bulleted lists. Some employers prefer the bullet résumé because they can skim the candidate's list of qualifications in a few seconds.

The following individuals would probably benefit from organizing their résumés by function or skill area instead of chronologically:

- nontraditional students who have had diverse job experiences
- people who are changing professions
- individuals who have changed jobs frequently
- ex-military personnel reentering the civilian marketplace

Note Dora Cooper Bolger's profitable use of a skills résumé format in Figure 7.7. She delayed attending college for several years to be a full-time parent, yet she uses the experiences she acquired during those years to her advantage in her résumé organized by "Skills." No gap of ten years interrupts her valuable marketable skills.

Preparing a Functional or Skills Résumé When you prepare a functional or skills résumé, start with your contact information and career objective, just as in a chronological résumé. To find the best two or three functional areas to include, use the prewriting strategies (especially clustering and brainstorming) discussed in Chapter 2 (see "Planning," pages 46–49).

After you discover and suitably revise the information to be included in your categories, briefly list your educational and work experiences, as Dora Cooper Bolger in Figure 7.7 and Anna Cassetti in Figure 7.8 (page 268) do.

TRANSITIONING INTO THE CIVILIAN WORKFORCE

Transitioning from the military into the civilian workforce is not easy. It may require you to greatly modify or adapt your military training or even to change careers altogether. Above all, you will have to ask yourself questions such as those in "Analyzing Your Strengths and Restricting Your Job Search" on pages 237–238 to find out what skills you learned in the service—technical, communication, interpersonal—that would readily transfer to the cvilian job market. Listing your skills will help you focus on the various kinds of jobs for which you can apply. Like other job seekers, you need to take advantage of networking sites such as LinkedIn and Facebook to find jobs and to make contacts. But also consult the following sites created to assist veterans in finding civilian employment.

- **MyNextMove.org**: directory of civilian occupations based on specific military job and experience
- **NRD.gov**: the National Resource Directory's Veterans Job Bank lists postings from companies looking to hire veterans
- **www.ebenefits.va.gov/ebenefits/jobs**: Links on this page include a skills translator that helps find transferable civilian skills for your military experience.
- **Military.com**: resources for transitioning to civilian life
- **veterans.linkedin.com**: networking microsite for veterans with tips, tools, and webinars
- **SimplyHired.com**; **BranchOut.com**; **VetCentral.us.jobs**; and **VetJobs .com**: jobs sites tagging positions specifically for veterans

FIGURE 7.7 Dora Cooper Bolger's Résumé Organized by Skills Areas

DORA COOPER BOLGER

 www.facebook.com/doracooperbolger
 www.linkedin.com/pub/dora-c-bolger

1215 Lakeview Avenue
Westhampton, MI 46532
Cell: 616-555-4773
dcbplanner@gmail.com

Objective	Seek full-time position as public affairs officer to promote the goals of a health care, educational, or charitable organization

Skills

Organizational Communication
- Delivered 24 presentations to civic groups on educational issues
- Recorded minutes and helped formulate agenda as president of large, local PTA (800 members) for past 6½ years
- Possess excellent computer skills in Microsoft Office 365 and Microsoft Dynamics CRM.
- Established and maintained the Facebook and Twitter accounts and wrote blog posts for Teens in Trouble.

Financial
- Spearheaded 3 major fund-raising drives (total of $225,000 collected)
- Prepared and implemented large family budget (3 children, 8 foster children)
- Planned budget, Foster Parents' Association
- Served as financial secretary, Faith United Methodist Church, for 4 years

Administrative
- Organized volunteers for National Kidney Foundation (2012–2016)
- Established and oversaw neighborhood carpool (17 drivers; more than 70 children) for 7 years
- Coordinated after-school tutoring program for Teens in Trouble; president since 2003
- Vice-president, Foster Parents' Association, 2014

Honors   "Volunteer of the Year," (2015) Michigan Child Placement Agency

Education   Metropolitan Community College, A.A., 2012
Mid-Michigan College, B.S., expected May 2016
Major: Public Administration; Minor: Psychology
GPA: 3.55 | Dean's List: 2014–2016

Work Experience   Secretary, 2004–2011 (full- and part-time): Merrymount Plastics; Foley and Wasson; Westhampton Health Dept.; G & K Electric

Restricted objective

Aptly features skill areas before education

Links achievements from volunteer and home-based activities most important to employer

Chooses strong, active verbs to convey image of a results-oriented professional

Places education after skills; includes major and related minor plus strong GPA

Excludes details about least recent jobs

© 2017 Cengage Learning

FIGURE 7.8 Anna Cassetti's Résumé Organized by Function or Skill Areas

---

ANNA C. CASSETTI
6457 Blackstone Avenue
Fort Worth, TX 76321-6733
(817) 555-5657
acassetti@netdor.com

Licensed Texas Realtor—756a2737
MacMurray Real Estate
1700 Ross Boulevard
Haltom City, TX 77320-1700
(817) 555-7211

www.facebook.com/annaccassetti • **@AnnaCassetti**
www.linkedin.com/pub/anna-c-cassetti

Begins with a clear and focused objective

OBJECTIVE
Sales position with real estate office in the Phoenix or Tucson area with opportunities to use proven skills in property appraisals and tax counseling

Groups accomplishments into three relevant and marketable skills areas for prospective employer

SALES/FINANCIAL
- Sold over $3 million of residential property (2012–present)
- Served as a tax consultant with special interest in real estate sales/market conditions
- Performed general banking procedures as chief teller
- Ordered and maintained ship's stores, U.S. Navy

PUBLIC RELATIONS
- Helped clients select appropriate property for their needs and income
- Counseled commercial and individual clients about taxes/benefits/liabilities
- Supervised, trained, and coordinated the activities of six full-time and two part-time bank tellers
- Commended for rapport in assisting customers with their banking needs

Uses bullets, strong verbs, and specific examples

COMMUNICATION
- Prepared detailed real estate appraisals
- Wrote in-depth business reports on appraisal procedures, property management problems, and banking policies affecting real estate transactions
- Achieved proficiency in CorpSheet and other spreadsheet programs
- Conducted small group training and sales sessions

Emphasizes written and oral skills

Stresses educational preparation after skills

EDUCATION
- B.S. in Real Estate Management, 2009, Texas Christian University, Fort Worth, Texas Advanced course work in business and real estate
- Diploma, Basic Income Tax Preparation, 2004, H&R Block, Westover Hills, Texas

EXPERIENCE
MacMurray Real Estate, Haltom City, Texas
2012–present; sales agent

Dallman Federal Savings and Loan, Inc., Fort Worth, Texas
2005–2011; Chief Teller

H&R Block, Westover Hills, Texas
2005 (Jan.–Apr.); consultant, tax preparer

Cruckshank's Hardware Store, Fort Worth, Texas
2002–2004; salesperson

Demonstrates professional commitment and successes

U.S. Navy, 1995–2001
Stores manager, 1998–2001; honorably discharged with rank of Petty Officer, Third Class

- www.ebenefits.va.gov/ebenefits/jobs: Links on this page include a skills translator that helps find transferable civilian skills for military experience.
- FedsHireVets.com: Run by the U.S. Office of Personnel Management, site contains federal veteran employment information and resources.

Veterans bring a wealth of experiences and competencies that can improve their chances of landing a job in the civilian sector. The skills listed here, common to all branches and divisions of the armed services, appeal to employers who want to hire individuals who possess a strong work ethic and a sense of duty and loyalty that the military stresses. Capitalize on these when preparing your résumé and drafting your letter of application:

1. Offering leadership by training and example
2. Excelling in building teamwork and efficiency
3. Meeting deadlines under stressful conditions
4. Working respectfully with individuals from diverse cultures
5. Adapting quickly to change
6. Paying attention to detail
7. Troubleshooting and solving problems quickly
8. Receiving specialized technical training
9. Managing budgets, equipment, supplies and other resources
10. Maintaining equipment
11. Exhibiting self-discipline
12. Being physically fit

Illustrate your accomplishments in these categories with specific examples when you write your résumé or letter of application. The more you match your military competencies to your employer's needs, the better your chances of landing an interview. Make your military service work for you in the civilian sector. See how Sandy Meagher did this in Figure 7.9 (page 270).

Using a Civilian Résumé Format, Language, and Context

While it is to your advantage to showcase the experience and technical skills you gained in the service, keep in mind that not all military duties automatically or even easily translate into civilian ones. You cannot prepare a résumé for a civilian boss the way you would your superior in the service. Study Figure 7.9, which contains a résumé prepared by a veteran, Sandy Meagher, who was discharged after eight years of service in the Marine Corps. As you prepare your civilian résumé, follow these guidelines:

1. Complete the Veterans Preference Document, and indicate that you have done so at the top of your résumé so that a prospective employer knows about your background, as Sandy Meagher has done in Figure 7.9.
2. When listing contact information, do not refer to yourself by your military rank, for example, Lance Cpl. Joseph Johns; Spec. E-3 Cathy Cookeston.
3. Avoid military abbreviations, and acronyms (Sitrep, FOB, LAV, MOS/MUC) that a civilian employer might not understand.
4. Provide a career objective consistent with the civilian job for which you are applying.
5. Describe your military job(s) in terms that an employer will easily understand. Rather than indicating you were a 1A2X1, simply say you were a cargo manager.

FIGURE 7.9 Sandy Meagher's Résumé Showing Transition from Military Service to Civilian Employment

Easy to see contact information

Sandy Meagher

301 65th St., Kansas City, KS 66083 • (703) 555-4309
sandy.meagher@gmail.com • [in] www.linkedin.com/pub/sandy-meagher

Completed Veterans Preference Document

Free from military jargon

Objective
A position in maintenance/vehicle repair for an urban mass transit system

Uses four skill areas thattransfer military accomplishments to civilian workforce

Supervising/Training
• Supervised/managed staff of 9 mechanics and transportation technicians
• Performed high-quality inspections on military wheeled and track vehicles
• Helped coordinate and maintain a "just-in-time" inventory of parts and products
   Received high ratings (96%) for unit efficiency and team building

Technical
• Fully trained mechanic on military wheeled and track vehicles
• Operated state-of-the-art diagnostic technologies equipment
• Responsible for both routine and extended vehicle/equipment repairs

Helpfully organized with bulleted items

Recordkeeping/Communications
• Monitored administrative actions regarding staff (finance, work schedules, etc.)
• Initiated and oversaw ordering and inventorying parts and products
• Maintained detailed records on vehicles serviced from start to finish

Chose effective strong verbs

Safety and Security
• Coordinated safety checks for motor pool and safety drills for staff
• Minimized shop environmental hazards by enforcing strong safety standards
• Decreased loss of parts/supplies by adhering to strict security codes

Education
A.S. Garden City Community College, 2016
U.S. Army, Wheeled Vehicle Mechanic, Track Vehicle Repairer, Basic
Non-Commissioned Officers School

Lists military honors to show dedication and service commitments

U.S. Decorations/Badges
Afghanistan Campaign Medal
Army Achievement Medal
Meritorious Service Medal

Employment
Walmart Auto Repair Technician, Kansas City, MO 2005–2006
U.S. Army, 2007–2015, Honorably discharged with rank of Sergeant First Class (E-5)
   Fort Riley, Kansas, 2007–2010
   Fort Benning, Georgia, 2011–2014
   Tour in Afghanistan, 2014–2015

6. Whether you use a chronological or functional résumé depends on the types of jobs you did in the military. If the job you performed involved immediately transferable skills and competencies, a chronological résumé may work well. But if your duties were diverse or appreciably different from those expected in a civilian job (for example, infantry, explosive detonation, warehousing surplus parts), then a functional résumé, like Dora Cooper Bolger's in Figure 7.7 or Sandy Meagher's in Figure 7.9 are preferable. (Meagher had other jobs in the military before being assigned to the motor pool.) It allows you to avoid any gaps that a chronological résumé shows and to summarize your military training and accomplishments spread over several enlistments and at various duty stations.

As the résumés in Figures 7.7, 7.8, and 7.9 do, quantify your accomplishments. Some possible skill/function categories from your tour(s) of duty you might use include:

Accounting/Finance	Maintenance
Administration	Public Information/Affairs
Communication	Purchasing
Criminal Justice	Recruiting
Cultural Diversity	Research
Engineering	Safety and Security
Health Care	Special skills (heavy equipment operations,
Human Resources	special truck/vehicle license, etc.)
Languages	Teamwork
Leadership	Training/Teaching

7. List your education, including any significant military training you received or schools you attended. Omit your high school or GED.
8. Briefly describe your computer skills (for example, Proficient in Office 365) or any specialized military software you used, but only if it is relevant to the civilian job for which you are applying and in terms a civilian employer can understand.
9. Emphasize languages you know (and indicate level of competency). But if you know only a few words or phrases, skip this category; however, if you have conversational skills (for example, basic conversational Arabic) or reading knowledge, then certainly note that.
10. List military awards, medals, or promotions (for example, Commendation for Efficiency, Meritorious Service Medal, Exceptional Leadership; promoted to E-5).
11. Mention any affiliations relevant to your job search (for example, professional societies or military organizations in your area of expertise), but do not include political affiliations or clubs.

THE DIGITAL RÉSUMÉ

In addition to drafting a hard copy of your résumé, expect to prepare multiple digital versions of it, including creating and posting it to the Web, formatting a scannable text, or emailing it. In today's highly competitive job market, where employers have differing requirements, it is to your advantage to use these various formats to attract the interest of prospective employers.

Things to Keep in Mind when Preparing a Digital Résumé

As you did with your hard copy résumé, your digital résumé has to be carefully organized and accurately written to meet a prospective employer's needs. But while the content of your résumé may remain the same when moving to a digital format, there are other things to keep in mind:

1. Always follow the employer's instructions when submitting or posting your digital résumé.
2. Employers generally prefer submission of digital résumé as either plain text (.txt) files, Microsoft Word files, or PDF files.
3. When preparing your digital résumé, be sure to use the exact keywords from the job posting, so you can match your job skills with the ones employers are searching for when they review possible candidates and help your résumé stand out if scanned by an applicant tracking system (ATS). If a job posting requires a person to have "supervised" co-workers, don't use "managed" instead of "supervised" in your résumé; keywords must be used exactly to be flagged by the applicant tracking system.

Ways to Submit Your Digital Résumé

Your digital résumé may be the most important document in your job search because employers determine who will make their interview list based on what they see in a résumé. There are five basic ways to create, post, or submit your digital résumé. But however you submit it, you must remember to make any changes in all versions of your résumé to be consistent. The following guidelines will help you prepare different digital versions of your résumé:

1. **Use the employer-provided application form.** Many employers have their own dedicated website where they accept applications for employment; this is one of the most widely used ways to get a prospective employer to look at your résumé. Applicants to these companies are asked to "paste" the text of their résumé into the online application form in order to submit it. In these situations, using a scannable version of a résumé, similar to the one in Figure 7.13 (page 278), is usually the best way to proceed. When filling out an online application form, take care to fill out every required field (and even the optional ones) with as many keywords from the job posting as possible.

2. **Post your résumé on the Web.** The Internet offers a variety of sites to disseminate your résumé. The main advantage of this strategy is that you will reach a large pool of potential employers. Here are some tips to help you post your résumé correctly for a potential employer.

   - Post it on one of the sites listed in Table 7.1 (page 240) to reach the maximum number of employers. If you have a Pinterest page, you can pin your résumé there, but classify it by your occupation; *IT résumé, practical nurse résumé,* etc.

- Post your résumé directly on an employer's website where it can be indexed and stored.
- Employers often print out the résumés of job seekers they are interested in, so be sure your résumé can be downloaded easily and quickly.
- If you post your résumé on your own website, do not provide more information than a prospective employer needs, and do not give out personal information. Protect your privacy by following the guidelines in "Making Your Résumé Cybersafe" (page 279).

3. Send your résumé via an email attachment. Many ads will ask you to email your résumé. To do so, save your résumé as a read-only PDF file. A PDF file will automatically retain the format, fonts, and graphics in your document, ensuring that it will look as you want it to no matter where and when it is printed. If you are given the option, email your résumé as a PDF document. Here are some practical guidelines to follow when emailing your résumé.

- Unless the employer instructs not to, send it as a PDF attachment.
- Include a short cover email, but also attach a longer application letter.
- An employer may ask you to send your résumé as a rich text format (rtf) document. If so, make sure you use a plain and simple design. Avoid underlining, boldface, italics, or shadowing, which can garble the text of your résumé, making it almost impossible for applicant tracking systems to read. Use all capital letters instead of bold or italics for emphasis and insert an asterisk (*) or a plus sign (+) in place of bullets (see Figure 7.10, page 274).
- Choose a simple, easy-to-read font like Arial, Times New Roman, or Verdana that is easy to scan and does not mask letters.

4. Create a scannable résumé. Many companies scan hard copy résumés (such as those in Figures 7.10 and 7.11) into their databases and applicant tracking systems so they can search for keywords (see "Making Your Digital Résumé Ready for Applicant Tracking Systems" pages 276–279). An increasing number of employers are now asking job candidates to paste the text of their résumé into a special submission window. To be successful, format your résumé so that key information is easy to locate and stands out clearly. Adhere to the following points when creating a scannable résumé:

- Follow all of the employer's instructions on formatting and submitting a résumé online. Otherwise, your application will be rejected.
- Choose and include nouns rather than action verbs to increase chance of keyword matches.
- Where possible, make your scannable résumé longer than your hard copy version to increase the number of keywords or matches with the employer's job description.
- Do not include accented letters, unusual symbols, graphics, icons, or photographs, as these will cause problems when your résumé is scanned.
- Use ample white space, which a scanner recognizes as separating one heading or section from another.
- If asked to submit hard copy of a scannable hard copy résumé, use a high-quality laser printer and put your résumé on white or off-white paper.

FIGURE 7.10 A Scannable, Electronic Version of Anthony Jones's Hard-Copy Résumé in Figure 7.4

All lines aligned flush with the left margin

Includes all information from traditional print résumé, but removes formatting

Uses both full names for all degrees and software programs so keywords are captured by applicant tracking systems

All caps rather than bold, italics, or fancy fonts used to highlight skill categories

Where possible, chooses and includes nouns rather than action verbs to increase chance of keyword matches

Uses variations of important keywords to maximize matches in an applicant tracking system ("website designer" and "web developer")

Asterisks rather than bullets mark beginning of lines

URL provided for webfolio but does not use hyperlinks or underlining, as this can cause scanning problems

---

Anthony H. Jones
ajdesigner@plat.com
Phone (707) 555-6390
www.facebook.com/anthonyhjones
@AnthonyHJones
www.linkedin.com/pub/anthony-h-jones

EDUCATION
Santa Rosa Junior College 2014–2016
Associate of Science (A.S.) degree to be awarded in June 2016
Dean's List in 2015; GPA 3.25
Commercial Graphics Illustration major
Specialty in design layout
Related courses included digital photography; graphics programs Adobe Illustrator CC, Adobe Dreamweaver CC, CorelDRAW Graphics Suite X7, Adobe Photoshop CC; desktop publishing programs Adobe InDesign CC and QuarkXPress 2015.

COMPUTER SKILLS
Excellent knowledge of web design, video editing, and graphic design software: Adobe InDesign CC, QuarkXPress 2015, Adobe Illustrator CC, Adobe Dreamweaver CC, XML, HTML, CorelDRAW Graphics Suite X7, Adobe Photoshop CC

EXPERIENCE
* Intern in layout and design department. Preparing page composition, photo archiving, and writing detailed assessment reports on digital photography, designs, and artwork used in Living in Sonoma County and Real Estate in Sonoma County magazines, McAdam Publishers, 8 Parkway Heights, Santa Rosa, CA, 2015–2016

* Salesperson; display designer for custom window displays, helped manage inventory database, Buchman's Department Store, Greenview Mall, Santa Rosa, 2013–2015

* Acted as website designer and developed and maintained a Facebook page for a successful fund drive that raised $5,600. Developed, Santa Rosa Humane Society, 2015.

* Web developer, graphic artist, and display designer

WEBFOLIO
A webfolio containing designs, photographs, illustrations, graphics, and graphic designs is available at www.plat.com/users/ajones/resume.html

© 2017 Cengage Learning

- Make all text flush to the left-hand margin.
- Avoid a script font. Use Times New Roman or Arial instead.
- Use at least 10- to 12-point type and allow a maximum width of 6½ inches to make your résumé easier to scan and read.
- Do not surround your résumé with a frame or border, or use lines, rules, or boxes, as this can lead to scanning difficulties.

FIGURE 7.11 A Scannable, Electronic Version of Dora Cooper Bolger's Hard-Copy Résumé in Figure 7.7

Dora Cooper Bolger
P.O. Box 3216
Westhampton, MI 46532
dcbplanner@gmail.com
www.facebook.com/doracooperbolger
www.linkedin.com/pub/dora-c-bolger

OBJECTIVE
Seek a full-time position as a public affairs officer to promote the goals of a health care, educational, or charitable organization

ORGANIZATIONAL COMMUNICATION EXPERIENCE
Presenter at 24 civic group functions on educational issues
Recorded minutes and helped formulate agenda as president of large, local PTA (800 members) for past 6 years
Excellent computer knowledge of Microsoft Office 365 and Microsoft Dynamics CRM
Established and maintained the Facebook and Twitter accounts and wrote blog posts for Teens in Trouble

FINANCIAL EXPERIENCE
Fundraiser for 3 major campaigns, over $225,000 collected
Prepared and implemented large family budget (3 children, 8 foster children)
Budget planner, Foster Parent's Association
Financial secretary and financial planner for 4 years, Faith United Methodist Church

ADMINISTRATIVE EXPERIENCE
Volunteer Coordinator/Leader, National Kidney Foundation, 2012–2016
Neighborhood carpool organizer for 17 drivers and more than 70 children for 7 years
President and coordinator of after-school tutoring program for Teens in Trouble since 2003
President and Secretary, local PTA, 2010–2016
Vice-president, Foster Parent's Association, 2014

HONORS
Volunteer of the Year, Michigan Child Placement Agency, 2015

EDUCATION
Metropolitan Community College, Associate of Arts (A.A.), 2012
Mid-Michigan College, Bachelor of Science (B.S.), expected May 2016
Public Administration major
Psychology minor
Dean's List 2014–2016, 3.55 GPA

COMPUTER SKILLS
Microsoft Office 365 and Microsoft Dynamics CRM

WORK EXPERIENCE
Secretary, 2004–2011 (full- and part-time), Merrymount Plastics, Foley and Wasson, Westhampton Health Department, G & K Electric

Avoids giving personal information; uses P.O. box, not address

Includes all information from traditional print résumé, but removes formatting

Where possible, chooses and includes nouns to list accomplishments, to increase chance of keyword matches

Uses variations of important keywords to maximize matches in an applicant tracking system ("budget planner" and "financial planner")

Avoids any symbols, boldfacing, or italics that could garble text

Documents acquired computer skills

- Include hyperlinks to your online résumé (if applicable), webfolio, and relevant social media or professional networking sites.
- Do not staple or fold the pages.

5. Create an HTML version of your résumé. You can post your résumé on your own website, social media page, or LinkedIn profile, and you can link to an HTML version of your résumé from other websites or from an email you send to a potential employer. In your online résumé you can include hyperlinks to your social media or professional networking sites, your own website, appropriate blogs you wrote, or to reviews of your professional work. If you include a webfolio, as in Figures 7.10 (page 274) or 7.12, hyperlinks will help an employer to access examples of your work quickly.

Making Your Digital Résumé Ready for Applicant Tracking Systems

As mentioned previously (see "Things to Keep in Mind When Preparing a Digital Résumé," page 272), prospective employers use databases and applicant tracking systems to scan résumés and find keywords they most want to see in the job seeker's description of his or her experience, education, and interpersonal skills. The more matches, or hits, they find between appropriate keywords in your résumé and those on their list, the better your chances are of being interviewed. List keywords throughout your résumé in appropriate places. Keywords should highlight your technical expertise, training and education, knowledge of a field, leadership ability, teamwork, writing/speaking skills, sales experience, and so on.

CASE STUDY

Creating a Digital Résumé for a Job Search

Beth Pryor recently earned her B.S. in marketing at Southern Ohio University. Because the competition for jobs is fierce, she has to prepare several versions of a persuasive résumé as well as a cover letter.

Different companies' requirements vary. Some companies want applicants to send their résumé as a PDF document attached to an email. Others require applicants to paste a text résumé into an online application form. And many employers ask candidates to submit digital portfolios of their work. The most useful advice she received from a former teacher was to: "Make certain your résumé emphasizes the skills that a marketing manager will want to have—teamwork, leadership, enthusiasm, creativity, and most of all your strong sense of visual design and thinking."

She created a version of her résumé in Microsoft Word first, then saved it as a PDF file (Figure 7.12). The scannable version of her résumé seen in Figure 7.13 on page 278 has removed the formatting and does not contain any boldface, italics, or indentations because these elements might prevent a scanner or the applicant tracking system from capturing her information. To accompany her résumé, Pryor developed a webfolio to display logo designs and advertising artwork plus copies of documents from her college marketing courses and an internship.

FIGURE 7.12 A PDF File of Beth Pryor's Résumé

Beth Pryor   PO Box 5112, Oxford, OH 45056
bethpryor@hotmail.com
in www.linkedin.com/pub/beth-pryor

Phone number
not given
because résumé
posted on Web

Objective   A position with an international marketing firm emphasizing analysis of
E- and M-Commerce strategies, management, and leadership skills

Education   **Southern Ohio University**, Jamesville, OH
B.S. in Marketing; Minor: Spanish
Graduation: June 2016 — GPA in major: 3.36

Relevant Areas of Study
• Buyer Behavior
• E- and M-Commerce Ethics
• Management: Leadership and Learning
• Marketing Analysis
• Collaborating in the Workplace
• International Business
• Promotional Strategies

PDF file retains
all formatting—
boldface,
bullets, etc.

Study Abroad, Summer 2015, Southern Ohio University
Business Administration Program in Santiago, Chile
• Completed 10-week program
• Developed second-language skills in Spanish

**Business
Internship**   **Archer Media Associates**, Marketing Assistant, Spring 2014
• Drafting marketing copy for Archer's largest client,
  Techsure, Ltd.
• Led a team that created a marketing plan for 3 Amazon.com
  clients
• Prepared 8 major press releases for clients in health care, food
  service management, IT
• Tracked media coverage for clients
• Participated in corporate training seminars

Information
chunked into
logically divided
sections

**Retail
Experience**   **The Boutique**, Sales Representative, 2012–2014
• Promoted to "key holder" (opened and closed store; supervised
  store short-term, Summer 2014)
• Helped train staff of 4 in weekly meetings
• Chaired 2-3 weekly meetings per quarter
• Implemented goal-oriented management strategies

Information is
easy to access
for employer
through
bulleted lists

Software Skills   • IBM Notes, Microsoft Access 2013, Adobe InDesign CC, Adobe
  Illustrator CC, Adobe Photoshop CC, Microsoft Office 365

Profiles   • LinkedIn: www.linkedin.com/pub/beth-pryor
• MarketingEdge: www.ms.marketingedge.com/profiles/bpryor

Hyperlinks allow
employer to
access further
relevant
information
about candidate

Memberships   Student Marketing Association, Southern Ohio University
• Treasurer, 2015–2016
• Public Relations Committee, 2013–2015

Webfolio   www.bethpryor.com/portfolio

(Continued)

FIGURE 7.13 A Scannable Version of Beth Pryor's Résumé in Figure 7.12

Omits personal details

BETH PRYOR
PO Box 5112
Jamesville, OH 45056
bethpryor@hotmail.com
www.linkedin.com/pub/beth-pryor

Simple text easily scanned into company's HR database, which will search for keywords

OBJECTIVE
A position with an international marketing firm emphasizing analysis of E- and M-Commerce strategies, management, and leadership skills

EDUCATION
Southern Ohio University, Jamesville, OH
Bachelor of Science (B.S.) in Marketing
Spanish minor
Graduation June 2014
3.36 GPA in major

Does not use boldfacing, italics, etc.

RELEVANT AREAS OF STUDY
Buyer Behavior
E- and M-Commerce Ethics
International Business
Management Leadership and Learning
Market Analysis
Workplace Collaboration
Promotional Strategies

All text formatted flush left for easy scanning

Key sections are separated with extra spacing and all caps

STUDY ABROAD, Summer 2015
Southern Ohio University Business Administration Program in Santiago, Chile
Graduate of 10-week program
Reader, speaker, intermediate Spanish

BUSINESS INTERNSHIP, Archer Media Associates, Spring 2014
Marketing copywriter for Archer's largest client, Techsure, Ltd.
Team leader for marketing group that created a plan for 3 Amazon.com clients.
Writer of 8 major press releases and copy for clients in health care, food service management, and information technology (IT).
Researcher of media coverage and visual designs for clients.
Participant in corporate training seminars.

Where possible, uses nouns to increase chance of keyword matches

SALES MANAGEMENT EXPERIENCE, The Boutique, 2012–2014
Sales Representative
Promotion to key holder, short-term store supervisor, Summer 2014
Staff trainer of 4 employees
Chair for 2–3 weekly meetings per quarter
Developer of goal-oriented management strategies

Uses numbers instead of words when quantifying achievements

SOFTWARE
IBM Notes, Microsoft Access 2013, Adobe InDesign CC, Adobe Illustrator CC, Adobe Photoshop CC, Microsoft Office 365

PROFILES
LinkedIn www.linkedin.com/pub/beth-pryor
MarketingEdge www.ms.marketingedge.com/profiles/bpryor

Includes relevant URLs to professional networking sites and webfolio

PROFESSIONAL MEMBERSHIP
Student Marketing Association, Southern Ohio University
Treasurer, 2015–2016
Public Relations Committee, 2013–2015

WEBFOLIO
www.bethpryor.com/portfolio

Here are a few tips to help you select and use appropriate keywords:

1. Include the descriptive keywords found in the employer's ad and website throughout your résumé to increase your chances of landing an interview.
2. Do not be afraid of using the shoptalk (or jargon) of your profession. An employer will expect you to be familiar with current terminology.
3. Provide both full names and acronyms for software, degrees, and organizations, in case the employer uses one or the other in the job announcement.
4. Use variations of important keywords to maximize matches in an applicant tracking system (for example, try to use both "website designer" and "web developer").
5. Replace the action verbs found in conventional résumé (on the left in the following list) with keyword nouns in digital résumé. Here are some examples:

Conventional Résumé	Digital Résumé
Wrote business report	Business report writer
Performed laboratory tests	Laboratory technician
Solved consumer complaints	Consumer advocate
Responsible for managing accounts	Accounts manager
Won three awards	Award winner
Edited company newsletter	Newsletter editor
Solved software problem	Software specialist

© 2017 Cengage Learning

Making Your Résumé Cybersafe

Whether you use a database service or post your résumé on your own website, protect your identity and your current job. Be careful about revealing personal information.

- Post your résumé only on legitimate sites. Avoid those that say they will flood the market. You don't know where your résumé will end up. Review Table 7.2 (page 250) regarding the Do's and Don'ts when creating your online profile.
- Do not put personal information in your résumé—home address, Social Security number, birthday, health status, or photograph.
- Never put the names of your references or their contact information online.
- Never use your present employer's company name or business email address.

Testing, Proofreading, and Sending Your Digital Résumé

Never underestimate the negative impact of errors in your résumé, email, or application letter. Many prospective employers will discard a résumé if they spot a typo.

1. Test your formatting. Send your résumé to a friend to be sure your file is readable and formatted correctly.
2. Print out your résumé and proofread the hard copy carefully. Do not rely on spell-check alone. It is easy to overlook mistakes if you only proofread what is on your computer screen.

3. Don't just put "résumé" as the subject of your email when sending your résumé to an employer. List the title, number, or code of the position for which you are applying.
4. Simply submitting your résumé online is sometimes not enough. If requested, also send a scannable hard copy and a letter of application (discussed next) to prospective employers. Do not fold or staple your résumé. Send it, along with your letter, in a large envelope (8½ × 11 inches).
5. Always keep a log of where you have posted your résumé online (see "Keep a Job Search Record," page 294).

LETTERS OF APPLICATION

Along with your résumé, expect to send your prospective employer a letter of application (also known as a cover letter), one of the most important pieces of correspondence you may ever write. Its goal is to get you an interview and ultimately the job. Letters you write in applying for jobs should be *personable, professional*, and *persuasive*—the three *P*'s. Knowing how the letter of application and résumé work together and how they differ can give you a better idea of how to compose your letter. Different companies have different policies about how they want letters of application sent to them; some prefer hard copy, some attachments, and some in the body of an email. You should be prepared for any of these methods.

How Application Letters and Résumés Differ

The résumé is a persuasive record of dates, important achievements, skills, names, places, addresses, and jobs. As noted earlier, you may prepare several different résumés, depending on your experience and the job market.

Your letter of application, however, is much more personal. It introduces you to a prospective employer. Because you must write a new, original letter to each prospective employer, you may write (or adapt) many different letters. Each letter of application should be tailored to a specific job. It should respond precisely to the qualifications the employer seeks.

The letter of application is a sales letter that emphasizes and applies the most relevant details (of education, experience, and talents) in your résumé. In short, the résumé contains the raw material that the letter of application transforms into a finished and highly marketable product—you.

Résumé Facts to Exclude from Letters of Application

The letter of application should not simply repeat the details listed in your résumé. In fact, the following details that you would include in your résumé should not be restated in the letter:

- personal data, including license or certificate numbers
- specific course numbers
- names and addresses of all your previous employers

Writing the Letter of Application

The letter of application, such as those in Figures 7.14–7.16, can make the difference between your getting an interview and your being eliminated early from consideration. It should convince a prospective employer that you will use the experience and education listed on your résumé in the job he or she is hoping to fill. You want your letter to be placed in the "definitely interview" category. As you prepare your letter, use the following general guidelines.

1. **Follow the standard conventions of letter writing.** There are a variety of ways to send a letter (see "Different Ways to Send Letters," pages 154–155). No matter how your letter is sent, proofread meticulously; a spelling error, typo, or grammatical mistake will make you look careless. As with your résumés, don't rely only on your spell-checker. (See "The Appearance of Your Letter," pages 162–163).

2. **Supply all contact information as part of your heading.** Include home address, phone numbers, email address, and links to your website or social media and professional networking profiles, if you have one. (See also "Heading," page 159.)

3. **Make sure your letter looks attractive.** Use wide margins, and don't crowd your page. Keep your paragraphs short and readable—no more than four or five sentences each.

4. **Send your letter to a specific person.** Never address an application letter "To Whom It May Concern," "Dear Sir or Madam," or "Dear Director of Human Resources." Get an individual's name from the company's website or by calling the company's main office, and be sure to verify the spelling of the person's name and his or her title.

5. **Don't send a form letter to every potential employer.** Stay away from generic application letter templates. Customize your letter to make sure you address the employer's specific needs.

6. **Be concise.** A one-page letter is standard in today's job market.

7. **Emphasize the "you attitude."** (See "Achieving the 'You Attitude': Four Guidelines," pages 167–168.) See yourself as an employer sees you. Focus on how your qualifications meet the employer's needs, not the other way around. Employers are not impressed by vain boasts ("I am the most efficient and effective safety engineer"). Convince prospective employers that you will be a valuable addition to their organization—a team player, a problem solver, an energetic representative, a skilled professional. (See "Making a Good Impression on Your Reader," pages 164–168.)

8. **Don't be tempted to send out your first draft.** Write and rewrite your letter of application until you are convinced it presents you in the best possible light. Getting the job may depend on it. A first or even second draft rarely sells your abilities as well as a third, fourth, or even fifth revision does.

9. **Tell the truth.** Don't exaggerate the importance of any previous job experience or academic work. Never mislead a potential employer by lying about anything

relating to degrees, continuing education units (CEUs), licenses, certificates, permits, or other professional qualifications.

The sections that follow give you some suggestions on how to prepare the various parts of an application letter successfully.

Your Opening Paragraph

The first paragraph of your letter of application is your introduction. It must get your reader's attention by answering four questions:

1. Why are you writing?
2. Where or how did you learn of the vacancy, the company, or the job?
3. What is the specific job title for which you are applying?
4. What is your most important qualification for the job?

Begin your letter by stating directly that you are writing to apply for a job. Don't say that you "want to apply for the job"; such an opening raises the question, "Why don't you, then?"

Avoid an unconventional or arrogant opening: "Are you looking for a dynamic, young, and talented accountant?" Do not begin with a question; be more positive and professional.

If you learned about the job through a newspaper or journal, make sure you italicize its title.

> I am applying for the food service manager position you advertised in the May 10 edition of the *Los Angeles Times* online.

Always check a company's website or social media pages first to see if their position is listed online, as Anthony Jones did in Figure 7.14.

If you learned of the job from a professor, a friend, or an employee at the firm, indicate that. Take advantage of a personal (networking) contact who is confident that you are qualified for and interested in the position, as María López (Figure 7.15, page 285) and Dora Cooper Bolger (Figure 7.16, page 286) did. But first confirm that your contact gives you permission to use his or her name.

You have to attract the reader's attention quickly and persuasively. In a sentence or two, tell the reader how your education and experience qualify you for the job. Use keywords from the job announcement.

The Body of Your Letter

The body of your letter, comprising one or two paragraphs, cites evidence from your résumé to prove you are qualified for the job. You might want to spend one paragraph on your education and one on your experience or combine your accomplishments into one paragraph.

Follow these guidelines for the body of your letter:

1. Keep your paragraphs short and readable—four or five sentences. Avoid long, complex sentences. Use the active voice to emphasize yourself as a doer. Review the action verbs in Table 7.3 (page 256) and, again, use keywords found in the employer's ad.

FIGURE 7.14 Letter of Application from Anthony Jones, a Recent Graduate with Little Job Experience

Anthony H. Jones

WEBSITE DEVELOPER
DESIGNER
GRAPHIC ARTIST

73 Allenwood Boulevard   www.plat.com/users/ajones/resume.html
Santa Rosa, CA 95401-1074   f www.facebook.com/anthonyhjones
707-555-6390   🐦 @AnthonyHJones
ajdesigner@plat.com   in www.linkedin.com/pub/anthony-h-jones

Clear and professional–looking letterhead

May 16, 2016

Ms. Jocelyn Nogasaki
Human Resources Manager
Megalith Publishing Company
1001 Heathcliff Row
San Francisco, CA 94123-7707

Writes to a specific person

Dear Ms. Nogasaki:

I am applying for the layout editor position advertised on your Linkedin page, which I accessed on May 14. Early next month, I will receive an A.S. degree in commercial graphics illustration from Santa Rosa Junior College.

Identifies position and source of ad

With a special interest in publishing, I have successfully completed more than 40 credit hours in courses directly related to layout design and gained experience using Adobe InDesign, Illustrator, and Photoshop CC, as well as QuarkXPress 2015. You might like to know that many Megalith publications were used as design and layout models in my graphics communications and digital photography courses.

Applies education directly to employer's business

My studies have also given me practical experience at McAdam Publishers as part of my Santa Rosa internship program. While working at McAdam, I was responsible for assisting the design department in page composition and archiving photos. Other related experiences I have include creating a website and developing and maintaining a Facebook page for the Santa Rosa Humane Society, and designing and executing custom window displays at Buchman's Department Store. As the enclosed résumé indicates, a webfolio containing designs, photographs, illustrations, graphics, and graphic designs is available at **www.plat.com/users/ajones/resume.html.**

Convincingly cites related job experience

Refers to résumé/webfolio

I would welcome the opportunity to discuss my qualifications in graphic design with you. My contact information is listed above. After June 8, I will be available for an interview at any time convenient for you.

Asks for an interview and thanks employer

Thank you for considering my application.

Sincerely yours,

Anthony H Jones

Anthony H. Jones
Encl.: Résumé

2. Don't begin each sentence with "I." Vary your sentence structure. Write reader-centered sentences, even those beginning with "I."

3. Concentrate on seeing yourself as a potential employer sees you. Prove that you can help an employer's sales and service, promote an organization's mission and goals, and be a reliable team player.

4. Highlight your qualifications by citing specific accomplishments. Tell your reader exactly how your education and job experience qualify you to perform and advance in the job advertised. Show how you can make a positive contribution to the employer's company. Don't simply say you are a great salesperson. Demonstrate your accomplishments by stressing that you increased the sales volume in your department by 18 percent within six months, you won an award or received a promotion for customer service, or you reduced costs by 10 percent. Employers are not impressed by boasting or arrogance. They want hard facts to prove you are the right person for the job.

5. Mention you are enclosing your résumé. Put an "Encl." notation at the bottom of your letter.

Education Recent graduates with little work experience, such as Anthony Jones in Figure 7.14, will, of course, spend more time discussing their education. Emphasize why and how your most significant educational accomplishments—course work, degrees, certificates, licenses, training—are relevant for the particular job. Mention significant extracurricular activities if they relate to the job description. Employers want to know which specific skills from your education translate into benefits for their company.

Only saying you will graduate with a degree in criminal justice does not explain how you, unlike all the other graduates of such programs, are best suited for a particular job. Ask yourself which classes you took are most relevant for the employer. Consider grouping classes to show how and why you are the best qualified applicant for the job. For example, when you indicate that you have completed 36 credit hours in software security and have another 12 credit hours in global business, you prove you have an expertise other job candidates may not have. Note how Anthony Jones in Figure 7.14 and María López in Figure 7.15 establish their educational qualifications with specific details about their training. Be sure to also mention internships or clinical training, as Jones and López do.

Experience After you discuss your educational qualifications, turn to your job experience. But if your experience is your most valuable and extensive qualification for the job, put it before education and stress any previous experience similar to what a new position calls for. Be sure to stress any promotions or other leadership roles you have had. If you are switching careers or returning to a career after years away from the workplace (because of military service, for example), start the body of your letter with your experience or your community and civic service, as Dora Cooper Bolger does in Figure 7.16 (page 286). Her volunteer work convincingly demonstrates she has the organizational and communication skills her prospective employer seeks. Never minimize such contributions.

FIGURE 7.15 Letter of Application from María López, a Recent Graduate with Some Job Experience

MARÍA LÓPEZ

1725 Brooke Street
Miami, FL 32701-2121
(305) 555-3429
mlopez@gmail.com
in www.linkedin.com/pub/maria-lopez

Uses professional– looking letterhead with contact information

May 15, 2016

Dr. Marvin Henrady
Medical/Dental Plaza, Suite 34
839 Causeway Drive
Miami, FL 32706-2468

Dear Dr. Henrady:

Mr. Mitchell Pelbourne, my clinical instructor at Miami-Dade Community College, informs me you are looking for a dental hygienist to work in your northside office. My education and experience qualify me for that position. This month I will graduate with an A.S. degree in the dental hygienist program, and I will take the Dental Assisting National Board exams in early June.

Begins with personal contact

Verifies she will have necessary licensure

I have successfully completed all course work and clinical programs in oral hygiene, anatomy, and prophylaxis techniques. During my clinical training, I received intensive practical instruction from several local dentists, including Dr. Tia Gutiérrez. Since your northside office specializes in pediatric dental care, you might find the subject of my major project—proper nutrition and dental care for preschoolers— especially relevant.

Links training to job responsibilities; demonstrates knowledge of employer's office

My related job experience working with children in a health care setting would be both relevant for and helpful to your office. For over two years, I was a unit assistant on the pediatric unit at St. Francis Hospital, and have experience in greeting patients, transcribing medical orders and surgical notes, and assisting the nursing staff. An additional job strength I would bring to your office is my bilingual (Spanish/English) communication skills. You will find more detailed information about my accomplishments in the enclosed résumé.

Relates previous experience to employer's needs; refers to résumé

I would appreciate the opportunity to talk with you about the position and my interest in pediatric dental care. I am available for an interview any time after 2:00 pm until June 9th, but after that I could visit your office at your convenience. Thank you for your consideration.

Ends with a polite request for an interview and thanks reader

Sincerely yours,

María López

María López

Encl. Résumé

FIGURE 7.16 Letter of Application from Dora Cooper Bolger, a Job Candidate with Years of Community and Civic Experience

Email address emphasizing professional achievement

DORA COOPER BOLGER
f www.facebook.com/doracooperbolger
in www.linkedin.com/pub/dora-c-bolger

1215 Lakeview Avenue
Westhampton, MI 46532
Cell: 616-555-4773
dcbplanner@aol.com

February 10, 2016

Dr. Lindsay Bafaloukos, Director
Tanselle Mental Health Agency
4400 West Gallagher Drive
Tanselle, MI 46932-3106

Dear Dr. Bafaloukos:

Begins with contact made at professional meeting, highlighting her qualifications

At a recent meeting of the County Services Council, a member of your staff, Homer Steen, told me that you will soon be hiring a public affairs coordinator. Because of my extensive experience in and commitment to community affairs, I would appreciate your considering me for this opening. I expect to receive my B.S. in Public Administration from Mid-Michigan College later this year.

Relates proven past successes to employer's needs; gives concrete examples of her skills

For the past ten years, I have organized community groups with outreach programs similar to Tanselle's. I have held administrative positions in the PTA and the Foster Parents' Association and served as president of Teens in Trouble, a volunteer group providing assistance to dysfunctional teens. My responsibilities with Teens have included coordinating counseling activities with various school programs, scheduling tutorials, maintaining the group's Facebook page, and representing the orgnization before local and state governmental agencies. I have been commended for my organizational and communication skills. My twenty-four presentations on foster home care and Teens in Trouble also demonstrate that I am an effective speaker, a skill I could put to work for Tanselle immediately.

Encourages reader to see her as best-prepared candidate; includes résumé

Because of my work at Mid-Michigan as well as for Teens and Foster Parents, I have the practical experience in communication and psychology to promote Tanselle's goals successfully. The enclosed résumé provides details about my experience, education, and honors I have received.

Requests interview and thanks reader

I would welcome an opportunity to discuss my work with Teens and other organizations I represented and how I might help Tanselle promote its programs. I am available for an interview at your convenience. Thank you for considering me for your public affairs coordinator position.

Sincerely yours,

Dora Cooper Bolger

Dora Cooper Bolger

Encl. Résumé

Relate Your Education and Experience to the Job Link your education and experience as benefits to the particular job you apply for. Persuasively show a prospective employer how your previous accomplishments, especially teamwork and responsibility, have prepared you for future success on the job. Relate your course work in computer science to being an efficient programmer. Indicate how your summer work for a local park district reinforced your exemplary skills in customer service. Connect your background to the prospective employer's company. Any homework you can do about the company's history, goals, or structure will pay off.

- By citing Megalith publications as a model in his courses, Anthony Jones stresses he is ready to start successfully from the first day on the job (Figure 7.14).
- Note how María López links her major school project and her work on a hospital pediatric unit to Dr. Henrady's specialty (Figure 7.15).
- Dora Cooper Bolger likewise proves that she is familiar with and can contribute to Tanselle's programs in community mental health though her extensive volunteer work and public speaking experience (Figure 7.16).

Closing

The purpose of your last paragraph is clear-cut—to convince the reader to call or email you for an interview. Keep your closing paragraph short—about two or three sentences—but be sure it fulfills the following four important functions:

1. briefly emphasizes once again your major qualifications
2. asks for an interview or a phone call
3. indicates when you are available for an interview
4. thanks the reader

End gracefully and professionally. Be straightforward. Don't leave the reader with a single weak, vague sentence: "I would like to have an interview at your convenience." That does nothing to sell you. Say that you would appreciate talking with the employer further to discuss your qualifications, as María López does in Figure 7.15. Then mention your chief talent. If you are applying for an international job or one far from home, you might request a phone interview instead of an in-person interview (see "Being Ready for a Phone Interview," page 288). You might also express your willingness to relocate if the job requires it.

After indicating your interest in the job, give the times you are available for an interview and specifically tell the reader where you can be reached. If you are going to a professional meeting that the employer might also attend, or if you are visiting the employer's city soon, say so.

The following samples show how *not* to close your letter and explain why.

Pushy: I would like to set up an interview with you. Please phone me to arrange a convenient time. [That's the employer's prerogative, not yours.]

Too Informal: I do not live far from your office. Let's meet for coffee sometime next week. [Say instead that because you live nearby, you will be available for an interview.]

Introduces New Subject: I would like to discuss other qualifications you have in mind for the job. [How do you know what the interviewer might have in mind?]

Note that the closing paragraphs in Figures 7.14, 7.15, and 7.16 avoid these errors.

GOING TO AN INTERVIEW

There are various ways for a prospective employer to conduct an interview. It might be a one-on-one meeting—you and the interviewer—or you may visit with a group of individuals or even with several groups from different divisions in the company to decide if you would fit in. You could have an interview over the telephone, or through a videoconference, or via Skype (see the Tech Note on page 289).

Being Ready for a Phone Interview

Often an employer has ten to fifteen viable candidates for a position and conducts a phone interview to narrow them down to the three or four they want to invite for a face-to-face interview. Be prepared for a phone interview by keeping the following in mind:

1. Indicate to the potential employer when you are available for a call, and specify your time zone—Central, Eastern, etc. If the call comes unexpectedly and you know you have a limited amount of time, ask the interviewer if it is possible to talk at another time, but offer alternative times within (at most) the next couple of hours or the next day, to stress your interest in the job.

2. Be prepared. Keep your résumé and information about the company at hand so that you can refer to them, if necessary, during the interview.

3. Find a quiet place for the call. Make sure your phone is charged and that there are no disturbing background noises. Music, a running appliance, or someone else talking in the same room are all distractions and can make you appear unprofessional.

4. Speak with confidence and poise. "Delivering Your Presentation" on pages 639–642 in Chapter 16 will give you tips on how to sound calm and professional.

5. Ask a couple of key questions about the job. Review "Questions You May Ask the Interviewer(s)" on pages 292–293). Impress the interviewer with your interest in his/her company and your enthusiasm about the job.

6. Always thank the interviewer. Be sure you get the interviewer's correct spelling of his/her name and the address where you can send a thank-you letter.

Preparing for an Interview

You should always be prepared to discuss *anything* listed on your résumé at an interview. If you can't recall the details about a job or activity listed on your résumé, refresh your memory so you won't be caught off-guard. Before you go to an interview, prepare by doing the following:

1. **Do your homework about the company.** Show you are interested in the company by learning as much as you can about it. Go to the corporate or agency website (or their Facebook page, or profile page on LinkedIn) to find out who founded the company, who the current CEO is, if it is a local firm or a subsidiary, its chief products or services, how many years it has been in business, how many employees it has, where its main office and plants are, and who its major clients and competitors are. Read company pages/boards on social media, its publications, blogs, and other news about it to get a sense of the corporate culture. If you know who is interviewing you, try to find out as much as possible about that person (looking up their LinkedIn profile is a good place to start). Also read recent stories about the company in leading business publications, such as the following:

- *The Wall Street Journal*—www.online.wsj.com
- *The New York Times*—www.nytimes.com
- *The Washington Post*—www.washingtonpost.com
- *USA Today*—www.usatoday.com
- *Bloomberg Businessweek*—www.businessweek.com
- *Fast Company*—www.fastcompany.com
- *Fortune*—www.fortune.com
- *Forbes*—www.forbes.com
- *Inc. Magazine*—www.inc.com

2. **Review the job description carefully.** Research the job—what does it entail? What skills do you have that relate directly to the job?

3. **Prepare a one- or two-minute summary of your chief qualifications.** You will most likely be asked to summarize your education, experience, teamwork, and professional goals during the job interview. In doing so, identify how specific

---

TECH NOTE

Skype Interviews

Prospective employers also conduct interviews over Skype (see "Videoconferencing with Skype," page 106). Less expensive than an on-site one, a Skype interview allows an employer to see you and assess your professional image. To have a successful Skype interview, be sure your webcam and Internet connections are working properly. Look directly into the webcam and do not stare at your computer screen. Eye contact is as important via Skype as in an on-site interview.

Be prepared. Keep a set of notes handy with the most crucial information you need to give to an employer. Dress professionally, too, even though the interview may be conducted from your dorm room or home. Position your webcam so that the background for your interview looks neat and business-like. Don't sit or stand in front of anything that detracts from your professional image. And remember to turn off all music, televisions, and phones and make sure you will not be interrupted, which can sink your chances of getting hired.

classes, course projects, jobs you have held, or community service have equipped you for the position the company wants to fill. Provide examples.

4. Take your portfolio, including three or four extra copies of your résumé, with you. Also bring a notepad and a pen (or your tablet) to write down essential details.

5. Practice your interview skills with a friend or job counselor. Be sure that this person asks tough questions about your education and experience so that you will get practice answering these questions realistically and convincingly.

6. Brush up on business etiquette. Silence your phone before your interview. Remember the name(s) of the interviewer(s) and others you may meet. Always be polite and respectful, saying "Thank you," "You're welcome," and so on. Pay special attention to acceptable ways of communicating with international audiences if your interview is with a multinational company or with a non-native speaker of English.

7. Bring your photo ID and Social Security card. Also bring any licenses or certificates you may be asked to present to a human resources office. If you are not a U.S. citizen, bring your work visa.

Questions to Expect at Your Interview

An interviewer may ask many questions that call for examples--illustrations of your handling of a problem with a co-worker, customer, or vendor. Be prepared with explicit instances that show you in a good light. The following questions are typical of those you can expect from interviewers, with advice on how to answer them.

- **Tell us something about yourself.** Emphasize achievements that show you are responsible (e.g., working to pay for your tuition), conscientious (participating in a community or service activity), and eager to contribute to and learn more about your profession and potential employer.
- **Why do you want to work for us?** Recall any job goals you have and apply them specifically to the job under discussion.
- **What qualifications do you have for the job?** Point to educational achievements and relevant work experience, especially IT skills.
- **What specific experience do you bring that can carry over to your job for us?** Mention any situations that are directly relevant to the duties and responsibilities that the prospective job will entail.
- **Describe your leadership strengths, skills, and accomplishments.** Describe specific instances when you have shown these qualities as part of your duties with any past employers or organizations.
- **What could you offer us that other candidates do not have? Why should we hire you?** Say enthusiasm, being a team player, problem-solving skills, ability to meet deadlines under stress. Emphasize that you are diplomatic yet goal oriented.
- **Why did you attend this school?** Be honest—location, costs, programs.

- **Why did you major in "X"?** Do not simply say financial benefits; concentrate on professional goals and interests.
- **In what course did you receive your lowest grade?** Don't say that you could have done better if you'd tried. Explain what the trouble was, and mention that you corrected it in a course in which you earned a B or an A.
- **What extracurricular activities did you participate in while in high school or college?** Indicate any responsibilities you had—managing money, preparing minutes, coordinating events. If you were unable to participate in such activities, tell the interviewer that a part-time job or community or church activities prevented you from participating. Such answers sound better than saying that you did not like sports or clubs in school.
- **Did you learn as much as you wanted from your course work?** This is a loaded question. Indicate that you learned a great deal but now look forward to the opportunity to gain more practical skills, to put into practice the principles and procedures you have learned.
- **What is your greatest strength?** Say being a team player, planning and organizing tasks efficiently, concerned about the environment, being cooperative and willing to learn, having the ability to grasp difficult concepts easily, wanting to find a more efficient or economical way of doing something, being proficient at managing time or money, taking criticism easily, and profiting from it.
- **What is your greatest shortcoming?** Be honest here and mention it, but then turn to ways in which you are improving. Don't say something deadly like, "I can never seem to finish what I start" or "I hate being criticized." You should neither dwell on your weaknesses nor keep silent about them. Saying "None" to this kind of question is as inadvisable as rattling off a list of faults.
- **How did you solve a problem or conflict with a co-worker, supervisor, or customer?** Describe a specific situation where you resolved a problem diplomatically and for the good of the company. Indicate what you learned that helped you on the job. Stress your ability to be courteous and honest and to work toward a productive resolution. State that you avoid language, tone of voice, or gestures that interfere with healthy dialogue.
- **How would you convince a co-worker about an issue?** Emphasize your ability to argue effectively for a proposal by providing an example from experience.
- **Why did you leave your last job?** Say "I returned to school full time" or "I moved from Jackson to Springfield," or say that you changed professions. *Never attack your previous employer.* That only makes you look bad.
- **Why would you leave your current job?** Again, never attack an individual or an organization. Say your current job has prepared you for the position you are now applying for. Emphasize your desire to work for a specific company because of its goals, work environment, and opportunities.
- **What can you do in the first sixty days to make a difference at our company?** Handle this question diplomatically and don't bring up a long list of things you would change. Instead, focus on how much you want to learn,

contribute to the overall effectiveness/efficiency of an office, department, or company, and that you are happy to have the opportunity to offer your perspective on the situation.

- **What are your career goals over the next three to five years?** State your career objectives in terms of what you would like to accomplish for the company, your profession, the community, and yourself. Be confident, not cocky.

What Do I Say About Salary?

Find out what the salary range is for your professional level in your area. Consult the U.S. Bureau of Labor Statistics' *Occupational Outlook Handbook* at www.bls.gov/ooh as well as www.salary.com. You can also ask your instructors or individuals you know who work for the company or call your professional organization for information. If the issue of salary comes up, ask if the company has established a salary range for the position and where you stand in relationship to that range. However, because many companies set fixed salaries for entry-level positions, it may be unwise to try to negotiate.

If you are asked what salary you expect for the job, do not give an exact figure. You may undercut yourself if the employer has a higher figure in mind. By doing your homework on salary ranges, you will have a better feel for the market when the employer does mention salary.

Factor other benifits into your salary calculations—health insurance, day care, housing, uniform/clothing allowances, product or service discounts, opportunities for travel and language instruction, and tuition reimbursement.

Questions You May Ask the Interviewer(s)

You will have a chance to ask the interviewer(s) questions. Watch for appropriate cues, and be prepared to say more than "No, I don't have any questions," which suggests either indifference or lack of preparation on your part. Here are some legitimate questions you can ask interviewers:

1. Will there be any safety, security, or proficiency requirements I will need to meet?
2. When is the starting date?
3. Is there a probationary period? If so, how long?
4. How often will my work be evaluated (monthly, quarterly, semiannually) and by whom (immediate superior, committee)?
5. What types of on-the-job or professional training are required or offered?
6. Are there any mentoring programs in place?
7. Is there any support for continuing my education to improve my job performance?
8. What do you regard as the top priority for this job?
9. Would you give me some examples of how or where I might collaborate with follow employees or even my boss?
10. How will I be evaluated in terms of success on the job? Who will do the evaluating?

11. What are the most important things I can accomplish or work toward during my evaluation period on the job?
12. What is the next step in your hiring process?

Also, ask questions about the company's products and services, including a dedication to greening the environment.

What Interviewer(s) Can't Ask You

Federal and state laws limit the questions an interviewer can ask. Questions about your age, marital status, the number or names of any children, religion, race, national origin, disabilities, or sexual orientation violate equal opportunity employment laws. Here are a few examples of questions that cannot be asked in an interview and the types of diplomatic responses you might use:

- **How many children do you have? Are you planning on starting a family?** State that your family obligations will not interfere with your job, travel, overtime.
- **Are you a U.S. citizen?** Simply respond that you are authorized to work in the United States.
- **What is your maiden name?** This is a sneaky way of asking a woman about her marital status. You can answer by saying that the name on your résumé is the name on your professional license or other certification.
- **How far away from work do you live?** Employers cannot discriminate against you based on where you live or ask about how long it will take you to commute to work. Say "I am ready to be here at the start of the work day or at other times the job calls for."
- **Are you in the reserves or National Guard?** Employers cannot ask about your current or possible future position in the military. But they can ask if there any upcoming occasions where you would not be able to be present for a job-related function.

Confronted with questions like these, it is always better to answer them positively rather than bristling—"It's none of your business."

Ten Interview Do's and Don'ts

Keep in mind these other interview do's and don'ts:

1. Be on time. In fact, show up about fifteen minutes early in case the interviewer or human resources office wants you to complete some forms.
2. Turn off your cell phone and any other media device! The last thing you want is for your phone to ring or receive a text message during your interview. Never text during an interview.
3. Dress appropriately for the occasion and be well groomed. Avoid using strong perfume or cologne.
4. Be careful about tattoos. Job counselors warn that visible tattoos can hurt a job seeker's chance for success.

5. Greet the interviewer with a friendly and firm, but not vicelike, handshake. Don't offer a limp, fishy handshake either. Thank the interviewer for inviting you.

6. Don't sit down before the interviewer does. Wait for the interviewer to invite you to sit and to indicate where.

7. Speak slowly and distinctly; do not nervously hurry to finish your sentences, and never interrupt or finish an interviewer's sentences. Avoid one- or two-word answers, which sound unfriendly or unprepared. Do not use slang (e.g., "Awesome!" or "Chill") or overly casual language ("Like…" "You know?"). Don't monopolize the discussion by talking too much and always about yourself. And don't act arrogantly as if the job is yours already. Show a keen interest in the company and its products, services, employees, contributions to the environment.

8. Do not chew gum, click a ballpoint pen, fidget, twirl your hair, or tap your foot against the floor, a chair, or a desk.

9. Maintain appropriate eye contact with the interviewer; do not sheepishly stare at the floor or the desk. If you are interviewed by a group of individuals, make eye contact with each one of them. Body language is equally important. Don't fold your arms—a signal that you are closed to the interviewer's suggestions and comments. Sit up straight; do not slouch. Smile; it shows you are confident.

10. When the interview is over, thank the interviewer(s) for considering you for the job, and say you look forward to hearing from him or her.

The Follow-Up Letter

Within twenty-four hours of your interview, it is wise to send a follow-up letter thanking the interviewer for his or her time and interest in you. In your letter, reemphasize your qualifications for the job by showing how they apply to the requirements described by the interviewer. You might also ask for further information to show your interest in the job and the employer. The sample follow-up letter in Figure 7.17 accomplishes all of these things.

KEEP A JOB SEARCH RECORD

A critical component of any job search is keeping track of

- Where you sent your résumés/letters of application
- The version of your résumé sent for each opening
- Contact information for potential employers
- People you have networked with
- Responses you have received to job applications
- Any information about salary range or working conditions you may have received from the interviews you had

Tracking this information (either on paper or electronically) ensures you have the details you need.

FIGURE 7.17 A Follow-Up Letter

Marcia Le Borde
2739 East Street Latrobe, PA 17042-0312
(610) 555-6373 mlb@springboard.com

September 22, 2016

Mr. Jack Fukura, Director
Human Resources Dept.
Global Tech
1334 Ridge Road N.E.
Pittsburgh, PA 17122-3107

Dear Mr. Fukura:

I enjoyed talking with you yesterday and learning more about the security officer position available at Global Tech. It was especially helpful to take a tour of the plant's north gate to see the challenges it presents for the security officer stationed there.

Expresses gratitude for an interview and singles out main company feature

As you noted at the interview, my training in surveillance software has prepared me to operate the sophisticated equipment Global Tech has recently installed. Please thank Ms. Turner for me for taking time to demonstrate this technology.

Reemphasizes qualifications

I look forward to receiving the handbook about Global Tech's employee services. Would you also kindly email me a copy of the newsletter from last quarter that introduced the new security equipment to your employees?

Asks for newsletter to express future interest

Thank you, again, for interviewing me for the position and your hospitality. Please let me know if you have any other questions. I look forward to hearing from you.

Ends politely by thanking interviewer

Sincerely yours,

Marcia Le Borde

Marcia Le Borde

ACCEPTING OR DECLINING A JOB OFFER

If you accept a job, send the employer a letter within a week of the offer. Accepting verbally on the phone is not enough, and never accept or decline a job offer through an email, text, or tweet. Your letter will make your acceptance official and will be included in your permanent personnel file. Accepting a job is easy. Make the communication with your new employer a model of clarity and diplomacy.

Refusing a job requires tact. Inform an employer why you are not taking the job. But do not bluntly begin with the refusal. Instead, prepare the reader for bad news by finding something about the company or agency to compliment—its products, the friendly work environment, the interview process, etc. Then move to your refusal and supply an honest but not elaborate explanation of why you are not taking the job. Many students cite educational opportunities, work schedules, geographic preference, or additional professional opportunities. End on a friendly note because you may be interested in working for the company in the future and do not want to leave any bad feelings.

SEARCHING FOR THE RIGHT JOB PAYS

As we saw, finding the right job takes a lot of hard work (researching, organizing, networking, and writing). But all your efforts will pay off with your first and subsequent checks. May all your letters, résumés, portfolios/webfolios, and applications be models of successful writing at work.

✓ REVISION CHECKLIST

- [ ] Enhanced my professional image to apply for jobs for which I am qualified.
- [ ] Looked for relevant jobs on social and professional networking sites.
- [ ] Created a professional profile for Facebook and LinkedIn.
- [ ] Joined groups on LinkedIn to increase my network.
- [ ] Did not put personal information on a job board/the Internet.
- [ ] Prepared a dossier at school placement office, including supporting letters from professors, employers, and community officials.
- [ ] Identified places where relevant jobs are advertised.
- [ ] Networked with instructors, friends, relatives, and individuals who work for the companies I want to join; notified them that I am looking for a job.
- [ ] Researched the companies I am interested in—on the Internet, through printed sources, and by networking with current employees.
- [ ] Inventoried my strengths carefully to prepare résumé.
- [ ] Wrote a focused and persuasive career-objective statement.
- [ ] Determined the most beneficial format of résumé to use—chronological, functional, or both.
- [ ] Investigated creating a website for my job search–related documents.

☐ Prepared a portfolio/webfolio that includes documents demonstrating my professional skills and achievements relevant for the job.

☐ Made résumé attractive and easy to read, with logical and persuasive headings and descriptive keywords.

☐ Made sure résumé contains neither too much nor too little information.

☐ Proofread résumé to ensure everything is correct, consistent, and accurate.

☐ Adapted military experience for a civilian employer's job listing.

☐ Created properly formatted digital résumé to send to prospective employers.

☐ Wrote a letter of application that shows how my specific skills and background meet an employer's exact needs.

☐ Prepared a short oral presentation about myself and my accomplishments for an interview.

☐ Researched prospective employer's company or organization and salary range.

☐ Sent prospective employer a follow-up letter within a few days after interview to thank the interviewer and show interest in position.

☐ Maintained an accurate and up-to-date record of my job search, including where I sent my resumes and letters of application and contact information for people I have networked with and potential employers.

EXERCISES

1. Using at least four different sources, including social media/networking sites such as LinkedIn, compile a list of ten employers for whom you would like to work. Get their names, street and email addresses, phone numbers, and the names of the managers or human resources officers. Then select one company and profile it—locations, services, kinds of products or services offered, number of employees, clients served, awards, contributions to the community or environment, and any other pertinent facts.

2. Create an appropriate professional profile for LinkedIn.

3. Write a letter to a former employer, a community leader, or an instructor requesting a letter of recommendation.

4. Which of the following would belong on your résumé? Which would not belong? Why?

   a. your student ID number
   b. your driver's license number
   c. the zip codes of your references
   d. a list of all your English courses in college
   e. the section numbers of the courses in your major
   f. a statement that you are recently divorced
   g. subscriptions to journals in your field
   h. the titles of stories or poems you published in a high school literary magazine or newspaper
   i. your GPA for each year you were in college
   j. foreign languages you studied
   k. years you attended college
   l. the date you were discharged from the service

m. names of the neighbors you are using as references

n. your religion

o. job titles you held

p. your summer job waiting tables

q. your telephone number

r. the reason you changed schools

s. your current status with the National Guard

t. the URL of your website or blog

u. your volunteer work for the Red Cross

v. the number of hours per week you spend reading science fiction

w. the title of your last term paper in your major

x. the name of the agency or business where you worked last

5. Indicate what is wrong with the following career objectives, and rewrite them to make them more precise and professional.

a. Job in a lawyer's office

b. Position with a safety emphasis

c. Desire growth position in a large department store

d. Am looking for entry position in health sciences

e. Position in sales with fast promotion rate

f. Want a job working with semiconductor circuits

g. Desire a good-paying job, hours: 8–4:30, with time and a half for overtime. Would like to stay in the Omaha area

h. Insurance work

i. Working with media

j. Job with preschoolers

k. Full-time position with hospitality chain

l. I want a career in nursing

m. Police work, particularly in a suburb of a large city

n. Any position for a qualified dietitian

o. Although I have not made up my mind about which area of forestry I shall go into, I am looking for a job that offers me training and rewards based upon my potential

6. As part of a team or on your own, revise the following poor résumé to make it more precise and persuasive. Include additional details where necessary and exclude any details that would hurt the job seeker's chances. Also correct any inconsistencies.

RÉSUMÉ OF

Powell T. Harrison
8604 So. Kirkpatrick St.
Ardville, Ohio
345 37 8760
614 234 4587
harrison@gem.com

<u>PERSONAL</u>	Confidential
CAREER <u>OBJECTIVE</u>	Seek good paying position with progressive Sunbelt company.

EDUCATION

2014–2016   Will receive degree from Central Tech. Institute in Arch. St.
             Earned high average last semester. Took necessary courses
             for major; interested in systems, plans, and design develop-
             ment.

2012–2014   Attended Ardville High School, Ardville, OH; took all courses
             required. Served on several student committees.

EXPERIENCE   None, except for numerous part-time jobs and student
             apprenticeship in the Ardville area. As part of student app.
             worked with local firm for two months.

HOBBIES   Surfing the Net, playing Playstation, Member of Junior Achieve-
             ment.

REFERENCES   Please write for names and addresses.

7. Determine what is wrong with the following sentences in a letter of application. Rewrite them to eliminate any mistakes, to focus on the "you attitude," or to make them more precise.

   a. Even though I have very little actual job experience, I can make up for it in enthusiasm.
   b. My qualifications will prove that I am the best person for your job.
   c. I would enjoy working with your other employees.
   d. This email résumé is my application for any job you now have open or expect to fill in the near future.
   e. Next month, my family and I will be moving to Detroit, and I must get a job in the area. Will you have anything open?
   f. If you are interested in me, then I hope that we make some type of arrangements to interview each other soon.
   g. I have not included a résumé because all pertinent information about me is in this letter.
   h. My GPA is only 2.5, but I did make two B's in my last term.
   i. I hope to take state boards soon.
   j. Your company, or so I have heard through the grapevine, has excellent fringe ben-efits. That is what I care about most, so I am applying for any position that you may advertise.
   k. I am writing to ask you to kindly consider whether I would be a qualified person for the position you announced in the newspaper.
   l. I have made plans to further my education.
   m. My résumé speaks for itself.

    n. I could not possibly accept a position that required weekend work, and night work is out, too.

    o. In my own estimation, I am a go-getter—an eager beaver, so to speak.

    p. My last employer was dead wrong when he let me go. I think he regrets it now.

    q. When you want to arrange an interview time, give me a call. I am home every afternoon after 4:00.

8. Explain why the following letter of application is ineffective. Rewrite it to make it more precise and appropriate.

Apartment 32
Jeggler Drive
Talcott, Arizona
Monday
Grandt Corporation
Production Supervisor
Capital City, Arizona

Dear Sir:

I am writing to ask you if your company will consider me for the position you announced online recently. I believe that with my education (I have an associate degree) and experience (I have worked four years as a freight supervisor), I could fill your job.

My schoolwork was done at two junior colleges, and I took more than enough courses in business management and information technology. In fact, here is a list of some of my courses: Supervision, Materials Management, Work Experience in Management, E-commerce, Safety Tactics, Introduction to Software Analysis, Art Design, Contemporary Business Principles, and Small Business Management. In addition, I have worked as a loading dock supervisor for the last two years, and before that I worked in the military in the Quartermaster Corps.

Please let me know if you are interested in me. I would like to have an interview with you at the earliest possible date, since there are some other firms also interested in me, too.

Eagerly yours,

George D. Milhous

---

9. Select two sources discussed in "Looking in the Right Places for a Job" on pages 239–242, and find notices for two or three jobs you believe you are qualified to fill, and then write a letter of application for one of them.

10. Write a chronological résumé to accompany the letter you wrote for Exercise 9.

11. Write a functional résumé to accompany your application letter in Exercise 9.

12. Bring the two résumés you prepared for Exercises 10 and 11 to class to be critiqued by a collaborative writing team. After your résumés are reviewed, revise them. Write an email to your instructor about the revisions you made, and explain why they will help you in your job search. Attach your résumé to the email.

13. Prepare a digital version of the résumé you prepared in either Exercise 10 or Exercise 11.

PART III

Gathering and Summarizing Information

Part opening image: George Hammerstein/Fancy/Corbis

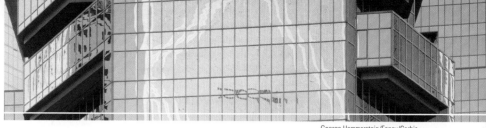

George Hammerstein/Fancy/Corbis

CHAPTER

8

Doing Research, Evaluating Sources, and Preparing Documentation in the Workplace

Being able to do research is crucial for success on the job, whatever company or department you work for and whatever your job title. Research is the lifeblood of a company. You can expect to spend as much as 25 to 30 percent of your time at work doing research. Companies use research to make major decisions that affect production, sales, service, hiring, promotions, and locations, as the research report at the end of this chapter illustrates (Figure 8.10, pages 349–363). Research follows a process. You have to gather, summarize, and organize information before you can interpret it. Then, in interpreting it, you must be able to answer questions and solve problems. Research does not always go as smoothly as you might expect it to. Don't get discouraged. Understand that such hurdles are temporary, and see them as opportunities to make sure your work is accurate, complete, and relevant.

SKILLS NECESSARY TO DO RESEARCH

To do effective research, you need to know how to

- network with people in your department, within your company, outside of your company, and potentially across the globe to gather relevant data
- read a host of print and online sources at your company or a library to find the most relevant studies/opinions on your topic
- do direct observations, perform tests, and make site visits
- interview one person or a carefully selected group of people
- prepare and send out surveys and analyze the results

- organize information into clear and accurate reports that answer questions and solve problems
- carefully and completely document your sources to give proper credit and to help readers find your sources

CHARACTERISTICS OF EFFECTIVE WORKPLACE RESEARCH

The research you do on the job needs to follow the highest professional and ethical standards. Businesses leave little margin for error and often do not give employees a second chance to get it right. To make sure your research meets your employer's expectations, it must be

1. Relevant. Job-related research must focus directly on providing specific answers and solutions to the key questions and problems affecting your company.

2. Current. Your information must be up-to-date. Markets and technologies change rapidly, and employers will insist that your research is on the cutting edge of your profession.

3. Accurate. Double- and triple-check all of the facts and figures, dates, addresses, names, regulations, URLs, and so on, used in your research. Don't substitute guesswork and unsupported estimates for hard facts. Make sure you record all information accurately.

4. Thorough. Look at a question or problem from all sides. Network with colleagues to look for any gaps or inconsistencies, as well as business opportunities. Confirm all options and opinions. Never omit important data.

5. Realistic. Base your research on realistic, profitable conclusions. Unsubstantiated recommendations that fly in the face of a company's protocol (e.g., drop a product line, hire or fire twenty-five people, or move a plant) may not be logical, profitable, or acceptable. Be sure that your research is consistent with your company's policies.

6. Ethical and legal. Obtain your findings ethically and lawfully so that you do not infringe on the rights of others. Plagiarism (see "What Must Be Cited," page 338), raiding someone's unpublished research, sharing confidential or privileged information with a third party, or skewing the results of a survey are all unethical acts. Be sure, too, that all of your recommendations are environmentally sound; follow a strong green philosophy.

THE RESEARCH PROCESS

As in the writing process, in doing research you may find yourself repeating certain steps. Say, for example, you are writing a business proposal and are incorporating information from several sources you've researched. At this stage of the process, you might think you've gathered enough information. However, as you work on the proposal, you may realize that it raises new questions. That may lead you back to repeating previous steps.

Let's look at the process in more detail:

Step 1. Confirm the purpose and audience of your report. Know who your audience is and why you are writing to them.

Step 2. Consult a variety of resources. Consult different sources in different media formats: print, online, and possibly audio and video. Don't rely on only a single source—one website or one trade journal.

Step 3. Evaluate sources, both in print and online. Given the explosion of information online, you have to be able to evaluate the content of what you read. Be prepared to read newspapers, journals, tests, surveys, interviews, websites, social media sites, blogs, and printed sources critically to see if the writers have a particular agenda or bias that might slant their opinion on the topic.

For more information, see "Evaluating Websites" on pages 331–333.

Step 4. Confer with appropriate resource people and experts at work, in your profession, and in your community. These can be individuals from different divisions of your company (IT, human resources, finance) or co-workers and members of your collaborative team. You might also consult various specialists who work for the local, state, or federal government.

Step 5. Continue to ask questions. Be sure to ask the right questions at each stage of your investigation. As you read, conduct an interview, make a site visit, send emails, or search databases, you may encounter dead ends, contradictions, and even new sources or leads you need to investigate.

Step 6. Document your sources. One of the most important steps in the research process is documenting—citing the various sources of information (online, in print, from interviews, site visits, etc.) on which your report or presentation is based. A later section of this chapter ("Documenting Sources," pages 337–347) will give you specific guidelines for how to do this.

TWO TYPES OF RESEARCH: PRIMARY AND SECONDARY

As we saw, you can expect to use many sources of information during the research process. But essentially your research will fall into two categories: **primary** and **secondary**. Both kinds of research are important to help you obtain a better understanding of your topic and provide your supervisor or customers with the careful and complete answers and recommendations they expect. You will often do both types of research, as the marketing report at the end of this chapter (Figure 8.10, pages 349–363) illustrates. In fact, one type of research sheds light on the other.

Conducting Primary Research

Doing primary research means consulting sources of information not found in printed documents or on the Web. It involves interacting directly with people, places, and things, and it is often done in the office, in the field, or in a laboratory. This type of research often requires gathering information from customers, clients, or other individuals who rely on your company's products or services.

Doing Secondary Research

Secondary research involves consulting existing print and online sources. When you conduct secondary research, you work with materials that someone else—an expert in your field, a government agency, even a competitor—has published, posted, or distributed.

Methods of Primary versus Secondary Research

Here are some examples of the different methods of doing primary and secondary research on the job:

Primary	Secondary
making direct observations	evaluating websites and social media sites
performing tests	searching databases
going on site visits/inspections	reading books, journals, and magazines
conducting interviews	consulting manuals and reference works
coordinating focus groups	examining product reviews
developing, sending, and analyzing surveys	using government documents

PRIMARY RESEARCH

There are several ways of doing primary research, including the following:

- direct observation, site visits, and tests
- interviews and focus groups
- surveys

Direct Observation, Site Visits, and Tests

Direct observation is seeing what is right in front of you—for instance, watching how an individual performs a task, determining how a piece of equipment works, or studying how a procedure is performed. The key to conducting effective research is observing actively, not passively.

Site visits require you to use the same keen attention to detail that you use in direct observation, except you will need to go to an off-site location to report what you find there. A site visit could take you to another department in your company, a prospective customer's office, the scene of an incident or accident, or an agricultural or manufacturing location relevant to your business report. See Figure 14.11 (see pages 585–586) for an example of an incident report based on visiting the site where a railroad accident occurred. Regardless of the location, you will have to describe for your boss precisely what you witnessed firsthand. Figure 14.8 (pages 576–577) contains an example of a trip report about opening a new restaurant based on information obtained from a site visit.

Conducting **tests** is another productive way to do primary research involving the observation of people, places, conditions, and things. A test can be as simple as examining two pieces of comparable office equipment side-by-side and noting how they compare, or trying out a new email marketing strategy. Or it can be as scientifically demanding as conducting a laboratory test. Figures 14.9 (page 580) and 14.10 (pages 581–583) are examples of reports based on laboratory tests conducted in the world of work.

Sometimes you may have to use all three types of research based on observation when preparing your report, as Kirk Smith did for a water-quality study in Figure 8.1. Not only did he observe and record the data-collection methods used at the three different municipal reservoirs, but he also visited these sites and conducted his own tests.

Interviews and Focus Groups

Two other important sources of primary information come from interviews and focus groups. You can do a one-on-one **interview** with an expert in the field, a co-worker, a client, or another resource person. Or you can hold a **focus group**, a question-and-answer session with multiple people—both company representatives and customers—attending. Interviews with employees as well as with focus groups allow you to gather essential information from and about a variety of customers.

Interviews

Interviews can be conducted in person, over the telephone, or through email, although Skype conversations and face-to-face meetings are the most productive way to generate relevant information. Figure 8.2 (page 310) contains an excerpt from an interview with a U.S. manager whose company transferred her to the company's Hongzhou, China, location for eighteen months. Note how the interviewer researched and structured his questions to help other employees who might be transferred to China.

Follow the process below when you have to conduct an interview for your workplace research.

1. Set Up the Interview

- Ask your supervisor or co-workers to help you identify experts or relevant customers you should interview, or consult other sources, such as business directories, client or customer lists, or professional organizations.
- Politely request an interview with the individual at his or her convenience. Be flexible. Your interviewee is giving you his or her time. Always let the individual know ahead of time exactly what you would like to discuss and why you are conducting the interview.
- Specify how much time you will need for the interview. Be realistic—fifteen minutes may be too short; two hours much too long.

FIGURE 8.1 A Report Based on Direct Observation, Site Visits, and Tests

---

Water Flow and Quality Evaluation of the Cambridge, Massachusetts, Drinking Water Source Area
Kirk P. Smith

The drinking water source for Cambridge, Massachusetts, consists of three primary storage reservoirs (Hobbs Brook Reservoir, Stony Brook Reservoir, and Fresh Pond), two principal streams (Hobbs Brook and Stony Brook), and nine small tributaries. Because previous investigations identified specific areas as potentially important sources of contaminants, several sites were selected for continuous monitoring to address the water supply regulations followed by the Cambridge Water Department (CWD). The purpose of this report is to evaluate the measurement methods used by the CWD.

    Reservoir altitude and meteorological measurement were recorded by monitoring stations installed at each reservoir. Water quality measurements of reservoir water were also recorded at USGS stations 01104880 and 42233020. These data were recorded at a frequency of 15 minutes, were uploaded to a U.S. Geological Survey (USGS) database on an hourly basis by phone modem, and were put on the Web at **http://ma.water.usgs.gov**. Stream-stage measurements were also recorded by monitoring stations on each principal stream and at the outlet of the Stony Brook Reservoir. These data were recorded every 15 minutes and were uploaded to a USGS database on an hourly basis by phone modem.

    In addition to measurements made on the principal streams, stream-stage and water-quality data were recorded by monitoring stations on 4 of the 9 small tributaries. My visits to these sites and independent water samplings confirm that CWD's measurements comply with USGS standards.

    Since the drainage areas of these sites are small and have large percentages of impervious surface, the risk of flooding, and often the quality of the water itself, can change rapidly. To document these responses effectively, the monitoring stations have recorded stream-stage and water-quality measurements at variable frequencies as high as 1 minute. These data were uploaded to a USGS database on an hourly basis and are available through **http://ma.water.usgs.gov**. I have found through visits and water sampling that CWD is not only compliant with, but exceeds, USGS standards in measuring drainage area water quality.

Margin annotations:
- *Provides key background information*
- *States purpose*
- *Explains methods using specific techniques to record accurate measurements*
- *Records data objectively*
- *Identifies variables important for tests*
- *Gives conclusion based on tests and observations*

Source: Adapted from *Hydrologic, Water-Quality, Bed-Sediment, Soil-Chemistry, and Statistical Summaries of Data for the Cambridge, Massachusetts, Drinking-Water Source Areas, Water Year 2004,* by Kirk P. Smith. U.S. Department of the Interior/U.S. Geological Survey. Open-File Report 2005–1383.

FIGURE 8.2 An Excerpt from an Interview Transcript

<table>
<tr>
<td>Logical opening question about preparation for visit</td>
<td>

Q: How did you prepare for your transfer to China?

A: Before I left for my eighteen-month stay, I profited most from participating in teleconferences with our other Chinese offices and attending China trade fairs in the United States and Canada. I also immersed myself in intensive, but admittedly very basic, conversational Chinese. And, of course, I partnered with several of I-Systems Chinese employees and managers here in Pittsburgh.

</td>
</tr>
<tr>
<td>Turns to problems in new job</td>
<td>

Q: What would you say was the biggest obstacle an American manager might face when working in China?

A: Seeing China through Western eyes.

</td>
</tr>
<tr>
<td>Asks for clarification</td>
<td>

Q: When you say "seeing China," what do you mean?

A: By that I mean looking at China from an American business perspective. We tend to think in U.S. terms about expanding and opening markets, that is, what we can do for China. But my Chinese colleagues reminded me about China's impact on American markets. While the United States accounts for only about 5 percent of the world's population, China has about 20 to 25 percent of it and can powerfully influence our company's decisions. Accordingly, we needed to shift our thinking about what China could do for us. To do this, we must have an appreciation of the Chinese way of doing business.

</td>
</tr>
<tr>
<td>Relevant follow-up question</td>
<td>

Q: What characterizes the Chinese way of doing business, as opposed to how we do it in the United States?

A: Americans have no problems mixing business and pleasure. In fact, we are famous for the business lunch or dinner. Banquets are great occasions to talk shop, to sell our products, services, and websites. But in China a dinner is strictly a social event, one for entertaining and not marketing. It is considered rude in China to inject talk about sales, quotas, operations, or e-markets at a dinner.

</td>
</tr>
<tr>
<td>Keeps interviewer focused on topic</td>
<td></td>
</tr>
<tr>
<td>Asks for further information</td>
<td>

Q: Do you have any other advice for U.S. workers whose companies relocate them to China?

A: Be careful about gestures and gifts.

</td>
</tr>
<tr>
<td>Good follow-up question</td>
<td>

Q: Why do you link the two?

A: To illustrate a major blunder, one of my colleagues kept patting a Chinese executive on the back, a sign in America of friendship and approval. Not so in China. It is seen as discourteous.

Q: And the gifts?

A: While some business gifts are appropriate, never give a Chinese executive a clock or stopwatch. It signals doom or death.

</td>
</tr>
</table>

2. Prepare for the Interview

- Continue to research your topic so that you have sufficient background information and do not waste time by requesting information available on the Web or from another source.
- Determine what information you need from the interview to help you solve the problem or answer the questions essential to your report. Be sure to prioritize getting the essential information you need.

3. Draft Your Questions Prepare your questions ahead of time, and take them to the interview. Never try to wing it. Your questions should be

- focused on the topic you want to find out about to avoid vague answers
- open-ended and designed to prompt thoughtful responses, not just yes or no answers
- objectively worded so that the interviewee is not forced to respond to loaded questions

Here are some examples of poorly written questions with effective revisions:

Vague Question	Restricted Question
How can a website help customers?	In what ways can we improve the navigational signals on our website to help customers find information quicker?

Yes or No Question	Open-Ended Question
Do you think big business is opposed to a healthy environment?	Would you identify two or three ways we could green our office space?

Loaded Question	Objectively Worded Question
Isn't the future of real estate security investments doomed to a bleak future?	What are your thoughts about the future of real estate security investments?

4. Conduct the Interview

- Show up for the interview on time, and dress appropriately.
- Always ask permission to record the interview or to take photographs.
- Stay focused. Don't stray from the topic or delve into personal matters.
- Be an attentive and appreciative listener. Let the interviewee do most of the talking.
- If the interviewee does not want to answer a question or has no further information to add, don't press the point. Move to the next question.
- If the interviewee(s) says that something is "off the record," respect his or her request and do not include it in your transcript or notes, or on tape.
- At the end of the interview, allow time for your interviewee to clarify any of his or her responses.

5. Follow Up After the Interview

- It's best to read through your notes immediately after the interview, while the conversation is still fresh in your mind.
- Thank the interviewee by letter or email within a day or two following the interview.
- If the interviewee requested a transcript of the interview, send it to him or her.
- Always request permission to quote anything from the interview in your report or presentation to your company or clients.

Focus Groups

Focus groups are typically composed of loyal or prospective customers who have been invited to give a company their opinions about a specific product, service, or future project. A company might also include paid consultants and even individuals selected from competitors' lists. Focus groups are used to obtain a wider variety of opinions than individual interviews may give and they are more personal and interactive than surveys. Businesses rely heavily on these groups to get honest, well-considered feedback from interested individuals and to incorporate that feedback into their research. Focus groups are usually conducted in face-to-face meetings, but virtual meeting technologies (see "Tech Note on Virtual Meetings," page 104) allow people outside of the area, even globally, to participate.

Follow the guidelines below to conduct a successful focus group:

1. Set Up the Focus Group

- Identify who should be invited to the focus group and how many individuals should be a part of that group. Effective focus groups usually consist of six to twelve participants to get a diversity of opinions but keep the group from being too crowded and unmanageable.
- Once you decide on the participants, give them with all of the details they need about the location, payment or reimbursement, and topics to be discussed.

2. Prepare for the Focus Group

- Formulate the specific questions you need to ask. As in a one-on-one interview, prepare your questions ahead of time, avoiding vague, yes or no, or loaded questions. Limit your questions to allow for ample discussion time.
- Plan to record the focus group and to bring in a co-leader or moderator to take notes. Unlike in a one-on-one interview, you will not be able to take effective notes while leading a focus group.

3. Conduct the Focus Group

- At the beginning of the meeting, establish reasonable ground rules, such as the importance of staying on topic, speaking in turn, and meeting the goals of the group (see "Sources of Conflict in Collaborative Groups and How to Solve Them," pages 81–83).

- Politely remind the group about confidentiality. Many companies have participants fill out confidentiality agreements before the group meets.
- Stick closely to the agenda. Don't stray off topic yourself or allow participants to do so.

4. Follow Up After the Focus Group Meets

- Record any observations about the group dynamic as a whole and about the individual participants, since this information may affect your results.
- Thank the participants again by letter or email within a day or two after the group meets.

Use of Social Networking Sites as a Recruiting Tool Many researchers and companies find social networking sites such as Facebook and Twitter useful for recruiting participants for research projects and for studying consumer trends. Companies or individuals wanting to organize a focus group, for example, can tweet a request to their customers on Twitter to generate participants, or have their followers participate in a tweet chat that takes place at a designated day/time and uses specially designated hashtags to allow participants to contribute their views. Questions can be posed and responses generated on Twitter, or you can direct participants to a more formal online survey outside of Twitter.

You can also use Facebook as a recruiting tool. By creating a Facebook "event" for a research project or focus group, companies and researchers can advertise the project or focus group session, distribute information, and even begin to collect data about participants, all from the same site. Twitter and Facebook are also useful for market researchers who need to find information about new products, services, technologies, and pricing. This type of research is especially helpful when you need to gather information within specific communities. Facebook, for example, allows users to create groups around virtually any topic, thus assisting researchers to find information, observe developing trends, or gauge reaction to new products by simply joining the group and following the posts already there.

Surveys

Surveys are among the most frequently used ways to conduct primary research in the world of work. Think of a survey as an interview with a relatively large number of people. The goal of a survey is simple — to collect and then quantify information about individuals' attitudes, habits, beliefs, product loyalty, knowledge, or opinions. You can conduct a survey over the phone, online, or by mail.

Five Steps for Using a Survey

There are five basic steps you need to follow when using a survey as a part of your research on the job:

1. Determine the Best Way to Deliver the Survey Surveys can be conducted over the phone, online, or by mail. Decide which medium you think will yield the best results and will work within your time frame and budget. If you need to receive detailed answers about a given topic, conduct a telephone survey, which gives you an opportunity to talk directly to the respondents and allows them to clarify their answers. But if your aim is to obtain results quickly and inexpensively, do an online survey.

2. Create the Survey Questionnaire There are many types of questions you can ask, as illustrated in Figure 8.3, including yes/no, ranking, rating, multiple-choice, and open-ended questions. Researchers advise asking questions that require the least amount of effort on the part of the respondents (yes/no, multiple-choice) to increase their chances of answering your questionnaire. Keep your survey to ten to fifteen questions in increase your response rate. Note how the WH eComm questionnaire in Figure 8.3 (pages 316–317) includes only twelve key questions, which the company needs to have answered to help it make important decisions. Finally, design your questionnaire to look inviting and streamlined. (See "The ABCs of Print Document Design" on pages 449–459 in Chapter 11 for guidelines to make your questionnaire look easy to complete.)

Here are some guidelines for writing specific questions to help you get the results you want—whether you are writing a mail or an online questionnaire or preparing a script for a telephone survey.

1. Phrase questions precisely. Vague questions only elicit answers that you cannot use or will be unable to analyze. Use valid, quantifiable questions.

> Ineffective: Are we open enough hours on Saturdays?
>   Yes____ No____
> Better: How many hours would you like us to be open on Saturdays?
>   4____ 5____ 6____ 7____ 8____

2. Ask only one question at a time. Avoid multiple questions within the same question, since you will not know the exact answer to each question.

> Ineffective: What is your overall impression of our customer support and delivery services?
>   poor___ fair____ good____ very good____ excellent____
> Better: (Turn the two questions above into two separate queries as follows.)
>   What is your overall impression of our customer support service?
>   poor___ fair____ good____ very good____ excellent____
>   How would you rate our delivery service?
>   poor___ fair____ good____ very good____ excellent____

3. Clearly differentiate each option in multiple-choice questions. If respondents are not sure of the differences among options, they may answer inappropriately because of question overlap, or they may skip the question altogether.

> Ineffective: When is the best time to call you?
>   Daytime___ Afternoon___ Weekday___ After work___ Evening___ Night___
> Better: When is the best time to call you?
>   Morning (8:00 a.m.–noon)___ Afternoon (noon–5:00 p.m.)___
>   Evening (5:00 p.m.–10:00 p.m.)___

4. Supply all of the necessary options in multiple-choice questions. If you omit an important option, respondents may choose a misleading answer or not answer at all.

Ineffective: Which types of nonalcoholic beverages would you like us to offer?

soda___ juice___ coffee/tea___ milk___

Better: Which types of nonalcoholic beverages would you like us to offer?

soda___ juice___ coffee/tea___ milk___ bottled water___ other (please specify)___

(The "bottled water" and "other" options give respondents a fuller range of answers.)

5. Do not use unfamiliar jargon or abbreviations. Don't assume that respondents will understand the jargon your company or profession uses.

Ineffective: What was your overall impression of the CGI in this film?

poor___ fair___ good___ very good___ excellent___

Better: What was your overall impression of the computer-generated imagery used in this film to create the global village scene?

poor___ fair___ good___ very good___ excellent___

6. Do not ask inappropriate questions. Refrain from asking questions about income, education level, or other personal matters such as age, ethnicity/race, gender, disability, religion, or sexual orientation unless these questions give you essential demographic information directly relevant to the topic of your survey.

7. Avoid leading or biased questions. Do not give your respondents slanted questions that bias their answer and thus the results of your survey.

Ineffective: Were you impressed by this award-winning product?

Yes___ No___

Better: Did you think this was an award-quality product?

Yes___ No___

8. Limit multiple-choice and ranking items to five items. The more complicated your list of multiple-choice or ranked items, the more difficult it will be for your respondents to give a clear and helpful answer and for you to analyze the survey results.

9. Limit rating ranges to a scale of 1 to 5. As with item 8 above, do not complicate your survey by providing a scale with such a wide range of options that respondents are unclear about how they differ or overlap.

CASE STUDY

The WH eComm Survey

Many online vendors ask customers, after a purchase, to rate their online shopping experience. Online customer feedback not only helps e-commerce companies learn about the level of their customers' satisfaction; it also helps them find out about customer preferences to make crucial business decisions.

Note how the WH eComm survey in Figure 8.3 (pages 316–317) asks both types of questions. Some questions ask about customer preferences (questions 1, 2, 5, 6, 8, and 9 fall into this category), while others ask about customer satisfaction (questions 3, 4, 7, and 10). The

(Continued)

FIGURE 8.3 An Example of an Online Survey

Cover email explains why survey is important to customers

Provides incentive to reply

Easy-to-read format

Fill-in option does not require a lengthy answer

Question is not phrased in a leading manner

WH eComm Customer Satisfaction Survey - Message (HTML)

FILE   MESSAGE   INSERT   OPTIONS   FORMAT TEXT   REVIEW

From: <Gregg_Laos@whecomm.com>

To: <Carol_Smith@acme.com>

Cc:

Subject: WH eComm Customer Satisfaction Survey

Dear Valued WH eComm Customer,

At WH eComm, we are committed to providing our customers with high-quality e-commerce software through an efficient and user-friendly website. Customer feedback is extremely important in helping us continue to improve our website. So that we may best meet your needs, please answer a few questions about your experience at WH eComm. You will find the survey on our website by clicking here. Your answers will help us continue to improve WH eComm online and to give you the efficient and prompt service you deserve.

To say thank you for filling out this short questionnaire, we want to offer you a 25 percent discount on your next purchase. When you have completed the survey, your discount will automatically be credited to your WH eComm online account.

Many thanks for your time and your confidence in us,

Gregg Laos
Manager
WH eComm

WH eComm
revolutionizing e-commerce

1. How many times have you visited our website?
○ First visit   ○ 2–4 times   ○ 5–7 times   ○ More than 7

2. How did you hear about our website?
○ Colleague
○ Advertisement in business journal
○ Another website
○ Search engine
○ Other (please specify) _____

3. Is the website easy to navigate?
○ Very easy   ○ Easy   ○ Somewhat easy   ○ Not easy

FIGURE 8.3 (Continued)

4. **How effective did you find the following sections of WH eComm?**

	Extremely effective	Effective	Could be improved	Ineffective
Web features	○	○	○	○
Search	○	○	○	○
FAQ	○	○	○	○
Online checkout	○	○	○	○

One question can elicit a great deal of consumer information

5. **How many times have you purchased our products?**
   ○ 1–2 times   ○ 3–4 times   ○ 5–7 times   ○ 8–9 times
   ○ More than 9

6. **What types of products have you purchased from WH eComm? (Check as many as apply.)**
   ○ E-commerce software   ○ Web design software
   ○ Networking software   ○ E-conferencing software

Multiple-choice items clearly differentiated

7. **How helpful did you find our customer service?**
   ○ Extremely helpful
   ○ Helpful
   ○ Could be improved
   ○ Not helpful

8. **How have you most often contacted our customer service center?**
   ○ Phone   ○ Email   ○ Fax   ○ Web

Provides non-overlapping choices

9. **How soon was your query answered (if applicable)?**
   ○ Same day   ○ Next day   ○ Within 3 days   ○ Within a week   ○ Longer

10. **How satisfied were you with the speed and efficiency of our customer service center?**
    ○ Very satisfied   ○ Somewhat satisfied   ○ Dissatisfied

Limits options

11. **Please rank, in order of importance, which factors most influence your online purchases.**

	Price	Shipping options/time	Returns policy	Website quality
Most important	○	○	○	○
	○	○	○	○
	○	○	○	○
	○	○	○	○
	○	○	○	○
Least important	○	○	○	○

Ranking question supplies all necessary options

12. **What would you most like to see changed or improved on our website?**

[   ]

Provides opportunity for respondent to elaborate

Thank you for taking the time to answer our questions.

Home

questions about customer preferences can be used to help the company decide where to advertise ("How did you hear about our website?") and to determine which products to promote ("What types of products have you purchased from WH eComm?"). The questions about customer satisfaction, meanwhile, elicit information to help the company improve its service by assessing such things as the usefulness of its website ("Is the website easy to navigate?") and the quality of its customer service ("How helpful did you find our customer service?").

In order to ensure that a meaningful number of customers replied to the survey, WH eComm made the questions easy to answer by simplifying the options as well as the format of the questions. Moreover, asking only twelve questions and providing an incentive (a 25% discount on the next purchase) also encouraged customers to respond.

3. Choose the Survey Recipients The success of a survey, of course, depends on targeting the right audience and in the right numbers. Sometimes that audience is small and easy to reach. For example, you might survey people within your own company, agency, or department (all of the nurses in ICU). But more often, the group you want to survey—all of your California customers or vendors, for example—is so large that you could not possibly survey the opinions of every member of that group. In that case, you need to gather information from enough people to make reliable and relevant judgments about the larger population, and you have to select a representative cross section of individuals from the larger group (by age, gender, background, experience, education, etc.).

4. Reach the Survey Recipients Don't expect all of your respondents, or even 40 or 50 percent, for that matter, to reply to your questionnaire. Researchers find that a response rate of 12 percent from a statistically chosen sample group is still valid. But to increase the chances of receiving replies from as many respondents as possible, follow these time-tested procedures:

- Provide a cover letter or email, as in Figure 8.3, asking recipients to reply and thanking them in advance for doing so.
- Offer respondents some incentive to answer the survey, such as the discount that WH eComm promises in Figure 8.3.
- Indicate whether respondents should identify themselves or remain anonymous.
- Clearly specify how the respondents are to answer the questions—using a check mark, circling the correct response, writing in a number, or just pointing and clicking.

5. Compile and Analyze the Survey Results The final step in conducting a survey is compiling and analyzing the results and to arrive at reliable and workable solutions. Here are some helpful tips to follow:

1. **Keep your completed surveys organized, and save them.** Don't throw away the completed surveys; you may need to refer to specific answers later, or your company or department may need to archive all surveys.

2. Create a data sheet. Originate a data sheet—for instance, an Excel spreadsheet—so that you can record all of the survey responses in one central document. Break the data sheet into logical categories, for instance, separate rows for each survey question and separate columns for each possible answer.

3. Record responses completely and accurately. Always record responses exactly as you receive them. If the response to a question is blank or illegible (or gives several answers to the same question), discard that response rather than making something up or guessing what the respondent meant.

4. Present your findings clearly and effectively. To help your boss or other readers understand your findings, create one or more simple tables in which you present key information in an easy-to-read format. Also supply a blank sample questionnaire for reference.

Online Survey Builders

There are a wide variety of free online survey-building websites, such as Survey Monkey (surveymonkey.com), Qualtrics (qualtrics.com), Free Online Surveys (freeonlinesurveys.com), and Kwik Surveys (kwiksurveys.com) that allow you to create, tally, and draw conclusions. These programs provide help on how to generate questions that will yield the best possible data, tabulate results automatically, and produce reports and graphics based upon those responses. An online program is especially helpful when you have to conduct a very large survey, reducing the amount of time it would take to compile and quantify responses. The automation of such programs further helps you to eliminate inaccuracies in the data that might otherwise occur as a result of human error.

SECONDARY RESEARCH

As we saw earlier ("Two Types of Research: Primary and Secondary," pages 306–307), secondary research requires you to consult sources that are already available (books, periodicals, reference works, websites, blogs, social media sites, etc.), as opposed to interacting directly with people, places, and things via direct observation, site visits, tests, interviews, focus groups, and surveys. Secondary research involves gathering documents and reading, summarizing, and incorporating them into your report.

Libraries

As part of your workplace research, you can expect to use one or more of the following types of libraries:

- corporate libraries
- public and academic libraries
- e-libraries

Corporate Libraries

One of the fastest, easiest, and most profitable ways to locate and collect crucial research data about your company is to consult your company or agency library.

Corporate libraries contain a vital history of a company's activities, past and present, and also houses business-specific and confidential documents not found in a public or academic library.

Types of Research Materials in a Corporate Library Regardless of the size of your company, the following documents and information are likely to be found in its corporate library, in its intranet archive, or in departmental files (e.g., IT, marketing, etc.):

- client and customer records
- corporate reports, studies, surveys, and proposals
- corporate newsletters—from inception to the present
- maps, diagrams, blueprints/specs
- legal records, including patents and contracts
- financial and operational information organized by month, year, or longer cycles
- books and trade periodicals directly related to your company's research and business
- product and service literature (catalogs, descriptions, technical specifications, training manuals, warranties, etc.) (See "Tech Note: Gray Literature," page 328.)
- competitor information, including comparative analyses, competitor catalogs, and sales information

Expect to supplement information from your corporate library with information from other sources and locations. Materials found in a corporate library may take you only part of the way toward what you need to learn. Supplement what you find in your corporate library with primary research, Web research, and trips to public or academic libraries.

Public and Academic Libraries

To start your library research using a public or academic library, access the home page for a full range of its services and for directions on how to conduct a search. Figure 8.4 shows the home page for one academic library, including links for reaching a librarian, accessing electronic resources, and locating relevant documents. Note how the library has made it easy for patrons to connect with the right department for assistance with their research. To make searching even more efficient and convenient, many libraries belong to a network, regional or global, of participating libraries, enabling patrons to access the catalogs of member libraries in the group, for instance the New Jersey State Library's Directory of Libraries. Also expect to consult WorldCat, a universal catalog of resources that lets you know whether the public and academic libraries in your area or the world over own a particular book, while Ex Libris Primo allows users to search their local library, regional, and international resources, as well as sources found with more standard web-based search engines like Google.

Start with your library's online catalog to make your research easier because of the powerful search options available as well as the various databases the library

FIGURE 8.4 An Academic Library's Home Page

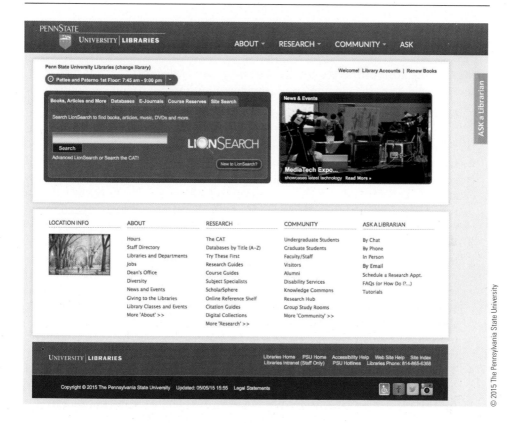

TECH NOTE

Intranets

As the name suggests, **intranets** are internal communication networks modeled after the Internet. They use passwords, directories, search engines, and multimedia content. Like the Internet, diversified companies, government agencies, and many large corporations use intranets to post documents, share and archive information, coordinate calendars, hold virtual meetings, conduct training sessions, make announcements, and post newsletters. (See Figure 4.5, page 128.) From a central directory, information is sent to, from, and within various divisions within the company—management, engineering, sales, human resources, environmental safety, public relations, and so forth. Documents might be designated as available to all employees or restricted, depending on the audience for and content of the document. Some files may, therefore, be closed to you because of confidentiality.

subscribes to. The library's online catalog lists all of the materials the library owns, subscribes to, or has access to. See the library home page in Figure 8.4, which lists (a) reference (research) works, (b) databases, (c) websites, (d) digital collections of resources, and (e) ways you can contact the staff at the library if you have any questions.

How Using Your Library's Online Catalog Can Help You Get Started

Here are guidelines to help you do research on your library's online catalog:

1. **Know your topic.** To get background information on your topic, start with an encyclopedia (print or online) or other general reference work so that you are aware of the various and relevant issues and subtopics involved.
2. **Use a range of keywords.** It is often difficult to know which keywords will generate the most complete or most useful search result. If your first attempts at using keywords don't yield any useful results, try other keywords or use the library catalog's own subject headings to try to find materials related to the topic you're researching.
3. **Restrict your subject.** Narrow your topic to find a manageable amount of information. For instance, suppose you are researching the use of lasers in cosmetic surgery. You might start your search with "medical uses of lasers." To narrow your subject, you might specify "use in cosmetic surgery." You could then further refine it by specifying "in ophthalmic cosmetic surgery." Using the "Advanced Search" function (see the link to the "Advanced LionSearch" in Figure 8.4) also allows you to restrict searches to specific date ranges and resource formats, among others.
4. **Take advantage of links.** An online catalog usually provides links to related materials that may be even more helpful to your search.
5. **Librarians are a resource.** Many libraries now feature a variety of ways to connect and interact with staff librarians: via web chats, text messages, email, phone, or in person. (See the tab for "ASK a Librarian" in Figure 8.4 as well as the list at the bottom right of the figure.) They are experts in both their own library's holdings and how to best search the catalog for your topic. They may have insights into resources you haven't even considered.

E-Libraries

E-libraries are designed to duplicate the experience of going to a library, as much as that is possible in a digital environment. They provide links to librarian-approved websites in a variety of subject areas, to books available online, and will connect you with general resources online (dictionaries, almanacs, encyclopedias, and more). They also make it easy to reach librarians who are available to answer reference questions online. Most public and academic libraries have duplicated their library resources online, including access to librarians via live web chats, text messages, email, or by phone. These sites offer a variety of helpful links as well.

There are a variety of e-libraries available online. A good starting point is the Internet Public Library (www.ipl.org), or ipl2. It is a well-known, comprehensive, and academically reliable e-library that not only provides the resources listed above, but also includes

- links to online periodical databases
- links to online newspapers around the world
- links to reliable blogs, exhibits of images, and much more

Other useful e-libraries include:

- Library of Congress Online Catalog (catalog.loc.gov)
- National Archives (www.archives.gov)
- Internet Archive (archive.org)
- Smithsonian Digital Library (library.si.edu/digital-library)

Databases

Databases are among the most helpful resources for doing research in your library. These online indexes allow you to search for and retrieve a wealth of magazine, journal, and newspaper articles, as well as reviews of books, films, art, music, etc., cataloged and classified by various search engines. These databases can be located through a library's online catalog or through a databases link at an e-library such as ipl2. Some libraries allow you to access their databases from a remote location.

Because most databases are available only by subscription, you need a library card to access them at a public library or an access code at a corporate library. To use an academic library, you have to be a registered student or alumnus. With these databases, you can search through thousands of articles in a few seconds. Many databases are updated often—daily, weekly, or monthly.

Information Found in Databases

Thousands of periodical databases are available from many different information services. They vary in terms of how they list information and what they offer. But most of them provide the following information, crucial for on-the-job research, when you do a keyword search to locate a particular article:

- Bibliographic citation, including author, title, publication date, source information, and perhaps subject categories.
- Keywords, which guide users to the main subjects that the article, poem, review, or op-ed covers to help them determine if it is useful in their research.
- The full text of the article, either retyped for the database or scanned in as a PDF version of the original document. You may need to click on a further link to get past the informational page and open the complete article.

Frequently Used Databases

You need to find out which databases are most relevant to your job-related research. Here are a few full-text databases that your corporate or community library will likely subscribe to:

1. **EBSCOhost.** This database provides full-text articles from thousands of popular magazines, professional journals, and newspapers and claims to offer the largest full-text collection of professional and academic articles in the world.

2. **Lexis/Nexis Academic.** This database is helpful for locating articles, as far back as the 1940s, in business and law.
3. **InfoTrac.** One of the largest periodical databases, InfoTrac contains a variety of articles from both academic journals and general-interest magazines.
4. **NewsBank.** NewsBank's database supplies over 70,000 news articles annually — from over 500 U.S. and Canadian newspapers.
5. **ProQuest.** Indexing more than 7,400 publications, this database includes newspapers and scholarly and general-interest sources in business, news, medicine, humanities, social sciences, hard sciences, and technology.
6. **JSTOR.** This resource provides full-text searches for almost 2,000 journals in the humanities, social sciences, and physical/biological sciences. JSTOR also will give you free access to public domain content from more than 200 journals published before 1923 in the United States and before 1870 in other countries.
7. **ERIC (Education Resources Information Center).** Run by the United States Department of Education, this digital library allows users access to education-related research, technical reports, journals, and other related materials.
8. **USA.gov.** Official database of the United States federal government, housing files, documents, and reports from all government agencies.

Business and Other Specialized Databases

Many libraries, including corporate ones, subscribe not only to the most popular databases above, but also to several business and specialized databases. Almost every professional discipline has its own database. In addition to these databases, international companies frequently develop their own databases to assist employees in their research. GlaxoSmithKline, the international pharmaceutical manufacturer, for instance, prepared and archived a password-protected periodical database of its research studies for use by its 100,000 employees in labs and offices worldwide.

Reference Materials

In addition to finding articles in databases reference works, available in print or online, are useful for workplace research. These include encyclopedias, dictionaries, almanacs, and atlases, as well as government documents, industry directories, handbooks and manuals, and statistics. These reference works will give you up-to-date information when you just need a quick and accurate overview of a topic or specific statistical, historical, or financial data.

But use general reference works such as encyclopedias cautiously. While they supply basic information and are easily accessible, do not confine your research to them, because they are limited in scope. A wise rule of thumb is to always double-check the facts you garner from a general reference work against those you find in more specialized works.

Encyclopedias

A general print encyclopedia, such as the *Columbia Encyclopedia* or the *Encyclopaedia Britannica*, is a useful starting point for research because it contains knowledgeable introductions to topics, summarizes events or processes, explains key terms, and includes recent updates, along with lists of further readings. Online encyclopedias include *Wikipedia* (www.wikipedia.org), an encyclopedia written and updated by volunteers that contains over 2 million entries, and the *Encyclopaedia Britannica Online* (www.britannica.com).

For your workplace research, you may consult a more specialized business or technology encyclopedia, such as one of the following:

- *Blackwell Encyclopedia of Management*—www.managementencyclopedia.com/
- *The Encyclopedia of Banking and Finance*—www.eagletraders.com/books/int_fin_encyclopedia.htm
- *Webopedia* (online technology dictionary for IT professionals)—www.webopedia.com/

Be especially careful when using *Wikipedia*. Unlike the more traditional encyclopedias above, which are authored by scholars and overseen by professional editors, *Wikipedia* articles are written by general readers and are not checked for accuracy or for bias by experts in the area.

Dictionaries

Rather than relying exclusively on general dictionaries, such as *The American Heritage Dictionary of the English Language* (available online at www.ahdictionary.com), you will have to use business and industry-specific dictionaries that define the words and phrases (jargon) of your profession. Most general and specialized dictionaries are available in print and online. Use only those specialized dictionaries that are officially endorsed by your profession. The following are two reliable online business dictionaries:

- *Deardorff's Glossary of International Economics*—www-personal.umich.edu/~alandear/glossary/
- *The Washington Post Business Glossary*—www.washingtonpost.com/wp-dyn/business/specials/glossary/index.html

Almanacs

An almanac is a collection of statistical data—charts, tables, graphs, and lists—published annually and carefully organized by general topics such as geography, awards/prizes, and science and technology. Here are some useful almanacs:

- *Infoplease*—www.infoplease.com
- *Plunkett Research*—www.plunkettresearch.com
- *FedStats*—fedstats.sites.usa.gov/
- *International Statistical Agencies*—www.bls.gov/bls/other.htm

Atlases

Atlases are collections of worldwide maps. Many types of workplace research involve consulting an atlas for locations as well as for statistical information about specific geographical areas. While print atlases are limited in what they can show, online atlases provide much more detail, including three-dimensional images, shading, and elevations. Among the most widely used print atlases are the *Times Atlas of the World* and the *National Geographic Atlas*. Here are some other handy online atlases:

- *Google Earth*—www.google.com/earth
- *Mapquest*—www.mapquest.com
- *National Geographic Map Machine*—maps.nationalgeographic.com/map-machine

Government Documents

Many government documents are available through the website of the department or agency that created them. But you can access all of these websites via **www.USA.gov**, the official government Web portal. You can use this link to take advantage of the millions of federal Web resources. Figure 8.5 shows the USA.gov Reference Center and General Government page, listing by category a variety of sites. Other major sites that provide access to government documents include

- *American Fact Finder*—http://factfinder2.census.gov
- *Library of Congress*—www.loc.gov

Directories

If in your job-related research you need to find information about specific companies and their decision makers, turn to one of the many industry-specific directories. They include a wide range of companies along with links to those

FIGURE 8.5 USA.gov Reference Center and General Government Page

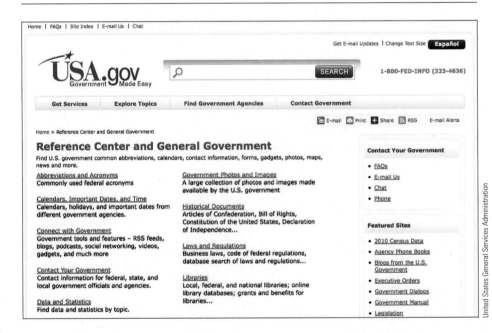

United States General Services Administration

companies' websites, or, more helpfully, staff-written overviews of companies, contact information, lists of key people, and financial statistics. Directories are invaluable in helping you find and build email lists and lists of prospective clients. Figure 8.6 shows the home page for Hoover's (http://www.hoovers.com) which provides industry overviews, company contact information, business statistics, and lists of competing companies. Other useful online directories include these:

- Corporate Information—www.corporateinformation.com. Similar to Hoover's, Corporate Information provides snapshots of over 35,000 companies in 65 countries.
- Zacks—www.zacks.com. Intended for investment purposes, Zacks supplies financial information about many companies.

Handbooks and Manuals

Handbooks and manuals include explanations of procedures, definitions of terms and concepts, descriptions of industry standards, and overviews of professional issues within the field. The *Occupational Outlook Handbook* (www.bls.gov/ooh), produced by the U.S. Bureau of Labor Statistics, for instance, "describes what workers do on the job, working conditions, the training and education needed, earnings, and expected job prospects in a wide range of occupations."

FIGURE 8.6 Home Page for Hoover's

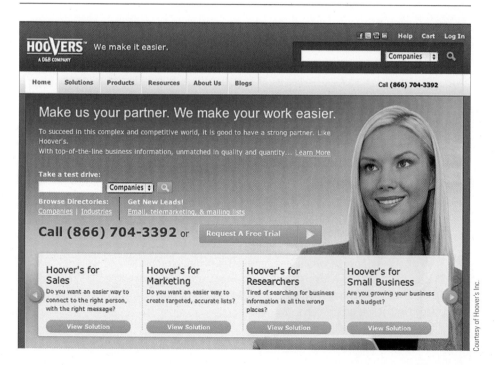

Courtesy of Hoover's Inc.

Among the most frequently consulted handbooks and manuals for workplace research are *Moody's Manuals* and *Standard and Poor's Corporate Descriptions*, both of which give information on the history of a company, descriptions of products and services, and basic financial details (stocks, earnings, and mergers).

Statistics

Statistical reference works give you valuable numerical data on a wide range of business-related subjects—employment, housing, immigration, population, pollution, technology, and overseas markets, among others. Statistical data are generated from numerous sources, mostly from the U.S. government, private agencies, international organizations, and colleges and universities. Here are several U.S. government websites that provide valuable statistical references to assist you in your workplace research:

- Federal Trade Commission—www.ftc.gov
- Fedstats—fedstats.sites.usa.gov
- Minority Business Development Agency—www.mbda.gov
- Small Business Administration—www.sba.gov
- U.S. Bureau of Economic Analysis—www.bea.gov
- U.S. Bureau of Labor Statistics—www.bls.gov
- U.S. Census Bureau—www.census.gov
- U.S. Data and Statistics—www.usa.gov/Topics/Reference_Shelf/Data.shtml
- U.S. Department of Education—www.eddataexpress.ed.gov
- U.S. Department of Housing and Urban Development—www.huduser.org

---

TECH NOTE

Gray Literature

Gray literature refers to documents prepared by a company, industry, or agency but not readily available through databases or online catalogs. Examples of gray literature include internal reports, newsletters, fact sheets, conference proceedings, and instruction booklets. Government agencies, special interest groups, and professional associations also produce gray literature.

Gray literature is an important resource for workplace research because it often provides information unavailable in books, journals, or newspapers or in scholarly publications. It includes public health information leaflets; appliance repair manuals; consumer product ratings; and business and industry reports on such topics as annual stockholder meetings, promotions, and new markets. Consult these resources when you compare your product or service with a competitor's.

North Dakota State University has provided a helpful compilation of websites that host gray literature (**library.ndsu.edu/gray-literature-resources**). Keep in mind that gray literature reflects the viewpoints and preferences of the company or industry that produced it; consult other sources as well.

Source: Sherry Laughlin, Librarian, William Carey University.

Internet Searches

The enormous amount of information available on the Internet grows larger every day. Acting as a "network of networks," the Internet gives you access to hundreds of millions of websites, databases, libraries, newsgroups, chat rooms, blogs, and other online sources. As a result, it is one of the quickest, easiest, and most effective ways to do secondary research. It is also one that requires caution. Just like conducting any other kind of research, your Internet research needs to be carefully planned and focused.

Subject Directories

Subject directories allow users to locate appropriate websites (as opposed to articles, which are located via periodical databases). Subject directories are organized into logical categories (e.g., Business) and subcategories (e.g., International Business and Trade) for easy navigation. Typically, each subcategory is annotated. Here are two examples of reliable subject directories:

- Library of Congress Virtual Reference Shelf (www.loc.gov/rr/askalib /virtualref.html)
- The WWW Virtual Library (vlib.org)

Search Engines

When you begin your research, start by using a search engine. A search engine scans webpages to find the keywords most relevant for your research. It then indexes the information it finds to create a frequently updated database of results. Search engines rank the results of your search using a computer algorithm that takes into account the popularity of websites, their contents, where the keywords appear on the page, and other sites that link to that page, presenting you with the most relevant matches for your keywords.

Since the Internet is vast, it only makes sense that multiple search engines are available, as Table 8.1 (page 330) shows. These include general and metasearch engines (which combine multiple search engines) as well as specialized, subject-specific search engines. Like the Web itself, search engines are constantly expanding as they index more pages in cyberspace each second. No single search engine is comprehensive. Researchers estimate that almost 40 percent of the Web is not even indexed by the most popular search engines. But by using a variety of search engines to conduct keyword searches, you will access a broader scope of sources and thereby increase your chances of finding the information you need.

Following are descriptions of three of the most frequently used search engines listed in Table 8.1.

1. **Google** (www.google.com) is currently one of the world's largest and easiest-to-use search engines, indexing over 8 billion pages. Google offers specialized engines such as Google Books, Google Images, and Google Videos.
2. **Yahoo!** (www.yahoo.com), one of the earliest search engines, Yahoo! suggests related keywords and allows you to open links in new windows.
3. **Bing** (www.bing.com) provides one of the most comprehensive searches, including image, audio, and video links, and divides findings into categories.

TABLE 8.1 Different Types of Internet Search Engines

Search Engines	Metasearch Engines
Bing	Dogpile
DuckDuckGo	Mamma
Google	Search.com
Yahoo	WebCrawler
	Zoo Search

Specialized Search Engines	
General	*News*
allsearchengines.co.uk (UK directory of subject-specific search engines)	Google News (news.google.com)
searchenginecolossus.com (an international directory of search engines)	Newspapers.com (directory of international, national, college, and business papers)
	World News Network (wn.com)
	Yahoo! News (news.yahoo.com)
Media	
Google Images (images.google.com)	*Business*
Google Videos (www.google.com/videohp)	allbusiness.com
Yahoo! Image Search (images.search.yahoo.com)	business.com
Yahoo! Video Search (video.search.yahoo.com)	

How to Conduct Keyword Searches: Some Guidelines

To use search engines effectively, you need to know how to conduct a keyword search. As you saw, when you enter a keyword into a search engine, it goes through its indexed websites and presents you with those that feature your keyword in the title, heading, meta tags, or text of the page. Follow the guidelines below to conduct successful keyword searches:

- **Be specific.** Although it might be tempting to start off with a broad subject like *business travel*, you may find yourself confronted with millions (if not billions) of hits that range from earning travel miles to news about corporate balance sheets. Before you start your search, narrow your focus to two or three significant keywords (and omitting *of*, *to*, *in*, *from*, and *on*, which most search engines exclude).
- **Modify your keywords.** Unlike the vague keywords *business travel*, specify the type of information you want to receive by refining your topic to reflect your specific need for information. Search for *business travel train Los Angeles* to net more precise, pertinent information. Try using synonyms if your original or modified keywords do not yield useful results.
- **Use Boolean connectors.** Boolean connectors, such as AND, OR, and NOT, are essential to limit and guide your search by reducing unrelated search results. For example, *business AND travel AND Los Angeles OR Santa Monica*

AND train NOT airplane NOT automobile would yield pages that included the terms business *and* travel, *and* Los Angeles or Santa Monica, *and* specifically via train (as opposed to by car or airplane).

- **Use delimiters.** To refine your search even further, use the following delimiters, sometimes called wildcard characters:
  - Quotation marks around a string of keywords limit your term to that particular phrase.
  - A plus sign (+) between terms can be used to replace the Boolean AND command, and a minus sign (−) can replace the OR command in many search engines.
  - An asterisk (*) at the end of a term broadens your search beyond that afforded by the keyword. For example, the term *employ** will return all terms that use employ as the stem of a keyword, such as *employment, employer,* and *employability.*
  - Some search engines, such as Google, allow you to use an asterisk within quotation marks to indicate a missing word. Searching for *"Australian * technology"* will find results including keyword phrases ranging from *Australian medical technology* to *Australian information technology.*
  - Enter advanced delimiters to specify the exact type of domain you want to search. Searching Google for *"internet security" site:gov* will retrieve all .gov (government) sites with information on Internet security. Similarly, searching for *"international training" site:edu* will pull up all .edu (education) sites with information on international training.

- **Use Shortcuts.** There are a number of shortcuts that allow users to access frequently requested information quickly and easily on the Internet. The following is not by any means a comprehensive list but does give you some additional ways to access information faster and more efficiently.
  - To find sites in a particular language, file format (Word, PDF, PowerPoint), or date, use the *Advanced Search* options available on most search engines.
  - To locate a map, type in the street address of the area you want, and a street map will automatically appear.
  - To receive a selection of web definitions taken from a variety of respected sources, type in "define" and then your keyword into Google.
  - Choose country-specific search engines, such as those available at Yahoo! or Google, to access information about companies, laws, news, and international relations essential for communicating with international readers.

Evaluating Websites

The criteria used to evaluate websites are similar to those you follow to assess print documents (see "Evaluate sources, both in print and online" on page 306). Just as not everything you read in print is accurate and unbiased, not everything on the Internet will be correct, up-to-date, objective, or useful. The fact that something is posted on the Web does not make it correct—after all, anyone can post practically anything. Remember that much of the information on the Internet is placed there without a peer-review process—that is, facts may not have been checked, sources may not be authoritative, and ideas and opinions may be biased and not be backed up by solid evidence. Overall, the quality of information you find on the Internet can range from unsupported, slanted, unethical, or just plain wrong, to authoritative, well supported, and objective.

Here are some questions to determine whether websites (and print sources, too) are credible, accurate, up-to-date, relevant, and objective.

Credible

- What credentials does the author or the organization post? Read the "About Us" or "About Me" page of any website critically to learn more about the author's qualifications and awards or the organization's history, mission statement, and track record.
- Does the website refer to the most respected and current research being done in the field?
- Is the author cited in other sources, including reference works and highly respected websites? Are there links to or from the author's or company's website to those sites?

Accurate

- How have the data been gathered, recorded, and interpreted? Are they complete, valid, logical, and consistent with the procedures and protocols of your profession?
- Do the facts, dates, and statistical information match those found in other sources, such as on other websites or in traditional research sources such as almanacs and encyclopedias (see "Encyclopedias," pages 324–325 and "Almanacs," page 325)? Again, do not rely on only one website for your facts and figures.
- Are visuals clear and undistorted (see "Choosing Effective Visuals," pages 402–406)?

Up-to-Date

- When was the content written and placed on the website? Does the website provide "Last updated on…" information?
- Does the website contain materials referring to current events, studies, and experiments, or do all the references go back many months or years?
- Is the information given on the website contradicted, supplemented, or labeled out-of-date on other more recent websites and in print reference works?

Relevant

- Is the website's content directly related to the subject of your report, or is it only remotely close to your topic.
- Does the website offer enough of the right type of data to be useful, or is it sketchy?

- How does the website help or hurt the case you are trying to build? Even a respected competitor's figures can give you valid and relevant information you can convincingly apply to your report.

Objective

- Does the website openly and clearly state its purpose and the audience for whom it is intended? Does it claim to give objective information, or is it really just trying to sell something or present a biased point of view? Again, read the "About Me" or "About Us" page carefully.
- Is the website legitimate? Verify whether a company or organization is legitimate by checking with the National Consumers League, www.nclnet.org.
- Does the website acknowledge opposing viewpoints and theories, and does it freely and clearly admit its own limitations and agendas?
- Does the author use a professional, objective tone and avoid using sexist, racist, and other demeaning stereotypical language or visuals?
- Is this website part of a reputable online discussion community (a listserv or chat room), or is it a platform for one individual's or organization's viewpoints?

THE IMPORTANCE OF NOTE TAKING

Note taking is the crucial link between finding sources, reading and responding to them, and writing your business report. At this stage, you are gathering crucial background information to build and support your report. Never trust your memory to keep all of your research facts straight. Taking notes is time well spent.

Notice how the business research report at the end of this chapter (Figure 8.10, pages 349–363) and the one in Chapter 15 on international employees in the workforce (Figure 15.3, pages 607–621)) incorporate a variety of important quotations, statistics, and even visuals from the notes from the sources that the writers consulted, including blogs, surveys, and interviews.

How to Take Effective Notes

Effective note taking requires you to (a) identify only the most relevant points, (b) exclude irrelevant or inessential ones, (c) summarize key information concisely and accurately, and (d) document the results. Follow these guidelines to make note taking easier and more efficient:

1. Photocopy or scan hard copy or download print or online articles, sections of books, reports, and other sources that you consult and mark relevant quotations, statistics, and other information you may incorporate into your work.
2. Record all quotations verbatim.
3. Bookmark any sites on the Internet that you know will be important for your work and that you may be likely to return to.
4. Cut and paste information from online sources directly into your word-processing program for reference, being careful to include exact source information.

What to Record

To take effective notes, you have to know how to summarize a great deal of information accurately. Study the guidelines on writing summaries in Chapter 9 (see "Contents of a Summary," pages 373–374). Here are the types of information you need to record in your notes.

1. **Include full bibliographic information for each source.** For *books*, list author, title, city of publication, publisher, date of publication, edition (if not the first), and page numbers. For *journal articles,* include author, title, publisher, volume number, date, and page numbers. For *websites*, record author, title, name of the site, URL, and the date you accessed the site.
2. **Copy quotations, names, facts, dates, and statistics accurately from the source.** Compare your notes with the original.
3. **Distinguish quotations from paraphrases.** Place quotation marks around any words, sentences, or extended quotations you record directly to avoid plagiarizing (see "What Must Be Cited," page 338).
4. **Indicate in your notes why the material you quoted or paraphrased is significant.** You may not remember later why the material is significant, so help your memory by leaving yourself a reminder—"Use in introduction"; "provides most current data."
5. **Clearly mark separate works by the same author.** If you are using two or more works by the same author in your research, be sure to indicate which quotations or paraphrases apply to which works.
6. **Identify and record only the most relevant and useful points.** You cannot copy down everything in your notes. Include only what you plan to actually use in your report.

To Quote or Not to Quote

Before recording information from sources, ask yourself three questions:

1. How much do I need to quote directly?
2. Where can I shorten a quote by using ellipses?
3. When should I paraphrase instead of quote?

Incorporating Quotes

A safe rule to follow is this: Quote sparingly. Do not be a human scanner. If you incorporate too many quotations in your report, you will simply be transferring the author's words from the book, article, or website to your paper. Do not use direct quotations simply as filler. Save them for when they count most:

- When an author has summarized a great deal of significant information concisely into a few well-chosen sentences
- When a writer has clarified a difficult concept exceedingly well
- When an author has made his or her chief statement or thesis

For example, the note in Figure 8.7 contains a brief, well-worded, and significant statement by an author. It is not necessary to quote verbatim all the evidence leading to that statement. The note stands well on its own.

TECH NOTE

Electronic Note-Taking Software

Electronic note-taking software offers a fast and convenient way to organize your notes, saving you from worrying about losing note cards or scraps of paper. Some popular electronic note-taking programs include Evernote, Microsoft OneNote, and Google Keep. Although each is slightly different (some allow users to download or upload audio and video), most have the following features in common to help researchers input, organize, search, save, print, and share their notes:

- Copy and paste text and images from Internet sources. Many programs automatically include the URL.
- Keyboard your own notes or, if you have neat handwriting, write directly on the tablet with a stylus. First check that your tablet has handwriting recognition software.
- Flag or color-code your notes to highlight and differentiate them.
- Organize your notes into categories, folders, or outlines.
- Reorganize your notes using a drag-and-drop feature.
- Search your notes for keywords or flags to locate relevant information.
- Back up your notes to make sure you don't lose them.
- Print your notes, export them to your office program, or email them to others.
- Collaborate with others using the same program.

If you are uncertain about exactly how much to quote verbatim, keep in mind that no more than 10 to 15 percent of your report should be made up of direct quotations. Remember that when you quote someone directly, you are telling your readers that these words are the most important part of the author's work as far as you are concerned. Be a selective filter, not a large funnel.

FIGURE 8.7 Note Containing a Direct Quotation

Jacquiline Betz, "Importance of Internet Medicine," *Journal of Community Medicine* 15 (Sept. 2015): 32.

"The Internet is a primary source of medical information for consumers. CybMed, an Internet marketing firm, estimates that more than 80 million people in 2015 consulted the Web for a variety of health-related information. Most users searched popular sites such as WebMD and Medscape to look up the signs and symptoms of their medical problems. Consumers also flocked to Drugs@FDA, an FDA website, to find information on new drugs and their possible side effects. These websites are the closest thing to a doctor who makes house calls."

© 2017 Cengage Learning

Using Ellipses

Sometimes a sentence or passage is particularly useful, but you may not want to quote it fully. You may want to delete some words that are not really necessary for your purpose. These omissions are indicated by using an **ellipsis** (three spaced dots within the sentence to indicate where words have been omitted). Here are some examples.

Full Quotation: "Diet and nutrition, which researchers have studied exten-sively, significantly affect oral health."

Quotation with Ellipsis: "Diet and nutrition . . . significantly affect oral health."

When the omission occurs at the end of the sentence, you must include the end-of-sentence punctuation after the ellipsis. In the following example, note how the shortened sentence ends with four spaced dots: the closing period and the three dots for the ellipsis.

Full Quotation: "Decisions on how to operate the company should be based on the most accurate and relevant information available from both within the company and from the specific community that the establishment serves."

Quotation with Ellipsis: "Decisions on how to operate the company should be based on the most accurate and relevant information available. . . ."

At times you may have to insert your own information within a quotation. This addition, known as an **interpolation**, is made by enclosing your clarifying identification or remark in brackets inside the quotation; for example, "It [the new transportation network] has been thoroughly tested and approved." Anything in brackets is not part of the original quotation.

Paraphrasing

A **paraphrase** is a restatement in your own words of the author's ideas. Even though you are using your own words to translate or restate, you still must document the paraphrase because you are using the author's facts and interpretations. You do not use quotation marks, though. When you include a paraphrase be careful to do three things:

1. Be faithful to the author's meaning. Do not alter facts or introduce new ideas.
2. Follow the order in which the author presents the information.
3. Use paraphrases in your report selectively. You do not want your report to be merely a restatement of someone else's ideas.

Paraphrased material can be introduced in your paper with an appropriate iden-tifying phrase, such as "According to Dampier's study," "To paraphrase Dampier," or "As Dampier observes." The note shown in Figure 8.8 paraphrases the following quotation:

While the effects of acid rain are felt first in lakes, which act as natural collection points, some scientists fear there may be extensive damage to forests as well. In the process de-scribed by one researcher as "premature senescence," trees exposed to acid sprays lose their leaves, wilt, and finally die. New trees may not grow to replace them. Deprived of natural cover, wildlife may flee or die. The extent of the damage to forest lands is extremely difficult

FIGURE 8.8 Note Containing a Paraphrase

Acid rain (body of report)
damage to forests

Dampier, www.rainenviron.com

Acid rain is as dangerous to the forests as to the lakes. Victims of "premature senescence," the trees become defoliated and die with no new trees taking their place. Without the trees' protection, wildlife vanishes. Although the exact damage is hard to measure, Swedish scientists have observed that in their country forest products decreased by 1 percent yearly.

© 2013 Cengage Learning

to determine, but scientists find the trend worrisome. In Sweden, for example, one estimate calculates that the yield in forest products decreased by about one percent each year.[1]

DOCUMENTING SOURCES

Documentation is at the heart of all the research you will do in school and on the job. To document means to furnish readers with information about the print and electronic sources you have used for the factual support of your statements, including books, journals, newspapers, surveys, reports, websites, and other resources such as listservs and email.

Documentation is an essential part of any research you do for four key reasons:

1. It demonstrates that you have done your homework by consulting experts on the subject and relying on the most authoritative sources to build your case persuasively.
2. It shows that you are aware of the latest research in your field, thus lending credibility and authority to your conclusions and recommendations.
3. It gives proper credit to those sources and avoids plagiarism (see "What Must Be Cited," page 338). Citing works by name and date is not a simple act of courtesy; it is an ethical requirement and, because so much material is protected by copyright, a point of law.
4. It informs readers about specific books, articles, surveys, blogs, or websites you used so they can locate your source and verify your facts or quotations.

The Ethics of Documentation: Determining What to Cite

As a researcher, you have to be sure about what information you must document and what information you do not. Before you start consulting sources, you have to

---

[1]Bill Dampier, "Now Even the Rain Is Dangerous," *International Wildlife* 10, pp. 18–19.

be very clear about the ethical standards involved in documentation. The following sections will give you a useful overview to make the documentation process more understandable and easier to follow.

What Must Be Cited

To ensure that your business report avoids plagiarism and maintains high ethical and professional standards, follow these guidelines:

- If you use a source and take something from it, document it. Document any direct quotations, even a single phrase or keyword.
- Stay away from **patchworking**—using bits and pieces of information and passing them off as your own—which is also an act of plagiarism. Always put quotation marks around anything you take verbatim, and document it.
- If any opinions, interpretations, and conclusions expressed verbally or in writing are not your own (e.g., you could not have reached them without the help of another source), you must document them.
- Even if you do not use an author's exact words but still get an idea, concept, or point of view from a source, document that work in your report.
- Never alter any original material to have it suit your argument. Changing any information—names, dates, times, test results—is a serious offense.
- If you use statistical data you have not compiled yourself, document them.
- Always document any visuals—photographs, graphs, tables, charts, images, even clip art downloaded from the Internet (and if you construct a visual based on someone else's data, you must acknowledge that source, too).
- Never submit the same research paper for one course that you wrote for another course without first obtaining permission from the second instructor.
- Do not delete an author's name when you are citing or forwarding an Internet document. You are obligated to give the Internet author full credit.

What Does Not Need to Be Cited

Be careful not to distract readers with unnecessary citations that only demonstrate your lack of understanding of the documentation process and can undercut the professionalism of your report. There is no need to cite the following:

- Common-knowledge scientific facts and formulas, such as "The normal human body temperature is 98.6 degrees Fahrenheit" or "H_2O is the chemical formula for water."
- Readily available geographical data, such as elevation of mountains; depths of lakes, rivers, etc.; population; mileage between two places; and so on.
- Well-known dates, such as the date of the first moon landing in 1969.
- Factual historical information, such as "George W. Bush was the 43rd President of the United States."
- Proverbs from folklore, such as "The hand is quicker than the eye."
- Well-known quotations, such as "We hold these truths to be self-evident . . . ," although it may be helpful to the reader if you mention the name of the person being quoted.

- The Bible, the Koran, or other religious texts, but provide a reference to the text and to the portion of the text quoted in parentheses (for instance, *New Jerusalem Bible*, Exod. 2.3).
- Classic literary works, but again reference the original author and the name of the work parenthetically—for instance, Mark Twain, *The Adventures of Huckleberry Finn* (Chapter 4), or Shakespeare, *The Merchant of Venice* (5.3.15). Indicate, though, from which edition you took the quotation.

Parenthetical Documentation

Two frequently used systems of parenthetical documentation are MLA (Modern Language Association) and APA (American Psychological Association):

- *MLA Handbook for Writers of Research Papers*, 7th ed. (New York: Modern Language Association, 2009), www.mla.org/style
- *Publication Manual of the American Psychological Association*, 6th ed. (Washington, DC: American Psychological Association, 2010), www .apastyle.org

MLA is used primarily in the humanities while APA is used in psychology, nursing, social sciences, and several technological/scientific fields. In business, however, your employer will determine whether you will follow MLA or APA. Because MLA and APA are the most well-known and accessible documentation styles, many businesses prefer to rely on one or the other, or they adapt or modify these methods to suit the company's needs and those of its clients. Both MLA and APA use parenthetical, or in-text documentation. That is, the writer tells readers directly in the text of the report what source is being quoted or referenced.

> MLA: "Creating an interactive website was among the top three priorities businesses have had over the last two years" (Morgan 203).
>
> APA: "Creating an interactive website was among the top three priorities businesses have had over the last two years" (Morgan, 2015, p. 203).

The MLA citation "(Morgan 203)" or the APA "(Morgan, 2015, p. 203)" informs readers that the writer has borrowed information from a work by Morgan, specifically from page 203. APA also includes the year Morgan's work was published. Such a source (author's last name, year, and page number) obviously does not supply complete documentation. Instead, the parenthetical reference points readers to an alphabetical list of works that appears at the end of the report. The list, called "Works Cited" in MLA or "References" in APA, contains full bibliographic data—titles, dates, web addresses, publishers, page numbers, and so on—about each source cited in your report.

Every work that appears in your report must be listed in your references section. (The only exceptions are personal communications such as emails and texts or well-known works like the Bible; these do not have to appear in an APA-style References section.) To provide accurate parenthetical documentation for your readers, first carefully prepare your Works Cited or References list (see "Preparing MLA Works Cited and APA References Lists" on page 340) so that you know which sources you are going to cite in the right form and at the right place in your text.

Keep your documentation brief and to the point so that you do not interrupt the reader's train of thought. In most cases, all you will need to include is the author's last name, date, and appropriate page number(s) in parentheses, usually at the end of sentences. When you mention the author's name in your sentence, though, MLA and APA both advise that you do not redundantly cite it again parenthetically; for example:

> MLA: Moscovi claims that "tourism has increased 17 percent this quarter" (76).
> APA: Moscovi (2015) claims that "tourism has increased by 17 percent this quarter" (p. 76).

For unsigned articles, use a shortened title in place of an author's name parenthetically.

> MLA: Shrewd bosses know that "chain-of-command meetings provide the opportunity to pass information up as well as down the administrative ladder" ("Working Smarter" 33).
> APA: Shrewd bosses know that "chain-of-command meetings provide the opportunity to pass information up as well as down the administrative ladder" ("Working Smarter," 2015, p.33).

Similarly, if you list the title of a reference work in the text of your paper, do not repeat it in your documentation.

> MLA: According to the *Encyclopedia Britannica*, Cecil B. DeMille's *King of Kings* was seen by nearly 800,000,000 individuals (3: 458).
> APA: According to the *Encyclopedia Britannica* (2014), Cecil B. DeMille's *King of Kings* was seen by nearly 800,000,000 individuals (3, p. 458).

The first number in parentheses in both versions refers to the volume number of the *Encyclopedia Britannica*; the second is the page number in that volume.

Preparing MLA Works Cited and APA References Lists

Whether you follow MLA or APA, you will need to list your sources at the end of your report, on a new page, under the title of "Works Cited" or "References" at the top and then arrange the list alphabetically by authors' last names (except when no author is listed). Both MLA and APA advise that you begin each citation flush to the left margin (but indent subsequent lines one-half inch) and that you double-space within and between the entries. But, as Table 8.2 points out, there are major differences between the MLA and APA guidelines on where to place information, punctuation, the use of italics and quotation marks, and capitalization. The following sections provide examples, following both MLA and APA, of some of the references you are most likely to include.

Sample Entries in MLA Works Cited and APA References Lists

Book by One Author

> MLA: Spinello, Richard. *Cyberethics: Morality and Law in Cyberspace*. Burlington: Jones & Bartlett, 2013. Print.
> APA: Spinello, R. (2013). *Cyberethics: Morality and law in cyberspace*. Burlington, MA: Jones & Bartlett.

TABLE 8.2 Basic Differences Between Preparing an MLA Works Cited List and an APA References List

	MLA	APA
Author	• List author's last name first, followed by a comma, and then first name and (if applicable) middle name or initial. • For two or three authors, invert only the first author's name (e.g., Smith, John, and Jose Alvarez), and connect the last two authors' names with *and*. • For more than three authors, cite just the first author listed on the work (Smith, John) and add *et al.* ("and others"), or you can provide all names in full in the order in which they appear on the title page or byline.	• List author's last name first, followed by a comma, and then cite only his/her first initial and middle initial (if known). • For multiple authors, invert all authors' names, separate the last two names with an ampersand (&), and still use only an initial for first names of authors. • For more than seven authors, invert the first six authors' names, insert an ellipsis (. . .) and then list the name of the last author (also inverted).
Title	• Italicize the full title of the book, newspaper, journal, or magazine, including any subtitles. • Capitalize the initial letters of all words in the title except for prepositions, articles, and coordinating conjunctions, unless the book or journal begins or ends with one of these. • Enclose titles of journal, newspaper, and magazine articles in double quotation marks. • Capitalize the initial letters of all words in the journal, newspaper, or magazine article title except for prepositions, articles, and coordinating conjunctions, unless the book or journal begins or ends with one of these.	• For a book, italicize the full title, and capitalize only the first word of the title and any proper names. If there is a subtitle, place it after the main title, followed by a colon, and capitalize only the first word of the subtitle. • For articles in newspapers, journals, or magazines, the title is not italicized. • Do not enclose titles of newspaper, journal, or magazine articles in quotation marks. • Capitalize only the first word of the article title (even if it is a preposition) and any proper nouns.
Volume and Page Numbers	• For articles, cite the volume and the issue number (separated by a period), followed by the year in parentheses: 52.1 (2015). For newspapers and magazines, use only the date—12 Aug. 2015. (Note that the day is listed first, followed by the month.) Then include page numbers **without** a "p." or "pp.": 91–100.	• Put the volume number of the journal or magazine in italics, with the issue number (not in italics) in parentheses immediately following, without a space. Then insert a comma and include page numbers: *12*(3), 87–102.

(*Continued*)

TABLE 8.2 (Continued)

	MLA	APA
Publication	• For books, give the city of publication. Then, after a colon, supply the publisher's name, followed by a comma, the year of publication, and a period. • Include the publication medium for all entries (e.g., Print, PDF, DVD, Radio, Web, etc.) at the end of the publication information.	• Place the date of publication in parentheses immediately after the author's name. Then add a period after the closing parenthesis. • For books, provide the city and two-letter abbreviation for the state, and then include the publisher's name after a colon—for example, Detroit, MI: MegaPress.
Web Sources (Websites, Blogs, Social Media, etc.)	• You do not need to include URLs, but indicate the website name, sponsor or publisher, date of publication, and medium of publication, followed by the date of access.	• Insert URLs in place of page numbers with the following designation: Retrieved from [and then list the URL]. • If a DOI (digital object identifier) has been assigned to the source, provide the DOI instead of the URL, as follows: doi:xxxxx
Personal Interview	• Provide the name of the person interviewed (last name first), followed by the type of interview that was conducted (email; in person) and the date.	• Interviews, conversations, and personal communications such as email are not included in APA reference lists, but you must still cite them within your paper.

© 2017 Cengage Learning

Book by Two Authors

MLA: Wu, Melody, and Tren Tucker. *China's Role in the Global Economy.* Denver: Tradevision P, 2015. Print.

APA: Wu, M., & Tucker, T. (2015). *China's role in the global economy.* Denver, CO: Tradevision Press.

Book by Three Authors

MLA: Barsh, Joanna, Cranston, Susie, and Geoffrey Lewis. *How Remarkable Women Lead: The Breakthrough Model for Work and Life.* New York: Crown, 2011. Print.

APA: Barsh, J., Cranston, S., and Lewis, G. (2011). *How remarkable women lead: The breakthrough model for work and life.* New York, NY: Crown.

Book by Four or More Authors (MLA)

MLA: Del Guidice, Manlio, et al. *Cross-Cultural Management: Fostering Innovation and Collaboration Inside the Multicultural Enterprise.* New York: Springer, 2012. Print.

Book by Eight or More Authors (APA)

APA: Berkowitz, H. A., Barner, P. L., Choi, D. G., Osler, T. O., Ruiz, J., Rowell, C. F., . . . Emmons, W. D. (2015). *Collaborating effectively and efficiently: A case study.* Los Angeles, CA: Ridgeway.

Electronic Version of a Printed Book

MLA: Martin, Dick. *OtherWise: The Wisdom You Need to Succeed in a Diverse World.* AMA COM, 2012. Books 24×7. Web. 19 Mar. 2015.

APA: Martin, D. (2012). *OtherWise: The wisdom you need to succeed in a diverseworld.* [Books 24×7 version]. Retrieved from http://library.books24×7.com.logon.lynx.lib.usm.edu/toc.aspx?site=PB3FH&bookid=45534

Edited Collection of Essays

MLA: Yang, Harrison Hao, and Shuyan Wang, eds. *Cases on E-Learning Management: Development and Implementation.* Hershey: Information Science Research, 2012. Print.

APA: Yang, H.H., & Wang, S. (Eds.). (2012). *Cases on e-learning management: development and implementation.* Hershey, PA: Information Science Research.

Work Included in a Collection of Essays

MLA: Maque, Isabelle, et al. "Profiting from Diversity in the Bank Sector." *Lessons on Profiting from Diversity.* Ed. Gloria Moss. New York: Palgrave Macmillan, 2012. 186–212. Print.

APA: Maque, I., Becuwe, A., Prim-Allaz, I., & Garnier, A. (2012). Profiting from diversity in the bank sector. In Gloria Moss (Ed.), *Lessons on profiting from diversity* (pp. 186–212). New York, NY: Palgrave Macmillan.

Book by a Corporate Author

MLA: African Development Bank. *African Economic Outlook: 2014.* Washington: Organisation for Economic Co-Operation and Development, 2014. Print.

APA: African Development Bank (2014). *African economic outlook: 2014.* Washington, D.C., Organisation for Economic Co-Operation and Development.

Article in a Professional Journal

MLA: Freeman, Douglas C. "Veterans in Corporate America: A New Source of World Class Diverse Talent." *Black Enterprise* 43.5 (2012): 82-84. Print.

APA: Freeman, D.C. (2012). Veterans in corporate America: A new source of world class diverse talent. *Black Enterprise, 43*(5), 82-84.

Article in a Print Magazine

MLA: Kurowska, Teresa. "Is the Boss Watching Every Keystroke You Make?" *Today's Workplace* Oct. 2015: 47+. Print.

APA: Kurowska, T. (2015, October). Is the boss watching every keystroke you make? *Today's Workplace, 47,* 72–73.

Article in a Professional Online Journal

MLA: Sayburn, Anna. "Health Campaigns that Have Changed Public Understanding." *British Medical Journal Online* 344 (2012). Web. 25 April 2012.

APA: Sayburn, A. (2012, April 25). Health campaigns that have changed public understanding. *British Medical Journal Online, 344.* doi: 10.1136 /bmj.e2866

Article in a Print Newspaper

MLA: Moss, Caroline. "The First Family of Instagram." *The New York Times* 1 January 2015: E1. Print.

APA: Moss, C. (2015, January 1). The first family of instagram. *The New York Times,* p. E1.

Online Encyclopedia Article

MLA: Kling, Arnold. "International Trade." *Concise Encyclopedia of Economics.* 2nd ed. Library of Economics and Liberty, 2008. Web. 27 Mar. 2010.

APA: Kling, A. (2008). International trade. In *Concise encyclopedia of economics* (2nd ed.). Retrieved March 27, 2010, from http://www.econlib.org /library/CEE/html

Online Unsigned Encyclopedia Article

MLA: "Link Sharing." *Small Business Encyclopedia.* Entrepreneur, 2013. Web. 20 Sept. 2013.

APA: Link Sharing. (2013). In *Small business encyclopedia.* Retrieved from http://www.entrepreneur.com/encyclopedia/

Unsigned Article in a Print Magazine or Newspaper

MLA: "The Green Machine." *Economist* 11 Mar. 2010: 7–8. Print.

APA: The green machine. (2010, March 11). *Economist,* 7–8.

Article in an Online Newspaper or Magazine

MLA: King, David Lee. "Revamping Social Media for 2013." *Business Review USA.* 6 Nov. 2012. Web. 20 Mar. 2013.

APA: King, D.L. (2012, November 6). Revamping social media for 2013. *Business Review USA.* Retrieved from http://www.businessreviewusa .com/marketing/social-media/revamping-social-media-for-2013

Government Document

MLA: Committee on Banking, Housing, and Urban Affairs. *Greener Communities, Greater Opportunities: New Ideas for Sustainable Development and Economic Growth.* Washington: GPO, 2010. Web. 12 Dec. 2010.

APA: Committee on Banking, Housing, and Urban Affairs (2010). *Greener communities, greater opportunities: New ideas for sustainable development and economic growth.* (Publication No. 1035-E online). Washington, D.C.: U.S. Government Printing Office.

Website

MLA: Natl. Council of La Raza. Home Page, 2015. Web. 17 May 2015.

APA: When referencing an *entire* website, APA style is to provide the URL in the body of the text and not list it in the References section.

Radio

MLA: "What Do Employers Really Want from College Grads." Reporter Amy Scott. *Marketplace.* American Public Media. WHYY, Philadelphia, 4 Mar. 2013. Radio.

APA: Scott, A. (Reporter). (2013, March 4). What do employers really want from college grads [Radio]. In *Marketplace.* Philadelphia, PA: WHYY American Public Media.

Television

MLA: "How Will Employment Change as U.S. Job Market Recovers?" Prod. Russ Clarkson. *NewsHour.* PBS. 8 Mar. 2013. Television.

APA: Clarkson, R. (Producer). (2013, Mar 8). How will employment change as U.S. job market recovers? [Television series episode.] In *NewsHour.* Arlington, VA: PBS.

Podcast

MLA: Coughlin, Chrissy, host. "60: Why climate change is a matter of policy for insurers." *Nature of Business Radio.* GreenBiz Group. 11 Nov. 2012. Web. 17 May 2013.

APA: Coughlin, Chrissy (Host). (2012, November 25). *Why climate change is a matter of policy for insurers* [Audio podcast]. Retrieved from http://www.greenbiz.com/blog/2012/11/25/why-climate -change-matter-policy-insurers

Blogs

MLA: Hamilton, Tina. "How to Really Make Twitter Work for Your Business." *Successful Blog.* N.p., 8 Mar. 2013. Web. 20 Mar. 2013.

APA: Hamilton, T. (2013, March 8). How to really make Twitter work for your business [Blog post]. Retrieved from http://www.successful-blog .com/1/how-to-really-make-twitter-work-for-your-business/

Personal Interview

MLA: Alvarez, José. E-mail interview. 15 Feb. 2016.

APA: Interviews, conversations, and presentations are not included in APA Reference lists, but you must still cite them within your paper as follows: (J. Alvarez, personal communication, February 15, 2016).

Email

MLA: Frazer, Tim. "Site Inspection Report for Landsdowne Corners." Message to the author. 12 July 2015. Email.

APA: Emails are not included in the References list. They are cited in the text as a personal communication.

Facebook Post

MLA: Snap Power. "Great review of our Chargers!" *Facebook*. Facebook, 31 Mar. 2015. Web. 15 May 2015.

APA: Snap Power (2015, March 31). Great review of our Chargers! [Facebook status update]. Retrieved from https://www.facebook.com/snaprays /posts/791412980936977

Tweet

MLA: NYU Langone Medical (@NYULMC). "Our nurses are making a difference—from aiding disaster relief at home to helping kids around the world bit. ly/1JBVHA8 #NursesWeek." 11 May 2015, 9:41 a.m. Tweet.

APA: NYU Langone Medical [@NYULMC] (2015, May 11). Our nurses are making a difference—from aiding disaster relief at home to helping kids around the world bit.ly/1JBVHA8 #NursesWeek. [Tweet]. Retrieved from https://twitter.com/NYULMC/status/597803705686163456

Brochure

MLA: Gao, Hubert. *Coping with Carpal Tunnel Syndrome*. New York: Beth Israel Hospital, 2015. Print.

APA: Gao, H. (2015). Coping with carpal tunnel syndrome [Brochure]. New York: NY: Beth Israel Hospital.

Survey

MLA: Guttierez, Joseph. "Market Survey for Duron, Inc." Survey. n.p. 10 Apr. 2015. Print.

APA: Surveys are unpublished personal communications not included in the References list.

Lecture or Speech

MLA: Phillips-Ricks, Jonathan. National Association of Black Business Leaders Conference. New York, 15 Aug. 2015. Lecture.

APA: Phillips-Ricks, J. (2015, August 15). Lecture presented at the National Association of Black Business Leaders Conference, New York, NY.

Press Release

MLA: American Council of Organic Farmers. *New Ways to Eliminate Chemicals from Home Gardens*. Omaha: ACOF, 31 Mar. 2015. Print.

APA: American Council of Organic Farmers. (2015, March 31). *New ways to eliminate chemicals from home gardens* [Press release]. Retrieved from aaof.org

Map

MLA: Fineberg, Donald. *Sonoma, California*. Map. Sonoma: Professional Maps, 2015. Print.

APA: Fineberg, D. (2015). *Sonoma, California* [Map]. Sonoma: Professional Maps.

Motion Picture

MLA: *Understanding Diabetes: From Diagnosis to Cure*. Dir. Jayne T. Cahill. Healthcare Videos. 2015. DVD.

APA: Cahill, J. T. (Director). (2015). *Understanding diabetes: From diagnosis to cure* [DVD]. Allentown, PA: Healthcare Videos.

A BUSINESS RESEARCH REPORT

The rest of this chapter consists of a business report written by members of the marketing team at New Horizons Development, Inc., a real estate group with holdings across the country. The marketing team was asked to solve a frequent workplace problem—how to sell a new product, location, and so on. To do so, the team created a plan to attract tenants to Sawmill Ridge, a new apartment complex that New Horizons was constructing in the Dallas/Fort Worth area, and submitted it both as a PDF attachment to an email and in hard copy form. Study the report in Figures 8.9 and 8.10 (pages 348–363) to see how the team members successfully combined primary and secondary sources to research and write their business report. Also note how the report documents these sources in the text and references them on the Works Cited list using the MLA format. Compare the documentation style in this report to the long report in Chapter 15 (see Figure 15.3, pages 607–621), which uses APA in-text documentation and includes a References list.

FIGURE 8.9 Transmittal Letter for a Long Report

Distinctive, relevant letterhead

New Horizons

Building Apartment Homes Since 1984

2800 Taylor Blvd.
Fort Worth, TX 76003
817-555-3300
www.newhorizons.com

Formal inside address style used, as the letter was submitted both in hard copy form and as a PDF attachment to an email

April 13, 2015

Talia Martinez-Ryals, Director
New Horizons, Southeast
170 Waters Drive
Tucson, AZ 85749-3001

Dear Director Martinez-Ryals:

Indicates that plan was requested by the reader

Specifies purpose, scope, and importance of the plan

We are happy to include the attached marketing plan for Sawmill Ridge that you commissioned. The development is scheduled to open in three months in this rapidly growing community of South Arlington, Texas.

Our plan projects launching both an online and a print campaign to market Sawmill Ridge for its community atmosphere and benefits as well as its proximity to expanding major employers and retail centers. We have determined that our most appropriate target audience will be young professionals, and will utilize Facebook, Twitter, YouTube, and our own website to reach them.

Emphasizes that the plan is based upon careful research

Our report is based on extensive demographic and market research. For the last two months, we have thoroughly investigated the South Arlington area, interviewed numerous business and community leaders, conducted focus groups, and explored current and projected demographics.

Invites reader's questions

Thank you for asking us to prepare this report for New Horizons and you. We would be happy to answer any questions you have about this report or supply you with further information. We look forward to hearing from you.

Respectfully,

Adrienne Hong
Adrienne Hong

Tyrell Carpenter
Tyrell Carpenter

Margarita Gonzales
Margarita Gonzales

Enclosure: A Marketing Plan for Sawmill Ridge, 2015

© 2017 Cengage Learning

FIGURE 8.10 A Long Report

A Marketing Plan for Sawmill Ridge, 2015

Adrienne Hong, Tyrell Carpenter,
and Margarita Gonzales

Prepared for
Talia Martinez-Ryals, Project Director, New Horizons
Southeast, Inc.

April 13, 2015

*Title page
provides
report title,
authors, date of
submission, and
company name*

*Information
is clearly
formatted and
listed*

*Gives date
submitted*

(Continued)

FIGURE 8.10 (Continued)

Abstract

This report contains a marketing strategy for our new Sawmill Ridge development in South Arlington, scheduled to open in three months. Based upon extensive primary and secondary research, our strategy for long-term success is to promote this new apartment complex by fostering a sense of community and emphasizing the proximity of the complex to businesses, schools, and shopping. These benefits will attract our target audience of young professionals (ages 24–34) whose jobs, income, family demographics, and lifestyle will also help guide us in determining how and where we advertise Sawmill Ridge. We need to take advantage of both online and print media, including Facebook, Twitter, YouTube, and developing a customized Sawmill Ridge website that will provide links to our social media sites and offer news about weekly and monthly activities. Essential to our strategy is developing a follow-up program to retain renters (and thus reduce turnover expenses) by providing the services and amenities that our target audience appreciates and expects. If accepted, our plan promises maximum occupancy at Sawmill Ridge with a minimum attrition when leases expire.

The purpose of the report is stated clearly and presented first

Describes research methods used in generating the report and the conclusions drawn

Lists recommendations for actions that support the conclusions presented

Footer uses Roman numerals in front matter pages

ii

FIGURE 8.10 (Continued)

Table of Contents

Logically divides report into sections

Gives readers a quick glance at the organization of the report

Headings clearly distinguished through strategic and consistent use of boldface and italics

© 2017 Cengage Learning

(Continued)

FIGURE 8.10 (Continued)

1

Introduction: Strategic Plan

Uses headers for page numbers

Two years ago, New Horizons Development, Inc., purchased a large tract of land (21.2 acres) in South Arlington to develop Sawmill Ridge, a Class A apartment community with a 54-building complex. The opening of Sawmill Ridge is scheduled for completion in three months. To fulfill our objectives for this project, we have created a marketing plan for the next phase of Sawmill Ridge to attract tenants.

Introduction clearly states the purpose and organization of the report

Our plan, described in this report, is based on a key marketing strategy linking Sawmill Ridge to community development. We provide background information about market conditions and location, describe the target audience, and outline plans for both print and online advertising, including the use of Facebook, Twitter, YouTube, and our own website. Our report also covers how to follow up inquiries and how to retain residents.

Building Community

Succinctly spells out marketing plan and how it will be developed in report

To attract and retain tenants to Sawmill Ridge, our plan is based on the marketing approach developed by Juanita Lagares and her team at the Tuscon, Arizona branch of New Horizons, "Building Community by Offering Neighborhood Convenience." Having access to neighborhood conveniences is essential to our target audience, described below. Consequently, the theme of community involvement is woven throughout our plan.

Background

The rental market conditions in the Arlington area, as well as Sawmill Ridge's proximity to three major employers and many new retail establishments, have shaped the focus and goals of our marketing plan.

Rental Market Conditions: Supply and Demand

Typical MLA in-text citation includes author and page(s)

Statistics backed up by current secondary sources

No page number for Web source—North Central Texas Council

Sawmill Ridge is opening at a favorable time. The Arlington rental market has continued to thrive for over three decades (D'Argento 211-13), and apartment net leasing activity in this area is the highest it has been in the past three years, with the annual absorption reaching 5,225 units (Evinson 211). As Figure 1 on page 2 shows, during the fourth quarter of 2014 occupancy in the Arlington area tightened significantly, standing at 92.7%. These figures point to a steady and impressive increase since the beginning of 2014. The Donnelley Realty Group (**donneleyrg.com**), which provides monthly data on apartment trends, record a healthy 4.7 percent growth in apartment occupancy in South Arlington throughout 2014. Further contributing to this strong demand, apartment communities have lost fewer residents to first-time home purchases over the last year (North Central Texas Council).

FIGURE 8.10 (Continued)

2

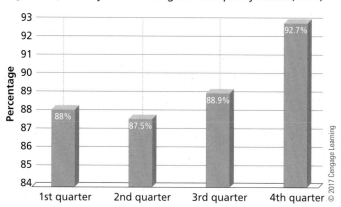

Figure 1 Quarterly South Arlington Occupancy Rates (2014)

Most important, though, in fueling this sizable demand for apartments, the greater Dallas/Fort Worth metro area has added a large block of new jobs. The U.S. Bureau of Labor Statistics reported that from October 2013 to October 2014, more than 111,000 jobs were generated in the area (U.S. Dept. of Labor). According to Betty Costinga, a Texas real estate expert frequently appearing on *Dallas This Morning*, "The single most important factor when selecting housing in the state of Texas is the location of jobs in the area." Corroborating this view, a recent article in *Time* magazine declared that Texas was "the job leader ... adding more jobs faster than any other state." ("Texas Boom Times" 20). We can take advantage of this increase in jobs.

Location: Selling the Community

As the map in Figure 2 illustrates, Sawmill Ridge is located in South Arlington, near the intersection of Pike Blvd. and Interstate 20, a major east-west corridor in the Metro area (South Arlington). Dallas is 9 miles to the east, while Fort Worth is 11 miles to the west. Moreover, Sawmill Ridge is close to major retail centers and several large businesses.

Proximity to Retail Centers

Sawmill Ridge is conveniently located near two major retail centers. Table 1 illustrates the proximity and size of the Parks Mall and the Highlands (which just opened).

Table 1 Retail Centers Near Sawmill Ridge

	Distance from Sawmill Ridge (miles)	Retail Space (square feet)
Parks Mall	1.2	2,000,000
Highlands	1.8	900,000

FIGURE 8.10 (Continued)

3

Figure 2   Map of Sawmill Ridge and the South Arlington Area

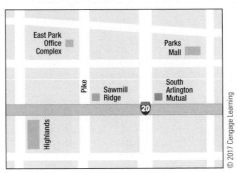

© 2017 Cengage Learning

Map provides readers with a clear visual of the site location

Based on our interview with Highlands' Associate Director, companies like Ethan Allen, Golf Galaxy, Talbot's, and Studio Movie Grill have already leased retail space in the new center (Weir). Other retailers—possibly the Body Shop, Gemstone Jewelers, Filene's Basement, and Media, Inc.—have been negotiating for retail space and are leasing units quickly (Stratton 341). Having so many diverse retailers nearby substantially increases the attractiveness of Sawmill Ridge and further emphasizes the neighborhood ethos for our subdivision.

Successful blend of primary research (interview) and secondary research (articles)

Our Arlington Area Quality of Life survey (available on our intranet) of over 700 area residents, conducted between November 15 of last year and January 31 of this year, highlights this fact. Response rate was high—over 30% of those surveyed responded. Ninety-five percent of the area residents indicated that they visit the Parks Mall weekly, and an additional 86% plan to visit the Highlands just as frequently after it opens. Only 12% were concerned that the Highlands would not cater to their needs (Hong, Carpenter, and Gonzales, "Survey").

Primary research (survey) provides useful statistics not available elsewhere

Proximity to Employers

Sawmill Ridge's proximity to major employers is also a tremendous advantage in terms of rental appeal. Our campaign will make maximum use of this benefit. Among the area's largest employers is South Arlington Mutual, whose central office with 1,500 employees is within easy driving distance of Sawmill Ridge. Another major group of employers is located at East Park Office Complex. A recent study revealed that over forty tenants employ more than 1,100 individuals there, a highly convenient location since the complex is less than a mile from Sawmill Ridge (D'Argento, "Booming Market").

Report supplies essential data to support the plan

We can also target our campaign to current employees at these firms. Our semiannual focus group, which surveyed 14 employees from

Second work by previously cited author requires title

© 2017 Cengage Learning

FIGURE 8.10 (Continued)

4

South Arlington Mutual, and 12 employees at the three largest firms at the East Park Office Complex, concluded that more than half of the employees at these companies are dissatisfied with their long commute to work and would strongly consider relocating to Sawmill Ridge. (Hong, Carpenter, and Gonzales, "Notes").

Targeting the Right Demographics

Based on the large numbers of varied retailers and businesses found in the South Arlington area, we will tailor our marketing strategy to attract young professionals (ages 24–34) with per capita incomes between $43,200 and $54,600 per year, individuals already working at these businesses or most likely to be employed there. Because many individuals in this group are young single professionals or have small children, Sawmill Ridge will emphasize the security and satisfaction with the community that our development offers. (Three top-rated elementary schools and one junior high school are within 2.4 miles of Sawmill Ridge.)

Our plan is firmly based on the demographics of the area. The U.S. Census Bureau report (U.S. Dept. of Commerce) and local real estate studies (Kearny-Schwartz 15-16; Evinson 211) provide the statistics in the infograph below, relevant to the 5-mile area surrounding Sawmill Ridge, reinforcing why and how our plan needs to reach this target audience:

Total Population:* 380,085 *within 2.5 miles of Sawmill Ridge

2.56 Average household size for renter-occupied units

Percent of population that is a single-earner or a dual-earner household

37.4% with children under 12 years old

9.4% with teenage children

$60,142 average household income

+13% than the national average

17.1% in entry level office jobs

25.7% in non-management level office jobs

33.2% in management level office jobs

© 2017 Cengage Learning

Based on these South Arlington demographics, we should easily be able to attract this target group to Sawmill Ridge, offering them the comfort,

Margin notes:
Focus group provides otherwise unavailable information

Identifies target audience

Primary research cited

Goverment agency listed like a corporate author

Target demographic solidly backed up by federal and local statistics

© 2017 Cengage Learning

FIGURE 8.10 (Continued)

5

*Work with no
author listed*

convenience, and security they demand from a large home apartment developer such as New Horizons. ("New Complex" D11).

Advertising Strategy

We plan to advertise online and through print media and to also use social media to reach the maximum number of potential tenants for Sawmill Ridge.

Online Advertising

*All statistics
and key points
solidly backed
by research*

Based upon our research, potential renters use all three media platforms: print, online, and mobile. Yun Je-mun points out that 91% of professionals looking for rentals rely on Web-based media as their resource versus 7% who only use print resources. Yet Alvarez and Pick find that 62% use Web *and* print resources, with many moving toward using apps on their mobile phones (4–5). According to Harold Slavens, in his posting at **forrentpress .com**, "Mobile marketing is a leading method of communication to engage consumers." Similarly, Sue McCallister (par. 4) claims that showcasing apartment rentals via ads in mobile apps clearly and persuasively directs traffic to developers' sites. We need to explore the options/costs of contracting with a Web-based mobile provider.

Regardless of the route, if an inquiry is followed up within the first eight hours of being received, a leasing professional has a 75% chance of renting the space to that client, a higher success rate than with prospective tenants responding to print advertisements (Bruckner).

Costs In terms of bottom-line costs, while advertising through online rental sites is highly adventageous, most local newspapers offer combined print/ online advertising contracts that help us reach the widest audience possible at an affordable cost. A combined print/online advertising contract is, on average, 35% less than doing either option separately, which provides us with substantial savings. Additionally, there are some print-only options that are worth pursuing because they reach our target audience in ways that compliment our online advertising options (see pages 6–7). Table 2 on page 6 shows the cost of running a full-color, quarter-page advertisement for one-month via the most preferred media options.

Social media promotion of Sawmill Ridge can also be achieved at very little cost, as the expense has already been accounted for as part of the yearly operating budget. We will use New Horizon's presence on Facebook, Twitter, and YouTube to promote Sawmill Ridge to our target audience of young professionals.

FIGURE 8.10 (Continued)

6

Table 2 Rates for a Full-Color, One-Quarter Page Advertisement (or Equivalent) in Various Media for 30 days (rates current as of April 1, 2015)

Type of Media	Cost	Notes
Online Only		
www.rent.com	$170	Monthly rate
www.apartments.com	$182	Monthly rate
www.DFWapartments.com	$185	Monthly rate
Newspaper + Online		
Dallas Monitor	$865	4 Sunday print ads + 1 month of internet ads
Dallas Tribune	$825	4 Sunday print ads + 1 month of internet ads
El Mundo (Hispanic weekly)	$585	4 weeks + 1 month of internet ads
Alt Dallas (alternative culture weekly)	$495	4 weeks + 1 month of internet ads
Print Only		
The Arlington Advocate (local weekly)	$350	4 consecutive weeks
Apartment Guide Magazine	$850	Monthly rate

The Most Effective Online Rental Sites To determine the most attractive Internet sites, we met with consultants at E-Pointe, a firm New Horizons has consulted with successfully on previous projects. Our team also attended a seminar regarding the top Internet rental sites in the Dallas/Fort Worth area to determine which were most frequently accessed by renters (Je-mun). Based on the information we gathered from these sources, we believe that the following three real estate-specific sites are the most effective avenues for advertising Sawmill Ridge (see Table 2 for details on cost):

- **www.rent.com**—The number one national rental source with a popular Arlington area section.
- **www.apartments.com**—The number two rental source in America, again with an Arlington area section.
- **www.DFWapartments.com**—A rental source accessed more often than any other site by Dallas/Fort Worth residents.

Creating a Custom Website In addition to advertising the sites above and through our social media outlets, we need to follow through with our "Creating Community" theme by designing our own website aimed at reaching our target audience. Creating our own website is essential to target our audience

Table clearly spells out differences between print and Internet ad rates

Table appears at right place in report and is easy to find and follow

No source line listed for table because it is original work

Attending seminar represents an important part of secondary research

Speech cited by speaker's name

Bulleted list breaks up text and improves readability

© 2017 Cengage Learning

FIGURE 8.10 (Continued)

7

and enhance our professional image (Punji par. 7). Developing our website will help us by:

Numbered list is easy to follow

1. Ensuring that New Horizons will surpass other developers whose Internet presence is less robust in the Arlington area.

Interview with expert backs up authors' plan

2. Providing our on-site personnel with a powerful marketing tool (Gilbert). All of our print media, social media sites, signage, and stationary will include the Sawmill Ridge URL for maximum exposure.

3. Reflecting New Horizons' green philosophy, through a virtual tour of Sawmill Ridge's eco-friendly landscapes and energy-saving features. Videos of the tour will be posted on YouTube and our website, and we will cross-promote the virtual tour on both Facebook and Twitter.

4. Making it easy for prospective tenants to fill out application forms and submit them online, considerably simplifying the leasing process. When potential customers complete the form online, we can waive the application fee of $50.00, thus "encouraging the Web shopper to action," as Alvarez and Pick describe it (224).

No need to cite authors mentioned in sentence

5. Giving prospective tenants the convenient option of paying their security deposit and monthly rent online.

Includes the use of social media to help market the development

6. Featuring a Sawmill Ridge Twitter feed and a link out to the Sawmill Ridge Facebook page and Instagram account, enabling rapid communication with residents about things like building-related issues or upcoming events in the South Arlington area, further fostering our emphasis on "building community."

In designing our South Arlington website, we can profit from and be consistent with similar sites that other divisions in our company have created. Figure 3, for instance, shows the homepage, located at **www.newhorizonstucson.com**, for a comparable development in Tucson, Arizona, which has targeted a similar audience. This website receives over 3,100 hits a week and incorporates the following features we would include on the Sawmill Ridge website

Uses privileged (internal) company information to create similar website in South Arlington

- Advertisements for discounts and specials at local businesses
- Information and links to area social, recreational, and educational resources
- A "Residents' Page" with uploaded pictures from parties, comments from residents, and news about upcoming events at Sawmill Ridge
- Design and feature updates on a regular basis

Print Advertising

Even though we can use online and print/online marketing as our major platforms to attract new tenants, targeted, strategic print-only advertising remains

FIGURE 8.10 (Continued)

8

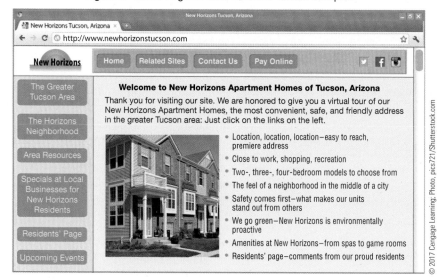

Figure 3   Home Page for New Horizons Tucson Complex

Welcome to New Horizons Apartment Homes of Tucson, Arizona

Thank you for visiting our site. We are honored to give you a virtual tour of our New Horizons Apartment Homes, the most convenient, safe, and friendly address in the greater Tucson area: Just click on the links on the left.

- Location, location, location–easy to reach, premiere address
- Close to work, shopping, recreation
- Two-, three-, four-bedroom models to choose from
- The feel of a neighborhood in the middle of a city
- Safety comes first–what makes our units stand out from others
- We go green–New Horizons is environmentally proactive
- Amenities at New Horizons–from spas to game rooms
- Residents' page–comments from our proud residents

© 2017 Cengage Learning. Photo, pics721/Shutterstock.com

Social media icons included to provide easy links to pages/feeds

Easy-to-navigate, user-friendly site

Provides relevant links

Writing is clean and concise

Light background color makes writing easy to read

useful as well. Camille D'Argento points out that 60% of the area's young professionals still pick up the local print-only newspaper for information on area cultural events (311). Our own research shows that when these young professionals are looking for housing, 36% of them will utilize the free glossy apartment guides found in area salons, market-places, restaurants, and bars (Hong, Carpenter, and Gonzales, "Survey"). Studying this print market, we believe that the following are the chief publications in which ads for Sawmill Ridge should be run:

Assures reader that print media will not be neglected

- ***The Arlington Advocate***. As Table 1 indicates, the cost for ads in most newspapers is very high. *The Arlington Advocate* charges are reasonable by comparison, and though it doesn't have the same extended reach as some of the other options, the newspaper can boast a dedicated, loyal readership of Arlington residents. After interviewing Darius Tant, manager of *The Arlington Advocate's* advertising department, we negotiated favorable terms for a three-month contract. We can run ads every week for 12 weeks for only $750 (a savings of $300 over the usual fee for that time frame).
- ***Apartment Guide Magazine***. One of the most popular rental publications for prospects in the Arlington area, with a circulation of 125,000, the *AGM* is readily available at many locations in the Sawmill Ridge area. A free advertisement on their website, located at **www .apartmentguide.com**, is included with the cost of a print ad in

Lists in easy-to-read bulleted segments the top five print advertising options

Research on price and circulation backs up argument and convinces reader to accept plan

© 2017 Cengage Learning

© 2017 Cengage Learning

FIGURE 8.10 (Continued)

9

Gives reader clear idea about quantities, distribution, and importance of publications

Apartment Guide. A one-page ad in *Apartment Guide* costs $850 per month.

- **Brochures**. Visually appealing brochures will be given to potential tenants during property tours and can also be distributed to local businesses relatively inexpensively.

Creating a Follow-Up Program

Authors plan ahead for second phase of marketing strategy

Responding to every telephone call, email inquiry, or text communication from potential tenants is crucial. When we receive a query, an expression of interest, or a referral, we need to follow up by gathering all relevant contact information from potential clients, including cell, home, and work phone numbers; email address; and street address. In addition, we should try to set up appointments at the prospective tenant's convenience.

Uses secondary research (published article) to document consequences of not following plan

Follow-up contact is also critical for prospective tenants who have visited Sawmill Ridge. Accordingly, we propose that each visitor to our develop-receives both a follow-up phone call (or email) and a thank-you card. As Kelly Talos emphasizes in her survey in *Rental Professionals Today*, 47% of rental communities do not respond to prospective residents effectively, resulting in numerous missed opportunities (90).

Retaining Renters

Research goes beyond just renting units

Our marketing plan also takes into account ways to retain residents at Sawmill Ridge. Roger Cho, in *Resident Developer's Monthly*, emphasized that developers need to link keeping residents with initial lease signing:

Long quotation indented 1 inch with no quotation marks

Ellipses tell reader part of quotation omitted

> Developers and renters often neglect the importance of retaining residents, perhaps the most basic ingredient in the leasing recipe. . . . Retention is particularly important in apartment complexes, where, depending on monthly rental rates, the owners can expect to lose as much as 15% of their annual revenue as a result of turnover . . . and as much as 8% of annual revenue due to residents withholding rent when their satisfaction is low and repairs are neglected. Those numbers may seem

FIGURE 8.10 (Continued)

10

standard, but add them together and you stand to lose nearly 25% annually—a percentage you can drastically reduce with a smart retention plan. (34)

To minimize turnover and maximize occupancy, our plan of "Creating Community" is geared to fulfill the expectations of our audience:

- To accommodate our residents' schedules, the office will open early (6:00 a.m.) and close late (7:00 p.m.) five days a week. This policy should help residents unable to visit the office during typical nine-to-five business hours.
- Sawmill Ridge will host at least four functions each month, including a monthly resident brunch, all announced on our Facebook page, Twitter feed, and Instagram account. In months with greater chances for decreased occupancy, the number of activities could increase by two to three.
- Thanks to an agreement we made with the Pet Motel in South Arlington, Sawmill Ridge residents will receive a 15% discount on kennel care.
- Emergency maintenance service will be provided 24/7. Maintenance technicians will be instructed to leave follow-up cards in each apartment home after they complete the service request.
- A monthly online newsletter, similar to that used at New Horizons Tucson, can supplement our website, showing our appreciation to tenants, providing information about upcoming events and announcing policy changes.

Conclusion

Our twofold approach—building a sense of community and emphasizing the proximity of the complex to businesses, schools, and shopping—is vital to attracting our target audience of young professionals to Sawmill Ridge. As part of this approach, we will market Sawmill Ridge in online, print, and social media to reach potential renters. Customer follow-up and our commitment to foster a sense of community and professionalism can ensure sustained, maximum occupancy.

Focuses on marketing strategy consistently

Gives reader carefully thought-out procedures staff must follow; ideas stem from primary research and collaborative thinking

In-house research is essential for preparing a new, related document

Conclusion succinctly summarizes report, listing only main points

© 2017 Cengage Learning

(Continued)

FIGURE 8.10 (Continued)

11

Works Cited list begins on a new page with the title centered at the top

List ordered alphabetically by author

Second and subsequent lines indented one-half inch. (Note this is approximated here in the figure.)

Two works by the same author team

Volume numbers and issue numbers for journals are separated by a period

Works Cited

Alvarez, Jesus, and Mary Ellen Pick. *eMarketing Tools for Interactive Communication*. Columbus, OH: Capital City P, 2014. Print.

Bruckner, Hans. "Don't Forget to Follow Up." *Real Estate Today* Mar. 2015: 45. Print.

Cho, Roger. "Retaining Renters." *Resident Developer's Monthly* Oct. 2014: 34+. Print.

Costinga, Betty. "The Texas Real Estate Market." Prod. Victor Jenkins. *Dallas This Morning*. KXAS, Dallas. 27 Feb. 2015. Television.

D'Argento, Camille. *A Contemporary Assessment of Dallas/Fort Worth Real Estate*. Dallas: Dallas UP, 2015. Print.

---. "South Arlington's Booming Market." *Dallas Real Estate Journal Online* 5.1 (2015): n. pag. Web. 2 Feb. 2015.

Donnelley Realty Group. "South Arlington Market Update." 29 Dec. 2014. Print.

Evinson, Lakita. "Leasing is Three-Year High in Arlington." *Dallas/Fort Worth Today* Jan. 2015: 211. Print.

Gilbert, Ray. Personal interview. 3 Oct. 2014.

Hong, Adrienne, Tyrell Carpenter, and Margarita Gonzales. "Arlington Area Quality of Life Survey." Survey. Arlington, TX. 30 Jan. 2015. Print.

---. "Notes." Focus group. Arlington, TX. 12 Dec. 2014. Print.

Je-mun, Yun. "Selling Dallas on the Web." Dallas Association of Real Estate Brokers conference, Dallas. 14 Sept. 2014. Lecture.

Kearney-Schwartz, Marianne. "2014 Local Real Estate Statistics." *Dallas Real Estate Journal* 6.1 (2015): 15–19. Print.

McCallister, Sue. "Mobile Apps Can Assist Homebuyers, Renters." *The Mobile Dallas News*. May 2014: n. pag. Web. 7 Nov. 2014.

"New Complex State of the Art." *Dallas Times* 20 Jan. 2015: D11+. Print.

North Central Texas Council of Governments. *2014 Population Estimates*. Arlington, TX: Author, 2014. Web. 7 Jan. 2015.

Punji, Kamlesh, "Your Internet Image." *Punji's Picks: Blog*. N.p., 30 Oct. 2014. Web. 16 Dec. 2014

Slovick, Harold. "ForRent Launches New Mobile App." *Forrent.com Press Blog*. 30 June 2014. Web. 14 Dec. 2014.

FIGURE 8.10 (Continued)

12

South Arlington, Texas. Map. Dallas: MapMakers, 2014. Web. 8 Apr. 2015.

Stratton, Daniella-Kay. "Highlands Center on the Move." *Dallas Life* Nov. 2010: 341. Print.

Tant, Darius. Personal interview. 18 Mar. 2015.

Talos, Kelly. The Importance of Brokerage Follow-Through." *Rental Professionals Today* 16.5 (2014): 90. Print.

"Texas Boom Times." *Time*, 23 Mar. 2015: 20-22. Print.

United States Dept. of Labor, Bureau of Labor Statistics. (2014). *Dallas-Fort Worth Area Economic Summary*. PDF. 5 Jan. 2015.

United States Dept. of Commerce, Census Bureau. *American FactFinder*. 16 June 2014. Web. 3 Nov. 2014.

Weir, Heidi. Personal interview. 25 Mar. 2015.

Unsigned map listed by map title

Organizations listed alphabetically by name

© 2017 Cengage Learning

CONCLUSION

This chapter has introduced you to some basic yet essential strategies and tools for doing primary and secondary research on the job. Clearly, you will need to rely on a host of resources—print and online reference works, databases, various search engines, websites, blogs, social media posts, interviews, and surveys. Relying on these sources, research tools, and strategies, you will have the most up-to-date, thorough, and relevant answers to the questions you are asked to investigate and the problems you need to solve on the job. Exploring these resources will prepare you to write the types of documents—websites, instructions, short and long reports, proposals—discussed in later chapters. The business report included in this chapter documents the types of research your employer will expect you to do.

✓ REVISION CHECKLIST

Process of Research

☐ Identified ways to research a significant, timely, and restricted topic.

☐ Formulated a mission statement to develop a clear sense of the purpose of research for employer.

☐ Consulted a wide variety of research materials, including social media posts.

(Continued)

☐ Conducted database, online catalog, and Internet searches.

☐ Used both primary and secondary research methods as needed.

☐ Evaluated the relevance and validity of my sources.

☐ Met with employers, reference librarians, or experts in my field.

☐ Networked with colleagues and boss to meet all deadlines.

☐ Documented sources accurately and completely.

Primary Research

☐ Conducted, or observed directly, an experiment or visited a site to describe and evaluate events, places needed for research.

☐ Set up an appointment with an authority on my topic. Prepared a list of appropriate questions beforehand.

☐ Interviewed experts, customers, and relevant government officials, used prepared questions, and stayed focused on the subject. Asked important follow-up questions.

☐ Identified a target audience for surveys.

☐ Created and distributed surveys using only valid, accurate questions and then interpreted my respondents' answers.

Secondary Research

☐ Searched online catalogs and databases for relevant articles and necessary research materials.

☐ Obtained full text of appropriate articles and other materials in hard or electronic copy.

☐ Checked relevant reference materials, such as almanacs, abstracts, encyclopedias, maps.

☐ Located relevant government sources using USA.gov, the Library of Congress, or the U.S. Government Printing Office.

☐ Read and evaluated periodicals, books, government documents, blogs, websites, and social media sites.

Internet Searches

☐ Searched for pertinent information using several search engines.

☐ Used multiple specific, concrete keywords to conduct Internet searches.

☐ Used search strategies such as Boolean connectors or delimiters to narrow and focus my keyword searches.

☐ Conducted a directory search or used e-library sources.

☐ Downloaded electronic sources available via library's online catalog or databases.

☐ Located webpages relating to my topic.

☐ Continued to refine my search using synonyms, alternative keywords, or more specific terms to access only the most useful material for my project.

☐ Joined a newsgroup, explored social media, or surveyed corporate blogs to extend my research.

Taking Notes

☐ Took careful notes and identified precisely the source from which my information came.

☐ Recorded all quotations accurately.

☐ Paraphrased fairly, ethically representing original material.

☐ Distinguished my comments and responses clearly from those of my sources.

☐ Incorporated information from notes into appropriate places in my document.

☐ Used correct punctuation with direct quotations, especially ellipses and brackets for interpolations.

Documentation

☐ Gave full and proper credit to sources consulted and cited in my work.

☐ Avoided plagiarism by supplying complete and accurate documentation of all sources quoted, paraphrased, or consulted for the paper or report.

☐ Recorded all direct quotations accurately; included page references where applicable.

☐ Paraphrased information correctly and acknowledged sources fully and accurately.

☐ Double-checked spelling of authors' and publishers' names and accuracy of all pertinent publication information.

☐ Followed MLA or APA documentation method (or whatever method your workplace requires) consistently in preparing Works Cited or References lists.

☐ Included all necessary in-text (parenthetical) references; cited each parenthetical reference fully and in correct alphabetical order in Works Cited or References lists.

☐ Made sure all works, including Internet sources, referred to in my report were included in Works Cited or References lists and alphabetized properly.

EXERCISES

1. Choose, define, and restrict a topic based on a problem or issue you might deal with in one of the following divisions of a company:

   a. IT
   b. human resources/diversity
   c. security
   d. marketing
   e. accounting

   f. health care/health risks
   g. energy/utilities
   h. animal rights
   i. transportation
   j. environment

   Discuss the steps you took to narrow the topic, the audience you would be writing for, and the types of questions that audience may have.

2. Based on the problem you identified in Exercise 1, select an expert relevant to that field to interview for primary research. Confer with classmates or co-workers to decide on

whom to interview. Prepare a list of ten questions for the interview, remembering to stay focused on your topic.

3. Visit an appropriate office, plant, agency, environmental site, or other location relevant to the topic you chose in Exercise 1.

4. Plan a direct observation experiment in a laboratory or other appropriate location to further investigate the topic you selected in Exercise 1. Construct an outline for this experiment, considering the types of information you expect to record and how it will enhance your research.

5. Construct a questionnaire to gather more information about the topic you selected in Exercise 1 or one of the following:

    a. mobile app security   **d.** safety in the workplace
    b. greening the workplace   **e.** global business trade
    c. international business etiquette   **f.** corporate image/mission

Prepare a list of ten questions and vary the format to include multiple-choice, yes/no, ranking, and open-ended questions. Think about how you will select your participants, the type of information you want to gather, and how it will enhance your research.

6. Working in a group, assume you are employed by a company that is marketing a new product or service. Your group is conducting market research into possible competitors. Choose three or four different brands of a product or service that is comparable to yours. Write a short report in which your group observes, tests, and analyzes these competing products or services, including packaging, contents, pricing, and endorsements. Make recommendations about how the product or service offered by your company can excel in the marketplace.

7. Gather a focus group to plan an advertising campaign for the product or service you selected in Exercise 6. Write a short report to your instructor on outcomes.

8. Prepare a list (providing full bibliographic information) of fifteen articles for the restricted topic you selected in Exercise 1. Use at least one of the online databases discussed in this chapter (see "Databases," pages 323–324).

9. Using the secondary research strategies explained in this chapter (see "Secondary Research," pages 319–333), investigate recent developments in online credit card fraud. Narrow your topic to a specific aspect of credit card fraud, such as prevention, detection, prosecution, and so on. Find the following:

    a. two recent and reliable Web sources using one of the resources mentioned in "Search Engines" (pages 329–330).
    b. two government sources (e.g., articles, reports, statistics, handbooks) using USA.gov.
    c. two online articles using one of the resources listed in the "E-Libraries" section (pages 322–323).
    d. two online newspaper articles.
    e. one corporate website using one of the sites listed in the "Directories" section (pages 326–327).
    f. one piece of gray literature (see "Tech Note: Gray Literature," page 328).

10. Using the search tools discussed in this chapter, locate the following items related to your major or job. Select titles that are most closely related to your career and explain how and why they would be useful to you. Prepare a separate bibliographic citation for each title.

a. titles of three important journals that are available in print and online
b. an abstract of an article appearing in one of the journals
c. a term in a specialized dictionary
d. a description or an illustration in a specialized encyclopedia
e. an article in an international newspaper available online
f. a training film or recording made after 2013
g. three U.S. government documents released after 2014

11. Assume you have to write a blog post about one of the following topics, introducing it to an audience of consumers. Using the resources and databases discussed in this chapter, prepare a working bibliography that contains at least ten relevant sources. After gathering and reading those sources, prepare the text and a visual for the blog post and submit them with your bibliography to your instructor. This assignment may be done as a collaborative writing exercise.

a. social media
b. fiber optics
c. online home security systems
d. 3-D television
e. robotics in medicine
f. the greenhouse effect
g. computer dating
h. laser surgery
i. globalization
j. diversity in the workplace
k. DNA testing
l. ethics of business blogging
m. airport security
n. latest generation of the iPhone

12. Using appropriate references discussed in this chapter, answer any five of the following questions. After your answer, list the specific works you consulted. Supply complete bibliographic information. For books, indicate author or editor, title, edition, place of publication and publisher, date, and volume and page numbers. For journals and magazines, include volume and page numbers; for newspapers, precise date and page numbers. For Internet sites, provide complete URL.

a. What is nanotechnology?
b. How many calories are there in an orange?
c. List three interviews that Hillary Clinton granted in 2014.
d. What is the boiling point of coal tar?
e. What was the headline in the *New York Times* the day you were born?
f. List three publications on outdoor recreation issued by the U.S. Department of the Interior from 2014 to the present.
g. What was the population of Spokane, Washington, in 2010?
h. List three articles, published between 2014 and 2015, on the advantages of electronic signatures.
i. Who discovered the neutrino?
j. What is the first recorded (printed) use of the word *ozone*?
k. Who edited the second edition of the *Encyclopedia of Psychology*, published in 1994?
l. What is the total number of Ebola cases reported in Sierre Leone in 2014–2015?
m. How many factories does Toyota have in the United States?

n. Who is the head of public relations for the Red Cross?

o. Name five plants that have the word *fly* as part of their common name.

p. What are the names and addresses of all the four-year colleges in the state of South Dakota?

q. Who is India's current head of state?

r. What is the current membership of the American Dental Association?

s. What are the names of the justices who currently serve on the U.S. Supreme Court?

13. Write a paraphrase of two of the following paragraphs:

a. Deep-fat frying is a mainstay of any successful fast-food operation and is one of the most commonly used procedures for the preparation and production of foods in the world. During the deep-frying process, oxidation and hydrolysis take place in the shortening and eventually change its functional, sensory, and nutritional quality. Current fat tests available to food operation managers for determining when used shortening should be discarded typically require identification of a change in some physical attribute of the shortening, such as color, smoke, foam development, etc. However, by the time these changes become evident, a considerable amount of degradation has usually taken place.[2]

b. Phishing is a form of identity theft in which victims are tricked into turning over their personal information to criminals through bogus email and websites. Phishing schemes, which rely on spam email, emerged in 2004 as a method of capturing personal information to use in identity theft. In phishing schemes, consumers receive email that purports to convey some urgent message about their financial accounts. Recipients are encouraged to respond promptly by clicking a link in the message to what are imitations of legitimate, trusted websites. As a result, the online consumer, believing he or she is connected to a legitimate enterprise, divulges personal financial information, which is diverted to the location of the criminal perpetrator. Essentially, phishers have hijacked the trusted brands of well-known banks, credit card issuers, and online retailers, to obtain valuable personal financial information that can be misused or sold to others for the same purpose. Although later phishing attacks have been more generic, they are based on a similar pretext.

Spam email easily reaches thousands if not millions of unsuspecting consumers at a time. With perhaps 5 percent of recipients estimated to divulge personal financial information, the spam scams are lucrative. In November 2004, the Anti-Phishing Working Group (APWG) reported over 1,500 new phishing attacks that month and a 28 percent average monthly growth rate in phishing sites from July through November. The APWG also identified a new form of fraud-based websites that pose as generic e-commerce sites, rather than brand-name sites, and perpetrate loan scams, mortgage frauds, online pharmacy frauds, and other banking frauds. While the United States hosts the largest number of phishing sites,

---

[2]Vincent J. Graziano, "Portable Instrument Rapidly Measures Quality of Frying Fat in Food Service Operations," *Food Technology* 33, page 50. Copyright © by Institute of Food Technologists. Reprinted by permission.

South Korea, China, Russia, Nigeria, Mexico, and Taiwan have also been identified as hosts. Federal law enforcement and others work with foreign counterparts to take down offending sites.

Thus, phishing attacks and "spoofed" email afford criminals an easy and cheap means of obtaining sensitive personal information from consumers, which can be very lucrative even if the false website is shut down within 48 to 72 hours.[3]

14. Ask a professor in your major what he or she regards as the most widely respected periodical in your field. Find a copy of the periodical, and explain its method of documentation (providing examples). How does it differ from the MLA method?

15. Put the following pieces of bibliographic information in proper form according to the MLA method of documentation for Works Cited. Correct errors in formatting, punctuation, and so on.

   a. *New York Times*. "Cisco and Texas Instruments Adapt to a New Tech World." Bits blog post. February 12, 2015. Quentin Hardy.

   b. Enterprise & Society. 16(1)2015. "Green Pastures of Plenty from Dry Desert Ground": Nature, Labor, and the Growth and Structure of a California Grape Company. Gabriel Winant. Pages 109 to 140.

   c. *EDN Network*. Access date: 10 July 2015. Simon Moffatt. "Handling Privacy and Security Concerns in the IoT: The Importance of Identity." http://www.edn.com/electronics-blogs/eye-on-iot-/4439853/Handling-Privacy-and-Security-Concerns-in-the-IoT–The-Importance-of-Identity

   d. "Managing Your Time." Blog post. Aug. 10, 2015. Being Smart at Work Blog. Debra Horowitz. www.bsaw@yahoo.com.

   e. "Bill Gates Gives $500 Million to Fight Malaria." Post Date: 11/3/2014. http://www.forbes.com/sites/danalexander/2014/11/03/bill-gates-gives-500-million-to-fight-malaria-other-diseases/. *Forbes*. Access Date: August 21, 2015. Dan Alexander.

   f. "Recycling Electronic Waste Responsibly: Excuses Dwindle." http://www.nytimes.com/2015/01/01/technology/personaltech/recycling-electronic-waste-responsibly-excuses-dwindle.html&assetType=nyt_now. *The New York Times*. Molly Wood. Access Date: May 18, 2015. Post Date: December 31, 2014.

   g. "401(k) Plans for Small Businesses." http://www.dol.gov/ebsa/publications/401kplans.html. U.S. Department of Labor. Access Date: 11 April 2015.

   h. "Artificial Intelligence and Data Mining." Pages 323–341. Newton Lee. *Counterterrorism and Cybersecurity: Total Information Awareness*. Published in 2015 by Springer Press in New York.

   i. "Social Dollars: The Economic Impact of Customer Participation in a Firm-Sponsored Online Customer Community." *Marketing Science*. Puneet Manchanda, Grant Packard, Adithya Pattabhiramaiah. Volume 34, Issue 3. May/June 2015.

   j. Volume 38, Issue 7. "Green Havens and Pollution Havens." *The World Economy*. Steven Poelhekke and Frederick van der Ploeg. Pages 1159-1178. July 2015.

---

[3]Anti-Phishing Working Group (APWG), "Phishing Attack Trends Report" (July 2004). See http://www.antiphishing.org. APWG is an industry association focused on eliminating the identity theft and fraud resulting from phishing. It reports regularly on the form and volume of phishing scams.

   k. "Google to Unleash Its Self-Driving Cars on California Roads." http://www
     .bloomberg.com/news/articles/2015-05-15/google-s-own-self-driving-cars
     -set-for-public-road-test. Brian Womack. *Bloomberg Business Week*. May 15,
     2015.

   l. Inc.com. Access Date: 23 October 2015. Post Date: 16 July 2015. "8 Tips to
     Running an Actually Successful Social Media Campaign." http://www.inc.com
     /ed-zitron/8-tips-to-running-an-actually-successful-social-media-campaign.html
     .Ed Zitron.

   m. Personal interview. 13 Sept. 2015. Marsha Keys, CEO, Biltmore Polymers,
     Chicago, IL.

   n. *The Nation*. April 22, 2014. "Where Have All the Green Jobs Gone?" http://www
     .thenation.com/blog/179439/where-have-all-green-jobs-gone. Blog post.
     Michelle Chen.

   o. *The International Trade Journal*. "Foreign Direct Investment, Pollution, and
     the Environmental Quality: A Model with Empirical Evidence from the Chinese
     Regions." 2015. Volume 29, Issue 3. Yanqing Jiang. Pages 212–227.

   p. November 2015, Volume 63, Issue 11. *New Investor Magazine*. "Why Purchase
     Trouble?" Veronica Braverman and Beth Crewes. Pages 78–83.

   q. "Introducing the Apple Watch." Pages B1–B3. Kevin Seitzer. April 20, 2015. *The
     Wall Street Journal*.

   r. Theodore Brandon. July 2015. Pages 26–28. "Greece's Economic Folly." Rochester
     Daily News.

   s. *EH.Net Encyclopedia*. Mushin, Jerry. http://eh.net/encyclopedia/the-euro-and-its
     -antecedents/ "The Euro and Its Antecedents." Edited by Robert Whaples. January
     1, 2015. Access Date: August 23, 2015.

   t. William D. Cohan. *The Atlantic Monthly*. May 2015. "Can Bankers Behave?" http://
     www.theatlantic.com/magazine/archive/2015/05/can-bankers-behave/389558/.
     Accessed June 12, 2015.

   u. "Workplace culture a benefits differentiator." Andrea Davis. *Employee Benefit
     News*. July 1, 2015.

   v. "What Is Code?" *Bloomberg Businessweek*. June 11, 2015. Paul Ford.

16. Put the bibliographic references you listed in MLA format in Exercise 15 into APA format
   for a References list.

17. Select one article from the periodical you chose for Exercise 14. Convert the bibliographic
   information for that article into the MLA parenthetical style.

18. The following passage contains mistakes in the MLA method of documentation. Find the
   mistakes and explain how to correct them.

   More and more companies are allowing employees to "telecommute" (see Smith;
   Dawson; Brown; Gura and Keith; and Allen). One expert defines telecommuting as
   "home-based work" (13). Having terminals in their homes "allows employees to work
   at a variety of jobs" ("New Employment Opportunities"). It has been estimated that currently 900,000 employees work out of their homes (Pennington, p. 56). That number
   is sure to increase as computer-based businesses multiply in the late 1990s (Brown). In
   one of her recent articles on telecommuting, Holcomb (167) found that "in the last year

alone 43 companies in the metropolitan Phoenix area made this option available to their employees."

Employees who telecommute cite a variety of benefits for such an arrangement (see in particular articles by Gura, Smith, and Kaplan). One employee of a mail order company whose opinion was quoted observed that "I can save about 15–17 hours a week in driving time" (from Allen). Working at home allows the telecommuting employee to work at his or her optimum times ("The Day Does Not Have to Start at 9:00 a.m."). Also, in articles by Kaplan and Keith the benefits of not having to leave home are emphasized: "A telecommuting parent does not have to worry about child care" (39). Telecommuting may "be here to stay" (quoted in a number of different website sources).

19. Submit your preliminary list of references (your tentative Works Cited page) for a long report to your instructor.

CHAPTER

9

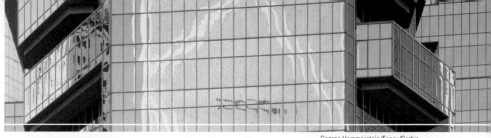

Summarizing Information at Work

Summaries are vital in the world of work. They get to the main points—the bottom line—right away for busy readers, giving them the big picture. A summary is a brief restatement of the main points of a book, report, website, article, laboratory test, PowerPoint presentation, or meeting. A summary saves readers hours of time because they do not have to study the original work or attend a conference. A summary can reduce a report or an article by 85 to 95 percent (or even more) and can capture the essential points of a three-day convention in a one-page memo. Finally, since only the most important points of a work are included in a summary, readers will know they have been given the crucial information they need.

SUMMARIES IN THE INFORMATION AGE

Thanks to the Web and other communication technologies, we have an abundance of information. It would be impossible to locate, classify, understand, and assess all this information without the help of summaries. They can be found all around you.

- Google retrieves positive "hits" by looking for keywords that summarize a source and help users determine whether the material is relevant for their purpose.
- A home page on the Web is in essence a summary of the various pages to which it is connected.
- Television and radio stations regularly air one- or two-minute "news breaks" that summarize in a few paragraphs the major stories of the day.
- A blog, such as that shown in Figure 4.7 (pages 134–135) often summarizes the results of many weeks of research and decision making.
- IMs, tweets, and text messages, require you to summarize information concisely for readers who have small screens and tight schedules.

THE IMPORTANCE OF SUMMARIES IN BUSINESS

On the job, writing summaries for employers, co-workers, and customers is a regular and important responsibility. Chapter 14 discusses a variety of reports—periodic, sales, progress, trip, test, and incident—whose effectiveness depends on a faithful summary of events. You may have to condense a proposal to fit a one-page format for an organization. Or you may be asked to summarize the main features of a competitor's product or a new model you saw at a trade show. You may be asked to write a news release—another type of summary vital for your organization's image (see "Writing Successful News Releases," pages 390–392)—for your employer's website.

Figure 9.1 is a summary of a long report evaluating workplace child care facilities. Note how it concisely identifies the main purpose and conclusions of the report.

CONTENTS OF A SUMMARY

The chief objective in writing a summary is deciding what to include and what to omit. Determine what is most relevant for your audience and its purpose. As we have seen, a summary is a streamlined review of *only* the most significant points. You will not save your readers time if you simply rephrase large sections of the original. That will simply supply readers with another report, not a summary.

Make your summary lean and useful by briefly telling readers the main points: purpose, scope, conclusions, and recommendations. A summary should straightforwardly and accurately answer readers' two most important questions:

1. What are the findings of the report or meeting?
2. How do the findings apply to my business, research, or job?

FIGURE 9.1 A Summary of a Long Report on Workplace Child Care Facilities

---

BENEFITS TO EMPLOYERS WHO OFFER ON-SITE CHILD CARE

Every week, close to 12.5 million children between the ages of six weeks to five years were in some kind of child care. According to a new study by The Pennabe Group, the 643 workplaces that offered accredited on-site care, were ten times more likely to reap major benefits, including:

- On average, workers use 35% less sick days than companies that do not offer on-site facilities.
- Year-to-year employee retention is 22% higher at workplaces that offer on-site child care.
- Employee satisfaction scores are 31% greater at these workplaces.
- Workplaces voted among the most favorable in a *Forbes* survey.

© 2017 Cengage Learning

What to Include in a Summary

1. **Purpose.** Why was the article or report written or hearing or meeting held? Give readers a brief introduction (even one sentence will do) indicating the main purpose of the report or event.
2. **Essential specifics.** Include only the essential names, costs, titles, places, or dates.
3. **Conclusions or results.** Emphasize what the final vote was, the result of the tests, or the proposed solution to the problem.
4. **Recommendations or implications.** What they are, when can they be carried out, and why they are necessary, or why a plan will not work.

What to Omit from a Summary

1. **Opinion.** Avoid injecting opinions—your own, the author's, or the speaker's. A later section of this chapter (pages 385–387) will deal with evaluative summaries that require you to state your views.
2. **New data.** Stick to the original article, report, book, or meeting. Avoid introducing comparisons with other works or conferences; readers will expect an unbiased digest of only the material being summarized.
3. **Irrelevant specifics.** Do not include biographical details about the author of an article that might be included in "Notes on Contributors."
4. **Examples.** Readers will want to know outcomes, results, and recommendations, not the illustrative details supporting or elaborating on those results.
5. **Background.** Readers want the big picture, not supporting or technical details.
6. **Jargon.** Technical definitions or jargon in the original document may confuse rather than clarify the essential information for general readers.
7. **Reference data.** Exclude information found in footnotes, bibliographies, appendixes, tables, or graphs.

PREPARING A SUMMARY

To write an effective summary, you need to proceed through a series of steps to identify the major points, and, finally, to put the essence of the material into your own words. Follow these steps to prepare a concise, useful summary.

1. **Read the material once in its entirety to get an overall impression of what it is about.** Become familiar with large issues, such as the purpose and organization of the work and the audience for whom it was written. Visual cues—headings, subheadings, words in italic or boldface type, sidebars—can help you to identify main ideas. Also look for a conclusion and any mini-summaries within the article or report.

2. **Reread the material.** Read it a second time or more if necessary. Locate all of the main points, and underline them. Pay attention to the key transitional words, which often fall into predictable categories:

- Words that enumerate: *first, second, third, initially, subsequently, finally, next, another*

- Words that express causation: *accordingly, as a result, because, consequently, subsequently, therefore, thus*
- Words that express contrasts and comparisons: *although, by the same token, despite, different from, furthermore, however, in comparison, in contrast, in addition, less than, likewise, more readily, more than, not only . . . but also, on the other hand, the same is true for, similar, unlike*
- Words that signal essentials: *basically, best, central, crucial, foremost, fundamental, important, indispensable, in general, leading, major, obviously, principal, significant*

Pay special attention to the first and last sentences of each paragraph. Often the first sentence of a paragraph contains the topic sentence, and the last sentence summarizes the paragraph or provides a transition to the next paragraph.

3. Collect your highlighted material or notes and organize the information into a draft summary. At this stage do not be concerned about how your sentences read. Use the language of the original, together with any necessary connective words or phrases of your own. *Expect to have more material here than will appear in the final version.* Do not worry; you are engaged in a process of selection and exclusion. Your purpose at this stage is to extract the principal ideas.

4. Read through and revise your draft(s) and delete whatever information you can. As you revise, see how many of your highlighted points can be condensed, combined, or eliminated. You may find that you have repeated a point. Be sure to be faithful to the original by preserving its emphases and sequence. Put quotation marks around any direct quotations. But try to avoid direct quotation wherever possible at this stage.

5. Now put the revised version into your own words. Again, make sure that your reworded summary has eliminated nonessential words. Connect your sentences with words that show relationships between ideas in the original (*also, although, because, consequently, however, nevertheless, since*).

TECH NOTE

Using Software to Summarize Documents

Your word-processing software can help you prepare your summary. First, download and open an existing digital file of the material (article, report, technical paper) you need to summarize. Then, "save as" a new file with a new filename. If all you have is hard copy, do an OCR scan so you can create a digital file to edit. As you read through it on your screen, cut nonessential material. The first time through, it is easier to cut what you don't want than it is to select exactly what you do want. Using this method of editing, you can delete single sentences or several paragraphs at a time. Also, highlight key points as you read through the original material. Highlighting during the first pass can guide you on your second reading as you attempt to include only relevant material for your summary and to start putting it into your own words (see "Paraphrasing," pages 336–337).

6. Edit your summary to make sure it is fair, clear, and concise. Compare your summary with the original to make sure you have captured the key points, especially those in the conclusion and recommendation sections. Your summary also needs to be brief and to the point.

7. Identify the source you have just summarized. Include pertinent bibliographic information in the title of your summary or in a footnote or an endnote. This gives proper credit to the original source and informs your readers where they can find the complete text if they want more details.

Make Sure Your Summary Is Ethical

Your supervisor will expect your summary to be honest, fair, and accurate, identifying the most crucial points of the article. Figure 9.5 on page 383 contains an unethical summary of Figure 9.2 that distorts the meaning and intention of the original by leading the reader to conclude that virtual reality is not valuable for law enforcement administrators—the very opposite point the author makes.

You can write an ethical summary by doing the following:

- Make sure your summary agrees with the original.
- Emphasize the main points the author makes.
- Do not omit key points.
- Be fair in expressing the author's conclusions/recommendations.
- Do not dwell on minor points to the exclusion of major ones.
- Do not let your own opinions distort or contradict the message of the original document.

CASE STUDY

Summarizing an Original Article

Figure 9.2, a 2,500-word article entitled "Virtual Reality: Essential in Law Enforcement Training," appeared in the *The Law Enforcement Bulletin* and hence is of primary interest to individuals in law enforcement administration. Assume you have been asked to write a summary of the article for your boss, a police chief in a medium-sized city who would be interested in increasing the use of virtual reality in the city's police academy training program.

By following the steps outlined above, you would first read the article carefully two or three times, highlighting the most important points, signaled by key words. Note what has been highlighted in the article. Also study the comments in the margins to see why certain information is to be included or excluded from the summary.

After you have identified the main points, extract them from the article and, still using the language of the article, join them into a coherent working draft summary, as in Figure 9.3. Then shorten and rewrite the working draft in your own words to produce the compact final version of your summary, as shown in Figure 9.4. Only 164 words long, the final summary is 6 percent of the length of the original article and records only major conclusions relevant to the audience for the article.

FIGURE 9.2 An Original Article with Important Points Highlighted for Use in a Summary

---

Virtual Reality: Essential in Law Enforcement Training

George P. Burroughs

A late night police pursuit of a suspected drunk driver winds through abandoned city streets. The short vehicle chase ends in a warehouse district where the suspect abandons his vehicle and runs into an unoccupied building. The suspect stops, pulls out a rifle, and fires at the pursuing officer before disappearing. The officer, shaken but uninjured, radios in his location and follows the suspect into the building.

> *Omit scenario— example of background; an opener*

Whether the officer's decision to pursue proves right or wrong, the training gained from this experience is immeasurable. Fortunately for this officer, the scenario occurred in the realm of virtual reality, where training can have a real-life impact without the accompanying risk.

> *Include important observation*

Traditional Training Limitations

In real life, police officers may not get a chance to learn from their mistakes. To survive, they must receive training that prepares them for most situations they might encounter on the street. However, because many training programs emphasize repetition to produce desired behaviors, they may not achieve the intended results, especially after students leave the training environment. Thus, the more realistic the training, the greater the lessons learned.

> *Major distinction*

Additionally, newer officers have less on-site crime experience. The key to teaching this new breed is to provide fast-paced, attention-getting instruction that is clear, concise, and relevant.

> *Include significant qualification*

Training with Virtual Reality

Years of data have proven that virtual reality simulations can provide the type of training that today's law enforcement officers need. By fully immersing the senses in a computer-generated environment, the artificial world becomes reality to users and greatly enhances their training experiences.

> *Emphasize author's main point*
>
> *Important reason for its neglect by law enforcement*

Considerable research has been conducted about the importance of virtual reality training for police departments, but the technology has not been as widely used as it needs to be. The apparent reason simply is that, for the most part, law enforcement has not asked for it.

Because virtual reality technologies are complex systems, they can be seen as both difficult to implement and expensive, and, thus, most law enforcement administrators have not utilized virtual reality technologies in a systematic, comprehensive way for training exercises. By understanding how virtual reality works, its cost efficiency, and its adaptability as a training tool, law enforcement administrators can significantly improve their officers' readiness in the field.

> *Restatement of main point above*
>
> *Note parallel items with key words signaling important applications*

Source: © Cengage Learning / Adapted from Hormann, J.S. (1995). Virtual Reality: The Future of Law Enforcement Training. FBI Law Enforcement Bulletin, 64(7), 7–12.

(Continued)

FIGURE 9.2 (Continued)

Significant phrase

Omit specific pieces of equipment

Omit example

How Does Virtual Reality Work?

Using complex coding and algorithms, modern virtual reality systems create realistic, three-dimensional environments. In earlier versions of virtual reality systems, users viewed images through a head-mounted device such as a helmet, goggles, or other apparatus that restricted their vision to two small video monitors, one in front of each eye. Contemporary programs, however, can offer a 360-degree, physically immersive, multi-participant, real-time environment. Some systems even use full-body sensors on each trainee to create avatars–virtual, but lifelike, digitally-rendered people–for each participant that reproduces exactly a user's height, weight, and overall body type. These avatars, controlled by the trainees, then move through the virtual space and scenario created for the training exercise.

Omit further examples

Major conclusion

While the recent improvements in virtual reality technologies have been impressive, the systems still have trouble with properly showing realistic recoil on firearms, or the variety of random noises that will accompany many law enforcement situations. However, the systems do allow for simulations in certain close-quarter situations–interior room searches, confined or tight indoor spaces–that are impractical (or even impossible) to carry out in normal training sessions, due to real-world limitations.

Major value to audience of administrators

Emphasize significant advantages in training

Use only main points relevant to target audience of administrators

Uses for Virtual Reality

Virtual reality is an excellent method for providing realistic, safe, and cost-effective training. For example, a police officer can struggle with virtual shoot/don't shoot dilemnas, or use it to learn how to best respond to crime scenes.

Within a virtual environment, students can make decisions and act upon them without risk to themselves or others. By the same token, instructors can critique students' actions, enabling students to review and learn from their mistakes. This ability gives virtual reality a great advantage over most conventional training methods.

The Department of Defense (DOD) lead public and private industry in developing virtual reality training. Since the early 1980s, DOD has actively researched, developed, and implemented virtual reality to train members of the armed forces to fight effectively in combat.

Note main military advantage

DOD's approach to virtual reality training emphasizes team tactics, and allows groups of military personnel to engage in combat safely on a virtual battlefield. Virtual battlefields can easily re-create real-world locations with interchangeable characteristics that would be expensive or impossible to reproduce in the real world. To explore "what if" scenarios, participants can modify enemy capabilities, terrain, weather, and weapon systems. Consequently this form of training has proven quite cost-effective.

FIGURE 9.2 (Continued)

Studies also show that military units perform better following virtual reality training. Even though virtual environments are only simulations, the complete immersion of the senses literally overwhelms users, totally immersing them in the simulated action. The realism provided by today's state-of-the-art systems plays a major role in the program's success. In fact, due to its past success, DOD trains infantry with virtual reality skill simulators.

Law Enforcement Training

Just as virtual reality is valuable as a training and planning tool for the military, incorporating virtual reality training systems nonetheless offers law enforcement an effective and cost-efficient tool for training in pursuit driving, firearms, stealth tactics in close-quarter situations, high-risk incident management, incident re-creation, and crime scene processing.

Unfortunately, few police forces have implemented virtual reality in law enforcement training in a systematic, comprehensive way. Previous encounters with earlier, inferior versions of the technology discouraged many law enforcement administrators, and the perception in many departments is that the current technology, while vastly improved, is too complex to implement on the local level. With start-up costs averaging $100,000 to $200,000, there are also budgetary limitations to implementation in many departments.

Modern virtual reality systems, however, have never been easier to use and customize for individualized training. While most systems offer prebuilt training scenarios, many systems also allow departments to build their own unique scenarios based on common encounters or buildings and structures in their own community. Most companies also offer installment payment options to help cash-strapped departments, offer 24/7 technical support, and will provide free training on how to utilize their systems to all key stakeholders. Significantly, studies have shown that use of a virtual reality simulator in law enforcement training is cheaper in the long term than constantly retooling and repairing more conventional training areas.

Pursuit Driving

Pursuit driving represents another area where virtual reality systems have benefited law enforcement. Simulators provide realistic feedback about road feel, steering capabilities, and other vehicle motions. As noted in demonstrations, the immersive experience features a 360-degree field of view and can feature one or more drivers. Environments can change between city streets and rural back roads, or be customized to represent specific streets and topographies. The vehicle itself can also be tailored to match that of a specific police force's cruisers.

Virtual reality driving simulators provide police departments with invaluable training at a fraction of the long-term cost of using actual vehicles. In fact,

Omit example

Key word "major" signals relevant idea for audience

Omit military application

Significant parallel points

Omit statistics

Note cost benefit again

Major conclusion signaled by key word "significantly"

Include application but omit examples

Include major advantage but exclude specific example

Note cost efficiency again

(Continued)

FIGURE 9.2 (Continued)

Include major
advantage
but exclude
specific
example

Note major
distinction
for training
purposes

New subtopic;
include
advantages
but omit
examples

Include
significant
points on
advantages

Next three
reasons
to adopt
virtual reality
systems
signaled by
keywords "in
addition,"
"also," and
"likewise"

simulators are being used by a number of police departments around the country. The Los Angeles County Sheriff's Office Emergency Vehicle Operations Center (EVOC) reports that simulators help police cadets develop more sensitive informal judgment and decision-making skills compared to cadets trained by more conventional methods. Still, as the EVOC supervisor cautions, virtual reality training should complement, not replace, actual behind-the-wheel instruction.

Firearms Training

Virtual reality systems also greatly enhance shoot/don't shoot training scenarios. Many systems feature a weapons simulator that allows a user to chose any of his or her department's current weapon options (whether it be a high-powered repeating rifle, a shotgun, a TASER, OC [pepper] spray, or even a flashlight), and realistically portrays outcomes based on a thorough assessment of the cadet's firing techniques, including cant angle, trigger squeeze, and butt pressure.

Evaluators can also alter the effectiveness of each weapon, including malfunctions that cadets might encounter. Assessors also have the benefit of observing the training program from any perspective, including stopping criminal activity. The training scenarios can involve actual building floor plans or local city streets, and criteria such as the weather or the number of participants can be altered easily.

High-Risk Incident Management

In addition to force option training, virtual reality has also proven to be invaluable for SWAT team members before high-risk tactical assaults. Floor plans and other known facts about a structure or area can be entered into a virtual reality system to re-create the exact environment for commanders and team members to analyze prior to action, and the systems excel at depicting close-quarter situations that are very hard to replicate in real-world settings.

Incident Re-creation

Law enforcement agencies can also collect data from victims, witnesses, suspects, and crime scenes to re-create traffic accidents, shootings, and other crimes. The virtual environment created from the data can be used to refresh the memories of victims and witnesses, to solve crimes, and, ultimately, to prosecute offenders.

FIGURE 9.2 (Continued)

Crime Scene Processing

Virtual reality crime scenes can likewise be used to train both detectives and patrol officers. First, officers can search the site and analyze evidence without ever leaving the station. Then, actual crime scenes can be realistically re-created, helping police departments to evaluate previous protocols and make any necessary modifications.

Omit examples

Is Virtual Reality Virtually Perfect?

Though virtual reality systems may appear to be the ideal law enforcement tool, as with any technology, some drawbacks exist. Currently, areas of concern range from the near-impossibility of simulating hard surfaces such as walls in a three-dimensional, immersive environment to the "giggle factor" for participants in the first few minutes of a training exercise that use full-body sensors and avatars. Fortunately, however, technologies are evolving and improving constantly, and as the use of virtual reality models increases, many of these concerns should be dispelled.

Crucial qualification and justification for expanding the use of virtual reality systems in law enforcement training

FIGURE 9.3 A Working Draft Summary of the "Virtual Reality" Article in Figure 9.2

Law enforcement officers put their lives on the line every day, yet their training does not fully allow them to anticipate what they will find on the streets. Virtual reality gives them realistic, high-tech benefits of encountering criminals without any risks. Traditional training methods, which work through repetition, cannot equal the advantages of virtual reality when it comes to teaching officers the lessons they must learn to survive in the field. Cadets today benefit from the attention-getting, highly realistic training that virtual reality affords them. Yet even though research has proven that virtual reality simulations can provide excellent training, law enforcement officials have not used it as often as necessary. Moreover, the perceived complexities of the systems and cost have created barriers to their extended use. It is essential that administrators know how virtual reality works, its flexibility, and cost efficiency. Working through complex coding and algorithms, virtual reality gives users a fully-immersible, three-dimensional environment. Some systems even use full-body sensors to create avatars fully controllable by cadets. But these devices do have problems; they have trouble simulating some aspects of firearms, and the random noise of law-enforcement situations. Even so, virtual reality programs provide cost-effective and life-saving benefits for law

FIGURE 9.3 (Continued)

enforcement officers. Thanks to this technology, new officers will be able to make quicker and better decisions in the field. Virtual reality was developed by the Department of Defense; armed forces used it to re-create battlefield conditions, helping troops better understand enemy position and tactics. Similarly, virtual reality holds great appeal for law enforcement training. Unfortunately, few police forces have adopted virtual reality in training in a systematic, comprehensive way. Yet virtual reality systems are cheaper in the long term than more conventional training methods. Driving simulators help officers prepare for high-speed chases. In Los Angeles County, such simulators complement more traditional training. Virtual reality can help officers in a variety of training missions—firearms, high-risk incidents, re-creating crimes, understanding the crime scene. Using virtual reality systems, officers never have to leave the station to achieve top-quality training. Admittedly, virtual reality has drawbacks, but as computer processing power increases, users should face fewer problems.

FIGURE 9.4 A Final, Effective Summary of the Article in Figure 9.2

Virtual reality offers benefits for law enforcement training that traditional methods cannot provide. This computer-generated technology simulates and re-creates real-life crime scenes without placing officers at risk. Thanks to virtual reality's fully-immersive, three-dimensional environment, officers enter the criminals' world to gain invaluable experience interacting with them. Because virtual reality systems are perceived as complex to use and expensive, administrators have not fully utilized them in training programs. Yet they provide a cost-effective, realistic way to conduct police training. The applications of virtual reality systems far exceed its military use of simulating battlefield conditions. They allow administrators to give trainees hands-on experience in pursuit driving, firearms training, SWAT team assaults, incident re-creation, and crime scene processing. Officers achieve top-quality training without ever leaving the station. Although virtual reality, like any technology, has limitations, increases in computer processing power provides constant improvements. Administrators need to fully embrace and adopt virtual reality systems to give officers field-translatable experiences.

FIGURE 9.5 An Unethical, Misleading Summary of the Article in Figure 9.2

A rookie police officer makes many mistakes in pursuing subjects. Training can cover many realistic situations, but young officers have inadequate experience. Given its complexity and cost, virtual reality holds little promise for law enforcement training. Virtual reality has too many limitations, including unrealistic firearm recoil, the fact that hard surfaces are impossible to replicate, and the random noises that distract trainees and causes a so-called "giggle factor." Instructors can gain much from virtual reality because they can better criticize their cadets. In the early 1980s, the DOD used virtual reality to duplicate battlefield conditions, but the complete immersion in the virtual world overwhelmed soldiers. Police forces have also recognized the limitations of virtual reality systems and have avoided using them to train recruits. The Los Angeles Sheriff's EVOC used a driving simulator but expressed their caution about it. There appear to be too many options in virtual reality systems for firearms training, causing confusion, though floor plans might have helped SWAT teams. Witnesses may need to refresh their memories with virtual reality. Again drawbacks exist. Computers have not evolved and improved the way they need to for these systems to be effective tools in law enforcement training.

Nonessential introductory material

Distorts article

Dwells on limitations at the expense of the main advantages

Misrepresents one of the limitations

Misrepresents the role of virtual reality

Comes to an erroneous conclusion

One-sided; omits success of simulation

Misrepresents the usefulness of the technology

Does not subordinate flaws

© 2017 Cengage Learning

EXECUTIVE SUMMARIES

An **executive summary,** found at the beginning of a proposal (Chapter 13) or a long report (Chapter 15), is usually one or two pages long (four to six concise paragraphs) and condenses the most important points from the proposal or report for a busy manager—the executive. An executive summary is written to help the reader reach a major decision based on the report or proposal. Your goal is to tell your employer concisely what findings the report includes, what those findings mean for the company or organization, and what action, if any, needs to be taken. Figure 9.6 (page 384), an executive summary of a report on software for a safety training program, directly advises a decision maker to purchase a safety software package.

What Managers Want to See in an Executive Summary

Managers use executive summaries so they will not have to wade through entire reports. They are most concerned with issues such as costs, profits, resources, personnel, timetables, and feasibility. Your summary must supply key information on the executive's four *E*'s: *evaluation, economy, efficiency,* and *expediency.*

Organization of an Executive Summary

An executive summary must be faithful to the report while giving readers what they need (Figure 9.6). First, read the report carefully, plan what you want to include, and then draft and revise using valuable connective words (see "Combine short,

FIGURE 9.6 An Executive Summary

A Report on Providing Better Training at Techtron Sites

Starts with purpose of report

Management has commissioned this report to investigate ways to prepare for the OSHA audits scheduled between February and June 2015, at our seven regional Techtron plants. Most directly, this report focuses on our ability to complete Phase One of ISO 14001 certification.

Identifies problem the report investigates and why it is important

Currently, the Techtron safety training programs are inadequate; they are neither comprehensive nor up-to-date. We lack necessary software to instruct employees about the EPA and OSHA regulations and requirements that apply to hazardous materials or procedures used in our company. Consequently, safety violations have occurred with lockouts, confined spaces, fall protection, and the "Right to Know Law" concerning labeling of chemicals.

Explains the solution tested

Exploring better ways to conduct our training sessions, we purchased a copy of the software program **EPA/OSHA Trainer**, regarded as the best on the market (available from EDI @ $1,300 per copy). The **Trainer** offers effective guidelines on developing safety meetings and giving demonstrations. It also includes instructions, written in clear, nontechnical language, on how to identify, collect, and document hazardous materials. Additionally, the **Trainer** supplies the full text of EPA/OSHA regulations, with updates issued quarterly.

Highlights benefits of trainer

Verifies effectiveness of solution

To test the effectiveness of the **Trainer** software, we scheduled an internal audit at our Hendersonville site last month. After progressing through the **Trainer** module, a core group of employees interviewed by management successfully completed all required regulatory training. Subsequently, employees who had undergone such training were able to instruct and monitor the performance of other employees in the program.

Ends by stressing action to be taken and by when

To ensure the safety of our employees and to compete in a global marketplace, Techtron must pass the OSHA 14001 certification. Purchasing seven additional copies of the **EPA/OSHA Trainer** software (7 @ $1,300 = $9,100) in the next month is a wise and necessary investment.

choppy sentences," page 61). Clearly you cannot write an executive summary of your report until after you have written the report itself.

Follow this organizational plan when you write an executive summary:

1. **Begin with the purpose and the scope of the report.** For example, a report might be written to study new marketing strategies, to identify inadequate software, or to relocate a store.
2. **Relate your purpose to a key problem.** Identify the source (background) and seriousness of the problem.
3. **Identify the criteria used to solve the problem.** Cite why and how the strategies used relate to solving the problems.
4. **Condense the findings of your report.** Specify what tests or surveys revealed. Be careful not to include too many details.
5. **Stress conclusions and possible solutions.** Be precise and clear.
6. **Provide recommendations.** For example, buy, sell, hire more personnel, relocate, or choose among alternative solutions. Also indicate when a decision needs to be made.

The order of information in an executive summary does not have to follow strictly the order of the report itself. In fact, some executive summaries start with recommendations. Find out your boss's preference.

EVALUATIVE SUMMARIES

You may also have to write an **evaluative summary,** also called a **critique**. As with executive summaries, you will be expected to provide a commentary on the material (that is, give your opinion). For example, you may have to condense and judge the merits of a report, paying special attention to whether its recommendations should be followed, modified, or ignored. Your company or agency may also ask you to write short evaluative summaries of job candidates, applications, sales proposals, or conferences.

Guidelines for Writing a Successful Evaluative Summary

To write a careful evaluative summary, follow the guidelines below:

- Keep the summary short—5 to 10 percent of the length of the original.
- Blend your evaluations with your summary; do not save your evaluations for the end of the summary.
- Place each evaluation near the summarized points to which it applies so readers will see your remarks in context.
- Include a pertinent quotation from the original to emphasize your recommendation.
- Comment on both the content and the style of the original.

Evaluating the Content

Answer these questions on content for your readers:

1. **How carefully and completely is the subject researched?** Is the material accurate and up-to-date? Are important details missing? Exactly what has the writer left out? Where could the reader find the missing information? If the material is inaccurate or incomplete, is the whole work affected or just part of it?
2. **Is the writer or speaker objective?** Are conclusions supported by evidence? Is the writer or speaker following a particular theory, program, or school of thought? Is that fact made clear in the source? Has the writer or speaker emphasized one point at the expense of others? What are the writer's qualifications and background?
3. **Does the work achieve its goal?** Is the topic too large to be usefully discussed in a single talk, article, or report? Is the work sketchy? Are there digressions, tangents, or irrelevant materials? Do the recommendations make sense?
4. **Is the material relevant to your audience?** How would the audience use it? Is the entire work relevant or just part of it? Why? Would the work be useful for all employees of your company or only for those working in certain areas? Why? What answers offered by the work would help to solve a specific problem you or others have encountered on the job?

You may want to review "Evaluating Websites" on pages 331–333.

Evaluating the Style

Answer these questions on style for the readers of your evaluative summary:

1. **Is the material readable?** Is it well written and easy to follow? Does it contain helpful headings, careful summaries, and appropriate examples?
2. **Is the material organized and free of errors?** Is each paragraph well-developed and does the author handle transitions well between paragraphs? Does it follow proper grammatical conventions (see Appendix, pages A-1–A-19)?
3. **What kind of vocabulary does the writer or speaker use?** Are there too many technical terms or too much jargon? Is it written for the layperson? Is the language precise or vague? Would readers have to skip certain sections that are too complicated?
4. **What visuals are included?** Infographs? Photographs? Videos? How are they used? Are they used effectively? Are there too many or too few?

Figures 9.7 and 9.8 (page 388) contain evaluative summaries. Note how the writers' assessments are woven into the condensed versions of the originals. Figure 9.7 is a student's opinion of an article summarized for a class in information management. Figure 9.8 is an evaluative summary in memo format collaboratively written by two employees who have just returned from a seminar. They have divided their labor, one writing the opening paragraph and the summary of "Techniques of Health Assessment" and the other doing the summaries of "Assessment of the Heart and Lungs" and "Assessment of the Abdomen." Together they drafted and revised the "Recommendations" and prepared the final copy of the memo.

FIGURE 9.7 An Evaluative Summary of an Article

Abbasi, Sami M., Kenneth W. Hollman, and Robert Hayes. "Bad Bosses and How Not to Be One." *Information Management Journal* 42.1 (2008): 52–56.

According to this practical and convincing article, the way employees are managed determines a company's success. The authors helpfully begin by describing the new twenty-first-century workplace where power has shifted from a top-down authoritative management style to one respecting employees as "knowledge workers" whose professional contributions are essential in a digital culture. The article then turns to a classifying six types of difficult bosses, ranging from incompetents, crooks, and bullies to dodgers, know-it-alls, and "walking policy manual[s]" who stick to a policy, however dated or contradictory. These bad bosses use intimidation, manipulation, blame, conflict, and cover-ups to exert or protect their power. Effective bosses, on the other hand, remove fear from the workplace, build trust, encourage feedback, and act as advocates for their employees with upper management. Although aimed at information managers, the guidelines in this readable article apply to anyone who wants to be a good—or better—boss.

Identifies purpose of article

Comments on style and organization

Indicates why and how article is useful to diverse audiences

ABSTRACTS

In addition to summaries, your employer may ask you to write abstracts. Abstracts are found in several key documents in the world of work and are a staple of the Internet.

Differences Between a Summary and an Abstract

The terms *summary* and *abstract* are often used interchangeably, resulting in some confusion. That problem arises because there are two distinct types of abstracts: **descriptive abstracts** and **informative abstracts.** An informative abstract is the same as a summary; it indicates what research was done, what conclusions were reached, and what recommendations were made. Look at the summary in Figure 9.4. It explains why the use of virtual reality should be incorporated in law enforcement training: because virtual reality gives officers field-translatable training. Informative abstracts are found at the beginning of long reports. Descriptive abstracts, however, do not give conclusions.

All abstracts share two characteristics: the writer never uses "I" and avoids footnotes.

FIGURE 9.8 A Collaboratively Written Evaluative Summary of a Seminar

SABINE MEMORIAL HOSPITAL
7200 MEDICAL BLVD.
SABINE, TX 77231-0011
(512) 555-6734
WWW.SABINEMEMORIAL.ORG

TO: Mohammed Lau, M.S.N.   SUBJECT: Evaluation of Physical
        Director of Nurses   Assessment Seminar

FROM: Elena Roja, R.N.   DATE: September 14, 2015
      Lee Schoppe, R.N.

Gives overall structure of seminar

On September 7, Doris Fujimoto, R.N., and Rick Poncé, R.N., both on the staff of Houston Presbyterian Hospital, conducted a practical and beneficial seminar on physical assessment. The one-day seminar was divided into three units: (1) **Techniques of Health Assessment**, (2) **Assessment of the Heart and Lungs**, and (3) **Assessment of the Abdomen**.

Techniques of Health Assessment

Describes and evaluates each part of seminar

Four procedures used in physical assessment—inspection, percussion, palpation, and auscultation—were defined and demonstrated. Return demonstrations, used throughout the seminar, meant we did not have to wait until we went back to work to practice our skills. The instructors stressed the proper use of the stethoscope and the seven primary methods of taking a patient's pulse (and the reasons why some methods are more useful than others). Participants were also asked to take the pulse of the person next to him/her using the methods discussed.

Assessment of the Heart and Lungs

Explains why one part was unsuccessful

After we inspected the chest externally, the seminar covered the proper placement of hands for percussion and palpation and the interpretation of various breath sounds. The instructors helped us find areas of the lung and identify heart sounds. However, the film, "Cardiopulmonary Receptors," on examining the heart and lungs was ineffective because it included too much information.

Assessment of the Abdomen

Continues to emphasize practical benefits of seminar

The instructors warned that the order of examination of the abdoman differs from that of the chest cavity. Auscultation, not percussion, follows inspection so that bowel sounds are not activated. The instructors clearly identified how to detect bowel sounds and how to locate the abdomen and palpate organs.

Recommendations

Ends with endorsement by offering suggestions for improving seminar

We strongly recommend a seminar like this for all nurses whose expanding role in the health care system requires more physical assessments. Although the seminar covered a wealth of information, the instructors admitted that they discussed only basics. In the future, however, it would be better to offer follow-up seminars on specific body systems (e.g., chest cavity, abdomen, central nervous system) instead of combining topics because of the amount of information involved and the time required for demonstrations.

Photo by Mikecphoto/Shutterstock.com

Writing an Informative Abstract

An informative abstract is not as long as an executive summary, which gives more supporting details. As a part of your course work or your job, you will probably have to write informative abstracts for long reports (Chapter 15).

One way to approach writing the abstract of a report is to think of it as a table of contents in sentence form. A table of contents is, in effect, a final outline; it is easily fleshed out into an abstract.

Writing a Descriptive Abstract

Unlike an informative abstract, a descriptive abstract is usually only a few sentences long; it does not go into any detail or give conclusions. As the name implies, a descriptive abstract provides information on what topics a work discusses but not how or why they are discussed. Here is a descriptive abstract of the article summarized in Figure 9.4:

> Virtual reality can be used to teach law enforcement officers firearms training, SWAT team assaults, incident re-creation, and crime location processing. This training technology should be used extensively by law enforcement administrators to better train police recruits.

Figure 9.9 reproduces two descriptive abstracts from the *Journal of Interactive Marketing*, a publication that includes abstracts as a way to help readers learn about research in this specialized discipline.

FIGURE 9.9 Descriptive Abstracts of Journal Articles

Strategic and Ethical Considerations in Managing Digital Privacy

Ravi Sarathy and Christopher J. Robinson (August 2003), *Journal of Business Ethics,* 46(2), pp. 111–126.

Information about customers and prospects is readily available through a variety of digital sources. The questions a marketer must answer is how much of this available data should be used for commercial purposes and how much should remain privileged and off limits. In this paper the authors develop a model of the factors influencing privacy strategy. This model incorporates external, ethical, and firm-specific factors that impact customer privacy protection strategy formulation. The model is then applied to various scenarios to determine the firm's most likely customer privacy strategy. International implications of the model are also discussed.

Scovotti. (8, 13)

The Professional Service Encounter in the Age of the Internet: An Exploratory Study

Gillian Hogg, Angus Laing, and Dan Winkelman (2003), *The Journal of Services Marketing,* 17(5), pp. 476–495.

The Internet, by providing access to an unprecedented amount of healthcare-related information, is changing the balance of power in the relationship between healthcare consumers and professionals. Patients play a more active role in the relationship, interacting with healthcare professionals and other consumers to understand their illnesses. This situation changes the nature of the doctor/patient relationship—where the doctor becomes only one of the *advisors* in the service encounter. The implications of this research extend to other types of service encounters, where consumers may be engaging in virtual, parallel service encounters.

Short, 3-4 sentence paragraph

Uses objective language

WRITING SUCCESSFUL NEWS RELEASES

A **news release,** sometimes called a **press release** or **media release,** is another type of on-the-job document that requires you to summarize key information for a variety of readers. Basically, a news release is an announcement (usually one page or a single screen on the Web) about your company's or agency's specific product, services, or personnel. It should be crisp and highlight only the most important and relevant facts clearly and straightforwardly, as the other summaries you have studied in this chapter do.

Figure 9.10 contains a sample news release distributed over the Internet.

Subjects Appropriate for News Releases

News releases should be written only about newsworthy subjects, such as these:

1. New products, services, or publications
2. New policies or procedures
3. Personnel changes and awards
4. New construction and developments
5. Financial and business news
6. Ecofriendly (green) news
7. Special events

News Releases About Bad News

While the topics above focus on a company's or organization's achievements, not all the news you may be asked to announce will be positive. You may have to report on events that concern product recalls, work stoppages or strikes, layoffs, plant closures, limited availability or unavailability of products or parts, fires, computer viruses, alerts, higher prices, declining enrollment, or canceled events.

Even when you have to write about these difficult events, portray your company honestly and professionally. Be accurate, ethical, honest and straightforward, and available.

Organization of a News Release

The following sections contain guidelines for organizing and writing the different parts of your news release. Note how these various parts flow together in the news release in Figure 9.10.

The cardinal rule in writing a news release is to put the most important piece of news first. Don't bury it in the middle or wait until the end. Everything in a news release should be arranged in descending order of importance so that your first paragraph contains only the most significant facts and ideas.

The Three Parts of a News Release

The three components of a news release are the slug (headline), lead, and body.

FIGURE 9.10 A News Release from the Web

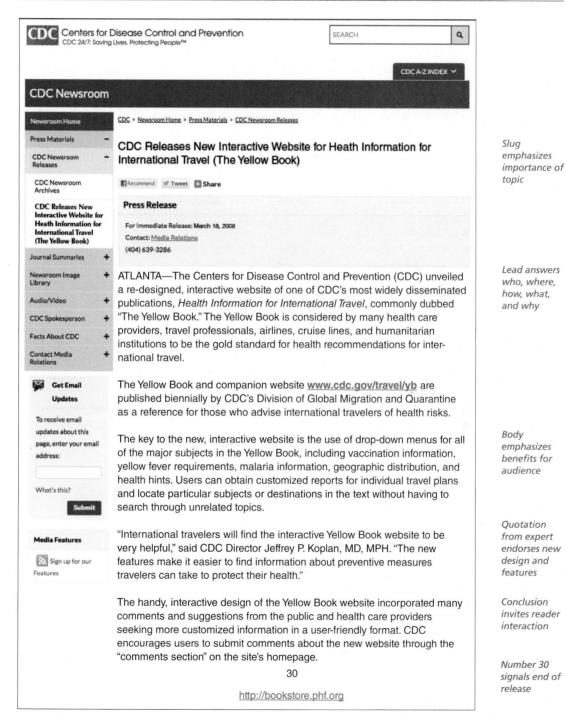

Slug emphasizes importance of topic

Lead answers who, where, how, what, and why

Body emphasizes benefits for audience

Quotation from expert endorses new design and features

Conclusion invites reader interaction

Number 30 signals end of release

Centers for Disease Control and Prevention (CDC).

The Slug, or Headline One of the most crucial parts of your release is the headline, or **slug.** It should announce a specific subject for readers and draw them into it. Write a slug that entices or grabs your readers, but also informs them quickly and clearly.

The Lead The first (and most significant) sentence of a news release is called the **lead.** It introduces and aptly summarizes your topic, sets the tone, and continues to keep readers' attention. For that reason it is also called the *hook.* The best leads easily answer the basic questions *Who? What? When? Where? Why?* — the five *W*'s — and *How?* (or *How much?*). Here is an effective lead that answers these crucial questions:

> *who*   *what*
> Maryville Engineering, Inc., has been awarded a contract by Aerodynamics, Inc.,
>
>   *why*
> to develop an acoustical system to measure and monitor stress levels at the
>
>   *where*   *when*
> Knoxville aircraft plant, district manager Carmelita Stinn, P.E., announced today.

The Body If the five *W*'s are answered in your lead, the following paragraphs can fill in only the most necessary supporting details. Regard your lead as a summary of a summary. The **body** of your release then amplifies the *Why?* and *How?* and may also get into the *So what?*

But avoid filling your news release with unnecessary technical details. Instead, relate your product or service to your targeted audience's needs by emphasizing the benefits to them without loading your news release with hype.

Use quotations selectively to clarify and highlight, not to apple-polish. Use a quotation only to report vital facts or to cite an authority. Do not turn your release into an interview with your employer or customer.

CONCLUSION

Summaries are a vital part of workplace writing, and knowing how to summarize a document—a report, proposal, or presentation—and select only the most important and relevant points for your audience is a prized job skill. Busy managers, clients, and even co-workers will depend on your summaries to give them the big picture, the bottom-line conclusions and recommendations they need to get the job done. Your summaries, including executive and evaluative ones, must be accurate, concise, relevant, and ethical.

✓ REVISION CHECKLIST

☐ Read and reread the original thoroughly to gain a clear understanding of the purpose and scope of the work.

☐ Highlighted key transitional words, main points, significant findings, applications, solutions, conclusions, and recommendations.

☐ Separated main points clearly from minor ones, background information, illustrations, and inconclusive findings.

☐ Omitted examples, explanations, and statistics from summary or abstract.

☐ Deleted information not useful to the audience because it is too technical or irrelevant.

☐ Changed language of original to my own words to avoid plagiarism.

☐ Made sure that emphasis of summary matches emphasis of original.

☐ Determined that sequence of information in the summary follows sequence of original.

☐ Added necessary connective words that accurately convey relationships between main points in original.

☐ Edited summary to eliminate repetition.

☐ Cited source of original correctly and completely.

☐ Avoided phrases that draw attention to the fact that I am writing a summary or an abstract.

☐ Summarized material in informative summary objectively without adding commentary.

☐ Commented on both content and style in an evaluative summary.

☐ Interspersed evaluative commentary throughout the summary so that assessments appear near relevant points.

☐ Included a direct quotation in the evaluative summary or news release to illustrate or reinforce my recommendation.

☐ Ensured that descriptive abstract is short and to the point and does not offer a judgment.

☐ Prepared news release that projects a professional image of my employer.

☐ Arranged information from top down, with most important information first.

EXERCISES

1. Summarize a chapter of a textbook you are now using for a course in your major field. Provide an accurate bibliographic reference for that chapter (author of the textbook, title of the chapter, title of the book, place of publication, publisher's name, date of publication, and page numbers of the chapter).

2. Summarize a lecture you heard recently. Limit your summary to one page. Identify in a bibliographic citation the speaker's name, the date, and the place of delivery.

3. Listen to a television network evening newscast and to a later news update on the same station. Select one major story covered on the evening news and indicate which details from it were omitted in the news update.

4. Write a summary of the marketing report in Chapter 8 (see Figure 8.10, pages 349–363) or the business report in Chapter 15 on non-native speakers of English in the workforce (see Figure 15.3, pages 607–621).

5. Bring to class an article from *Reader's Digest* and the original material it condensed, usually an article in a journal or magazine published six months to a year earlier. In a paragraph or two indicate what the *Digest* article omits from the original. Also point out how the condensed version is written so that the omitted material is not missed and how the condensation does not misrepresent the main points of the article.

6. Assume that you are applying for a job and that the human resources manager asks you to summarize your qualifications. In two or three paragraphs, indicate how your background and interests make you suited for the job. Mention the job by title at the beginning of your first paragraph.

7. Write a summary of one of the following articles.

   a. "The Mouse That Knows You" in Chapter 1 (pages 40–41)
   b. "Mobile App Developers: Start with Security," below

Mobile App Developers: Start with Security[1]

Smartphones and tablets are powerful and popular, with more than a thousand new mobile apps hitting the market each day. In this fast-moving era of entrepreneurship and creativity, is security keeping up? Apps and mobile devices often rely on consumer data — including contact information, photos, and location to name a few — and can be vulnerable to digital snoops, data breaches, and real-world thieves. The Federal Trade Commission (FTC), the nation's consumer protection agency, offers these tips to help developers approach mobile app security.

Aim for reasonable data security

There is no checklist for securing all apps. Different apps have different security needs. For example, an alarm clock app that collects little or no data will likely raise fewer security considerations than a location-based social network. Apps that are more complex may rely on remote servers for storing and manipulating users' data, meaning that developers must be familiar with securing software, securing transmissions of data, *and* securing servers. Adding to the challenge: Security threats and best practices evolve quickly.

The FTC expects app developers to adopt and maintain reasonable data security practices and doesn't prescribe a one-size-fits-all approach. This brochure offers a starting point to help you provide a secure experience for your users. If applied thoughtfully and consistently, these tips can help protect you, your users, and the reputation of your app.

---

[1]*Adapted from* Federal Trade Commission. (2013, February). *Mobile App Developers: Start with Security*. Retrieved from https://www.ftc.gov/tips-advice/business-center/guidance/mobile-app -developers-start-security

Tips for mobile app security

Your team should include at least one person responsible for considering security at every stage of your app's development. If you're running a solo operation, that person is you. It's easy to assume someone else is handling security — whether that someone is a mobile operating system provider, a device manufacturer, or another member of the development team. It's true that everyone has a role to play, but as the developer, you're the final line of defense.

Practice data minimization: Don't collect or keep data you don't need. For example, if your photo-editing app doesn't require access to a user's contact info, don't ask for it. Simply put, data you don't collect is data you don't need to worry about protecting. Avoid keeping data longer than you need to. For example, if you offer a location-based mobile game, get rid of the location data when it's no longer relevant.

Research the mobile platforms you work with. Each mobile operating system uses different application programming interface (APIs), provides you with different security-related features, and handles permissions its own way. Don't expect that one platform works exactly like another. Do your research and adapt your code accordingly.

Mobile platforms often provide helpful security features. But it's your job to understand those features (and their limitations), implement them properly, and take other measures necessary to protect your users. In addition, while platform-based permissions might be helpful in conveying security information to your customers, they're no substitute for your own effective communication. Talk to your users in your own words.

If you create credentials for your users (like usernames and passwords), create them securely. For example, a short number string might be an appropriate token for authenticating a user on a game score board, but the same credential wouldn't be appropriate for a social networking app.

Use transit encryption for usernames, passwords, and other important data; perform due diligence on libraries and third-party code.

Anytime your app transmits usernames, passwords, API keys, or other types of important data, use transit encryption. Mobile devices commonly rely on unsecure Wi-Fi access points at coffee shops, airports, and the like — and it's easy for troublemakers to snoop and intercept connections.

To protect users, developers often deploy SSL/TLS in the form of HTTPS. Consider using HTTPS or another industry-standard method. There's no need to reinvent the wheel. If you use HTTPS, use a digital certificate and ensure your app checks it properly. A no-frills digital certificate from a reputable vendor is inexpensive and helps your customers ensure they're communicating with your servers, and not someone else's. But standards change, so keep an eye on current technologies, and make sure you're using the latest and greatest security features.

Before using someone else's code to build or augment your app, do your research. Does this library or SDK have known security vulnerabilities? Has it been tested in real-world settings? Have other developers reported problems? Third-party libraries can save time, but make sure you stay accountable for your app.

Protect your data, servers, and passwords.

If your app handles personal information, consider protecting or obscuring the data — for example, by using encryption. Some platforms have special storage schemes for sensitive data like passwords and keys. Use them if they're available. This helps protect your users in the event of viruses, malware, or a lost device.

If you maintain a server that communicates with your app, take appropriate security measures to protect it. If you rely on a commercial cloud provider, understand the divisions of responsibility for securing and updating software on the server. While some commercial services will monitor and update your servers' security, others leave you in control.

Server security is its own complex topic, so do some research. Take steps to protect yourself from common vulnerabilities, including injection attacks, cross-site scripting, and other threats.

Don't store passwords in plaintext on your server. Instead, consider using an iterated cryptographic hash function to hash users' passwords and then verify against these hash values. (Your users can simply reset their passwords if they forget.) That way, if your server suffers a data breach, passwords aren't left completely exposed.

Even after you ship your app, stay involved. New vulnerabilities arise daily, and even the most reputable software libraries require security updates. Follow general and library-specific mailing lists and have a plan for shipping security updates if needed. Check your inbox, too. User feedback can help you spot and fix security vulnerabilities. When they discover vulnerabilities, researchers often try to resolve the issue with developers before publishing their findings. It's best to be part of that discussion early on.

8. Write a descriptive abstract of the article you selected in Exercise 7.

9. Write an executive summary of the proposal in Figure 13.5 (pages 530–534) to purchase updated inventory software.

10. Write an evaluative summary of "The Mouse That Knows You" in Chapter 1 (pages 40–41).

11. Write an informative abstract of the report in Figure 15.3 (pages 607–621).

12. Write an appropriate news release on one of the following newsworthy topics to be included on your company's website:

   a. premiering a new product or service
   b. acquiring a smaller firm whose products and services are very different from those of your company
   c. providing an environmentally sensitive service that enhances life in the community in which your employer's headquarters is located
   d. offering highly competitive warranties on a new line of products
   e. protecting a section of wetlands adjoining one of your company's construction sites

13. Write a news release on one of the following unpleasant topics, while still projecting a positive image of your company:

    a. inconveniences because of recent construction

    b. a reduction in the hours of operation of a store or plant

    c. an increase in insurance premiums

    d. an order page is down on a frequently visited e-business site because of a computer virus

    e. a sports injury that has benched a star player on a local team for the next month

    f. a boil-water notice issued for a subdivision that depends on a local reservoir for its water supply

PART IV

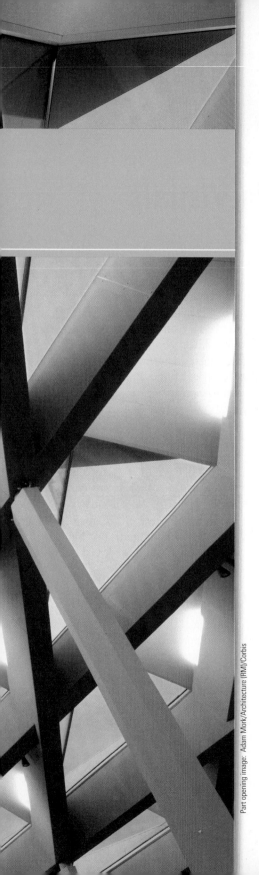

Part opening image: Adam Mork/Architecture (RM)/Corbis

Preparing Documents and Visuals

CHAPTER

10

Designing Clear Visuals

Visuals are essential in the world of work. No matter where you work—in a health care facility, government agency, retail business, bank, and so on—your employer will expect you to be visually competent. That means you will have to interpret, use, and create visuals and graphics. Visuals often explain the job you have to do and help you report on how well you did it. Tables, charts, graphs, drawings, diagrams, maps, and photographs are an important, functional part of almost every workplace document, including employee handbooks, instructions, proposals, reports, blogs, newsletters, and websites.

Visuals work in conjunction with your writing to summarize, inform, illustrate, and persuade. The tables, graphs, and charts you use to simplify financial and other statistical information in a report, and the photos and other graphics you incorporate in them, have a major impact on how readers will see and judge your work. Effective visuals can drive traffic to your website. But a poorly designed visual, either in a hard copy or an e-document—one that is incorrect, incomplete, unclear, or unethical—signals to readers that your research and writing may also be flawed.

VISUAL THINKING IN THE GLOBAL WORKPLACE

Our web-based, global culture highly prizes visual thinking, or seeing and presenting information in terms of spatial and organizational appearance. Experts estimate that as much as 80 percent of our learning comes through our sense of sight. The way we process information visually helps us to develop ideas, organize them, and even solve problems when they occur. As we saw in Chapter 2 (see "Planning," pages 46–49), visual devices such as clustering, mindmapping, and outlining help writers to discover, develop, and organize their ideas.

In our digital culture, whether we are navigating a website, using a media device, collaborating with colleagues, or communicating with clients, visuals play a major role in conveying information. Animation, color, icons, graphs, illustrations, charts, photographs, and infographs

all contribute to our understanding and evaluation. Visuals make documents informative, inviting, and easy to read.

Visuals also play a powerful role in symbolizing corporate identity and reinforcing brand loyalty in the minds of consumers across the globe; consider McDonald's golden arches, Nike's swoosh, Starbucks' mermaid, or Ralph Lauren's polo pony and rider. A company's own logo reveals a great deal visually about its image, values, and mission.

Chapter 10 surveys the kinds of visuals you will encounter most frequently in the world of work. It shows you how to read, locate, create, and write about them, and it also describes the types of visuals and visual configurations you can create with graphics software packages. Finally, this chapter discusses the ethical ways to use visuals and explains how to select the most appropriate ones for global audiences. But as you have already seen, the discussion of visuals in this book is not confined just to this chapter. Visuals are discussed in other chapters as part of the process of preparing a variety of business documents—letters, memos, instructions, proposals, reports, blogs, websites, and presentations.

THE PURPOSE OF VISUALS

Visuals are essential in the world of work. They are vital to the success of reports, proposals, instructions, PowerPoint presentations, websites, blogs, and many other documents. Even your company logo reveals a great deal about your firm's or organization's image and mission. Here are several reasons visuals can improve your work; each point is graphically reinforced in Figure 10.1 (page 402).

1. Visuals condense and summarize a large quantity of information/text into a relatively small space. They can record data in far less space than it would take to describe those facts in words alone. Note how in Figure 10.1 a simple graph summarizes and documents the market shares of two different types of computer sales.

2. Visuals can simplify and communicate concepts. A visual shows ideas while a verbal description only tells about them. Visuals help readers more clearly see and understand percentages, trends, comparisons, contrasts, and reduce the chances of a reader misunderstanding a concept. Figure 10.1, for example, shows at a glance the growth of online computer sales.

3. Visuals arouse a reader's immediate interest. They catch the reader's eye quickly by setting important information apart and giving relief from having to wade through a page of monotonous text with only sentences and paragraphs. Visuals also have tremendous sales appeal, persuading readers to buy a product or service or accept your point of view.

4. Visuals help readers find key information quickly. They highlight, separate, or show relationships/data to emphasize points for readers so they do not have to hunt through text to find them. Visuals separate main points from supporting details.

FIGURE 10.1 A Line-and-Bar Chart Comparing Market Share of Online Computer Purchases with Those Purchased at Brick-and-Mortar Stores

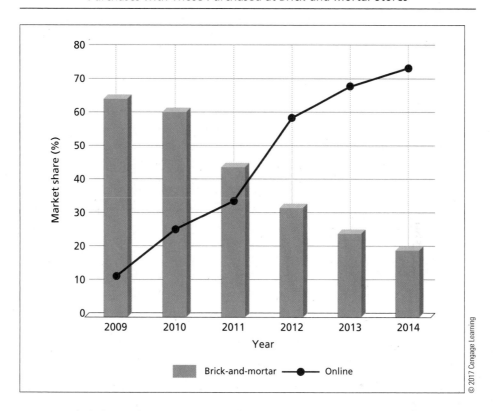

© 2017 Cengage Learning

5. Visuals help readers remember information longer. Their impact reinforces a message and emphasizes what's most important for readers. Well-chosen and designed visuals can motivate your reader to understand and accept your ideas.

TYPES OF VISUALS AND THEIR FUNCTIONS

Table 10.1 shows some of the most common types of visuals found in workplace writing and explains how you can use them. Each of these visuals is discussed in this chapter.

CHOOSING EFFECTIVE VISUALS

Select your visuals carefully. Here are some suggestions that will guide you when choosing a visual:

1. Supply a visual only when it is relevant for your purpose and audience. Never include a visual simply for decoration. Tell your readers why you are including it and what to look for in it. A short report on fire drills does not need a picture of a fire station.

TABLE 10.1 Types of Workplace Visuals

Table	**Table 1. Charting the Lesson** Lesson Page Page Page A 1 3 6 B 2 2 5 C 3 1 4 © Cengage Learning	• Presents large amounts of data in a compact space • Organizes data (figures, facts) into easy-to-read categories using rows and columns • Gives statistical data or verbal descriptions clearly and concisely • Allows readers to see comparisons and contrasts more quickly when numbers are embedded
Line graph	© Cengage Learning	• Transforms numbers into a picture (curves, shapes, patterns) that represents movement over time or in space • Displays data that change often—costs, sales, rates, employment, production, temperature, etc. • Forecasts trends in terms of variables
Circle or pie chart	© Cengage Learning	• Uses wedges to show the parts/percentages (budgets, shares, time allotments, etc.) that make up the whole • Shows the proportion of each part to another; relates each part to the whole • Effective visual to show data from tables or charts • Easily understood by audiences worldwide
Bar chart	© Cengage Learning	• Uses vertical or horizontal bars to measure different data in space or time • Represents comparisons/changes through the comparative length of bars • Can be segmented (divided) to show multiple percentages within a single bar • Less technical than a graph
Flow chart	© Cengage Learning	• Reveals stages in an activity or process • Arrows provide accurate directions on the order in which steps are to be taken • Blueprints the actual steps to take, first to last, to complete a process/job • Identifies places where retracing or skipping steps is required
Organizational chart	© Cengage Learning	• Illustrates the relationship of one part of an organization to another • Shows structure of an organization from chief executive to divisions and departments to employees • Provides quick view of areas of authority and responsibility • Helps in routing material to appropriate readers

(Continued)

TABLE 10.1 (Continued)

Pictograph	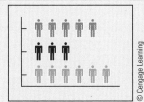	• Represents statistical data by means of pictures varying in size, numbers, or color
		• Easy for a global audience to understand if the symbols/icons (pictograms) are chosen carefully
		• Must supply a key stating how much each symbol represents

Map		• Details specific geographic features (elevation, lakes/rivers, forests, etc.)
		• Identifies roads, businesses (company locations, TV station, etc.)
		• Displays census data (population density, number of households with children)
		• Reveals location, distance, relationship of one place to another

Cutaway drawing	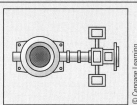	• Explains how something looks or works
		• Reveals the interior view of an object by removing the exterior view
		• Uncovers an internal mechanism that a photo or simple drawing cannot

Exploded drawing	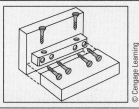	• Shows an object with parts separated to indicate the relationship of the parts to one another
		• Illustrates how parts fit together
		• Explains how a piece of equipment is constructed and should be assembled or disassembled

Photograph		• Demonstrates the actual appearance of something
		• Accurately shows "before" and "after" scenes
		• Pinpoints color accurately—no guesswork
		• Cannot reveal interior parts

Clip art		• Provides ready-made icons, images, symbols, and pictures
		• Available online or in print form
		• Must be appropriate for audience, especially international readers
		• Should not look unprofessional or cartoonish

FIGURE 10.2 A Visual Used in Conjunction with Written Work

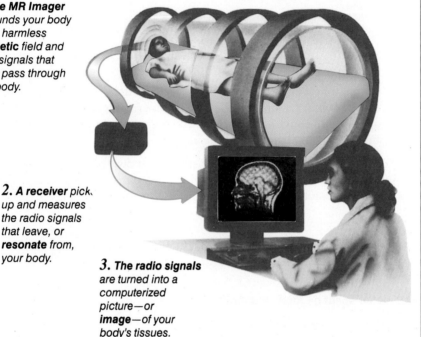

A PICTURE FROM THE INSIDE OUT

At the heart of the magnetic resonance imager is a large magnet that is big enough for you to lie inside. Look at the picture below. The **magnet** directs radio signals to surround sections of your body. When the signals pass through your body, they **resonate** (release a signal). Then your body's response is picked up by a receiver and sent to a computer. The computer analyzes the signal and converts it into a visual **image** of your tissues on a video screen.

1. **The MR Imager** surrounds your body with a harmless **magnetic** field and radio signals that safely pass through your body.

2. **A receiver** picks up and measures the radio signals that leave, or **resonate** from, your body.

3. **The radio signals** are turned into a computerized picture—or **image**—of your body's tissues.

Source: Krames Communications.

2. Don't include more detail in your visual than your reader needs. Unnecessary details complicate and slow down any process.

3. Use visuals in conjunction with—not as a substitute for—your written work. Visuals do not take the place of words. Giving readers a set of illustrations or a table alone may not meet their need for a summary or recommendations. See how the visual of an MRI, along with a description of its function in Figure 10.2, makes the procedure easier to understand for a general audience.

4. Visuals should not simply repeat what is in your text. If your text is clear and concise without a visual, don't include one.

5. Size your visuals carefully. Do not try to cram a visual onto a page or allow it to spill over the text or margins. Also, do not resize an image so that it becomes hard to read or distorted.

Ineffective Visuals: What *Not* to Do

Here are some guidelines on what to avoid with visuals:

- Avoid visuals that include more details than your audience needs.
- Never use a visual that distracts from your work (for example, one that is too small, too large, does not use the right type of shading, etc.).
- Never use a visual that presents information that contradicts your work.
- Never distort a visual for emphasis or decoration by adding unnecessary lines, patterns, or bars (see "Using Visuals Ethically," pages 433–438).
- Be careful that you don't omit anything when you reproduce an existing visual.
- Never use visuals that stereotype (for example, avoid pictures of a workforce that excludes female employees).
- Don't use a visual that looks fuzzy, dotted, or streaked. Choose the correct resolution for your image to make sure it appears sharp and contains the level of detail needed. The **dpi** of an image (or "dots per inch") is one method of determining resolution. Getting the dpi right is crucial when printing images in hard copy form. Check with your employer regarding the resolution needed for any images you generate.

See how Figure 10.3 violates many of these rules. It divides an image of a U.S. dollar bill into too many slices. Confronted with so many different wedges the reader would have trouble identifying, separating, comparing, and understanding the costs.

FIGURE 10.3 An Ineffective Visual: Too Much Information Is Crowded into One Graphic

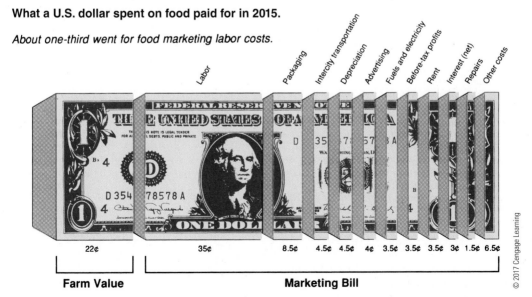

What a U.S. dollar spent on food paid for in 2015.

About one-third went for food marketing labor costs.

GENERATING, SCANNING, AND UPLOADING VISUALS

Here are three ways to incorporate a visual into your work.

1. You can easily generate charts, graphs, or tables through the templates in your software, such as Microsoft Word or Excel. By selecting, for instance, Insert Chart or Insert Table, you can insert your raw numerical data into the appropriate template and then add titles, labels, and color-coded keys, etc. This software also shows visuals from different perspectives, adds shading or three-dimensional effects, etc., and can help you insert the visual in your text.

2. With a scanner you can produce a high-resolution digital copy of an image or a document and then archive it for use it in any of your print or online documents. Scanners also help you incorporate visuals that are unavailable in digital form, such as older photographs, diagrams, etc.

3. You can upload visuals into documents or presentations, often with just a few short clicks, with the right software. But always make sure when uploading a file with a visual that you've selected the highest-quality version available. That way, the visual is clear and sharp.

Regardless of how you incorporate a visual, always request permission if you did not create the visual yourself. Otherwise, you are guilty of plagiarism.

INSERTING AND WRITING ABOUT VISUALS: SOME GUIDELINES

Using a visual requires more of you as a writer than simply inserting it into your written work. You need to use visuals in conjunction with what you write. The following guidelines will help you to (1) identify, (2) cite, (3) insert, (4) introduce, and (5) interpret visuals for your readers.

Identify Your Visuals

Give each visual a number and caption (title) that indicates the subject or explains what the visual illustrates. An unidentified visual is meaningless. A caption helps your audience interpret your visual—to see it with your purpose in mind. Tell your readers what you want them to look for by doing the following:

- Use a different typeface (**bold**) and size in your caption than what you use in the visual itself.
- Include key words about the function and the subject of your visual in a caption.
- Make sure any terms you cite in a caption are consistent with the units of measurement and the scope (years, months, seasons) of your visual.
- Use arrows or lead lines to point to key parts of your visual and include labels to clearly identify important elements.

Tables and figures should be numbered separately throughout the text—Table 1 or Figure 3.5, for example. (In the latter case, Figure 3.5 is the fifth figure to appear in Chapter 3.)

Cite the Source for Your Visuals

If you use a visual that is not your own work, give credit to your source (newspaper, magazine, textbook, company, federal agency, individual, blog, social media site, or website). If your paper or report is intended for publication (either in print or online), you must first obtain permission to reproduce copyrighted visuals from the copyright holder.

Insert Your Visuals Appropriately

Since many of the images you use will come from outside sources, especially the Web, you have to incorporate them clearly and in appropriate places in your written work.

Here are some guidelines to help you incorporate the visuals in the most appropriate places for your readers:

- Always plan ahead when you need to place a visual. They need to work in conjunction with your text (see "Choosing Effective Visuals," pages 402–406). Determine why and how you need a particular visual.
- Never insert a visual *before* a discussion of it; readers will wonder why it is there. Use a sentence or two to introduce your visuals before they appear in your document.
- Do not insert a visual without a reference to it in the text, and do not refer to a visual in your text and then fail to include it.
- Mention in the text of your paper or report that you are including a visual. Tell readers where it is found: "below," "on the following page," "to the right," "at the bottom of page 3."
- Place visuals as close as possible to the first mention of them in the text. Try not to put a visual more than one page after the discussion of it. Never wait two or three pages to present it. By inserting a visual near the beginning of your discussion, you help readers better understand your explanation.
- Use an appropriate size for your visual. Don't make it too large or too small. There is no need to enlarge a photograph if a smaller image is understandable. Gauge size by determining how much data you need to present and where the visual best fits into your discussion of it (see "Ineffective Visuals: What *Not* to Do," page 406).
- If the visual is small enough, insert it directly in the text rather than on a separate page. If your visual occupies an entire page, place that page containing your visual on the facing page or immediately after the page on which the first reference to it appears.
- Center your visual and, if necessary, box it. Leave at least 1 inch of white space around it. Squeezing visuals toward the left or right margins looks unprofessional.

- Never collect all your visuals and put them in an appendix. Readers need to see them at the points in your discussion where they are most pertinent.

Introduce Your Visuals

Refer to each visual by its number, and if necessary, mention the title as well. In introducing the visual, though, do not just insert a reference to it, such as "See Figure 3.4" or "Look at Table 1." Relate the visual to the text it illustrates or helps explain. Here are two ways of writing a lead-in sentence for a visual.

Poor: Our store saw a dramatic rise in the shipment of electric ranges over the five-year period as opposed to the less impressive increase in washing machines. (See Figure 3.)

This sentence does not tie the visual (Figure 3) into the sentence where it belongs. The visual just trails insignificantly behind.

Better: As Figure 3 shows, our store saw a dramatic rise in the shipment of electric ranges over the five-year period as opposed to the less impressive increase in washing machines.

Mentioning the visual in this way alerts readers to its presence and function in your work and helps them to more easily understand your message. Explain why you are including a visual and how it will help your readers understand your work.

Interpret Your Visuals

Tell readers what to look for and why. Let them know what is most significant about the visual. Point out any distinctive features, major parts, or crucial relationships. Do not expect the visual to explain itself. Inform readers what the numbers or images in your visual mean, how they make or prove a key point. What conclusions do you want readers to reach after seeing your visual?

In a report on the benefits of vanpooling, the writer supplied the following visual, a table:

TABLE 14 Travel Time (in minutes): Automobile versus Vanpool

Individual Automobile	Vanpool
25	32.5
30	39.0
35	45.5
40	52.0
45	58.5
50	65.0
55	71.5
60	78.0

Source: U.S. Department of Transportation. *Increased Transportation Efficiency Through Ridesharing: The Brokerage Approach* (Washington, D.C., DOT-OS—40096): 45.

To interpret the table, the writer called attention to it in the context of a discussion on transportation efficiency.

> Although, as Table 14 suggests, the travel time in a vanpool may be as much as 30 percent longer than in an automobile (to allow for pickups), the total trip time for the vanpool user can be about the same as with an automobile because vanpools eliminate the need to search for parking spaces and to walk to the employment site entrance.[1]

TWO CATEGORIES OF VISUALS: TABLES AND FIGURES

Visuals can be divided into two categories—tables and figures. A **table** organizes information—numbers and/or words—in parallel columns and rows for easy comparison of data. Any visual that is not a table is considered a figure. **Figures** include graphs, circle charts, bar charts, organizational charts, flow charts, pictographs, maps, photographs, drawings, and infographs. Expect to use both tables and figures in your work.

TABLES

Tables contain parallel columns and rows of information organized and arranged into categories to show, in a compact space, changes in time, distance, cost, employment, or some other distinguishable or quantifiable variable. Tables also summarize material for easy recall—causes of wars; provisions of a law; or differences between a common cold, flu, and pneumonia. See how Table 10.2 on sources of protein condenses much information and arranges it in quickly identifiable categories.

Parts of a Table

To use a table properly, you need to know the parts that constitute it. Refer to Table 10.2, which labels these parts, as you read the following:

- The main **column** is "Amount Needed to Satisfy Minimum Daily Requirement," and the **subcolumns** are the protein sources for which the table gives data.
- The **stub** is the first column on the left-hand side, below the column heading "Source." The stub lists the foods for which information is broken down in the subcolumns.
- A **rule** (or line) across the top of the table separates the title from the column headings and the column headings from the body of the table.

Guidelines for Using Tables

When you include a table in your work, follow these guidelines.

- Number the tables according to the order in which they are discussed (Table 1, Table 2, Table 3). Tables should be numbered separately from figures (charts, graphs, photos) in your text.

---

[1]James A. Devine, "Vanpooling: A New Economic Tool," *AIDC Journal*.

- Keep the table on the page where it is most appropriate. It is hard for readers to follow a table spread across different pages.
- Give each table a concise and descriptive title to show exactly what is being represented or compared.
- Use words in the stub (a list of items about which information is given), but put numbers under column headings.
- Supply footnotes, often indicated by small raised letters ([a], [b]), if something in the table needs to be qualified, for example, the number of cups of milk in Table 10.2, then put that information below the table.
- List items in alphabetical, chronological, or other logical order.
- Arrange the data you want to compare vertically, not horizontally; it is easier to read down a column than across a series of rows.
- Place tables at the top (preferable) or bottom of the page, and center them on the page rather than placing them up against the right or left margin.
- Don't use more than five or six columns; tables wider than that are more difficult for readers to understand.
- When possible, round off numbers in your columns to the nearest whole number to assist readers in following and retaining information.
- Always credit the source (the supplier of the statistical information) on which your table is based.

TABLE 10.2 Parts of a Table

TABLE 1 Efficiency of Some Protein Sources in Meeting an Adult's Minimum Daily Requirements

Source	Percent of Protein	Percent of Amino Acids	Amount Needed to Satisfy Minimum Daily Requirement	
			(grams)	(ounces)
Cheese[a]	27	70	227	7.2
Corn	10	50	860	30.0
Eggs	11	97	403	14.1
Fish[a]	22	80	244	8.5
Kidney beans	23	40	468	16.4
Meat[a]	25	68	253	8.8
Milk	4	82	1,311	45.9[b]
Soybeans	34	60	210	7.3

Labels pointing to table parts: Table number, Title, Rule, Column heading, Subheading, Stub, Origin of data, Footnotes

Source: From Starr/Taggart, Biology: *The Unity and Diversity of Life*, 4E. © 1987 Cengage Learning.

[a] = Average value
[b] = Equivalent of 6 cups

FIGURES

As we saw, any visual that is not a table is classified as a **figure.** The types of figures we will examine next are

- graphs
- circle, or pie, charts
- bar charts
- organizational charts
- flow charts
- pictographs
- maps
- photographs
- drawings
- clip art
- infographics

Graphs

Graphs transform numbers into pictures with shapes, patterns, and shading. They take statistical data presented in tables and put them into rising and falling lines or steep or gentle curves. The two main types of graphs are simple line graphs and multiple-line graphs.

Functions of Graphs

Graphs vividly portray information that changes, such as

- costs
- distributions
- employment
- energy levels
- population
- sales
- temperatures
- tourism/travel
- trends

Graphs not only describe past and current situations but also forecast trends over time.

Graphs versus Tables

Because graphs actually show change, they are more dramatic than tables. You will make the reader's job easier by using a graph rather than a table. Many financial websites and print publications—the *Wall Street Journal* and *USA Today*, for example—open with a graph for the benefit of busy readers who want a great deal of financial information summarized quickly.

Simple Line Graphs

Basically, a **simple line graph** consists of two sides—a **vertical** or **y-axis** and a **horizontal** or **x-axis**—that intersect to form a right angle, as in Figure 10.4. The space between the two axes contains the picture made by the graph—the amount of snowfall in Springfield between November 2014 and April 2015. The vertical line represents the **dependent variable** (the snowfall in inches); the horizontal line, the **independent variable** (time in months). The dependent variable is influenced most directly by the independent variable, which almost always is expressed in terms of time or distance. The vertical axis is read from bottom to top; the horizontal axis from left to right. Simple line graphs such as the one in Figure 10.4 can easily be created using spreadsheet software such as Microsoft Excel or Google Sheets.

Multiple-Line Graphs

The graph in Figure 10.4 contains only one line of data. But a **multiple-line graph** can show how a number of dependent variables (different conditions, products, etc.)

FIGURE 10.4 A Simple Line Graph Showing the Amount of Snowfall in Springfield from November 2014 to April 2015

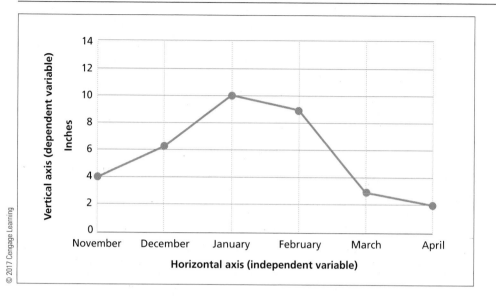

Graph is easy to read and follow

Variables clearly labeled

© 2017 Cengage Learning

compare with one another. The six-month sales figures for three salespeople can be seen in the graph in Figure 10.5 (page 414). The graph contains a separate line for each of the three salespeople. At a glance, readers can see how the three compare and how many dollars each salesperson generated per month. Note how the line representing each person is clearly differentiated from the others by symbols and colors. Each line is clearly tied to a **legend** (an explanatory key below the graph) identifying the three salespeople.

Guidelines on Creating Graphs

1. Use no more than three lines in a multiple-line graph, so readers can interpret the graph more easily. If the lines run close together, use a legend to identify individual lines.
2. Label each line or color to identify what it represents for readers. Include a legend, as in Figure 10.5.
3. In a multiple-line graph, keep each line distinct by using different colors, dots or dashes, or symbols. Note the different symbols in Figure 10.5.
4. Make sure you plot enough points to show a reasonable and ethical range of the data. Using only three or four points may distort the evidence. (See "Guidelines for Using Visuals Ethically," pages 434–436.)
5. Keep the scale consistent and realistic. If you start with hours, do not switch to days or vice versa. If you are recording annual rates or accounts, do not skip a year or two in order to save time or be more concise.

FIGURE 10.5 A Multiple-Line Graph Showing Sales Figures for the First Six Months of 2016 for Three Salespeople

Uses different symbols and colors to represent each salesperson

Legend explains what different symbols and colors represent

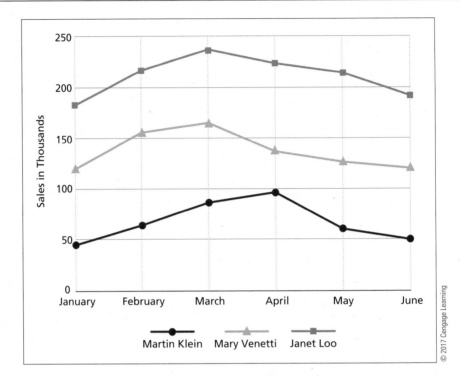

© 2017 Cengage Learning

6. For some graphs, there is no need to begin with a zero. A **suppressed zero graph** automatically begins with a larger number when it would be impossible to start with zero. For others, you may not have to include numbers beyond a certain point. Your subject and purpose will determine the range of data you need to show. If you use a suppressed zero graph, make sure you do so ethically. (See "Using Visuals Ethically," pages 433–437.)

Charts

Although charts and graphs may seem similar, there is a big difference between them. Graphs are usually more complex and plotted according to specific mathematical coordinates. **Charts,** however, do not display exact and complex mathematical data found in tables and graphs. Instead, they present an overall picture of how individual pieces of data (from a graph or table) relate to each other as parts of a whole.

Among the most frequently used charts are (1) pie, or circle, charts, (2) bar charts, (3) organizational charts, and (4) flow charts.

Pie Charts

Pie charts are also known as circle charts, a name that descriptively points to their construction and interpretation. Tables are more technical and detailed than pie

FIGURE 10.6 A Three-Dimensional Pie Chart Showing the Breakdown by Department of a Proposed City Budget for 2016

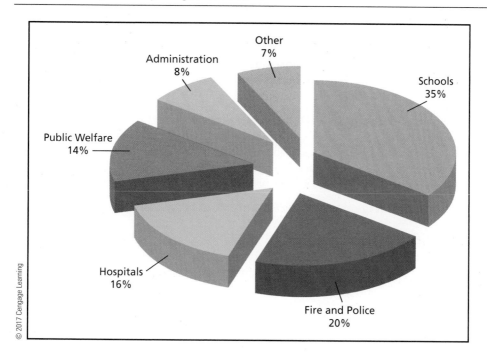

Other
7%

Administration
8%

Schools
35%

Public Welfare
14%

*Puts largest
slice first*

*Size of slice
determined by
percentage;
totals 100%*

Hospitals
16%

*Uses a
different,
easily
contrasted
color for each
category*

Fire and Police
20%

© 2017 Cengage Learning

charts. Figure 10.6 shows an example of a pie chart used in a government document. A table or graph with a more detailed breakdown of, say, a city's budget would be much more appropriate for a technical audience (auditors, budget and city planners).

The full circle, or pie, represents the whole amount (100 percent or 360 degrees) of the data being represented; the entire budget of a company or a family, a population group, an area of land, the resources of an organization or institution. Each slice or wedge represents a percentage or portion of the whole.

A pie chart effectively allows readers to see two things at once: the relationship of the parts to one another and the relationship of the parts to the whole.

Preparing a Pie Chart

Follow these six rules to create and present your pie chart.

1. Make sure the individual slices total 100 percent, or 360 degrees. Check your math.

2. Put the largest slice first, at the 12 o'clock position, and then move clockwise with proportionately smaller slices. Schools occupy the largest slice in Figure 10.6 because they receive the biggest share of taxes.

3. Do not divide a circle, or pie, into too few or too many slices. If you have only three wedges, use another visual to display them (a bar chart, for example, discussed next). If you have more than seven or eight wedges, you will destroy the dramatic effect. Instead, combine several slices of small percentages (2 percent, 3 percent, 4 percent) into one slice labeled "Other," "Miscellaneous," or "Related Items."

4. Label each slice of the pie horizontally. Do not put in a label upside down or slide it in vertically. If the individual slice of the pie is small, draw a connecting line from the slice to a label positioned outside the pie.

5. Shade, color, or cross-hatch slices of the pie to further separate and distinguish the parts. Note how Figure 10.6 effectively uses color. But be careful not to obscure labels and percentages; also make certain that adjacent slices can be distinguished readily from each other. Do not use the same color or similar colors for two adjacent slices.

6. Give percentages for each slice to further assist readers, as in Figure 10.6.

Bar Charts

A **bar chart** consists of a series of vertical or horizontal bars that indicate comparisons of statistical data. For instance, in Figure 10.7 vertical bars depict increases

FIGURE 10.7 A Vertical Bar Chart

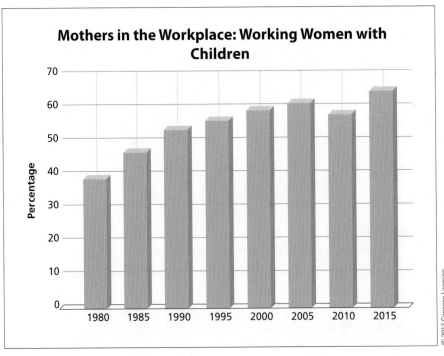

Bars are evenly spaced and clearly labeled

Length of bar determined by the percentages listed on the left-hand side of visual

Years clearly marked at bottom of columns

© 2017 Cengage Learning

FIGURE 10.8 A Horizontal Bar Chart

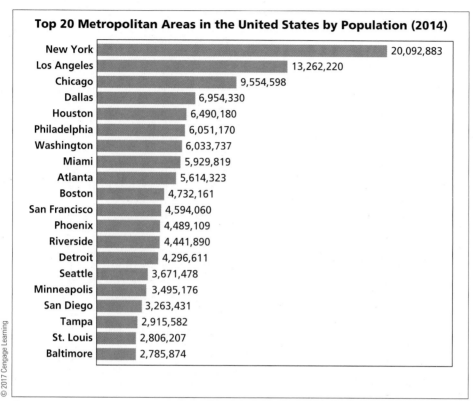

Top 20 Metropolitan Areas in the United States by Population (2014)

New York	20,092,883
Los Angeles	13,262,220
Chicago	9,554,598
Dallas	6,954,330
Houston	6,490,180
Philadelphia	6,051,170
Washington	6,033,737
Miami	5,929,819
Atlanta	5,614,323
Boston	4,732,161
San Francisco	4,594,060
Phoenix	4,489,109
Riverside	4,441,890
Detroit	4,296,611
Seattle	3,671,478
Minneapolis	3,495,176
San Diego	3,263,431
Tampa	2,915,582
St. Louis	2,806,207
Baltimore	2,785,874

Arranges bars in decreasing order

Name of city precedes bar for easier reference

Provides exact numbers after each bar

Visual summarizes a large amount of information concisely

Source: U.S. Census Bureau

in the number of working mothers. Figure 10.8 uses horizontal bars to depict the nation's top 20 metropolitan areas in 2014. The length of the bars is determined according to a scale that your computer software can easily compute.

Bar Charts, Graphs, and Tables—Which Should You Use? When should you use a bar chart rather than a table or a line graph? Your audience will help you decide. If you are asked to present statistics on costs for the company accountant, use a table. Because a bar chart is limited to a few columns, it cannot convey as much information as a table or graph. However, if you are presenting the same information to a group of stockholders or to a diverse group of employees, a bar chart may be more relevant and persuasive.

Types of Bar Charts There are three types of bar charts. Regardless of which type you use, leave adequate space between each bar.

    1. Simple bar charts. Figure 10.7 is the most basic form of bar chart. Each bar represents the percentage of working women with children, and the height of the bar corresponds to the number of percentage points for a given year.

FIGURE 10.9 A Multiple-Bar Chart Showing the Preferred Social Media Site of Teenagers, 2012–2015

Legend explains what each bar represents

Avoids confusion by using only four bars in a group

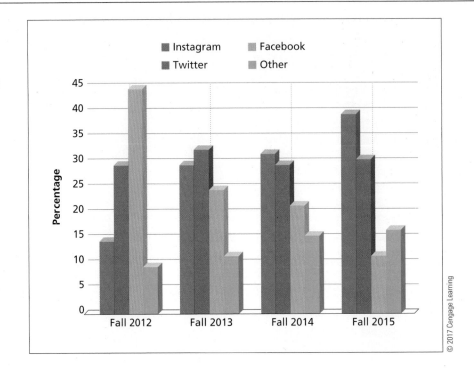

© 2017 Cengage Learning

2. Multiple-bar charts. Figure 10.9 shows a variation of the simple, vertical bar chart. Four different colored bars are used for each year to represent the amount of money spent on different types of advertising from 2012 to 2015. A legend at the top of the chart explains what each bar stands for. Avoid using more than four bars in a group. More bars will make your chart crowded and difficult to read.

3. Segmented, or cross-hatched (divided), bar charts. To show the different components that constitute a measured whole, use a segmented bar chart like the one in Figure 10.10. A single segmented bar lists the travel expenses of Weemco Communications, a small firm, in January 2016. The entire bar equals the travel total—$274,000—which was spent in four areas: airfare, ground transportation, lodging, and meals. Each of these expenses is represented by a different type of shading on the single column. A group of segmented bars can be used to show multiple comparisons among many categories, as in Figure 10.11, which depicts energy consumption by sector in five states.

Organizational Charts

An **organizational chart** pictures the chain of command in a company or agency, with the lines of authority stretching down from the chief executive, manager, or

FIGURE 10.10 A Segmented Bar Chart Representing Total Travel Expenditures for Weemco
Communications, January 2016

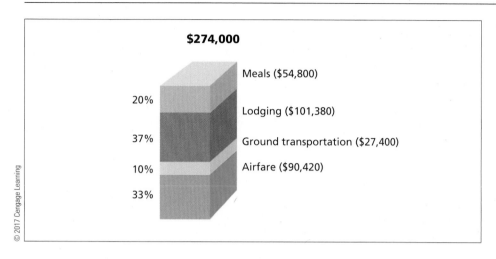

*Entire bar
equals the
travel total*

FIGURE 10.11 A Multiple-Bar, Segmented Bar Chart Showing Energy Consumption by Sector in
Five States

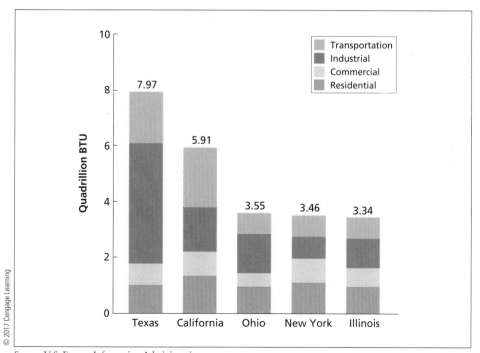

*Shows
multiple
comparisons
among many
categories*

Source: U.S. Energy Information Administration.

FIGURE 10.12 An Organizational Chart Representing Critical Care Nursing Services at Union General Hospital

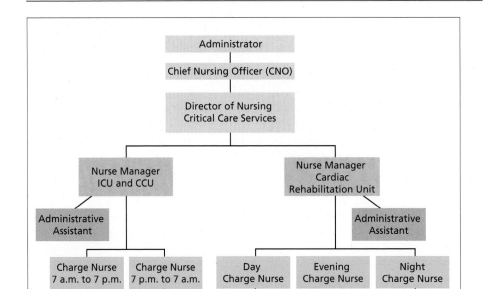

© 2017 Cengage Learning

administrator to the assistant manager, department heads, or supervisors to the workforce of employees. Figure 10.12 shows a hospital's organizational chart for its nursing services.

Organizational charts have these functions:

- to inform employees and customers about the makeup of a company
- to depict the various offices, departments, and units
- to show where people work in relationship to one another in a business

Flow Charts

A **flow chart** displays the stages in which something is manufactured, is accomplished, develops, or operates. Flow charts are highly effective in showing the steps of a procedure.

Flow charts often proceed from left to right and back again, as in the one appearing on the next page, showing the steps students must take to graduate

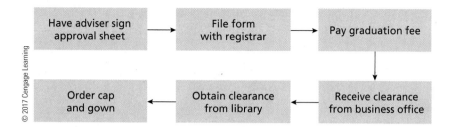

Flow charts can also be constructed to read from top to bottom. Computer programming instructions often are written that way. See, for example, Figure 10.13, which like a computer programming chart lists the steps that a **customer** must follow when ordering products online.

Pictographs

A **pictograph** uses picture symbols (called **pictograms**) to represent differences in statistical data, as in Figure 10.14 (page 422). Each symbol or icon stands for a specific number, quantity, or value.

FIGURE 10.13 A Flow Chart for Ordering Products Online

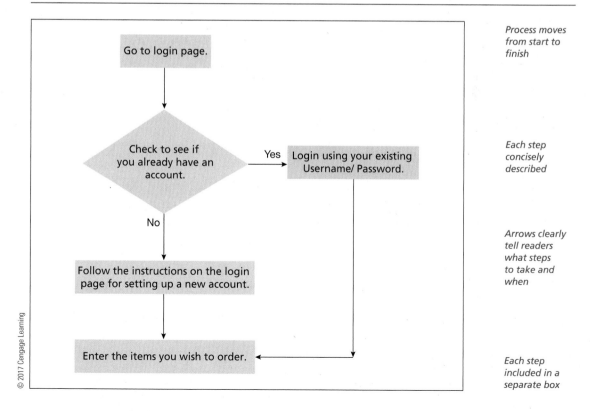

FIGURE 10.14 A Pictograph Showing Financial Details from One Pension Fund

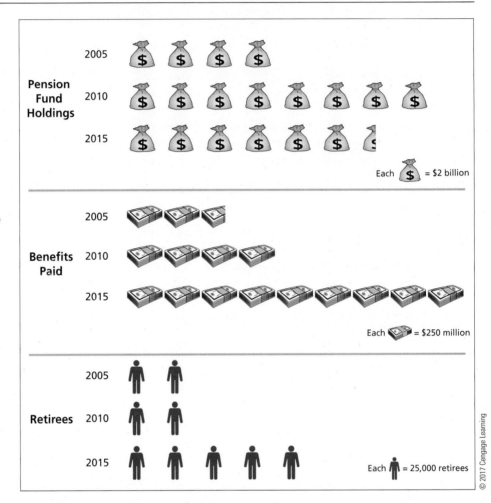

Guidelines for Creating a Pictograph When you create a pictograph, follow these three guidelines:

1. Choose an appropriate symbol for the topic—such as a smartphone icon to represent the increase in the number of sales of iPhones.
2. Always indicate the precise quantities involved by placing numbers after the pictures or at the top of the visual.
3. Increase the number of symbols rather than their sizes because differences in size are often difficult to construct accurately and harder for readers to interpret.

Maps

The **maps** you use on the job may range from highly sophisticated and detailed geographic tools to simple sketches such as the map in Figure 10.15, which shows the location of a town's water filter plants and pumping stations.

You may have to construct your own map, like the one in Figure 10.15, or scan one in a printed source or copy one from the Internet. If you use a map from an outside source (such as Google Maps), be sure to obtain permission to use it from the copyright holder.

Guidelines for Creating a Map

Follow these steps when you create a map:

1. Always acknowledge your source if you did not construct the map yourself.
2. Use distinct lines, colors, symbols, and shading to indicate features.
3. Include a legend, or map key, explaining dotted lines, colors, shading, and symbols, as in Figure 10.15.
4. Exclude features (rivers, elevations, county seats) that do not directly relate to your topic. For example, a map showing the crops grown in two adjacent counties need not show all the roads and highways in those counties.
5. Indicate direction. Conventionally, maps show north, often by including a compass icon, such as that in Figure 10.15.

FIGURE 10.15 A Map Showing the Location of Smithville Water Department's Water Filter Plants and Pumping Stations

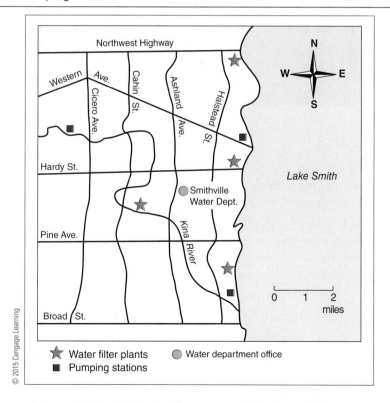

© 2015 Cengage Learning

FIGURE 10.16 A Photo Showing What a Piece of Equipment Looks Like

Corbis

Photographs

Correctly taken or scanned, **photographs** are an extremely helpful addition to job-related writing. A photograph's chief virtues are realism and clarity. Among its many advantages, a photo can

- show what an object looks like (Figure 10.16)
- demonstrate how to perform a certain procedure (Figure 10.17)
- compare relative sizes and shapes of objects (Figure 10.17)
- compare and contrast scenes or procedures (Figure 10.18, page 426)

Guidelines for Taking Photographs

Digital cameras and smartphones allow you to supply professional-looking, customized photos easily with your written work. One of the primary advantages of working with digital images is that they can be uploaded and shared quickly and

FIGURE 10.17 A Photo Showing How to Perform a Procedure and Comparing
Relative Sizes and Shapes of Objects

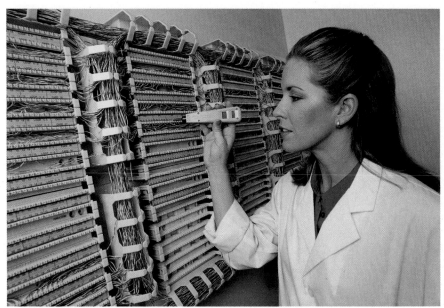

Corbis

easily over the Internet, but you still have to follow these guidelines when taking
photographs:

1. **Take the photo from the most appropriate distance.** Decide how much foreground and background information your audience needs. For example, if you
   are photographing a three-story office building, your picture may misleadingly
   show only one or two stories if you are standing too close to the building.
2. **Select the correct angle.** Take the photo from an angle that makes sense, usually straight on so that the object or person photographed can be viewed in full.
3. **Include only the details that are necessary and relevant for your purpose.**
   Crop (edit out) any unnecessary details from the photograph (see "Tech Note:
   Using Photoshop," page 427, and Figure 10.19, page 427).
4. **Provide a sense of scale.** So that readers understand the size of the object, include in the photograph a person (if the object is very large), a hand (if the object is small), or a ruler.
5. **Make sure you consider lighting and resolution.** Take your photograph in appropriate light so that the subject of your photograph is clear and crisp, and use
   the highest resolution possible for mximum clarity.
6. **Always ask for permission before you take a photograph of a person, place, or**
   thing, unless you are photographing a public park or building. Do not take photographs of copyrighted materials, for instance, a work of art, a page from a copyrighted book, or a movie or television screen. Also obtain permission from your
   boss if you are photographing your own company's equipment, sites, or designs.

FIGURE 10.18 Photos Showing Comparison/Contrast of Using Gasoline versus Electricity to Power an Automobile

moodboard/Super Value Royalty-Free/Corbis

Dean Siracusa/Corbis

TECH NOTE

Using Photoshop®

Photoshop®, a software program from Adobe (**www.photoshop.com**), is used throughout the world of work to edit, combine, and manipulate images in various media, including digital, mobile, print, and on the Web. With Photoshop you can

- edit photographs for color, sharpness, contrast, brightness, size, and resolution—you can also edit out unnecessary details, and eliminate "red eye." The original photo in Figure 10.19, for example, was changed to remove cars and bags of trash, to show the effects of a downtown beautification effort more clearly.
- greatly improve the visual quality of your photographs with custom-made images that establish or enhance your company's brands.
- design impressive graphics, illustrations, logos, and letterheads.
- supply navigational bars and color-coordinated photos for your websites or blogs.
- work with customizable templates for social media.

While Photoshop offers all of these benefits and more, you must still prepare a preliminary sketch or copy (similar to an outline or draft for a report) to create a framework for your final image. When working in Photoshop you also have to apply photography skills such as knowledge of the type and angle of the light source (see "Guidelines for Taking Photographs," pages 424–425). You need to select the highest-resolution images possible; otherwise your image may become blurry (or "pixilated") and not reproduce at a high quality (see "Ineffective Visuals: What *Not* to Do," page 406).

Photoshop offers all of these features at a relatively low cost, but it does require some technical skill to use it effectively. The software is primarily used by graphic design professionals, but you can learn some of the basic functions quickly. As with other types of graphics software, though, you need to follow all the ethical guidelines found on pages 433–438 (see "Using Visuals Ethically").

FIGURE 10.19 Removing Unnecessary Details from a Photograph Using Photoshop

Before

After

FIGURE 10.20 A Poor Photograph—Taken from the Wrong Angle So That Everything Merges and Becomes Confusing

Goldenjack/Shutterstock.com

To get a graphic sense of the effects of taking a photo the wrong and right way, study the photographs in Figures 10.20 and 10.21. In Figure 10.20, everything merges because the shot was taken from the wrong angle. The reader has no sense of the parts of the truck, their size, or their function. A clear and useful picture of a hydraulic truck (often called a "cherry picker") used to cut high branches can be seen in Figure 10.21. The photographer rightly placed the truck in the foreground but included enough background information to indicate the truck's function. The worker in the bucket helps to show the relative size of the truck and the function of the equipment.

Drawings

Drawings can show where an object is located, how a tool or machine is put together. A drawing can be simple, such as the **schematic drawing** in Figure 10.22 (page 430), which shows readers exactly where to place smoke detectors depending on the size of their homes.

A more detailed drawing can reveal the interior of an object. Such sketches are called **cutaway drawings** because they show internal parts normally concealed

FIGURE 10.21 An Effective Photograph—Truck in Foreground, Enough Background Information, and a Worker to Show the Size and Function of the Truck

iStockphoto.com/Allister Clark

from view. Figure 10.23 (page 431) is a cutaway drawing of an extended-range electric vehicle, the Chevrolet Volt.

Another kind of sketch is an **exploded drawing**, which blows the entire object up and apart, as in Figure 10.24 (page 432), to show how the individual parts of a computer are arranged. An exploded drawing comes with many owner's guide for equipment or devices, and uses **callouts**, or labels, to identify the components.

Guidelines for Using Drawings

1. Include only as much detail as your reader will need to understand what to do, be it to assemble or to operate a mechanism.
2. Clearly, label all parts so that your reader can identify and separate them.
3. Decide on the most appropriate view of the object to illustrate—aerial, frontal, lateral, reverse, exterior, interior—and indicate in the title which view it is.
4. Keep the parts of the drawing proportionate unless you are purposely enlarging one section (see Figure 12.9, pages 500–509).

FIGURE 10.22 A Schematic Drawing Showing Where to Place Smoke Detectors in a House

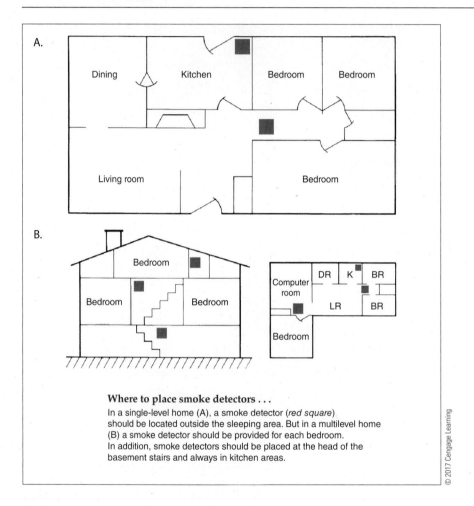

Where to place smoke detectors . . .
In a single-level home (A), a smoke detector (*red square*)
should be located outside the sleeping area. But in a multilevel home
(B) a smoke detector should be provided for each bedroom.
In addition, smoke detectors should be placed at the head of the
basement stairs and always in kitchen areas.

© 2017 Cengage Learning

Clip Art

Clip art (or icons) refers to ready-to-use electronic images. These small cartoon-style representations and photographs, such as the ones shown in Figure 10.25 (page 432), depict almost any workplace subject. Free clip art and photo-illustration databases can be found at the following websites (among others): **www.wpclipart .com**; **www.reusableart.com**; and freerangestock.com.

Guidelines for Using Clip Art

When you use clip art, follow these guidelines:

1. **Choose simple, easy-to-understand icons.** Select an image that conveys your idea quickly and directly. Avoid using an icon of an unfamiliar object

FIGURE 10.23 Cutaway Drawing of an Electric Car

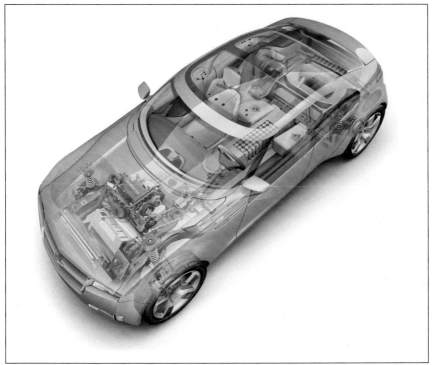

Source: General Motors Corporation. Used with permission, GM Media Archives.

or of a drawing or silhouette that might confuse your audience, especially a global one.

2. **Use clip art functionally.** Do not insert clip art as decorations. Make sure each has a specific function. Including too many will make your work look unprofessional.

3. **Be sure the clip art is relevant for your audience and your message.** A clip art airplane does not belong in a technical report on fuel capacity or jet engine design.

4. **Make sure your clip art is professional.** Some clip art is humorous, even silly, which may not be appropriate for a professional business report or proposal.

Infographics

An **infograph** (*information* plus *graphic*) combines a variety of visuals (for example, bar charts, graphs, icons, photographs) with numerical data (for example, statistics) to give readers an easy-to-understand overview or timeline of a complex process. Infographs tell a story. Influenced by the Web, an infograph such as the

FIGURE 10.24 Exploded Drawing of a Notebook Computer

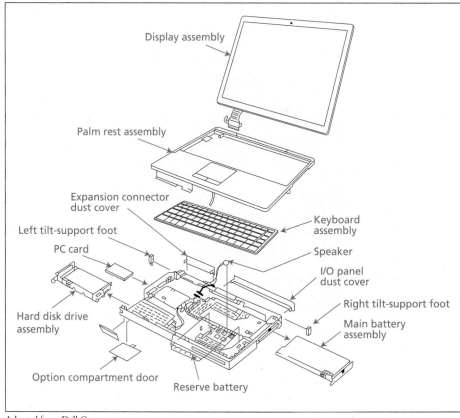

Adapted from Dell Computers

FIGURE 10.25 Examples of Clip Art

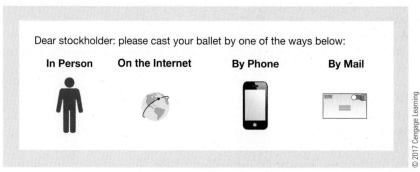

© 2017 Cengage Learning

FIGURE 10.26 Example of an Infograph

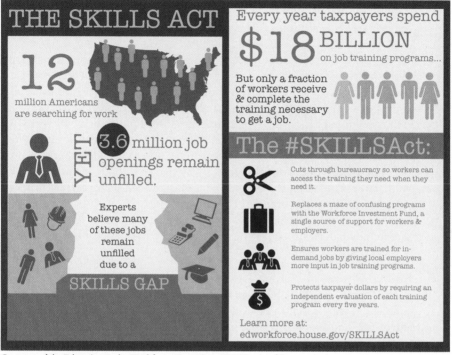

Combines numbers with images

Includes statistics

Uses appropriate icons

Helps readers understand a complex law quickly

Courtesy of the Education & the Workforce Committee, U.S. House of Representatives.

one in Figure 10.26 summarizes information that otherwise would require many visuals and pages of text to explain. As with the other visuals discussed in this chapter, use only the highest-quality graphics, and make sure text and image work together, not in opposition to each other; words, numbers, pictographs, and visuals all need to reinforce your message.

USING VISUALS ETHICALLY

Make sure your visuals, whether you create or import them, are ethical. Ethical visuals convey and interpret statistical information and other types of data, products and equipment, locations, and even individuals without misinterpretation. Ethical visuals should be:

- accurate
- honest, fair
- complete
- appropriate
- easy to read
- clearly labeled
- uncluttered
- consistent with conventions

Guidelines for Using Visuals Ethically

To ensure that your visuals are ethical, honest, accurate, and easy to read, avoid the following unethical practices no matter what type of visual you use.

Photos

- Don't distort a photo by omitting key details or by misrepresenting dimensions, angles, sizes, or surroundings or by superimposing one image over another.
- Don't take a photo of your most expensive, top-of-the-line product/model but then place the cost of your lowest-priced product/model under it.
- Don't misrepresent location—for example, taking a photo in a "doctored" or off-site location, studio, or lab and then claiming it as an "actual" location shot.
- Don't counterfeit or subtly alter a company's logo to sell, distribute, or promote an imitation as the real thing.
- Avoid stereotypes (e.g., showing only caucasian men using certain types of equipment or wearing a brand of clothing).
- Never take a photo of an individual for business purposes (e.g., for a newsletter, an ad, the company's website or social media site) without his or her permission.

Graphs

- Don't distort a graph by plotting it in misleading or unequal intervals—for example, omitting certain years or dates to hide a decline in profits. Contrast Figure 10.27, and its misleading interpretation, with the ethical revision in Figure 10.28.
- Include information in correct chronological sequence along the horizontal axis. Note how Figure 10.27 omits key years.
- Don't switch the type of information usually given along the vertical axis with the horizontal axis.
- Don't project any growth or increase on your graph without having reliable and valid reasons.
- Don't misrepresent data or trends by making increments along the vertical axis too limited, leaving a much smaller (and incomplete) area to represent. When data are plotted wrongly this way, readers are unethically led to misinterpret the numbers—to read that there was little loss in revenue, or no change in sales, for example. For instance, if the horizontal axis begins at $5 and advances to $6 a share, you leave only an intentionally small and misleading area to measure. If stocks fell below $5 a share, your graph would unethically not represent those declines.

Bar Charts

- Don't use color or shading to mislead or distort—for example, shading one bar to make it more prominent than the others.
- Make sure the height and width of each bar truthfully represents the data it purports to. That is, don't make one of the bars larger to maximize the profits, products, or sales in any one year.

FIGURE 10.27 An Unethical Graph and Misleading Interpretation

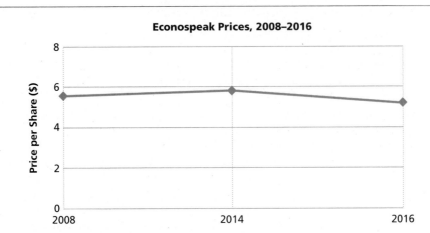

Econospeak's stock prices during 2008–2016 have been stable, resting securely at about $5.60. The graph above illustrates the stability of Econospeak's stock. Given our steady market, we believe shareholders will be confident in our recent decision to proceed with Econospeak's further expansion into global markets.

© 2017 Cengage Learning

FIGURE 10.28 An Ethical Revision of Figure 10.27

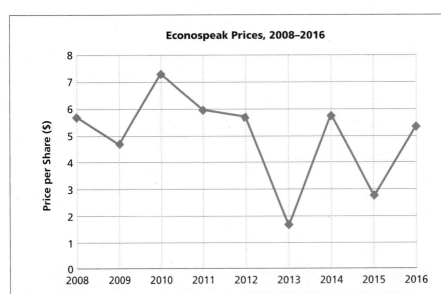

Econospeak's stock prices have not been as stable over 2008–2016 as we would have liked. The graph above illustrates the challenges the company has faced in the market in the past decade, resulting in fluctuation of prices. We believe, however, that Econospeak's further expansion into global markets will increase dividends by 2017.

© 2017 Cengage Learning

- Show bars for every year (or other sales period) covered. Note how the un-ethical bar chart (and accompanying text) in Figure 10.29 violates this rule, but the chart in Figure 10.30 ethically represents the data.

Pie Charts

- Don't use 3-D to distort the thickness of one slice of the pie and thereby misleadingly deemphasize other slices.
- Avoid concealing negative information (losses, expenses, etc.) by including the information in another category, or slice, or lumping it into a category marked "Other" or "Miscellaneous."
- Make sure percentages match the size of the slices of the pie chart. Study Figures 10.31 and 10.32 (page 438). Note how a larger expense for guest speakers (35% of budget) is unethically misrepresented in Figure 10.31 by using a smaller-sized wedge, while the expenses for venue rental (14%) are actually less than for guest speaker expenses but are drawn larger to misrepresent costs.

Drawings

- Avoid any clutter that hides features.
- Label all parts correctly.
- Do not omit or shadow any necessary parts.
- Tell readers what to look for, as in Figure 10.22.
- Draw an object accurately. Indicate if your drawing is the actual size of the object or equipment or if it is drawn to scale. Provide a scale.

Pictographs

- Choose icons that are culturally and ethnically appropriate, tasteful, and free from stereotyping (see Figure 10.14, page 422, and Figure 10.26, page 433).
- Make sure the size or shape of your pictograph accurately represents the financial or other statistical information it is meant to represent.
- Do not distort the size of a pictograph, increasing or decreasing its height or width, to suggest a larger or smaller quantity, whether in sales, population, services, etc.

USING APPROPRIATE VISUALS FOR INTERNATIONAL AUDIENCES

Whether you are writing for an expanding international business community in India or China, or for multicultural readers in the United States, you will have to prepare numerous documents that require visuals. These can range from instructions

FIGURE 10.29 An Unethical Bar Chart that Misrepresents Key Data

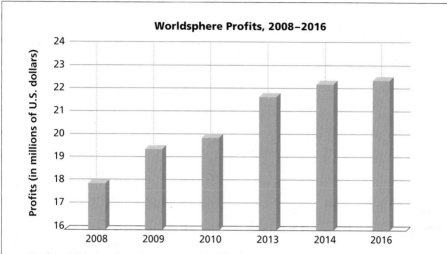

Profits at Worldsphere have seen a healthy increase over recent years. This bar chart demonstrates the steady increase in profits, which have risen $4.5 million since 2008. Given the profit history of Worldsphere, our investors can be confident of future growth and the security of their stock in our company.

© 2017 Cengage Learning

FIGURE 10.30 An Ethical Revision of Figure 10.29

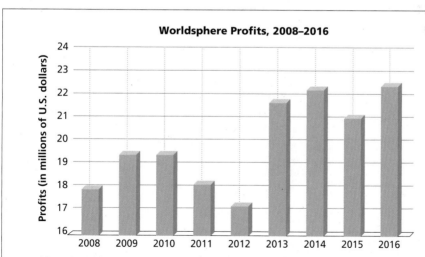

Although profits at Worldsphere have been volatile recently, we are now at our highest profit margin of the last eight years. This bar chart shows the effects of market difficulties for the period 2008–2016, when the economy suffered major cutbacks. However, Worldsphere achieved a successful turnaround in 2013, with profits regaining strength due to our advances in research and technology.

© 2017 Cengage Learning

FIGURE 10.31 An Unethical Pie Chart with Inappropriately-Sized Wedges

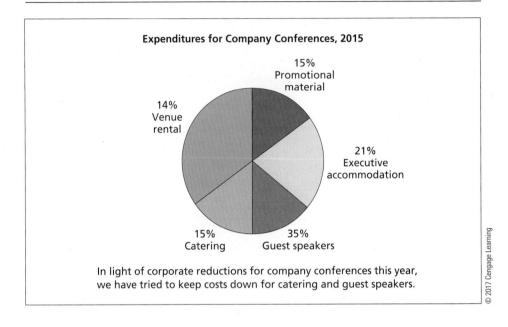

Expenditures for Company Conferences, 2015

15%
Promotional
material

14%
Venue
rental

21%
Executive
accommodation

15%
Catering

35%
Guest speakers

In light of corporate reductions for company conferences this year, we have tried to keep costs down for catering and guest speakers.

© 2017 Cengage Learning

FIGURE 10.32 An Ethical Revision of Figure 10.31

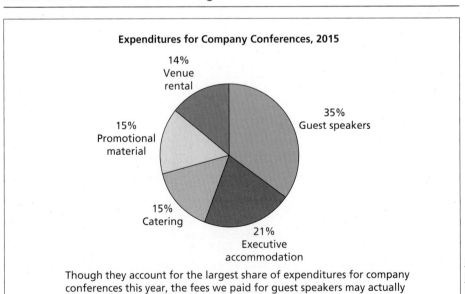

Expenditures for Company Conferences, 2015

14%
Venue
rental

35%
Guest speakers

15%
Promotional
material

15%
Catering

21%
Executive
accommodation

Though they account for the largest share of expenditures for company conferences this year, the fees we paid for guest speakers may actually be our greatest advantage. These speakers have shown us ways to maximize our profits in expanding markets.

© 2017 Cengage Learning

FIGURE 10.33 Internationally Recognized Icons

© 2017 Cengage Learning

containing warning and caution statements to tables, graphs, charts, and photos for proposals, reports, presentations, websites, and social media.

Visuals Do Not Always Translate from One Culture to Another

While there are internationally recognized icons, such as those in Figure 10.33, visuals do not automatically transfer from one culture to another. Visuals and other graphic devices may have one meaning or use in the United States and a radically different one in other countries around the world. To avoid confusing or offending your international audience, consult a native speaker from your audience's country to see if your visuals are culturally acceptable.

Guidelines for Using Visuals for International Audiences

To communicate appropriately and respectfully with international readers through visuals and other graphics, follow these guidelines:

1. Do not use images that ethnically or racially stereotype your readers. Depicting Native Americans through clip art images of red-faced chiefs is insulting. Rather than using an ethnic or racial pictograph, use neutral stick figures or nonbiased clip art. See, for example, the human figure in Figure 10.25.

2. Be respectful of religious symbols and images. Portraying a smiling Buddha to sell products is considered disrespectful to residents in Southeast Asia.

3. Be careful when using political imagery. Using the Statue of Liberty to signify freedom to an international audience may prove confusing because the audience is not sure what this American-centric icon is supposed to symbolize. If you do include political symbols, make certain you are using them correctly and respectfully. Including the Indian flag in a presentation, for example, may be necessary and appropriate, but displaying it hanging upside down is certain to anger Indian audiences.

4. Avoid using culturally insensitive or objectionable photographs. A photograph portraying men and women eating together at a business conference is unacceptable in Saudi Arabia. Moreover, sitting with one leg crossed over the other is seen as disrespectful in many countries in the world.

5. Avoid icons or clip art that international readers would misunderstand. In the United States, an owl can stand for wisdom, thrift, and memory while in Japan, Romania, and some African countries it is a symbol for death. A software program showing an icon of a mailbox (shown here) to represent email confused readers in other countries who thought the icon represented a birdhouse. A better alternative would be an icon of an envelope.

Similarly, the Apple icon for "trash" (a garbage can) confused some international readers because not all garbage cans look alike.

6. Be cautious about using images or photos with hand gestures, especially in manuals or other instructional materials. Many gestures are culture-specific; they do not necessarily mean the same thing in other countries that they do in the United States. Table 10.3 lists cultural differences around the globe for some common gestures.

7. Don't offend international readers by using colors that are culturally inappropriate. Red in China symbolizes happiness while yellow in Saudi Arabia signifies strength. Green is regarded as a sacred color in Saudi Arabia.

Always research (on the Internet or by consulting a representative from the audience you want to reach) if the color scheme you have chosen is appropriate for your target audience. For example, purple is the color of death and mourning in Thailand as white is in China. Although orange is the symbolic color of Northern Ireland, avoid using it when writing to readers whose culture does not value that color.

TABLE 10.3 Different Cultural Meanings of Various Gestures

Gesture	Meaning in the United States	Meaning in Other Countries
OK sign (index finger joined to thumb in a circle)	All right; agreement	Sexual insult in Brazil, Germany, Russia; sign for zero, worthlessness in France
Thumbs-up	A winning gesture; good job; approval	Offensive gesture in Muslim countries
Waving or holding out open palm	Stop	Obscene in Greece—equivalent to throwing garbage at someone
Pointing with the index finger	This way; pay attention; turn the page	Rude, insulting in Japan, Sri Lanka, and Venezuela; in Saudi Arabia used only for animals, not for people
Nodding head up and down	Agreement, saying yes	Greek version of saying "no"; in China means "I understand," not "I agree"

8. Be careful when using directional signs and shapes. While road signs tend to be fairly recognizable throughout the world—for example, the octagon is generally understood as the shape for the stop sign—there are country-specific signs and code books. For instance, a pennant-shaped sign, signaling a no-passing zone on American highways, may not have the same meaning in Nigeria or India. The following symbol points to a railroad crossing for American readers but would baffle an audience in the Czech Republic.

9. Refrain from using sports-related imagery and symbols. While international audiences may know images related to soccer (or *football*, as it is called in most other countries), they may not know what a baseball diamond, bat, or glove is, or what the goalposts or end zone in American football looks like. It is better to stay away from such visual images (See also "Ten Guidelines for Communicating with International Readers," pages 169–173).

10. Avoid confusing an international audience with punctuation and other writing symbols employed in the United States. Not all cultures use a question mark (?) to end a sentence asking a question, to represent the Help function in a computer program, or for an FAQ link on a website. Similarly, ellipses (. . .) and slashes (and/or) may not be a part of the language your international audience reads and writes. Be careful, too, about using the following graphic symbols, familiar to writers and speakers of U.S. English but not necessarily to an international audience:

#	pound	&	ampersand (and)
©	copyright	*	asterisk

Include a glossary or a key to these symbols or any other graphics your reader may not understand, or revise your sentences to avoid these symbols.

CONCLUSION

This chapter has introduced you to the types of visuals you can expect to use frequently in the world of work and has given you guidelines on how to construct or import, label, insert, introduce, and cite them in your writing. Following the guidelines in this chapter will make your documents more businesslike, more persuasive, and easier for your readers to follow. Equally important, whenever you use a visual, always keep in mind the same ethical standards that you follow in your written work. Intentionally distorting a visual is akin to plagiarizing. You also need to be respectful of your audience's culture and the context in which your visual will be included.

✓ REVISION CHECKLIST

☐ Selected most effective type of visual (table, chart, graph, drawing, photograph, infograph) to represent information the audience needs.

☐ Drafted and edited visual until it met readers' needs.

☐ Determined right amount of detail to include in visual.

☐ Made sure every visual is attractive, clear, complete, and relevant.

☐ Gave each visual a number, a caption (title), and, where necessary, a legend and callouts.

☐ Inserted visual close to the description or commentary accompanying it.

☐ Planned where to best place visual and surrounded each one with adequate white space.

☐ Inserted page number where visual can be found.

☐ Introduced and interpreted each visual in appropriate place in report or proposal.

☐ Explained what visual shows and why it is important.

☐ Made sure every photograph is clear and relevant.

☐ Acknowledged sources for any copyrighted visuals and gave credit to individuals whose statistical data are the basis of a visual.

☐ Secured written permission to use visual in published work, whether in print or in an e-document (such as a website).

☐ Used and interpreted visuals ethically and appropriately.

☐ Did not distort or skew any visual to misrepresent data.

☐ Selected visuals and colors that respect the cultural traditions of international readers.

EXERCISES

1. Bring to class printouts or screen shots of three or four home pages that use especially effective visuals. In a short memo or email (three or four paragraphs) to your instructor, indicate why and how each visual is appropriate for and convincing to a particular audience. What would each home page look like without its visual?

2. Find a website you think includes poorly designed or inappropriate visuals. Explain to your instructor why these visuals are ineffective, and redesign two of them.

3. Locate a print document that is visual-poor, and select an appropriate visual to accompany it. Justify your choice of visual and its inclusion in an email to your instructor.

4. Record the highest temperature reached in your town for the next five days. Then collect data on the highest temperature reached in three of the following cities over the same period: Boston, Chicago, Dallas, Denver, Los Angeles, Miami, New Orleans, New York, Philadelphia, Phoenix, Salt Lake City, San Francisco, Seattle. (You can get this information on the Internet.) Prepare a table showing the differences for the five-day period.

5. Go to a supermarket and get the prices of four different brands of the same product (a candy bar, a soft drink, a box of cereal). Present your findings in the form of a table.

6. Recently, a government agency supplied statistics on the world production of oranges (including tangerines) in thousands of metric tons for the following countries during the years 2011–2015: Brazil, 2,098, 2,132, 2,760, 2,872; Israel, 909, 1,076, 1,148, 1,221; Italy, 1,669, 1,599, 1,766, 1,604; Japan, 2,424, 2,994, 2,885, 4,070; Mexico, 937, 1,405, 1,114, 1,270; Spain, 2,135, 2,005, 2,179, 2,642; and the United States, 7,658, 7,875, 7,889, 9,245. Prepare a table with that information and then write a paragraph in which you introduce and refer to the table and draw conclusions from it.

7. Keep a record for one week of the number of miles you walk, ride, or drive each day. Then prepare a line graph depicting that information.

8. Prepare a table to show the following statistical data: According to the 2000 census, the town of Ardmore had a population of 34,567. By the 2010 census, the town's population had decreased by 4,500. In the 2000 census, the town of Morrison had a population of 23,809, but by the 2010 census, the population had increased by 3,689. The 2010 census figure for the town of Berkesville was 25,675, which was an increase of 2,768 from the 2000 census.

9. Prepare a line graph for the information in Exercise 8.

10. Prepare a bar graph for the information in Exercise 8.

11. Write a paragraph (four to five sentences) introducing and interpreting the following table for a website aimed at general readers.

Year	Soft Drink Companies	Bottling Plants	Per Capita Consumption (Gallons)
1945	750	750	10.3
1950	578	611	12.5
1955	457	466	18.6
1960	380	407	17.2
1965	231	292	15.9
1970	171	229	15.4
1975	118	197	16.0
1980	92	154	18.7
1985	54	102	21.1
1990	43	88	23.1
1995	45	82	25.3
2000	37	78	27.6
2005	34	72	30.1
2010	31	70	32.3
2015	30	69	31.4

12. According to a municipal study in 2015, the distribution of all companies classified in each enterprise in that city was as follows: minerals, 0.4 percent; selected services, 33.3 percent; e- and brick-and-mortar sales, 36.7 percent; wholesale trade, 6.5 percent; manufacturing, 5.3 percent; and construction, 17.8 percent. Make a pie chart to

represent the distribution, and write a one- or two-paragraph interpretation to accompany (and explain the significance of) your visual.

13. Construct a segmented bar chart to represent the kinds and numbers of courses you took in a two-semester period or during your last year in high school.

14. Prepare a bar chart for the different brands of the product you selected in Exercise 5. Write a paragraph introducing your chart.

15. Find a pictograph in a math or business textbook, in a magazine, or on a website from the Census Bureau or the Department of Labor Statistics. Make a bar graph from the information contained in the pictograph, and then write a paragraph introducing the bar graph and drawing conclusions from it.

16. Make an organizational chart for a business or an agency you worked for recently. Include part-time and full-time employees, but indicate their titles or functions with different kinds of shapes or lines. Then write a brief letter to your employer explaining why your organizational chart should be distributed to all employees. Focus on the types of problems that could be avoided if employees had access to such a visual.

17. Prepare a flow chart for one of the following activities:

    a. jumping a "dead" car battery
    b. giving an injection
    c. making a reservation online
    d. using an iPhone to check the status of a flight
    e. checking your credit online
    f. putting out an electrical fire
    g. changing your email password
    h. preparing a visual using a graphics software package
    i. uploading a video to a social media site
    j. joining a chat group
    k. filing for an extension to pay state taxes
    l. any job you do

18. Prepare a drawing of one of the following simple tools, and include appropriate callouts with your visual.

    a. high-definition TV
    b. iPad
    c. pliers
    d. stethoscope
    e. swivel chair
    f. Galaxy S6
    g. Compact fluorescent lightbulb
    h. Makita circular saw

19. Draw an interior view of a piece of equipment you use in your major or on your job, and then identify the relevant parts using callouts.

20. Prepare appropriate visuals to illustrate the data listed in parts (a) and (b). In a paragraph immediately after the visual, explain why the type of visual you selected is appropriate for the information.

    a. Life expectancy is increasing in the United States. This growth can be dramatically measured by comparing the number of teenagers with the number of older adults (over age 65) in the United States during the last few years and then projecting those figures. In 1970, there were approximately 28 million teenagers and 20 million older adults. By 1990, the number of teenagers climbed to 30 million, and the number of older adults increased to 25 million. In 2000, there were 27 million teenagers and 31 million older adults. In 2010, the number of teenagers had leveled off to 23 million, but the number of older adults soared to more than 36 million.

b. Researchers estimate that for every adult in the United States 3,985 cigarettes were purchased in 1990; 4,100 in 1995; 3,875 in 2000; 3,490 in 2005; 2,910 in 2010; and 2,720 in 2015.

21. Find a photograph that contains some irrelevant clutter. The marketing department of your company wants to use the photograph. Write a letter to the department head explaining what to delete and why.

22. Below are three examples of poorly prepared visuals with brief explanations of how they were intended to be used. Redo one of the visuals to make it easier to read and to better organize the information. Write a paragraph to accompany your new visual.

a. To illustrate a report on problems that pilots have encountered with a particular model of jet engine.

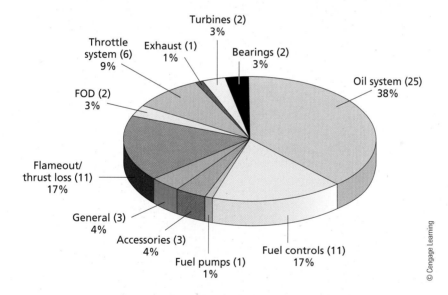

b. To show that a hiking trail is compatible with wheelchair access laws.

c. to encourage programmers to write applications for the Android operating system.

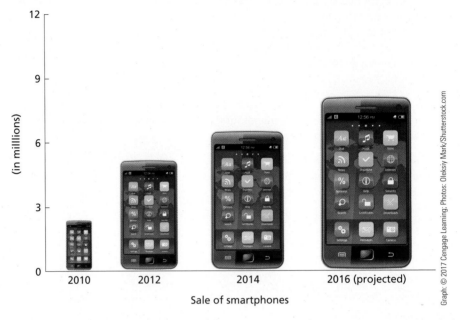

23. You work for a large manufacturer of industrial heat pumps and have been asked to help write a section of a report on the increased business your firm has been doing overseas. Based on the sales figures below for the years 2013, 2014, and 2015 (listed in that order) for each of the following countries, prepare two different yet complementary visuals. Also, supply a one-page description and interpretation of the statistics represented in your visuals. You may work collaboratively with one or more students in your class to prepare the visuals and to write the section of the report on international sales.

Argentina, 45, 53, 34; Australia, 78, 90, 115; Bolivia, 23, 43, 52; Brazil, 29, 34, 35; Canada, 116, 234, 256; China, 7, 100, 296; Denmark, 65, 54, 87; England, 256, 345, 476; France, 198, 167, 345; Germany, 234, 398, 429; Holland, 65, 80, 89; Italy, 49, 52, 97; Japan, 67, 43, 29; Korea, 55, 43, 28; New Zealand, 12, 69, 114; Norway, 33, 92, 104; Switzerland, 164, 266, 306; Sweden, 145, 217, 266.

In your written report, take into account trends, shifts in sales, and possible consequences for further marketing, and conclude with a specific recommendation to your employer.

24. You have been asked to create a logo, including a visual, for one of the following new businesses opening in your town. Explain your design and why you think it is effective.

    a. solar panel installation firm

    b. home health care company

    c. studio offering musical instrument lessons

    d. outdoor apparel manufacturer

    e. toxic waste removal company

    f. math and science tutor

25. Explain why the following visuals and graphic symbols would be inappropriate in communicating with an international audience and how you would revise a document containing them:

   a. clip art showing a string tied around an index finger
   b. a picture of a man with a sombrero on a website for Pronto Check Cashing Company
   c. clip art of a lightbulb and the logo "Smart Ideas" for a CPA firm
   d. clip art showing someone crossing the middle finger over the index finger (wishing sign)
   e. a drawing of a cupid figure for a caterer
   f. a sales brochure showing a white and blue flag for a French audience
   g. a poster showing a women's track and field team used to advertise a brand of footware to an Arabic-speaking audience
   h. a satisfied customer making the "okay" gesture in an ad aimed at a Japanese audience
   i. an image of a rabbit on a website for an automobile manufacturer to stress how fast its cars are
   j. a photograph of a roll of Scotch tape to show international readers that your company can solve problems quickly
   k. a photograph of a baseball umpire holding up his hands to ask readers to repeat a step in a set of instructions
   l. a drawing of a white glove to sell home and carpet cleaning supplies
   m. a piece of clip art showing a rooster for a business that opens early in the day
   n. the letters *a*, *b*, *c* in a box to indicate that a directory is alphabetically arranged
   o. a pair of scissors moving along a rectangle of dotted lines to indicate a merchant offers prospective customers a money-saving coupon

CHAPTER 11

Designing Successful Documents and Websites

The success of your documents and websites depend as much on how they look as on what they say. As we saw, in the workplace, you will be expected to design professional-looking memos, letters, instructions, and reports; you may also be asked to create or contribute content to blogs and websites. This chapter gives you practical advice for making your work more reader-friendly and visually appealing.

CHARACTERISTICS OF EFFECTIVE DESIGN

In designing documents and websites, you need to project a positive, professional image of yourself, your company, and your product or service. A report or website filled with nothing but thick, unbroken long paragraphs crowded to the margins, with no visual clues to break them up or to make information stand out, is sure to intimidate readers and turn them away. They will conclude that your work is too complex and not worth their effort or time. Readers expect documents and websites to be interactive, to use color images, and to include easy-to-scan texts and visuals. Your company, too, will win or lose points because of your design choices. A visually appealing document or website will enhance a company's reputation and improve its sales. A poorly designed one will not.

Make your documents look user-friendly—clear, logical, and consistent—by signaling to your audience that your message is

- easy to read
- easy to follow and understand
- easy to find and recall

This chapter will show you how to design professional-looking, reader-friendly documents and websites that are a credit to you and your company.

ORGANIZING INFORMATION VISUALLY

Today's web-based culture prizes visual thinking when you design all kinds of documents. The way you organize and visualize information can help readers move quickly and clearly through your document. Take a quick look at Figures 11.1 and 11.2 (pages 450–453). The same information is contained in each figure. Which visually appeals to you more? Which do you think would be easier to read? Which is better designed? As the two figures show, design or layout plays a crucial role in an audience's overall acceptance of your work.

Figure 11.2 exemplifies the effective design characteristics (on the left) while Figure 11.1 sadly displays the ineffective ones (on the right).

Effective Design	Ineffective Design
• visually appealing	• crowded
• logically organized	• disorganized/cluttered
• clear/simplicity	• hard to follow
• accessible/scannable	• difficult to read
• varied/contrasting	• boring, repetitious
• relevant	• inconsistent

Study the annotations to these figures to see how the errors in Figure 11.1 are corrected in Figure 11.2. By modeling your written work after the document in Figure 11.2, you can guarantee that your readers will appreciate your layout.

THE ABCS OF PRINT DOCUMENT DESIGN

The basic elements of effective document design are

- page layout
- typography, or type design
- heads and subheads
- graphics
- color

The proper arrangement and balance of type, white space, and graphics involve the same level of preparation that you would spend on your research, drafting, revising, and editing. Just as you do research to find information, you have to research and experiment in order to adopt the most effective design for your document.

Page Layout

Each of your pages needs to coordinate space and text pleasingly. Too much or too little of one or the other can jeopardize the reader's acceptance of your message. To design an effective page layout, pay attention to the following elements.

   1. White space. White space (blank space) refers to open areas on a page, such as margins and space around images, is free of text, visuals, or other design features, e.g., headings. It can help you increase the impact and tone of your message;

FIGURE 11.1 A Poorly Designed Document

No title

Single-spacing makes document difficult to read

Lack of headings in color or boldface makes it hard for readers to organize material

Using so many different fonts may confuse readers and not be effective in emphasizing or highlighting information.

Uneven presentation of numbers

Lack of adequate margins makes document look dense and complex

Unnecessary italics are confusing

Inconsistent use of italics and boldfacing

The results for the recent cholesterol screening at *our company's Health Fair* were distributed to each employee last week. Many employees wanted to know more about cholesterol in general, the different types of cholesterol, what the results mean, and the foods that are high or low in cholesterol.

We hope the information provided below will help employees better answer their questions concerning cholesterol and our cholesterol screening program.

High cholesterol, along with high blood pressure and obesity, is one of the primary risk factors that may contribute to the development of coronary heart disease and may eventually lead to a heart attack or stroke. Cholesterol is a fatty, sticky substance found in the bloodstream. Excessive amounts of the bad type of cholesterol can deposit on the walls of the heart arteries. *This deposit is called plaque, and over a long period of time plaque can narrow or even block the blood flow through the arteries.*

Total cholesterol is divided into three parts—LDL (low-density lipoprotein), or bad cholesterol; HDL (high-density lipoprotein), or good cholesterol; and VLDL (very low-density lipoprotein), a much smaller component of cholesterol you don't have to worry about. Bad (LDL) cholesterol forms on the walls of your arteries and can cause a lot of damage. Good cholesterol, on the other hand, functions like a sponge, mopping up cholesterol and carrying it out of the bloodstream.

You should have received *three cholesterol numbers.* One is for your HDL (or good cholesterol) and the other is for your LDL, or bad cholesterol, reading. These two numbers are added to give you the third, or composite, level of your total cholesterol.

As you can see, a total cholesterol reading of below 200 is considered safe. Continue what you have been doing. If your reading falls in the moderate risk range of 200–239, you need to modify your diet, get more exercise, and have your cholesterol checked again in six months. *If your reading is above 240, see your doctor.* You may need to take cholesterol-lowering medication, if your doctor prescribes it. Reducing your total cholesterol by even as little as 25% can decrease your risk of a heart attack by 50%.

The Surgeon General recommends that your LDL, or bad cholesterol, should at least be below 100; and your HDL, or good cholesterol, needs to be at least above 40. Ideally, the ratio between your HDL and overall cholesterol numbers should be between 3.5 and 5 to 1. That is, your HDL should be at least 20% of your total cholesterol number. The higher your HDL is, the better, of course. So even if you have a high LDL reading, if your HDL is correspondingly high you will be at less risk.

One of the easiest ways to decrease your cholesterol is to modify your diet. Cholesterol is found in foods that are high in saturated fat. Saturated fat *comes from animal sources and also from certain vegetable sources.* Foods high in bad cholesterol that you should restrict or avoid, include whole milk, red meat, eggs, cheese, butter, shrimp, oils such as palm and coconut, and avocados. Generally, food groups low in cholesterol include fruits, vegetables, and whole grains (assorted wheat breads, oatmeal, and certain cereals), *lean meats (fish, chicken)*, and beans.

The goal of our cholesterol screening is to help each employee lower his or her cholesterol level and eventually reduce the risk of heart disease. **Besides the advice given above,** you can do the following: get regular aerobic exercise—bicycling, brisk walking, swimming, rowing—for at least 30 minutes 3–4 times a week. But get your doctor's approval first. *Eat foods low in cholesterol* but high in dietary fiber (beans, oatmeal, brown rice). Maintain a healthy weight for your frame to lower your body fat. Minimize stress, which can increase cholesterol. Learn relaxation techniques.

FIGURE 11.2 An Effectively Designed Document with the Same Text as Figure 11.1

Cholesterol Screening

The results for the recent cholesterol screening at our company's Health Fair were distributed to each employee last week. Many employees wanted to know more about cholesterol in general, the different types of cholesterol, what the results mean, and the foods that are high or low in cholesterol. We hope the information provided below will help employees better answer their questions concerning cholesterol and our cholesterol screening program.

Determining Risk Factors

High cholesterol, along with high blood pressure and obesity, is one of the primary risk factors that may contribute to the development of coronary heart disease and may eventually lead to a heart attack or stroke. Cholesterol is a fatty, sticky substance found in the bloodstream. Excessive amounts of the bad type of cholesterol can deposit on the walls of the heart arteries. This deposit is called **plaque** and over a long period of time plaque can narrow or even block the blood flow through the arteries.

Separating Types of Cholesterol

Total cholesterol is divided into three parts: (1) **LDL** (low-density lipoprotein), or bad cholesterol; (2) **HDL** (high-density lipoprotein), or good cholesterol; and (3) **VLDL** (very low-density lipoprotein), a much smaller component of cholesterol you don't have to worry about. Bad (LDL) cholesterol forms on the walls of your arteries and can cause a lot of damage. Good cholesterol, on the other hand, functions like a sponge, mopping up cholesterol and carrying it out of the bloodstream.

1

Title clearly set apart from text with capitalization, larger font, and use of color

Text is double-spaced with more ample margins, making it more readable

Headings in color and larger font divide material into easy-to-follow units for readers

Consistent use of one typeface for text

Only key words being defined are boldfaced

Page does not look cluttered

Types of cholesterol are helpfully labeled with numbers

(Continued)

FIGURE 11.2 (Continued)

Understanding Your Cholesterol Results

You should have received three cholesterol numbers. One is for your **HDL** (or good cholesterol), and the other is for your **LDL** (or bad cholesterol) reading. These two numbers are added to give you the third, or composite, level of your total cholesterol.

Cholesterol levels can be classified as follows:

Minimal Risk	Moderate Risk	High Risk
below 200	200–239	above 240

As you can see, a total cholesterol reading of below 200 is considered safe. You are doing fine. Continue what you have been doing. If your reading falls in the moderate risk range of 200–239, you need to modify your diet, get more exercise, and have your cholesterol checked again in six months. If your reading is above 240, see your doctor. You may need to take cholesterol-lowering medication, if your doctor prescribes it. Reducing your total cholesterol by even as little as 25% can decrease your risk of a heart attack by 50%.

Knowing the Relationship Between Bad and Good Cholesterol

The Surgeon General recommends that your **LDL**, or bad cholesterol, should at least be below 100. And your **HDL**, or good cholesterol, needs to be at least above 40. Ideally, the ratio between your HDL and overall cholesterol numbers should be between 3.5 and 5 to 1. That is, your **HDL** should be at least 20% of your total cholesterol number. The higher your **HDL** is, the better, of course. So even if you have a high **LDL** reading, if your **HDL** is correspondingly high you will be at less risk.

Recognizing Food Sources of Cholesterol

One of the easiest ways to decrease your cholesterol is to modify your diet. Cholesterol is found in foods that are high in saturated fat. Saturated fat

FIGURE 11.2 (Continued)

comes from animal sources and also from certain vegetable sources. Foods high in bad cholesterol that you should restrict include:

1. whole milk

2. red meat

3. eggs

4. cheese

5. butter

6. shrimp

7. oils such as palm and coconut

8. avocados

Generally, food groups low in cholesterol include fruits, vegetables, and whole grains (wheat breads, oatmeal, and certain cereals), lean meats (fish, chicken), and beans.

Realizing It Is Up to You

The goal of our cholesterol screening program is to help each employee lower his or her cholesterol level and eventually reduce the risk of heart disease. Besides the advice given above, you can do the following:

- Get regular aerobic exercise—bicycling, brisk walking, swimming, rowing—for at least 30 minutes 3–4 times a week. But get your doctor's approval first.

- Eat foods low in cholesterol but high in dietary fiber (beans, oatmeal, brown rice).

- Maintain a healthy weight for your frame to lower your body fat.

- Minimize stress, which can increase cholesterol. Learn relaxation techniques.

3

A double-spaced, numbered list helps readers easily identify foods with bad cholesterol

Easy-to-follow examples of foods low in cholesterol in parentheses

Heading signals conclusion

Bulleted list serves as both conclusion and plan for future action

Source: Thanks to Sgt. Mannie E. Hall of the U.S. Army for his advice in drafting this document

use white space between paragraphs and sections to signal beginnings and endings. Skimping on white space by packing too much print on the page only distracts the reader from the message you want to convey. White space, on the other hand, can entice, comfort, and appeal to your audience's "psychology of space" by

- attracting and sustaining the reader's attention
- assuring the reader that information is presented logically
- announcing that information is easy to follow
- assisting the reader to organize information visually
- allowing the reader to highlight important information

Again, compare Figures 11.1 and 11.2. Which document shows that it was designed by someone who understands the importance of white space?

2. Margins. Use wide margins, usually 1 to 1 ½ inches, to "frame" your document with white space surrounding text and visuals. Margins prevent your document from looking cluttered or overcrowded. If your document requires binding, you may have to leave a wider left margin (2 inches).

3. Line length. Most readers find a text line of 10 to 14 words, or 50 to 70 characters (depending on the type size you choose), comfortable and pleasing to read. Excessively long lines that bump into the margins signal that your work is difficult to read. In the following example, note how the extra-long lines unsettle your reading and tax your eye movement; they signal rough going.

To succeed in the world of business, workers must brush up on their networking skills. The network process has many benefits that you need to be aware of. These benefits range from finding a better job to accomplishing your job more easily and efficiently. Through networking you are able to expand the number of contacts who can help you. Networking means sharing news and opportunities. The Internet is the key to successful networking.

Conversely, do not print a document with overly short or extremely uneven lines.

> To succeed in today's busy world of
> business, workers must
> brush up on their networking skills. The
> network process has many
> benefits you need to be
> aware of.

Readers will suspect your ideas are incomplete, superficial, or even simple-minded.

4. Columns. Document text can be organized in either single-column or multicolumn formats. Memos, letters, and reports are usually formatted without columns, whereas documents that intersperse text and visuals (such as newsletters and magazines) work better in multicolumn formats. Smaller typefaces also work well in multicolumn formats.

Typography

Typography consists of font (also called **typeface**), font size, font styles, justification, heads and subheads. Take a look at Figure 11.3, which illustrates different typefaces and sizes.

FIGURE 11.3 Sample Typefaces and Type Sizes

---

8 point Georgia works well for endnotes and footnotes

12 point Times New Roman works well for main text and figure legends

14 point Arial works well for section headings

18 point Georgia works well for chapter titles

Font

The readability of your text is crucial. Select a font, therefore, that ensures your text is

- legible
- attractive
- functional
- appropriate for your message
- complementary with accompanying graphics

Fonts are also characterized as **serif** (the short cross-lines at the ends of some letters, such as the top of the G in "Georgia" in Figure 11.3) or **sans serif** (without the serifs). The font you use can make your document look businesslike or too casual. Avoid using a font that looks like script or cursive, and don't mix and switch fonts. The result makes your work look amateurish and disorganized, as in Figure 11.1. Although Times New Roman and Arial are preferred for most workplace documents, other fonts have different visual impacts, and designers often employ them in both printed documents and websites.

Font Size

Font size options are almost unlimited. Font size is measured in units called **points**. There are 72 points to the inch. The larger the point size, the larger the type. Never print your letter or report in 6- or 8-point type, like classified ads in a newspaper, or in a size larger than 12-point type unless you are designing for readers with visual difficulties (see "Tech Note: Website Accessibility," pages 471–472)

Font Styles

Font styles include roman, boldface, italics, underlining, and small caps.

Roman

Boldface

Italics

<u>Underlining</u>

SMALL CAPS

Avoid overusing boldface and italics. Use them only when necessary and not just for decoration. Do *not* underline the text unless absolutely necessary. Not only will too many special visual effects make your work harder to read, but you will also lose the dramatic impact these features have to distinguish and emphasize key points that rightfully deserve to be set in boldface or italic type.

Justification

Sometimes referred to as **alignment**, **justification** consists of left, right, full, and centered options. Left-justified (also called **unjustified** or **ragged right**) text is preferred because it allows the space between words to remain constant, making the text easier to read. In full-justified text (both left and right margins are aligned) the word spacing varies from line to line. Left justification gives a document a less formal look than full justification. Narrow columns of text should be set left-justified to avoid awkward gaps between words and excessive hyphenation.

Our website offers consumers a mall on the Internet. It gives shoppers access to our products and services and makes buying easy and fun.	Our website offers consumers a mall on the Internet. It gives shoppers access to our products and services and makes buying easy and fun.
Left-justified text	**Right-justified text**
Our website offers consumers a mall on the Internet. It gives shoppers access to our products and services and makes buying easy and fun.	Our website offers consumers a mall on the Internet. It gives shoppers access to our products and services and makes buying easy and fun.
Full-justified text	**Centered text**

Heads and Subheads

Heads (e.g., titles) and **subheads** (e.g., subtitles) are brief descriptive phrases that signal starting points or major divisions in your document. They provide helpful road signs for readers charting their course through a document, as in Figure 11.2. Heads divide, or chunk, your document into its major parts, sections, or segments. Note how many of the figures in this book include heads and subheads. Heads immediately attract attention and quickly inform readers about the function, scope, purpose, or contents of your document and its individual sections, or that one section is finishing and another starting. Moreover, they help readers prioritize information by emphasizing the main points they need to look for and remember. Without heads and subheads your work will look unorganized and cluttered.

How to Write Heads and Subheads

It takes time to write appropriate heads and subheads and determine where to place them in your document. Following the writing process described in Chapter 2, first map out what you want to say. By carefully outlining your work and then revising it, you can determine how many sections you will need and what kinds of information each should contain. In your final copy, every major section will require a head; and each subdivision will use a subhead. Look at the "Table of Contents" section (page 601) and Figure 15.3 (page 608) to see how the writer logically divided her work.

How to Format Heads and Subheads

To design a document with logical heads and subheads, follow these guidelines.

1. Insert white space between the sections to make room for the head. Leave at least two additional spaces above and below a head to set it off from a previous section.
2. Use consistent typeface for headings and subheadings. Be consistent in the way you key each type of head—that is, center each head or align it flush with the left margin.
3. Use larger type size for heads and subheads than for text; major heads should be larger than subheads. If your text is in 10-point type, your heads may be in 16-point type and your subheads in 12- or 14-point type.
4. To further differentiate heads from subheads, use all capital letters, initial capital letters (capitalize the first letter of each important word), boldface, italics, or different colors (see "Guidelines on Using Color Effectively," page 459).

Note how the long reports in Figures 8.10 (pages 349–363) and 15.3 (pages 607–621) incorporate heads and subheads to divide and highlight information.

How to Keep Heads and Subheads Grammatically Parallel

Heads and subheads should parallel each other grammatically. Note how the following headings, from a poorly organized proposal from the Acme Company, are not parallel:

- What Is the Problem?
- Describing What Acme Can Do to Solve the Problem
- It's a Matter of Time. . . .
- Fees Acme Will Charge
- When You Need to Pay
- Finding Out Who's Who

Revised, the heads are parallel and easier for readers to understand and follow:

- A Brief History of the Problem
- A Description of Acme's Solutions
- A Timetable Acme Can Follow
- A Breakdown of Acme's Fees
- A Payment Plan
- A Listing of Acme's Staff

Grammatically parallel heads are easier to follow and further demonstrate that you have logically structured your document.

How to Make Heads Functional

Heads not only alert readers to major sections of your work, but they also summarize what readers will find in each section. To make sure your heads and subheads are functional, follow these three guidelines:

1. Keep your heads and subheads concise, but avoid using vague, one-word titles such as "Conditions." Readers will not know if you are referring to the weather, financial markets, or the terms of an agreement.
2. Don't overuse heads; having too many heads is as bad as having too few (e.g., don't start each paragraph with a head or subhead). Note how even in a short document such as Figure 11.2, several heads help readers better follow the discussion about watching their cholesterol.
3. Make sure each of your heads and subheads matches the divisions and subdivisions, as well as page references, found in your table of contents (see "Table of Contents," page 601).

Lists

Placing items in a list helps readers by dividing, organizing, and ranking information. Lists emphasize important points and make your page easy to read. Lists can also be numbered (as in Figure 11.2), lettered, or bulleted. Take a look at Figures 6.16 (page 223), 13.5 (pages 530–534), and 15.3 (pages 607–621), which effectively use lists.

Captions

Captions are titles that can be found either above or below figures and help readers identify or explain a visual, a photograph, or other graphic. Captions also can provide information about the source or copyright holder for an image. (Chapter 10 discusses using captions with visuals in a document.)

Graphics

The following list identifies some common graphics elements used when designing documents. (Use of specific visuals in documents is covered in Chapter 10; see pages 400–447.)

1. **Boxes.** Boxes isolate or highlight text or visuals. Figure 11.3 (page 455) is enclosed within a box to help set its content apart from the text around it.
2. **Rules.** Rules are classified as either vertical or horizontal. Vertical rules might be used to separate columns of text, while horizontal rules might separate sections introduced by subheads.
3. **Letterhead and logo.** A company's corporate image is represented and symbolized by its letterhead, usually consisting of a graphic, or icon, integrated with the company name. Notice the variety of letterheads and logos used in letters in Chapters 5 and 6, especially Figures 5.7 (page 170) and 6.12 (page 214). Often

the company's street address, email address, website, and social media URLs are part of the letterhead. Company letterhead conveys the firm's message and symbolizes its mission statement and goals. Typically, logos and sometimes the entire letterhead are imported as graphics files. Letterhead and logos should creatively set one company apart from others.

Using Color

Using other types of color: shading, highlighting, background color in workplace documents is a good way to enhance readability, break up long segments of text, contrast sections/images, and tie important ideas together. Tastefully done, color can help sell ideas more effectively than black and white alone. You can use color for borders and graphic accents, headings, titles, and keywords. Addresses, sidebars, rules, and boxes that link related facts, figures, or information in websites are often in color. But first determine if using color serves a functional purpose, as in Figure 11.2, or if it is merely a decoration. If it is window-dressing, stick with black and white.

Guidelines on Using Color Effectively

Here are some guidelines to follow when you use color in your documents or websites:

- Estimate how the color will look on the page—colors look different on the screen than they do on a sheet of paper. Print a sample page to get a clear idea.
- Make sure text colors contrast sharply with background colors in both print and web-based documents.
- Use no more than two or three colors on a page or screen unless there are photographs, illustrations, or graphics. Too many colors are confusing and can clutter your message.
- Too many bright colors overwhelm the eye, so use them sparingly—only to call attention to important elements.
- Select "cool" colors, such as blue, turquoise, purple, and magenta, for backgrounds. However, avoid light blue text, which is hard to read against a dark background, or yellow text on a light blue background.
- Use colors that respect an international reader's cultural heritage. (See "Guidelines for Using Visuals for International Audiences," pages 439–441).

DESKTOP PUBLISHING

Desktop publishing programs, sometimes referred to as **page layout software**, provide an inexpensive alternative to a professional print shop. Because desktop publishing software permits users to design page layouts, include visuals, and produce high-quality final copies, you can create printed documents right in your own home or office.

With desktop publishing you can

- select from templates specifically designed for reports, newsletters, brochures, and other formats
- design your own templates if you create similar documents often

- take advantage of numerous font choices, type sizes, and styles (such as bold-face, italics, and underlining).
- delete, insert, and move entire blocks of text
- justify margins
- change line spacing
- center words, titles, or lines of text
- break and number pages
- arrange text in multiple columns
- insert sidebars, tables, footnotes, headers, footers, and sidebar quotes
- create graphics, such as illustrations, charts, and graphs that you have created using the drawing tools of your software program.
- import graphics such as drawings, photographs, icons, and logos

Study the advice given in the Case Study (see page 462) by a publications manager who designs her company's newsletter

Type

While Times New Roman and Arial are preferred in the world of work, there are many different styles of type (see "Typography," pages 454–456). All computers equipped with software that contains a large number of typefaces. Additionally, thousands of high-quality fonts are available over the Internet at such sites as http://1001freefonts.com and www.fonts.com.

Templates

Desktop publishing software sometimes includes predesigned templates. Templates, like those shown in Figure 11.4, are page layout patterns for reports, newsletters, brochures, and other marketing and communications documents. A template for a report, for example, would contain all the headings and divisions you need. You can also create and save your own template for an original format you use frequently.

Graphics

Like other visuals, graphics work in conjunction with your words. A document without visuals or graphics may look boring, confusing, or unattractive. You will have to judge how and when a graphic can improve your message and help you convince your reader. (For more on creating effective visuals, see Chapter 10, pages 400–447.)

A graphics program allows you to draw shapes and lines that can be manipulated (skewed, enlarged) and offers options for sophisticated use of color and shading. With a drawing program, you can create diagrams, charts, and illustrations that can be saved and imported into word-processing or desktop publishing documents.

You can move and place graphics anywhere in a document. Graphic design programs provide customized graphs, charts, tables, and expanded font sizes and shapes.

FIGURE 11.4 Examples of Templates

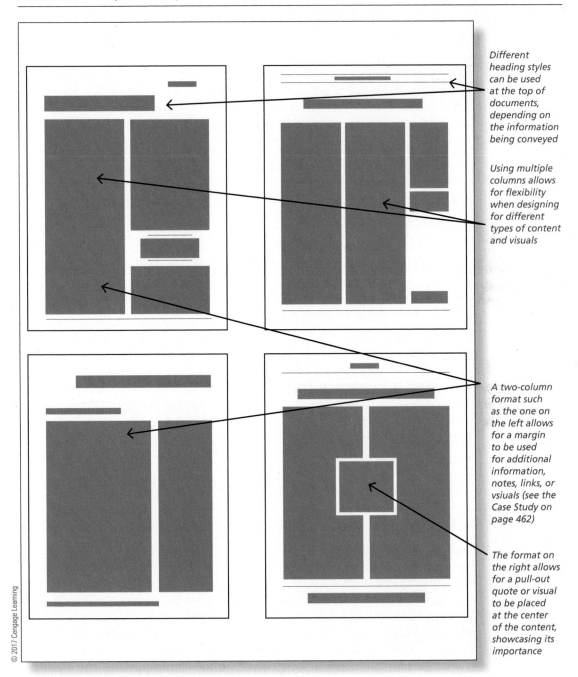

Different heading styles can be used at the top of documents, depending on the information being conveyed

Using multiple columns allows for flexibility when designing for different types of content and visuals

A two-column format such as the one on the left allows for a margin to be used for additional information, notes, links, or vsiuals (see the Case Study on page 462)

The format on the right allows for a pull-out quote or visual to be placed at the center of the content, showcasing its importance

© 2017 Cengage Learning

CASE STUDY

Designing a Company Newsletter: Advice from a Pro

My name is Jameka Harris, the publications manager at Mellon IT, a firm that has a strong commitment to designing professional-looking documents. I oversee the publication of the company's monthly newsletter, available in a variety of formats—electronically, posted on our website, and printed in a limited number of hard copies to save paper and reduce costs. I make sure that the text is readable and the visuals are crisp, clear, and relevant.

Doing the Layout for Each Issue

The first thing I do is to plan the way each issue will look—that is, the layout of both text and graphics. I use a template with a two-column vertical grid (see Figure 11.4, page 461) on each page. Into the grid I fit three or four stories as well as our regular features, including

- a question-and-answer section
- a staff profile
- a calendar
- a boxed insert with a safety tip

I have to calculate how much space to give each of these items so that the newsletter look balanced, uncrowded, and aligned.

Sequencing Each Issue

The most important story is inserted in the left column, where readers often start looking at the issue. I make sure each story is in the same typeface (font) and type size. The title is in a boldface color type to stand out, followed by a byline in small caps. If a story is continued on another page, a "jumpline" in italics tells readers where, and, of course, I must save room for it on the continuing page.

Using Space

But I do more than fit text into the available space. I also have to fit space in and around each story or feature. Double-spacing between paragraphs gives our newsletter an uncrowded look. I leave 3 picas of space between columns on a page so that the text in one column does not crash text or graphics in the other column. I also leave room for a header, which carries the page number and the title of the newsletter, and for a generous footer, or bottom margin, to frame the contents.

Using Visuals and Color

Every visual needs to relate to the right story or feature, be clear, and be properly sized. While a visual too big dwarfs a story, one that is too small is hard to read. But if a reader's browser does not have the right plug-in installed, he or she will see "Image cannot be displayed." To avoid this, I translate text and graphics into HTML and plain text. In photo captions, I always verify the names of individuals in the photo to identify them for our readers. I leave plenty of space around each photo and other visuals to set them apart from the text.

Like visuals, color can make or break a newsletter. Color has to be tasteful, improve readability, be functional, not used just for decoration. The question-and-answer section, for instance, carries a blue banner, while the safety tip is aptly framed in red.

Design thus works in conjunction with the overall message of our newsletter.

Here are some types of graphic tools available to you:

1. Drawing tools. Desktop publishing programs allow you to create a variety of shapes, rules, borders, and arrows. Having drawn a shape, you can use other tools to fill in or alter the appearance of the shape or to add words to it. You can also arrange all the elements into a graphic that communicates quickly and effectively.

2. Icons. Icons are symbols or visual representations of concepts or actions. The skull and crossbones on a container of poison is an icon that warns of danger (see "Cautions," page 498). **Graphic icons** are simply pictures that communicate directly. Using a combination of image and color (see "Guidelines on Using Color Effectively," page 459), they tell us at a glance which restroom to use or how to fasten the seat belt in an airplane. Examples of public service information icons are shown below:

  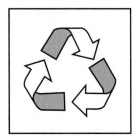

3. Clip art. Clip art is a type of simple drawing, often classified by themes, that can be imported to your document. (See "Clip Art," pages 430–431.) Some clip art packages and websites offer tens of thousands of images, arranged into such diverse categories as animals, computers, holidays, famous people, food, and various businesses and technologies. Clip art is widely used to make business documents attractive and appealing.

4. Stock photos and art. Stock photos and art can be imported for use in your documents or on your website. Popular low-cost stock image websites are istockphoto.com and shutterstock.com.

BEFORE CHOOSING A DESIGN

Before you begin designing a document, you need to know exactly what you are designing, for whom, and how. Note that planning is the first thing the publications manager does in the Case Study on page 462. Think carefully about how your work will look on the page, what you want to achieve, and what your resources are. Always get your plans approved by your boss or the publications committee. Here are questions to ask:

1. Who is your target audience? Will your readers be local residents or global consumers? What do they have in common—gender, location, educational level? You must consider how to reach and appeal to this group before you decide on a

"look and feel" for your document. Print size, style, and so forth should be selected based on the audience's characteristics and needs.

2. What is the purpose of your document? Will you have to motivate readers to look at it? Use an eye-catching cover page, attractive colors, and short paragraphs. Or is your document required reading for co-workers and therefore subject to "house style"? Are you designing a newsletter for a professional group? If so, must you comply with a set of guidelines about how, for example, your newsletter should be laid out?

3. How will your document be reproduced? Will it be set by a professional printer, posted on the company website, or is it a document that can be printed out and distributed? This will affect the number and type of colors you use, the layout of the document, and the type and size of paper you select.

4. How will it be distributed? Will it fit in a standard size envelope? Will it need to be folded more than once? Do you need larger envelopes or a smaller page size? Or will the document be posted or distributed electronically?

5. How much will it cost? Financial decisions are crucial in making design choices. Color printing can be more expensive than standard black-and-white printing. If you use color, try to stick to one or two colors throughout to keep the costs down. Talk to your boss about the costs of reproduction before you decide on anything.

WRITING FOR AND DESIGNING WEBSITES*

In the global marketplace, you need to apply the skills you have just learned in designing documents and visuals to an online environment (websites, blogs, etc.). In fact, companies often ask their employees to write for and prepare visuals for a corporate website, and while you may not be expected to construct a website on your own, you will likely be part of a team of specialists in information technology, graphics, and marketing responsible for your firm's web presence. To be a helpful member of this team, you have to keep up with the latest features of website design and information on how your company can incorporate them. You may also be asked to critique a competitor's website or to assist a client in preparing his/her website. This section of Chapter 11 stresses the principles and guidelines you need to follow to

- help readers navigate your website quickly, moving from one part to another easily
- ensure that your site is current
- make your site user friendly (for global readers as well as English-speaking audiences)
- create a visually attractive site
- keep your design and content ethical

---

*I am grateful to Father Michael Tracey, of Bay St. Louis, Mississippi, for his invaluable advice on designing websites.

Web Versus Print Readers

To help design and write for the web, you need to recognize how webpages are read differently from the way print documents are.

1. Readers do not generally go through a website word for word hunting for information, carefully studying each sentence. They want to find information at a glance. On the average, web readers spend ten to eighty seconds scanning a page. If they don't find what they need, they'll click to another site.

2. Web readers want articles, news stories, and features to be more condensed, and more strategically arranged. They want only essential information.

CASE STUDY

Differences between Print Document Organization and Website Organization

The organization of a print document differs greatly from the organization of a website. To illustrate this difference, look again at the article in Figure 9.2, "Virtual Reality: Essential in Law Enforcement Training" (pages 377–381). The article has eleven sections presented in the following order:

1. Traditional Training Limitations
2. Training with Virtual Reality
3. How Does Virtual Reality Work?
4. Uses for Virtual Reality
5. Law Enforcement Training
6. Pursuit Driving
7. Firearms Training
8. High-Risk Incident Management
9. Incident Re-creation
10. Crime Scene Processing
11. Is Virtual Reality Virtually Perfect?

This is not how information looks on the Web or how it is processed by Web readers. A print document is usually read sequentially, page for page, whereas information on a website can be "navigated" using the search function or hyperlinks or both. This allows readers to customize their experience and focus on specific information. When an article like that in Figure 9.2 appears online, it has to be organized like a web-based document, as in Figure 11.5.

When determining the best way to present the article online, you should first create a storyboard to decide how and what information is to be presented (see "Creating Storyboards for Websites and Other Documents," pages 473–474), including a home page with a URL address, an eye-catching but professional image or photo, and navigational tools such as menus and hyperlinks. You might want to start the article on your home page and provide a "More" link to guide readers into your site.

You could convert each of the eleven headings from the print article into hyperlinks, grouped under a navigation bar on the left side of the screen (as in Figure 11.5). Instead of turning pages, readers will click on the hyperlinks to jump to any section of the website.

To allow visitors to comment on the site, you will need to provide a comment form or an email address for readers to send in their responses. You will also want to provide a link for contact information, so that interested readers can get in touch by mail, phone, or email.

(Continued)

FIGURE 11.5 The Home Page for a Website Based on the Virtual Reality Article in Figure 9.2

General information about the website, contact information, and search functionality are set in the top navigational bar

Hyperlinks allow for easy navigation

Uses appropriate visual to catch reader's attention

Short chunk of text designed to guide reading

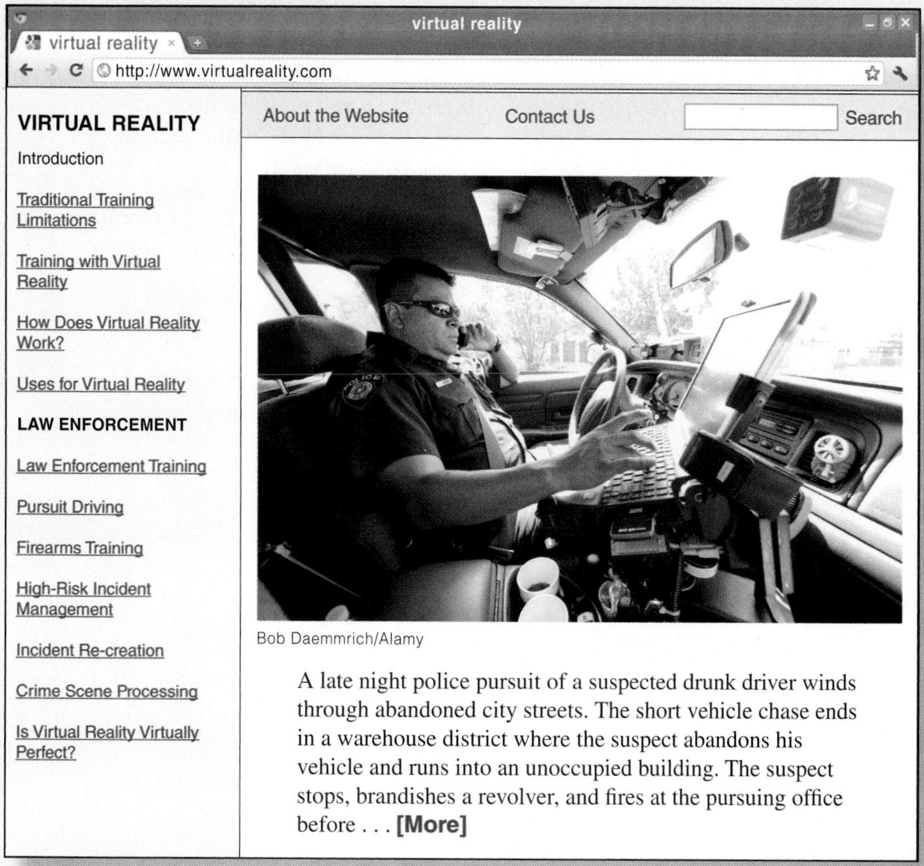

virtual reality

virtual reality ×

← → C http://www.virtualreality.com

VIRTUAL REALITY

Introduction

Traditional Training Limitations

Training with Virtual Reality

How Does Virtual Reality Work?

Uses for Virtual Reality

LAW ENFORCEMENT

Law Enforcement Training

Pursuit Driving

Firearms Training

High-Risk Incident Management

Incident Re-creation

Crime Scene Processing

Is Virtual Reality Virtually Perfect?

About the Website   Contact Us   Search

Bob Daemmrich/Alamy

A late night police pursuit of a suspected drunk driver winds through abandoned city streets. The short vehicle chase ends in a warehouse district where the suspect abandons his vehicle and runs into an unoccupied building. The suspect stops, brandishes a revolver, and fires at the pursuing office before . . . **[More]**

© 2017 Cengage Learning

3. A web audience will not necessarily read your entire website. Because they may not have even begun their search at your site, your web audience may not navigate through your pages in any predetermined order, or even read all of its parts.

4. Web readers will expect navigational cues that readers of a print source do not have. A web audience will be looking for visual markers such as highlighted keywords to click on or bulleted lists, different colored text, commands such as *search, click here, go to, go back, contact us,* arrows and crosses, or hyperlinks of other sites to visit. Note how these cues are incorporated into the website in Figure 11.6.

FIGURE 11.6 A Well-Designed Home Page

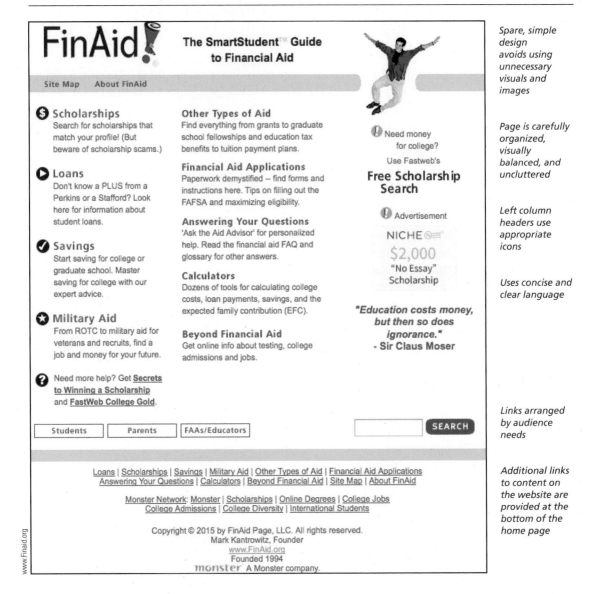

Preparing a Successful Home Page

Successful home pages need to catch a visitor's attention and sell a product or service, and/or introduce your organization clearly and effectively. For example, students applying for financial aid can find it a daunting process, but the design of the FinAid home page, Figure 11.6 helps to keep the research process upbeat

and easy to follow. Even the image of the student "jumping for joy" contributes to the site's user-friendliness. The writing style and tone, for example, are also appropriately conversational, friendly, and helpful—"Find everything from grants to . . . tuition payment plans"; "Beware scholarship scams." The FinAid home page also provides clear links to the other related websites. Similarly, the CDC home page in Figure 11.7 uses appropriate images for the "Health & Safety Topics"—an airplane for "Travelers' Health" and a pictograph of a family for "Life Stages & Populations."

Designing and Writing for the Web: Eight Guidelines

By adhering to the following eight guidelines, you can create an effectively designed and written website that will capture your audience's attention.

1. **Make your site easy to find.**

   - Choose a professional domain name that clearly and quickly tells readers what you do. Avoid cute spellings and fanciful names, e.g., happihouse.com. Instead, use a clear, easy-to-remember name, e.g., toledohousepainters.com. A good place to start is the InterNIC website (www.internic.net) which provides updated information on domain name registrations.
   - To optimize your chances of being listed by search engines, use keywords that sell your business or organization. Use Google's AdWords' Keyword Tool (https://adwords.google.com/KeywordPlanner) for help in choosing terms that will increase traffic to your site. The website featured in Figure 11.6, for example, uses dozens of keywords (including ones such as student aid, student financial aid, student loans, federal student aid, and college financial aid) to improve the possibility the site will be listed by search engines. Make sure you cross-link to relevant pages on your website as well.

2. **Make your site easy to navigate.**

   - Help your visitors find their way easily through your site with logical and effective navigation tools such as

hyperlinks	search engines
navigation bars	button links
indexes and menus	rollover icons
site maps and tables of contents	previous, next, and back links

     Provide multiple navigation aids such as clearly labeled sections, each illustrated with icons, and links to multimedia and tools, as in Figures 11.6 and 11.7.

   - The main navigation menu needs to be absolutely consistent on every page of your website so users don't get lost.
   - Test every link to make sure it is current, that it works, and that it connects to related sites.

FIGURE 11.7 The CDC Home Page with Examples of Navigational Links

Provides means to search site

Animated banner changes to highlight 5 different stories

Uses appropriate icons

Easy to navigate because of images and menus

White space ensures page does not look crowded

Writing is concise, clear, easy to understand

Courtesy of the CDC.

- Don't overload your page with images, making it look crowded. Note how the FinAid website in Figure 11.6 uses a single image, five smaller icons, and boxes at the bottom left of the home page to help readers.
- Don't have your website to autoplay videos or make any noise at all without the user's permission. This is a mistake that amateurs make, and it will alienate potential customers who may be browsing the site at work, on a bus or train, or in a crowded environment.

3. **Make your site informative.**

- Provide essential information on your home page, including your company's name, address, email, phone number, and links to social media sites and your corporate blog. The more helpful your site is, the more likely it will draw repeat visitors.
- Tell visitors what products or services you offer. Figure 11.6 offers tailor-made services (such as "Calculators") to students, parents, and educators.
- Indicate what type of information can be obtained through your website, including links to your customer service and technical support. The FinAid website in Figure 11.6 provides information quickly on scholarships, savings, military aid, and more.
- Offer readers different types of interaction—FAQs, bulletin boards, animated product demonstrations, and free email subscriptions. For example, the FinAid site offers a "Free Scholarship Search" (see Figure 11.6).

4. **Make your site easy to read for both native English speakers and international readers.**

- Not only does the writing need to be concise, but lines of text should contain no more than twelve to fifteen words, as it's much harder to read long lines on a computer screen than it is in print since you don't have your hands to guide you. Avoid squeezing lots of text, clip art, and images onto a webpage.
- Put the most important point first in a seven- to eight-word headline (e.g., "The SmartStudent^{TM} Guide to Financial Aid").
- Write short descriptions of content—no more than three to four lines, as in the FinAid site in Figure 11.6.
- Provide headings with attention-grabbing keywords, bulleted lists, and numbered lists to help readers locate information quickly, (e.g., Scholarships, Loans, Military).
- Include plenty of white space between sections.
- Insert scannable terms and hyperlinks (such as the buttons or text underlined and in blue in Figure 11.6).
- Select fonts that are easy to read (see "Typography," pages 454–456). The more different fonts you use, the more unprofessional your site will look. Choose one or two standard fonts and stick with them throughout the site. Ditto with text color and font sizes.
- Select background colors that make your text easy to read. For example, don't use dark green lettering on a black background.

5. **Keep your site updated.**

- New information is vital for selling your product or service on a company website. Feature a blog, updates about your business, or preproduction information on products, services, community projects, and environmental efforts. Build in hyperlinks to product reviews, conferences, awards, and so on.
- Broken links are a complete disaster for a business, because users will feel if the business is not professional enough to keep its website in working order,

what guarantee do they have that the product will work well and be delivered on time? There are free link-checkers online that you can use to go through your site line by line to make sure all links are working.

- Revise the design of your home page if your company offers a new product or service or a new promotion. A revised home page alerts customers to the latest products and services.
- Indicate when your site was last updated so readers will know your information is kept current.

6. **Use images and icons effectively.**

- Arrange images and photos so they do not interfere with text.
- Choose appropriate icons or images to illustrate menus and page sections. Figure 11.6 uses easy-to-recognize icons for money and military assistance.
- Be careful of putting things on your website that will take a long time to load, like huge, high-resolution images, fancy fonts, animations, or video backgrounds. Users lose patience quickly and may move on to another site before your home page is even done loading.
- Keep images proportional so that they are neither too big nor too small for the page.

TECH NOTE

Website Accessibility

The Americans with Disabilities Act (ADA) (see http://www.ada.gov/2010_regs.htm) and Section 508 of the Rehabilitation Act (see http://www.section508.gov/section508 -laws) ensure equal access online for individuals with disabilities who are blind or have low vision and use screen readers (a type of assistive technology which "verbalizes" text). It also applies to deaf or hard of hearing individuals (who thus may need other types of assistive technologies).

Making sure your website is accessible to customers, clients, fellow employees, and the general public who may have disabilities should be a top priority when planning website design and implementation. Making your website accessible enables all users to learn about your company's website, regardless of their different needs, connection speeds, platforms, or technological set-ups.

The website Web Content Accessibility Guidelines (WCAG) (http://www.w3.org /WAI/intro/wcag) provides extensive information on how to make your website accessible. There are also accessibility checkers available online that can be used, such as the IDI Web Accessibility Checker (http://achecker.ca/) and the WAVE Web Accessibility Tool (http://wave.webaim.org/). But here are just a few general guidelines you can to follow:

- **Keyboard access.** Since some users are unable to operate a mouse or a track pad, accessible websites should allow these readers to navigate using only a keyboard.

(Continued)

- **Background/foreground colors.** Make sure there is ample contrast between the two on your website (see "Using Color," page 459) to help those with visual impairments.
- **Document format.** "Text only" is the most accessible format for documents online, allowing for easy use by screen readers. This format can be used in both Word and Google Doc documents.
- **PDF's should be "tagged" for access.** Tags allow screen readers to read text accurately and help individuals who are blind or have low vision to access content that would otherwise be inaccessible. Tagging needs to include not only text but headings, tables, and captions for images as well.
- **Captions.** Any videos or audio files posted on websites should be captioned. Where necessary, provide printed transcripts of any audio or video content.
- **Alternative text for images.** Any images (photos, graphs, figures) on a website should also include text descriptions.

7. **Encourage visitor interaction by soliciting feedback.**

   - Ask readers to email or contact you on social media about your product, service, or website. Make sure a procedure for handling that feedback is developed within your organization.
   - Include a feedback form or survey with specifically targeted questions — including multiple-choice, pull-down menus, and comment boxes — about your website to encourage visitors to leave useful comments, such as the "eCards" section in Figure 11.7. (See "Surveys," pages 313–319.)

8. **Make sure your website is ethical.**

   - Never post confidential or proprietary information.
   - Never post anything insulting or harassing, and never attack a competitor, a colleague, another department in your company, or a government agency.
   - Do not plagiarize from another web (or print) source. Just because images are freely available on another site doesn't mean you can use them on your own website. If you don't have original images that you created, you will need to purchase licenses to use images from stock photo sites like Shutterstock, iStockphoto, dreamstime, or 123rf. If you include any information from another site — including quotations, visuals, or statistics — obtain permission, and acknowledge the source on your site.
   - Do not use sexist, racist, or other biased forms of language. Moreover, do not offend an international audience by using terms, names, or visuals that are insulting, stereotypical, or condescending. (See "Using Appropriate Visuals for International Audiences," pages 438–441.)
   - Never make false or exaggerated claims. Be honest and accurate. Earn your readers' and employer's trust.

Website Design Templates

While professional website designers might use powerful commercial software like Adobe Dreamweaver, Microsoft FrontPage, or NetObjects Fusion to create a company's website, there are several online, template-based website design programs available for those who are not designers or who are without any specialized software knowledge. Such template-based programs, including Weebly, Wix, Squarespace, and WordPress (among others), come with customizable designs and are organized to help users navigate through them. Most importantly, perhaps, website design templates allow you to just focus on the content and not have to worry about HTML coding, functionality, or navigation.

CREATING STORYBOARDS FOR WEBSITES AND OTHER DOCUMENTS

To help you plan the design of a website or a print document such as a brochure, newsletter, or even a handbook, you may find it useful to create a storyboard. The concept of **storyboarding** originated in the film industry as a way for directors to visualize scenes in their films before actually shooting them. Figure 11.8 (page 474) illustrates successive versions of a storyboard for the home page of a website.

Acting as a map to your site or as a preliminary layout of a document, a storyboard gives you a clearer idea about the structure and navigation of each page of your website or document, and it allows you to plan the interplay between text and visuals. Like a draft of a report or proposal, your storyboard will become fuller the more you revise it—adding, moving, and linking content and graphics.

Here are some guidelines for effective storyboarding:

1. **Map out the site or document pages.** Label them according to various pages of the site or sections of the document, for example, Home Page, About Our Company, Contact Us, Place an Order.

2. **Plan the layout of each page.** Consider what content each page must have and how that information can be signaled through graphics and typography. For instance, a home page should include your company's logo, a brief introduction to or history of the company, and information about the goods or services it offers.

3. **Determine basic design elements.** Decide which fonts, backgrounds, and frames will look professional and appealing to customers. Then decide on size and height and where to place columns, images, sidebars, or highlighted areas.

FIGURE 11.8 Successive Versions of a Storyboard for a Home Page

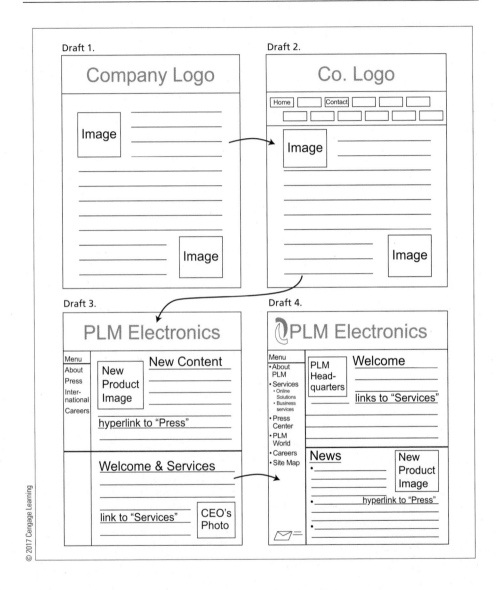

© 2017 Cengage Learning

4. Build in navigational aids. Make searching your website quick and effective. Always include hyperlinks to an email form so that readers can contact you. Ensure that your website is easy to navigate by using a clear, concise menu for each of the separate areas of your website, and make sure that every page links back to your home page. For brochures or other documents, make sure you insert clear and concise headings and subheadings, and provide contact information.

FOUR RULES OF EFFECTIVE PAGE DESIGN: A WRAP-UP

The following four rules summarize the basic principles of effective document and Web design. If you adhere to them, your work, online or in print, will be professional looking.

1. Keep it straightforward. Do not overuse graphic effects and type fonts in an effort to impress your audience; keep it straightforward so that you do not lose sight of the purpose of the document or website by using an over-the-top design.

2. Be consistent. Use your layout and design elements consistently throughout your document and website. Repeat your design elements on each page, including fonts, text alignment, colors, borders, and headings.

3. Make it clear. Make your message easy to read. Fancy designs may look good, but they do not always add to the clarity of your document or website.

4. Remember that less is more. Limit the number of items on your page. An item can be a paragraph of text or a picture, as long as it provides a focal point on the page. Too much information on a Web or document page can make it difficult to digest, and in the process information can be lost in the clutter.

✔ REVISION CHECKLIST

Printed Documents

- [ ] Arranged information in the most logical, easy-to-grasp order.
- [ ] Included only relevant visuals—clip art, icons, stock photos.
- [ ] Left adequate, eye-pleasing white space in text and margins to frame document.
- [ ] Maintained pleasing, easy-to-read line length and spacing.
- [ ] Chose appropriate typeface for message and document and did not mix typefaces.
- [ ] Used effective type size, neither too small (under 10 point) nor too large (over 12 point), for body of text.
- [ ] Incorporated appropriate visual cues (for example, italics or boldface) for readers.
- [ ] Inserted heads and subheads to organize information for the reader.
- [ ] Used lists, bullets, and numbers to divide information.
- [ ] Chose colors to make sure they look professional, contrast with background, and are appropriate for international readers.
- [ ] Learned features of desktop publishing program.

Websites

- [ ] Planned location of text and visuals with a storyboard.
- [ ] Designed website so that it is easy to find on major search engines.

(Continued)

☐ Made sure navigation is clear and logical, not overly complex.

☐ Identified all pages either with headings or with text that explains the purpose of each page.

☐ Ensured that the site is informative and relevant and that the content is current.

☐ Kept the site current by revising it frequently and including the most recent research.

☐ Used headings, subheadings, and white space to break information into readable chunks.

☐ Encouraged visitor interaction by soliciting feedback.

☐ Provided ways for reader to interact with the site, whether via email, a feedback page, social media, or a blog where comments can be posted.

☐ Did not crowd images and text on the same page.

☐ Chose appropriate background colors so text is clear and easy to read.

☐ Strove to make sure the site is ethical.

EXERCISES

1. Find an ineffectively designed print document—a form, a set of instructions, a brochure, a section of a manual, a catalog, a newsletter—and assume that you are a document design consultant. Write a sales letter (see "Sales Letters," pages 192–198) to the company or agency that prepared and distributed the document, offering to redesign it and any other documents they have. Stress your qualifications, and include a sample of your work. You will have to be convincing and diplomatic; precisely and professionally persuade your readers that they need your services to improve their corporate image, customer relations, and sales or services.

2. Provide two or three poorly designed print documents or websites. Working with a team of three or four students, determine which of the documents and/or websites the group provided is the hardest to follow, the most unappealing, and the least logically arranged. After selecting that document or website, collaboratively write a memo to your instructor on what is wrong with the design and what you would do to improve its appearance and organization.

3. As a group, redesign the document or website your group selected for Exercise 2. (Reformat it; add headings, spacing, and visual clues; include relevant visuals; and so on.) Submit both the original and the redesigned document or website to your instructor.

4. Redesign the document in Figure 11.9 to make it conform to the guidelines specified in this chapter.

5. Redesign the document in Figure 11.10 to make it conform to the guidelines specified in this chapter. Reformat it; add headings, spacing, and visual clues; and provide a short introduction.

FIGURE 11.9 The "Before" Document for Exercise 4

7

TTI's in the loop on effective detector placement

Ever sit in bumper-to-bumper traffic and wish they'd widen the roads so people could get through more quickly? Well, that costs a lot of money. Which is why transportation engineers who deal with traffic congestion and the problems it causes look for more cost-effective alternatives to get you where you're going—and faster.

TTI researchers recently completed a TxDOT/FHWA-sponsored study entitled *Effective Detector Placement for Computerized Traffic Management.* The research sought to expand and improve the use of inductance loop detectors (ILDs) to complement traffic signals, signal systems and other advanced traffic management systems. This is a cheaper congestion solution than building or widening a road.

An ILD is an electrical circuit containing a loop of copper wire embedded in the pavement. As a vehicle passes over the wire loop, it takes energy from the loop. If that change is large enough, a detection is recorded. Thus, we are able to collect data on the movement or presence of vehicles on the roadway. Advanced traffic management systems operate best with accurate information on how many vehicles are present and how fast they are traveling.

The primary goal of the recent project was to use loop detectors as an integral part of the congestion-reduction system. Traditional problems with ILDs were addressed—like crosstalk, or interference between two adjacent loops—and innovative new applications for ILDs in advanced traffic systems—like detecting wrong-way HOV-lane movements.

Other applications include using ILDs to move traffic more

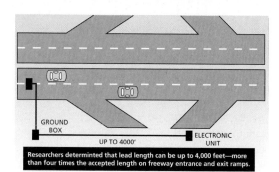

Researchers determinted that lead length can be up to 4,000 feet—more than four times the accepted length on freeway entrance and exit ramps.

GROUND BOX — UP TO 4000' — ELECTRONIC UNIT

efficiently at diamond interchanges, at high-volume, high-speed approaches and on the freeway entrance ramps. The long-range contribution of the study is a set of guidelines for using ILDs in the situations listed above. As freeway management systems continue to evolve, the guidelines developed through the nine study reports will provide designers with practical information on the most effective placement of ILDs.

A major finding of the research deals with lead length, or the length of wire necessary to connect the loop to the detector electronic unit. The study showed that the loop can be placed more than 4,000 feet from the point of control—four times the currently accepted distance. This information will give traffic designers much more flexibility when integrating ILDs into their traffic system designs.

The researchers also made some important discoveries about using ILDs to measure speed. They found that the best speed trap is nine meters (two loops interconnected

with a timing device and spaced nine meters apart). They also determined that to get reasonably accurate and consistent speeds with an ILD, some things must be the same between a pair of loops: make, type or model of the detector units, sensitivity settings and loop configuration.

The findings from this research facilitate the use of loop detectors in managing traffic. And better management of driver frustration— just as important, even if less measurable than the congestion that causes it—is bound to follow.

Ultimately the three watchwords for this project were optimization, innovation, and implementation. Taking the tried-and-true and finding a better way to use it is, after all, the underlying building block for all engineering endeavors.

To order TTI Research Report 1392-9F, see the back page order form of this issue. For more information on loop detectors, contact Don Woods, 409/845-5792, FAX 409/845-6481 (E-mail: d-woods@tamu.edu).

Source: Texas Transportation Institute's Researcher; article author, Chris Pourteau. Reprinted with permission of the Texas Transportation Institute.

FIGURE 11.10 A Poorly Designed Document for Exercise 5

WHY SHOULD YOU WASH YOUR HANDS?
Bacteria and viruses (germs) that cause illnesses are spread when you don't wash your hands.
If you don't wash your hands, you risk acquiring:
The common cold or flu
Gastrointestinal illnesses Shigella or hepatitis A
Respiratory illnesses
Should you wash your hands?
You need to wash your hands several times every day. Some important times to wash your hands are:
BEFORE
Preparing or eating food.
Treating a cut wound.
Tending to someone who is sick.
Inserting or removing contacts.
After
Using the bathroom.
Changing a diaper or helping a child use the bathroom (don't forget the child's hands)
Handling raw meats/poultry/eggs
Touching pets, especially reptiles
handling garbage
Sneezing or blowing your nose, or helping a child blow his/her nose
Touching any body fluids like blood or mucus
Being in contact with a sick person
Playing outside or with children and their toys
WHEN SHOULD YOU WASH YOUR HANDS?
There is a right way to wash your hands.
Follow these steps and you will help protect yourself and your family from illness.
Like any good habit, proper hand washing must be taught.
Take the time to teach it to your children and make sure they practice.

© 2017 Cengage Learning

6. The home page of Stanley's Accounting Temps in Figure 11.11 violates the guidelines for web designs given in this chapter. Write a one-page memo to your instructor specifying how Stanley's Accounting Temps might better address its online customers. Group your recommendations under the headings of content, design, and navigation. As a supporting document for your memo, design a new home page for the company by creating a storyboard for it.

7. Locate two websites that advertise a similar product, service, or industry. Analyze some of the webpage elements each one uses, comparing the strengths and weaknesses of each site. Write a one-page memo to your instructor explaining which is the more effective site and why.

FIGURE 11.11 A Poorly Designed Home Page for Exercise 6

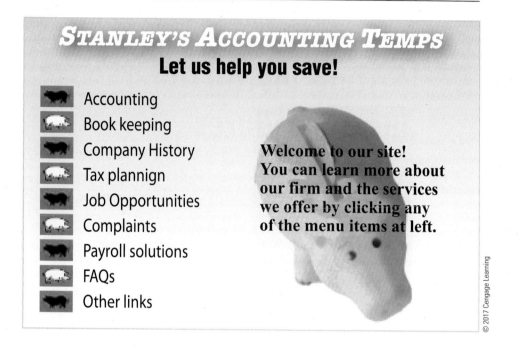

8. Find a website that you believe is ineffective. Using "The Four Keys to Effective Writing" (pages 11–20), as well as your knowledge of webpage elements, write a one-page assessment of the site, discussing three or four changes you think would make it more effective. Attach a printed hard copy of the website's home page with your assessment.

CHAPTER

12

Writing Instructions and Procedures

Clear and accurate instructions and procedures are essential to the world of work. Instructions tell—and frequently show—how to do something: perform a specific task (draw blood; install new software); operate a machine (a pH meter); construct, install, maintain, monitor, adjust, or repair equipment (an incubator; a scanner).

While the purpose of writing **instructions** is to explain how to perform a task in a step-by-step manner, the purpose of writing procedures is slightly different. Often the two terms are incorrectly used interchangeably. **Procedures** refers to policies, duties, protocols, and guidelines that a business or organization expects its employees to follow.

INSTRUCTIONS, PROCEDURES, AND YOUR JOB

As part of your job, you may be asked to write instructions and procedures, alone or with a group, for your co-workers or for your customers who use your company's services or products. Your employer stands to gain or lose much from the quality and the accuracy of these documents you prepare. Well-written instructions and procedures are important because they ensure safety and efficiency at your workplace. They help you and your colleagues

- assemble a product
- know what problems are present in a process
- carry out the duties your employer expects

This chapter will first show you how to develop, draft, illustrate, edit, and design a variety of instructions. Then it will move into a discussion of writing procedures about job-related duties.

WHY INSTRUCTIONS ARE IMPORTANT

Perhaps no other type of occupational writing demands more from the writer than do instructions because so much is at stake—for both you and your reader. The reader has to understand what you write and be able to perform the steps. You cannot afford to be unclear, inaccurate, or incomplete. Instructions are significant for many reasons, including safety, efficiency, and convenience.

Safety

Carefully written instructions get a job done without damage or injury. Poorly written instructions can cause an injury and may result in costly damage claims or even lawsuits. Notice how the product labels in your medicine cabinet inform consumers how to take a medication safely. Without those instructions, consumers would be endangered by taking too much or too little medicine or by not administering it properly. To make sure your instructions are safe, they must be

- accurate
- consistent
- thorough
- clearly written
- effectively illustrated
- carefully organized

Your instructions also have to be legally proper. Companies have a legal and ethical obligation to prepare instructions that protect readers' safety. Instructions must

- specify what constitutes normal and proper use
- warn about misuse and identify potential risks and hazards
- signal any cautions, risks, or dangers through prominently displayed symbols, warnings, and cautions
- inform readers how to obtain further help

Failure to provide such information in plain, clear language that readers can understand and easily follow is regarded by the courts to be as serious as manufacturing a defective product or not meeting code specifications. Several government agencies such as the U.S. Consumer Product Safety Commission (www.cpsc.gov) notify consumers about products that have been found to be unsafe.

Efficiency

Well-written instructions help businesses run smoothly and efficiently. No work would be done if employees did not have clear instructions to follow. For example, without instructions on how to operate a piece of equipment, employees would not know how to get a job done. Imagine how inefficient it would be for a business if employees had to stop their work each time they did not have or could not understand a set of instructions. Equally alarming, what if employees made a number of serious mistakes because of confusing directions, costing a business sales, decreasing productivity, and increasing expenses? Giving readers helpful tips to make their work easier will increase their efficiency in doing it.

Convenience

Clear, easy-to-follow instructions make a customer's job easier and less frustrating. Instructions reflect a product's or service's quality and convenience. They can create goodwill or destroy it. How many times have you heard complaints about a company because its instructions were hard to follow? Poorly written and illustrated instructions will cost your customers time and you their business. Customers want instructions that are written in clear, plain language and that use helpful photographs or drawings so they can assemble, install, or use a product right away. Instructions are also a vital part of "service after the sale." Owners' manuals, for example, help buyers avoid a product breakdown and help them keep the product in good working order.

THE VARIETY OF INSTRUCTIONS: A BRIEF OVERVIEW

Instructions vary in length, complexity, and format. Wordless instructions such as those in Figure 12.1 from an airline safety card can be quickly understood by a large international audience. Other instructions are one word long: *stop, lift, rotate, print, erase.* Others are a few sentences long: "Insert blank disk in external disk drive"; "Close tightly after using"; "Store in an upright position."

Instructions can be given in a variety of formats, both in print and online, and can include

- numbered steps (see Figures 12.2; 12.3, page 484; and 12.4, page 485)
- bulleted steps (see Figure 12.4)
- concise paragraphs (see Figures 12.2–12.4)
- online instructions (see Figure 12.4 and Figure 12.9, pages 500–509)

You will have to determine which of the above formats are most appropriate for the kinds of instructions you are to write.

Many instructions are given online. If you purchase a new iPad, for instance, online instructions will guide you in setting up and registering it. Figure 12.4 shows a set of instructions posted online to help its customers repair a leaky faucet. Websites for products and services often include hyperlinks to "help screens" that give consumers information on assembly and use. The long set of instructions on installing the Epson WorkForce 610 series printer in Figure 12.9 combines print and online instructions.

Instructions are also provided through videos on YouTube and other sites that actually show viewers how to assemble or install a product or perform another task.

FIGURE 12.1 Wordless Instructions on How to Use an Oxygen Mask on an Airplane

© 2017 Cengage Learning

FIGURE 12.2 Instructions That Supply a Visual with Each Written Step

Proper Brushing

Proper brushing is essential for cleaning teeth and gums effectively. Use a toothbrush with soft, nylon, round-ended bristles that will not scratch and irritate teeth or damage gums.

1

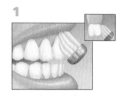

Place bristles along the gumline at a 45-degree angle. Bristles should contact both the tooth surface and the gumline.

Uses easy-to-follow steps with ample space between each one

2

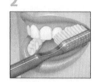

Gently brush the outer tooth surfaces of 2–3 teeth using a vibrating back and forth rolling motion. Move brush to the next group of 2–3 teeth and repeat.

Clear, numbered visuals help readers follow directions

3

Maintain a 45-degree angle with bristles contacting the tooth surface and gumline. Gently brush, using back, forth, and rolling motion along all of the inner tooth surfaces.

Begins each step with strong, active verbs listed in color

4

Tilt brush vertically behind the front teeth. Make several up and down strokes using the front half of the brush.

Offers helpful hints

5

Place the brush against the biting surface of the teeth and use a gentle back and forth scrubbing motion. Brush the tongue from back to front to remove odor-producing bacteria.

Explains why a step is important

Source: Reprinted by permission of American Dental Hygienists' Association. Illustrations adapted and used courtesy of the John O. Butler Company, makers of *GUM* Healthcare products.

In these online instructions, someone talks you through each step, alerts you to potential problems, and gives helpful tips at various stages of the process. One smoke detector manufacturer, for example, hired a New Jersey fire chief to demonstrate how to properly assemble, locate and mount, maintain, and test its product.

FIGURE 12.3 Instructions in a Numbered List

How to Copy Files to a USB Flash Drive from Your Laptop or Notebook

Follow these instructions to copy your files to a flash drive from your laptop or notebook. As you perform these instructions, refer to the photo of a USB flash drive below:

Uses numbered steps

1. Insert the USB flash drive into a USB portal of your laptop or notebook.

Strong, active verbs give readers clear directions

2. Find the folder or file to be copied to the USB flash drive, and right-click on it. NOTE: The folder or file will be highlighted, and a menu with "Open" at the top will appear.

3. Within the menu, move your cursor down to the "Send To" option. Here you will see a list of locations where you may send the selected folder or file.

Provides photograph to assist readers

4. Choose the USB flash drive location. Your folder or file will be automatically copied over. CAUTION: DO NOT REMOVE THE USB FLASH DRIVE AT THIS POINT, OR YOU WILL RISK DAMAGING IT.

Inserts "CAUTION" statement at proper place

5. Go to "My Computer" from the "Start" menu, and double-click on the USB flash drive. If the folder or files you selected in Step 2 are listed here, your copying was successful.

Tells reader how to determine if he/she did step accurately

6. Eject the USB flash drive before removing it from the computer. To do so, go to "My Computer" again, right-click on the USB flash drive, and select the "Eject" option from the menu.

7. Remove the USB flash drive from the USB portal.

Text: © 2017 Cengage Learning; Photo: Microsoft Clip Art

ASSESSING AND MEETING YOUR AUDIENCE'S NEEDS

To assess your audience's needs, put yourself in your readers' position. Do not assume that your readers have performed the process before or have operated the equipment as many times as you have. (If they had, there would be no need for your instructions.) No one who has written a set of instructions ever disappointed readers by making directions too clear or too easy to follow. Remember, too, that your audience will often include non-native speakers of English, a worldwide audience of potential consumers. The more you know about how and why your reader will use your instructions, the steps likely to cause problems, and the background information you need to supply, the easier and clearer your instructions will be to follow.

FIGURE 12.4 Online Instructions on How to Repair a Leaky Faucet, Using a Numbered List, a Sequence of Steps, and an Exploded Drawing

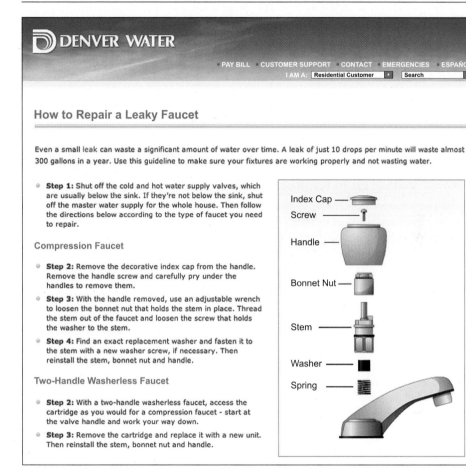

The company's home page helpfully includes links to customer support and emergency contact information, and also makes the website available in Spanish

Begins with helpful information about the importance of the instructions

Easy-to-follow boldfaced numbered steps

Exploded drawing shows relationship of parts to one another making disassembling easier

Alerts reader to differences in faucets

Courtesy of Denver Water.

Key Questions to Ask About Your Audience

The more you know about your audience, the better your instructions can be. To determine your readers' needs, ask yourself the following questions:

- How and why will my readers use my instructions? (Co-workers, consumers, and experts in the field all have different expectations.)
- What language skills do they possess? Is English their first (native) language?
- How much do my readers already know about the product or service?
- How much background information will I have to supply?
- What steps will most likely cause readers trouble?
- What types of visuals do I need to supply (photographs for consumers; diagrams and spec sheets for technicians)?

- How often will readers refer back to my instructions—every day or just as a refresher?
- Where will my audience most likely be following my instructions—in the workplace, outdoors, in a workshop equipped with tools, or in their homes?
- What resources, such as special equipment or energy sources, will my readers need to perform my instructions successfully?

Writing Instructions for International Audiences

Your instructions will often be aimed at a worldwide audience of potential customers, many of whom do not use English as their first language and may be following your instructions through a translation of them into their native language. Here are some useful guidelines when writing instructions for this diverse group of readers:

1. **Write in plain, simple language.** Use international English (see "International Business Correspondence," pages 169–180).
2. **Use terms and units of measurement that your readers will understand.** Avoid abbreviations, acronyms, and jargon, and don't assume that international readers will use or understand the units of measurement common in the United States.
3. **Make sure all of your visuals are clear and culturally appropriate.** In some instances, your instructions may be given exclusively through visuals (as in Figure 12.1).
4. **Be aware that colors can have different meanings.** Red, yellow, and green, for instance, may not convey the same meaning in other cultures that they do in the United States. (See "Guidelines for Using Visuals for International Audiences," pages 439–441.)
5. **Ask a non-native speaker to review your instructions.** This will ensure that your instructions are easy to understand for international readers and culturally sensitive.

USING WORD-PROCESSING SOFTWARE TO HELP YOU DESIGN INSTRUCTIONS

Take advantage of the following word-processing features to help you draft, revise, and format your instructions:

1. **Brainstorm and cluster to get ideas and steps down.** Find and compile the information you will need to include in the steps of your instructions, and think ahead about possible warnings, cautions, and any helpful hints that users may need to complete the steps (see "Planning," pages 46–49).
2. **Take advantage of the Outline feature.** This feature of word-processing programs makes it easy to identify, order, and change the steps in a set of instructions, allowing you to try out different options quickly and easily.
3. **Choose a font that is easy to read.** Fonts like Arial or Times New Roman provide clean and easy-to-read text for your instructions. (See "Typography," pages 454–456.)

4. **Use numbered and bulleted lists.** Numbered steps help readers follow the sequence of your instructions, and bulleted lists break up text to make it easier to read.

5. **Provide adequate spacing.** Always double-space between steps to set each apart and to make following the steps easier. See "The ABCs of Print Document Design," pages 449–459.

6. **Put any notes, cautions, or warnings right next to the step to which they pertain.**

7. **Employ boldface sparingly.** Use it to emphasize warnings, cautions, and notes (see "Font Styles," pages 455–456) so readers will not overlook the crucial messages they contain.

8. **Include icons/visuals that will be easy to understand for a broad range of readers.** Put them as close to the steps they apply to as possible. Size any image correctly—neither so big that it will look unprofessional, nor so small that it cannot be seen clearly.

9. **Avoid the use of underlining for emphasis.** Underlined text may introduce confusion to your readers because it could be interpreted as a hyperlink.

10. **Give readers hyperlinks within instructions when they will make their jobs easier.**

THE PROCESS OF WRITING INSTRUCTIONS

As we saw in Chapter 2, clear and concise writing evolves when you follow a process. To make sure your instructions are accurate and easy for your audience to perform, you must plan your steps, perform a trial run, write and test your draft, and revise and edit.

Plan Your Steps

Before writing, do some research to understand completely the process you are asking someone else to perform. Make sure you know

- the reason for doing something
- the parts or tools required
- the steps to follow in the right order to get the job done
- the results of the job
- the potential risks or dangers

If you are not absolutely sure about the process, ask an expert for a demonstration. Do some background reading and talk to or email colleagues who may have written or followed a similar instruction.

Perform a Trial Run

Actually perform the job (assembling, repairing, maintaining, servicing, dissecting) yourself or with your writing team. Go through a number of trial runs. Take notes as you go along, and be sure to divide the job into simple, distinct steps for readers to follow. Don't give readers too much to do in any one step. Each step should be *complete*, *sequential*, *concise*, and *easy* for your audience to understand and perform.

CASE STUDY

Meeting Your Audience's Needs

The instructions contained in the United Solar Power memo in Figure 12.5 were sent to a technical audience—photovoltaic (PV) technicians—who needed instructions on a special process. Even though the instructions are for a technical audience, they still have a clearly defined and focused introduction, use numbered steps, include a visual, and have a caution or warning statement.

FIGURE 12.5 Instructions Alerting a Technical Audience to Special Circumstances

UNITED SOLAR POWER

Because the instructions are written for technicians, there is no need to explain that "PV" means "photovoltaic"

TO: All PV Technicians

FROM: Linda Swarski, Vice-President, Service Department
SUBJECT: Safely Mounting and Wiring the PV Modules in the US6000 System
DATE: April 5, 2016

Explains why the instructions are important

The following policy has been formulated to help you safely and effectively mount and wire the PV modules in the US6000 system. The steps to perform are as follows:

Lists directions in numbered steps

Step 1
Review the **NEC Article 110, Chapter 2; Article 250, Chapter 3; and Articles 300, 310, 480, and 690.** Follow these provisions exactly to ensure a safe electrical installation.

High level of specificity needed because the instructions are aimed at a specialist

Step 2
Map out the base plate grid and ensure that the array layout is **at least** 12" away from the sides and top of the roof, and **at least** 16" away from the eave of the roof (see Figure 1).

Uses boldface to indicate important points

FIGURE 12.5 (Continued)

At least 12" from the
sides and top of roof

At least 16"
from eave

Hill120/Shutterstock.com

Figure 1

Step 3
When installing the PV panels to the base plates, **never** allow the output cable to be wedged in between the mount and the panel frame, as this can cause short circuits and fire.

Clear visual illustrates one of the steps

Step 4
Make sure each PV panel's connectors are pushed in all the way; they will malfunction if not fully inserted.

Identifies important conditions

Step 5
Properly secure the output cable to the mount, as high winds will cause damage to loose-fitting cables and result in substandard energy generation.

CAUTION: *PV panels generate electricity whenever they are exposed to sunlight. Be extremely careful handling the panels during the installation process. You could experience an electrical shock if you touch the wires or connectors of the panel's electrical cable.*

Indicates a dangerous situation with a red CAUTION and use of boldface

If you have any questions about the above, please feel free to text me at **(609) 559-1002** or **linda.swarski@unitedsolar.com**.

Contact information prominently displayed in boldface

Write and Test Your Draft

Transform your notes into a draft (or drafts) of the instructions you want readers to follow. Then conduct a **usability test** by asking individuals from the intended audience (consumers, technicians) to follow your instructions as you have written them. Ask participants to read your instructions aloud and ask questions. Observe where they run into difficulty—or get results different from yours.

Revise and Edit

Based on your observations and user feedback, revise your instructions to avoid

- missing steps
- too many activities in one step
- steps that are out of order
- unclear or incomplete steps

Consider whether your instructions would be easier to accomplish if you included visuals.

Analyzing the needs and the background of your audience will help you choose appropriate words and details. A set of instructions accompanying an environmentally safe floor cleaner would obviously use different terminology, abbreviations, and level of detail than would a set of instructions a professor gives a class in organic chemistry.

> General Audience: Place 8 drops of vinegar in a test tube with a piece of limestone about the size of a pea.
>
> Specialized Audience: Place 8 gtts of CH_3COOH in a test tube, and add 1 mg of $CaCO_3$.

USING THE RIGHT STYLE

To write instructions that readers can understand and turn into effective action, observe the following guidelines.

1. Make sure verbs are in the present tense and imperative mood. Imperatives are commands without the pronoun *you*. Note how the instructions in Figures 12.2, 12.3, and 12.4 contain imperatives—"Reinstall the stem" instead of "You reinstall the stem." In instructions, deleting the *you* is not discourteous, as it would be in a business letter or report. The command tells readers, "These steps work, so do them exactly as stated." Choose imperative verbs such as those listed in Table 12.1.

2. Write clear, short sentences in the active voice. Keep sentences short and uncomplicated. Sentences under twenty words (preferably under fifteen) are easy to read. Note that the sentences in Figures 12.2, 12.3, and 12.4 are, for the most part, under fifteen words. But do not omit articles (*a*, *an*, *the*) or any connective words (such as *and*, *but*, and *however*) which will make your instructions harder to follow.

3. Use precise terms for measurements, distances, and times. Indefinite, vague directions leave users wondering whether they are doing the right thing. Avoid vague words such as *frequently*, *occasionally*, *probably*, and *possibly*. The following vague direction is better expressed through precise revision.

> Vague: Turn the distributor cap a little. (*How much is a little?*)
> Precise: Turn the distributor cap one quarter of a rotation.

TABLE 12.1 Some Helpful Imperative Verbs Used in Instructions

add	determine	hold	pass	rotate	tear
adjust	dig	include	paste	rub	thread
apply	display	increase	peel	run	tie
attach	double-click	insert	pick up	save	tighten
back up	download	inspect	plug	scan	tilt
blow	drag	install	point	scroll	trace
boldface	drain	lift	pour	scrub	transect
call up	drill	link on	press	select	transfer
change	drop	load	prevent	send	trim
check	ease	log on	print	set	turn
choose	eject	loosen	provide	shake	twist
clean	eliminate	lower	pry	shift	type
click	enter	lubricate	pull	shut off	unplug
clip	exit	maintain	push	slide	use
close	fasten	measure	raise	slip	ventilate
connect	find	mix	reboot	spread	verify
contact	flip	mount	release	squeeze	wash
copy	flush	move	remove	start	weigh
cover	follow	navigate	replace	stop	wind
create	forward	notify	reply	strain	wipe
cut	gather	oil	review	switch	wire
delete	group	open	roll	tab down	wrap

© Cengage Learning

4. Include connective words as signposts. Connective words specify the exact order in which something is to be done (especially when your instructions are written in paragraphs). Words such as *first*, *then*, and *before* help readers stay on course, reinforcing the sequence of the procedures.

5. Number each step when you present your instructions in a list. You also can use bullets. Plenty of white space between steps also distinctly separates them for the reader.

USING VISUALS EFFECTIVELY

Readers welcome visuals in almost any set of instructions. A visual can help readers get a job done more quickly and increase their confidence to

- see what an object or piece of equipment looks like fully assembled
- identify the size and placement of parts
- understand how to assemble parts effectively and easily
- illustrate the right and wrong way to do something
- see if a piece of equipment works properly
- identify possible sources of danger, injury, or malfunction
- determine whether a problem is serious, minor, or even not a problem.

The number and kinds of visuals you include will, of course, depend on the process or equipment you are explaining and on your audience's background and needs. Some instructions may require only one or two visuals. The instructions in

Figure 12.3 telling users how to copy files using a USB flash drive show what a USB flash drive looks like. In Figure 12.2, however, each step is accompanied by a visual demonstrating a proper technique for brushing teeth.

One frequently used visual in instructions is an exploded drawing, like the one in Figure 12.4, which helps consumers see how various parts of a faucet fit together, or the one in Figure 12.6, which labels and shows the relationship of the parts of an industrial extension cord.

Guidelines for Using Visuals in Instructions

Follow these guidelines to use visuals effectively in your instructions:

1. Set visuals off with white space so they are easy to find and read.
2. Place each visual next to the step it illustrates, not next to another step, buried at the bottom of the page, or on another page.
3. Select a visual that is appropriate for your audience. For example, a photo of a person demonstrating a proper stretch technique is sufficient for a general audience, which does not need an elaborate medical illustration of the muscular system.
4. Assign each visual a number (Figures 1 and 2), and refer to it by figure number in your instructions.

FIGURE 12.6 Exploded Drawing Showing How to Assemble an Industrial Extension Cord

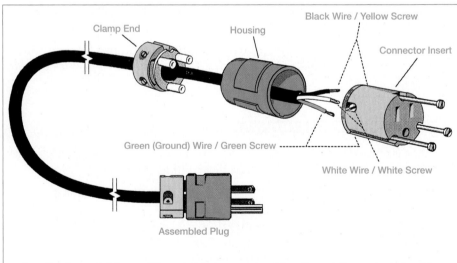

1. Run the end of the cord through the clamp end and then through the center hole of the housing.
2. Pull the cord through until it extends 2 inches beyond the housing.
3. Strip about 1¼ inches of outer insulation from the end of the cord.
4. Twist the exposed ends to prevent stray strands.

Source: Drawing courtesy of Sally Eddy.

5. Make sure the visual looks exactly like the object the user must assemble, run, maintain, or repair. Using a photo of a different model might confuse readers.
6. Always inform readers if a part is missing or is reduced in your visual.
7. Where necessary, label or number parts of the visual, as in Figure 12.2.

Refer to Chapter 10 for further guidelines on numbering visuals (see "Identify Your Visuals," pages 407–408) and inserting them in your document (see "Introduce Your Visuals," page 409).

THE SIX PARTS OF INSTRUCTIONS

Except for very short instructions, such as those illustrated in Figures 12.1 through 12.6, a set of instructions generally contains six main parts: (1) an introduction; (2) a list of equipment and materials; (3) the actual steps to perform the process; (4) warnings, cautions, and notes; (5) a conclusion (when necessary); and (6) a troubleshooting guide. The long set of instructions on installing a printer in Figure 12.9 contains most of these.

Introduction

The function of your introduction is to provide readers with enough *necessary* background information to understand why and how your instructions work. An introduction must make readers feel comfortable and well prepared before they turn to the actual steps.

What to Include in an Introduction

Not every introduction to a set of instructions will contain all six categories of information listed here. Some instructions will require less detail. You will have to judge how much background information to give your readers for the specific instructions you write.

1. **State why the instructions are useful for a specific audience.** Many instructions begin with introductions that stress safety, educational, or occupational benefits. Here is an introduction from a set of safety instructions describing protective lockout of equipment.

> The purpose of these instructions is to provide plant electrical technicians with a uniform method of locking out machinery or equipment. This will prevent the possibility of setting moving parts in motion, energizing electrical lines; or opening valves while repair, setup, or cleaning work is in progress.

Note how Figure 12.7 (page 495) highlights the safety and convenience of using an infusion pump, helping the nursing staff meet their patients' needs.

2. **Indicate how a particular piece of equipment or process works.** An introduction can briefly discuss the "theory of operation" to help readers understand why something works the way your instructions say it should. Such a discussion sometimes describes a scientific law or principle. An introduction to instructions on

how to run an autoclave begins by explaining the function of the machine: "These instructions will teach you how to operate an autoclave, which is used to sterilize surgical instruments through the live additive-free stream."

The introduction in Figure 12.7 describes the function and features of the LifeCare Provider 5500 System and pump.

3. Point out any safety measures or precautions a reader may need to be aware of. By alerting readers early in your instructions, you help them perform the process much more safely and efficiently. The introduction in Figure 12.7 cautions the nursing staff about an audible alarm signal in the event of a malfunction.

4. Stress any advantages or benefits the reader will gain by performing the instructions. Make the reader feel good about buying or using the product by explaining how it will make a job easier to perform, save the reader time and money, or allow the reader to accomplish a job with fewer mistakes or false starts. Again, the introduction in Figure 12.7 informs nurses that the infusion pump can be quickly programmed.

5. Provide hyperlinks. When readers will be following your instructions online (as in parts of Figure 12.9), provide hyperlinks to any sites or materials they need to know about. Similarly, provide relevant cross-references in printed instructions.

List of Equipment and Materials

Clearly, some instructions, as in Figure 12.2, do not need to list all of the materials readers will need. But when you do, make your list complete and clear. Do not wait until the readers are actually performing one of the steps to tell them that a certain type of drill or a specific kind of chemical is required. They may have to stop what they are doing to find the equipment or material; moreover, the procedure may fail or present hazards if users do not have the right equipment at the right time. For example, if a Phillips screwdriver is essential to complete one step, specify that type of screwdriver under the heading "Equipment and Materials"; do not list just "screwdriver." See Figure 12.8 (page 496), which shows images of the types of tools and screws necessary to remove a refrigerator door.

Steps for Your Instructions

The heart of your instructions will consist of clearly distinguished steps that readers must follow to achieve the desired results. Figure 12.9 (pages 500–509) contains a model set of steps on how to set up an all-in-one printer. Note how each step is precisely keyed to the visual, further helping readers perform the procedure. Refer to Figure 12.9 as you study this section.

Guidelines for Writing Steps

To help your readers understand your steps, observe the following rules.

1. Put the steps in their correct order, and number them. If a step is out of order or is missing, the entire set of instructions can be wrong or, worse yet, dangerous.

FIGURE 12.7 Introduction to a Guide for Using an Infusion Pump

1 Overview Orientation

The LifeCare PROVIDER 5500 System is a portable infusion pump, specially designed to deliver analgesic drugs, antibiotics, and chemotherapeutics.

The pump can be programmed in either milligrams or cubic centimeters, and in four different delivery configurations for greater nursing convenience and to tailor precisely the most effective regimen for each patient.

Bolus Mode allows your patient to self-administer analgesia within programmed limits.

This is the traditional PCA delivery, "analgesia-on-demand," based on the patient's need.

Continuous Mode delivers a continuous "background" infusion with no additional PCA doses permitted.

Continuous-plus-Bolus Mode allows the patient to self-administer a Bolus dose in addition to receiving a simultaneous Continuous dose infusion.

Intermittent Mode delivers a specific dose (in cc or mg) at intermittent intervals over 24 hours.

You can also establish the "lockout" interval, the frequency with which a patient may receive a Bolus dose of analgesic drug.

The PROVIDER 5500 System records all settings in memory and can be quickly re-programmed to save nursing time when repeating established protocols or changing fluid reservoirs.

The portable system operates on battery power.

To minimize tampering and discourage theft, there is an optional locking security lockbox that also secures the system to an IV pole.

The audible alarm signals in the event of a malfunction, and the digital readout describes the malfunction.

- Compact and lightweight.
- Delivery rates between 0.1 cc and 250 cc per hour, in 0.1-cc increments.

Display Panel

- Individual display indicators appear only during programming and operation.
- Only on a *selective* basis.
- Tone sounds when activated.
- Runs on BATTERY POWER ONLY.
- Disposable Primary IV set with integral infusion cartridge.

Gives function of equipment

Points out time-saving features

Explains security option

Describes different modes or options

Calls attention to convenience features

Emphasizes safety features

Use of color to distinguish parts, various modes

Source: Reprinted by permission of Abbott Laboratories Hospital Products Division.

Double-check every step, and number each one to indicate its correct place in the sequence of tasks you are describing (see Figure 12.9, pages 500–509).

  2. Include the right amount of information in each step. Make each step short and simple. Giving readers too much information can be as risky as giving them

FIGURE 12.8 List of Tools Needed for Instructions on How to Remove a Refrigerator Door

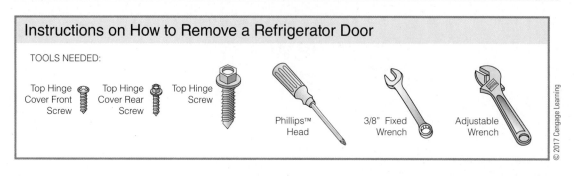

too little. Keep in mind that each step should ask readers to perform a single task in the entire process. In the following example showing how to access voice mail, note how the first version combines too many steps, while the revision corrects the problem:

Incorrect:	1.	To access your voice mail, make sure you've listened to old messages and then press "1" to obtain your new messages.
	2.	When each new message is finished, press "7" to delete the message or "8" to store it in the archives. Press "2" to replay the message.
	3.	To review your saved messages, press "9." To end the call, press "#."

Correct:	1.	To access your voice mail, press "1" to obtain your new messages.
	2.	When each new message is finished, press "7" to delete the message or "8" to store it in the archives. Press "2" to replay the message.
	3.	To review your saved messages, press "9."
	4.	To end the call, press "#."

3. Group closely related activities into one step. Sometimes closely related actions do belong in one step to help the reader coordinate activities and to emphasize their being done at the same time, in the same place, or with the same equipment.

Don't divide an action into two steps if it has to be done in one. For example, instructions showing how to light a gas furnace would not list as two steps actions that must be performed simultaneously to avoid a possible explosion:

| Incorrect: | 1. | Depress the lighting valve. |
| | 2. | Hold a match to the pilot light. |

| Correct: | 1. | Depress the lighting valve while holding a match to the pilot light. |

Similarly, do not separate two steps of a computer command that must be performed simultaneously.

| Incorrect: | 1. | Press the CONTROL key. |
| | 2. | Press the ALT key. |

| Correct: | 1. | While holding down the CONTROL key, press the ALT key. |

4. Give the reader hints on how best to accomplish the procedure. Obviously, you cannot do that for every step, but if there is a chance that the reader might run into difficulties, provide some helpful advice to make the step easier to perform: "If there is blood on the transducer diaphragm, dip the transducer in blood solvent, such as hydrogen peroxide or Hemosol." You can also tell readers if they have a choice of materials and techniques or how they might obtain the best results: "Several thin coats of paint will give a better finish than one heavy coat."

5. State whether one step directly influences (or jeopardizes) the outcome of another. Because all steps in a set of instructions are interrelated, you do not have to tell readers how every step affects every other. But stating specific relationships is particularly helpful when dangerous or highly intricate operations are involved. You will save the reader time, and you will stress the need for care. Forewarned is forearmed. Here is an example:

> Step 2:   Tighten the fan belt. Failure to tighten the fan belt now will cause it to loosen and come off when the lever is turned on in Step 5.

Do not wait until Step 5 to tell readers that you hope they did a good job tightening the fan belt in Step 2. Information that comes after the fact is not helpful and could potentially be dangerous.

6. Where necessary, insert graphics to assist readers in carrying out the step. Almost every step in the set of long instructions in Figure 12.9 (pages 500–009) is illustrated with a drawing of the printer, an enlargement of a part, or a screenshot.

7. Your instructions might be translated into an international reader's language, as you can see in the warning statements in the next section.

Warnings, Cautions, and Notes

At appropriate places in the steps of your instructions, you may have to stop the reader to issue a warning, a caution, or a note. Warnings and cautions are mandatory texts that you must provide to protect the user of the equipment from injury, or to protect hardware or software from costly damage to your company. A note usually provides related information, such as an explanation, a tip, a comment, or other useful, but not life-threatening or equipment-damaging information. Study the following examples as well as those in Figure 12.9, especially for Step 4, pages 504–505, "Install ink cartridges."

Warnings

A warning ensures a reader's safety. It tells readers that a step, if not prepared for or performed properly, could seriously injure them, as the following warning does, or even endanger their lives.

WARNING: UNPLUG MACHINE BEFORE REMOVING PLATEN GLASS.

ADVERTENCIA: DESENCHUFE LA MAQUINA ANTES DE QUITAR EL VIDRIO.

Spanish translation

Cautions

A caution tells readers how to avoid a mistake that could damage equipment or cause the process to fail—for instance, "Do not force the plug."

 ### Caution: Formatting erases all data on the disk

小心： 格式化会删除磁盘的所有资料

Even diligent readers sometimes only skim or glance at a document. But some icons, like those below, universally convey "warning" or "caution" without requiring any text or explanation.

Notes

A note does not comment on the safety of the user or the equipment but does provide clarification, options, or a helpful hint on how to do the step quicker or more efficiently.

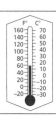 At 20 degrees F, a battery uses about 68 percent of its power.

Eksi 7 derecede, bir pil enerjisinin yaklasik yuzde 68 ini kullanir.

Guidelines for Using Warnings, Cautions, and Notes

1. **Do not regard warnings and cautions as optional.** They are vital for legal and safety reasons to protect lives and property. In fact, you and your company can be sued if you fail to notify the users of your product or service of dangerous conditions that could result in injury or death.

2. **Put warnings and cautions as close as possible to the step to which they pertain.** (The exact placement may vary depending on the context and nature of the warning.) If you insert a warning or caution statement too early, readers may forget it by the time they come to the step to which it applies. Putting the notification too late exposes the reader, and possibly equipment as well, to risk.

3. **Graphically set warnings and cautions apart from the rest of the instructions.** Use icons such as those shown earlier. Print such statements in capital letters,

boldface, or different colors. Red is especially effective for warnings and cautions if your readers are native speakers of English. But remember that colors have different meanings in other countries (see "Guidelines for Using Visuals for International Artists," pages 439–441). If you expect your product to be used globally, you might consider rendering cautions using a different (but distinct) color, such as in Figure 12.9, where green is used to set cautions apart from the rest of the text.

4. Include relevant explanations to help readers know what to watch out for and what precautions to take. Do not just insert the word *WARNING* or *CAUTION*. Explain what the dangerous condition is and how to avoid it. Look at the examples of cautions in Figure 12.9.

5. Do not include a warning or a caution just to emphasize a point. Putting too many warnings or cautions in your instructions will decrease their impact on readers. Use them sparingly — only when absolutely necessary — so readers will not be tempted to ignore them.

6. Use notes only when the procedure calls for them and when they help readers. See how functional the notes are in Figure 12.9.

Conclusion

Not every set of instructions requires a conclusion. For short instructions containing only a few simple steps, such as those in Figures 12.1 through 12.6, no conclusion is necessary. For longer, more involved jobs, a conclusion can provide a succinct wrap-up of what the reader has done, end with a single sentence of congratulations, or reassure readers. A conclusion might also tell readers what to expect once a job is finished, describe the results of a test, or explain how a piece of equipment is supposed to look or operate. Figure 12.9 ends with an "Any questions?" section that supplies a comprehensive list of ways readers can receive further help and guidance. Always supply contact information and hyperlinks, should a reader need further information.

Troubleshooting Guide

Instructions can also come with a section on troubleshooting to help readers when they encounter a problem. Often formatted as a table or chart, troubleshooting guides describe the problems that are most likely to occur and explain the easiest ways to correct them. Troubleshooting tips can also be found within various steps of a set of instructions, or online, as shown on the last page of Figure 12.9. Troubleshooting guides and tips help consumers avoid frustration and the expense of a service call.

MODEL OF FULL SET OF INSTRUCTIONS

Study Figure 12.9, which is a full set of instructions for setting up an Epson all-in-one printer. It includes most of the parts discussed in this chapter: an introduction; a list of materials; numbered steps; cautions and notes; and a conclusion.

Intended for a global audience, these instructions are a model of a user-friendly document. They are written and formatted for consumers to be easy to read and to perform. The language is clear and concise. Sentences are short and direct, yet the tone is free from any cultural bias.

Pay special attention to how these instructions coordinate words, visuals, and colors to assist readers. Each step is clearly numbered and accompanied by an appropriate visual (e.g., enlarged drawing) or visual device (arrows, icons, directional symbols). Screen shots are inserted to help readers understand various steps they need to perform instructions online. Finally, caution statements and notes are inserted in the appropriate places to make sure readers install and set up their Epson all-in-one printer safely.

FIGURE 12.9 Complete Set of Instructions with Visuals Showing Parts Included

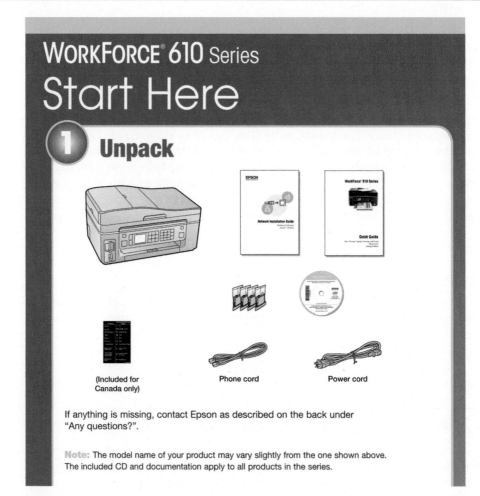

Visuals show contents

Unpacking serves as an introduction to the product

Note reassures readers about use of different model names

Courtesy of Seiko Epson Corp.

FIGURE 12.9 (Continued)

Caution: Do not open ink cartridge packages until you are ready to install the ink. Cartridges are vacuum packed to maintain reliability.

Canada only: For French speakers, remove stickers from the backing sheet and place over corresponding text on the control panel.

Remove all protective materials.

Caution notice alerts readers to possible product damage

Colored arrows assist readers in unpacking contents

② **Turn on and adjust**

1 Connect the power cable.

Caution: Do not connect to your computer yet.

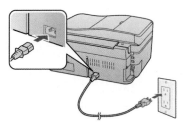

Uses two-level numbering— large circled numbers for the major sections and smaller boldfaced numbers for each step in those sections

2 Lift the control panel to raise it, then press the ⏻ **On** button.

Enlarged drawing and contrasting colors assist readers to identify, connect, and move parts

Note: To lower the control panel, squeeze the release lever underneath and push the control panel down. For more information on using and adjusting the control panel, see your *Quick Guide*.

Uses color to have note stand out

Courtesy of Seiko Epson Corp.

(Continued)

FIGURE 12.9 (Continued)

Make settings

1   Select your language.

Press ▲ or ▼ to select the desired option.

Press **OK** when done.

Uses symbols, screens, and keypads to visualize and reinforce each step

2   Select your country/region, then press **OK**.

Specifies and explains options

3   For the Daylight Saving Time setting, select **Summer** if your region uses Daylight Saving Time and it's currently in effect. (DST is effective from spring through summer.) Otherwise, select **Winter** to turn off the setting. Press **OK**.

Each step begins with imperative verb

4   Press ▲ or ▼ to select the date format, then press ▶. Don't press **OK** yet.

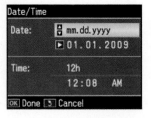

Courtesy of Seiko Epson Corp.

FIGURE 12.9 (Continued)

5   Use the numeric keypad to set the date. Don't press **OK** yet.

 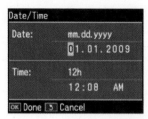

Repeated use of red print alerts reader not to perform a step yet

6   Press ▲ or ▼ to select the time format, then press ▶. Don't press **OK** yet.

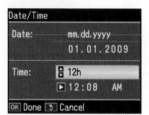

Each step includes written directions and often an appropriate visual

7   Use the numeric keypad to set the time.

 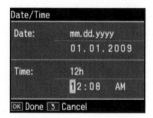

8   If you selected **12h** as the time format, press ▲ or ▼ to select **AM** or **PM**.

Uses boldface for emphasis

9   Press **OK** when done.

Note: You can change the date and time settings by pressing the **Home** button, selecting **Setup**, selecting **Printer Setup**, then selecting **Date/Time**.

Provides helpful tip on changing date and time settings

Courtesy of Seiko Epson Corp.   *(Continued)*

FIGURE 12.9 (Continued)

Gives important information before readers perform the steps

④ Install ink cartridges

Note: Don't load paper before installing the ink cartridges.

1 Lift up the scanner.

2 Open the cartridge cover.

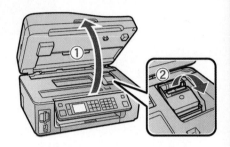

Directional arrows illustrate correct movement of parts

3 Shake the ink cartridges gently 4 or 5 times, then unpack them.

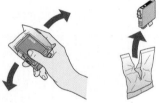

Specifies number of repetitions

4 Remove only the yellow tape from each cartridge.

Caution notice inserted in appropriate place with symbols showing wrong way to perform step

Caution: Don't remove any other seals or the cartridges may leak.

5 Insert the cartridges in the holder for each color.

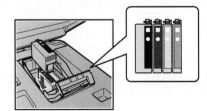

Courtesy of Seiko Epson Corp.

FIGURE 12.9 (Continued)

6 Press each cartridge down until it clicks.

Visual clues reinforce the right way to perform step

7 Close the ink cartridge cover and press it down until it clicks.

Helps reader know when step is carried out successfully

8 Lower the scanner.

Uses concise language

9 Press the **OK** button to charge the ink. Charging takes about 3 minutes.

Note: Your product ships with full cartridges and part of the ink from the first cartridges is used for priming the product.

Caution: Don't turn off the product while the ink system is charging or you'll waste ink.

Note and caution notices help readers use product more economically and efficiently

Courtesy of Seiko Epson Corp.

(Continued)

FIGURE 12.9 (Continued)

> ## 5 Load paper
>
> *Generous white space makes steps easier to distinguish and to follow*
>
> **1**   Open the paper support and pull up the extensions.
>
>
>
> *Groups related activities in one step*
>
> **2**   Extend the output tray and raise the stopper.
>
>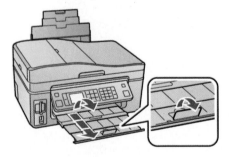
>
> *Supplies helpful information on best way to use product*
>
> **Note:** If you are using legal-size paper, do not raise the stopper.
>
> *Includes three visuals, two of them enlarged drawings, pinpointing exact places reader needs to recognize to perform the step*
>
> **3**   Hold the feeder guard forward, then squeeze the edge guide and slide it to the left.
>
>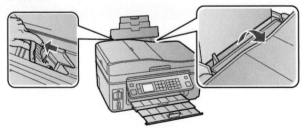

Courtesy of Seiko Epson Corp.

FIGURE 12.9 (Continued)

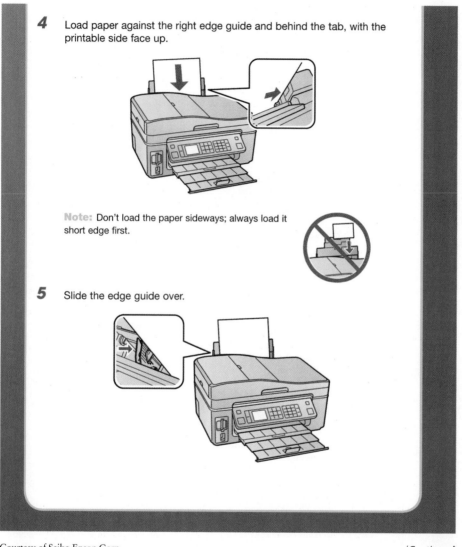

4 Load paper against the right edge guide and behind the tab, with the printable side face up.

Visuals show right and wrong ways to load paper

Note: Don't load the paper sideways; always load it short edge first.

5 Slide the edge guide over.

Instructions written in concise and clear language

Courtesy of Seiko Epson Corp.

(Continued)

FIGURE 12.9 (Continued)

Instructions
clearly
indicate
product
options

Section 7
alerts readers
that they can
use different
types of
connections

Arrows point
to where
instructions
for each type
of connection
can be found

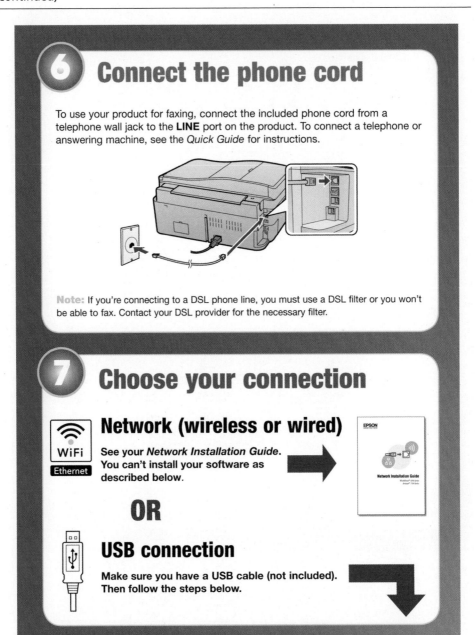

Courtesy of Seiko Epson Corp.

FIGURE 12.9 (Continued)

Any questions?

Quick Guide

Basic instructions for printing, copying, scanning, and faxing.

Online *Epson Information Center*

Click the desktop shortcut for easy access to the user's guide, FAQs, online troubleshooting advice, and software downloads. You can also purchase paper and ink.

Provides information on how and where readers can receive further help

Network Installation Guide and Video

Instructions on configuring the product for a network. For a video tutorial and other information about setting up a wireless network, go to: **epson.com/support/wireless**

On-screen help with your software

Select **Help** or **?** when you're using your software.

Color helps to identify options for readers

Epson Technical Support

Internet Support

Visit Epson's support website at **epson.com/support** and select your product for solutions to common problems. You can download drivers and documentation, get FAQs and troubleshooting advice, or e-mail Epson with your questions.

Speak to a Support Representative

Call (562) 276-4382 (U.S.) or (905) 709-3839 (Canada), 6 AM to 6 PM, Pacific Time, Monday through Friday. Days and hours of support are subject to change without notice. Toll or long distance charges may apply.

Indicates further support available online; supplies hyperlinks

Boilerplate information that appears with all Epson products

Courtesy of Seiko Epson Corp.

WRITING PROCEDURES FOR POLICIES AND REGULATIONS

Up to this point, we have concentrated primarily on instructions dealing with how to put things together; how to install, repair, or use equipment; and how to alert readers to mechanical or even personal danger.

But there is another type of writing that provides guidelines for getting things done in the world of work: procedures. These concern policies and regulations found in employee handbooks and other internal corporate communications, such as on websites, in memos, in email messages, or on a company's intranet (a private computer network). Note, however, that some companies do not disseminate policy via email because it is perceived as less formal than hard copy and can accidentally be deleted. Figure 12.10 (pages 512–513) shows an example of a company's flextime procedures written in a memo format.

Some Examples of Procedures

Procedures deal with a wide range of "how-to" activities within an organization, including the following:

- accessing a company file or database

- preparing for an audit, a transition, a merger

- applying for family or medical leave

- dressing professionally at work or at a job site

- forwarding and routing information

- reserving a company vehicle or facility

- submitting a work-related grievance, e.g, bullying, discrimination

- requesting travel expense reimbursement

- fulfilling promotion requirements

- requesting a transfer within the company

- using company email

- posting to one of the company's social media websites

Policy procedures have a major impact on a company and its workers. They affect schedules, payrolls, acceptable and unacceptable behaviors at work, and a range of protocols governing the way the organization does business internally and externally. Procedures also help an organization run smoothly and consistently. Adhering to them, all employees follow the same regulations and standards.

Meeting the Needs of Your Marketplace

As with instructions, you will have to plan carefully when you write a set of procedures. A mistake in business procedures can be as wide ranging and as costly as an error in a set of assembly instructions because poorly written procedures can land a company or its employees in significant financial and legal trouble.

To avoid such difficulties, spell out precisely what is expected of employees—how, when, where, and why they are to perform or adhere to a certain policy. Use the same strategies as for instructions discussed earlier in this chapter. Leave no chance for misunderstanding or ambiguity; be straightforward and clear-cut. Determine what information employees need in order to comply with your company's regulations.

Many times procedures involve a policy or a change in the work environment. Help readers by including, whenever necessary, definitions, headings, some prefatory explanations, and an offer to assist employees with any questions they may have. Always present the procedures to management to approve or to revise before sending them to employees via hard copy or as an e-document.

CASE STUDY

Writing Procedures at Work

Scheduling employees' time is a major consideration in the world of work. Figure 12.10 shows a memo from Tequina Bowers, a human resources manager, notifying employees how they can take advantage of a new flextime schedule. Note how Bowers divides her procedures into an introduction explaining when flextime will go into effect and what choices employees have, a section that clearly defines flextime, and finally the specific guidelines. Her job is to make sure the procedures are clear, do not contradict current company policy, and explicitly identify actions that a company will not tolerate; for example, switching hours with another employee.

The various regulations about what employees cannot do in flextime might be seen as the equivalents of the warning and caution statements discussed earlier (see "Warnings, Cautions, and Notes," pages 497–499). But note that Bowers's memo does not veer off to discuss benefits to the employer or to examine where flextime has been used elsewhere. Finally, this example of procedural writing protects NewTech, Inc. legally by establishing the policies by which an employee's scheduled work time is clearly defined, delineated, and assessed.

FIGURE 12.10 Memo Outlining Procedures to Follow Regarding a New Scheduling Policy

Notifies readers of new policy and states purpose of the memo

Spells out precisely how company defines flextime—uses boldface for most important information

Provides helpful examples

Stresses employee responsibilities and consequences of violating rules

NewTech, Inc.
● ● ●

4300 Ames Boulevard, Gunderson, CO 81230-0999
303.555.9721 **www.newtechinc.com**
f **www.facebook.com/NewTechInc**

TO: All Employees
FROM: Tequina Bowers T.B.
                 Human Resources Schedule
DATE: March 21, 2016
SUBJECT: Procedures for Opting for a Flextime Schedule

Effective 60 days from now, on May 20, 2016, employees will have the opportunity to switch to a flextime schedule or to remain on their current 8-hour fixed schedule. This memo explains the new flextime option and sets out the procedures you must follow if you choose this new schedule.

What is Flextime?

Flextime is based on a certain number of **core hours** and **flexible hours**. Our company will be open twelve hours, from 6:00 a.m. to 6:00 p.m. weekdays, to accommodate both fixed and flextime schedules. During this 12-hour period, all employees on flextime will be expected to work **8½ consecutive hours**, which includes a half-hour for lunch.

Regardless of schedule options, all employees must work a **common core time from 10:00 a.m. to 4:00 p.m.**, but flextime employees will be free to choose their own starting and quitting times. For instance, they might elect to arrive at 8:00 a.m. and leave at 4:30 p.m., or they may want to start at 9:30 a.m. and leave at 6:00 p.m.

Flextime Guidelines and Rules

Employees are expected to understand their individual responsibilities and adjust their schedules accordingly. All flextime employees must adhere strictly to the following regulations and realize that the option of a flextime schedule will be revoked for violations.

FIGURE 12.10 (Continued)

page 2

What Flextime Employees Must Do

(1) Be present during core time, but arriving and leaving the facility during their flexible work hours.
(2) Observe a minimum unpaid half-hour lunch break each working day.
(3) Cooperate with their supervisors to make sure adequate coverage is provided for their department from 6:00 a.m. to 6:00 p.m.
(4) Notify supervisors at once if you know you will be absent.
(5) Attend monthly corporate meetings even though such meetings may be outside their chosen flextime schedules.
(6) Adhere to company dress codes during any time they are at work, regardless of their flextime schedule.
(7) Agree to work on a flextime schedule for a minimum 6-month period.

What Flextime Employees Can't Do

(1) Be tardy during core time.
(2) Switch, bank, borrow, or trade flextime hours with other employees without the written approval of an immediate supervisor.
(3) File for overtime without a supervisor's approval.
(4) Self-schedule a vacation or leave by expanding flextime hours.
(5) Alternate between fixed time and flextime.

How Do You Sign Up for Flextime?

If you opt for a flextime schedule, first you need to obtain and complete a transfer of hours form from your supervisor. Next, you must sign up on the Human Resources department website to participate officially in this program.

I will be happy to talk to you about this new work schedule and to answer any questions. Please call me at ext. 5121, email me at **tbowers@newtechinc.com,** or visit the Human Resources Dept in Admin. 201. Thank you for your cooperation.

Carefully outlines what is acceptable according to new policy

Numbered points make policy easier to understand, follow, and refer to in the future

Stipulates what new policy will not allow in clear and concise language

Explains steps to begin flextime

Encourages feedback and questions

© 2017 Cengage Learning

SOME FINAL ADVICE

Perhaps the most important piece of advice to leave you with is this: Do not take *anything* for granted when you have to write a set of instructions or procedures. It is wrong and sometimes dangerous to assume that your readers have performed the procedures before, that they will automatically supply missing or "obvious" information, or that they will easily anticipate your next step or know what is expected of them at work without being informed. No one ever complained that a set of instructions was too clear or too easy to follow. Similarly, make sure that the procedures you may be called upon to write are easy to understand and to follow.

✓ REVISION CHECKLIST

- [ ] Analyzed my intended audience's background, especially why and how they will use my instructions.
- [ ] Tested my instructions to make sure they include all the necessary steps in their proper sequence.
- [ ] Ensured all measurements, distances, times, and relationships are precise and correct.
- [ ] Avoided technical terms if my audience is not a group of specialists in my field.
- [ ] Used the imperative mood for verbs and wrote clear, short sentences.
- [ ] Made my instructions easy to read and follow for an international audience.
- [ ] Chose effective visuals, labeled them, and placed them next to the step(s) to which they apply.
- [ ] Included relevant hyperlinks in online instructions to provide readers with help screens or further information.
- [ ] Made my introduction proportionate to the length and complexity of my instructions and suitable for my readers' needs.
- [ ] Included necessary background, safety, and operational information in the introduction.
- [ ] Provided a complete list of tools and materials my audience needs to carry out the instructions.
- [ ] Put the instructions in easy-to-follow steps and in the correct chronological/ sequential order.
- [ ] Used numbers or bullets to label the steps and inserted connective words to reinforce order.
- [ ] Inserted warnings, cautions, and notes where necessary and included culturally appropriate icons and colors that make them easy to find and to understand.
- [ ] Supplied a conclusion that summarizes what readers should have done or reassures them that they have completed the job satisfactorily.
- [ ] Provided troubleshooting guide to help readers identify a problem and take appropriate steps to fix it.
- [ ] Clearly spelled out policies, protocols, responsibilities, restrictions, and consequences of procedures for readers.

☐ Defined any terms readers may be unfamiliar with in procedures and, where helpful, provided an example.

☐ Submitted a copy of procedures to administrators for their approval before distributing to employees.

EXERCISES

1. Find a set of instructions that does not contain any visuals but that you think should to make the directions clearer. Design those visuals yourself, and indicate where they should be inserted in the instructions.

2. In a technical manual in your field or in an owner's manual, locate a set of instructions that you think is poorly written and illustrated. In a memo to your instructor, explain why the instructions are unclear, confusing, or badly formatted. Then, revise the instructions to make them easier for the reader to carry out. Submit the original instructions with your revision.

3. Write a short set of instructions in numbered steps (or in paragraph format) on one of the following relatively simple activities.

   a. tying a shoe
   b. using an ATM to withdraw money
   c. setting a DVR to record a television show
   d. sending a text message
   e. planting a tree or a shrub
   f. sewing a button on a shirt
   g. removing a stain from clothing
   h. pumping gas into a car
   i. creating a blog
   j. logging onto your college library's server
   k. polishing a floor
   l. shifting gears in a car
   m. taking a photograph with a mobile phone
   n. posting a video to your Facebook account

4. Write an appropriate introduction and conclusion for the set of instructions you wrote for Exercise 3.

5. Write a set of full instructions on one of the following more complex topics. Identify your audience. Include an appropriate introduction; a list of equipment and materials; numbered steps with necessary warnings, cautions, and notes; a troubleshooting guide; and an effective conclusion. Also include whatever visuals you think will help your audience.

   a. scanning a document
   b. accurately collecting a specimen or lab sample

    c. testing chlorine in a swimming pool

    d. shaving a patient for surgery

    e. removing "red eye" from a digital photo

    f. surveying a parcel of land

    g. creating a slideshow of the digital photos you took on a job

    h. jumping a dead car battery

    i. using the Heimlich maneuver to help a choking individual

    j. testing a circuit

    k. setting up a video conference call using Skype

    l. taking someone's blood pressure

    m. editing digital video

    n. welding a V-joint

    o. recording a podcast

    p. establishing the right dpi/resolution for an image you are using in a set of instructions

    q. backing up your computer files to an external hard drive

    r. building a backyard composting system

    s. decontaminating a doctor's exam room after an infectious patient leaves

6. The following set of instructions is confusing, vague, and out of order. Rewrite the instructions to make them clear, easy to follow, and correct. Make sure that each step follows the guidelines outlined in this chapter.

Reupholstering a Piece of Furniture

(1) Although it might be difficult to match the worn material with the new material, you might as well try.

(2) If you cannot, remove the old material.

(3) Take out the padding.

(4) Take out all of the tacks before removing the old covering. You might want to save the old covering.

(5) Measure the new material with the old, if you are able to.

(6) Check the frame, springs, webbing, and padding.

(7) Put the new material over the old.

(8) Check to see if it matches.

(9) You must have the same size as before.

(10) Look at the padding inside. If it is lumpy, smooth it out.

(11) You will need to tack all the sides down. Space your tacks a good distance apart.

(12) When you spot wrinkles, remove the tacks.

(13) Caution: in step 11, do not drive your tacks all the way through. Leave some room.

(14) Work from the center to the edge in step 11.

(15) Put the new material over the old furniture.

P.S. Use strong cords whenever there are tacks. Put the cords under the nails so that they hold.

---

7. Write a set of procedures on "greening" a student union or an employee rest area. This exercise can be done collaboratively, with each member of the team taking a key area: lighting, heating/cooling, recycling, noise pollution, food services. Include a relevant visual with your procedure.

8. Write a set of procedures, similar to Figure 12.10, for one of the following policies or regulations:

   a. offering quality customer service over the phone or via the Web
   b. filing a claim for a personal injury on the job
   c. decorating an employee's personal space—what is and is not allowed?
   d. checking social media at work
   e. ensuring confidentiality at work
   f. enrolling in mandatory courses to maintain a license or certificate
   g. playing music in the workplace
   h. going through an orientation procedure before beginning a new job
   i. following an acceptable company dress code
   j. allowing tattoos and body piercings in the workplace
   k. registering a domain name for a sponsored group at work or school
   l. receiving reimbursement for carpooling, taking public transportation, or riding a bicycle to work
   m. using a company vehicle
   n. going on a service call to a customer's home
   o. changing filters, parts, etc., on a periodic basis at work
   p. representing your company/organization at a professional meeting
   q. greening an office space
   r. submitting documentation for a promotion
   s. traveling with a pet on an airplane or a train
   t. requesting a refund for inadequate service

CHAPTER

13

Writing Winning Proposals

A **proposal** is a detailed plan of action submitted to a reader or group of readers for approval. The readers are usually in a position of authority — supervisors, managers, department heads, company buyers, elected officials, military or civic leaders — to endorse or reject the plan. Your proposal must convince these readers that your plan will help them improve their business, save them money, enhance their image on social media, improve customer satisfaction, make the environment safer, or all of these.

Proposals are written for many purposes and many different audiences. You can write an internal proposal, for example, to your boss, seeking authorization to hire staff, change a procedure, or purchase new equipment or software. Or you can write a sales proposal to potential customers, offering a product or a service (such as providing training with new, special firefighting gear or selling an office manager a line of ergonomically designed furniture).

Grant proposals, when writers apply for funding — to staff a community center or run a rural clinic — must follow the detailed guidelines found in RFPs (see "Solicited Proposals and Requests for Proposals (RFPs)," pages 520–523) specified by the funding agency, which is often a government office or charitable foundation.

Depending on the job, proposals can vary greatly in size and in scope. A formal proposal can be a very long and complex document running into hundreds of pages. A proposal to your employer, however, about redesigning the company website could easily be conveyed in a few pages, the length of a short report. To propose doing a small job for a prospective client — for example, establishing an electronic record retrieval system — a letter with information on costs, materials, and a timetable might suffice. The sales letter in Figure 6.3 (page 195) illustrates a short proposal in letter format. Proposals can be **unsolicited** — that is, they originate with you — or they can be **solicited**, requested by a company or organization, as in Figure 13.6 (pages 537–539).

PROPOSALS ARE PERSUASIVE PLANS

Proposals, whether large or small, must be highly persuasive to succeed. Without your audience's approval, your plan will never go into effect, however accurate and important you think it is. Your enthusiasm is not enough; you have to supply hard evidence. Your proposals must convince readers that your plan is relevant, practical, based upon careful research, and designed to benefit the reader and his or her company.

Every proposal you write must exhibit a "can do" attitude, putting the reader and his or her company's needs at the center of your work. Show readers how approving your plan will save them time and money, increase productivity, enhance corporate image, improve employee morale, or attract new business. The tone of your proposal should be "Here is what I can do for you." Yates Engineering has won millions of dollars of business through its reader-centered proposals. Its slogan is "On time... within budget ... to your satisfaction." Time, budget, and your readers' satisfaction and convenience are among the key ingredients of a winning proposal.

Customize your proposal by personalizing it. Use online surveys (see "Online Survey Builders, page 319) and social media feedback to help you gauge your audience's needs. Take into account also comments on review sites such as Yelp, TripAdvisor, and Angie's List. Advertisements such as the ones in Figure 1.7 (page 24) often contain mini-proposals appealing to a customer's need for a more economical and efficient way to do things. Notice how the advertisement in Figure 13.1 encourages potential clients to purchase a security package based on a

FIGURE 13.1 An Example of a "Can Do" Attitude

variety of available options from motion detection systems to video surveillance to well-trained officers.

PROPOSALS FREQUENTLY ARE COLLABORATIVE EFFORTS

Like many other examples of business and technical writing, proposals often are the product of teamwork. Even a short in-house proposal, such as the one in Figure 13.5 (pages 530–534), is often researched and put together by more than one individual in the company or agency.

Many times, individual employees will pull together information from their separate areas (such as graphics and design, finance, marketing, technology, transportation, and even legal) and put it into a proposal that each member of the team then reads and revises until the team agrees that the document is ready to be released.

TYPES OF PROPOSALS

Proposals are classified according to (1) how they originate and (2) where they are sent after they are written. Distinctions are made between *solicited* and *unsolicited* proposals based on how they originate and between **internal** and **external** proposals based on where they are sent. Depending on your audience and your purpose, you may write an internal solicited or unsolicited proposal, or you may write an external solicited or unsolicited proposal. Solicited proposals often involve requests for proposals. Figure 13.2 provides a visual representation of the various types of proposals.

Solicited Proposals and Requests for Proposals (RFPs)

When a company has a particular problem to be solved or a job to be done, it will solicit, or invite, proposals. Accordingly, you do not have to spend time identifying the company's problem. The company will notify you and other competitors by preparing a **request for proposals** (RFP), which is a set of instructions that specifies the exact type of work to be done, along with guidelines on how and when the company wants the work completed.

FIGURE 13.2 Types of Proposals

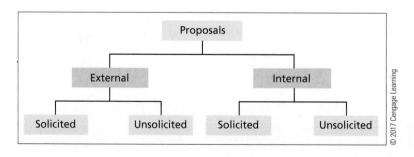

© 2017 Cengage Learning

Some RFPs are long and full of legal requirements and conditions. Others, like the examples in Figures 13.3 and 13.4 (page 522), are more concise. RFPs are sent to firms with track records in the relevant field. RFPs are also printed in trade publications, posted on a company's website or a site such as rfpzone.com, or even posted on a social media site like Facebook to attract the highest number of qualified bidders for the job. The U.S. government publishes RFPs in the *Federal Register* (www.federalregister.gov) or *Federal Business Opportunities* (also known as *FedBizOpps*) (www.fbo.gov). No two RFPs are alike.

An RFP helps you understand what the customer wants. It is often extremely detailed and even tells you how the company wants the proposal prepared, for example, what information is to be included (on backgrounds, personnel, equipment, budgets), where it needs to appear, and how many copies of the proposal you have to submit.

Your proposal will be evaluated according to how well you fulfill the terms of the RFP. For that reason, follow the directions in the RFP exactly. Note that the solicited proposal in Figure 13.6 (pages 537–539) directly refers to the terms of the RFP. You should even use the language (specialized terms, specifically stated needs) of the RFP in your proposal to convince readers that you understand their

FIGURE 13.3 A Sample RFP for a Smaller Project

REQUEST FOR PROPOSALS

Mesa Community College is soliciting proposals to construct and to install 50 individual study carrels in its Holmes Memorial Library. These carrels must be highly serviceable, include a 32-inch Internet-ready touch screen, be electronically wired for assistive technologies, and conform to all specification standards of the American Library Association (ALA) and the Americans with Disabilities Act. Proposals should include the precise measurements of the carrels to be installed, the specific acoustical and lighting benefits, and the types and amount of storage space offered, and an analysis of the annual environmental impact for each unit.

Work on constructing and installing the carrels must be completed no later than the start of the Fall Semester, August 21, 2016. Proposals should include a schedule of when different phases of work will be completed and an itemized budget for labor, materials, equipment, and necessary tests to ensure high-quality acoustical performance. Contractors should detail their qualifications, including a description of similar recent work and a list of references. Proposals should be submitted in triplicate no later than March 2, 2016 to:

Dr. Barbara Feldstein
Director of the Library
Mesa Community College
Mesa, CO 80932-0617
BFeldstein@Mesa.edu

FIGURE 13.4 A Section of an RFP for a Larger Project

An RFP for the Fund for Rural America

The Fund for Rural America program supports competitively awarded research, extension, and education grants addressing key issues that contribute to the economic diversification and development of rural areas. The amount available for support of this program is approximately $9,500,000, from which approximately 15–20 awards will be made.

Program Description

Preservation of the economic viability of rural communities is the chief focus of the Fund for Rural America. The program focuses attention on rural communities' twin challenges of rural community innovation and demographic change. Challenges of an aging population, the arrival of new immigrant populations, . . . and workforce development all are critical issues that affect rural economies. Rural communities may propose research, education, and extension/outreach projects that will increase our understanding of these demographic forces and develop the capacity to turn these challenges into economic promise.

Rural Community Innovation

This program solicits research, education, and extension proposals that will help rural Americans address existing and new problems in innovative ways. The goals of this program area are to generate relevant knowledge and transfer that knowledge to assist rural communities to diversify their economies, to develop and maintain profitable farms, firms, and businesses, to build community, to aid growth, to protect natural resources, and to increase family financial security.

Projects such as the following combine multiple strategies for innovation that Fund for Rural America encourages in order to:

- help a community move to a more bio-based economy (carbon control credits, promoting locally based bio-based industries, linking bio-based materials to a diverse agriculture and community);
- include using land that offers development options (farmland preservation, farming on the urban fringe, rural-urban land use issues);
- institute policies that increase profits of small and minority farmers;
- use e-commerce applications for remote rural areas and minority populations, develop community information networks to support e-commerce and e-communities, and adapt e-commerce strategies for planning and social capital development;
- expand network capabilities among producers, businesses, entrepreneurs, families, individuals, nonprofit groups, community institutions, local government, and state and federal agencies;
- develop a new generation of Internet-based planning tools (geospatial analysis, information stores, economic and land use blueprints) and the ability to apply and tailor them for place-sensitive development.

Source: U.S. Department of Agriculture.

requirements and to get them to accept your plan. If you have any questions, by all means call the agency or company so you do not waste your time or theirs by including irrelevant or unnecessary details in your proposal.

Unsolicited Proposals

With an unsolicited proposal, you—not the reader—make the first move. Unlike a solicited proposal, in which the company to which you are submitting the proposal knows about the problem, your unsolicited proposal has to convince readers that (1) there is a problem, (2) it is important enough to be corrected, and (3) you and your firm are the ones to solve it.

Doing all this is not as difficult as it sounds. If your readers accept your identification of the problem, you have greatly increased the chances of their accepting your plan to solve it. Just remember that you will have to prove that solving the problem carries major benefits for your readers.

Internal and External Proposals

An internal proposal is written to one or several decision makers in your own organization who have to sign off or approve your plan. As you will see in Figure 13.5 (pages 530–534), an internal proposal can deal with a variety of topics, including changing a policy or procedure, requesting additional personnel, or purchasing or updating equipment or software.

An external proposal is sent to a decision maker outside your company. It might go to a potential client you have never worked for (see Figure 13.6, pages 537–539) or to a previous or current client. An external proposal can also be submitted to a government funding agency, such as the Department of Agriculture, in response to its RFP (see Figure 13.4). External proposals tend to be more formal than internal ones.

TECH NOTE

Finding U.S. Government RFPs Online

The U.S. government, through its many departments and agencies, is an important source for RFPs. FedBizOpps (**www.fbo.gov**) claims that it offers "a comprehensive listing of government RFP's." In addition, the *Federal Register* (**www.federalregister .gov**), published daily by the U.S. government, issues hundreds of legal regulations as well as requests for proposals from various agencies.

Another site to search for government RFPs on the Internet is *Commerce Business Daily* (*CBD*), which "lists notices of proposed government procurement actions, contract awards, sales of government property and other procurement information. A new edition of the *CBD* is issued every business day, and each edition contains approximately 500–1000 notices." The *CBD* website (**www.cbd-net.com**) lists the government's requests for, among other things, equipment, supplies, and a variety of services from assembling to maintaining equipment to dredging.

EIGHT GUIDELINES FOR WRITING A SUCCESSFUL PROPOSAL

The following guidelines will help you persuade your audience to approve your plan. Refer to these guidelines and Figures 13.5 and 13.6 both before and while you formulate your plan.

1. Approach writing a proposal as a problem-solving activity. Your purpose should reflect your ability to identify and solve problems. Convince your audience that you know what their needs are and that you will meet them, as Alissa Bond and Stacy Holton do in Figure 13.5, and as Neelow Singh and Jack Rosen do in Figure 13.6.

2. Regard your audience as skeptical. Even though you offer a plan that you think will benefit readers, do not be overconfident that they will automatically accept it as the best and only way to proceed. Brainstorm, alone or with your collaborative team, to anticipate and answer your readers' questions and objections. Use social media and online surveys to find customer information you can incorporate in your proposal. To determine whether your proposal is feasible, readers will study it carefully. If your proposal contains errors or inconsistencies, omits information, or deviates from what they are looking for, your readers will reject it.

3. Research your proposal topic thoroughly. A winning proposal is *not* based on a few well-meaning, general suggestions. To provide the detailed information necessary and to convince readers, you will have to do your homework. Research your topic by studying the latest technology in the field (as Alissa Bond and Stacy Holton do in Figure 13.5), shopping for the best prices, comparing your prices and services with what the competition offers, verifying schedules, visiting customers, making site visits, and interviewing key individuals. Make sure that any technology or equipment you use or sell complies with all codes, specifications, and standards.

4. Scout out what your competitors are doing. Become familiar with your competitors' products or services, have a fair idea about their market costs, and be able to show how your company's work is better overall. Provide examples; offer a demonstration. Read competitors' websites, social media posts on Facebook, Twitter, and Pinterest, and print publications very carefully. Let readers know you have done your homework on their behalf. See how the employees who wrote the internal proposal in Figure 13.5 researched the industry average for losses due to unsold inventory and inventory discounts. Note, too, how the writers in Figure 13.6 prove that their product and service are superior to those of their competitors.

5. Prove that your proposal is workable. The bottom-line question from your readers is "Will this plan work?" Your proposal should contain no statements that say, "Let's see what happens if we do *X* or *Y*." Analyze and test each part of your proposal to eliminate any quirks and to revise the proposal appropriately before readers evaluate it. What you propose should be consistent with the organization and capabilities of the company and should respect its corporate mission and culture. See how Alissa Bond and Stacy Holton argue how relevant, user friendly, and compatible Inventech is for their sporting goods company. For instance, recommending that a small company of eighteen employees triple its workforce to implement your plan would be foolish and risky.

6. Be sure your proposal is financially realistic. "Is it worth the money?" is another bottom-line question you can expect from your readers. For example, recommending that your company spend $20,000 to solve a $2,000 problem is just not feasible. Note how Figure 13.5 details both the cost of inaction and the amount needed to correct the problem and how Figure 13.6 stresses that the costs are in line with what the customer wants to spend. Above all, make readers believe that the benefits are worth the costs.

7. Be ethical. Your proposal needs to follow all the guidelines for ethical conduct (see "Ethical Writing in the Workplace," pages 26–37). You must be trustworthy and truthful about all the claims you make about products, services, and contracts and that you will be professional and respond to any questions or problems your readers voice. Later sections of this chapter discuss the ethical standards you must adhere to when writing either an internal proposal (pages 526–536) or a sales proposal (pages 536–541).

8. Package your proposal attractively. Make sure that your proposal is well presented (professional looking, inviting, and easy to read) and that all visuals are clear and appropriately placed. The visual appearance of your proposal can contribute greatly to whether it is accepted.

TECH NOTE

Document Design and Your Proposal

As we saw in Chapter 11, the overall design and layout of a document play a major role in its acceptance by an audience. This is especially true of a proposal—a key sales document for you and your company. Your proposal will be competing with many (perhaps 50 or 100) other proposals, and the first impression it makes should be attractive, logically organized, and reader friendly. If it is designed professionally and pleasingly, it will remain in the running. If not, your proposal may be rejected before your audience reads your first sentence.

Here are some guidelines to help you prepare an attractive and carefully designed proposal.

- Make sure you follow the RFP guidelines to the letter—in terms of spacing, title page, number of copies, appendixes, exhibits, and so on.
- Double-check to make sure your proposal looks professional. If you have to submit a printed document, use good-quality paper and a sturdy binding. If you have to submit your proposal electronically, make sure you follow the instructions exactly.

(Continued)

- Organize your proposal into sections that help readers identify and follow its various parts—for example, problem, solution, budget, timetable, personnel. If the RFP asks you to include certain sections, follow these instructions exactly. Otherwise your proposal could be rejected.
- Use clearly marked, logically ordered, and consistent headings (or, if necessary, subheadings) to separate sections of your proposal to help readers follow and understand your work easily, quickly, and clearly.
- Insert extra spacing between sections of your proposal so they stand out and show readers your work is organized.
- Use a professional-looking and easy-to-read font and type size. Do not try to cram more information in by resorting to an 8-point type.
- Include easy-to-follow indented lists, each item preceded by a bullet or an asterisk.
- Clearly label and insert all visuals in the most appropriate places in your proposal. See Figure 13.5, which does an especially effective job.
- Put budgets in easy-to-read tables; do not bury numbers in a paragraph of prose. Make sure each item in a budget is identified and highlighted or relegated to a footnote or an appendix.
- Keep your paragraphs to five to six sentences. Heavy blocks of prose slow readers down and make them think your work is dense and hard to follow. Consider your readers' comfort level.
- Do not fail to include and label any supporting documents or materials that are not a part of your proposal proper, for example, schedules, surveys, or samples, as in Figure 13.6.

INTERNAL PROPOSALS

The primary purpose of an internal proposal, such as the one shown in Figure 13.5 (pages 530–534), is to offer a realistic and constructive plan to help your company run its business more efficiently and economically.

On your job you may discover a better way of doing something or a more efficient way to correct a problem. You believe that your proposed change will save your employer time, money, or further trouble. (Note how Alissa Bond and Stacy Holton indentified and researched a more effective and efficient way for Challenger Sports to manage its inventory and to satisfy its customers in Figure 13.5.) Or your department head, manager, or supervisor may call your attention to a problem and ask you for specific ways to solve it.

Regardless of who identifies the problem, your proposal, generally speaking, will be an informal, in-house message. A brief (one- to three- or four-page) memo, as in Figure 13.5, or even a shorter email, should be appropriate.

Some Common Topics for Internal Proposals

An internal proposal can be written about a variety of topics, including the following:

- purchasing new or more advanced equipment to replace obsolete or inefficient computers, appliances, vehicles, and the like, or upgrading equipment technology
- obtaining new software and offering training sessions to show employees how to use it
- recruiting new employees or retraining current ones on a new technique or process
- eliminating a dangerous condition or reducing an environmental risk to prevent accidents—for employees, customers, or the community at large
- cutting costs—for services, supplies, transportation, advertising, etc.
- improving technology/communication within or between departments of a company or agency
- expanding work space or making it greener, more private, ergonomically comfortable and efficient for employees, or more inviting to customers
- providing better safety and security, safeguarding a company's records

As this bulleted list shows, internal proposals cover almost every activity or policy that can affect the day-to-day operations of a company or an agency.

Following the Proper Chain of Command

Writing an internal proposal requires you to be sensitive to office politics. It may be wise first to meet with your boss to see if she or he has already identified the problem or has specific suggestions on how to solve it. If given the go-ahead, then you and your team need to provide your boss with a draft and ask for feedback.

But do not assume that your readers will automatically agree that there is a problem or that your plan is the only way to tackle it. Remember that your employer will expect you to be very convincing about both the problem you say exists and the changes you are advocating in the workplace under his or her supervision. Don't rock the corporate boat by going over your supervisor's head, questioning his or her authority, or suggesting a plan that is too costly.

Ethically Anticipating and Resolving Corporate Readers' Problems

When you prepare an internal proposal, you need to be aware of the ethical obligations you have and the ways to meet them. Here are some important guidelines:

1. **Consider the company wide implications of your plan.** The change you propose (transfers, new budgets or technology, new hires) may have sweeping and potentially disruptive implications for another office or division in your company.

2. **Do not discount the possible impact of your change on co-workers from cultural traditions other than your own.** In addition to speaking to your employer, consult your human resources or cultural diversity director.

3. **Find out whether your proposed plan is within your company's budget.** How much can your department, branch, or office spend (e.g., on hardware,

software, updates)? Check with your boss, and always monitor the price of your company's stock orders to make sure any expenditures are likely to be approved.

4. Realize that your reader may feel threatened by your plan. Your plan may sound just right to you, but your boss may regard it as criticism leveled at him or her, your department, or even the company as a whole.

5. Take into account that your reader may have "pet projects" or predetermined ways of doing things. Address them respectfully. You may even find a way to build on or complement such projects or procedures.

6. Keep in mind that your boss may have to take your proposal farther up the organizational ladder for commentary and approval. You cannot disregard the chain of command at your company or organization.

7. Never rely on someone else to supply the specific details on how your proposal will work. For example, do not write an internal proposal that says the marketing, technical support, or human resources department could supply the necessary details for your proposal to work. That unfairly pushes the responsibility onto others.

CASE STUDY

Drafting an Internal Proposal to Create a Mobile App for a Health Food Store

Jaclyn Tan, an evening shift supervisor for a small chain of health food stores, realized from conversations with staff and customers, as well as from marketing surveys conducted through the company website and posts to blogs and Facebook, that her employer was missing many opportunities for sales by not having a free mobile app available for customers.

Tan sent a memo through email to her boss, district manager Arnold Maddox, identifying some of the benefits to the company in having its own app and requested permission to investigate more formally the options and costs involved in creating the app. After several discussions with Maddox, in person and online, Tan got approval to draft an internal proposal to create a customer app.

Brainstorming with her fellow employees, she identified the key functionalities needed for the app, such as allowing customers to

- check the availability of favorite products
- pre-order/pre-pay for items that were difficult to keep in stock
- alert them to sales and new products
- establish and maintain a charge account status

She also found that their customers would appreciate

- information on relevant Food and Drug Administration (FDA) and United States Department of Agriculture (USDA) reports
- special events, such as the store hosting speakers and sponsoring healthy cooking classes
- community events where her company's products might be promoted.

Armed with this information, she contacted several mobile app consultants to investigate the time and costs involved in creating an app to meet her customer's needs and respect her company's history and mission.

Working with the consultants via Skype and email, Tan was able to estimate the following:

Estimated hours of work needed to create the app, test it, and link it to the store's website	150
IT consultants cost	x $75/hr. (on average)
TOTAL COST	**$11,250**

Having gathered relevant technical and financial information, she shared her findings with her co-workers. She was then ready to write an internal proposal that respected her employer's chain of command and that would better promote her company's products and services.

Organization of an Internal Proposal

A short internal proposal follows a relatively straightforward plan of organization, from identifying the problem to solving it. Internal proposals usually contain four parts, as shown in Figure 13.5: *purpose*, *problem*, *solution*, and *conclusion*. Refer to the figure as you read the following discussion.

Purpose

Begin your proposal with a brief statement as Alissa Bond and Stacy Holton do to their supervisor: "I propose that . . ." State right away why you think a specific change is necessary now. Then succinctly define the problem and emphasize that your plan, if approved by the reader, will solve that problem.

Problem

In this section, prove that a problem exists. Document its importance for your boss and your company; as a matter of fact, the more you show, with concrete evidence, how the problem affects your boss's work (and area of supervision), the more likely you are to persuade him or her to act.

Here are some guidelines for documenting a problem:

- Avoid vague (and unsupported) generalizations such as these: "We're losing money each day with this procedure." "Costs continue to escalate." "The trouble occurs frequently in a number of places." "Numerous complaints have come in." "If something isn't done soon, more problems will result." Figure 13.5 focuses on an inventory tracking system.
- Provide quantifiable details about the problem, such as the amount of money or time a company is actually losing per day, week, or month. Document

FIGURE 13.5 An Internal Unsolicited Proposal to Purchase Updated Inventory Software

www.challengersports.com
Waveland 591-727-6079
Addison 591-650-2362
Turnersville 591-936-2290

 www.facebook.com

 @challengersports

www.pinterest.com/challengersp

Date: October 1, 2015
To: Michael Sapientia, Owner
From: Alissa Bond and Stacy Holton
RE: A proposal to purchase and implement new inventory-tracking
software within the next 30 days

Purpose

We propose a cost-effective solution for a growing problem at our stores: the
lack of an accurate, easy-to-use inventory tracking system. We propose that
you approve the purchase and installation, within the next month, of the
Inventech software program as well as the necessary hardware to make the
system operable. Our company will benefit from an up-to-date inventory
system that serves customers better and regains lost revenue because of
inadequate inventory procedures.

The Problem with Current Inventory Systems

Since we expanded last year from just our Waveland store to two additional
locations, our inventory ordering methods have not accurately reflected
customer demand. Up until now, we have relied on our employees to gauge
ordering needs, but because of our recent expansion, the salesforce we had last
year at our Waveland store is now divided among all three Challenger stores.
To staff these new locations, we hired 15 part-time employees (most of whom
are new to the retail sporting goods business). Table 1 below shows our
current staffing situation compared to last year.

Table 1

Last Year	This Year
Waveland (6 full-time, 3 part-time)	Waveland (2 full-time, 6 part-time)
	Addison (2 full-time, 6 part-time)
	Turnersville (2 full-time, 6 part-time)

Because we had to spread our experienced full-time staff among three stores
we have not been able to gauge our inventory needs as accurately as before
our expansion. The problem of effectively tracking and ordering adequate
inventory was compounded by assuming that the two new stores would
mirror the purchasing decisions of customers at the Waveland site. Instead, our
records show that customer demands have differed greatly from store to store,
and often by a disturbingly large amount. For example:

- The Addison store sells three times the number of football-related
  jerseys and gear than Waveland does.
- The Turnersville store sells almost four times as many
  fishing-related items as either the Waveland or Addison stores do.
- The Waveland store sells almost double the amount of golf-related
  items as the Addison and Turnersville stores do combined.

*Clearly states
why proposal is
being sent*

*Acknowledges
company's
stated goals
and projects
outcome of
adopting their
recommen-
dation*

*Identifies
problem by
giving reader
essential
background
information
based on
primary research*

*Table provides
quick synopsis of
current staffing
situation*

*Divides the
problem into
parts: financial
and customer
service*

*Bulleted list
of succinct
examples of
basis for the
inventory
problem*

FIGURE 13.5 (Continued)

Page 2

By stocking the Addison and Turnersville locations with the same inventory as Waveland, we fell short of meeting customer demand during the key Fall and Christmas selling seasons. Moreover, even when employees referred customers to one of our other two stores, we often lost business to competitors, as only 35 percent of our same-store referrals would up purchasing an item from us. We also saw a surge in negative tweets and posts on Facebook. Research shows that when consumers have a negative buying experience the first time they try a new business, more than half of them will not give this business "a second chance to make a first impression" (Maynard et al., 2014).*

Cites important research

But having too much inventory is as unprofitable as stocking too little. A surplus of merchandise takes up costly warehouse and showroom space, while stocking too few items can drive our customers elsewhere. But whatever the case, we are losing business and revenue because of the dated and inefficient ways we purchase and stock merchandise.

Provides sourcing and background information for the table that follows

Table 2 below, based on a detailed internal audit (made on September 14th in preparation for the 2015 tax year), breaks down the losses we have incurred since January 2015 due to overstocking in all three stores.

Note that in the table,

- *Revenue Loss from Discounting* represents the loss we actually experienced when we sold these items at a deep and necessary discount as opposed to their full retail prices.
- *Revenue Loss from Unsold Inventory* documents the revenue forfeited when the inventoried items did not sell at all.

Table 2

Accumulates important financial information in easy-to-read table

Sport	Revenue Loss from Discounting	Revenue Loss from Unsold Inventory	Total Loss
Golf	$17,835	$7,715	$25,550
Football	$16,545	$4,455	$21,000
Fishing	$8,355	$11,390	$19,745
Soccer	$9,650	$3,850	$13,500
Cycling	$8,625	$3,570	$12,195
Baseball	$5,225	$3,730	$8,955
Basketball	$4,010	$4,715	$8,725
Swimming	$7,110	$890	$8,000
Hockey	$5,135	$2,680	$7,815
TOTAL	**$82,490**	**$42,995**	**$125,485**

(*Continued*)

*To save space the references section has been omitted.

FIGURE 13.5 (Continued)

Lost revenue comes from discounting plus unsold inventory. Our total losses amount to 12.6% of our expected revenue from all these items, or $125,485 across the three stores. In our city-wide sales area, competing sporting goods stores lost only 6.6% of expected revenue, as opposed to our 12.6%, because of unsold inventory or deep discounting.

The explanation for such losses is our not having a comprehensive inventory tracking system, compounded by our opening two new stores. This not only hurts the Challenger brand in the marketplace; it cumulatively means greater losses this coming fiscal year. Deep discounting undermines our marketing strategy of being a premiere sporting goods store that gives customers a one-stop-shopping experience. It also jeopardizes our long-term goal to expand our customer base effectively through the two new stores in Addison and Turnersville.

A Solution to the Problem

Purchasing and installing a comprehensive inventory tracking system will allow Challenger to reclaim a sizable percentage of the revenue we have lost by upgrading our inventory procedures and considerably reducing discounting and carrying unsold inventory. A relevant study of small businesses by Lapka and Harper (2014) found that when businesses began using a tracking system, they were able to reclaim almost 33% of revenue losses due to inventory issues in the first year.

We believe that by switching to an updated, comprehensive inventory tracking system our company will benefit in several ways:

- Based on the study above (Lapka and Harper, 2014), we could conservatively reclaim 28% of the revenue lost this year due to inventory problems
- We could recoup maximum use of display room and warehouse space.
- Eliminating a large percentage of surplus stock, we would reduce a lower profit margin from discount sales.
- We would provide better possibilities for each store to specialize based on sales/customer needs.
- We would be better positioned to expand and maintain our customer base at all three locations.
- Our rating on social review sites like Yelp would improve as customer complaints about lack of products decreased.

Feasibility of Installing New Inventory Tracking Software

We researched several tracking software programs and believe that Inventech Inventory Tracking (**www.inventech.com/inventory**) offers the best and most cost-effective software for Challenger's inventory problems. Inventech will allow us to track, record, and calculate our merchandise efficiently and be in a better position to project orders in fiscal year 2016.

Diplomatically identifies cause of the problem without assigning blame

Emphasizes possible future problems

Problem is clearly stated before giving reader supporting evidence

Relates solution to both parts of the inventory problem

Bulleted list makes benefits and recommendations easy to follow

FIGURE 13.5 (Continued)

Page 4

A further benefit is that Inventech allows us to retain historical sales data and to perform many inventory audits that we are currently unable to perform such as:

- Track inventory for each item from each store at the end of every business day.
- Project required inventory levels for the next 7 days based on historical sales data and current inventory levels.
- Automatically place orders for items that we are low on with suppliers who can promise delivery with only a 2-day lead.
- Generate daily recommended transfers of items from high-inventory locations to low-inventory ones, again based on historical sales data and current inventory levels.
- Assist us through customized software to grow and expand as we increase our stores in the future.

Shows problem can be solved and how

Training

Training for all employees can begin as soon as the software is purchased, the necessary hardware and network upgrades are implemented, and the software installed. Another benefit of going with Inventech is that they offer on-site, 6-hour training programs at a cost of $520 per employee; these programs can be scheduled at our convenience with 2 week's notice—in plenty of time for holiday shopping. Given Inventech's solid reputation for training (verified by checking their references, as well as posts to blogs and Facebook and reviews on Yelp), the system can be fully in-place within the next 30 days.

Provides an overview of the steps required to implement the proposal, and a timeline for carrying it out

Costs

The costs of implementing our proposal are as follows:

Site license and IT Service Plan for Inventech (Version 7.1)	$5,757.00 ($1,919.00 per year per store × 3 stores)
6-hour training for all staff (24 employees)	$12,480.00 ($520 each × 24 employees)
New external hard drives for each store to run software and keep secure inventory records	$10,788.00 ($899 each × 12 registers)
Installation of software and increasing the capacity of the computer network for the company	$11,200
TOTAL	**$40,225**

Itemizes costs

(Continued)

FIGURE 13.5 (Continued)

<table>
<tr>
<td>

Interprets costs for the reader

</td>
<td>

Page 5

There are other financial advantages in purchasing the new Inventech software. We would also be able to amortize, for tax purposes, the cost of the installation of the inventory tracking software ($40,225) over 5 years. Our annual expenses would, therefore, actually be:

$34,468 ($12,480 for training + $10,788 for hard drives + $11,200 for network upgrades) ÷ 5 years = $6,893.60
+ $5,757.00 (annual site license)
$12,650.60 **per year**

</td>
</tr>
</table>

Proves change is cost effective; provides specific financial evidence

Compared with the **$125,485** we lost in revenue last year because of insufficient inventory procedures, the amount of annual depreciated costs for the new Inventech system is significantly smaller and well worth our investment. Using the Inventech software will allow us to recoup 28% of the revenue lost due to inventory problems, which means that purchasing the Inventech system will also bring in additional revenue of at least **$35,136** for 2016.

Conclusion

Succinctly recaps all major benefits of buying the updated software

Purchasing the Inventech software is necessary, feasible, and cost effective for Challenger. By approving our proposal, the company can realistically expect to generate at least **$35,136** in additional revenue annually, increase customer satisfaction and patronage at all three stores. We will be happy to discuss this proposal with you at your convenience, and look forward to answering any questions. Thank you.

Thanks reader

the financial trouble so that you can show in the next section how your plan offers an efficient and workable solution. See Table 2 in Figure 13.5.

- Indicate how many employees (or work-hours) are involved or how many customers are inconvenienced or endangered by a procedure or condition. The writers in Figure 13.5 researched industry standards for losses related to inventory and used this information to document the importance of the problem.
- Verify how widespread a problem is or how frequently it occurs by citing specific times it occurs. (See the bulleted list at the bottom of page 1 of Figure 13.5.)
- Relate the problem to an organization's image, corporate reputation, or influence (where appropriate). Pinpoint exactly how and where the problem lessens your company's effectiveness or hurts its standing in the market or on social media. Indicate who is affected and how the problem affects your company's business, as the writers do in the problem statement in Figure 13.5.

Solution or Plan

In this section, describe the change you propose and want approved. Tie your solution (the change) directly to the problem you have just documented. Each part of your plan should help eliminate the problem or should help increase the productivity, efficiency, or safety you think is possible.

Your reader will again expect to find factual evidence. Be specific. Do not give merely an outline of your plan or say that details can be worked out later. Supply evidence that answers the following questions: (1) Is the plan workable? and (2) Is it cost-effective? See how the writers of the proposal in Figure 13.5 do that.

To get the reader to say "Yes" to both questions, supply the facts you have gathered as a result of your research. For example, if you propose that your firm buy new software or equipment, do the necessary homework to find the most efficient and cost-effective model available, as the proposal writers in Figure 13.5 do.

- Supply the vendors' names, the costs, major conditions of service and training contracts, and warranties.
- Describe how your firm could use the equipment or technology to obtain better or quicker results.
- Document specific tasks the new equipment can perform more efficiently at a lower cost than the equipment now in use.

A proposal to change or establish new procedures must address the following questions:

- How does the new (or revised) procedure work?
- How many employees or customers will be affected by it?
- When can it go into operation?
- How much will it cost the employer to change procedures?
- What delays or losses in business might be expected while the company switches from one procedure to another?
- What employees, equipment, technology, or locations are already available to accomplish the change?

Beyond a doubt, costs will be of utmost importance to your decision-maker reader. Make sure you supply a careful and accurate budget. Moreover, make the costs attractive by emphasizing how inexpensive they are compared with the cost of not making the change, as Bond and Holton do persuasively in the section labeled "Costs" in Figure 13.5. Link costs to savings and other benefits. And always be sure to double-check your math.

It is also wise to raise alternative solutions before the reader does—and to discuss their disadvantages.

Conclusion

Your conclusion should be short—a paragraph or two at the most. Remind readers that (1) the problem is ongoing and serious, (2) the reason for change is justified and beneficial to your organization, and (3) action needs to be taken. Reemphasize the most important benefits in the conclusion, as in Figure 13.5. Also, indicate that you are willing to discuss your plan with the reader and want his or her feedback, a necessity in arguing for a corporate change at any level.

SALES PROPOSALS

A **sales proposal** is the most common external proposal. Its purpose is to sell your company's brand, its products or services for a set fee. Whether short or long, a sales proposal is a marketing tool that includes a detailed description of the work you propose to do. Figure 13.6 on pages 537–539 is an example of a sales proposal.

Knowing Your Audience and Meeting Its Needs

Your audience will usually be one or more executives who have the power to approve or reject a proposal. This audience may be even more skeptical than readers of an internal proposal, because they may not know you or your work. To increase your chances of success, follow the company you're sending your proposal to on social media to get a better sense of its customers' views and its needs. Try to anticipate an audience's questions, such as:

- Does the writer's firm understand our problem?
- Can the writer's firm deliver what it promises?
- Can the job be completed on time?
- Is the budget reasonable and realistic?
- Will the job be done exactly as we proposed?
- Has the writer demonstrated his or her qualifications and trustworthiness?

Answer each of these questions by demonstrating how your product or service is tailored to the customer's needs.

Be sure, too, that your proposal has a competitive edge. Your proposal has to convince readers that the product or service your company offers is more reliable, economical, efficient, and up-to-date than another company's. Whenever relevant, stress that your company offers state-of-the-art technology, exemplary service, and after-the-sale assistance and warranty. Here is where your homework will pay off. See how Neelow Singh and Jack Rosen emphasize the range of advantages their flooring offers a prospective customer in Figure 13.6.

Being Ethical and Legal

In addition to the guidelines in Chapter 1 (see "Some Guidelines to Help You Reach Ethical Decisions," pages 32–34), here are some ways to make sure your sales proposal follows the highest ethical standards:

- **View your proposal as a contract.** If you omit information, misrepresent claims, or minimize risks, you can be taken to court and sued for damages.
- **Submit a complete, accurate, and fair budget.** Break down all costs in your budget. Indicate if your fees are by the job, weekly, or hourly. Always alert readers to any possible additional charges (e.g., the fees for permits, an increase in the price of materials).

FIGURE 13.6 PDF of a Sales Proposal in Response to a Request from a Company

Reynolds Interiors

250 Commence Avenue • Edison, NJ 08837-2129
www.reynolds.com • 732-777-8733 • Fax: 732-777-8833

FOLLOW US ON FACEBOOK (www.facebook.com/reynoldsinteriors)

AND TWITTER (@reynoldsinteriors)

January 18, 2016

Mr. Floyd Tompkins, Manager
General Appliances
140 Kilmer Road
Edison, NJ 08817-7639

Dear Mr. Tompkins:

In response to your request for bid #GA01012012 posted on your website for an appropriate floor covering at your new showroom, Reynolds Interiors is pleased to submit the following proposal to meet your specific needs. We appreciated the opportunity to visit your showroom on January 15 in order to gather information to prepare this proposal.

After carefully reviewing your requirements for a floor covering and inspecting your new facility, we believe that **Armstrong Classic Corlon 900** is the most suitable choice. Traffic tests conducted by the independent Contemporary Flooring Institute have repeatedly proved the superiority of Corlon's construction and resistance. Please go to the Institute's website (**www.cfi.org**) for a streaming video demonstration of how beautiful, durable, and versatile Classic Corlon flooring is.

Corlon's Advantages

Guaranteed against defects for a full three years, Corlon is one of the finest and most durable floor coverings manufactured by Armstrong. It is a heavy-duty commercial floor 0.085-inch thick for protection and durability. Twenty-five percent of the material consists of interface backing; the other 75 percent is an inlaid wear layer that offers exceptionally high resistance to the heavy, everyday traffic your showroom will see.

Another important feature of Corlon is the size of its rolls. Unlike other leading brands of commercial flooring—Remington or Treadmaster—Corlon comes in 12-foot-wide rather than 6-foot-wide rolls. This extra width will significantly reduce the number of seams on your floor, thus increasing its attractiveness and eliminating the dangers of splitting or bulging.

Letterhead advertises company's presence on social-networking sites

Proposal sent as a PDF attachment to an email in accordance for the request for bid

Begins with a reference to company's request for bids

Acknowledges site visit

Identifies best solution

Cites an independent source to corroborate the benefits of the product

Describes product features that will benefit reader

Distinguishes product from competitors'

(Continued)

FIGURE 13.6 (Continued)

Page 2

Explains how job is done professionally

Installation Procedures

The Classic Corlon 900 requires an inlaid seaming process, a technical procedure requiring the skill of a highly trained floor mechanic. Herman Goshen, our certified chief floor mechanic, has more than eighteen years of experience working with the inlaid seam process. His professional work and keen sense of layout and design have been consistently praised by our many customers on Google+ Local and Angie's List, and I am proud of our 5-star rating on Yelp (**www.yelp.com/biz/reynolds-interiors**). To see a video demonstration of the installation process, please visit our website: **www.reynolds.com/inlaid_installation**.

Cites a video embedded on their website

Installation Schedule

Gives realistic timetable

We can install the Classic Corlon 900 on your showroom floor during the first week of March, which fits the timetable specified in your request. The material will take 3½ days for my 4-person crew to install, but will be ready to walk on immediately. Be assured that your floor will be installed no later than March 7th. We recommend, though, that you do not move heavy equipment onto the floor for 24 hours after installation.

Costs

The following costs include the Classic Corlon floor, labor, and taxes:

Itemizes all costs based on market conditions and reader's bid

750 sq. yards of Classic Corlon at $31.25/sq. yd.	$ 23,437.50
Labor (4 people × 28 hrs. @ $20.00/hr.)	$ 2,240.00
Sealing fluid (10 gals. @ $20.00/gal.)	$ 200.00
Subtotal	$ 25,877.50
Sales tax (7 percent)	$ 1,811.43
GRAND TOTAL	$ 27,688.93

Points out proposal comes in under budget—always a major consideration for buyers

Our costs are more than $1,300.00 below those specified in your bid.

Reynolds' Qualifications

Establishes history of service and provides documented evidence of quality work

Reynolds Interiors has been in business for more than 28 years. In that time, we have installed more than 2,500 commercial floors in Trenton and its suburbs. In the last year alone, we have served more than 60 satisfied customers, including the new multipurpose Tech Mart facility in downtown New Brunswick. Our designs have also been included in several commercial properties that have won awards from the

FIGURE 13.6 (Continued)

Page 3

Architectural Review Board and have been showcased in such publications as *New Jersey Homes* and *Best Housing Plans, 2015–2016*. Reynolds has also repeatedly received high commendations from our customers on our Facebook page. We would be happy to furnish you with a list of our references.

Thank you for the opportunity to submit this proposal to General Appliances. We are confident that you will be pleased with the appearance and durability of the Armstrong Classic Corlon 900 floor and our installation process. If we can provide you with further information about our service or Corlon flooring, or if you have any questions, please call us at 732-777-8733 or visit us at our website (**www.reynolds.com**) or on Facebook (**www.facebook.com/reynoldsinteriors**).

Sincerely yours,

Neelow Singh

Neelow Singh
Sales Consultant

Jack Rosen

Jack Rosen
Installation Supervisor

Thanks reader and encourages him to accept the proposal

© 2017 Cengage Learning

- **Estimate a realistic timeframe to do the work.** It would be unethical to say a job takes more time than necessary so you can then charge more.
- **Stipulate precisely what your product can (or cannot) do and what a service contract includes and excludes.** Don't make false claims. Always identify exceptions, limitations, and restrictions.

Organization of a Sales Proposal

Most sales proposals include the following elements: *introduction, description of the proposed product or service, timetable, costs, qualifications of your company,* and *conclusion.*

Introduction

The introduction to a sales proposal can be a single paragraph in a brief proposal or several pages in a more complex one. Basically, your introduction should persuasively prepare readers for everything that follows in your proposal. The introduction itself may contain the following sections, which sometimes may be combined.

1. **Statement of purpose and subject of proposal.** Tell readers why you are writing, and identify the specific subject of your work. Refer to the request for proposals or bids the reader has issued, as the writers in Figure 13.6 do. Briefly define the solution you propose. Tell readers exactly what you propose to do for them. Be clear about what your plan covers and, if there could be any doubt, what it does not.

2. **Background of the problem you propose to solve.** Show readers that you are familiar with their problem and why it is important. In a solicited proposal like the one in Figure 13.6, this section is usually unnecessary because the potential client has already identified the problem and wants to know how you would address it. In that case, just point out how your company would solve the problem, mentioning your superiority over your competitors (see the section "Corlon's Advantages" in Figure 13.6).

In an unsolicited proposal, you need to describe the problem in convincing detail, identifying the specific trouble areas. Depending on the type of proposal you submit, you may want to focus briefly on the dimensions of the problem—when it was first observed, who/what it most acutely affects, and the specific organizational/community/environmental context in which the problem is most troubling.

Description of the Proposed Product or Service

This section is the heart of your proposal. Before spending their money, customers will demand hard, factual evidence of what you claim can and should be done. Here are some points that your proposal should cover.

1. **Carefully show potential customers that your product or service is right for them.** Stress particular benefits of your product or service most relevant to your reader. Blend sales talk with descriptions of hardware. Where possible, utilize the Internet to convey information that isn't possible in a written proposal. Note how the proposal in Figure 13.6 references the online results of an independent testing agency to stress the benefits of the product it sells, and it also points the reader to a streaming video on the company's website that demonstrates the installation process that will be used.

2. **Describe your work in appropriate detail.** Specify what the product looks like; what it does; and how consistently and well it will perform in the readers' office, plant, hospital, or agency. You might include a brochure, picture, diagram, or, as the writers of the proposal in Figure 13.6 do, a few samples of your product for customers to study.

3. **Stress any special features, maintenance advantages, installation or warranty benefits.** Convince readers that your product is the most up-to-date and efficient one they could select. Highlight features that show the quality, consistency, or security of your work. See how Neelow Singh and Jack Rosen in Figure 13.6 demonstrate why and how Corlon is the best choice for the heavy traffic of the General Appliances showroom. For a service, emphasize the procedures you use, the terms of the service, the quality assurance tests you run, and especially any state-of-the-art equipment.

Timetable

A carefully planned timetable assures readers that you know your job and that you can accomplish it in the deadline set forth in the call for proposals or bids. Your dates should match any listed in a company's proposal request. Provide specific dates to indicate

- when the work will begin
- how the work will be divided into phases or stages
- when you will be finished
- whether any follow-up visits or services are involved

For proposals offering a service, specify how many times — an hour, a week, a month — customers can expect to receive your help; for example, spraying three times a month if your company offers exterminating services, or 24-hour-a-day monitoring of social media sites to provide off-hours feedback for customer complaints. The proposal writers in Figure 13.6 assure their reader that installation will be done by a specified date.

Costs

Make your budget accurate, complete, and convincing. But give customers more than merely the bottom-line cost. Show exactly what readers are getting for their money so that they can determine if everything they need is included. Itemize costs for

- specific services
- equipment and materials
- labor (by the hour or by the job)
- transportation/travel
- training

To further persuade readers to accept their proposal, the writers in Figure 13.5 stress how customers' positive reviews on review sites like Yelp and Angie's List are crucial to growing their business. In Figure 13.6, the authors point out how their work comes in under the specified budget.

If something is not included or is considered optional, say so — additional hours of training, replacement of parts, upgrades, and the like. If you anticipate a price increase, let the customer know how long current prices will stay in effect. That information may spur them to act favorably now.

Qualifications of Your Company

Emphasize your company's accomplishments and expertise in providing similar services and/or equipment. Mention the names of a few local firms for whom you have worked that would be able to recommend you and cite any awards or commendations, as the writers do in Figure 13.6, e.g., the Tech Mart facility.

Conclusion

This is the "call to action" section of your sales proposal. Encourage your reader to approve your plan by stressing its major benefits. Offer to answer any questions the reader may have. And take the opportunity to refer the reader to any samples, visuals, or sites on social media.

PROPOSALS FOR RESEARCH REPORTS

You may also be required to write a proposal to your boss seeking her or his authorization to do research, or to your instructor to get a paper or report topic approved, as in Figure 13.7.

The principles guiding internal and sales proposals also apply to research proposals. As with internal and sales proposals, you will be writing to convince the reader—your boss or instructor—to approve a major piece of work. Your boss will read your proposal to make sure you write the best possible report to solve a company problem and to increase company profits. Your instructor will look at your report to make sure it meets the course objectives. In drafting any research proposal, make sure of four things:

- that you have chosen a significant topic
- that you have sufficiently restricted the topic
- that you will investigate important sources of information about that topic
- that you can accomplish your work in the specified time

Your proposal will give your reader an opportunity to spot omissions or inconsistencies and to provide helpful suggestions.

To prepare an effective proposal for a research project, you have to do so preliminary research. You cannot just pick any topic that comes to mind or guess about procedures, sources, or conclusions. As other proposal readers will, your boss or instructor will want convincing and specific evidence about why you are researching this topic and your approach to it. Be prepared to cite key facts to show that you are familiar with the subject and that you are prepared to write about it knowledgeably.

Be very clear about the research you will do and what resources you intend to use. For example, you need to do some preliminary research using the following sources before you write a research proposal:

- Internet—list relevant websites, blogs, and social media sites you have consulted
- Search engines or databases—for a working bibliography
- Books and articles, online and print—but only those that bear directly on your topic
- Interviews—in person, email, over the telephone, and so on
- Proposed visits to relevant sites—laboratories, salt marshes, health care facilities, plants, offices, and so on

Review Chapter 8 on primary and secondary research methods.

Organization of a Proposal for a Research Report

Your proposal for an in-house report or for a school research project can be a memo or an email divided into six sections, as illustrated in Figure 13.7: *purpose* (introduction), *background of the problem* (why it is important), *questions to be investigated*, *methods of research*, *timetable*, and *request for approval*. However, be ready to reorder or expand these sections if your reader wants you to follow a different organizational plan.

FIGURE 13.7 A Proposal to Write a Research Report for a Class

To: Professor Marisol Vegas
From: Anna Beth Rowe
Date: February 6, 2015
Subject: Proposal to write a report on the ethical issues involved in using apps in customer surveillance in m-commerce

Purpose

To increase consumers' awareness of the implications of using their smartphones and other mobile devices, I propose to research and write a background report on the ethical issues involved in customer surveillance in mobile marketing (or m-commerce).

Concisely states purpose

Background of the Problem

Smartphones and other mobile devices from Apple, Samsung, and other vendors have become a vital part of the shopping experience. The reason is clear. As Delores Pentoney claims, "More people around the globe use iPhones than computers" (par. 1). The trend will definitely continue. MasterCard's CMO Raja Rajamannar predicts that by 2020 there will be "50-billion connected devices [in use]" (par. 1), and as Alvin Alvarez, executive vice president of National Commerce Corporation, observes, "By leveraging the convenience of a consumer's mobile phone, merchants can drive loyalty, brand affinity, and simplify the transaction process through the new product capability" (par. 3).

Demonstrates importance of topic with statistics and quotation from m-commerce executive

But iPhones, iPads, and other mobile devices pose major ethical challenges. Essential to m-commerce technology is what Sara Holes, an influential m-commerce security writer, refers to as "hotspots that trigger a message or ad delivered to your device if you walk or drive into a given area" (134). Each device includes a UDID, or unique device identity, that sends and time stamps data about the consumers' whereabouts and online activities, visits, how much time they spend in a location, etc. Technology expert Rob Lever points out that "By tracking users' smartphones and their identities, retailers can tell how often a customer visits" (par. 8). M-commerce retailers use a UDID to alert consumers to a sale or to a new product in a nearby store. Marketers can also text a consumer as he or she drives by a restaurant, a mall, an auto dealership, or even a yard sale. What is disturbing is that cellular service providers can track and store this data indefinitely.

Provides further details about scope and significance of problem to be investigated

Even more threatening, though, a UDID can be used for purposes other than promoting a particular brand or service. Security experts and members of Congress are concerned that m-commerce strategies violate

References the research of a security expert

(Continued)

FIGURE 13.7 (Continued)

Convincingly shows widespread implications of problem

consumer privacy. Granted, consumers have to divulge their location to receive mobile sales alerts. But Taylor Sloane, whose research is often cited in the literature on m-commerce, still worries about the ethics of tracking an individual's trips, locations, and driving habits, which allows cell phone service providers to predict where he or she goes and when. That information, Sloane contends, could be "collected and sold to unintended customers such as . . . divorce lawyers, debt collectors, or even industrial spies" (par. 5), not to mention hackers.

Identifies audience for whom report is intended

Understanding the ethical consequences consumers face in using their smartphones is vital for evaluating the terms of their service agreements and assessing the risks they run in using these devices. To ensure that consumers have the latest information, I request permission to do research for a background report on the privacy risks involved in m-commerce.

Questions to Be Investigated

At this preliminary stage of my research, I think my report will need to address the following questions related to the ethics of apps in m-commerce:

Formulates specific questions report will address

1. What marketing strategies are unique to m-commerce?
2. What have providers done with the data they collect about consumers' driving and shopping habits?
3. What specific risks to privacy do consumers face in using their smartphones?
4. What obligations do cellular service providers have to protect consumers' data and identity?
5. Can ethical m-commerce apps compete by clearly addressing a consumer's right to privacy?
6. What rights do consumers have to protect their identity and location when using their smartphones or other mobile devices?
7. What specific changes need to be legislated to safeguard cell phone alerts for legitimate reasons (e.g., warnings about natural disasters)?

Outlines tentative organization of report

I propose to divide the body of my paper according to three key issues of m-commerce: *Mobile Surveillance, Consumer Security,* and *Proposed Changes for End-User License Agreements.*

Methods of Research

I intend to find and read recent literature dealing with m-commerce and ethics and interview one or two m-commerce experts and one or two branch managers of local smartphone service providers. Judging from

FIGURE 13.7 (Continued)

my initial research, there are a large number of entries found on privacy issues in the mobile marketplace through Google, Bing, Academic Search Premier, and Business Source Complete.

To restrict my topic, though, I have narrowed my keyword search to the most important issues of *apps*, *tracking*, *consent*, *surveillance*, *privacy risks*, *M-consumer*, and *protection*. From a preliminary check of documents available at our college library and through its online databases, I believe the following book, articles, and blogs may be most helpful in my research.

Alvarez, Alvin. "Mobile Marketing Strategies Drive Sales." m-merchants. blogger.com. 25 January 2015. Web. 2 Feb. 2015.

Chan, Felix T.S., and Alain Yee-Loong Zheng. "Analysis of the Determinants of Consumers' M-commerce Usage Activities." *Online Information Review* 37.3 (2013): 443–61. Web. 31 Jan. 2015.

Clifford, Stephanie, and Quentin Hardy. "Attention, Shoppers: Store Is Tracking Your Cell." *The New York Times*. The New York Times, 14 July 2013. Web. 02 Feb. 2015.

Hofler, Drew. "Will 2015 Usher In a New Era for B2B Commerce?" *Forbes*. Forbes Magazine, 7 Jan. 2015. Web. 02 Feb. 2015.

Holes, Sara. "Watch for Hotspots when You Use Your Apps." *Springfield Herald*. 8 Feb. 2015. 133+. Print.

Kao, Danny Tengti. "The Impact of Transaction Trust on Consumers' Intentions to Adopt M-Commerce: A Cross-Cultural Investigation." *CyberPsychology & Behavior* 12.2 (2009): 225–29. Web. 28 Jan. 2015.

Lever, Rob. "Retailers Smarten up with Smartphone Shoppers." *Phys.org*. N.p., 1 Nov. 2013. Web. 3 Feb. 2015.

Marshall, Aarian. "NYC's Smartphone-Tracking Phone Booths Do Not Mark the Data Privacy Apocalypse." *CityLab.com*. The Atlantic, 6 Oct. 2014. Web. 02 Feb. 2015.

Pentoney, Delores. "Mobile Apps Sour." *Business World*. Oct. 2014. Web. 2 Feb. 2015.

Porter, Patricia. *Technology and Risk*. Chicago: Watsin, 2013. Print.

Rajamannar, Raja. "15 Mobile Trends to Watch in 2015." *Mashable*. N.p., 2 Jan. 2015. Web. 02 Feb. 2015.

Shin, Dong-Hee. "Towards an Understanding of the Consumer Acceptance of Mobile Wallet." *Computers in Human Behavior* 25.6 (2009): 1343–354. Web. 3 Feb. 2015.

Sloane, Taylor. "iPhone Applications and Consumer Privacy." *iTech World*. 30 Sept. 2014. Web. 20 Jan. 2015.

Gives detailed lists of primary and secondary sources to be consulted, with rationale

Demonstrates how and why topic is restricted

Uses proper MLA style for documentation

Cites only most relevant and current sources

Includes both print and Web-based research

(Continued)

FIGURE 13.7 (Continued)

"10 Things You May Have Missed." *Stores Magazine* 94.12 (2012): 15. *Business Source Complete*. Web. 2 Feb. 2015.

Thompson, Betty. "The M-Commerce Blogger." *blogspot365.com*. 13 January 2015. Web. 25 Jan. 2015.

Watkins, María. "Comment." *Facebook*. Facebook, 21 Aug. 2014. Web. 31 Jan. 2015.

Identifies need for additional interviews

I also plan to interview at least two marketing experts in the Springfield area to learn how they assess ethical issues involving mobile apps. My first choice is Katarina Kuhn at M-Trade, who has prepared several webinars on M-security and ethics in the past year. If she is unavailable, I will try to interview HR directors with credentials in the field such as Paul Goya at Consumer Advocacy Rights and Jen Holka at Tech Consultants, Inc. Further, I have a list of four or five branch managers at Apple, Samsung, and other providers and intend to email or visit them to get their views on m-security and privacy.

Timetable

Specifies schedule and how to meet it

I hope to complete my research by March 13 and my interviews by March 20. Then I will spend the following two weeks working on a draft, which I will turn in, as you asked, by April 3. After receiving your comments on my draft, I will work on revising the final copy of my background report and submit it by May 1, the date you specified. I will also send to you two progress reports—one when I finish my research and another when I decide on the final organization of my report

Request for Approval

Politely requests approval and feedback

Thank you for approving my plan for this background report. I welcome any further suggestions on how you think I might best proceed.

Purpose (Introduction)

Keep your introduction short—a paragraph, maybe two, pinpointing the subject and purpose of your work.

> I propose to research and write a report about the "hot knife" laser used in treating portwine stains and other birthmarks.

> I intend to investigate the relationship that exists between office space and our employees' need for "psychological space."

Then briefly indicate why the topic or the problem you propose to study is significant—why you have chosen that topic and why research on it is relevant or worthwhile for a specific audience or objective. Study how Anna Beth Rowe in Figure 13.7 states how and why her background report will be useful for consumers.

Supply your boss with a few background details about your topic—for example, the importance of using a laser as opposed to conventional ways of treating birthmarks. Prove that you have thought carefully about selecting a significant, relevant topic.

Background of the Problem

In this second section, give your reader information about why the problem is important. Cite evidence from your preliminary research and explain key terms or ideas. Show how you propose to break the topic into meaningful units. Tell your reader what specific issues, points, or areas you hope to explore.

Questions to Be Investigated

In this section, formulate a list of questions you intend your research report to answer. The topics included in such questions might later become major sections of the report. Make sure your issues or questions do not overlap and that each relates directly to and supports your restricted topic. See how in Figure 13.7, Rowe proposes to divide her report on m-commerce into three distinct yet related areas.

Methods of Research

In the fourth section of your proposal inform your boss how you expect to find the answers to the questions you raised in the previous section or how you intend to locate information about your list of subtopics. It's not enough to write, "I will gather appropriate information and analyze it." Specify what data you hope to include, where they are located, and how you intend to retrieve them.

In researching information about the problem, and any proposed solutions, you can expect to use both primary and secondary research methods and tools. Review relevant sections of Chapter 8. Certainly, you will gather data from the Web and from literature published in print sources. (In fact, research reports can be based exclusively on literature searches.) The literature can include

- websites, blogs, webfolios
- social media sites (such as Twitter and Facebook)
- books
- encyclopedias or other reference materials, such as statistical data found in manuals or almanacs, online and in print
- articles in professional journals and trade publications, online and in print
- newspapers and magazines, online and in print
- personal interviews
- company gray literature
- reviews

Inform your reader what indexes, abstracts, or Internet searches you intend to use as part of your research (review "Internet Searches," pages 329–330). To document your preliminary work, provide your reader with a list of appropriate titles on your topic, and follow the style of documentation used for an MLA Works Cited page (discussed in "Preparing MLA Works Cited and APA References List," on page 340) or in another style preferred by your supervisor or employer.

In addition to these online and print materials, you might also collect information from primary research, including lab experiments, field tests, interviews with experts, surveys, or a combination of any of those sources.

Timetable

Indicate when and in what order you expect to complete the different phases of your project. Your boss or instructor needs that information to keep track of your progress and to make sure you will complete your work on time. Specify tentative dates for completing your research, draft(s), revisions, and final copy.

You may have to submit progress reports (see "Progess Reports," pages 567–571) at regular intervals. If you are asked to do that, indicate when you will submit the progress reports, as Rowe does in Figure 13.7.

Request for Approval

End your proposal with a request for approval of your topic and a plan of action. You might also invite suggestions from your employer or instructor on how to restrict, research, or organize your topic.

A FINAL REMINDER

This chapter has given you some basic information and specific strategies for writing winning proposals. Keep in mind that a proposal presents a plan to decision makers for their approval. To win that approval, your proposal must be (1) realistic, (2) carefully researched, (3) highly persuasive, (4) ethical, and (5) visually appealing and easy to follow. Those essential characteristics apply to internal proposals in memo format written to your employer, more formal sales proposals submitted online to a potential customer, and research proposals submitted to your instructor through email.

✓ REVISION CHECKLIST

General Guidelines

☐ Established and distinguished the roles of the collaborative team members involved in the preparation of the proposal.

☐ Researched appropriate sources for RFPs, and followed their instructions.

☐ Identified a realistic problem in my proposal—one that is restricted and relevant to my audience's needs.

☐ Effectively convinced audience that the problem exists and that it needs to be solved.

☐ Incorporated the scope and importance of the problem.

☐ Persuasively emphasized benefits of solving the problem according to the proposal, and incorporated the "you attitude" throughout.

☐ Offered a solution that can be realistically implemented—that is, it is both appropriate and feasible, economically and strategically, for the audience.

☐ Wrote clearly so the audience can understand how and why my proposal would work.

☐ Researched the background of the problem.

☐ Used specific figures about costs, personnel, technology, and concrete details to show how the proposal saves time and money.

☐ Double-checked the proposal to catch errors, omissions, and inconsistencies.

☐ Avoided exaggerations and underbidding.

☐ Presented information ethically.

☐ Organized the proposal with appropriate headings for clarity and ease of reading.

☐ Used white space, lists, graphics, and a professional-looking font to make my proposal visually attractive and reader friendly.

For Internal Proposals

☐ Demonstrated how the proposal benefits my company and my supervisor.

☐ Took into account office politics in describing the problem and offering a solution.

☐ Discussed the proposal with co-workers or supervisors who may be affected.

For Sales Proposals

☐ Related my product or service to the prospective customer's needs and showed a clear understanding of those needs.

☐ Prepared a comprehensive, realistic, and ethical budget; accounted for all expenses; and itemized costs of products and services.

☐ Linked costs to benefits.

☐ Provided a timetable with exact dates for implementing the proposal.

☐ Cited other successful jobs, satisfied clients, and positive reviews on social media to show my company's track record.

☐ Concluded the proposal with a summary of the main benefits to readers and a call to action.

For Research Papers/Reports

☐ Proved to my supervisor or instructor that I researched the problem by supplying a list of possible references and sources, including ones from the Internet, personal interviews, and social media posts.

☐ Selected a major problem to investigate in my report.

☐ Supplied relevant and restricted questions my report will answer.

EXERCISES

1. In two or three paragraphs, identify and document a problem (in services, safety, ecology, communication, traffic, scheduling) that you see in your office or your community. Make sure you give your reader—a civic official or an employer—specific evidence that a problem does exist and that it needs to be corrected.

2. Write a short internal proposal, modeled after Figure 13.5, based on the problem you identified in Exercise 1.

3. As a collaborative group project, prepare a short internal proposal, similar to that in Figure 13.5 (pages 530–534), recommending to a company or a college a specific change in procedure, technology, training, transportation, safety, personnel, or policy. Make sure your team provides an appropriate audience (college administrator, department manager, or section chief) with specific evidence about the existence of the problem and your solution of it. Possible topics include these:

   a. providing more and safer parking or lighting
   b. instituting job sharing for mothers
   c. converting existing clients over to using new smart chip credit cards
   d. purchasing new office or laboratory equipment or software
   e. hiring more faculty, student workers, or office help
   f. allowing employees to telecommute
   g. changing the lighting or furniture in a student or company lounge or kitchen to make it more eco-friendly
   h. installing wireless routers and signal enhancers to boost the range of the company's wireless network
   i. increasing the number of weekend, night, or online classes in your major
   j. adding more health-conscious offerings to the school or company cafeteria menu
   k. develop an app that lets customers order goods and services remotely

4. Write a sales proposal as a collaborative group, similar to the one in Figure 13.6 (pages 537–539), on one of the following services or products or on a topic your instructor approves:

   a. providing exterminating or trash removal service to a store or restaurant
   b. supplying a hospital with rental tablet devices for patients' rooms
   c. designing websites or blogs
   d. obtaining temporary office help or nursing care
   e. supplying landscaping and lawn care work
   f. testing for noise, air, or water pollution in your community or neighborhood
   g. furnishing transportation for students, employees, or members of a community group
   h. offering technical consulting service to save a company money
   i. digging a well for a small apartment complex
   j. supplying insurance coverage to a small firm (five to ten employees)
   k. cleaning the parking lot and outside walkways at a shopping center

       l. making a work area safer or greener

       m. preparing an IT seminar or training program for employees

       n. increasing donations to a community or charitable fund

       o. offering discounted memberships at a fitness center

5. Write a solicited proposal for one of the topics listed in Exercise 4 or for a topic that your instructor approves. Do this exercise as a collaborative project. Review Figure 13.6.

6. Write an appropriate proposal—internal, solicited sales, or unsolicited sales—based on the information contained in one of the following two articles. Assume that your or your prospective customer's company or community faces a problem similar to one discussed in one of these articles. Use as much of the information in the article as you need, and add any details of your own that you think are necessary. This exercise can be done as an individual or a collaborative assignment

a. Multiuse Campuses: A Plan That Works

Gaylord Community School in Gaylord, Michigan, is a bustling center of activity from the first light of dawn to well after dusk. People of all ages come and go until late into the evening for a multitude of activities that include attending classes and meetings, catching up with friends, getting a flu shot, and seeing a play. That's because in addition to a high school, the campus also includes senior and day-care centers, classrooms for adult education, an auditorium for the performing arts, a community health care site, and even a space that can be booked for weddings and other special occasions.

In Big Lake, Minnesota, elementary, middle, and high school buildings are all situated on one centrally located campus that makes up the entire Big Lake School District. Also included in this innovative layout are a state-of-the-art theater, a community resource center, and a multipurpose athletic arena, all of which are used extensively by the entire community.

Both the Gaylord and Big Lake schools are models of a growing movement toward multiuse community campuses that serve as "anchor[s] in the civic life of our nation," according to U.S. Secretary of Education Richard W. Riley. I recently had the pleasure of visiting Secretary Riley in his office. Also present were AARP President Joe Perkins and National Retired Teachers Association Director Annette Norsman, both of whom are involved in many facets of education and lifelong learning.

We discussed many things, including our concerns about the current increase in the number of students caused by the Baby Boom echo (children of the Boomers) and how that population is going to further stress the already crumbling infrastructure of American schools. We also talked about the need for resources—to employ more teachers, bring technology into the classroom, strengthen educational curriculum and opportunities for all ages—and the pressing need to build and renovate schools. That led to a discussion about the necessity and benefit of involving the whole community in the design and use of new school facilities.

I always thought that it was a shame that the majority of schools are used only a third of the day, three fourths of the year, by only a fifth of the population. Considering that there will be more school construction over the next decade than at any time since the 1950s, it just makes sense to consider the intergenerational and community benefits of multiuse spaces, benefits that include everything from establishing better learning environments to getting more bang for the tax buck.

There are many additional bonuses for multiuse educational complexes: They create an exciting community hub, bring life and culture to a central area, and revitalize and nourish the neighborhood in which they are located.

It's a win-win situation for everyone involved.

b. Self-Illuminating Exit Signs

The Marine Corps Development and Education Center (MCDEC), Quantico, Virginia, submitted a project recently, to replace incandescent illumination exit signs with self-illuminating exit signs for a cost of $97,238. The first-year savings were anticipated to be about $37,171 with an anticipated payback time of 2.6 years—making this an excellent way to save money.

The primary benefit of these self-illuminating exit signs is that virtually all operation and maintenance expense is eliminated for the life of the device, normally from 10 to 12 years. Power failures or other disturbances will not cause them to go out. In new construction, expensive electrical circuits can be totally eliminated. In retrofits, the release of a dedicated circuit for other use may be of considerable benefit. Initial total cost of installing circuits and conventional devices approximately equals the cost of the self-illuminating signs. Installation labor and expense for the self-illuminating signs is about that of hanging a picture.

The amount of electricity saved varies and depends on whether your existing fixtures are fluorescent (13 to 26 watts) or incandescent (50 to 100 watts). Multiply the number of fixtures $\times$ wattage/fixture $\times$ hours operated/day $\times$ days/year = kWh/year savings. For example, assume:

400 incandescent fixtures

$0.10/kWh

0.04 kW/fixture

24 hours/day, 365 days/year operation

$400 \times 0.04 \times 24 \times 365 = 140,160$ kWh/year

$140,160 \times \$0.10 = \$14,016$/year for electricity

Now add in savings achieved from reducing labor to change bulbs; avoiding bulb material, stocking, and storage costs; avoiding transportation costs involved in bulb changes; and reusing existing bulbs.

The above savings can be significant. For the MCDEC Quantico project, estimates of bulb change interval and savings were 700 hours (29 days) and $13,512/ year when all factors were considered.

The cost of a self-illuminating sign depends on whether one or two faces are illuminated primarily and varies between different suppliers. Single-face prices will likely be $200 to $250 while double-face prices may be $450 to $500. The contractor at Quantico found better prices than these ranges indicate. The labor cost should be about $10 per sign.

If you can use an exit-sign system with high dependability, no maintenance, and zero operations cost in your retrofit or new construction projects, try a self-illuminating exit-sign system in your economic analysis today. "Isolite" signs, by Safety Light Corp., are listed as FSC (Fire Safety Code) Group 99, Part IV, Section A, Class 9905 signs and are available through GSA contract. Contact Gerald Harnett, Safety Light Corp., P.O. Box 266, Greenbelt, MD 20070 for more information.

7. Write a research proposal on which the report on recruiting and retaining multinational workers in Figure 15.3 (pages 607–621) could have been based.

8. Write a research proposal, similar to the one in Figure 13.7 (pages 543–546), to your instructor seeking approval for a research-based long report. Do the necessary preliminary research to show that you have selected a suitable topic, narrowed it, and identified the sources of information you have to consult. List at least six relevant and recent articles, two recent books (since 2014), several websites, and two or three professional blogs pertinent to your topic.

9. Write a proposal in letter format (similar to Figure 5.7 on page 170) for a business you manage to attract new international clients. As part of your letter, stress any new equipment or services you offer and provide any background/history about your business that might appeal to a particular group's international customers.

Adam Mork/Architecture (RM)/Corbis

Writing Effective Short Reports

This chapter shows you how to write short reports, which are among the most important and frequent types of business communications you may be called upon to prepare. Short, informal reports give up-to-date information (and sometimes what it means and what should be done about it) to help a company or organization run smoothly, efficiently, and profitably. These reports, which cover a wide range of topics, can help a company fulfill its obligations and plan for its future. Short reports are crucial to day-to-day operations of any company or organization, and are designed for an audience of busy decision makers.

WHY SHORT REPORTS ARE IMPORTANT

A short report can be defined as an organized presentation of relevant data on any topic—money, travel, time, technology, personnel, service equipment, weather, the environment—that a company or agency tracks in its ongoing operations. Short reports are practical and to the point. They show that work is being done, and they also show your boss that you are alert, professional, and reliable. Short reports are written to co-workers, employers, vendors, and clients. When they are intended for individuals within your organization, these reports can be sent as either hard copy memos, as attachments to emails, or simply sent in the body of an email. For clients, you will usually send your reports out as letters (or as a PDF letter attached to an email).

Businesses cannot function without short written reports. Reports tell whether

- work is being completed
- schedules are being met
- costs have been contained
- sales projections are being met
- trips or conferences/trade shows have been successful
- meetings with customers are profitable

- locations have been selected
- problems have been solved

You may write an occasional report for a special purpose, in response to a specific question, or you may be required to write a daily, weekly, or monthly report about routine activities. For example, a short report can update your manager or client about the status of a project, provide feedback about a customer survey, prove you followed the regulations of a state or federal agency, or assess your own or someone else's accomplishments at work.

TYPES OF SHORT REPORTS

To give you a sense of some of the topics you may be required to write about, here is a list of various types of short reports common in the business world.

appraisal report	incident report	progress/activity report
audit report	inventory report	recommendation report
budget report	investigative report	research report
compliance report	laboratory report	sales report
construction report	management trainee report	site inspection report
design report	manager's report	status report
employee activity/	marketing report	survey report
performance report	medicine/treatment	test report
environmental assessment	error report	travel report
evaluation report	operations report	
experiment report	periodic report	
feasibility report	production report	

This chapter concentrates on seven of the most common types of reports you are likely to encounter on your job.

1. periodic reports
2. sales reports
3. progress reports
4. employee activity/performance reports
5. trip/travel reports
6. test reports
7. incident reports

Although there are many kinds of short reports, they all are written for readers who need factual information so that they can get a job accomplished. Never think of the reports you write as a series of casual notes jotted down for *your* convenience.

EIGHT GUIDELINES FOR WRITING SHORT REPORTS

Although there are many short reports, the following eight guidelines will help you write any type of short report successfully.

1. Anticipate How an Audience Will Use Your Report

Knowing who will read your report and why is crucial to your success as a writer. Readers will want to know what the reason for the report is and how you found your information. Consider how much your audience knows about your project and what types of information they need most. A co-worker or someone else in your field may be familiar with technical information. But managers, who will constitute the largest audience for your report, may not always understand or be interested in such technical information. Instead, they will want bottom-line details about costs,

---

TECH NOTE

Creating Templates for Short Reports

You can use your word processor's template function to create professional-looking reports. Templates are predesigned formats for page layouts that specify style elements of a document. They allow you to automate designs for periodic, sales, progress, incident, and other types of reports. An existing template will format information to create a professional-looking report. Using templates, you reduce the risk of errors, omissions, and inconsistencies and ensure that you follow your company's style and format.

To create a specific report template, simply set the format options (such as font, margins, and line spacing) for a new document, type place markers for your text (including headers, footers, and titles), import custom visuals (such as a company logo), and save the document as a template. When you need to create a new report using the template, simply open it, insert the content of your report, and save the document under a new file name. You can customize the formatting of any or all of the following elements:

- Headers, footers for a company address, titles, and dates
- List formatting, such as bullet-point style and numbered lists
- Line spacing and text justification
- Font style, size, and color
- Standard graphics, e.g., a flowchart, organizational charts, or infographs
- Margin size, paragraph indentation, and columns
- Standard visual elements such as tables, which can also be filled with the data appropriate to your report
- Automatic table of contents based on the titles used in your report

But when using templates keep the following precautions in mind:

- Be sure to follow your company's style when creating templates, particularly those including a company logo.
- Double-check everything in the template to be sure it is appropriate for the kind of report you're writing. Differences between reports may require visual adjustments, to margins, headers, footers, line spacing, list formatting, etc.
- When creating a template with place markers to indicate the position of certain textual elements, insert them in boldface for emphasis. Using brackets (for example, **[type title here]** or **[body of text here]**) will highlight and thus emphasize these place holders.

personnel, and schedules, for example. Similarly, audiences outside of your company (clients, media, community agencies, etc.) will likely not be interested in technical information. Rather, they want information that helps them understand your company, how it works or serves customers, and how to interact with it.

All audiences, however, want clear and concise information about the topics these readers need to know. For more information on how to make your reports concise and easy to follow, see "Write Clearly and Concisely," page 560.

2. Do the Necessary Research

An effective short report needs the same careful research that goes into other on-the-job writing. Your research may be as simple as messaging, tweeting, emailing, or leaving a voicemail for a colleague or checking a piece of equipment. Or you may have to test or inspect a product or service or assess the relative merits of one plan over another. Some frequent types of research you can expect to do on the job include:

- verifying data in reference manuals or code books
- searching online archives and databases for recent discussions of a problem or procedure
- comparing and contrasting competitor's products or services on social media and other sources
- reading background information in professional and trade journals
- pricing equipment
- preparing a budget
- reviewing and updating a client's file
- testing equipment
- performing an experiment or procedure
- conferring with or interviewing colleagues, managers, vendors, or clients
- visiting and describing a site
- attending a conference, trade show, or workshop

Never trust your memory to keep track of all the details that go into making a successful short report. Take notes, either by hand or on your mobile device. Collect all the relevant data you will need—names, model numbers, costs, places, technology, etc.—and organize this information carefully into an outline, which will help you interpret these facts for your readers. (Review Chapter 8 for the variety of research methods used in the world of work.)

3. Be Objective and Ethical

Your readers will expect you to report the facts objectively and impartially—locations, costs, sales, weather conditions, eyewitness accounts, observations, statistics, test measurements, and descriptions. Your reports should be truthful, accurate, and complete. Here are some guidelines to follow:

- Omit irrelevant information.
- Make sure it is up-to-date.

Using the Web to Do Research for Short Reports

Many government agencies provide the statistical raw data that go into various types of short reports—employment figures, population data, environmental statistics, and so on. Incorporating information from these and other relevant sites give readers the necessary documentation they need to accept a conclusion or recommendation.

Other businesses also post information that may be relevant to your report for your company. Large corporations such as General Motors or IBM help you see the progress of stocks and mutual funds or obtain other industry-wide information on their websites. Finally, ConsumerReports.org (**www.consumerreports.org**) evaluates different brands of products so that you don't have to do testing yourself.

Here are some sites that publish appropriate information for short reports:

- BizStats, **www.bizstats.com**
- U.S. Bureau of Labor Statistics, **www.bls.gov**
- U.S. Bureau of Transportation, **www.bts.gov**
- Federal Reserve, **www.federalreserve.gov**
- National Center for Educational Statistics, **http://nces.ed.gov**
- National Center for Health Statistics, **www.cdc.gov/nchs**
- New York Stock Exchange, **www.nyse.com**
- UNESCO Institute for Statistics, **www.uis.unesco.org**
- United Nations Statistics Division, **http://unstats.un.org/unsd**
- U.S. Census Bureau, **www.census.gov**

- Avoid guesswork. If you don't know or have not yet found out, say so and indicate how, where, and when you'll try to find out.
- Do not substitute impressions or unsupported personal opinions for careful research. Your report should be unbiased and based on hard, factual evidence.
- Be ethical. Don't use biased, skewed, or incomplete data. Provide a balanced, straightforward, and honest account; don't exaggerate or minimize. Don't omit key facts. If a project is over budget or late, state so but indicate why and what might be done to correct the problem.
- Make sure your report is relevant, accurate, and reliable. Double-check your details against other sources, and make sure you have sufficient information to reach your conclusions or provide recommendations.

Review "Ethical Writing in the Workplace" in Chapter 1 (pages 26–37).

4. Organize Carefully

Organizing a short report effectively means including the right amount of information in the most appropriate places for your audience. You cannot just jot down some random ideas and details and submit those as your report. Make your report easy to read and to follow. Many times a simple chronological or sequential organization is best. But, regardless of how you organized your report, readers will expect your report to contain information on such topics as *purpose, findings, conclusions,* and, in many reports, *recommendations,* as described in the following sections.

Purpose

Always begin by telling readers why you are writing (your purpose) and by alerting them to what you will discuss and why it is significant. You may have to refer to their giving you authorization to do the report, as in Figures 14.5 or 14.8. Give your readers a summary of key events and details at the beginning to help them follow the remainder of the report quickly. Essential background information alerts readers to the importance of your report. When you establish the scope (or limits) of your report, you help readers zero in on specific times, costs, places, or problems.

Findings

This should be the longest part of your report and contain the data (the results) you have collected—facts about prices, personnel, equipment, events, locations, incidents, or tests. Gather the data from your research, site visits, interviews, or discussions with co-workers, employers, or clients. Use statistical sources, as in "Tech Note: Using the Web to Do Research for Short Reports." (See also "Two Types of Research: Primary and Secondary," pages 306–307.) Again, choose only those details that have the greatest importance and relevance to your reader. Separate major points from minor ones.

Conclusion

Your conclusion tells readers what your data mean. It can summarize what has happened; review what actions were taken; or explain the outcome or results of a test, a visit, or a program. Be aware, though, that readers are skeptical and may ask why you didn't reach a different conclusion. Anticipate possible objections and explain why other conclusions are unworkable.

Recommendations

A recommendation informs readers what specific actions you think your company or client should take, for example, market a new product, hire more staff, institute safety measures, update software, select among alternative plans or procedures, and so on. Recommendations must be based on the data you collected, the resources (budget) and schedule that your company or department follows, and the conclusions you have reached. They need to show persuasively how all the pieces fit together.

Note how the periodic report in Figure 14.1 (page 562) fails to help readers see and understand the organization and importance of the information. But the revised version of the report, Figure 14.2 (page 563–564), clearly illustrates effective report writing.

Note that because of the deadlines executives face, some companies prefer that recommendations come at the beginning of the report (as in Figure 14.8), followed by supporting documentation.

5. Write Clearly and Concisely

Writing clearly and concisely is essential in all business reports. Ask your boss or experienced co-workers about the appropriate style your company prefers. Also look at previous, similar reports to get a sense of your company's style and tone.

Here are a few guidelines to help you write clearly and concisely.

- **Use an informative title or subject line that gets to the point right away.** "Software Options" is not as clear as "Most Economical Options for Customer Relationship Management (CRM) Software."
- **Write in plain English.** Make every word count, avoid jargon, and keep your writing simple, yet precise and straightforward. Prune business clichés such as "at the end of the day" or "let's circle back."
- **For global readers, make sure you use international English.** Keep your sentences short, and write in the active voice. Do not use U.S. idioms, slang, or abbreviations. (See "Ten Guidelines for Communicating with International Readers," in Chapter 5, pages 169–173.)
- **Adopt a professional yet personal tone.** Avoid being overly formal or too casual—strike a balance between these two extremes. Don't sound arrogant by adopting a tone that suggests you alone have the final authority.
- **Keep your report as concise as possible to give readers essential information.** Don't burden them with lengthy project histories when all they ask for is a quick update on a project, and don't pad the report with unnecessary details to sound important. A short report is usually no longer than one to three pages.

6. Create a Reader-Centered Design

The appearance of your report will influence how your readers will respond to it and to you. Here are some useful guidelines. (You may also want to review Chapters 10 and 11 on visuals and document design.)

- **Help readers locate and digest information quickly.** Use headings, subheadings, bullets, and numbered lists to guide readers through your report. Doing this, you break large portions of text into easy-to-read parts. Your headings and subheadings give readers the big picture at a glance. Many reports in this chapter demonstrate how headings and bulleted or numbered lists assist readers. For instance, see Figures 14.2, 14.3, and 14.5.
- **If you are submitting your report as an electronic document, use hyperlinks where appropriate to help readers find information quickly.**
- **Make your report look professional, readable, and easy to follow.** Don't flood your report with color. (See "Tech Note: Creating Templates for Short Reports" on page 556.) Avoid using flashy color or fancy fonts that are hard to read. Also, don't try to squeeze too much text onto the page. Always leave comfortable margins.
- **Be consistent in your design and format.** Use the same font throughout the text of your report and choose a consistent typeface for headings and subheadings.

7. Include visuals/graphics/tables only when they are needed.

Visuals can help readers see trends, explain a process, assimilate factual/statistical data, etc. Here are a few guidelines for how to appropriately and successfully include visuals in your short reports:

- **Include only the most essential visuals.** Don't go overboard. Use visuals only if they make the reader's job easier, reinforcing or summarizing key data quickly, as the table in Figure 14.2 and the map in Figure 14.8 do. Keep visuals simple and relevant, e.g., a picture or drawing to illustrate a major point.
- **Never include a visual without explaining why it is there, what it contains, and how it is useful.**
- **Make sure that you place your visual as close as possible to the text it will help to explain or illustrate.**

8. Choose the Most Appropriate Format

Depending on your company's or organization's policies, you can send your short report as an email (as in Figure 14.6), a memo, a PDF attachment (as in Figure 14.4), or a letter. For routine reports to your boss or others inside your company, you will likely use a memo format, as in Figures 14.2, 14.3, and 14.8. Note that with a memo format your readers will not expect you to include an inside address or formal salutation and complimentary close. Incident reports, however, are often submitted as hard-copy memos for legal reasons; but they can also be written as a memo, as in Figure 14.11, or by completing a special form. Some incident reports, to save the reader's time, are scanned and sent as an email attachment. When writing to clients and other readers outside your company or organization, it is best to send your report as a formal letter (including a salutation and complimentary close, as in Figure 14.5).

PERIODIC REPORTS

Periodic reports, as their name signifies, provide readers with information at regularly scheduled intervals—daily, weekly, bimonthly (twice a month), monthly, or quarterly. They help a company or an agency monitor the quantity and quality of the services it provides and the amount and types of work done by employees. Information in periodic reports helps managers plan schedules; hire, train, assign, and reassign staff; budget funds; determine needs and goals; and fulfill a corporate mission. The following case study (pages 562–565) shows a poor draft of a periodic report (Figure 14.1) and a successful revision (Figure 14.2).

SALES REPORTS

Sales reports provide businesses with a necessary and ongoing record of accounts, online and mail purchases, losses, and profits over a specified period of time. They help businesses assess past performance and plan for the future. As a financial record, sales reports list costs per unit, discounts or special reductions, and subtotals and totals. Sales reports also show gains and losses. They may also provide statistics for comparing two quarters' sales.

A Poor and an Effective Short Report

Sergeants Daniel Huxley, Jennifer Chavez, and Ivor Paz of the Springdale Police Department were responsible for writing a monthly periodic report for the second quarter of 2016 for Captain J.T. Martin, their boss. Confronted with a mass of data about various crimes and misdemeanors, they had to organize, compare, and contrast this data as well as draw conclusions and make recommendations. Figure 14.1, an early draft of their report, does not follow the guidelines in "Eight Guidelines for Writing Short Reports," pages 555–561. But Figure 14.2, a revised version of Figure 14.1, does. Read through both reports, keeping in mind the following differences:

- **Research.** Although Figure 14.1 includes statistics, it does not explain or provide recommendations based on them. Figure 14.2, however, provides explanations, supplies more detail, and gives concrete recommendations.
- **Audience analysis.** Figure 14.1 simply throws facts at the reader. Figure 14.2, however, consistently takes the reader's needs into account by focusing on how Captain Martin will use the statistical information about the crime rate during the second quarter of the year. To help Captain Martin, Figure 14.2 presents the most important information first, then explains and analyzes the numbers for her and provides realistic and direct recommendations.
- **Objectivity/ethics.** In Figure 14.1, details have not been checked against any other sources, so the report is incomplete and possibly inaccurate. Figure 14.2, however, eliminates the guesswork and, more ethically, offers solutions, careful analysis, and a variety of relevant sources.
- **Organization.** Figure 14.1 makes no attempt to organize the report so it is reader-friendly. It contains three dense and disorganized paragraphs and does not summarize the facts. But Figure 14.2 supplies a clear purpose statement, organizes and summarizes the facts concisely, and helpfully groups recommendations.
- **Writing style and tone.** Figure 14.1 is just an accumulation of numbers, making it hard for Capt. Martin to access or understand their importance. The tone is smug and arrogant. Figure 14.2, on the other hand, is easy to follow and to understand. It uses helpful connective words and phrases ("compared to last quarter," "overall") and includes important contexts ("were less than last quarter").
- **Format and visuals.** Figure 14.1 lacks headers, bullets, visuals, or consistent paragraph indentation, and uses italics and boldface unnecessarily. Figure 14.2 instead supplies clear heads, breaks the text into easy-to-digest subheads, places numerical data in visual form (Table 1), and uses bulleted lists.

FIGURE 14.1 An Example of a Poorly Written, Poorly Organized, and Poorly Formatted Periodic Report

Springdale Police Department

Emergency 555-1000   **Administration** 555-1001   **Traffic** 555-1002

www.springdalepd.gov

TO: Captain J. T. Martin
FROM: Sergeants Daniel Huxley, Jennifer Chavez,
              and Ivor Paz
SUBJECT: Crimes
DATE: July 11, 2016

This report will let you know what happened this quarter as opposed to what happened last quarter as far as crimes are concerned in Springdale. This **report is based on statistics** the department has given us over the quarter.

    Here we'll let the facts speak for themselves. From Jan.–Mar. we saw 132 robberies while from Apr.–June we had 158. Home burglaries for this period: 43; last period: 36. 33 cars were stolen in the period before this one; now we have 40. Interestingly enough, **last year at this time we had only 27** thefts. *Four of them involved heirlooms.*

Homicides were 4 this time versus 5 last quarter; assault and battery charges were 92 this time, 77 last time. Carrying a concealed weapon, 11 (10 last quarter). We had 47 arrests (55 last quarter) for charges of possession of **a controlled substance**. Rape charges were 8, **1 less than last quarter**. 360 citations this time for moving violations: **speeding** 197/165, and failing to observe the signals 118/102 last quarter. DUIs this quarter—only 45, or 23 fewer than last quarter.

    Misdemeanors this quarter: disturbing the peace 53; vagrancy/public drunkenness 88; violating leash laws 32; violating city codes 39, including **dumping trash**. Last quarter the figures were **48, 59, 21, 43**.

We believe this report is **complete and up-to-date**. We further hope that this report has given you all the facts you will need.

Vague subject line

Introduction doesn't give overall picture

Inconsistent and confusing use of boldface and italic

Throws facts out without any sense of reader's needs

Includes irrelevant detail

No analysis or commentary

Gives undigested numbers

Poor, inconsistent format

Hard-to-follow comparisons and contrasts

Conclusion provides no summary or recommendations

FIGURE 14.2 A Well-Prepared Report, Revised from Figure 14.1

Springdale Police Department

Emergency 555-1000 **Administration** 555-1001 **Traffic** 555-1002

www.springdalepd.gov

TO: Captain J. T. Martin
FROM: Sergeants Daniel Huxley, Jennifer Chavez, and Ivor Paz
SUBJECT: Crime rate for the second quarter of 2016
DATE: July 11, 2016

From April 1 to June 30, 852 crimes were reported in Springdale, representing a 5 percent increase over the 815 crimes recorded during the previous quarter.

TYPES OF CRIMES

The following report, based on the table below, discusses the specific types of crimes, organized into four categories: **robberies and theft**, **felonies**, **traffic**, and **misdemeanors**.

Table 1 Comparison of the 1st and 2nd Quarter Crime Rates in Springdale

Category	1st Quarter	2nd Quarter
ROBBERIES AND THEFT		
Commercial	63	75
Domestic	36	43
Auto	33	40
FELONIES		
Homicide	5	4
Assault and battery	77	92
Carrying a concealed weapon	10	11
Possession of a controlled substance	55	47
Rape	9	8
TRAFFIC		
Speeding	165	197
Failure to observe signals	102	118
DUI	78	45
MISDEMEANORS		
Disturbing the peace	48	53
Vagrancy	40	48
Public drunkenness	19	40
Leash law violations	21	32
Dumping trash	43	39
Other	8	12

Robberies and Theft

The greatest increase in crime was in robberies, 20 percent more than last quarter. Downtown merchants reported 75 burglaries, exceeding $985,000. The biggest theft

Precise subject line

Begins with concise overview of report

Organizes crimes into categories

Supplies easy-to-follow visual

Table is boxed, making it easier to read

Uses clear headings to show organization of report

FIGURE 14.2 (Continued)

Page 2

occurred on May 21 at Paterson's Jewelers, when three armed robbers stole more than $217,000 in merchandise. (Suspects were apprehended two days later.) Home burglaries accounted for 43 crimes, though the thefts were not confined to any one residential area. We also had 40 car thefts reported and investigated.

Felonies
Homicides decreased slightly from last quarter—from 5 to 4. Charges for battery, however, increased—15 more than we had last quarter. Arrests for carrying a concealed weapon were nearly identical this quarter to last quarter's total. But the 47 arrests for possession of a controlled substance were appreciably down from the first quarter. Arrests for rape for this quarter also were less than last quarter's. Three of those rapes happened within one week (May 6–12) and have been attributed to the same suspect, now in custody.

Traffic
Traffic violations were higher (4 percent) than those last quarter—360 as opposed to 345. Most of the citations were issued for speeding (197) or for failing to observe signals (118). Officers issued 45 citations to motorists for DUIs, a significant decrease from the 78 DUIs issued last quarter. The new state penalty of withholding a driver's license for six months of anyone convicted of driving while under the influence appears to have been an effective deterrent.

Misdemeanors
The largest number of arrests in this category were for disturbing the peace—53. Compared to last quarter, this is an increase of 10 percent. There were 88 arrests for vagrancy and public drunkenness, an increase from the 59 charges made last quarter. We issued 32 citations for violations of leash laws, which represents a sizable increase over last quarter's 21 citations. Thirty-nine citations were issued for dumping trash at the Mason Reservoir.

CONCLUSION
Overall, while the crime rate has decreased for traffic violations (especially DUIs) and possession of controlled substances this quarter, we have seen a marked increase in arrests for robberies and battery.

RECOMMENDATIONS
To help deter robberies in the downtown area, we recommend the following:

• increasing surveillance units to 15 rather than the 10 now in the area
• offering businesses our workshop on safety and security precautions, as we did during the first quarter

Historically, battery arrests have risen during the second quarter. Our recommendations to counter this trend include:

• continuing to work closely with the Springdale Anti-Crime League
• providing more foot and bicycle patrols in the neighborhoods with the highest incidence of battery complaints

Documents effective actions

Provides essential background and statistical information and comparative analyses

Easy-to-read sentences

Draws logical conclusion

Includes only data reader needs

Summarizes findings of report

Offers specific actions/ changes based on conclusion of report in bulleted lists

Recommendations are realistic and valid

Sales reports are also a managerial tool because they help businesses make both short- and long-range plans. The restaurant manager's sales report illustrated in Figure 14.3 guides the owners to decide which popular entrées to highlight and

FIGURE 14.3 A Sales Report

Eye-catching logo

Dayton, OH 43210 ● (813) 555-4000 ● (813) 555-4100 fax
www.theoaks.com ● ⨍ www.facebook.com/theoaks

THE OAKS

TO:	Gina Smeltzer Alfonso Zapatta, Owners	DATE:	June 20, 2016
FROM:	Sam Jelinek S J Manager	SUBJECT:	Analysis of entrée sales, June 6–10 and 13–17

Restricted subject line

Begins with purpose and scope of report

As we agreed at our monthly meeting on June 3, here is my analysis of entrée sales for two weeks to assist us in our menu planning. Below is a record of entrée sales for the weeks of June 6–10 and 13–17 that I compiled and put in the table for easier comparisons.

Organizes findings of the report in helpful table

	Portion Size	June 6–10 Amount	June 6–10 Percentage	June 13–17 Amount	June 13–17 Percentage	Both Weeks Amount	Both Weeks Percentage
Cornish Hen	6 oz.	238	17	307	17	545	17
Stuffed Young Turkey	8 oz.	112	8	182	10	294	9
Broiled Salmon Steak	8 oz.	154	11	217	12	371	12
Brook Trout	12 oz.	182	13	252	14	434	13
Prime Rib	10 oz.	168	12	198	11	366	11
Lobster Tails	2–4 oz.	147	10	161	9	308	10
Delmonico Steak	10 oz.	56	4	70	4	126	4
Moroccan Chicken	6 oz.	343	25	413	23	756	24
		1,400	**100**	**1,800**	**100**	**3,200**	**100**

Boldfaces totals

Recommendations
Based on the figures in the table above, I recommend that we do the following:

1. Order at least 100 more pounds of prime rib each two-week period to be eligible for further quantity discounts from the Northern Meat Company.
2. Remove the Delmonico Steak entrée because of its low acceptance.
3. Introduce a new chicken or fish entrée to take the place of the Delmonico Steak; I would suggest grilled lemon chicken to accommodate those patrons interested in a tasty, low-fat, lower-cholesterol, reduced sodium entrée.

Offers precise and relevant recommendations

Please give me your responses within the next week. It shouldn't take more than a few days to implement these changes. Thank you.

Requests authorization to implement recommendations

which unpopular ones to modify or delete. Note how the recommendations follow logically from the figures manager Sam Jelinek gives to Gina Smeltzer and Alfonso Zapatta, the owners of The Oaks. Because readers are familiar with the subject of the report, Jelinek did not have to supply background information on the entire offerings.

PROGRESS REPORTS

A **progress report,** such as those in Figures 14.4 (page 569) and 14.5 (page 570), informs readers about the status of an ongoing project. It lets them know how much and what type of work has been done by a particular date, by whom, how well, and how close the entire job is to being completed. A progress report reveals whether you are

- specifying what work has been done
- keeping on your schedule
- staying within your budget
- using the proper technology or equipment
- making the right assignments
- identifying an unexpected problem
- providing adjustments in schedules, personnel, and so on
- indicating what work remains to be done
- completing the job efficiently, correctly, and according to codes

Almost any kind of ongoing work can be described in a progress report—research for a paper, construction of an apartment complex, preparation of a website, documentation of a patient's rehabilitation. Progress reports are often prepared at key phases, or milestones, in a project.

Audience for Progress Reports

A progress report is intended for people who generally are not working alongside you but who need a record of your activities to coordinate them with other individuals' efforts and to learn about problems or changes in plans. For example, supervisors who do not work in a field or branch office (and non-native speakers of English who manage overseas offices) will rely on your progress reports for much of their information. Customers, such as a contractor's clients, expect reports on how carefully their money is being spent, if schedules are being met, and whether there is a risk of going over the budget.

The length of a progress report will depend on your audience and on the complexity of the project. A short email to a supervisor about organizing a time management workshop might be all that is necessary. A report to an instructor about the progress a student is making on a research report easily could be handled in a memo, such as Anna Beth Rowe's progress report in Figure 14.4 (page 569) on the research report described in her proposal in Chapter 13 (Figure 13.7, pages 543–546). Dale Brandt's assessment of the progress his construction company is making in renovating Dr. Burke's office is given in a letter in Figure 14.5 (page 570).

Frequency of Progress Reports

Progress reports can be written at any regular interval, even annually. Your specific job and your employer's needs will dictate how often you have to keep others informed of your progress. Anna Beth Rowe was asked to submit two progress reports, the first of which is found in Figure 14.4. Contractor Dale Brandt determined that three reports, spaced four to six weeks apart, would be necessary to keep Dr. Burke posted; Figure 14.5 (page 570) is the second of those reports.

Parts of a Progress Report

Progress reports should contain information on (1) the work you have done, (2) the work you are currently doing, and (3) the work you will do.

How to Begin a Progress Report

In a brief introduction,

- indicate why you are writing the report
- provide any necessary project titles or codes and specify dates
- help readers recall the job you are doing for them

If you are writing an initial progress report, supply brief background information in the opening. Anna Beth Rowe states the purpose and scope of her work in the first paragraph in Figure 14.4.

If you are submitting a subsequent progress report, inform your reader about where your previous report left off and where the current one begins. Make sure you clearly specify the period covered by each report. Note how Dale Brandt's first paragraph in Figure 14.5 calls attention to the continuity of his work.

How to Write the Body of a Progress Report

The body of the report should provide significant details about costs, materials, personnel, and times for the major stages of the project.

- Emphasize completed tasks, not false starts. If you report that the carpentry work or painting is finished, readers do not need an explanation of paint viscosity or geometrical patterns.
- Omit routine or well-known details ("I had to use the library when I wanted to read the back issues of *Safety News* that were not archived on the Web").
- Describe in the body of your report any snags you encountered that may affect the work in progress. See Anna Beth Rowe's explanation of replacing a planned interview subject, or Dale Brandt's section on electrical problems in Figure 14.5. Ethically, the reader needs to know about trouble early in the project, so appropriate changes or corrections can be made.

How to End a Progress Report

The conclusion should give a timetable for the completion of duties or the submission of the next progress report. Give the date by which you expect work to be completed. Be realistic; do not promise to have a job done in less time than you

FIGURE 14.4 A Progress Report for a Student's Research Report Sent as a PDF

TO: Professor Marisol Vega
FROM: Anna Beth Rowe
DATE: March 21, 2015
SUBJECT: First Progress Report on Research Report

This is the first of two progress reports that you asked me to submit about my background report on the ethical issues involved in using apps in m-commerce.

From February 6 until March 20, I gathered information from library holdings, the Internet, and one interview. Of the sixteen references listed in my proposal, I've so far found only thirteen. The text by Patricia Porter (*Technology and Risk*) and the article by Sara Holes ("Watch for Hotspots when You Use Your Apps") are not available at our campus library, and I'm working with Document Delivery to receive these texts as soon as possible. One of my Internet sources, *blogspot365.com,* has been down for the past several days, but according to their webmaster, service should be restored in the next 4–5 days.

On March 18, I had an extended interview (1½ hours) with Katrina Kuhn, a marketing specialist and M-security consultant. She gave me some helpful handouts from her m-commerce seminars, as well as a copy of a webinar presentation she'd recently delivered on how consumers can better safeguard their privacy when using mobile apps — which I hope to include in the research for my report.

Because of an extended trip to Denver, Paul Goya could not meet with me. At his suggestion, though, I am trying to schedule an interview with Robert Sims, the manager at Mobile General here in Springfield. Sims has made numerous sales presentations and in-house briefings on the mobile apps his company developed to improve customer service and provide better monitoring. Even if Mr. Goya cannot meet with me, Ms. Kuhn gave me a great deal of information about the legal and ethical foundations of m-commerce. Also, there is a chance I might interview Jen Holka at Tech Consultants in early May when her schedule clears. Not currently having the secondary sources listed above may temporarily slow, but not stop, my work.

Starting tomorrow, I will begin my report and will submit my final copy May 1. As you requested, you will receive a second progress report and a draft of my research report on April 3.

Clearly states purpose of report

Provides updates by citing individual references and actions taken

Details results of primary research

Gives detailed descriptions of steps in the research process

Anticipates problem

Concludes with next steps

FIGURE 14.5 The Second of Three Progress Reports from a Contractor to a Customer

Brandt Construction Company

"Building a Greener Tomorrow"

Halsted at Roosevelt, Chicago, Illinois 60608-0999 • 312-555-3700 • Fax: 312-555-1731
www.brandtcon.com ▪ 🄵 www.facebook.com/brandtconstruction/

April 29, 2016

Dr. Pamela Burke
1439 Grand Avenue
Mount Prospect, IL 60045-1003

Dear Dr. Burke:

Here is my second progress report you asked me to submit about the renovation work being done at your new clinic at Hacienda and Donohue. I am pleased to report that work proceeded satisfactorily in April according to the plans you had approved in March.

Review of Work Completed in March
As I informed you in my first progress report on March 31, we tore down the walls, pulled the old wiring, and removed existing plumbing lines. All the gutting work was finished in March.

Work Completed During April
By April 4, we had laid the new pipes and connected them to the main septic line. We also installed the two commodes, four standard sinks, and a utility basin. The heating and air-conditioning ducts were installed by April 8. From April 11–15, we erected soundproof walls in the four examination rooms, the reception area, your office, and the laboratory. Throughout your clinic we used environmentally safe (green) materials. To further conserve energy, we installed solar panels on the roof, as you requested.

Problems with the Electrical System
We had difficulty with the electrical work, however. The outlets and the generator for the laboratory equipment required extra-duty power lines that Con Edison and Cook County inspectors had to approve, which slowed us down by three days. Also, Midtown Electric failed to deliver the recessed lighting fixtures by April 22. Those fixtures and the generator are now installed. Nevertheless, the cost of those fixtures increased the material budget by **$5,288.00**. But the overall cost for labor remains as we had projected—**$94,550**.

Work Remaining
The finishing work is scheduled for May. By May 13, the floors in the examination rooms, laboratory, washrooms, and hallways should be tiled and the reception area and your office carpeted. By May 16, the reception area and your office should be paneled and painted. If everything stays on schedule, touch-up work is planned for May 16–20. You should be able to move into your new clinic by May 23.

You will receive a third and final progress report by May 16. Thank you again for the confidence you have placed in our company.

Sincerely yours,

Dale Brandt

Dale Brandt

Professional-looking letterhead emphasizing ecology

Begins with key information: project status

Recaps activities for background

Summarizes current accomplish-ments

Attention to greening the building

Identifies problems, how they were solved

Specifies work remaining

Projects successful completion

Promises to keep reader informed

know it will take. Readers will not expect miracles, only informed estimates. Even so, any conclusion must be tentative. Note that the good news Dale Brandt gives Dr. Burke about moving into her new clinic is qualified by the words "If everything stays on schedule." He also employs the "you attitude" by thanking Dr. Burke again for her business.

EMPLOYEE ACTIVITY/PERFORMANCE REPORTS

An **employee activity/performance report** informs your boss about what you did during a specified period (weekly, monthly, quarterly). He/she will expect you to explain how you managed your time and fulfilled the requirements of your job. Accountability is a major objective in the world of work and, as we saw in Chapter 1 (see "Ethical Requirements on the Job," pages 27–29), employers closely monitor employees, even online. An activity report is a vital indication of an employee's performance. Your supervisor or manager will want to know about the specific tasks you accomplished, how many of them, when, and why, as well as any ongoing projects in which you are involved. Activity reports will play a role in assessing your job performance and determining whether you should be promoted.

Figure 14.6 (page 572) shows an employee activity report written by Carey Lewis, an administrative assistant, for his supervisor, Beth-Anne Prohaska. Note how he classifies his accomplishments into four major categories and provides an honest, objective, and concise explanation of what he has done and why. Each of Lewis's accomplishments squares with his job responsibility.

Guidelines for Writing an Activity Report

To write a reliable and efficient activity report, you need to document what you have done. Keep track of your accomplishments by using an electronic or hard copy log, recording and saving job-related duties and correlating the hours you spent on a project with your timesheets. Here are some guidelines to follow when you write an activity/performance report:

- **Use the format that your employer or agency dictates.** This might be a special form, a memo, an email, or an email with an attachment, such as an annotated day-to-day calendar.
- **Make sure you are honest, objective, and accurate.** It is unethical to misrepresent what you did—for example, saying a job took longer than it did or exaggerating the number of tasks you actually performed. Do not claim credit for tasks you did not accomplish or finish. But do give credit to coworkers with whom you collaborated, as Carey Lewis does in Figure 14.6.
- **Describe your major accomplishments.** Quantify and give dates, if necessary. But be careful that you do not dwell on smaller duties ("I answered the phone every day") at the expense of omitting tasks that demonstrate your writing, organizational, and collaborative skills at work.
- **Be sure that each of your accomplishments squares with your job description.** Indicate how your performance meets the goals your employer set for

FIGURE 14.6 An Employee Activity Report Sent as an Email with Attachments

Includes attachment

Gives background and briefly summarizes purpose of report

Uses boldfaced headings to group activities

Uses strong verbs to convey type of work

Provides key dates

Describes job duties clearly

References attachment

Specifies length and topic of presentation

Acknowledges collaboration

Promises continuity and politely requests feedback

To: Carey Lewis (clewis@wdynamics.com)
Cc: Beth-Anne Prohaska (baprohaska@wdynamics.com)
Bcc: Gloria Arrelo (garrelo@starinstruments.com)
Subject: Monthly Activity Report for August

📎 🔲 Purchase Orders   📎 🔲 Workflow

Dear Ms. Prohaska:

During the past pay cycle (August 1–August 31), I worked on several projects that I believe helped to ensure, and even increase, the efficiency of our department. Below I have categorized my activities (all of which are specified in my job description), included completion dates for major tasks, and attached relevant documentation.

Oversaw Day-to-Day Management of Office
- Maintained adequate office supplies (see attachment: "Purchase Orders")
- Researched costs and features of new all-in-one printer and priced models for purchase
- Submitted recommendation for all-in-one printer (August 5)
- Trained two new interns (Loretta Bauer, Scott Chu)

Prepared and Delivered Documents
- Edited and posted the monthly newsletter to the company's website (August 17)
- Compiled, printed, and distributed monthly sales report (August 24)
- Updated, archived, and retrieved records

Planned Schedules
- Managed office calendar of events and meetings and posted it to the website
- Arranged travel plans for 4 staff on sales visits; two of these were overseas trips
- Coordinated workflow charts (see attachment: "Workflow")
- Logged staff timesheets in master file

Organized Meetings
- Presented short report (15 minutes) at HR meeting on August 5 about our department's successes in marketing new products on our Facebook and Pinterest sites
- Created—with assistant manager Richard Fleming—and distributed agenda for monthly staff meeting (August 26)
- Took minutes for monthly meeting and shared them on company intranet (August 30)

For the coming month I will continue to fulfill my ongoing responsibilities as well as meet our department's goals for any new assignments. I look forward to any comments you may have about my past or current performance.

Respectfully,

Carey Lewis
Administrative Assistant

© 2017 Cengage Learning

you. Specify how your tasks assist, improve, or contribute to your department or division. Emphasize how your achievements benefit your employer.
- **Include training sessions or workshops you attended, licensure/ certification updates, committee memberships, and presentations you**

made. List and describe any meetings, classes, continuing education sessions that help you to do your job more efficiently, accurately, or promptly.

- **Stress how your job accomplishments benefited the company, your department, or your community.** Link what you have done to the goals your company or department hopes to meet, such as sharing minutes in Figures 14.6.

- **Be prepared to verify your activities with copies of relevant documents, emails, and even messages.** Maintain a folder of all these documents so you can compile them for yearly evaluations.

TRIP/TRAVEL REPORTS

Reporting on the trips you take is an important professional responsibility in the world of work. Basically, you are on a fact-finding mission. In documenting what you did and saw, **trip reports** (also called **travel reports**) keep readers informed about your efforts and how they affect ongoing or future business, as Figure 14.8 shows. Moreover, such reports help you better understand your job and develop your networking skills. Trip reports also should be written immediately after you attend a convention or sales meeting or call on customers when your memory of events is fresh.

Questions Your Trip/Travel Report Needs to Answer

Specifically, a trip report should answer the following questions for your readers:

- Where did you go?
- When did you go?
- Why did you go?
- What did you see?
- How did your trip financially benefit your company?
- Whom did you see?
- What did they tell you?
- What did you do about it?
- Any problems or setbacks encountered?
- Do you have any recommendations?

For a business trip, you are also likely to have to inform readers how much it cost and to supply them with receipts for all of your business expenses.

Common Types of Trip/Travel Reports

Trip reports can cover a wide range of activities and are called by different names to characterize those activities. Most likely, you will encounter the following four types of trip reports.

1. Field trip reports. These reports, often assigned in a course, are written after a visit to a laboratory, hospital, detention center, or other location to show what you have learned about the operation of a facility. You will be expected to describe how an institution is organized, the technical procedures and/or equipment used, pertinent ecological conditions, or the ratio of one group to another. The emphasis in such reports is on the educational value of the trip, as nursing student Mark Tourneur's report in Figure 14.7 (page 574–575) demonstrates.

FIGURE 14.7 A Field Trip Report

TO: Katherine Holmes, RN, MSN
           Director, RN Program
FROM: Mark Tourneur M.T.
           RN Student
DATE: November 12, 2015
SUBJECT: Field Trip to Water Valley Extended Care Center

Explains purpose of trip

On Monday, November 9, I visited the Water Valley Extended Care Center, 1400 Medford Boulevard, as part of my preparation for my internship in an extended care facility next semester.

Philosophy and Organization

Describes the mission and organization of the facility

Before my tour started, the director, Sue LaFrance, explained the holistic philosophy of health care at Water Valley and emphasized the diverse kinds of nursing practiced there. She stressed that the agency is not restricted to geriatric clients but admits anyone requiring extended care. She pointed out that Water Valley is a medium-sized facility (150 beds) and contains three wings: (1) the Infirmary, (2) the General Nursing Unit, and (3) the Ambulatory Unit.

Primary Client Services

My tour began with the Infirmary, staffed by one RN and two LPNs, where I observed a number of life-support systems in operation:

Summarizes what he observed, whom he met, and the various units of the facility

- IVs
- oxygen setups
- feeding tubes
- cardiac monitors

Then I was shown the General Nursing Unit (40 beds), staffed by three LPNs and four aides. Clients can have private or semiprivate rooms; bathrooms have wide doors and lowered sinks for patients using wheelchairs or walkers. The Ambulatory Unit serves 90 clients who can provide their own daily care.

Additional Client Services
Dietetics

Usefully provides subheads to organize his report

Before lunch in the main dining room, I was introduced to Jack Isoke, the dietitian, who explained the different menus he coordinates. The most common are low-sodium and ADA (American Diabetic Association) restricted-calorie. Staff members eat with the clients, reinforcing the holistic focus of the agency.

Pharmacy

Documents conferences with staff

After lunch, Kendra Tishner, the pharmacist, discussed the agency's procedures for ordering and delivering medications. She also described the client teaching she does and the in-service workshops she conducts.

FIGURE 14.7 (Continued)

Katherine Holmes
November 12, 2015
Page 2

Physical/Spiritual Therapy
I then observed clients in both recreational and physical therapy. Water Valley's full-time physical therapist, Tracy Cook, works with stroke and arthritic clients and helps those with broken bones regain the use of their limbs. In addition to a weight room, Water Valley has a small sauna that most of the clients use at least twice a week.

The clients' spiritual needs are not neglected, either. A small interdenominational chapel is located just south of the Ambulatory Unit.

Benefits for My Internship
From my visit to Water Valley, I learned a great deal about the health care delivery system at an extended care facility. I was especially pleased to have been given so much information on emergency procedures, medication orders, and physical therapy programs. My forthcoming internship should be even more productive, as I now have firsthand knowledge about these various services.

Describes the function of various locations in the facility

Concludes with the advantages of the trip

2. Site inspection reports. These reports inform managers about conditions at a branch office or plant, a customer's business, or the advisability of relocating an office or other facility. After visiting the site, you will determine whether it meets your employer's (or customer's) needs. Site inspection reports can provide information about the physical plant, the environment (air, soil, water, vegetation), safety, IT, or financial operations.

Figure 14.8 (page 576–577), which begins with a recommendation, is a report written to a district manager interested in acquiring a new site for a fast-food restaurant.

3. Home health or social work visit reports. Nurses, social workers, and probation officers, for instance, report routinely on their visits to patients, clients, and parolees. Their reports describe clients' lifestyles, assess needs, and make recommendations based on a variety of sources—clients, health care professionals, charitable organizations, and the like. These reports are often divided into *Purpose of the Visit, Description of the Visit,* and *Action Taken as a Result of the Visit.*

4. Sales/customer visit reports. Visiting current or prospective customers at their place of business or at trade shows can result in further business opportunities for you and your company. Your supervisor will need to know the following about your sales call:

(a) What are the customer's needs and history of transactions with your company?
(b) Which products or services that your company provides best meet those needs?

FIGURE 14.8 A Site Inspection Repost Using a Map

VAIL's CHICKEN HOUSE
"CHICKEN WITH STYLE"

 www.facebook.com/vailschicken/
 @vailschicken

TO: Pretha Bandi   *B.A.R.*
FROM: Beth Armando-Ruiz
Development Department

DATE: March 28, 2016
SUBJECT: New Site for Vail's #7

Begins with most important details about the writer's recommendation

Recommendation
To follow up on our discussions earlier this month, as you requested, I think the best location for the new Vail's Chicken House is the vacant Dairy World restaurant at the northeast corner of Smith and Fairfax Avenues—1701 Fairfax. I inspected this property on March 21 and 22 and also talked to Kim Shao, the broker at Crescent Realty **(kims@crescent.org)**, representing the Dairy World Company. The location, parking facilities, and building at the Dairy World site all present the best opportunity for future growth and increased sales for Vail's.

Gives essential contact information

Provides necessary background details

The Location
Please refer to the map below. Located at the intersection of the two busiest streets on the southeast side of the city, the property will allow us to take advantage of the traffic flow to attract customers. Being only one block west of the Cloverleaf Mall should also help increase our business.

Includes map and traffic flow information essential for reader's purpose

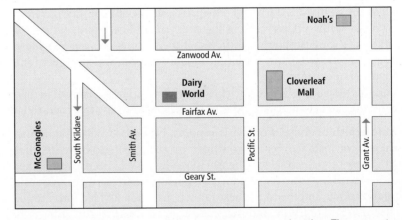

Clearly transitions to another advantage

Another benefit is that customers will have easy access to our location. They can enter or exit the Dairy World site from either Smith or Fairfax Avenues. Left turns onto Smith are prohibited from 7 a.m. to 9 a.m., but since most of our business is done after 11 a.m., the restriction poses few problems.

Denver, CO 87123   (303) 555-7200   www.vails.com

FIGURE 14.8 (Continued)

Area Competition

Only two other fast food establishments are within a one-mile vicinity. McGonagles, 1534 South Kildare, specializes in hamburgers; and Noah's, 703 Grant Ave., serves primarily seafood entrées. Their offerings will not directly compete with ours. The closest fast food restaurant serving chicken is Johnson's, 1.8 miles away.

Assesses the location, in light of the competition

Parking Facilities

The parking lot has space for 18 cars, and the area at the south end of the property (70 feet × 54 feet) could accommodate 14–15 more vehicles. The driveways and parking lot were paved with asphalt last July and appear to be in excellent condition. We will also be able to use the drive-up window on the north side of the building.

Gives only the most essential facts audience needs on parking, seating capacity, and alterations

The Building

The building has 3,993 square feet of heated and cooled space. The four Fujitsu air-conditioning units and heating units were installed within the last fifteen months and seem to be in good working order; nine more months of transferable warranty remain on all these units.

Writer has done research on equipment

The only major changes we must make are in the kitchen. To prepare items on the Vail's menu, we must add at least three more exhaust fans (there is only one now) and to expand the grill and cooking areas by 80 square feet. The kitchen also has three relatively new sinks and offers ample storage space in the 16 cabinets.

Paragraphs are easy to follow with precise topic sentences

The restaurant has a seating capacity of up to 34 persons; 10 booths are covered with red vinyl and are comfortably padded. A color-coordinated serving counter could seat 8 to 10 patrons. The floor does not need to be retiled, but the walls will have to be painted to match Vail's decor.

Does not overwhelm reader with petty details

(c) What types of demonstrations, samples, or written materials (brochures) did you give the customer?

(d) What questions or reservations does the customer have about your products or services?

(e) Who are your company's chief competitors and how do their products and services stack up against your firm's?

(f) How does your firm stand in terms of landing a contract?

(g) What kinds of follow-up visits, calls, or information might be necessary to clinch the deal?

(h) What business/market trends have you observed?

Make sure you spell out precisely how you successfully represented your company and its products or services.

How to Gather Information for a Trip/Travel Report

Regardless of the kind of trip report you have to write, your assignment will be easier and your report better organized if you follow these suggestions.

1. Before you leave on the site inspection, field trip, or other business trip, make sure you have your employer's authorization to travel, use a company vehicle, and submit expenses. Be sure you are prepared:

   a. Obtain all necessary names; street, email, and website addresses; and relevant telephone and cell numbers, as well as any necessary URLs and social media site information.

   b. Check files for previous correspondence, case studies, warranties, or contracts or agreements.

   c. Download or obtain hard copies of any work orders, instructions, or other documents pertinent to your visit.

   d. Bring a laptop, tablet, or other mobile device with you. Keep a journal of what you saw and heard.

   e. Locate a map of the area and get the directions you'll need beforehand. (Both maps and directions can be obtained easily at www.mapquest.com, maps.yahoo.com, and maps.google.com).

   f. Keep a record of appointment times and locations as well as the names and job titles of the people whom you expect to meet.

   g. Save all receipts.

   h. Bring a videorecorder, camera, audio recorder, smartphone, laptop, or tablet, if necessary, to record important data. You may be asked to post photographs from your trip on your company's website.

2. When you return from your trip, keep the following hints in mind as you compile your report:

   a. Write your report promptly; otherwise you may forget important details.

   b. When a trip takes you to two or more widely separated places, note in your report when you arrived at each place and how long you stayed.

   c. Exclude irrelevant details, such as whether the trip was enjoyable, what you ate, or how delighted you were to meet people. Concentrate on the information your reader needs to make a decision, meet a goal, or receive a timely update.

d. Be objective about what you saw and heard. Indicate when you quote someone as part of an interview.

e. Offer to answer any questions your reader may have about the trip and its outcomes.

f. Include any relevant financial information from your trip: expenses incurred, budget information or impact, etc.

TEST REPORTS

Much physical research (the discovery and documentation of facts) is communicated through short reports variously called **experiment, investigation, laboratory**, or **operations reports**. They all record the results of tests, whether the tests were conducted in a forest, computer center, laboratory, shopping mall, or soybean field. You may be asked to test an existing or a new product or procedure or verify certain physical or environmental conditions for a class or an employer. Figures 14.9 and 14.10 contain two test reports.

CASE STUDY

Two Sample Test Reports

Figure 14.9 (page 580) is a relatively simple and short test report in memo format regarding sanitary conditions at a hospital psychiatric unit. The report follows a direct and useful pattern of organization:

- statement of purpose—*why?*
- findings—*what happened?*
- recommendations—*what next?*

Submitted by an infection control officer, the report does not provide elaborate details about the particular laboratory procedures used to determine whether bacteria were present, nor does it describe the pathogenic (disease-causing) properties of the bacteria. Such descriptions are unnecessary for the audience (the housekeeping department) to do its job.

A more complex short test report can be found in Figure 14.10 (pages 581–583), which studies the effects of four light periods on the growth of paulownia seedlings (a flowering tree cultivated in China). The report, published in a scientific journal, is addressed to specialists in forestry and agronomy. Such a test report follows a different, more detailed pattern of organization than the report in Figure 14.9 and includes an informative abstract (see "Abstracts," pages 387–389), an introduction, a materials and methods section, a results and discussion section, and a conclusion.

To meet the needs of an expert audience, the writers of the report in Figure 14.10 had to include much more information than did Janeen Cufaude, the infection control officer who wrote the report in Figure 14.9, about the way the test was conducted and the types of scientific data the audience expects and needs. The researchers did not have to define technical terms for their audience, and they could confidently use scientific symbols and formulas as well.

FIGURE 14.9 A Short, Informal Test Report

Charleston, WV 25324-0114 / (304) 555-1800 / www.charlestongeneral.com

TO: James Dill, Supervisor   FROM: Janeen Cufaude *JC*
          Housekeeping   Infection Control Officer

DATE: December 14, 2015   SUBJECT: Routine sanitation inspection,
                                             December 11, 2015

States why tests were performed and how

As part of the monthly check of the psychiatric unit (11A) on December 11, five areas were swabbed and tested for bacterial growth. The results of the lab tests of these samples are as follows:

Gives results of tests conducted in different locations

AREA	**FINDINGS**
1. cabinet in patients' kitchen	1. positive for 2 colonies of strep germs
2. rug in eating area	2. positive for food particles and yeasts and molds
3. baseboard in dayroom	3. positive for particles of dust
4. medicine counter in nurses' station	4. negative for bacteria—no growth after 48 hours
5. corridor by south elevator	5. positive for 4 colonies of staph germs isolated

ACTIONS TO BE TAKEN AT ONCE

Provides detailed directions based on results

1. Clean the kitchen cabinets with K-504 liquid daily, 3:1 dilution.
2. Shampoo rug areas bimonthly with heavy-duty shampoo, and clean visibly soiled areas with Safetec Sanizide Plus as often as needed.
3. Wipe all baseboards weekly with K-12 spray cleanser.
4. Mop heavily traveled corridors and access areas with K-504 cleanser daily, 1:1 dilution.

FIGURE 14.10 A Test Report Published in a Scientific Journal

Paulownia Seedlings Respond to Increased Daylength

M. J. Immel, E. M. Tackett, and S. B. Carpenter

Abstract

Paulownia seedlings grown under four photoperiods were evaluated after a growing period of 97 days. Height growth and total dry weight production were both significantly increased in the 16- and 24-hour photoperiods.

Begins with informative abstract

Introduction

Paulownia (*Paulownia tomentosa* [Thunb.] Steud.), a native of China, is a little known species in the United States. Recently, however, there has been increased interest in this species for surface mine reclamation (*1*).* Paulownia seems to be especially well adapted to harsh micro-climates of surface mines; it grows very rapidly and appears to be drought-resistant. In Kentucky and surrounding states, paulownia wood is actively sought by Japanese buyers and has brought prices comparable to black walnut (*2*).

This increased interest in paulownia has resulted in several attempts to direct seed it on surface mines, but little success has been achieved. The high light requirements and the extremely small size of paulownia seed (approximately 6,000 per gram) may be the limiting factors. Planting paulownia seedlings is preferred; but, because of their succulent nature, seedlings are usually produced and outplanted as container stock rather than bareroot seedlings. Daylength is an important factor in the production of vigorous container plants (*5*).

Our study compares the effects that four photoperiods—8, 12, 16, and 24 hours—had on the early growth of container-grown paulownia seedlings over a period of 97 days.

Gives background, purpose, and scope of study

Materials and Methods

Seeds used in this study were stratified in a 1:1 mixture of peat moss and sand at 4°C for 2 years. Following cold storage, seeds were placed on a 1:1 potting soil–sand mix and mulched with cheesecloth. They were then placed under continuous light until germination occurred. Germination percentages were high, indicating paulownia seeds can survive long periods of storage with little loss of viability (*3*).

Thirty days after germination, 3- to 4-centimeter seedlings were transplanted into 8-quart plastic pots filled with an equal mixture of potting soil, sand, and peat moss. Seventy-five seedlings were randomly assigned to each of the four treatments. Treatments were for 4 photoperiods—8, 12, 16, and 24 hours—and were replicated three times in 12 light chambers. Each chamber was 1.2- by 1.2-meters with an artificial light source 71 centimeters above the chamber floor.

The light source consisted of eight fluorescent lights: four 40-watt plant growth lamps alternated with four 40-watt cool white lamps. Light intensity averaged 550 foot-candles (1340μ einsteins/m²/s) at the top of each pot and the temperature averaged 550 foot-candles (1340 einsteins/m²/s) at the top of each pot and the temperature averaged 23°C (+2°C).

Seedlings were watered and fertilized after transplanting with a 6-gram 14-4-6 agriform container tablet. Beginning 1 month after transplanting, two seedlings were randomly selected and harvested from each chamber for a total of 24 trees.

Describes steps taken: procedures, conditions, and equipment used

Uses technical terms and symbols audience expects

---

*To save space, the references have been omitted.

(Continued)

FIGURE 14.10 (Continued)

Height, root collar diameter, length of longest root, and oven-dry weight (at 65°C) were determined for each seedling. Harvests continued every week for 5 additional weeks.

Results and Discussion

Results indicate that early growth of paulownia is influenced by photoperiod, as shown in Table 1 below:

Includes a visual to summarize results and then explains what happened

TABLE 1. Height Diameter, Root Length, Total Dry Weight, and R/S Ratio for Paulownia Seedlings Grown Under Four Photoperiods After 97 Days.

Photo period (hrs.)	Height (cm)	Diameter (cm)	Root length (cm)	Total dry weight (gm)	R/S ratio
8	13.1	0.48	16.0	1.65	0.18
12	17.8	0.67	34.7	7.27	0.32
16	27.3	0.93	31.1	15.92	0.39
24	29.2	0.90	43.9	18.66	0.33

Expanding the photoperiod from 8 to either 16 or 24 hours increased height growth by 100 percent. Height growth in the 12-hour treatment also increased, but did not differ significantly from the 8-hour treatment. Heights under photoperiods of 8, 12, 16, and 24 hours were 13.1, 17.8, 27.3, and 29.2 centimeters, respectively.

Cites related studies

Previous studies have also shown that photoperiod affects the growth of paulownia seedlings (4, 6). Sanderson (6), for example, found that paulownia seedlings grown under continuous light averaged 27.2 centimeters in height after 101 days compared with 29.2 centimeters for our 24-hour seedlings. Other corresponding photoperiods were equally comparable. Downs and Borthwick (4) also concluded that height growth of paulownia was affected by extending the photoperiod.

The great treatment differences were shown in total dry weight production. Refer again to Table 1. The mean weight of 1.65 grams for seedlings in the 8-hour treatment was significantly less than that of any of the other photoperiods. The 16- and 24-hour treatments did not differ significantly. In fact, they more than doubled the average weight for seedlings in the 12-hour treatment.

Provides accurate measurements in a clear, objective tone

Root-to-shoot ratio (R/S) indicates the relative proportion of growth allocated to roots versus shoots for the seedlings in each photoperiod. In this study, shoots were developing at nearly three times the rate of the roots for seedlings in the 12-, 16-, and 24-hour treatments.

The 0.18 R/S ratio for seedlings in the 8-hour treatment was much lower, indicating that relative growth of the shoot is approximately five times that of the root. The shorter photoperiod, therefore, decreased root development relative to shoot development as well as significantly reduced total dry weight production.

Although root collar diameter and root length did not significantly differ under the different photoperiods after 97 days, there was a trend for greater diameter and root growth when exposed to longer photoperiods.

FIGURE 14.10 (Continued)

Page 3

Conclusions

    Results indicate that the growth of paulownia seedlings is affected by changes in the photoperiod. Increasing the photoperiod significantly increased height growth and total dry matter production. The distribution of dry matter (R/S ratio) was altered by increasing the photoperiod; as a consequence, the ratio was larger in the longer photoperiods. In contrast to earlier studies (*4*), we found paulownia seedlings subjected to extended photoperiods were still growing after 97 days.

Interprets the significance of the results

Adapted from M. J. Immel, E. M. Tackett, and S. B. Carpenter, "Paulownia Seedlings Respond to Increased Daylength," *Tree Planters' Notes* 31(*1*): 3–5. United States Department of Agriculture, Forest Service.

    Objectivity and accuracy are essential ingredients in a test report. Readers want to know about your empirical research (the facts), not about your feelings. Record your observations without bias or guesswork in a laboratory journal, log book, or electronically and always document the results with precise measurements using the standard symbols and abbreviations of your profession.

Questions Your Test Report Needs to Answer

Readers will expect your test report to supply the following information:

- why you performed the test—an explanation of the reasons, your goals, and who authorized you to perform the test
- how you performed the test—under what circumstances or controls you conducted the test, what procedures and equipment you used, etc.
- what the outcomes were—your conclusions
- what implications or recommendations follow from your test—what you learned, discovered, confirmed, or disproved or rejected

When you sign the final copy of your report, you certify that things happened exactly when, how, and why you say they did.

INCIDENT REPORTS

The short reports discussed thus far in this chapter have dealt with routine work. They have described events that were anticipated or supervised. But every business or agency runs into unexpected trouble that delays routine work, damages equipment or property, or may result in personal injury. These circumstances need to be documented in an **incident** (or **accident**) **report**. The audience for an incident report can be within your organization or outside it, or both. Employers use incident reports to make changes so that the problem does not occur again or so that a job can be done more effectively and safely. On some occasions, government inspectors, insurance agents, and attorneys must be informed about those events that have interfered with or threatened normal, safe operations.

When to Submit an Incident Report

An incident report is submitted when there is, for example,

- an accident—fire, automobile, physical injury
- a law enforcement offense
- an environmental danger
- a computer virus
- a machine breakdown
- a delivery delay
- a cost overrun
- a production slowdown

Figure 14.11 is an incident report about a train derailment submitted by the engineer on duty. This report is in memo format, but some companies or agencies require you to fill out a special form. While many organizations require a hard copy of an incident report to be sent or filed, others ask you to include it as an attachment to an email. Always check with your supervisor about your company's preferred method.

Parts of an Incident Report

Include the following information in your incident report. Note how Figure 14.11 includes precise and accurate information for each of these parts.

1. Identification details. Specify who and what was involved, and gather all relevant data—names, contact information, model/serial numbers, and so on. Record titles, department, and employment identification numbers. Indicate if you or your fellow employees were working alone. For customers or victims, record home addresses, home and cell phone numbers, email addresses, and places of employment. Insurance companies will also require policy numbers.

2. Type of incident. Briefly identify the incident—personal injury, fire, burglary, equipment failure. Identify any part(s) of the body precisely. "Eye injury" is not enough; "injury to the right eye, causing bleeding" is better. "Dislocated right shoulder" or "punctured left forearm" is descriptive and exact. A report on damaged equipment should list make and model numbers.

3. Time and location of the incident. Include precise date (not "Thursday") and time (a.m. or p.m.).

FIGURE 14.11 An Incident Report in Memo Format

THE GREAT HARVESTER RAILROAD
Des Moines, IA 50306-4005
www.ghrr.com

TO: Angela O'Brien, District Manager
             James Hwang, Safety Inspector
FROM: Nick Roane, Engineer *Nick Roane*
DATE: October 6, 2015
SUBJECT: Derailment of Train 26 on October 5, 2015

Signs report to verify account of incident

Type of Incident
Two grain cars went off the track while I was driving Engine 457 of Train 26 on October 5, 2015. There were no injuries to the crew.

Begins with most important details

Description of Incident
At 7:20 a.m., I was traveling north at a speed of 30 miles an hour on the single main line track four miles east of Ridgeville, Illinois. Weather conditions and visibility were excellent. Suddenly, the last two grain cars, 3022 and 3053, jumped the track. The train automatically went into emergency braking and came to a stop. But it did not stop before both grain cars turned at a 45° angle. After checking these cars, I found that half the contents of their loads had spilled. The train was not carrying any hazardous chemicals or other environmentally damaging shipments.

Gives precise time, location

Describes what happened

I notified Supervisor Bill Purvis at 7:40 a.m., and within 45 minutes he and a section crew arrived at the scene with rerailing equipment. The crew removed the two grain cars from the track, put in new ties, and made the main line track passable by 11:25 a.m. At 1:25 p.m. a vacuum car arrived with Engine 372 from Hazlehurst, Illinois, and its crew proceeded with the clean-up operation. By 3:25 p.m. all the spilled grain was loaded onto the cars brought by the Hazlehurst train. Bill Purvis notified Barnwell Granary that their shipment would be at least eight hours late.

Explains what was done

Causes of Incident
Supervisor Purvis and I checked the stretch of train track where the cars derailed and found it to be heavily worn. We believe that a fisher joint slipped when the grain cars hit it, and the track broke. You can see the location of the cracked fisher joint in the graphic below.

Determines likely cause

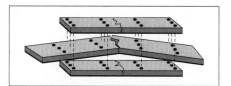

Supplies easy-to-follow exploded visual

(Continued)

FIGURE 14.11 (Continued)

*Records
precise steps
taken*

Angela O'Brien
James Hwang
October 6, 2015
Page 2

Actions Taken
We performed the following procedures after the accident:

1. Checked the section of track for 8 miles on either side of Ridgeville for any signs of defective fisher joints.
2. Repaired at once any defective joints we saw.
3. Instructed all engineers to slow down to 5 to 10 mph over this section of the track until the rail check is completed for 20 miles on either side of the accident site.

© 2017 Cengage Learning

4. Description of what happened. This section is the longest part of the report. Let readers know exactly what took place and why, how it occurred, and what led up to the incident.

5. What was done after the incident. Describe the action you took to correct conditions, how things got back to normal, and what was done to treat the injured, make the environment safer, speed a delivery, or repair damaged equipment.

6. What caused the incident. Make sure your explanation is consistent with your description of what happened. Pinpoint the trouble. In Figure 14.11, for example, the defective fisher joint is listed under the heading "Causes of Incident."

7. Actions taken. Specify any actions taken to prevent the problem from recurring. They may involve repairing any broken parts, as in Figure 14.11, calling a special safety meeting, asking for further training, adapting existing equipment, doing emergency planning, or modifying schedules.

Protecting Yourself Legally

An incident report can be admitted as legal evidence, and it then becomes part of a permanent legal record that can be used by law enforcement and attorneys in court to establish negligence and liability on your and your company's part. It can also be used by an employer to determine employee responsibility. An incident report frequently concerns the two topics over which powerful legal battles are waged— health and property. You could lose a case in court if your report is not written competently, clearly, accurately, and completely.

You have to be very careful about collecting and recording details. Make sure your report is not sketchy, confusing, or incomplete. To avoid these errors, you may have to interview employees or bystanders; travel to the incident site; check manuals, code books, or other guides; consult safety experts; collect and describe evidence; or research records/archives.

To ensure that what you write is legally proper, follow these guidelines:

1. Submit your report promptly, and sign or initial it. Any delay might be seen as a cover-up. Send your report to the appropriate parties immediately after you have gathered the necessary information and had it reviewed by your supervisor. You may have to post photographs as well.

2. Double-check your spelling (individuals' names, pieces of equipment, etc.), your math, and your punctuation. An error here calls the accuracy and validity of your whole report into question.

3. Be accurate, objective, and complete. Give readers sufficient information to know exactly what happened and the order in which it occurred. Never omit or distort facts; the information may surface later, and you could be accused of a cover-up. Do not simply write "I do not know" for an answer. If you are not sure, state why. Also be careful that there are no discrepancies or inconsistencies in your report.

4. Give facts, not opinions. Provide a factual account of what actually happened, not a biased interpretation of events or one based on speculation or hearsay. Vague responses such as "I guess," "I wonder," "apparently," "perhaps," or "possibly" weaken your objectivity. Indicate who discovered, reported, or witnessed the incident. But stick to details you witnessed or that were seen by eyewitnesses. Identify witnesses or victims by giving complete names, contact information, places of employment, and so on. Keep in mind that stating what someone else saw is regarded as hearsay and therefore is not admissible in a court of law. State only what *you* saw or heard. When you describe what happened, avoid drawing uncalled-for conclusions. Consider the following statements of opinion versus fact:

> Opinion: The patient seemed confused and caught himself in his IV tubing.
> Fact: The patient caught himself in his IV tubing.

> Opinion: The equipment was defective.
> Fact: The bolt was cracked.

Be careful, too, about blaming someone. Statements such as "Baxter was incompetent" or "The company knew of the problem but did nothing about it" are libelous remarks.

5. Do not exceed your professional responsibilities. Answer only those questions you are qualified to answer. Do not presume to speak as a first responder, a detective, an inspector, a physician, a supervisor, or a judge. Do not represent yourself as an attorney or a claims adjuster in writing the report. And don't take sides.

SHORT REPORTS: SOME FINAL THOUGHTS

To prepare successful short reports, keep in mind the rules of short report writing discussed in this chapter. Always take into account your readers' needs and expectations at every stage of your writing, take accurate and complete notes, document carefully what you write about, write objectively and ethically, present complicated data clearly and concisely, provide background and context where necessary, and provide specific recommendations, where called for, based upon the facts. Remembering these basic rules will earn you praise and possibly promotions at work.

✔ REVISION CHECKLIST

- ☐ Understood why short reports are important for my company or organization.
- ☐ Made sure reader understood reason for report.
- ☐ Recognized the type of report (e.g., periodic, progress, employee activity, etc.) I need to write.
- ☐ Chose the report format that is most appropriate for my audience (memos or emails for supervisor or co-workers; letters for clients).
- ☐ Put all the information in the right section.
- ☐ Did appropriate research to give my readers enough information to help them make careful decisions.
- ☐ Provided significant information about costs, materials, personnel, locations, environmental conditions, and times, so readers will know that my work consists of facts, not impressions.
- ☐ Double-checked all data—names, costs, figures, dates, places, and equipment models and numbers.
- ☐ Made sure all my comments and recommendations were ethical.
- ☐ Followed all organization guidelines.
- ☐ Adhered to all legal requirements.
- ☐ Eliminated unnecessary details or those too technical for my audience.
- ☐ Kept report concise, to the point, readable, and easy to read.
- ☐ Used headings whenever feasible to organize and categorize information.
- ☐ Supplied relevant visuals to help readers understand my message and crunch any numbers.
- ☐ Employed underlining, boldface, or italics to set headings apart or to emphasize key ideas.
- ☐ Began report with a statement of purpose that clearly described the scope and significance of my work.
- ☐ Incorporated tables, maps, graphs, and other pertinent visuals to dislplay data whenever appropriate.
- ☐ Explained clearly what the data meant in a conclusion section.
- ☐ Determined that recommendations logically follow from the data and that they are relevant and realistic.

Periodic/Sales Reports
- ☐ Submitted my report at scheduled intervals.
- ☐ Provided accurate data on quantities sold or services provided.

☐ Documented, organized, described, and explained the importance of the data, including sales figures.

☐ Verified necessary statistics and trends so that my report is thorough and accurate.

Progress Reports

☐ Reported at key stages of the project.

☐ Gave readers bottom-line information on costs, equipment, personnel, and schedules.

☐ Described the work or projects to be completed.

☐ Alerted readers about any problems—delays or cost overruns.

Employee Activity/Performance Reports

☐ Accounted for how I spent my time at work for a given period.

☐ Categorized types of projects and tasks accomplished.

☐ Indicated when a job was a collaborative effort—with whom I worked and when.

☐ Identified projects and tasks that continue into the next scheduled evaluation period (monthly, quarterly, etc.).

Trip/Travel Reports

☐ Explained the purpose of the trip—where and when I went and whom I visited, interviewed, made a presentation for, or saw at a conference.

☐ Recorded all names, places, dates, costs, etc., accurately.

☐ Supplied relevant visuals, such as photographs and charts.

☐ Included findings and recommendations.

☐ Indicated I am available for questions or clarifications.

Test Reports

☐ Recorded data accurately and objectively.

☐ Specified why the test was performed and which procedures and equipment were used.

☐ Explained the significance of results and outcomes, emphasizing how the information can be applied to meet my company's needs.

Incident Reports

☐ Identified the type of incident, time, place, victims and eyewitnesses, injuries, and so on.

☐ Provided a factual, objective, and accurate account of the incident in a logical or chronological order.

☐ Stated without bias what may have caused the incident; did not draw unjustified conclusions.

☐ Explained what has been or can be done to correct the problem and prevent it from recurring.

EXERCISES

1. Bring to class an example of a periodic report from your present or previous job or from any community, religious, or social organization to which you belong. In an accompanying memo to your instructor, indicate who the audience is and why such a report is necessary, stressing how it is organized, what kinds of factual data it contains, what visuals were used, and how it might be improved in content, organization, style, and design.

2. Assume that you are the manager of an apartment complex (300 units). Write a periodic report based on the following information: 26 units are vacant, 38 soon will be vacant, and 27 soon will be leased (by June 1). Also add a section of recommendations to your supervisor (the head of the management company for which you work) on how vacant apartments might be leased more quickly and perhaps at increased rents. Consider such important information as decorating, advertising, installing a new security system, providing Wi-Fi access, and amenities such as a pool, fitness center, or clubhouse, and first-month discounts.

3. Assume you work for a household appliance store. Prepare a sales report based on the information contained in the following table. Include a section on recommendations for your manager.

	Number Sold	
Product	October	November
Kitchen Appliances		
Refrigerators	72	103
Dishwashers	27	14
Freezers	10	36
Electric ranges	26	26
Gas ranges	10	3
Microwaves	31	46
Laundry Appliances		
Washers	50	75
Dryers	24	36
Air Treatments		
Room air conditioners	41	69
Dehumidifiers	7	2

4. Write a progress report on the wins and losses (and, if applicable, ties) of your favorite sports team for the past season. Address the report to the director of publicity for the

team and stress how the director might use those facts for future publicity. As part of your report, indicate what might be an effective lead for a press release about the team's efforts.

5. Submit a progress report to your writing instructor on what you have learned in his or her course so far this term, specifying which formatting and writing skills you want to develop in greater detail, and how you propose doing so. Mention specific memos, emails, letters, instructions, reports, summaries, websites, social media posts, blogs, or proposals you have written or will soon write.

6. Prepare a site inspection report on any part of the college campus or plant, hospital, office, store, or other facility in which you work that might need remodeling, expansion, rewiring, or new or additional air-conditioning, plumbing, and/or heating work.

7. You and your collaborative team have been asked to write a short preliminary inspection report on the condition of a historic building for your state historical society. Inspecting the building, the home of a famous late-nineteenth-century governor, you discover the problems listed below. Include all these details in your report. Also supply recommendations for your readers: a director of the state historical society, a state architect, and four representatives of the subcommittee on finance from your state legislature. Design two appropriate visuals to include in your report.

   - The eight front columns are all in need of repair; two of them may have to be replaced.
   - The area below each bottom window casement needs to be excavated for waterproofing.
   - The slate tile on the roof has deteriorated and needs immediate replacement.
   - The front stairs show signs of mortar leaching and require attention at once.
   - Sections of gutter on the northwest and northeast sides of the house must be changed; other gutters are in fair shape.
   - Wood shutters need to be repainted; four of the twelve may even need to be replaced.
   - All trees around the house need pruning; an old elm in the backyard shows signs of decay.
   - The siding is in desperate need of preparation and painting.
   - The brick near the front entrance is dirty and moss-covered.

8. Write a report to an instructor in your major or to an employer about a trip you have taken recently—to a museum, laboratory, health care agency, correctional facility, radio or television station, plant or factory, or office. Indicate why you took the trip, name the individuals (with their job titles) you met on the trip, and stress what you learned and how that information will help you in course work or on your job. Include a relevant visual as part of your report.

9. Write an employee activity/performance report on what you accomplished at your job, full or part time, during the last month. In your introduction, indicate how the work you did helps your employer meet his or her goals. In your conclusion, forecast how the work you expect to do next month illustrates your dedication to doing an effective job.

10. Submit a test report on the purpose, procedures, results, conclusions, and recommendations of an experiment you conducted on one of the following topics:

   a. soil
   b. Wi-Fi access in an airport or bus station
   c. water
   d. automobiles
   e. textiles/clothing
   f. animals
   g. recreational facilities
   h. mobile device hardware or software
   i. forests
   j. food
   k. air quality
   l. hybrid electric fuel cell vehicles
   m. blood
   n. noise levels

11. Write an incident report about a problem you encountered in your work or at home in the last year. Document the problem and provide a solution. Use the memo format shown in Figure 14.11.

12. Write an incident report about one of the following problems. Assume that it has happened to you. Supply relevant details and visuals in your report. Identify the audience for whom you are writing and the agency you are representing or trying to reach.

   a. After hydroplaning, your company car hits a tree and has a damaged front fender.
   b. You have been the victim of an electrical shock because an electrical tool was not grounded.
   c. You twist your back lifting a bulky package in the office or plant.
   d. A virus has infected your company's intranet, and it will have to be shut down for 12 hours to debug it.
   e. The crane (or other piece of equipment) you are operating breaks down, and you lose a half-day's work.
   f. The vendor has been unable to repair the corrupted software on your computer, and you cannot complete a job without buying a more expensive software package.
   g. An electrical storm knocked out your computer; you lost 1,000 mailing label addresses and will have to hire additional help to complete a mandatory mailing by the end of the week.
   h. A scammer has stolen some sensitive files (documents) about a new product your company hoped to launch next month.
   i. An irate customer threatens one of your sales staff, but there was no physical violence, though the daily routine of your business was disrupted and several other customers walked out.
   j. After attending a trade show for your company, you find out that you have been a victim of identity theft, and that your company-issued credit card has been compromised.

13. Choose one of the following descriptions of an incident, and write a report based on it. The descriptions contain unnecessary details, vague words, insufficient information, unclear cause-and-effect relationships, or a combination of those errors. In writing your report, correct the errors by adding or deleting whatever information you believe is necessary. You may also want to rearrange the order in which information is listed. Use a memo format, like that in Figure 14.11, to write the report.

a. After sliding across the slippery road late at night, my car ran into another vehicle, one of those fancy imported cars. The driver of that car must have been asleep at the wheel. The paint and glass chips were all over. I was driving back from our regional meeting and wanted to report to the home office the next day. The accident will slow me down.

b. Whoever packed the glass mugs did not know what he or she was doing. The tape was not the right type, nor was it sealed correctly. The carton was too flimsy as well. It could have been better packed to hold all those mugs. Moreover, since the bus had to travel across some pretty hilly country, the package would have broken anyhow. The best way to ship these kinds of goods is in specially marked and packed boxes. The value of the box contents was listed at $575.

CHAPTER 15

Writing Careful Long Reports

This chapter introduces you to long reports—how and why they are written and organized. It is appropriate to discuss long reports in one of the last chapters of *Successful Writing at Work* because they require you to use and combine many of the writing skills and research strategies you have already learned. In the world of global business, a long report is the culmination of many weeks or months of hard work on an important company project.

The following skills will be most helpful to you as you study long reports; appropriate page numbers appear for the topics that have already been discussed:

- functioning as a member of a collaborative writing team (see "Collaboration is Crucial to the Writing Process," pages 75–76)
- respecting corporate image and mission and adhering to corporate guidelines on preparing and routing reports (see "Ethical Requirements on the Job," pages 27–29)
- assessing and meeting your audience's multiple needs (see "Identifying Your Audience," pages 11–13)
- gathering and summarizing information from print and online sources, and conducting interviews (see Chapter 8, pages 304–337)
- generating, drafting, revising, and editing your ideas and those of your team (see Chapter 2, pages 44–70)
- reporting the results of your research accurately and concisely (see "Characteristics of Effective Workplace Research," page 305)
- creating and introducing visuals and designing documents (see Chapter 11, pages 448–464)
- using appropriate documentation (see "Documenting Sources," pages 337–347)
- preparing an informative abstract (see "Abstracts," pages 387–389)

Having developed these skills, you should be ready to write a successful long report. The collaborative team of writers of the model long report in Figure 15.3 (pages 607–621) uses all of the above skills in their work for RPM Technologies.

CHARACTERISTICS OF A LONG REPORT

The following sections explain some of the key elements in a long report. You will find a model long report (Figure 15.3) at the end of the chapter (pages 607-621).

Scope

A long report is a major study that provides an in-depth view of a key problem or idea. It might be eight to twenty pages long or even much longer, depending on the scope of the subject. The implications of a long report are wide-ranging for a business or organization—relocating a plant, adding a new network, changing a programming operation, or adapting the workplace for multinational employees, as in Figure 15.3.

Unlike a short report, a long report may discuss not just one or two current events but, rather, a major problem in detail, the continuing history of a problem, or an idea (and the background information necessary to understand it in perspective).

The titles of some typical long reports suggest their extensive (and in some cases exhaustive) coverage:

- The Transportation Problems in Kingford, Oregon, and the Use of Rapid Transit
- Promoting More Effective E-Commerce and E-Tailing at TechWorld Inc.
- Virtual Reality Attractions in Theme Parks in Jersey City, New Jersey
- Expanding Health Care Delivery Systems in Tate County
- Internet Medicine in Providing Health Care in Rural Areas: Ways to Serve Southern Montana

Research

A long, comprehensive report requires much more extensive research than a short report does. Information can be gathered over time from primary and secondary research—Internet searches, listservs, books, articles, blogs, social media, government documents, laboratory experiments, on-site visits and tests, conferences with your boss and co-workers, interviews, and the writer's own observations. For a long report, you will have to do a great deal of research and possibly interviewing to track down relevant background information and to discover what experts have said about the subject and what they propose should be suggested or have even done. Make sure all your sources are accurate, current, and relevant. Note how much research went into the business report in Figure 8.10 (pages 349–363) and the long report in Figure 15.3.

For a report for class, you will be asked to identify a major problem or topic, while in the business world the topic and even your approach to it will more than likely be dictated to you by your boss and company policy, as the cover letter (see Figure 15.2, page 606) to the long report in Figure 15.3 indicates.

Format

A long report is too detailed and complex to be adequately organized in a memo or letter format. And while long reports are often presented in hard copy form, they may also be requested as an e-document (such as a PDF file posted to a company's intranet). The product of thorough research and analysis, the long report gives readers detailed discussions and interpretations of large quantities of data. To present the information in a logical and orderly fashion, the long report contains various parts, sections, headings, subheadings, documentation, and supplements (appendices) that would never be included in a short report. Look at the sections of a report in the Table of Contents (page 608) for the long report in Figure 15.3. Also, note how this long report gives readers a variety of visuals, including charts, a graph, and even a multicultural calendar.

Timetable

A long report is generally commissioned by a company or an agency to explore with extensive documentation a subject involving personnel, locations, technology, costs, safety, or the environment. Many times a long report is required by law—for example, investigating the feasibility of a project that will affect the ecosystem. When you prepare a long report for a class project, select a topic that really interests you and/or your collaborative group, because you will spend a good portion of the term working on it. Here is a possible timeline for a long report to give you a sense of the process of preparing one.

Audience

The audience for a long report usually consists of individuals in the top levels of management—presidents, vice presidents, superintendents, directors, heads of departments—who make executive, financial, and organizational decisions. These individuals are responsible for long-range planning, or seeing the big picture, so to speak. A long report written about a campus issue or problem may at first be read by your instructor and then sent to an appropriate decision maker, such as a dean of students, a business manager, a director of athletics, or the head of campus security.

Collaborative Effort

Like many short reports, the long report in the world of business may be a collaborative effort, the product of a committee or team whose work is reviewed by a main editor to make sure that the final text is consistently and accurately written. Individuals in many departments within a company—IT, document design, engineering, sales, transportation, legal affairs, public relations, safety—may cooperate in planning, researching, drafting, revising, and editing a long report.

The team should estimate a realistic timeframe necessary to complete the various stages of their work—when drafts are due and when editing must be concluded, for example. A project schedule based on that estimate should then guide a writing team's work. But remember: Projects almost always take longer than initially planned. Prepare for a possible delay at any one stage. The team may have to submit written progress reports (see "Progress Reports," pages 567–571) to its members, as well as to management.

TECH NOTE

Using Government-Sponsored Research

The U.S. government conducts or sponsors a great deal of research that you might find relevant for your reports. The following is a short list of some major government and other relevant websites.

- **www.epa.gov** will lead you to press releases, test guidelines, and information about grants, contracts, and job opportunities at the Environmental Protection Agency.
- **www.osha.gov**, the website for the Occupational Safety and Health Administration, supplies information about OSHA standards, news releases and fact sheets, publications, technical information, and safety links.
- **www.sba.gov** leads to the Small Business Administration's website, where you'll find guides on beginning a small business, the opportunity to include your business in the national register, and contact information for local SBA offices.
- **www.bls.gov** is sponsored by the Bureau of Labor Statistics. This organization compiles and maintains financial information on inflation, growth or decline in the number of businesses, and wage increases.
- **www.gpo.gov/fdsys** is the Government Printing Office's Federal Digital System. It provides free electronic access to a variety of federal documents, including legislative, judicial, and executive resources.
- **www.ars.usda.gov** is the portal to the Agricultural Research Service (ARS), the U.S. Department of Agriculture's chief scientific research agency. ARS conducts research to ensure high-quality, safe food; assess the nutritional needs of Americans; sustain a competitive agricultural economy; and enhance the environment.

To be successful, a collaborative writing team (such as Teri Smith Ruckel's team in Figure 15.3) should observe the guidelines and procedures for collaborative writing in Chapter 3 (see "Collaborative Writing and the Writing Process," pages 77–79).

THE PROCESS OF WRITING A LONG REPORT

Because work on a long report will be spread over many weeks, you need to see it not as a series of static or isolated tasks but as an evolving project. Before you embark on that project, review the information on the writing process in Chapter 2 (see "The Writing Process," page 45). The following guidelines will also help you plan and write a long report.

   1. **Identify a significant topic.** While you won't usually get to choose the topic of your long report, when you write one for a class, make sure you select a topic that is important and worth exploring in detail. Choose a topic/problem that is relevant for your audience, whether it is a group of college administrators or community leaders, and something that will help them better understand or even solve a problem.

   2. **Conduct research.** You'll have to do some preliminary research—widespread reading, online searching, conferring with and interviewing experts, and possibly making site visits–to get an overview of key ideas and individuals involved, and the implications for your company and/or community. Note the kinds of research Terri Smith Ruckel and her collaborative team did for their long report (see Figure 15.3, pages 607–621).

   3. **Expect to confer regularly with your supervisor and team members.** In these meetings, be prepared to ask pertinent and researched questions to pin down exactly what your boss wants and how your writing team can accomplish this goal. Your supervisor may want you to submit an outline before you draft the report and may expect several more drafts for approval before you write the final version.

   4. **Revise your work often.** Be prepared to work on several outlines and drafts. Your revisions may sometimes be extensive, depending on what your boss or collaborative team recommends or what your research uncovers. You may have to consult new sources or delete older ones.

   5. **Keep the order flexible at first.** A long report is not written in "final" order— abstract to recommendations. Instead, expect to write in "loose" order to reflect the process whereby you gathered information and organized it into categories. Usually, the body of the report is written before the introduction so the authors can make sure they have not left anything out. Recommendations can be made only after you prepare your conclusion. And abstracts are always written last.

   6. **Prepare both a day-to-day calendar and a checklist.** Keep both posted where you do your work—above your desk or computer, or use your operating

system's calendar program—so that you can track your progress. The calendar should mark *milestones*—that is, dates by which each stage of your work must be completed.

PARTS OF A LONG REPORT

A long report may include some or all of the following 12 parts, which form three categories: **front matter** (letter of transmittal, title page, abstract, table of contents, list of illustrations), **report text** (introduction, body, conclusion, recommendations), and **back matter** (glossary, references cited, any appendices).

Numbering the Pages of a Long Report

You will use two sets of numbers for the pages of your long report, one for the front matter and another for the text and back matter of your report. See Figure 15.3 for an example of proper pagination in a long report. Use lowercase Roman numerals (e.g., i, ii, iii, iv) for the front matter. The title page counts as page i, but do not number it. Instead, start with the table of contents as page ii. Then number the list of illustrations as page iii and the abstract, if it appears on a separate page as in Figure 15.3, as page iv. Format all front matter page numbers as footers.

For the text and back matter of your report, use consecutive Arabic numerals in the headers, that is, in the upper right-hand side of each page. Keep in mind, though, that your instructor or employer may prefer you to use APA (American Psychological Association) or MLA (Modern Language Association) style, or for you to use a different placement for the page numbers—for example, putting all report page numbers in footers or in headers.

Front Matter

As the name implies, the front matter of a long report consists of everything that precedes the actual text of the report. Such elements introduce, explain, and summarize to help the reader locate various parts of the report.

Letter of Transmittal

This three- or four-paragraph (usually only one-page) letter states the purpose, scope, and major recommendation(s) of the report. If written to an instructor, the letter should additionally note that the report was done as a course assignment. Figure 15.1 (page 600) shows a sample letter of transmittal for a business report highlighting the main points of the report that will most interest readers. The first paragraph indicates why the report is being sent and points out why it is important. The second paragraph summarizes and justifies the recommendations in the report. The final paragraph thanks the reader for the opportunity to prepare the report and offers to answer any questions or discuss or clarify any parts of the document.

FIGURE 15.1 A Letter of Transmittal for a Long Report

ALPHA CONSULTANTS

1400 Ridge ■ Evanston, California 97214-1005

805-555-9200 ■ ◼ www.facebook.com/alphaconsultants

www.alphaconsultants.com

August 14, 2015

Dr. K. G. Lowry, President
Coastal College
San Diego, CA 93219-2619

Dear Dr. Lowry:

Indicates why report was done

We are happy to offer you the enclosed report, **A Study to Determine New Directions in Women's Athletics at Coastal College**, which you commissioned. Our report contains our recommendations about strengthening existing sports programs and creating new ones at Coastal College.

Gives three key recommenda- tions

Provides justification for recommenda- tions

We recommend that Coastal should engage in more aggressive recruitment to establish a more competitive women's baseball team, should offer additional athletic activities in women's track and field by August 2016, and should create a new interdisciplinary program between the Athletic Department and the Women's Studies Program. Based on the findings in our report, we believe that these recommendations are cost-effective, timely, and consistent with the mission of Coastal College.

Encourages response and questions

It has been an honor to prepare this report for you. We hope that you find it helpful in meeting students' needs at Coastal College. If you have any questions or if you would like to discuss any of our recommendations, please call us.

Sincerely yours,

Barbara Gilchrist

Barbara Gilchrist

Lee T. Sidell

Lee T. Sidell

Encl. Report

Title Page

Since MLA and APA have different formats for title pages, find out what your employer prefers. Basically, though, your title page should contain the following:

- the full title of your report. The title should tell readers what your topic is and how you have restricted it in time, space, or method. Avoid titles that are vague, too short, or too long.

Vague Title:	A Report on the Internet: Some Findings
Too Short:	The Internet
Too Long:	A Report on the Internet: A Study of Social Media Companies and Their Relationship with Consumer Preferences and Identity Protection Within the Past Five Years

- the name of the company or agency preparing the report
- the name(s) of the report writer(s)
- the date the report was submitted
- any agency, order, or grant number (if applicable)
- the name of the person, firm, or organization for which the report was prepared

Make sure that your title page looks professional. Center your title and graphically subordinate any subtitles. Do not use abbreviations (e.g., *bldgs.* for *buildings, gov't* for *government, bus.* for *business*) or acronyms (e.g., *AMS* for *Association of Marketing Students; PTAs* for *Physical Therapist Assistants*).

Table of Contents

The table of contents lists the major headings and subheadings of your report and tells readers on which pages they can be found (see Figure 15.3, pages 607–621). Make sure that your table of contents exactly matches the order and wording of your main headings and subheadings. It reveals the scope of your report and helps readers identify the parts of your report that are of most interest to them. Although the APA no longer recommends a table of contents or a list of illustrations, these pages are provided in Figure 15.3 as models for students whose instructors asked for these pages.

List of Illustrations

A list of all the visuals indicates where they can be found in your report. Note the variety of visuals found in Figure 15.3—a circle chart, a bar chart, a graph, a calendar.

Abstract

As discussed in Chapter 9 (see "Abstracts," pages 387–389), an abstract summarizes the report, presenting a brief overview of the problem and conclusions. Abstracts may be placed at various points in long reports—on the title page, on a separate page preceding or following the table of contents, or as the first page of the report text (see page iv of Figure 15.3 for an example of an abstract).

Begin your abstract with a sentence that identifies the subject, purpose, scope, and importance of your report. Then concentrate on the main points your report covers, briefly comment on the results and outcomes you reached, and clearly pinpoint your recommendations. See how the abstract Terri Smith Ruckel and her team prepared for their readers in Figure 15.3 (page 609) succinctly lists the team's conclusions, or findings.

Some information does not belong in an abstract. Do not give readers a detailed description of the methods you used or try to squeeze in every minor point. It is also unnecessary to repeat who commissioned the report and why. And never include information in your abstract not found in your report.

When you write your abstract, use complete sentences with keywords. Appropriate keywords make it easy for search engines to find your report if it is posted on the Web or if it will be archived on, say, a company intranet (see "How to Conduct Keyword Searches: Some Guidelines," pages 330–331).

Text of the Report

The text of a long report consists of an introduction, the body, a conclusion, and sometimes recommendations.

Introduction

The introduction may constitute as much as 20 percent of your report, but usually it is not any longer. If it were, the introduction would be disproportionate to the rest of your work, especially the body. The introduction is essential because it tells readers why your report was written and thus helps them to understand and interpret everything that follows. See how Terri Smith Ruckel emphasizes the importance of research for her employer, RPM Technologies, in the introduction to Figure 15.3. But make sure you do not put your findings, conclusion, or recommendations in your introduction.

Do not regard the introduction as one undivided block of information. It includes the following related parts, which should be labeled with subheadings. Keep in mind, though, that your employer may ask you to list these parts in a different order.

1. Background. To understand why your topic is significant and hence worthy of study, readers need to know about its history. This history may include information on such topics as who was originally involved, when, and where; how someone was affected by the issue; what opinions have been expressed on the issue; and what the implications of your study are. Note how the long report in Figure 15.3 provides useful background information on why multinational employees are a growing and important segment of the U.S. workforce.

2. Problem. Identify the problem or issue that led you to write the report. Keep in mind that your problem needs to be significant enough to warrant a long report. Because the problem or topic you investigated will determine everything in your report, you need to state it clearly and precisely. That statement may be restricted to a few sentences. Here is a problem statement from a report on how earlier construction designs failed to account for the requirements of Americans with disabilities:

> Every builder since the late 1990s has paid attention to codes on meeting needs of disabled residents. In the past, however, the building industry had not sufficiently met the needs for accessible workplaces and homes for all age and physical ability groups. The industry too often relied on expensive and specialized plans to modify existing structures rather than creating universally designed spaces that were accessible to everyone.

3. Purpose statement. The purpose statement, crucial to the success of the report, tells readers why you wrote the report and what you hope to accomplish or prove. It expresses the goal of all your research. In explaining why you gathered information about a particular problem or topic, indicate how such information might be useful to a specific audience, company, or group. Like the problem statement, the purpose statement does not have to be long or complex. A sentence or two will suffice. You might begin simply by saying, "The purpose of this report is. . . ."

4. Scope. This section informs readers about the specific limits—number and type of issues, time, money, locations, personnel, and so forth—you have placed on your investigation. You need to inform readers about what they will find in your report or what they won't through your statement about the scope of your work. The long report in Figure 15.3 concentrates on adapting the RPM workplace to meet the communication and cultural needs of a workforce of multinational employees, not on trends in the international employment market—two completely different topics.

Body

Fifty to seventy-five percent of your long report will be devoted to the body or *discussion*. Everything in this and all the other sections of your report grows out of your purpose and how you have limited your scope.

What to Include in the Body of a Report The body of a report contains

- statistical information
- any relevant figures, charts, tables, or other visuals
- details about the environment
- physical descriptions
- interpretations and comments of the authorities whose work you consulted or the individuals whom you have interviewed as part of your research
- a description of the range of options you surveyed and ones you feel are the most appropriate

In Figure 15.3 (pages 607–621), the body of the report spells out precisely what specific changes RPM must make to recruit and retain multinational employees—from offering cross-cultural training to making sure corporate documents are written in plain English.

The body of your report should

- be carefully organized to reveal a coherent and well-defined plan
- separate material into meaningful parts to identify the major issues as well as minor issues in your report
- clearly relate the parts to one another
- use headings to help your reader identify major sections more quickly

Headings Your organization is reflected in the different headings and subheadings included in your report. Use them to make your report easy to follow. Organizational headings will also enable someone skimming the report to find specific information quickly. The headings, of course, will be included in the table of contents. (Note how Figure 15.3 is carefully organized into sections.)

Transitions In addition to headings, use transitions to reveal the organization of the body of your report. At the beginning of each major section of the body, tell readers what they will find in that section and why. Summary sentences at the end of a section will tell readers where they have been and prepare them for any subsequent discussions. The report in Figure 15.3 does an effective job of providing internal summaries, e.g., on pages 612 and 614.

Conclusion

The conclusion should tie everything together for readers by presenting the findings of your report. Findings, of course, will vary depending on the type of research you do. For a report based on a study of sources located through various reference searches (see Figure 8.10, pages 349–363), the conclusion should summarize the main viewpoints of the authorities whose works you have cited. For a report done for a business, you must spell out the implications for your readers in terms of costs, personnel, products, location, and so forth.

Regardless of the type of research you do, your conclusions should

- be based on the information and documentation in the body of the report
- corroborate the evidence/information you gave in the body of your report
- grow out of the work you describe in the body of the report
- stick to the areas that your report covers, and not stray into areas it does not

Recommendations

The recommendation(s) section tells readers what should be done about the findings recorded in the conclusion. Your recommendation(s) tells readers how to solve the problem your report has focused on. Readers will expect you to advise them on a specific course of action—what new technology to purchase, when and where to expand a market, how to improve and safeguard a web presence, or who to recruit, hire, train, and retain multinationals for your company, as in Figure 15.3.

Back Matter

Included in the back matter of the report are all of the supporting data that, if included in the text of the report, would bog the reader down in details and cloud the main points the report makes.

Glossary

The glossary is an alphabetical list of the specialized vocabulary used in a long report and the definitions. A glossary might be unnecessary if your report does not use a highly technical vocabulary, as in Figure 15.3, or if *all* members of your audience are familiar with the specialized terms you do use.

Citations List

Any sources cited in your report—websites, books, articles, television programs, interviews, reviews, blogs, social media posts, graphics, podcasts, webinars—are usually listed in this section (see "Documenting Sources," pages 337–347). Always ask your employer or instructor how he or she wants information to be documented, that is, what method of documentation to follow (see "Parenthetical Documentation," pages 339–340). Note that the long report in Figure 15.3 follows the APA system of documentation (the business report in Figure 8.10 follows MLA style).

Appendix

An appendix contains supporting materials for the report—tables and charts too long to include in the discussion, sample questionnaires, budgets and cost estimates, correspondence about the preparation of the report, case histories, transcripts of telephone conversations, copies of relevant letters, documents upon which the report is based, and so forth.

A MODEL LONG REPORT

The long report in Figure 15.3 (starting on page 607) was written by a senior training specialist, Terri Smith Ruckel and her collaborative team, for the vice president of human resources who had commissioned it. Note that only Ruckel's name appears on the report, according to her company's policy. The main task facing Ruckel and her team was to demonstrate what RPM Technologies had to do to meet the needs of multinational workers and thus promote diversity in the workplace. She gathered relevant data from both primary research (interviews, direct observations, site visits, and tests; see "Primary Research, pages 307–319) and secondary research (consulting and commenting at times on sources already available, such as books, websites, journal articles, reference works, government documents, and even RPM in-house publications; see "Secondary Research," pages 319–333).

Figure 15.3 contains all the parts of a long report discussed in this chapter except a glossary and an appendix. Intended for a decision maker interested in learning more about the problems multinational workers face, the report does not contain the technical terms and data that would require a glossary or an appendix. Note how the cover letter (Figure 15.2, page 606) introduces the report and spells out its significance for RPM Technologies while the abstract succinctly identifies only the main points of the report.

FIGURE 15.2 Transmittal Letter for a Long Report

RPMTechnologies

4500 Florissant Drive   St. Louis, MO 63174

314.555.2121   **www.rpmtech.com**

 www.facebook.com/rpmtechnologies   **www.youtube.com/user/rpmtechnologies**

May 6, 2016

Jesse Butler
Vice President, Human Resources
RPM Technologies

Dear Vice President Butler:

Begins with major recommendation of report

With this letter I am enclosing the report my team and I prepared on effective ways to recruit and retain a multinational workforce for RPM Technologies, which you requested we submit by early May. The report argues for the necessity of adapting the RPM workplace to meet the needs of multinational employees, including promoting cultural sensitivity and ensuring that our written communications are easily understood by this audience.

Presents findings of report

Multinational workers undoubtedly will continue to play a major role in U.S. businesses and at RPM as well. With their technical skills and homeland contacts, these employees can help RPM Technologies successfully compete in today's global marketplace.

Alerts reader to major ways to solve problems

But businesses like RPM need to recruit qualified multinational workers more aggressively and then provide equal opportunities for them in the workplace. We must also be sensitive to the cultural diversity and communication demands of an international workforce. By including cross-cultural training—for native and non-native English-speaking employees alike—RPM can more effectively promote cultural sensitivity. Plain English or translated versions of key corporate documents can further improve the workplace environment for our multinational employees.

Offers to answer questions

I hope you find this report helpful in recruiting and retaining additional multinational employees for RPM Technologies. If you have any questions or want to discuss our recommendations or research, please let me know at **terri_ruckel@rpmtech.com.** I look forward to receiving your input.

Sincerely yours,

Terri Smith Ruckel

Terri Smith Ruckel
Senior Training Specialist

Enclosure notation specifies report is attached

Enclosure: Report

FIGURE 15.3 A Long Report

Adapting the RPM Workplace for Multinational Employees

Terri Smith Ruckel

**Senior Training Specialist
RPM Technologies**

Prepared for

**Jesse Butler
Vice President, Human Resources**

May 6, 2016

Title page is carefully formatted and uses boldface

Identifies writer and job title; Ruckel presents report from entire staff— writing for another's signature

RPM executive who assigned the report

Date submitted

Title page is not numbered

(Continued)

FIGURE 15.3 (Continued)

While APA does not include a table of contents, individual employers such as RPM may require one

Major divisions of report in all capital letters and boldface

Records key sections and subsections of report

Subheadings indicated by indentations and italics

Page numbers included for major sections of report

No subsections needed here

Lists references on separate pages

Uses Roman numeral for Table of Contents

Table of Contents

ii

FIGURE 15.3 (Continued)

List of Illustrations

iii

Identifies each figure by number, title, and page number

Provides a title for each visual

Abstract

This report investigates how U.S. businesses such as RPM must gain a competitive advantage in today's global marketplace by recruiting and retaining a multinational workforce. The recent wave of immigrants is in great demand for their technical skills and economic ties to their homeland. Yet many companies like ours still operate by policies designed for native speakers of English. Instead, we have to adapt RPM's company policies and environment to meet the cultural, religious, social, and communication needs of these multinational workers. To do this, we must promote cultural sensitivity training, both for multinatiols and employees who are native speakers of English. Additionally, as other U.S. firms have successfully done, RPM should adapt vacation sched-ules and daycare facilities for an expanding multicultural workforce. Equally important too, RPM has to ensure, either through translations or plain-English versions, that all company documents and signage can be easily understood by multinational workers.

iv

Concise, informative abstract that states purpose of report and why it is important for audience

Uses helpful transitional terms such as "additionally" and "equally important"

Footer uses Roman numerals for front matter pages

(Continued)

FIGURE 15.3 (Continued)

1

Introduction

Background

   The U.S. workforce has been undergoing a remarkable revolution. The
U.S. Bureau of Labor Statistics predicts that by 2022 our country's labor force
will comprise 173.5 million workers who must fill 177 million jobs (2015).
The most dramatic effect of filling this labor shortage will be in hiring greater
numbers of highly skilled multinational employees, including those joining RPM.
Currently, "one of every five IT specialists [and] one of every six persons in
engineering or science occupations . . . is foreign born" (Keshevi & Foley, 2014,
p. 210). In 2015, the number of international residents in the United States totaled
41.3 million, according to the U.S. Census Bureau (2015).This new wave of
immigrants comprises 16.3 percent of the labor force (U.S. BLS, 2013), and is
projected to go to nearly 30 percent by 2030 (Immigration Coalition, 2015, p. 8).
As Alexa Quincy aptly put it, "The United States is becoming the most multicul-
turally diverse country in the global economy" (2014, p. 5).

   Unlike earlier generations, immigrants today actively maintain ties with their
native countries. These new immigrants travel back and forth so regularly they
have become global citizens, exercising an enormous influence on the success of
a business like RPM. They provide business contacts with other markets,
enhancing a company's ability to trade and invest profitably abroad. Figure 1
below identifies these major groups.

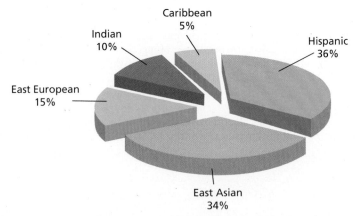

Figure 1
Major Ethnic Groups
Immigrating to the United States (2005–2015)

Caribbean 5%
Indian 10%
Hispanic 36%
East European 15%
East Asian 34%

Source: Brown, P. (2014, February). *History of U.S. immigration.*
Retrieved from http://immigration.ucn.edu

FIGURE 15.3 (Continued)

2

Undeniably, many immigrants today often possess advanced levels of technical expertise. A report by the Kaiser Foundation found that California's Silicon Valley had significantly benefited from the immigrants who have arrived with much needed technical training. Relocated Chinese, East Asian, and Indian scientists and engineers now hold more than 40 percent of the region's technical positions ("Immigrants Find," 2015, p. 37). Figure 2 below indicates the leading countries of origin for Silicon Valley's immigrants employed in technical fields in 2015, and records the percentage for each nationality (Joint Silicon Valley Regional Foundation, 2015, p. 12).

Problem

RPM, like other m-commerce companies, is experiencing a critical talent shortage of IT and other professionals, making the recruitment of a multinational workforce a vital priority for us. Meeting the cultural and communication demands of these workers, however, poses serious challenges for RPM. The traditional workplace needs to be transformed to respect the ways multinational employees communicate about business. Native English-speaking employees will also have to be better prepared to understand and to appreciate their international co-workers.

Identifies a major problem and explains why it exists

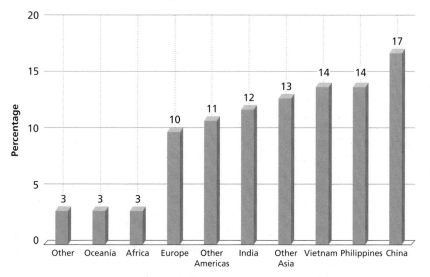

Figure 2
Country of Origin for Silicon Valley Immigrants Employed in Technical Fields in 2015

Bar chart identifies and quantifies major groups of immigrants

Relevant visual in appropriate place in text

Source: Joint Silicon Valley Regional Foundation. (2015). *2015 Silicon Valley Index*. Retrieved from http://www.svrf.org/sites/publications/2015-silicon-valley-index.pdf

(Continued)

FIGURE 15.3 (Continued)

3

Two separate, corroborating sources

Unfortunately, many corporate policies and programs at RPM, and at other U.S. companies as well, have been created for native-born, English-speaking employees (Morales, 2015; Reynolds, 2014, para. 4). Rather than rewarding multinational workers, such policies unintentionally punish them.

Purpose

Concisely states why the report was written

The purpose of this report is to show that to increase multicultural technical employees in the workplace, RPM must further adapt its business environment to recruit and retain this essential and diverse labor force. This report spells out specific steps RPM must take to accommodate this new multinational workforce.

Scope

Informs reader that report will focus directly on RPM's needs

This report explores cultural diversity in the current U.S. workplace and suggests ways for RPM to compete successfully in the global marketplace by providing equal employment opportunities for multinational workers. By doing this, we will foster cross-cultural literacy and improve training in intercultural communication at our firm.

Discussion

Providing Equal Workplace Opportunities for Multinational Employees

Discussion is organized into three main sections, each with subsections

Aggressive Recruitment of IT Professionals from Diverse Cultures

A multilingual workforce is vital if RPM wants to compete in a culturally diverse global market. But firms such as ours must be prepared to adapt or modify hiring policies and procedures to attract these multinational employees, beginning with rethinking our recruitment and retention policies. Routine visits to U.S. campuses by company recruiters or "specialized international recruiters" can help us identify and hire highly qualified multinational job candidates (Hamilton, 2015, p. 36).

Emphasizes recruiting multinational workers and suggests how to do so

Moreover, RPM should visit universities abroad with distinguished IT programs to attract talented multinational employees. We need to encourage students and recent graduates from these universities to apply for a J-1 visa to learn more about RPM through an internship program. As Marissa Bolanos reported, "Tansen Electronics went to Russia for software engineers with the experience they couldn't readily find among U.S. workers." (2015, para. 3). These searches, along with articles on our website, posts to our Facebook page, tweets, and executive blogs, should emphasize RPM's commitment to globalization and help attract international workers to RPM. Lobbying more actively to increase the number of H1-B visas for skilled workers will also help RPM.

Identifies specific benefits for RPM

Capitalizing on a diverse workforce, RPM can more effectively increase our multicultural customer base worldwide. Logically, customers buy from individuals they can relate to culturally. RPM might take a lead from Visions Bank of California, a business serving a diverse population, especially its Asian and

FIGURE 15.3 (Continued)

4

Hispanic customers. The bank has a successful recruitment history of hiring employees with language skills in Hindi, Vietnamese, Korean, and Spanish. In fact, Visions Bank ranked fourth as an employer of minorities (Visions Bank of California, 2014, para. 8). Figure 3 charts the increase in multinational employees hired by Visions Bank over an 8-year period.

Another highly competitive business, Auto-Drive, selected Hector Reyes, a Hispanic, to serve as its CEO. The nation's third-largest automotive parts retailer, with 2,627 locations nationwide, Auto-Drive under Reyes's leadership has hired more international employees—totaling more than 25 percent of its workforce—than it had in previous years. Many top Fortune 500 companies, such as Cisco and Intel, can also claim that 40% or more of their workforce is comprised of multinationals ("100 Best Companies," 2016). Closer to RPM in St. Louis, Whitney Abernathy—manager of Netshop, Inc.—found that contracts from Indonesia increased by 17 percent after she hired Jakarta native Safja Jacoef (personal communication, April 2, 2016).

Personal communications (such as interviews and emails) not included in APA References list

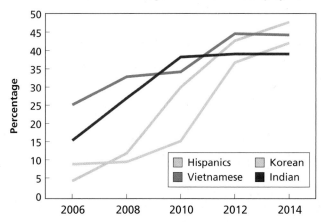

Figure 3
Visions Bank of California
Growth in Percentage of Multinational Employees

Source: Hamilton, B. E. (2015). Diversity is the answer for today's work force. *Journal of Business Diversity, 10*(38), 35–37.

Tracks key information in a clear and concise graph

Supplies necessary legend

Provides source

Commitment to Ethnic Representation

Many companies have mission statements on diversity and multinational employees in the workplace. G.E., American Airlines, IBM, and Walmart promote multinationals as mentors and interpreters. Eastman Kodak has eight employee cultural network groups, including the Hispanic Organization for Leadership and Advocacy, or HOLA, which is "committed to foster excellence and leadership

Stresses other business precedents that encourage recruiting these employees

© 2017 Cengage Learning

(Continued)

FIGURE 15.3 (Continued)

5

among Hispanics by providing personal growth and development opportunities through informal mentoring, training, and interaction with management" ("Employee Networks," 2015, para. 6).

Such a proactive program, which we might incorporate at RPM, recognizes the leadership abilities of multinational employees. Moreover, "glass ceilings," which in the past have prevented women and ethnic employees from moving up the corporate ladder, are being shattered. Tesfaye Aklilu, Vice President at United Technologies, astutely observes:

> In a global business environment, diversity is an ... imperative. Diversity of cultures, ideas, perspectives, and values is the norm of today's international companies. The exchange of ideas from different cultural perspectives gives a business additional, valuable information. Every employee can see his/her position from a global vantage point. (Aklilu, 2016, para. 1)

RPM would also do well to follow the lead of one of our chief competitors, Ablex Polymers, that recently won an award from the International Business Foundation for hiring more Hispanic American women managers ("Ablex Wins Award," 2016, para. 1).

Promoting and Incorporating Cultural Awareness Within the Company

Cross-cultural Training

Many of RPM's competitors have created cultural awareness programs for international employees as well as native speakers. Committed to diversity, Aetna (2008) offers online courses on ethnicity (e.g., "A Bridge to Asia") to "promote an atmosphere of openness and trust" (p. 14) while Johnson & Johnson conducts Diversity University "to help employees . . . understand and value differences and the benefits of working collaboratively . . . to meet business goals" (2015, Diversity University section, para. 1). Employees find it easier to work with someone whose values and beliefs they understand, while employers benefit from collaboration.

Such a program could have prevented the problem RPM experienced when a non-native English-speaking employee was offended by a cultural misunderstanding ("RPM First Quarter," 2016, p. 7). We would do well to model our programs after those at American Express, which has a workforce representing 40 nations, or those at Extel Communications with its large percentage of Hispanic and Vietnamese employees. United Parcel Service (UPS) profitably pairs a native English-speaking employee with an international employee to improve on-the-job problem solving and communication skills. For instance, Jamie Allen, a UPS employee since 2006, found her work with Lekha Nfara-Kahn to be one of the most rewarding experiences of her job (Johnson, 2015, p. 45).

Although they need to encourage cultural sensitivity training, U.S. firms like RPM should also be cautious about severing international workers' cultural

Marginal annotations:

Indents quotation of forty or more words

Second major section

Cites business incentive to adapt as competitors did

References internal document from company intranet

Transition to new subdivision—networking of employees with similar cultural backgrounds

FIGURE 15.3 (Continued)

6

ties—a delicate balance. When management actively promotes bonds among employees from similar cultures, workers are less fearful about losing their identity. Encouraging such contacts, Globe Citizens Bank has profitably mobilized culturally similar groups by asking workers of shared ethnic heritages to network with each other (Gordon & Rao, 2015, p. 39). Employees of Turkish ancestry from Globe's main New York office go to lunch twice a month with Turkish-born employees from the Newark branches. Globe hosts these luncheons and in return receives a bimonthly evaluation of the bank's Turkish and Middle Eastern policies (Hamilton, 2015, p. 36).

Cultural education must go both ways, though. The U.S. business culture has conventions, too, and few international employees would want to ignore them, but they need to know what those conventions are (Johnson, 2015, p. 48). A frequent problem with U.S. corporations such as RPM is that we assume everyone knows how we do things and how we think—it never occurs to us to explain ourselves. For example,

- native speakers of English are typically comfortable within a space of around 1 to 1.5 feet for general personal interactions in business. But workers from Taiwan or Japan, who prefer a greater conversational distance, feel uncomfortable if their desks are less than a few feet away from another employee's workspace (Quincy, 2014; "Taiwanese Business Culture," 2015).
- Chinese use both hands when giving and receiving anything of value, including gifts and particularly business cards; you should do the same as this is one of the first points at which you will make an impression. (Canadian Trade Commissioner Service, 2015, Attending and Conducting Meetings section, para. 11).

Corporate efforts to validate diverse cultures might also include the recognition of an ethnic group's holidays. RPM has just begun to do this by hosting cultural events, including Cinco de Mayo and Chinese New Year celebrations, but we could add even more events, following the lead of other companies:

- Many companies honor National Hispanic Heritage Month in September, coinciding with the independence celebrations of five Latin American countries (Workplace Diversity Commission, 2015, p. 37).
- Wells Fargo has a long-standing relationship with the Chinese community and "has a long tradition of participating in Lunar New Year celebrations, including parades and the publication of special calendars, coin banks and red gift envelopes" (Mayer, 2015, para. 1).
- GRT Systems sends New Year's greetings at Waisak (the Buddhist Day of Enlightenment) to its employees who are Buddhist. (M. Saradayan, personal communication, February 28, 2016).
- "Flexi-time is being offered to some Muslims undertaking a daily fast for the 30 consecutive days of Ramadan. Other companies allow Muslims to begin their working day later so they can catch up on sleep after waking up at 3 am to eat" ("Ramadan: when does it end," 2014, para. 6).

Figure 4 (on page 7) provides a helpful multicultural calendar that RPM needs to adapt to establish our cultural sensitivity policies.

Relevant source on topic of immigration

Offers two examples RPM could follow

Another clear transitional sentence

Identifies key RPM problem

Gives cultural example

Spells out precise ways RPM can incorporate cultural sensitivity into the workplace

Includes appropriate calendar of ethnic holidays

(Continued)

FIGURE 15.3 (Continued)

7

Figure 4
A Multicultural Calendar

December 2015

◄ Nov 2015 | | | | | | Jan 2016►

Sun	Mon	Tue	Wed	Thu	Fri	Sat
		1	2 Arba'een (Shia Muslim)	3	4	5
6 Feast of St. Nicholas (some European countries)	7 Hanukkah begins (Jewish) (ends Dec.14) Utpanna/Utpatti Ekadashi (Hindu)	8 Bodhi Day (Rohatsu-Buddhism)	9	10	11	12 Feast of Our Lady of Guadalupe (Catholic)
13	14	15	16 Las Posadas begins (Hispanic) (ends Dec. 24)	17	18	19
20	21 Gita Jayanti (Hindu) Winter Solstice	22	23 Mawlid an-Nabi (Muslim)	24 Noche Buena (Hispanic) Dattatreya Jayanti (Hindu)	25 Christmas (Christian)	26 Kwanzaa begins (Interfaith) (ends Jan. 1)
27	28	29	30	31 New Year's Eve (Western)		

Source: Johnson, V.M. (2015). Growing multinational diversity in business sparks changes. *Business Across the Nation, 23*(7), 43–48.

Successful U.S. firms have been sensitive to the needs of their English-speaking employees for decades. Flexible scheduling, telecommuting options, daycare, and preventive health programs have become part of corporate benefit plans. Many of these options and benefits have been in place at RPM. But an international workforce presents additional cultural opportunities for RPM management. For example, our company cafeterias might easily accommodate the dietary restrictions of vegetarian workers or those who abstain from certain foods, such as dairy products. At GlobeTech, for example, soybean and fish entrees are always available (Reynolds, 2014, para. 8). Adding ethnic items at RPM would reinforce our cultural awareness and respect for multinational employees.

Day care remains a key issue in hiring and retaining skilled employees, whether they are native or non-native speakers of English. RPM's child care facilities at our offices in St. Louis and San Luis Obispo have brought us much positive publicity over the past eight years ("RPM Day Care Facilities," 2015, para. 3). But by modifying child care that reflects our workers' culturally diverse needs, RPM can

Major visual with a great deal of detail merits three-quarters of a page to make it readable

Pays attention to major world holidays

Visual helps to convince RPM to adopt similar policy

Identifies current RPM programs and how they could be easily modified to assist multinational workers

Cites company publication showing research within the organization

FIGURE 15.3 (Continued)

8

give a multinational workforce greater peace of mind and better enable them to do their jobs. A pacesetter in this field is DEJ Mobile, which insists that at least two or three of its daycare workers must be fluent in Korean or Hindi (Parker, 2015, para. 2). One of our competitors, ITCorp, hires Hispanic and East Asian bilingual day care workers and tries to serve foods the children customarily eat at home (Gordon & Rao, 2015).

Making Business Communication More Understandable for Multinational Employees

Translation of Written Communications

Among the essential documents causing trouble for multicultural readers are company handbooks, insurance and health care obligations, policy changes, and OSHA and EPA regulations (Hamilton, 2015). To ensure maximum understanding of these documents by a multinational workforce, RPM should provide a translation, or at least a plain English version, of them. To accomplish this, RPM could solicit the help of employees who are fluent in the non-native English speakers' languages as well as contract with professional translators to prepare appropriate work-related documents.

Workplace signs in particular, especially safety messages, must consider the language needs of international workers. In the best interest of corporate safety, RPM could have these signs translated into the languages represented by multinationals in the workplace and/or post signs that use global symbols. The American National Standards Institute (ANSI) declares "safety symbols can promote greater and more rapid communication of the safety message over text only signs" (Wunderling, 2014, p. 57). Unquestionably, we need to avoid signs that workers might find hard or even impossible to decipher. For example, a capital **P** for "Parking" or an **H** for "Hospital" might be unfamiliar to non-native speakers of English (Parker, 2015, para. 10).

Language Training Must Be Reciprocal

But language training has to be reciprocal—for native as well as non-native speakers—if communication is to succeed. A recent international survey of executive recruiters showed that being bilingual is critical to success in the international world of business ("Developing Foreign Language Skills," 2016). Twenty percent of households in the United States speak a language other than English (Youngston, 2016). Unfortunately, this is the case with so many of RPM's native-spreaking employees. However, many of the international workers RPM needs to recruit are bi- or even trilingual. In India, Israel, or South Africa, for example, the average worker speaks two or more languages every day to conduct business. We need to offer (and pay for) additional English instruction for our multinational workers if they need it. As Lindsay McMahon writes, when employees struggle with English in the workplace, companies lose "valuable time, potential new ideas and strategies, and teamwork between colleagues who have different points of view" (2013, para. 9).

Since RPM needs to recruit such workers, we have to learn more about the cultures and languages of these global employees. RPM management should consider contracting with one of the companies specializing in language instruction

Margin notes:

APA lists blogs in references

Third major section of discussion

Turns to written communication and multinational workers

Offers practical solution

Gives examples of what to avoid and why

Cites business survey to confirm the necessity of change at RPM

Argues that reader must consider both sides

Includes helpful link to assist reader

© 2017 Cengage Learning

(Continued)

FIGURE 15.3 (Continued)

9

for businesspeople (**www.selfgrowth.com/foreignlanguage.html**). We also need to network with international employee groups to solicit their help and advice.

Conclusion

To compete in the global marketplace, RPM must emphasize cultural diversity much more in its corporate mission and throughout the workplace. Through its policies and programs, RPM should aggressively recruit and retain an increasing number of technologically educated and experienced multinational workers. Such workers are in great demand today and will be even more so over the next ten to twenty years. They can help RPM increase our international customer base and advance the state of our technology. But the workplace must be sensitive to their cultural, religious, dietary, and communication needs. Providing equal opportunities, diversity training and networking, and easy-to-understand business documents will also keep RPM globally competitive in recruiting and retaining these essential employees

Recommendations

By implementing the following recommendations, based on the conclusions reached in this report, RPM Technologies can succeed in hiring and promoting the IT multinational professionals our company needs for future success in today's global economy.

1. Recruit multinational workers more effectively through our website and social media, international hiring specialists, and visits to college and university campuses here and abroad.
2. Work more closely with the Immigration and Naturalization Service (INS) to retain multinationals.
3. Establish a mentoring program to identify and foster leadership abilities in multinational employees, resulting in retaining and promoting these workers.
4. Promote cultural sensitivity and networking through groups compromising multinationals and native English-speaking employees.
5. Encourage a group's cultural ties by actively supporting such work-related organizations such as the Hispanic Organization for Advocacy and Leadership (HOLA).
6. Develop educational materials for employees who are native speakers of English about the cultural traditions of their multinational co-workers.
7. Reassess and adapt RPM's day care facilities to more effectively meet the needs of children of multinational employees.
8. Supply relevant translations and plain-English versions of company hand-books, manuals, new regulations, insurance policies, safety codes, and other human resource documents.
9. Support second-language training programs to enhance communication and collaboration between multinational and native speaker employees at RPM.

Conclusion concisely summarizes the highlights of the report without repeating the documentation

Forecasts continuing benefits for RPM

Provides specific, relevant recommen-dations, based on conclusions, to solve the problem at RPM

Numbered list format is easy for busy executives to read

Uses strong persuasive verbs to introduce each recommen-dation

© 2017 Cengage Learning

FIGURE 15.3 (Continued)

10

References

100 best companies to work for, 2016. (2016, February 8). *International Business Magazine*. Retrieved from http://archive.ibm.com/magazines/best -companies/2016/minorities

Ablex wins award. (2016, February). Retrieved from http://www.ablexinter.org

Aetna, Inc. (2008, March). *Diversity annual report: The strength of diversity*. Retrieved from http://www.aetna.com/about/aetna/diversity/data/AetnaEnglish_2008.pdf

Aklilu, T. (2016). *Diversity at UTC*. Retrieved from http://www.utc.com/careers /diversity/index4.htm

Mayer, A. (2015, February 16). Red envelopes. [Web log post]. Retrieved from http://blogs.wellsfargo.com/guidedbyhistory/2015/02/red-envelopes/

Bolanos, M. (2015, June 18). U.S. Companies think globally to survive locally in today's market. *Global Marketplace Journal*. Retrieved from http://www.globalmarketplacejournal/bolanos/1806_2015.htm

Brown, P. (2014, February). *History of U.S. immigration*. Retrieved from http://immigration.ucn.edu

Canadian Trade Commissioner Service. (2015, February 9). Business Etiquette in China. Retrieved from http://www.tradecommissioner.gc.ca/eng/document .jsp?did=107932&cid=512&oid=32

Developing foreign language skills is good business. (2016, February 3). *Business World*. Retrieved from http://www.businessworld.ca/article.cfm/newsID/7109.cfm

Employee Networks (Resource Groups). (2015, February). Retrieved from http://www.kodak.com/ek/US/en/Global_Sustainability/Stewardship/Global _Diversity/Employee_Networks.htm

Gordon, T., & Rao, P. (2015). Challenges ahead for American companies. *National Economics Review, 11*(3), 38–42, 56.

Hamilton, B. E. (2015). Diversity is the answer for today's work force. *Journal of Business Diversity, 10*(38), 35–37.

Immigrants find the American dream in California's Silicon Valley. (2015, March). *Silicon Valley News*, p. 37.

Immigration Coalition of the United States. (2015). *Employment Projections, 2015–2030*. Retrieved from http://immigrationcoalition.org /Employment_Projections_2015–2030.pdf

Includes only sources actually cited in report

Double-spaces between entries

Arranges all entries by author's last name or (if no author) by first word of title excluding articles ("a," "an," "the")

Specifies date of publication for every entry after author's name (or title, if author's name not given)

Capitalizes only first word and proper nouns in title

Provides page numbers for print sources

Indents second and subsequent lines ½ inch

(Continued)

FIGURE 15.3 (Continued)

Johnson & Johnson. (2015). *Diversity and Inclusion Programs and Activities*. Retrieved from http://http://www.jnj.com/about-jnj/diversity/programs

Johnson, V. M. (2015). Growing multinational diversity in business sparks changes. *Business Across the Nation, 23*(7), 43–48.

Joint Silicon Valley Regional Foundation. (2015). *2015 Silicon Valley Index*. Retrieved from http://www.svrf.org/sites/publications/2015-silicon-valley -index.pdf

Keshevi, T. & Foley, B. (2014). The contributions of high-skilled immigrants. In B. Foley (Ed.), *Immigration and U.S. technology* (pp. 210–214). Washington, DC: International Policy Institute.

McMahon, L. (2013, January 16). How to get your company to pay for your English classes. [Web log post]. Retrieved from http://www.englishandculture.com/blog/bid/90314/How-to-Get-Your -Company-to-Pay-for-Your-English-Classes

Morales, J. [J_Morales112]. (2013, February 26). US Corporations create policies and programs and forget they have non-English-speaking employees. #RememberUs http://tinyurl.com/ ou9t94d [Tweet]. Retrieved from https://twitter.com/J_Morales112/status/306195345845664356

Parker, M. (2015, May 26). Multinational hires—advice and advocacy [Web log post]. Retrieved from http://parkeronimmigration.blogspot.com /2015/05/26/multinational_hires-advice_and_advocacy.php

Quincy, A. (2014). Multiculturalism makes for a good business. *Workforce, Inc., 14*(2), 5–8.

Ramadan: When does it end, and other questions. (2014, July 24). *The Week*. Retrieved from http://www.theweek.co.uk/religion/54029/ramadan-when -does-it-end-and-other-questions

Reynolds, P. (2014, February 3). Serving up culture [Web log post]. Retrieved from http://www.culture.org/2014/02/serving_up_culture

RPM day care facilities rated high. (2015, November 15). *RPM News*. Retrieved from http://www.rpm.com/rpmnews/11_15_2015/rpm_daycare_facilities_rated_high

RPM first quarter activity report. (2016). *RPM Internal Reports*. Retrieved from http://www.rpm.com/internalreports/2016_firstquarter

Taiwanese business culture. (2015). *Executive Planet*. Retrieved from http://www.executiveplanet.com/business-culture-in/132438266669.html

References blog posts with proper APA citations

Gives full Web addresses for verification and to make source easy to find

Cites material available on company intranet

FIGURE 15.3 (Continued)

12

U.S. Bureau of Labor Statistics (2015, November 24). Foreign-Born Workers: Labor Force Characteristics-2013. [Press release]. Retrieved from http://www.bls.gov/news.release/pdf/forbrn.pdf

U.S. Census Bureau. (2011–2015). *2011–2015 American Community Survey 5-Year Estimates.* Retrieved from http://www.census.gov/acs/www/data_documentation/2015_release/

Visions Bank of California. (2014, June 23). Federation magazine ranks Visions Bank one of the best companies for minorities. Retrieved from http://www.vboc.com/about/main/0,3250,2485_11256_502261585,00.html

Workplace Diversity Commission, Hispanic Working Group. (2015). Report on the Hispanic workplace challenge in the United States. Retrieved from http://www.wdc/hwg/report/2015

Wunderling, A. (2014, December 10). Standards for workplace signs and symbols. *Workplace Safety, 23*(12), 56–57.

Youngston, Z. [@YoungstonZ] (2016, January 5). Twenty percent of households in the United States speak a language other than English. [Tweet]. Retrieved from https://twitter.com/YoungstonZ/status/597803705682263456

Italicizes title of government report

Government documents provide valuable statistics

Article about a company included on company website

FINAL WORDS OF ADVICE ABOUT LONG REPORTS

Perhaps no piece of writing you do on the job carries more weight than the long report. You can simplify your job and increase your chances for success by following these guidelines for scheduling, researching, and collaborating:

1. Plan and work early. Do not postpone work until a deadline draws near.
2. Confer often and carefully with others in your group.
3. Do a thorough search among Internet, print, and other resources.
4. Consult with specialists in other fields both in your company and in other organizations, including government officials.
5. Divide your workload into meaningful units. Reassure yourself that you do not have to write the report or even an entire section of the report in one day
6. Set up mini-deadlines for each phase of your work, and then meet them.

✔ REVISION CHECKLIST

☐ Concentrated on a major problem—one with significant implications for my school, neighborhood, city, or employer.

☐ Identified, justified, and described the significance of the main problem.

☐ Did sufficient research—in the library, on the Internet, or through interviewing, personal observation, or testing.

☐ Became familiar with key terms and major trends in the field.

☐ Anticipated how various managers and other decision makers will use and profit from my report for their long-range planning.

☐ Made sure I understood what my readers are looking for.

☐ Adhered to all specified schedules for completing various stages of the long report.

☐ Divided and labeled the parts of the long report to make it easy for readers to follow and to show a careful plan of organization.

☐ Supplied an informative abstract that leaves no doubt in readers' minds about what the report deals with and why.

☐ Designed an attractive title page that contains all the basic information—title, date, for whom the report is written, my name.

☐ Gave my readers all the necessary introductory information about background, problem, purpose of report, and scope.

☐ Included in the body of the report the weight of all my research—the facts, statistics, interview comments, and descriptions—that my readers need.

☐ Included subheadings to reflect the major divisions into which I have organized the research that forms the nucleus of the text.

☐ Wrapped up the report in a succinct conclusion. Told readers what the findings of my research are and accurately interpreted all data.

☐ Supplied a recommendations section (if required) that tells readers concretely how they can respond to the problem using the data. Offered recommendations that are realistic and practical and related directly to the research and topic.

☐ Included in the final copy of the report all the parts listed in the table of contents.

☐ Supplied a one-page transmittal letter informing readers why the report was written and describing its scope and findings.

EXERCISES

1. Send an email to your instructor describing how one of the short reports in Chapter 14 could be useful to someone who has to write a long report.

2. Using the information contained in Figure 15.1, draft an introduction for the report "A Study to Determine New Directions in Women's Athletics at Coastal College." Add any details you think will be relevant.

3. What kinds of research did Terri Smith Ruckel and her team need to do to write the long report in Figure 15.3? As part of your answer, include the titles of any specific reference works you think the writer may have consulted.

4. Study Figure 15.3 and answer the following questions based on it:

   a. Why can the abstract be termed informative rather than descriptive?
   b. How have Ruckel and her team successfully limited the scope of the report?
   c. Where have Ruckel and her team used internal summaries especially well?
   d. Where and how have the writers adapted their technical information for their audience (a general reader)?
   e. What visual devices do the writers use to separate parts of the report?
   f. How do the writers introduce, summarize, and draw conclusions from the expert opinions in order to substantiate the main points?
   g. How have the writers documented information?
   h. What functions does the conclusion serve for readers?
   i. How do the recommendations follow from the material presented in the report? How are they both distinct and interrelated?

5. Come to class prepared to discuss a major community problem suitable for a long report (e.g., traffic, crime, air and water pollution, housing, transportation). Then write a letter to an appropriate agency or business requesting a study of the problem and a report.

6. Write a report outline for the problem you selected in Exercise 5. Use major headings. Include a cover letter with your outline.

7. Have your instructor approve the outline you prepared for Exercise 6. Then write a long report based on the outline, either on your own or as part of a collaborative writing team.

Making Successful Presentations at Work

In today's web-based world of information, presentations play a vital role. According to the U.S. Department of Labor's Occupational Safety and Health Administration (OSHA) Office of Training and Education, "retention of information three days after a meeting or other event is six times greater when [it] is presented by visual and oral means than when the information is presented by the spoken word alone."[1] Almost every job requires employees to have and to use carefully developed speaking skills. In fact, to get hired, you have to be a persuasive speaker at your job interview. And to advance up the corporate ladder, you must continue to be a confident, well-prepared, and persuasive speaker.

The world of work receives and shares much of its information through informal briefings, collaborative discussions, PowerPoint or Prezi presentations, videoconfering, webinars, and formal presentations. Your employer will expect your oral communication skills in all these situations to be as effective and professional as your writing skills. The goal of this chapter is to help you be a more successful speaker on the job.

WRITING A DOCUMENT VERSUS MAKING A PRESENTATION

Writing a document and delivering a report both require you to (1) research your topic, (2) plan your organization, and (3) choose your language and visuals carefully. There are, nevertheless, some fundamental differences between these two ways of communicating in the world of work. When you make a presentation, you must focus on these additional items:

- Your appearance—how you dress, stand, move, and gesture
- Your delivery—whether you can be heard, your tone of voice, whether you sound confident or nervous

---

[1]McKay, M. How do audio/visual aids help in business communication? *Houston Chronicle*. Retrieved from http://smallbusiness.chron.com/audio-visual-aids-business -communication-694.html

- The complexity of your subject—your talk must be informative yet concise and easily understood the first (and likely only) time the audience hears it
- The amount of time you have been allotted
- Your audience's attention span—usually not more than fifteen or twenty minutes
- The layout of the room—lighting, capacity, acoustics, etc.
- The equipment necessary for your presentation—screen, monitors, computers, whiteboards, Skype, microphones
- Your visuals—they must be clear and easily seen, even from the back of the room
- Your interaction with the audience—questions, comments, and nonverbal responses including laughs, frowns, puzzled looks

TYPES OF PRESENTATIONS

You will make numerous presentations on the job that will vary in the amount of preparation they require, the time they last, and the audience and occasion for which they are intended. Here are some presentations you can expect to make frequently before different audiences in the world of work.

For Your Customers or Clients

- sales appeals stressing how and why your company's products or services meet your listeners' needs
- scenarios about why your company is better than the competition
- demonstrations of your products or services
- a persuasive overview of your company's contributions to the economy, the community, the environment
- tours of a company facility

For Your Boss

- progress or status reports on how a project is going
- an assessment of your job accomplishments
- a justification of a budget, your own position, or your department or division
- a summary of a conference or meeting you attended

For Your Co-Workers

- an end-of-shift report, such as those made by police officers and nurses
- an explanation of a new or revised company policy
- a training session on job safety, operating equipment, new software
- a briefing on new job assignments and tasks

For Community Leaders or Groups

- appeals before elected officials
- an explanation of your group's decision or activity
- an update on completing a public works project

INFORMAL BRIEFINGS

If you have ever given a book report or explained laboratory results in front of a class, you have given an **informal briefing**. Such reports are a routine part of many jobs. They usually last between ten and fifteen minutes and are given to a small group of co-workers and possibly your boss. Other topics for such briefings often focus on training, motivating a workforce, reviewing sales activities, and so on.

Whatever the topic, informal briefings bring people up-to-date by supplying them with key information. Figure 16.1 contains an outline for an informal briefing to the staff at a bank.

FIGURE 16.1 An Outline of Speaking Points for an Informal Briefing

Clearly focused topic

Uses short outline of main points to stress at briefing

Motivates audience

Includes a relevant slide to help tellers identify counterfeit currency

Gives precise directions

Supplies bank policy to staff via e-distribution.

Crime Alert Briefing: People's National Bank, Millersville, May 8, 2015

Topic of briefing: Crime alert about the increasing number of counterfeit $20 and $50 bills in the Millersville area.

I. **Introduction**
   A. Area banks have been asked to be on the lookout for an increased number of counterfeit $20 and $50 bills in circulation
   B. Our customers trust in us to protect their financial security
   C. We have a responsibility as tellers/bank officers to identify counterfeit bills and to keep them out of circulation

II. **Identifying Counterfeit Bills**
   A. Be especially vigilant of $20's and $50's left in our night depository
   B. Make sure you compare any suspected fraudulent bills with real currency
   C. Here are some telltale signs to look for:
      1. No watermark is visible when the bill is held up to the light
      2. The paper stains black when a counterfeit detector pen is used
      3. There are blurred lines and fuzzy scrolls along the border (edges) of each counterfeit bill
         SHOW SLIDE 1 (enlarged photo of counterfeit $20 bill)

III. **Conclusion**
   A. Thank you for your help
   B. If you have any questions, call a bank officer
   C. Review bank policy on reporting counterfeit currency (distributed to staff via email)

When you have to make an informal briefing, follow these guidelines:

1. **Prepare.** Though your talk is short, never speak off-the-cuff. Do some research, e.g., speak with your boss and team members, review procedures, etc.
2. **Decide on your main points.** Write down a few key items you want to cover, and keep this list or outline before you as you speak. Highlight key names, terms, dates, or places.
3. **Avoid information overload.** Do not crowd too many points into one briefing.
4. **Be highly focused.** Include only relevant examples that your audience can easily apply to solve a particular problem or clarify a work-related issue.
5. **Be concise.** Your audience may be on a strict timetable and have obligations to fulfill later in the day.
6. **Stay positive.** Even when you have unpleasant news to impart (e.g., a project delay), resist blaming or lecturing your audience. Instead, concentrate on the positive steps needed to resolve the problem.
7. **Don't overwhelm your listeners with visuals.** Target only two or three main points to illustrate.
8. **End on time.** Be sure to allow time at the end of your briefing for questions, comments, and suggestions. Thank listeners for their time and cooperation.

Note how the speaker's outline and slide in Figure 16.1 identifies key points, illustrates them with examples, inserts appropriate visuals (slides) in the most effective places, and makes sure the briefing is audience-focused and runs on schedule.

FORMAL PRESENTATIONS

While an informal briefing is likely to be short, generally conversational, and intended for a limited number of people, a **formal presentation** is much longer, far less conversational, and perhaps intended for a wider audience.

A formal presentation involves much more preparation. You cannot just dash it off. Just as you did with an informal briefing you will have to do the following; only more extensively and over a longer period of time:

- research the subject
- interview key resource individuals
- prepare, time, and sequence visuals
- coordinate your talk with presentations by your co-workers or boss
- rehearse your presentation

Many of us are uncomfortable in front of an audience because we feel frightened or embarrassed. Much of that anxiety can be eased if you know what to expect. The two areas you should investigate thoroughly before you begin to work on your presentation are (1) who will be in your audience and (2) why they are there.

Analyzing Your Audience

The more you learn about your audience, the better prepared you will be to give your listeners what they need. Just as you do for your written work, for your oral presentation you will have to do some research about the audience, emphasizing the "you attitude" and establishing your own credibility. Put yourself in your audience's place. They will ask: what is your main point, why is it relevant, what benefits are in your talk for them and their company?

Guidelines for Analyzing Your Audience

Here are seven key questions to ask when analyzing your audience.

1. **How much do they know about your topic?** Are they
   - consumers with little or no technical knowledge
   - technical individuals who understand terms, jargon, and background
   - business managers looking only for the bottom line

2. **What unites them as a group?** Are they
   - members of the same profession
   - customers using the same products
   - employees of the company you work for

3. **What do they want to receive from your presentation?** Do they want
   - a quick overview
   - bottom-line financial details
   - technical details on materials, methods, and conclusions (results)

4. **What is their interest or stake in your topic?** Are they
   - friendly and interested
   - neutral—waiting to be informed, entertained, or persuaded
   - uncooperative, antagonistic, or likely to challenge you

5. **What do you want them to do after hearing your presentation?**
   - buy a product or service
   - adopt a plan
   - change a schedule
   - learn more about your topic
   - sign a petition
   - follow a new policy (e.g., safety procedures)

6. **What questions are they likely to raise?** Will they be
   - about money, profits, expenses, salary
   - about personnel, hiring, training
   - about transfers, mergers, promotions
   - about new job responsibilities, accountability
   - about locations, new, remodeled, domestic, overseas
   - about schedules/timetables, effect on quotes, salary

7. **What considerations should you give to a multinational audience?**
   - use common, easily understood vocabulary
   - use simple sentences
   - don't use unfamiliar abbreviations, acronyms, contractions, or metaphors
   - use appropriate, culturally sensitive visuals and images

The Parts of Formal Presentations

As you read this section, refer to Marilyn Claire Ford's PowerPoint presentation in Figure 16.2 (pages 630–633). Note how effectively she used the PowerPoint format to convince a potential client, GTP Systems, to purchase a service contract provided by World Tech, her employer. Her presentation consists of seven slides that contain relevant images and concise text.

The Introduction

The most important part of a presentation is the introduction. You can capture your audience's attention by answering these questions: (1) Who are you? (2) What are your qualifications? (3) What specific topic are you speaking about? and (4) How is the topic relevant to the audience?

Your first and most immediate goal is to establish rapport with your listeners, win their confidence, and elicit their cooperation. Because your listeners are probably at their most attentive during the first few minutes of your presentation, they will pay close attention to everything about you and what you say. Seize the moment and build momentum.

An effective introduction should be proportional to the length of the presentation. A ten-minute speech requires no more than a sixty-second introduction; a twenty-minute speech needs no more than a two- or three-minute introduction. Notice how in slides 1 and 2 of Figure 16.2, Ford introduces herself, her company, and its benefits for GTP.

How to Begin You can begin by introducing yourself, emphasizing your professional qualifications and interests. (A self-introduction is unnecessary if someone else has introduced you or if you know everyone in the room.) Never apologize—for being nervous, unprepared, unqualified—or complain about the time or location for the presentation. Always ask if your audience can hear you.

Give Listeners a Road Map Indicate what your topic is and how you have organized what you have to say about it, for instance,

> My presentation today on greening the workplace will last about 20 minutes. I have divided it into three linked parts. First, I will outline our current greening initiatives. Second, I will give a detailed proposal for how we can green all the departments in our company. Third, I will show how our company can profitably implement those changes. At the end of my presentation, there will be time for your questions and comments.

The most informative presentations are the easiest to follow. Restrict your topic to ensure that you will be able to organize it carefully and sensibly—for example, a tasty diet under 1,000 calories a day or a course in learning Adobe InDesign or another software package.

Capture the Audience's Attention Use any of the following strategies to get your audience to "bite the hook":

- Ask a question. "Did you know that every 15 minutes a foreign-owned business opens in China?" or "Do you know what's in your bottled water besides water?"

FIGURE 16.2 A Sample PowerPoint Presentation

Slide 1

Clear, persuasive title

Background color contrasts well with text

Introduces speaker, provides reason for presentation and date

Type size and font make slide easy to read

Switching to Videoconferencing
A Wise Choice for

Marilyn Claire Ford
Sales Consultant

World Tech

November 15, 2015

Slide 2

Uses short title for each slide

Includes relevant visual emphasizing networking

Succinctly lists benefits in short, easy-to-read bulleted points

What We Offer

iStockphoto.com/Jacob Wackerhausen

- User-friendly videoconferencing
- Cutting-edge communication technology
- Flexible, low-cost networking
- Single network for data, voice, and video

FIGURE 16.2 (Continued)

Easy to Use

With a simple phone call, you can

- Arrange a meeting with colleagues at multiple sites
- Use your computer to access World Tech's conferencing system
- See, hear, and talk with all participants

Andrey_Popov/Shutterstock.com

© 2017 Cengage Learning

Cost Effective

- Dramatically reduces costs for travel
- Upgrades current computer system for less than the cost of buying a new computer
- Cuts data-processing expenses by 60%

iStockphoto.com/George Pchemyan

© 2017 Cengage Learning

(Continued)

FIGURE 16.2 (Continued)

Slide 5

Third sales feature appropriately describes specific technology

Leaves generous margins

Explains how product can increase efficiency

Visual shows benefits of staff interacting

Improves Staff Efficiency

- Brings people together at the right time
- Enhances communication when employees see and hear each other
- SMART Board technology aids collaboration

iStockphoto.com/Jacob Wackerhausen

© 2017 Cengage Learning

Slide 6

Stresses worldwide benefits

Visual reinforces global marketplace

Bulleted points all focus on single topic

Advantages in the Global Marketplace

- Connects all locations to one virtual office
- Increases sales worldwide
- Strengthens global networking

iStockphoto.com/Will Selarep

© 2017 Cengage Learning

FIGURE 16.2 (Continued)

Slide 7

Title signals end of presentation

Summarizes key advantages

Issues a call to action

Makes contact easy through website, email, and telephone

- Start with a quotation. "Winston Churchill said, 'We get things to make a living but we give things to have a life.'" (Consult *Bartlett's Familiar Quotations* online at www.bartleby.com/100)
- Use a relevant and memorable statistic. "In 2014, two million heart attack victims will live to tell about it." (Go to the *Information Please Almanac* at www.infoplease.com to find something relevant to your presentation topic.)

Be careful about using humor in a business talk. It could backfire; the audience may not get the point or could even be offended by it.

The Body
The body is the longest part of your presentation, just as it is in a long report. It should constitute about 60 to 70 percent of your presentation. Make it persuasive and relevant to your audience by (1) explaining a process, (2) describing a condition, (3) solving a problem, (4) arguing a case, or (5) doing all of these. See how the body of Marilyn Claire Ford's presentation in Figure 16.2 is organized around the benefits of GTP's switching to desktop videoconferencing. In slides 3 through 6 she outlines how easy, economical, and efficient such technology is to use in the global marketplace.

To get the right perspective, recall your own experiences as a member of an audience. How often did you feel bored or angry because a speaker tried to overload you with details or could not stick to the point?

Ways to Organize the Body Here are a few helpful ways you can present and organize information in the body of your presentation. When you write a report, you design your document to help readers visually, supplying headings, bullets, white space, and headers and footers (see "The ABCs of Print Document Design," pages 449–459). In a presentation, you need to switch from those purely visual devices to aural ones, such as the following:

1. **Give signals to show where you are going or where you have been.** Enumerate your points: *first, second, third.* Emphasize cause-and-effect relationships with *subsequently, therefore, furthermore.* When you tell a story, follow a chronological sequence and use signposts: *before, following, next, then.* (See Appendix: A Writer's Brief Guide, Table A.1, page A-3.)
2. **Comment on your own material.** Tell the audience if some point is especially significant, memorable, or relevant. "This next fact is the most important one I'll give you today."
3. **Provide internal summaries.** Spending a few seconds to recap what you have just covered will reassure your audience that you want them to be clear about what you have covered thus far.

We have already discussed the difficulties in creating a secure app that our sales force can use. Now we will need to turn to the options we recommend, from the most basic to those more complex.

The Conclusion

Plan your conclusion as carefully as you do your introduction. Stopping with a screeching halt is as bad as trailing off in a fading monotone. Never introduce a new subject or simply repeat your introduction. An effective conclusion should leave the audience feeling that you and they have come full circle and accomplished what you promised.

What to Put in a Conclusion Never introduce a new subject or simply repeat your introduction. A conclusion can contain the following:

- a fresh restatement of your three or four main points
- a call to action, just as in a sales letter—to buy, to note, to agree, to volunteer
- a final emphasis on a key statistic (for example, "The installation of the stainless steel heating tanks has, as we have seen, saved our firm 32 percent in energy costs.

End your presentation, as Marilyn Claire Ford does in slide 7, with a concise summary of the main points, and urge listeners to buy your product or service.

Mean It When You Say, "Finally" When you tell your audience you are concluding, make sure you mean it. Saying, "In conclusion," and then talking for another ten-minutes frustrates listeners and makes them less receptive to your message. When you finish, thank your audience for their time and, if the schedule allows, invite questions.

Always Leave Time for Questions Make sure you budget your time to give the audience an opportunity to ask questions, offer suggestions, or make comments.

Presentation Software

As Marilyn Claire Ford's presentation in Figure 16.2 demonstrates, business presentations very frequently rely on **PowerPoint** or other software such as **Corel Presentations, Apple's Keynote,** or the web-based **Prezi** (prezi.com). Knowing how to use these graphics packages is a crucial skill your employer will expect you to have. This software enables you to support and present your talk with concise text and carefully chosen visuals. They allow you to plan, write, and add visuals to your slides.

Presentation Software Capabilities

With PowerPoint, Prezi, Corel Presentation, and Keynote, you can

- format and edit text
- import visuals, photos, digital art, graphs, charts, pictograms, infographs
- incorporate a variety of shapes and symbols—arrows, asterisks, bullets, cylinders, pyramids, and flowcharts
- offer animation, sound bites, video clips
- insert icons, logos, and letterheads
- reuse and revise your presentation anytime

With the web-based presentation software such as Prezi, you can do all of the things listed above, as well as

- show a cohesive, complete presentation all at once, "zooming" into each key area as you make your presentation
- format your presentation into a "mental map" that you explore "slide-by-slide" in an animated, dynamic way
- help you work more easily with a group, using Prezi's web-based platform

While web-based presentation software like Prezi has gained in popularity recently, the overwhelming preference in the world of work is to use PowerPoint.

Presentation software can also help you as a speaker. For instance, in PowerPoint you can keyboard your notes so that they scroll at the bottom of your computer screen. These notes are not seen by the audience, but they are available if you need them. You also can print parts of your presentation or your entire program in color or gray scale (black and white) to reinforce your presentation with professional-looking handouts.

Editing with presentation software allows you to customize any text or visual. You can copy, move, alter, and delete text, graphics, or sound bites. You can also change the color or texture of a background, saving you time and effort in re-creating a visual.

Organize the Presentation

Map out your presentation before you actually create your slides. Prepare an outline (see "Outlining," pages 48–49) to help you discover and develop the ideas you want to discuss. Following this outline, you can organize your presentation carefully, which is as important as the details you show your audience.

1. Identify the main points you want to cover, as Ford did in presenting information to save GTP time and money, increase staff efficiency, and help the company compete in a global economy. Then you can organize your topics logically and persuasively.
2. Divide your presentation into major sections that best accomplish your objective, whether to inform, to persuade, or to document.
3. Include only those supporting details that relate directly to your topic and to your audience's needs. These key points should help you determine the number of slides and visuals to use.
4. Don't overload your audience with so much data on individual slides that you lose, bore, or turn them off. Note that Ford used only seven slides in Figure 16.2.
5. Choose your visuals carefully. Resist the temptation to dazzle your audience with electronic special effects. Your goal is not to create a glitzy show but to represent your company professionally.

Test the Technology

Find and eliminate any bugs at the rehearsal stage. Call in advance to confirm the room and any equipment you may need. Save and preview your presentation in the format in which you will be giving it. Bring your own computer to the meeting, and set up the projector and your notebook in advance. Make sure your software is compatible with the equipment you will use. Be sure any web links you plan to use are relevant and functioning, not broken links. It is also wise to have an alternative plan if the technology you use fails unexpectedly. Both iOS and Android phones allow users to store presentations on them in a variety of ways. More modern projectors and SMART boards allow for easy connection of technology via USB ports, allowing you to access your presentation via your smartphone if you run into any problems with your computer.

Prepare Handouts

It's always wise to have handouts with you in case you run into technical difficulties. Handouts of your slides (make sure you keep a copy for yourself) will allow you to continue with your presentation, and they will also help your audience follow your presentation and take notes about it while you speak. Make sure your handouts match your presentation exactly by providing your audience with a printout of each slide.

Do not distribute any handouts ahead of time. Wait until you are ready to use them. Otherwise, they may divert your audience's attention from your presentation.

Guidelines on Using Presentation Software Effectively

Here are some tips to ensure the best design and organization of your presentation, whether you use PowerPoint, Prezi, Keynote, or any other program. Refer to Figure 16.2 as you study these guidelines.

Readability

- Make sure each slide is easy to read—clear, concise, and uncluttered.
- Use a type size that is easy to see, even from a distance. For a small presentation on your notebook, use 24- to 28-point type or larger. Increase your type size for headings and titles to 32 point, as in Figure 16.2.
- Keep your design consistent. Don't switch from one font to another.
- Avoid ornate and script fonts, and do not put everything in boldface, italics, or all capital letters. Marilyn Claire Ford used boldface (and white type against a blue background) for only the headings in Figure 16.2.

Text

- Keep your text short and simple. Use easy-to-recall names, words, and phrases. Your audience will not have the time to read long, complex messages.
- Use bulleted lists instead of unbroken paragraphs. But put no more than five bulleted lines on a slide, and limit each line to seven or eight words. Don't squeeze words on a line. Include no more than forty words per slide.
- Double-space between bulleted items, and leave generous margins on all sides.
- Title each slide using a question, a statement, or a key name or phrase, as in Figure 16.2.

Sequencing Slides

- Keep your slides in the order in which you need to show them.
- Retain the same transition (cover left or straight right) from slide to slide to avoid visual confusion.
- In general, spend about one to two minutes per slide, but don't read each slide verbatim. Summarize main ideas or concisely expand them while looking at your audience, not the slide.
- Time your slides so your audience can read them. Never continue to show a slide after you have moved on to a new topic.
- If you invite audience participation and interaction, build in extra time between your slides. Leave time for questions and encourage returning to earlier slides if members of the audience have specific questions.

Background/Color

- Find a pleasant contrasting background to make your text easy to read. Avoid extremely light or dark backgrounds that may obscure your text. Stay away from stark backgrounds, e.g., cold white images on a black screen.
- Use the same background for each slide, as in Figure 16.2.
- Avoid shadowing your text for "decorative" visual effect.
- Use color sparingly, and make sure it is professionally appropriate. Don't turn each slide into a sizzling neon sign. Avoid hot red, pink, etc.

Graphics

- Keep graphics clear, simple, and positioned appropriately on the slide.
- Make certain all graphics are at a high-enough resolution that they will not seem "blurry" or "pixilated" when projected on a larger screen.
- Be sure visuals do not cover or shadow text.
- Show only those visuals that support your main points. Not every slide requires a visual. For example, slide 7 in Figure 16.2 does not use a visual.
- Include no more than one graphic per slide; otherwise, the slide will appear cluttered and your text will be more difficult to read.
- Include easy-to-follow graphs and charts instead of complicated tables, elaborate flow charts, or busy diagrams.
- Stay away from clip art; it can make your product or services look unprofessional.
- Incorporate animation, sound effects, or video clips only when they are persuasive, relevant, and professional. Otherwise they can distract your audience.
- Don't bother with borders; they do not make a slide clearer.

Quality Check

- Be sure your spelling, grammar, names, dates, costs, and sources are correct.
- Double-check all math, equations, and percentages.

Delivering the Presentation

- Don't just read the slides; your audience can do that.
- Regard the slides as keywords in your outline of the presentation or speech. As you present it, you will describe, explain, and elaborate with information not on the slides.

Noncomputerized Presentations

On the job you can expect to use a variety of visuals besides those included in PowerPoint presentations. There will be situations in which you may have to use a conventional chalkboard, a flip chart, or an overhead projector to make a presentation instead of your notebook. You will almost surely be asked to prepare handouts that include text, visuals, or a combination to distribute before or during your talk.

Regardless of the medium you use, make sure your visuals are

- easy to see
- easy to understand
- appropriately sized
- relevant
- accurate
- professional looking

Getting the Most from Your Noncomputerized Visuals

The following practical suggestions will help you get the most from your visuals when time and space may prohibit using computer setups.

1. Do not set up your visuals before your talk. The audience will wonder how you are going to use the graphics and so may not give you their full attention. When you are finished with a visual, put it away.

2. Firmly anchor any maps or illustrations. Having a map roll up or a picture fall off an easel during a presentation is embarrassing.

3. Never obstruct the audience's view by standing in front of your visuals. Use a pointer or a laser pointer to direct the audience's attention to your visual.

4. Avoid crowding too many images onto one visual. Use no more than one visual per page.

5. Do not put much writing on a visual. Elaborate labels or wordy descriptions are hard to read. Enlarge any writing on a visual so your audience can read it quickly and easily.

Rehearsing Your Presentation

All presentations require rehearsal. Don't skip rehearsing your presentation thinking it will save you time. Rehearsing will actually help you become more familiar with your topic and overall message, building your confidence. Rehearsing will also help you acquire more natural speech rhythms—pitch, pauses, and pacing. Here are some strategies to use as you rehearse your talk.

- Know your topic and the various parts of your presentation.
- If possible, practice in the room where you will make your presentation.
- Speak in front of a full-length mirror or before a friend or colleague for at least one rehearsal to see how an audience might view you.
- Talk into an audio recorder to determine whether you sound friendly or frantic, poised or pressured. You can also catch and correct yourself if you are speaking too quickly or too slowly. A normal conversation rate is about 120 to 140 words a minute, but for presentations it's best to speak slightly slower (100 to 120 words a minute) so it is easy for audiences to follow you.
- Time yourself so that you will not exceed your allotted time or fall far short of your audience's expectations.
- Practice with the presentation software, visuals, equipment, or projector that you intend to use in your speech for valuable hands-on experience.
- Monitor the types of gestures (neither too many nor too few) you use for clarity and emphasis in your talk.
- Check the room where you will make your presentation, if possible, to find out about acoustics, lighting, seating, and available equipment.
- Video-capture your final rehearsal and show it to a colleague or instructor for feedback.

Delivering Your Presentation

A poor delivery can ruin a good presentation. First impressions are crucial. Research shows that people decide what they think of you in the first two or three minutes of your presentation. You will be evaluated not only on what you say but on the image you project: how you look, how you talk, and how you move (your body language). Do you mumble into your notes, never looking at the audience? Do you clutch the lectern as if to keep it in place? Do you shift nervously from one foot to the other? Do you shuffle through your notes? All those actions betray your nervousness and detract from your presentation.

The following suggestions on how to deliver a presentation will help you be a well-prepared, poised speaker.

Settling Your Nerves Before You Speak

Being nervous before your presentation is normal—a faster heartbeat, cold, sweaty palms, shaking. But don't let your nerves stop you from delivering a highly successful talk.

Here are some ways you can calm yourself before you deliver your presentation:

- Give yourself plenty of time to get there. The more you have to rush, the more anxious you will be.
- Avoid caffeine for a few hours before your talk if it makes you jittery.
- Take some deep breaths, and then hold your breath while you count to ten. Exhale. This will slow your heart rate and lower your blood pressure.
- Remind yourself that you have spent hours preparing. Think positive. Your hard work will pull you through.
- Try to chat with one or two members of the audience ahead of time to relax. See your audience as friends—people who can help your career.

Guidelines for Making Your Presentation

Everyone is nervous before a talk. Accept that fact and even allow a few seconds of "panic time." Then put your nervous energy to work for you. Chances are, your audience will have no idea how anxious you are; they cannot see the butterflies in your stomach. Again, see your audience as friends, not enemies. Remember to do the following:

1. Establish eye contact with your listeners. Look at as many people in your audience as possible to establish a relationship with them. Never bury your head in your notes or keep your eyes fixed on a screen or keyboard. You will only signal your lack of interest in the audience or your fear of public speaking. Even during an informal presentation, try to establish rapport with each person in the room.

2. Repond to audience feedback. Watch your listeners' reactions and respond appropriately to them—nodding to agree, pausing a moment, paraphrasing to clarify a confusing point. Know your material well so that if someone asks you a question or wants you to return to a point, you are not fumbling through your notes or trying feverishly to locate the right screen.

3. Speak in a friendly, confident tone. Let the audience know that you are happy they are there. Speak in a natural, pleasant voice, but avoid verbal tics ("you know," "I mean") and fillers ("um," "ah," "er") repeated several times each minute. Such nervous habits will make your audience nervous and your speech less effective. Use pauses instead.

4. Vary the rate of your delivery. Vary your rate and inflection to help you emphasize key points and make transitions. Talk slowly enough for your audience to understand you, yet quickly enough so that you don't sound as if you are belaboring or emphasizing each word.

5. Adjust your volume appropriately. Talking in a monotone, never raising or lowering your voice, will lull your audience to sleep or at least inattention. Talk loudly enough for everyone to hear, but be careful if you are using a microphone. Your voice will be amplified, so if you speak too loudly, you will boom rather than project. Every word with a *b*, *p*, or *d* will sound like an explosive in your listeners' ears. Watch out for the other extreme—speaking so softly that only the first two rows can hear you.

6. Watch your posture. Don't shift from one foot to another. But do not slouch or look wooden either. If you stand motionless, looking as if *rigor mortis* has set in, your speech will be judged cold and lifeless, no matter how lively your words are.

7. Use appropriate body language. Be natural and consistent. Do not startle an audience by suddenly pounding on a desk for emphasis. Avoid gestures that will distract or alienate your audience. For example, don't fold your arms as you talk, a gesture that signals you are unreceptive (closed) to your audience's reactions. Also, avoid nervous habits that can divert the audience's attention: scratching your head, twirling your hair, pushing up your glasses, fumbling with your notes, or tapping your foot. Nor do you have to remain still or step with robotlike movements. The remote control for a PowerPoint or Prezi presentation allows you to casually walk around the room as you click and change screens.

8. Dress professionally. Do not wear clothes or clanking jewelry that call attention to themselves. Follow your company's dress code. Unless it specifies otherwise (e.g., "casual Fidays"), wear clothes that are the business norm for your profession.

Handling Interruptions

Be diplomatic if someone interrupts your presentation with a question. Thank the individual by saying, "That's a good question. I'll be happy to answer it at the end of the presentation when there'll be time for questions." If someone is disruptive during your talk or a question-and-answer session and wants to debate with you, offer to meet with him or her after the session to discuss the point in question. Moreover, if you cannot answer a particular question, say you'll be glad to get back to the person, and go on to other questions.

When You Have Finished

Don't just sit down, walk back to your place on the platform or in the audience, or, worse yet, march out of the room. Thank your listeners for their attention and stay at the lectern or at your laptop for audience applause or questions.

If a question-and-answer session is to follow your speech, anticipate questions your audience is likely to ask. But it's a good idea to give your audience a time limit. For example, you might say, "I'll be happy to answer your questions now before we break in ten minutes for lunch." By setting limits, you reduce the chances of a lengthy debate with members of the audience, and you can then politely leave after your time elapses.

Evaluating Presentations

This chapter has given you information on how to construct and deliver both an informal and formal business presentation. As a way of reviewing that advice, study Figure 16.3 below—an evaluation form similar to those used by instructors in colleges and universities. Note that the form gives equal emphasis to the speaker's performance or delivery and to the organization, content, and sequence of the presentation.

FIGURE 16.3 An Evaluation Form for a Presentation

Name of Speaker: _____	Date: _____
Title of Presentation: _____	Length: _____

PART I: THE SPEAKER'S DELIVERY
Circle the appropriate number using a 1 (lowest) to 5 (highest) scale.

1. Appearance	1 unprofessional	2	3	4	5 well-groomed
2. Eye contact	1 poor	2	3	4	5 effective
3. Tone of voice	1 monotonous	2	3	4	5 varied
4. Diction	1 slurred	2	3	4	5 clear
5. Posture	1 poor	2	3	4	5 natural
6. Gestures	1 distracting	2	3	4	5 appropriate
7. Self-confidence	1 nervous	2	3	4	5 poised
8. Interaction with audience	1 minimal	2	3	4	5 engaging

PART II: THE PRESENTATION ITSELF
Circle the appropriate number: 1 = poor; 5 = superior.

1. Made sure topic was relevant to audience	1	2	3	4	5

FIGURE 16.3 (Continued)

2. Began with clear statement of purpose	1	2	3	4	5
3. Followed logical organization	1	2	3	4	5
4. Gave audience cues to look for transitions between sections	1	2	3	4	5
5. Matched content to technical knowledge of audience	1	2	3	4	5
6. Provided convincing supporting evidence	1	2	3	4	5
7. Did not digress	1	2	3	4	5
8. Concluded with a summary of main points	1	2	3	4	5
9. Stayed within time limits	1	2	3	4	5
10. Allowed time for questions	1	2	3	4	5

PART III: USE OF VISUALS (SLIDES OR OTHER GRAPHICS)
Again, circle the appropriate number: = 1 poor; 5 = superior.

1. Used right number of visuals	1	2	3	4	5
2. Ensured all visuals were relevant	1	2	3	4	5
3. Carefully timed the sequence of visuals	1	2	3	4	5
4. Made sure audience could see visuals clearly	1	2	3	4	5
5. Selected visuals that clarified or simplified a point	1	2	3	4	5
6. Referred to visuals and indicated why they were important	1	2	3	4	5
7. Credited the source of visuals	1	2	3	4	5

✔ REVISION CHECKLIST

- ☐ Anticipated my audience's background, interest, and even potential resistance, as well as questions about the message of both informal and formal presentations.
- ☐ Organized an informal briefing to make it easy to understand and to incorporate it into the work routine.
- ☐ Prepared an outline and identified and corrected any weak or redundant areas.
- ☐ Drafted an introduction to provide a "road map" of the presentation and to arouse audience interest.
- ☐ Started with interesting and relevant statistics, a question, an anecdote, or a similar "hook" to capture audience attention.
- ☐ Limited the body of my presentation to the main points.
- ☐ Sequenced the main points logically and made connections among them.
- ☐ Used supporting examples and illustrations appropriate to my audience and message.
- ☐ Made sure my conclusion contains a summary of the main points of my presentation and a specific call to action.
- ☐ Designed visuals that are clear, easy to read, and relevant for my audience.
- ☐ Experimented successfully with presentation software before using it for my presentation.
- ☐ Used an appropriate number of slides and made sure they were readable.
- ☐ Showed slides in the correct, carefully timed sequence.
- ☐ Prepared handouts in case of equipment trouble.
- ☐ Rehearsed my presentation thoroughly to become familiar with its content, organization, and visuals.
- ☐ Monitored my volume, tone, and rate to vary my delivery and to emphasize my major points.
- ☐ Rehearsed my gestures to make them relevant and nonintrusive.
- ☐ Timed my presentation, complete with visuals, to run close to the allotted time.

EXERCISES

1. Prepare a three- to five-minute presentation explaining how a piece of equipment that you use on your job works. If the equipment is small enough, bring it with you to class. If it is too large, prepare an appropriate visual or two for use in your talk. Submit an outline similar to that in Figure 16.1.

2. You have just been asked to talk about the students at your school or the employees where you work. Narrow the topic and submit an outline to your instructor, showing how you have limited the topic and gathered and organized evidence. Incorporate two or three appropriate visuals (photographs, maps, charts, icons, or even videos) in your PowerPoint presentation. Follow the format of the presentation in Figure 16.2.

3. Prepare a ten-minute presentation on a controversial topic that you would present before a civic group—the PTA, the local chapter of an organization, a post of the Veterans of Foreign Wars, a synagogue, a mosque, or a church club.

4. Using the information contained in the internal unsolicited proposal in Chapter 13 (Figure 13.5, pages 530–534) or in the long report on multinational workers in Chapter 15 (Figure 15.3, pages 607–621), prepare a short presentation (five to seven minutes) for your class.

5. Deliver a formal presentation on one of the following topics. Restrict your topic, and divide it into four key issues, as in Figure 16.2. Use at least three visuals with your talk. Submit an outline to your instructor.

   a. new equipment at work
   b. Using the Internet to provide interactive health care in rural areas
   c. a major change in housing or traffic control in your city
   d. a paper or report you wrote in school or on your job
   e. "greening" your school's or company's vistor's center
   f. the budget or spending cuts planned for your department or your town's school district for a given year
   g. applying for and receiving financial aid

6. Using the evaluation form in Figure 16.3, evaluate a speaker—a speech class student, a local politician, or a co-worker delivering a report at work. Specify the time, place, and occasion of the speech. Pay special attention to any visuals the speaker uses.

Appendix

A Writer's Brief Guide to Paragraphs, Sentences, and Words

To write successfully, you must know how to create effective paragraphs, write and punctuate clear sentences, and use words correctly. This guide succinctly explains some of the basic elements of clear and accurate writing.

PARAGRAPHS

Writing a Well-Developed Paragraph

A paragraph is the basic building block for any piece of writing. It is (1) a group of related sentences (2) arranged in a logical order (3) supplying readers with detailed, appropriate information (4) on a single important topic.

A paragraph expresses one central idea, with each sentence contributing to the overall meaning of that idea. The paragraph does that by means of a **topic sentence,** which states the central idea, and **supporting information,** which explains the topic sentence.

Supply a Topic Sentence

The topic sentence is the most important sentence in your paragraph. Carefully worded and restricted, it helps you generate and control your information. An effective topic sentence also helps readers grasp your main idea quickly. As you draft your paragraphs, pay close attention to the following three guidelines.

   1. **Make sure you provide a topic sentence.** In their rush to supply readers with facts, some writers forget or neglect to include a topic sentence. The following paragraph, with no topic sentence, shows how fragmented such writing can be.

No topic sentence: Sensors found on each machine detect wind speed and direction and other important details such as ice loading and potential metal fatigue. The information is fed into a microprocessor in the nacelle (or engine housing). The microprocessor then automatically keeps the blades turned into the wind, starts and stops

A–1

the machine, and changes the pitch of the tips of the blades to increase power under varying wind conditions. Should any part of the wind turbine suffer damage or malfunction, the microprocessor will immediately shut the machine down.

Only when a suitable topic sentence is added—"The MOD-2 wind turbine features the latest technology"—can readers understand what the technical details have in common.

2. Put your topic sentence first. Place your topic sentence at the beginning of your paragraph because the first sentence occupies a commanding position. Burying the key idea in the middle or near the end of the paragraph makes it harder for readers to comprehend your purpose or act on your information.

3. Be sure your topic sentence is focused and discusses only one central idea. A broad or unrestricted topic sentence leads to a shaky, incomplete paragraph for two reasons:

- The paragraph will not contain enough information to support the topic sentence.
- A broad topic sentence will not summarize or forecast specific information in the paragraph.

The following example of a carefully constructed paragraph contains a clear topic sentence in an appropriate position (*italicized*) and adequate supporting details.

> *Fat is an important part of everyone's diet.* It is nutritionally present in the basic food groups we eat—meat and poultry, dairy products, and oils—to aid growth or development. The fats and fatty acids present in those foods ensure proper metabolism, thus helping to turn what we eat into the energy we need. Those same fats and fatty acids also act as carriers for important vitamins like A, D, E, and K. Another important role of fat is that it keeps us from feeling hungry by delaying digestion. Fat also enhances the flavor of the food we eat, making it more enjoyable.

Three Characteristics of an Effective Paragraph

Effective paragraphs have **unity, coherence,** and **completeness.**

Unity

A unified paragraph sticks to one topic without wandering. Every sentence and every detail supports, explains, or proves the central idea. A unified paragraph includes only relevant information and excludes unnecessary or irrelevant comments.

Coherence

In a coherent paragraph, all sentences flow smoothly and logically to and from each other like the links of a chain. Use these three techniques to achieve coherence.

1. Use transitional words and phrases. Some useful transitional, or connective, words and phrases, grouped according to the relationships they express, are listed in Table A.1.

TABLE A.1 Transitional, or Connective, Words and Phrases

Addition	additionally	besides	moreover
	again	first, second, third	next
	along with	furthermore	together with
	also	in addition	too
	and	many	what's more
	as well as	numerous	
Cause/effect	accordingly	consequently	on account of
	and so	due to	since
	as a result	hence	therefore
	because of	if	thus
Comparison/ contrast	but	in contrast	on the other hand
	conversely	in the same way	similarly
	equally	likewise	still
	however	on the contrary	yet
Conclusion	all in all	in brief	on the whole
	altogether	in conclusion	to conclude
	as we saw	in short	to put into perspective
	at last	in summary	to summarize
	finally	last	to wrap up
Condition	although	granted that	provided that
	depending	if	to be sure
	even though	of course	unless
Emphasis	above all	for emphasis	of course
	after all	indeed	surely
	again	in fact	to repeat
	as a matter of fact	in other words	to stress
	as I said	obviously	unquestionably
Illustration	for example	in other words	that is
	for instance	in particular	to demonstrate
	in effect	specifically	to illustrate
Place	across from	below	over
	adjacent to	beyond	there
	alongside of	here	under
	at this point	in front of	where
	behind	next to	wherever
Time	afterward	formerly	previously
	at length	hereafter	soon
	at the same time	later	simultaneously
	at times	meanwhile	subsequently
	beforehand	next	then
	currently	now	until
	during	once	when
	earlier	presently	while

Paragraph with connective words: Advertising a product on the radio has many advantages over using television. *For one thing*, radio rates are much cheaper. *For example*, a one-time 60-second spot on local television can cost $5,000. *For that money*, advertisers can purchase nine 30-second spots on the radio. *Equally attractive* are the low production costs for radio advertising. *In contrast*, television advertising often includes extra costs for actors and voice-overs. *Another* advantage radio offers advertisers is immediate scheduling. *Often* the ad appears during the same week a contract is signed. *On the other hand*, television stations are *frequently* booked up months in advance, so it may be a long time *before* an ad appears. *Furthermore*, radio gives advertisers a greater opportunity to reach potential buyers. *After all*, radio follows listeners everywhere—in their homes, at work, and in their cars. *Although* television is very popular, it cannot do that.

2. Use pronouns and demonstrative adjectives. Words like *he*, *she*, *him*, *her*, *they*, *their*, and so on, contribute to paragraph coherence and improve the flow of sentences.

> Paragraph with pronouns:
>
> Traffic studies are an important tool for store owners looking for a new location. *These* studies are relatively inexpensive and highly accurate. *They* can tell owners how much traffic passes by a particular location at a particular time and why. Moreover, *they* can help owners determine what particular characteristics the individuals have in common. Because of *their* helpfulness, *these* studies can save owners time and money and possibly prevent financial ruin.

3. Use parallel (coordinated) grammatical structures. Parallelism means using the same form of the word, phrase, clause, or sentence to express related concepts.

> Orientation sessions accomplish four useful goals for trainees. First, they introduce trainees to key personnel in accounting, IT, maintenance, and security. Second, they give trainees experience logging into the database system, selecting appropriate menus, editing core documents, and getting off the system. Third, they explain to trainees the company policies affecting the way supplies are ordered, used, and stored. Fourth, they help trainees understand their ethical responsibilities in such sensitive areas as computer security and use.

Parallelism is at work on a number of levels in the preceding paragraph, among them these:

- The four sentences about the four goals start in the same way grammatically ("... they introduce/give/explain/help ...") to help readers categorize the information.
- Within individual sentences, the repetition of **present participles** (*logging*, selec*ting*, edit*ing*, get*ting*) and of **past participles** (order*ed*, us*ed*, stor*ed*) helps the writer coordinate information.
- Transitional words—*first*, *second*, *third*, *fourth*—provide a clear-cut sequence.

Completeness

A complete paragraph provides readers with sufficient information to clarify, analyze, support, defend, or prove the central idea expressed in the topic sentence. The reader feels satisfied that the writer has given necessary details.

Skimpy paragraph:	Farmers are turning their crops and farm wastes into cost-effective fuels. Much that is grown on the farm is being converted to energy. This energy can have many uses and save farmers a lot of money in operating expenses.
Fully developed paragraph:	Farm crops and wastes are being turned into fuels to save farmers operating costs. Alcohol can be distilled from grain, sugar beets, and corn. Converted to ethanol (90 percent gasoline, 10 percent ethanol), this fuel runs such farm equipment as irrigation pumps, feed grinders, and tractors. Similarly, through a biomass digestion system, farmers can produce methane from animal or crop wastes as a natural gas for heating and cooking. Finally, cellulose pellets, derived from plant materials, become solid fuel that can save farmers money in heating barns.

SENTENCES

Constructing and Punctuating Sentences

The way you construct and punctuate your sentences can determine whether you succeed or fail in the world of work. Your sentences reveal a lot about you. They tell readers how clearly you can convey a message. And any message is only as effective and as thoughtful as the sentences of which it is made.

What Makes a Sentence

A sentence is a complete thought, expressed by a subject and a verb that can make sense standing alone.

> subject   verb
> Websites   sell   products.

The Difference Between Phrases and Clauses

The first step toward success in writing sentences is learning to recognize the difference between phrases and clauses. A **phrase** is a group of words that does not contain a subject and a verb; phrases cannot make sense standing alone. Phrases cannot be sentences.

> in the park   No subject: Who is in the park?
>   No verb: What was done in the park?
> for every patient in intensive care No subject: Who did something for every patient?
>   No verb: What was done for every patient?

A **clause** does contain a subject and a verb, but *not every clause is a sentence.* Only **independent** (or **main**) **clauses** can stand alone as sentences. Here is an example of an independent clause that is a complete sentence.

> subject   verb   object
> The president closed the college.

A **dependent** (or **subordinate**) **clause** also contains a subject and a verb, but it does not make complete sense and cannot stand alone. Why? A dependent clause contains a subordinating conjunction—*after, although, as, because, before, even though, if, since, unless, when, where, whereas, while*—at the beginning of the clause. Such conjunctions subordinate the clause in which they appear and make the clause dependent for meaning and completion on an independent clause.

After
Before
Because   }   the president closed the college
Even though
Unless

"After the president closed the college" is not a complete thought but a dependent clause that leaves us in suspense. It needs to be completed with an independent clause telling us what happened "after."

dependent clause (not a sentence)	subject	verb	phrase
After the president closed the college,	we	played	in the snow.

Avoiding Sentence Fragments

An incomplete sentence is called a **fragment.** Fragments can be phrases or dependent clauses. They either lack a verb or a subject or have broken away from an independent clause. A fragment is isolated: It needs an overhaul to supply missing parts to turn it into an independent clause or to glue it back to an independent clause to have it make sense.

To avoid writing fragments, follow these rules. *Note that incorrect examples are preceded by a minus sign, correct revisions by a plus sign.*

  1. Do not use a subordinate clause as a sentence. Even though it contains a subject and a verb, a subordinate clause standing alone is still a fragment. To avoid this kind of sentence fragment, simply join the two clauses (the independent clause and the dependent clause containing a subordinating conjunction) with a comma— *not* a period or semicolon.

    Bad: Unless we agreed to the plan. (What would happen?)
    Bad: Unless we agreed to the plan; the project manager would discontinue the operation. (A semicolon cannot set off the subordinate clause.)
  Good: Unless we agreed to the plan, the project manager would discontinue the operation.
    Bad: Because safety precautions were taken. (What happened?)
  Good: Because safety precautions were taken, ten construction workers escaped injury.

Sometimes subordinate clauses appear at the end of a sentence. They may be introduced by a subordinate conjunction, an adverb, or a relative pronoun (*that, which, who*). Do not separate these clauses from the preceding independent clause with a period, thus turning them into fragments.

    Bad: An all-volunteer fire department posed some problems. Especially for residents in the western part of town.

Good: An all-volunteer fire department posed some problems, especially for residents in the western part of town. (The word *especially* qualifies *posed*, referred to in the independent clause.)

2. Every sentence must have a subject telling the reader who does the action.

Bad: Being extra careful not to spill the solution. (Who?)
Good: The technician was being extra careful not to spill the solution.

3. Every sentence must have a complete verb. Watch especially for verbs ending in *-ing*. They need another verb (some form of *to be*) to make them complete.

Bad: The machine running in the computer department. (Did what?)

You can change that fragment into a sentence by supplying the correct form of the verb.

Good: The machine *is running* in the computer department.
Good: The machine *runs* in the computer department.

Or you can revise the entire sentence, adding a new thought.

Good: The machine running in the computer department processes all new accounts.

4. Do not detach prepositional phrases from independent clauses. Prepositional phrases (beginning with *at*, *by*, *for*, *from*, *in*, *to*, *with*, and so forth) are not complete thoughts and cannot stand alone. Correct the error by leaving the phrases attached to the sentence to which they belong.

Bad: By three o'clock the next day. (What was to happen?)
Good: The supervisor wanted our reports by three o'clock the next day.

Correcting Comma Splices

Fragments occur when you use only bits and pieces of complete sentences. Another common error that some writers commit involves just the reverse kind of action. They weakly and wrongly join two complete sentences (independent clauses) with a comma as if those two sentences were really only one sentence. Such an error is called a **comma splice.** Here is an example:

Bad: Gasoline prices have risen by 15 percent in the last month, we will drive the car less often.

Two independent clauses (complete sentences) exist:

Good: Gasoline prices have risen by 15 percent in the last month.
Good: We will drive the car less often.

A comma alone lacks the power to separate independent clauses.

As the preceding example shows, many pronouns—*I*, *he*, *she*, *it*, *we*, *they*—are used as the subjects of independent clauses. A comma splice will result if you place a comma instead of a semicolon or period between two independent clauses where the second clause opens with a pronoun.

> **Bad:**   Maria approved the plan, she liked its cost-effective approach.
> **Good:** Maria approved the plan; she liked its cost-effective approach.

However, relative pronouns (*who*, *whom*, *which*, *that*) are preceded by a comma, not a period or a semicolon, when they introduce subordinate clauses.

> **Bad:**   She approved the plan. Which had a cost-effective approach.
> **Good:** She approved the plan, which had a cost-effective approach.

Four Ways to Correct Comma Splices

1. Remove the comma separating two independent clauses and replace it with a period. Then capitalize the first letter of the first word of the new sentence.

> **Good:**   Gasoline prices have risen by 15 percent in the last month. We will drive the car less often.

2. Insert a coordinating conjunction (*and*, *but*, *or*, *nor*, *so*, *for*, *yet*) after the comma. Together, the conjunction and the comma properly separate the two independent clauses.

> **Good:**   Gasoline prices have risen by 15 percent in the last month, so we will drive the car less often.

3. Rewrite the sentence. If it makes sense to do so, turn the first independent clause into a dependent clause by adding a subordinate conjunction; then insert a comma and add the second independent clause.

> **Good:**   Because gasoline prices have risen by 10 percent in the last month, we will drive the car less often.

4. Delete the comma and insert a semicolon.

> **Good:**   Gasoline prices have risen by 15 percent in the last month; we will drive the car less often.

Of the four ways to correct the comma splice, sentences 3 and 4 are equally suitable, but sentence 3 reads more smoothly and so is the better choice.

The semicolon is an effective and forceful punctuation mark when two independent clauses are closely related—that is, when they announce contrasting or parallel views, as the two following examples reveal:

> **Good:**   The union favored the new legislation; the company opposed it. (contrasting views)
> **Good:**   Night classes help the college and the community; students can take more credit hours to advance their careers. (parallel views)

How Not to Correct Comma Splices

Some writers mistakenly try to correct comma splices by inserting a conjunctive adverb (*also*, *consequently*, *furthermore*, *however*, *moreover*, *nevertheless*, *then*, *therefore*) after the comma.

> **Bad:**   Gasoline prices have risen by 15 percent in the last month, consequently we will drive the car less often.

Because the conjunctive adverb (*consequently*) is not as powerful as the coordinating conjunction (*and, but, for*), the error is not eliminated. If you use a conjunctive adverb—*consequently, however, nevertheless*—you still must insert a semicolon or a period before it, as the following examples show:

Good: Gasoline prices have risen by 15 percent in the last month; consequently, we will drive the car less often.

Good: Gasoline prices have risen by 15 percent in the last month. Consequently, we will drive the car less often.

Making Subjects and Verbs Agree in Your Sentences

A subject and a verb must agree in number. A singular subject takes a singular verb, whereas a plural subject requires a plural verb.

Singular Subject	Plural Subject
the engineer calculates	engineers calculate
a report analyzes	reports analyze
a policy changes	policies change

You can avoid subject-verb agreement errors by following eight simple rules.

1. Disregard any words that come between the subject and its verb.

Faulty: The customer who ordered three parts want them shipped this afternoon.
Correct: The customer who ordered three parts wants them shipped this afternoon.

2. A compound subject takes a plural verb. (A compound subject has two parts connected by *and*.)

Faulty: The engineering department and the safety committee prefers to develop new guidelines.
Correct: The engineering department and the safety committee prefer to develop new guidelines.

3. When a compound subject contains *neither . . . nor* or *either . . . or*, the verb agrees with the subject closer to it.

Faulty: Either the residents or the manager are going to file the complaint.
Correct: Either the residents or the manager is going to file the complaint.
Correct: Either the manager or the residents are going to file the complaint.

4. Use a singular verb after collective nouns when the group functions as a single unit. (Collective nouns are words like *committee, crew, department, group, organization, staff, team*.)

Correct: The crew was available to repair the machine.
Correct: The committee asks that all recommendations be submitted by Friday.

However, in this situation:

Correct: The staff were unable to agree on the best model. (The staff acted as individuals, not a unit, so a plural verb is required.)

5. Use a singular verb with indefinite pronouns. (Indefinite pronouns are words such as *anybody, anyone, each, everyone, everything, no one, somebody, something*.)

> Each of the programmers has completed the seminar.
> Somebody usually volunteers for that duty.

Similarly, when *all*, *most*, *more*, or *part* is the subject, it requires a singular verb.

> Most of the money is allocated.
> Part of the equipment was salvageable.

6. Words like *scissors* and *pants* are plural when they are the true subject.

> Faulty: A pair of trousers were available in his size. (*Pair* is the true subject, and it is a singular noun.)
> Correct: The trousers were on sale.

7. Some foreign plurals always take a plural verb. Examples include *curricula, data, media, phenomena, strata, syllabi*.

> The data conclusively prove my point.
> The media are usually the first to point out a politician's weak points.

8. Use a singular verb with fractions.

> Three-fourths of her research proposal was finished.

Writing Sentences That Say What You Mean

Your sentences should say exactly what you mean, without double talk, misplaced humor, or nonsense. Sentences are composed of words and word groups that influence each other.

Writing Logical Sentences

Sentences should not contradict themselves or make outlandish claims. The following example contains an error in logic; note how easily the suggested revision solves the problem.

> Illogical: Steel roll-away shutters make it possible for the sun to be shaded in the summer and to have it shine in the winter. (The sun is far too large to shade; the writer means that a room or a house could be shaded with the shutters.)
> Revision: Steel roll-away shutters make it possible for owners to shade their living rooms in the summer and to admit sunshine during the winter.

Using Contextually Appropriate Words

Sentences should use the combination of words most appropriate for the subject.

> Inappropriate: The members of the Nuclear Regulatory Commission saw fear radiated on the faces of the residents. (The word *radiated* is obviously ill advised in this context; use a neutral term.)
> Revision: The members of the Nuclear Regulatory Commission saw fear reflected on the faces of the residents.

Writing Sentences with Well-Placed Modifiers

A **modifier** is a word, phrase, or clause that describes, limits, or qualifies the meaning of another word or word group. A modifier can consist of one word (a *blue* car), a prepositional phrase (the man *in the toll booth*), a relative clause (the woman *who won the marathon*), or an *-ing* or *-ed* phrase (*walking three miles a day*, the student was in good shape; *seated in the first row*, we saw everything on stage).

A **dangling modifier** is one that cannot logically modify any word in the sentence.

> Bad: When answering the question, his calculator fell off the table.

One way to correct the error is to insert the right subject after the *-ing* phrase.

> Good: When answering the question, he knocked his calculator off the table.

You can also turn the phrase into a subordinate clause.

> Good: When he answered the question, his calculator fell off the table.
> Good: His calculator fell off the table as he answered the question.

A **misplaced modifier** illogically modifies the wrong word or words in the sentence. The result is often comical.

> Bad: Hiding in the corner, growling and snarling, our guide spotted the frightened cub. (Is the guide growling and snarling in the corner?)
> Bad: All travel requests must be submitted by employees in red ink. (Are the employees covered in red ink?)

The problem with both of those examples is word order. The modifiers are misplaced because they are attached to the wrong words in the sentence. Correct the error by moving the modifier to where it belongs.

> Good: Hiding in the corner, growling and snarling, the frightened cub was spotted by our guide.
> Good: All travel requests by employees must be submitted in red ink.

Misplacing a relative clause (introduced by relative pronouns like *who, whom, that, which*) can also lead to problems with modification.

> Bad: The salesperson rang up the merchandise for the customer that the store had discounted. (The merchandise was discounted, not the customer.)
> Bad: The salesperson rang up the merchandise that the store had discounted for the customer. (The salesperson rang up the discount for the customer; the store did not discount the customer.)
> Good: The salesperson rang up for the customer the merchandise that the store had discounted.

Always place the relative clause immediately after the word it modifies.

Using Pronoun References Correctly

Sentences will be vague if they contain a faulty use of pronouns. When you use a pronoun whose **antecedent** (the person, place, or object the pronoun refers to) is unclear, you risk confusing your reader.

Unclear:	After the plants are clean, we separate the stems from the roots and place them in the sun to dry. (Is it the stems or the roots that lie in the sun?)
Revision:	After the plants are clean, we separate the stems from the roots and place the stems in the sun to dry.
Unclear:	The park ranger was pleased to see the workers planting new trees and installing new benches. This will attract more tourists. (The trees or the benches or both?)
Revision:	The park ranger was pleased to see the workers planting new trees and installing new benches, because additional trees and benches will attract more tourists.

WORDS

Spelling Words Correctly

A misspelled word may seem like a small matter, but on an employment application, an email, an incident report, a letter, a short or long report, or a PowerPoint slide, it can make you look careless or, even worse, uneducated. Readers will inevitably question your other skills if your spelling is incorrect.

The Benefits and Pitfalls of Spell-Checkers

Do not rely exclusively on a spell-checker to solve all your spelling and word-choice problems. Spell-checkers recognize only those words that have been listed in them. A proper name or a new, infrequently used word may be flagged as an error even though the word is spelled correctly. Moreover, a spell-checker cannot differentiate between such homonyms as *too* and *two* or *there* and *their.* A spell-checker identifies only misspelled words, not misused words.

Consulting a Dictionary

Always have a dictionary handy. Two useful online dictionaries to consult are *Merriam-Webster OnLine* (www.merriam-webster.com) and *Dictionary.com* (dictionary.reference.com).

Using Apostrophes Correctly

Apostrophes cause some writers special problems. Basically, apostrophes are used for three reasons: (1) contractions, (2) possessives, and (3) plurals of some abbreviations and letters used as nouns. The following guidelines will help you sort out these uses.

1. In a **contraction,** the apostrophe takes the place of the missing letter or letters: *I've = I have; doesn't = does not; he's = he is; it's = it is.* (*Its* is a possessive pronoun—the dog and *its* bone—not a contraction. There is no such form as *its'.*)

2. To form a **possessive,** follow these rules.

   a. If a singular or plural noun does not end in an *-s*, add *'s* to show possession.

Mary's locker	the woman's jacket
children's books	the women's jackets
the staff's dedication	the company's policy

   b. If a singular noun ends in *-s*, add *'s* to show possession.

the class's project	the boss's schedule

   c. If a plural noun ends in *-s*, add just the *'* to indicate possession.

employees' benefits	computers' speed
lawyers' fees	stores' prices

   d. If a proper name ends in *-s*, add *'s* to form the possessive.

Jones's account	Keats's poetry
Jill Williams's house	James's contract

   e. If it is a compound noun, add an *'* or *'s* to the end of the word.

my brother-in-law's business	Ms. Melek-Patel's order

   f. To indicate shared possession, add *'s* to just the final name.

Rao and Kline's website	Juan and Anne's major

   g. To indicate separate possession, add *'s* to each name.

Juan's and Tia's transcripts	Shakespeare's and Byron's poetry

3. For abbreviations with periods and for lowercase letters used as nouns, form the plural by adding *'s*.

his *p*'s and *q*'s	Q and A's	Ph.D.'s

   To form the plural of numbers and capital letters used as nouns, including abbreviations without periods, just add *s*. To avoid misreading some capital letters, however, you may need to add an apostrophe.

during the 1980s	all perfect 10s
their SATs	several local YMCAs
the 3 R's	straight A's

Inserting Hyphens Properly

Use a hyphen (-, as opposed to a dash, —) for

- **compound words**

four-part lecture	heavy-duty machine	long-term prospects

- **most words beginning with** *self*

self-starting	self-defense	self-regulating	self-governing

- **fractions used as adjectives**

at the three-quarter level	two-thirds majority

Using Ellipses

Sometimes a sentence or passage is particularly useful, but you may not want to quote it fully. You may want to delete some words that are not really necessary for your purpose. An omission is indicated by using an **ellipsis** (three spaced dots within the sentence to indicate where words have been omitted). Here is an example:

Full Quotation: "Diet and nutrition, which researchers have studied extensively, significantly affect oral health."

Quotation with Ellipsis: "Diet and nutrition . . . significantly affect oral health."

Using Numerals Versus Words

Write out numbers as words rather than numerals in these situations:

- **to begin a sentence**
Nineteen ninety-nine was the first year of our recruitment drive.

- **to indicate the first number when two numbers are used together**
The company needed eleven 9-foot slabs.

But use numerals, not words, in these situations:

- **with abbreviations, percentages, symbols, units of measurement, dates**

17 percent	11:30 a.m.	70 ml
December 3, 2012	$250.00	50 K

- **for page references**
pp. 56–59

- **for large numbers**

3,000,000	23,750	1,714

Use both numerals and words when you want to be as precise as possible in a contract or a proposal.

We agreed to pay the vendor an extra twenty-five dollars ($25.00) per hour to finish the job by May 18.

Matching the Right Word with the Right Meaning

The words in the following list frequently are mistaken for one another. Some are true homonyms; others are just similar in spelling, pronunciation, or usage. The part of speech is given after each word. Make sure you use the right word in the right context.

accept (v) to receive, to acknowledge: *We accept your proposal.*
except (prep) excluding, but: *Everyone attended the meeting except Neelou.*

advice (n) a recommendation: *I should have taken Xi's advice.*
advise (v) to counsel: *Our lawyers advised us not to sign the contract.*

affect (v) to change, to influence: *Does the detour on Route 22 affect your travel plans?*

effect (n) a result: *What was the effect of the new procedure?*
effect (v) to bring about: *We will try to effect a change in company policy.*

allot (v) to distribute, to assign: *The manager allotted the writing team two weeks to complete the report.*
a lot (n) a quantity: *They bought a lot of supplies for the trip.*

all ready (adj) two-word phrase *all + ready*; to be finished; to be prepared: *We are all ready for the inspector's visit.*
already (adv) previously, before a given time: *Our webmaster had already updated the site.*

altar (n) central place of worship: *There were fresh flowers on the altar.*
alter (v) to change, to amend: *The tailor altered the trousers.*

ascent (n) upward movement: *We watched the space shuttle's ascent.*
assent (n) agreement: *She won the teacher's assent.*
assent (v) to agree: *The committee asked the company to assent to the new terms.*

attain (v) to achieve, to reach: *We attained our sales goal this month.*
obtain (v) to get, to receive: *You can obtain a job application on their website.*

cite (v) to document: *Please cite several examples to support your claim.*
site (n) place, location: *They want to build a parking lot on the site of the old theater.*
sight (n) vision: *His sight improved with bifocals.*

coarse (adj) rough: *The sandpaper felt coarse.*
course (n) subject of study: *Sharonda took a course in calculus this fall.*

complement (v) to add to, enhance: *Her graphs and charts complemented my proposal.*
compliment (v) to praise: *The customer complimented us on our courteous staff.*

continually (adv) frequently and regularly: *This answering machine continually disconnects the caller in the middle of the message.*
continuously (adv) constantly; without stopping: *The air-conditioning is on continuously during the summer.*

council (n) government body: *The council voted to increase salaries for all city employees.*
counsel (n) advice: *She gave the trainee pertinent counsel.*

defer (v) To put off until later: *His student loan was deferred while he finished his degree.*
differ (v) to disagree, to be different: *The committee differed among its members about the bond issue.*

discreet (adj) showing respect, being tactful: *The manager was discreet in answering the complaint letter.*
discrete (adj) separate, distinct: *Put those figures into discrete categories for processing.*

dual (adj) double: *That report serves a dual purpose.*
duel (n) a fight, a battle: *The argument almost turned into a duel.*

eminent (adj) prominent, highly esteemed: *Dr. Felicia Rollins is the most eminent neurologist in our community.*
imminent (adj) about to happen: *A hostile takeover of that company is imminent.*

envelop (v) to surround: *The major feared that fog would envelop the city.*
envelope (n) container for a letter: *Always send letters in an envelope with our company logo on it.*

fair (n) convention, exhibition: *The technology fair featured a home theater with five satellite speakers.*
fair (adj) honest: *Their price was fair.*
fare (n) cost for a trip: *She was able to get a discount on a round-trip fare.*
fare (n) food: *They ate East Asian fare.*

foreword (n) preface to a book: *The foreword outlined the author's goals in her study of new global markets.*
forward (adv) toward a time or place; in advance: *We moved the time of the visit forward on the calendar so we could meet the overseas manager.*
forward (v) to send ahead: *We forwarded her email to her new server.*

imply (v) to suggest: *The supervisor implied that the mechanics had taken too long for their lunch break.*
infer (v) to draw a conclusion: *We can infer from these sales figures that the new advertising campaign is working.*

it's (pronoun + verb) contraction of *it* and *is*: *Do you think it's too early to tell?*
its (adj) possessive form of *it*: *That old printer is on its last legs.*

knew (v) (past tense of *know*): *She knew the new regulations.*
new (adj) never used before: *The subwoofer was new.*

lay/laid/laid (v) to put down: *Lay aside that project for now. He laid aside the project. He had already laid aside the project twice before.*
lie/lay/lain (v) to recline: *I think I'll lie down for a while. He lay there for only a few minutes before the firefighter rescued him. She has lain out in the sun too often.*

lean (adj) thin, skinny: *She asked for a lean slice of roast.*
lean (v) to rest against: *The shovel leaned against the fence.*
lien (n) a claim against: *There was a lien against his property for back taxes.*

lose (v) to misplace, to fail to win: *Be careful not to lose my calculator. I hope I don't lose my seat on the planning board.*
loose (adj) not tight: *The printer ribbon was too loose.*

miner (n) individual who works in a mine: *His uncle was a miner in West Virginia.*
minor (n) someone under legal age: *The law forbids the sale of tobacco to minors.*

overdo (v) to exceed, to do in excess: *The coach did not want her players to overdo their practice time.*
overdue (adj) past due: *The quarterly bill was overdue by three weeks.*

pare (v) to cut back: *Sandoval pared the skin from the apple.*
pair (n) a couple: *They offered a pair of resolutions.*
pear (n) a fruit: *Alphonso ate a pear with lunch.*

passed (v) went by (past tense of *pass*): *He passed me in the hall without recognizing me.*
past (n) time gone by: *We've never used their services in the past.*

peace (n) absence of war or conflict: *Joaquin enjoyed the peace he found in his new job.*
piece (n) a fragment, portion: *Each daycare child received a piece of Wanda's birthday cake.*

personal (adj) private: *The manager closes the door when she discusses personal matters with one of her staff.*
personnel (n) staff of employees: *All personnel must participate in the 401(k) retirement program.*

perspective (n) viewpoint: *From the customer's perspective, we are an honest and courteous company.*
prospective (adj) expected, likely to happen or become: *Email the prospective budget to district managers.*

plain (adj) simple, not fancy: *He ate plain food.*
plane (n) airplane: *The plane for Dallas leaves in an hour.*
plane (v) to make smooth: *The carpenter planed the wood.*

precede (v) to go before: *A presentation will precede the open discussion.*
proceed (v) to carry on, to go ahead: *Proceed as if we had never received that letter.*

principal (adj) main, chief: *Sales of new software constitute their principal source of revenue.*
principal (n) the head of a school: *She was a high school principal before she entered the business world.*
principal (n) money owed: *The principal on that loan totaled $32,800.*
principle (n) a policy, a belief: *Sales reps should operate on the principle that the customer is always right.*

quiet (adj) silent, not loud: *He liked to spend a quiet afternoon surfing the Net.*
quite (adv) to a degree: *The officer was quite encouraged by the recruit's performance.*

stationary (adj) not moving: *Miguel rides a stationary bicycle for an hour every morning.*
stationery (n) writing supplies, such as paper and envelopes: *Please stop off at the stationery store and buy some more address labels.*

than (conj) as opposed to (used in comparisons): *He is a faster keyboarder than his predecessor.*

then (adv) at that time: *First she called the vendor; then she summarized their conversation in an email to her boss.*

their (adj) possessive form of *they*: *All the lab technicians took their vacations during June and July.*

there (adv) in that place: *Please put the printer in there.*

they're (pronoun + verb) contraction of *they* and *are*: *They're our two best customer service representatives.*

to (prep): *They invited us to their new facility.*

too (adv) also, excessive: *The painters put too much enamel on the railings.*

two (n) the number: *Two new notebooks arrived today.*

waiver (n) intentional relinquishment of a right, claim, or privilege: *The company issued a waiver so that additional liability insurance would not have to be secured.*

waver (v) to shake, to move: *Our company would not waver in its commitment to safety.*

who's (pronoun + verb) contraction of *who* and *is*: *Who's up next for a promotion?*

whose (adj) possessive form of *who*: *Whose idea was that in the first place?*

you're (pronoun + verb) contraction of *you* and *are*: *You're going to like their decision.*

your (adj) possessive form of *you*: *They agree with your ideas.*

PROOFREADING MARKS

⌒o	Correct a typu.	Correct a typo.
r⌒/m⌒/⌒o	Correct nore than one typu.	Correct more than one typo.
t	Insert a leter.	Insert a letter.
or words	Insert a word.	Insert a word or words.
℘	Make a a deletion.	Make a deletion.
℘	Delette and close up space.	Delete and close up space.
◠	Close up ex tra space.	Close up extra space.
#	Insertproper spacing.	Insert proper spacing.
#/◠	Closeu p and insert space.	Close up and insert space.
eq #	Regularize proper ⌣ spacing.	Regularize proper spacing.
tr	Transpose letters injdcated.	Transpose letters indicated.
tr	Transpose as words indicated.	Transpose words as indicated.
tr	Reorder shown as words several.	Reorder several words as shown.
[[	Move text to left.	Move text to left.
]]	Move text to right.	Move text to right.
¶	Indent for paragraph.	Indent for paragraph.
no ¶	No paragraph indent.	No paragraph indent.
// //	Align type vertically.	Align type vertically.
run in	Run back turnover lines.	Run back turnover lines.
	Break line when it runs far too long.	Break line when it runs far too long.
⊙	Insert period here.	Insert period here.
⌃	Commas commas everywhere.	Commas, commas everywhere.
⌄	Its in need of an apostrophe.	It's in need of an apostrophe.
⌄/⌄	Add quotation marks, he begged.	"Add quotation marks," he begged.
;	Add a semicolon don't hesitate.	Add a semicolon; don't hesitate.
:	She advised "You need a colon."	She advised: "You need a colon."
?	How about a question mark.	How about a question mark?
(/)	Add parentheses as they say.	Add parentheses (as they say).
lc	Sometimes you want Lowercase.	Sometimes you want lowercase.
caps	Sometimes you want upperCASE.	Sometimes you want UPPERCASE.
ital	Add italics instantly.	Add italics *instantly*.
bf	Add boldface if necessary.	Add **boldface** if necessary.
wf	Fix a wrong font letter.	Fix a wrong font letter.
sp	Spell out all ③ terms.	Spell out all three terms.
⌄	Change x to a subscript.	Change $_x$ to a subscript.
⌄	Change y to a superscript.	Change ^{y} to a superscript.
stet	Let stand as is.	Let stand as is. (To retract a change already marked.)

Index

Guide to *Case Studies* and *Tech Notes*